HETEROGENEOUS
INTERNETWORKING

HETEROGENEOUS INTERNETWORKING

Networking Technically Diverse Operating Systems

HARRY SINGH

For book and bookstore information

http://www.prenhall.com

PRENTICE HALL PTR
Upper Saddle River, New Jersey 07458

Library of Congress Cataloging-in-Publication Data

Singh, Harry

    Heterogeneous internetworking: networking technically diverse
operating systems/Harry Singh.

      .p.   cm.

    Includes bibliographical references and index.

    ISBN 0-13-255696-0 (pbk.)

    1. Internetworking (Telecommunication) I. title.

TK5105.5.S5463 1996

  004.6—dc20   96-14943
                                             CIP

Production Editor: *Kerry Reardon*
Acquisitions Editor: *Michael Meehan*
Cover Design: *Design Source*
Cover Design Director: *Jerry Votta*
Manufacturing Manager: *Alexis R. Heydt*

©1996 Prentice Hall PTR
Prentice-Hall, Inc.
A Simon & Schuster Company
Upper Saddle River, New Jersey 07458

The publisher offers discounts on this book when ordered in bulk quantities.
For more information contact:

Corporate Sales Department
Prentice Hall PTR
One Lake Street
Upper Saddle River, N.J. 07458
Phone: 800-382-3419
FAX: 201-236-7141
E-mail: corpsales@prenhall.com

Printed in the United States of America

10 9 8 7 6 5 4 3 2 1

ISBN 0-13-255696-0

Prentice-Hall International (UK) Limited, *London*
Prentice-Hall of Australia Pty. Limited, *Sydney*
Prentice-Hall Canada Inc., *Toronto*
Prentice-Hall Hispanoamericana, S.A., *Mexico*
Prentice-Hall of India Private Limited, *New Delhi*
Prentice-Hall of Japan, *Tokyo*
Simon & Schuster Asia Pte. Ltd., *Singapore*
Editora Prentice-Hall do Brasil, Ltda., *Rio de Janeiro*

Dedication

To my brother, Shamsher, for his affection and encouragement,
To my daughters, Sarita, Sushila, and Samita, for their love,
To my son, Sanjay, for his inspiration, and
To my parents, for their patience and devotion.

Trademarks

The following are registered trademarks of International Business Machines Corporation:

MVS, AS/400, VM, AIX, AIX/6000, NetView, RACF, ESA/370, PC/DOS, AT, XT, NetBIOS, NCP, SAA, APPC, IBM 604, DOS-360, OS/2, IBM 360, IBM 370, PC-LAN, VTAM, LU6.2, SSP, NetView/6000.

The following are registered trademarks of Digital Equipment Corporation:
VAX, VAX, VMS, RMS, ULTRIX, DEC, PDP, Rdb, VT, OpenVMS,, All-IN-ONE, DECnet, PATHWORKS, Phase V.

The following are trademarks of Hitachi Data Systems: *Osiris*

The following are registered trademarks of Novell, Inc.: *NetWare, IPX/SPX, NetWare Lite, NetWare LANalyzer.*

The following are registered trademarks of AT&T: *AT&T, TLI.*

The following are registered trademarks of Xerox Corporation: *XEROX, XNS.*

The following are registered trademarks of Apple Computer Corporation: *Mac, Macintosh, AppleTalk, LocalTalk, EtherTalk, TokenTalk.*

The following are registered trademarks of Microsoft Corporation: *XENIX, Microsoft, Windows 3.1, NT, Windows NT, MS-DOS, NT Advanced Server.*

The following are registered trademarks of Hewlett-Packard Company: *Apollo, Hewlett-Packard, RPC, OpenView, StarLAN, NetMetrix.*

The following are registered trademarks of Sun Microsystems, Inc.: *Sun, Solaris, SunOS, NFS, SunNet Manager.*

The following are registered trademarks of X/Open: *UNIX.*

The following are registered trademarks of Massachusetts Institute of Technology: *X-Windows.*

The following are registered trademarks of Banyan Corporation: *VINES.*

The following are registered trademarks of Network General Corporation: *Expert Sniffer, Network General Reporter, Foundation Manager.*

The following are registered trademarks of Sperry Rand Corporation: *UNIVAC.*

The following are registered trademarks of Boreland International, Inc.: *dBASE.*

The following are registered trademarks of Cabletron Systems: *SPECTRUM.*

The following are registered trademarks of NetLabs, Inc.: *DiMONS, NerveCenter, DualManager.*

The following are registered trademarks of Digilog, Inc.: *LANVista, WANVista.*

The following are registered trademarks of FTP Software, Inc.: *LANWatch.*

The following are registered trademarks of Cisco Systems, Inc.: *NetScout.*

CONTENTS

PREFACE   *xv*

1   OVERVIEW   *1*

Introduction   1
Historical Perspectives   7
Technology Trends   21
Organization of This Text   22
Summary   23
Exercises   25

2   INTERNETWORKING BASIC CONCEPTS   *26*

Introduction   26
Environments   29
Prevalent Networks   52
Role of Standards   55
Summary   56
Exercises   58

3   *STANDARDS AND PROTOCOLS*   **59**

    Introduction   59
    Issues   60
    Standards   64
    Summary   91
    Exercises   92

4   *NETWORK BUILDING BLOCKS*   **93**

    Introduction   93
    Network Communications   94
    LAN Architecture   103
    Switching Techniques   106
    LAN Topologies   107
    LAN Components   111
    Transport Media Considerations   114
    Ethernet Technology   117
    Token Ring Technology   123
    Token Bus (IEEE 802.4)   126
    AppleTalk/LocalTalk   128
    Summary   130
    Exercises   130

5   *INTERNETWORKING PROTOCOLS–I*   **132**

    Introduction   132
    OSI Protocols   133
    Integrated Services Digital Network   148
    OSI and ISDN   149
    OSI and X/Open Standards   151
    TCP and IP Protocols   151
    Protocol Dependencies   164
    Summary   164
    Exercises   166

6 **INTERNETWORKING PROTOCOLS–II**   **167**

    Introduction   167
    Systems Network Architecture   168
    Other Protocols   181
    Internetworking with WANs   191
    Internetworking Examples   200
    Summary   205
    Exercises   205

7 **INTERNETWORKING TOOLS**   **207**

    Introduction   207
    Network Interconnection   208
    Repeaters   210
    Bridges   213
    Network Configurations with Bridges   221
    Routers and Layer 3 Devices   223
    Multiprotocol Routers   227
    Network Configuration Examples with Routers   227
    Gateways   228
    Network Configuration Examples with Gateways   231
    Backbones   233
    Seven-Layer Protocol Conversion   234
    Summary   239
    Exercises   241

8 **APPLICATIONS**   **242**

    Introduction   242
    Issues   243
    Application Types   249
    Applications and Utilities   251
    Incompatibility Solutions   264
    Applications of LANs and WANs   266
    Summary   268
    Exercises   269

9   UNIX INTERNETWORKING   270

Introduction   270
Networking with UNIX   271
UNIX Facilities   276
UNIX-to-UNIX Communications   279
UNIX-to-Non-UNIX Communications   284
LAN Implementations   293
Internetworking Scenarios   296
Summary   302
Exercises   303

10   INTEGRATING THE DESKTOP   304

Introduction   304
Environments   305
Running TCP/IP on a PC   324
Connecting with UNIX   335
Summary   339
Exercises   340

11   INTEGRATING UNIX AND THE PCS (X WINDOWS)   341

Introduction   341
Overview   342
The X Protocol   346
Implementing X Window System   351
TCP/IP: Network and Serial Connectivity   357
Network-to-UNIX Integration   361
Summary   362
An Example: How to Turn PC into an X Terminal   362
Exercises   363

12   INTERNETWORKING WITH MAC   364

Introduction   364
Overview   365

Networking Options   371
Mac-to-DOS Connectivity   375
Macs and the Enterprise Network   383
Network Administration and Maintenance   386
Summary   392
Exercises   393

13 INTEGRATING LEGACY NETWORKS   394

Introduction   394
SNA Networking   395
IBM Mainframe to UNIX   414
VMS-to-UNIX   425
AS/400-to-UNIX   430
Summary   432
Exercises   434

14 INTERNETWORK TROUBLESHOOTING AND MONITORING–I   435

Introduction   435
Troubleshooting Methodology   436
Remote Monitoring Tools   441
Third-Party Tools and Applications   446
Summary   463
Exercises   463

15 INTERNETWORK TROUBLESHOOTING AND MONITORING–II   464

Introduction   464
Getting Started   465
LAN/WAN Troubleshooting Problem Areas   468
Troubleshooting the TCP/IP Internetwork   478
Measurement and Testing   480
Multivendor Solutions   485
Summary   486
Exercises   486

16 TROUBLESHOOTING A GLOBAL NETWORK (AN EXAMPLE)   487

Introduction   487
Knowing Your Resources   488
Bottleneck Isolation   490
Looking for Trouble and Remedies   491
WAN Bandwidth Problems   493
Broadband Troubleshooting   494
T1 Problems   495
Summary   496
Exercises   497

17 MANAGING NETWORKS   498

Introduction   498
Functions of a Management System   500
Components of a Management System   507
Network Management Protocols   511
Comparisons of SNMP, CMIP, and CMOT   520
Management Strategies and Products   521
Summary   530
Exercises   531

18 SUMMARY AND CONCLUSIONS   532

Introduction   532
Internetworking Environments   533
Internetworking Configurations   534
Minimizing Network Failures   537
Strategies for Managing Networks and Security   538
Future of Internetworking   540
Finally   541

APPENDICES

1   TECHNICAL NOTES   *543*

Introduction	543
Address Resolution Protocol	544
Bridges	545
Carrier Sense Multiple Access/Collision Detect	545
Datagram	546
Domain Name System	546
Ethernet	547
FDDI	548
Filtering	550
Forwarding	550
Gateways	552
Internetworking	552
Internet Address Classes	552
Internet Protocol	553
LAN	554
LAN Media	554
Management Information Base	555
Multiport Bridges	556
NetView	556
Network Operating System	556
Open Systems Interconnection	557
Open Shortest Path First	561
Packet	561
Point-to-Point Protocol	562
Repeaters	562
Routers	564
SQL	565
Simple Network Management Protocol	567
Token Ring (802.5)	567
Transmission Control Protocol Suite	569
Transmission Control Protocol	570
WANs	572

II **ANSWERS TO EXERCISES** **576**

Chapter 1 Overview 576
Chapter 2 Internetworking Basic Concepts 577
Chapter 3 Standards and Protocols 579
Chapter 4 Network Building Blocks 579
Chapter 5 Internetworking Protocols–I 581
Chapter 6 Internetworking Protocols–II 582
Chapter 7 Internetworking Tools 583
Chapter 8 Applications 584
Chapter 9 UNIX Internetworking 585
Chapter 10 Integrating the Desktop 587
Chapter 11 Integrating UNIX and the PCs (X Windows) 589
Chapter 12 Internetworking with Mac 591
Chapter 13 Integrating Legacy Networks 592
Chapter 14 Internetwork Troubleshooting and Monitoring–I 594
Chapter 15 Internetwork Troubleshooting and Monitoring–II 596
Chapter 16 Troubleshooting a Global Network (An Example) 596
Chapter 17 Managing Networks 597

III **GLOSSARY** **600**

BIBLIOGRAPHY **625**

INDEX **631**

Preface

INTRODUCTION

A generation or two ago, who had even heard of e-mail? Today, who has not used it? As tools for the greatest technological revolution in our lifetime, they make our home and business only at arm's reach. Internetworks not only make our airline and hotel reservations, monitor astronauts or satellites in space, compute our payrolls, provide instant credit checks, control scientific experiments, and even help in our day-to-day communication. It is the computers, operating systems, and related technologies which provide the interconnectivity between desks, departments, cities, and countries. This is the technology of internetworking we have become so dependent upon.

Internetworks come in all shapes and sizes. Some are small and trivial. Some are diverse and complex. Some span a room, while others span the globe. But whatever they may look like and whatever their complexity, internetworks are the way of life today.

Throughout most of this book, the emphasis is on the internetworking technologies. It is the purpose of this book neither to underrate them, nor to overrate them; neither to glorify them, nor to abhor them, but rather to help you *understand* them. This book undertakes to investigate internetworking technologies in a complete and evenhanded way. It tries to show that heterogeneous internetworking is not just a "connectivity thing," but a set of concepts that stems from a number of technological constraints.

THE PURPOSES SERVED

The advent and growth of micro-processors have brought new challenges to the enterprise. This has generated the need for many companies to distribute their data, applications, and resources. The decentralization, cost of the microprocessors, and the growth of operating systems have caused heterogeneity of enormous proportions. But the enterprise must still be able to communicate and access the data/resources as if it was still one comprehensive system. This book addresses those concerns of the enterprise.

Many excellent books have been written discussing various theoretical facets of engineering design and analysis of computer networks. This book provides the basics that are needed for practical application of the concepts of internetworking. In addition, it leads the reader step by step to become self reliant in internetworking using differing hardware as well as operating systems and applications software.

Because of extensive examples, exercises, and illustrations, this book is intended to become a practical reference guide, a text book, or a cookbook for internetworking. The book is a comprehensive guide for internetworking from concepts to connectivity.

This text is intended as a self-administered course for a wide variety of computer professionals, network administrators, and technical staff who need an in-depth understanding of internetworking concepts and applications. It is well suited for the following audiences:

- Technical support groups.
- Network engineers and managers.
- Systems analysts.
- Network systems administrators.
- Application developers.
- Computer Science students.

The reader should be able to take away the following knowledge from this book:

- Basic internetworking concepts.
- Heterogeneous operating environments.
- Network connectivity, configurations, and installation options.
- Learn how, when, and what devices to use to enhance/monitor/ extend these networks.
- How to connect, operate, and manage these networks.
- Learn how various applications can take advantage of the underlying networks.
- Learn how to integrate or connect PC's, workstations, and mainframes, using varying operating systems like DOS, NT, Windows, OS/400, MVS, and many varieties of UNIX.

Extensive exercises provide a highly productive learning environment. The technical notes provide detailed topical information as valuable reference aids both during and after the book coverage, and provide the foundation for future technologies and higher level technical training.

THE TECHNOLOGIES DISCUSSED

The technology described in the book is evolving. Depending upon the enterprise internetworking needs, any existing or future networking software can be used. There are no specific software or particular release level requirements for adequately using this book. However, in order to interoperate between two hardware platforms or operating systems (UNIX, DOS, Windows, Windows NT, OS/400, etc.), proper media (Coax, Twisted pair, etc.), communication protocols (TCP/IP, SNA, DECnet, etc.), network technologies (Ethernet, Token Ring, FDDI, etc.), and connectors (repeaters, bridges, routers, gateways) are required. Windows NT or Windows Advanced Server is still evolving. Therefore, current knowledge of the technology will be beneficial.

ORGANIZATION OF THE BOOK

The book is organized in a modular fashion. If a reader has prior knowledge of certain subjects, the reader will not need to start from the beginning. For example, if the reader is already knowledgeable in OSI and/or TCP/IP protocols, the reader can directly proceed to the following chapters. In addition, the reader can learn about a specific topic from the "Technical Notes" in Appendix 1.

ACKNOWLEDGMENTS

This book began as an exercise to define client/server connectivity among various workstations and the mainframe. It soon grew into a project to cover connectivity options and solutions among diverse operating systems and hardware platforms.

Many thanks to the technical reviewers used by Prentice Hall. Their insight, comments, criticism, and suggestions added greatly to the final result.

Many thanks to Subodh Garg and Abha Gupta, who reviewed various sections of the manuscript. Thanks to Murty Susrala, who spent many hours helping me with the acquisition of research materials.

Special thanks to Derrick Bast, a friend in the internetworking world, who reviewed the complete manuscript, made one or two minor changes while covering each page, and made significant contributions to the accuracy and readability of the text.

Harry Singh

HETEROGENEOUS INTERNETWORKING

1

OVERVIEW

Introduction
  Objectives of Internetworking
  What Is Internetworking
  Need for Internetworking
  Terminology
  Issues
Historical Perspectives
  Pre-1950s
  1950s
  1960s
  Early 1970s

  Mid-1970s
  Late 1970s
  1980s (PCs)
  Mid-1980s (LANs)
  Late 1980s (WANs)
  1990s (Internetworking LANs and WANs)
  1990s (The Client/Server Revolution)
Technology Trends
Organization of This Text
Summary
Exercises

INTRODUCTION

One of the currently prevailing management doctrine states that "success is dictated by one's ability to manage change." If that is the case, management information systems (MIS) departments in an enterprise will succeed or fail based on their ability to manage the internetworking of dissimilar operating systems, the primary vehicle of change in the information technology industry today.

Unfortunately, an abundance of international standards, vendor innovations, industry partnerships, and technology advances has brought both chaos and opportunity to the world of connectivity. The challenge for users is taking advantage of the existing technology while avoiding the chaos. It is, indeed, a formidable challenge.

The promises of vendor internetworking solutions and the plethora of internetworking standards are alluring. Freed from the tyranny of proprietary vendor offerings in some cases and myriad of options in the others, users find themselves calling the shots in a competitive marketplace increasingly populated with low-cost, standardized offerings. But none of these solutions comes bundled in one neat, convenient, turnkey package. In reality, they are like so many loose pieces of a puzzle—a puzzle that must be assembled by the users.

This requires a diligent strategic plan that formulates guidelines and statements of direction. This plan must be carefully thought and based on an understanding of the disadvantages and advantages of available hardware and software solutions. To gain that knowledge, many tough questions must be asked. For instance, is it wise to build your enterprise network on existing de facto standards that may be controlled by monopolistic vendors? Or is it better to wait, possibly for months or years, for formal standards bodies to deliver truly interoperable results?

Examination of the existing technologies and the trends can help answer some of these questions. Designed to be more specific and tactical than strategic plans, they may address departmental, organizational, or even industrywide applications, no matter how large or small. These blueprints can always provide a constant baseline as systems, technologies, and internetworking demands expand. In the final analysis, users must coordinate the pressing need to interoperate with the more tangible requirements of the business enterprise.

Even though the computer industry is young as compared to other industries, computer technologies have made spectacular progress in a short time. During the first two decades, the computers were highly centralized, which came to be known as the glass house. However, the merging of communications and computer technologies has had a profound influence on the way the computer systems are being organized today.

The concept of users bringing work to the glass house is rapidly becoming obsolete as users want computer power on their desks. The old model of a single computer serving all the organization's computational needs is being rapidly replaced by one in which a large number of separate but interconnected computers do the job. These systems are called computer networks and internetworks, depending on the geographical and technological spans.

Objectives of Internetworking

Practically every business enterprise, large or small, has a substantial number of computers in operation. Some businesses have all their resources centralized in a building, while others have them scattered all over the globe. For example, a company with many offices, subsidiaries, or factories may have a computer system at each location or may depend upon the other location to meet some of its computing needs. Until the 1980s, these computers may have worked in isolation from the others, but with the revolution of the PCs and the desire to make the local staffs more productive, the businesses were forced to connect them together to extract and correlate information about the entire company. In order for an organization to be successful and competitive, there are a number of objectives that "internetworking" and "networking" must meet:

- The first objective of networking/internetworking is to make all applications, data, and computing hardware available to everyone on the network without regard to the physical location of the resource or the user. That has given rise to *resource sharing* or *resource distribution* and the information has been placed where it is more frequently used or manipulated.

- The second objective is to provide *economies of scale*. Mainframes are extremely expensive to buy and maintain. If these computers are not effectively used or accessible to the users, these could be replaced for smaller and more versatile workstations to achieve better *price* and *performance.*

- To create alternate sources of supply to provide *high reliability* and *availability*. All files or databases could be replicated on two or three machines, so if one of them is unavailable due to hardware failure or power stoppage, the other copies could be used. For mission-critical applications, such as airline reservations system, banking, and traffic control, the ability to continue operating even after hardware failures is of great importance.

- The *ability to link* local networks (local area networks, or LANs) in a given building with others in the same building or another building or across town or even across the continent.

- The *ability to increase system performance* as the workload grows by adding more processors. With central mainframe computing, when the system is full, it must be replaced by a more powerful one, usually at great disruption to the users.

Simply, a computer internetwork can provide a powerful communication media among widely separated people, especially via electronic mail or messaging, even among dissimilar operating systems and/or technologies.

What Is Internetworking

An internetwork consists of one or more linked networks. These networks may have to traverse diverse operating environments or diverse networking protocols. These networks can use AppleTalk, NetBIOS, Novell's Internetwork Packet Exchange/Sequenced Packet Exchange (IPX/SPX), Transmission Control Protocol/Internet Protocol (TCP/IP), NetBIOS, SNA, DECnet, or other network protocols. They can use token ring, fiber distributed data interface (FDDI), Ethernet, ARCnet, or other media access types. However, the major criteria to implement any type of internetwork is an understanding of the benefits, limitations, and configuration options available.

Internetworking encompasses the increasingly complex process of delivering data from one network segment to another. In distributed network environments, data traveling across internetwork links can traverse one or more intermediate network (e.g., wide area networks, or WANs) connections. The type of data that travel over internetwork links is rapidly expanding to include client/server applications, fax, video, and voice. Depending on budget and bandwidth requirements, internetwork equipment ranges from inexpensive dial-up modems, to bridges or routers with WAN interfaces, to sophisticated asynchronous transfer modes (ATMs) and like switches.

Today's enterprise networks consist of LANs of various protocols, supporting an array of media and architectures, connected to wide area networks consisting of a variety of communication systems. These complex networks span cities, countries, and continents and are being influenced by emerging technologies driven by user demands and vendor innovations. Managing these disparate systems can be challenging

Given the various types of data traversing the growing range of internetwork links, the task of designing and managing internetworks can appear overwhelmingly complex. Traffic must move efficiently between nodes, between LANs, and between LANs and WANs. To take advantage of the technologies and economies of scale, you need to understand the underlying technologies, protocols, and management of the fundamental parts of networks.

The emergence of parallel and distributed processing, client/server technologies, and the increasing use of high-bandwidth applications such as multimedia, full-motion video, graphics, and CAD/CAM have created additional demands on networking facilities. In modern offices, word processing, database, spreadsheet, and other nondata processing users demand equal access to network facilities with more critical applications.

Designing a LAN-to-WAN internetworking system using the more appropriate communications facilities and managing it successfully demand a variety of expertise. Designing an efficient internetwork is influenced by several facility-specific issues. These include the business activities of the organization, types of users and their access priorities, size of the network, geographical distribution of network nodes, frequency of use, and a host of other factors. This impacts the two basic design requirements that are common to all internetworks.

- *High-performance processing:* The increasing power of source entities, such as PCs, has increased the demand for efficient high-speed throughput rates. The ability to provide error-free throughput at required speed to network nodes is vital to the success of enterprise internetworks. High-performance processing depends on the design of the network, choice of media and internetworking devices, size of the facility, frequency of use, security, and so on. Users expect on-demand availability of network services from remote locations. This requires efficient traffic management to ensure bottleneck-free flow of traffic while providing adequate alternate routes in case of emergencies.
- *Flexible configurations:* User demands, mergers and acquisitions, and other priorities require frequent reconfiguration with minimum of service interruptions.

Need for Internetworking

As enterprises grow with acquisitions or mergers or in the number of employees, and in complexity, the desire to share information and resources drives the need for connecting systems. Companies link their local or remote networks primarily to

- Share files.
- Share network resources (printers, modems, disk drives, etc.).
- Access a centralized database.
- Use electronic mail.

Internetworks have also become a necessity as businesses decentralize their computer systems and begin to expand the number of offices and communication protocols. Data communication has become a fundamental part of computing. Worldwide networks gather data about such diverse subjects as atmospheric conditions, crop production, and airline traffic. Groups establish mailing lists so they can share information of common interest.

In the business world, data networks are essential because they allow the businesses to reconcile their accounts or inventories or global economies. In the scientific community, they allow the scientists to send programs and data to remote supercomputers for processing, to retrieve results of computation, and to exchange scientific information with colleagues. Unfortunately, most networks are independent entities, established to serve the needs of a single group.

The information managers choose a hardware technology appropriate to their communication problems. Some users need a high-speed network to connect machines, but such networks cannot be expanded to span large distances. Others settle for slower speed networks that connect machines thousands of miles apart, but they demand reliability and integrity. More important, it is impossible to build a universal network from a single hardware or software technology because no single network suffices for all uses.

The emergence of new technologies makes it possible to connect many disparate physical and logical networks. This new technology is known as internetworking, which accommodates multiple, diverse, underlying hardware technologies by adding both physical connectivity schemes, innovative devices like bridges and routers, and a set of conventions known as protocols. This technology attempts to hide the details of the complexity of the network hardware and software and permits users (and applications) to communicate independent of their physical network connections.

Terminology

Throughout this book, we will be using the term *internetwork* to mean an interconnection of *autonomous* computer networks and/or just computers. *Network* is a system of software and hardware connected in a manner to support data transmission. The *computer network* means that two or more computers are interconnected allowing them to exchange information. The interconnection may be via a twisted pair, fiber optic cables, coaxial cables, lasers, communication satellites, or microwaves. By *autonomous*, we mean that the computers and networks are *independent* systems when they are not connected. With a *computer network*, the user must be able to log into a machine or network of machines, move files, submit jobs remotely, and possibly perform network management tasks personally.

Another commonly used term will be *protocol*. Protocol or architecture is a standardized set of rules that specifies the format, timing, sequencing, and/or error checking for data transmissions. A protocol, therefore, is a description of data formats and procedures used for communication between nodes or computers or computer systems.

The term *distributed processing* is used to describe networks where computer processing is not centrally located at one computer but is physically distributed. Distributed processing is a term that became prevalent along with the advent of PC networks to describe the fact that all of the users had their own CPU and because of this required less work from the central unit. This allowed the central unit to control such things as printing and file sharing more efficiently.

In a complex field as *internetworking*, there are a lot of terms which the network specialists use. A comprehensive list of these terms is provided in the *glossary* section of this book.

Issues

Internetworking multiple vendors' devices, networks, and architectures is a complex job. MIS and telecommunications managers need to be aware of the following major management and technical issues:

- *Performance* decreases when networks are connected together. It is extremely difficult to compute network performance measures on an end-to-end basis. A major difficulty is that the data traffic to a destination may go through many local telephone companies, long-distance companies, and foreign companies. Computing an end-to-end performance of all vendors' equipment and networks are to be combined. Depending on the number of circuits between the originating and terminating nodes, the computation may be difficult.

  The performance measurement units also vary between device and network vendors. Therefore, enterprises must carefully select the networks to be interconnected (if they have a choice) so that the end user's performance objectives can be met.

- *Standardization* can decrease the choice of vendors, but reduce the potential obsolescence of a customer's devices and the need for relays to interconnect networks.

  Increased complications are introduced when a foreign telecommunications company is used since those companies network standards may not conform with the native set.

- Bandwidth, rerouting, and integration of backbone networks become important issues in LAN-WAN interconnection. The bandwidth available in LANs is on the order of megabytes per second, while equivalent bandwidth on long-distance networks costs much more. If a customer leases a backbone network to carry high-bandwidth WAN traffic among major cities, that customer frequently requests automatic rerouting in case of failure of a major facility. Sophisticated software and hardware are required for such functions.

  Many companies are also beginning to merge their data, voice, and video traffic onto a backbone network. This makes it possible to lease high-bandwidth at cheaper prices. The introduction of fiber optics in the long-distance networks has given common carriers global digital connectivity at high rates and cheaper prices.

- Some type of *security* must be provided for network users. Users on a LAN are often logged onto their personal computers, even though they are not using their terminals at that time. Such open terminals provide hackers with the opportunity to access computer systems using remote logins. When the traffic is transmitted using long-distance lines shared with other users and if the long-distance vendors do not provide their customers with transmission security, one customer's traffic can be tapped by other customers.

- Assuring *integrity* of corporate data is an important issue. LAN-WAN interconnection gives an end user the ability to access and change the databases remotely.

Internetworking makes it possible for an end user to corrupt the data in corporate databases.

- These issues multiply as different countries are internetworked. Standards are different in every country, and the equipment from such countries is not compatible. An organization must retain and recruit talented personnel to address such compatability issues.

HISTORICAL PERSPECTIVES

A single technology has dominated each of the past three centuries. The eighteenth century was the time of the great mechanical systems accompanying the Industrial Revolution. The nineteenth century was the age of the steam engine. During the twentieth century, the key technology has been information gathering, processing, and distribution. We have also seen unprecedented growth in the computer industry, radio, telephone, and television installations. As we move toward the final years of the twentieth century, these technologies are rapidly converging.

Pre-1950's

During the first half of the twentieth century, computers were mere curiosities used only for complex scientific and engineering calculations. Although they were powerful as compared to many mechanical calculators, computers of the time were built for specific purposes and were very limited in functionality.

In 1934, Dr. John V. Atanasoff, a professor of physics at Iowa State College (now Iowa State University), modified an IBM punched card machine to perform calculations mechanically. In 1942, he built a prototype of an electronic digital computer, called them ABC (Atanasoff Berry Computer). The ABC had a memory consisting of 45 vacuum tubes.

In 1946, the Electronic Numerical Integrator and Calculator (ENIAC) went into operation at the Moore School of Electrical Engineering of the University of Pennsylvania. This specialized computer was built to compute firing and ballistic tables to help guide army artillarymen in aiming their guns. ENIAC was invented by Dr. John W. Mauchly and J. Presper Eckert. ENIAC occupied 1500 square feet, weighed 30 tons, contained 19,000 vacuum tubes, and required 130 kW of power. The primary advantage of the ENIAC was that it could perform several operations, simultaneously—a capability that has only recently become possible with the advent of modern digital computer systems.

In 1948, IBM introduced a general-purpose electronic digital computer called the IBM 604. More than 4000 of these machines were built in the next 10 years. The IBM 604 contained an electronic arithmetic and storage unit with over 1400 vacuum tubes and a separate card-handling machine to perform input and output. As evidenced in Figure 1.1, these computers soon became obsolete, and were replaced with newer technologies.

General-purpose computers require large amounts of storage. Earlier machines used vacuum tubes which were neither economical nor easy to handle. This prompted developers to perfect the use of acoustic mercury delay lines as storage devices for memories. In

Figure 1.1 Came of age.

1946, EDSAC (Electronic Delay Storage Automatic Calculator) was the first machine, invented by Professor Wilkes of Cambridge University England, to perform completely automated calculations and use these storage devices.

1950s

The government played a very important role in the early days of the digital computer development. The National Bureau of Standard (NBS), now National Institute for Standards and Technology (NIST), gave a boost to the computer industry by developing computers of their own.

In the 1950s, *stored program* computers were invented. By loading instructions into the memory, stored program computers could carry out varied tasks based on the users' imagination. The modern computer age had just begun. In the beginning, computers were physically enormous, expensive, and very difficult to program and use. Memory was limited to a few thousand bytes, and communications with the machine took place through paper tapes, punched cards, or even handset toggle switches. Programming languages had not been invented, so even simple applications took extensive time to develop. During the entire decade of the 1950s, only a few dozen machines were sold, each costing hundreds of thousands of dollars.

In 1951, UNIVAC I, the first business data processing system, was delivered to the U.S. Bureau of Census. Not long after UNIVAC I was operational, *automatic program-*

ming techniques were developed to help users better utilize these machines. IBM 650 was the most popular, which consisted of three units: a punched card input-output unit, a console unit, and a power unit.

The single biggest computer achievement of the 1950s was the invention of *programming languages*. Before that invention occurred, programmers worked strictly with ones and zeros used by the computer itself. A programming language is a notation—sometimes similar to English, sometimes mathematical in appearance depending upon the language—designed to be understandable (nothing to do with the ease of use we clamor for today) by humans rather than computers. The whole idea of programming languages is to allow people to think in their own terms when working with computers instead of having to constantly deal with bits and bytes built into the machine. In fact, an intermediary processing step took the programming language and translated it into the machine understandable language.

By introducing languages as a high-level tool for programming computers, the 1950s made application development truly approachable for the first time. Even 40-plus years later, COBOL and FORTRAN are still two of the most extensively used programming languages in the world.

However, even with stored program capability and programming languages, computers in the 1950s were still very limited in function. Permanent storage, disks and tapes, had not been invented, so databases were not possible. Yet computers made it possible to build large models involving millions of calculations. Nonetheless, the idea of an electronic brain, somehow a window to the future, captured the imagination of the scientists and the lay public alike. Computers, previously mysterious, suddenly appeared understandable and became a fascination of all.

1960s

The evolution of information technology architectures has marched in lockstep with changing models. In the 1960s, businesses focused much of their efforts on growth—the more the better. In the 1960s, a decade of boundless hope, computers not only learned to walk, but to run. People began to view computers as artificial intelligence that may replace people one day, in all kinds of tasks.

During the 1960s, dozens of companies began to manufacture high-speed computers. All these machines were much faster and more reliable than the early computers. Most of the machines made during the late 1950s and early 1960s belonged to the *second* generation of computers. These machines were much smaller, required less power, and produced much less heat. The use of *transistors as basic components* of internal computer circuits was the main reason for this improvement.

By the middle of the 1960s, computer companies had realized that the potential marketplace was huge. With the introduction of permanent storage, particularly magnetic disks, databases became possible. The database, in turn, promoted a vision of an organization where the computer could act as a central coordinator for companywide activities. This vision made database a key corporate resource. For the first time, people were viewing computers not just as arcane predictive devices. Instead, they saw computers as a true competitive advantage. The idea of information systems for business took shape.

The *third* generation computers appeared in 1964 when IBM announced System/360. These employed miniature circuits, making them smaller, more reliable, and faster than earlier machines. Along with the third-generation computers, newer and faster equipment was also introduced for storage and handling of input-output. One fact remains true today that the development of peripherals (input-output–type devices) still lag the processor development.

Early in the 1960s, people still thought of computers as large calculating machines. Scientists started to think about them as potential artificial intelligences. However, by the end of the decade a new role was clear that a computer was a superb tool for automating complex business processes. The 1960s also saw the development of modern operating systems (a jungle in today's business environment). The fact remains that three of the four leading operating systems of the 1990s, MVS, UNIX, and DOS/360, were all developed in the 1960s. These operating systems allowed the computers to be a shared resource within an enterprise and allowed them to run processes automatically.

Although the computers in the 1960s did not fundamentally change business organizations, they played a major role in shaping their organization structure and subsequent growth. Large organizations that were previously drowning in paper suddenly found that computer technology allowed them to do more with the same.

The 1960s was a decade of multinational corporations, worldwide airline reservation systems, worldwide credit cards, and global banking. Conglomeration and acquisition became a normal route to corporate growth, with the computer at the center. By the end of the 1960s, the computers had truly become indispensable for any large organization. Along with big computers, organizations invested heavily in programming, professional and support staff, and custom applications.

Early 1970s

In the 1970s, information systems moved to the forefront as businesses took their first steps toward mission-critical systems. It was in this environment that airline reservation systems took off. Simultaneously, timesharing and on-line transaction processing provided immediate access to business applications—applications that were aimed directly at end-user functions.

In the early 1970s, the concept associated with the *on-line databases*—databases connected to and fed by networked terminals—suddenly appeared in the *Harvard Business Review*, proposing that management could eliminate all isolation by

- Viewing information as a key corporate resource.
- Building a totally consistent, companywide, integrated database.
- Ensuring that information was entered into and updated at an opportune time.

Now they could view sales information, customer complaints, inventory, and costs at the touch of a keyboard. Most of all, the 1970s produced a vision for the future that information is instantly available and is organized in a consistent database that allows a company to operate faster to stay in touch with the real world. In addition, the 1970s marked two key trends in management understanding of computers:

- They learned how the computers and on-line databases could make their enterprises more competitive.
- They also realized that building on-line organization was an expensive experience.

Computer networks as we know it today may have started in the late 1960s or early 1970s with the ARPANET development. Prior to that time, there were computer vendor "networks" primarily designed to connect terminals to a mainframe. Although the term *network architecture* was not yet widely used, the initial ARPANET design did have a structure and a concept of *protocol layering*, each upper layer building upon the services of the one below.

Mid-1970s

By the mid-1970s, business had big dreams: on-line corporations, wired desktops, and totally consistent databases. Now the pundits also realized that they needed to accommodate diverse types of interconnection between networks. Therefore, the vendors started designing (architecting) their own brand of network solutions: IBM's SNA, DEC's DECnet, and of course, DARPA's TCP/IP.

Late 1970s

After reaching a plateau, the entire computer world changed between 1968 and 1972. Databases, terminals, permanent storage, and networks became practical. This resulted in making the existing applications obsolete and created a need for a whole new class of applications that collectively defied everything that had come before in terms of usability, complexity, and cost. Until the revolution of the databases, the managers hardly understood the potential of computers.

By the late 1970s, the computer industry was beginning to mature. True, big computers, their databases, and related development tools had reached a plateau with little qualitative change. However, the focus and energy shifted from the computers and databases to the process of designing and building applications.

The late 1970s also saw networking conferences dominate debates over the relative merits of circuit versus packet switching to transmit data from one end to another and standardizing the way computers communicate with each other. But the computer vendors continued to support their proprietary networks and architectures.

During the same period, another major influence was emerging in the network community, namely, the realization that multivendor systems could no longer be avoided and would require action to be taken for interoperability. Thus grew the desire to develop a common architecture that would allow these disparate networks and systems to converse with each other, and thus the International Standards Organization (ISO) was born to define an "explicit" architecture for *open systems interconnection* (OSI).

Still in the 1970s, minicomputers became the distributed processor of choice for interactive computing.

1980s (PCs)

In the early 1980s the focus was on converting application development from an art to an engineering discipline—structured programming. Also the emphasis shifted as to how to connect the disparate hardware and operating systems together. Even IBM had so many different types of computers with so many different operating systems that could not communicate with each other. This was vigorously touted by Digital Equipment Corporation in their ads *"we connect IBM better than IBM."*

Another revolution was also brewing in the 1980s: the birth of the personal computer, or PC. During the initial ramp-up of the computer environment in the mid-1960s, the computers consisted of large mainframes with terminals attached directly to them. The large computers resided in environmentally controlled computer rooms which were (and still are) expensive to build and required specially trained personnel to maintain the computer system. In the business community, this was the "only" method of user-computer interface until around 1980, when the first personal computers were introduced on the market.

Referring to Figure 1.2, you will see that the early method of computing had many disadvantages and advantages. This computing environment allowed for multiple users on one computer, accessing the same applications and files, some messaging capability, and equal access to the associated peripheral devices, such as printers, modems, and disk drives. For system administrators, this allowed for centralized management of the computer. On the other hand, the cost of cabling for the user terminals represented the second most expensive aspect of installing a computer and of course, the cost of the computer itself.

This environment was known as centralized computing. If the mainframe or a minicomputer went down, all users were affected until the computers were operational again. The user's terminals were usually dumb terminals, that is, terminals having very little

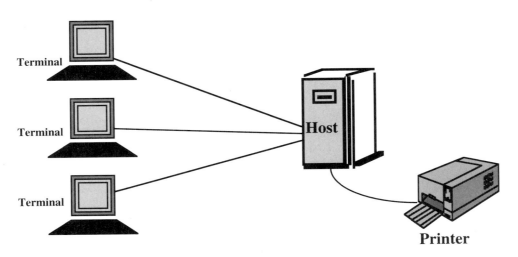

Figure 1.2 Centralized computing.

intelligence, since most of the processing was done at the mainframe. Multiple host connections were limited. When users wanted to connect to a host other than the one they were directly connected via their terminal, the choices were limited. Such an environment was effective at the time, but increasing demands were placed on it with very few other alternatives.

In 1981, IBM introduced the personal computer, and the computing environment was changed forever. The personal computer industry went through the same kind of birth process that mainframes went through in the 1950s. For the first half of the decade, management and MIS were convinced that personal computers were just a passing fad. After all, calculators were a big deal in the 1970s, and they hardly had any effect on the business environment. By 1985, it became clear that personal computers were here to stay and, in a way, different from the calculators.

The personal computer gave the user much more freedom. In effect, the personal computer brought the mainframe functionality to the desktop. It did not bring the power of the mainframe, but it did not need to since there was only one user working one application at a time. It did eliminate some of the disadvantages of the mainframe, such as centralized computing, high cabling costs, environmentally controlled computer rooms, expensive maintenance costs, and so on.

Now the users had complete control over their computing environments and enjoyed having personal application software (even solitaire) that would run on individual computers. But there were no capabilities to share applications, data, or mail. The original mainframe-PC connectivity was still accomplished using the original terminal cable. The PC was attached to the mainframe with this cable, and a terminal emulation software program was run on the PC to emulate the original dumb terminal. This openly provided limited access to the enterprise resources.

By 1985, another revolution started. Instead of depending on the mainframe, applications were being developed on the PC. Except for mission-critical applications, users took the development process into their own hands and developed applications like VisiCalc, Lotus 1-2-3, dBASE, and WordStar. While only addressing special needs, these applications were also dramatically easier to learn and use than mainframe applications.

Mid-1980s (LANs)

The 1980s also ushered in the era of end-user and team productivity. PCs and LANs became ubiquitous on the information processing landscape. Software geared toward servicing individuals and small teams of end users dominated IS departments. Word processing, spreadsheets, graphics, electronic mail, and network operating systems were the big-ticket items in many software budgets.

About the same time as the introduction of personal computers, the local area networks were introduced into the market. A LAN allowed not only connection from the host-terminal environment but also complete interconnection with the personal computer (Figure 1.3). All devices and associated peripherals could be shared across a single cabling scheme. At first, LANs were usually confined to the scientific and engineering communities, but it did not take long for networks to spread to the commercial community.

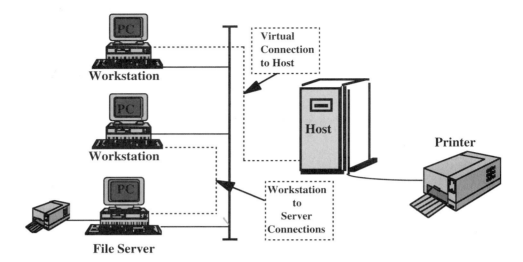

Figure 1.3 A local area network.

The advantages of a LAN were so great that they tended to overshadow the disadvantages. Not only did a network allow personal computers to work with each other, the mainframe or minicomputer was now integrated with the personal computer without the use of a terminal cable. Lower cable costs, ease of transition, and reduced maintenance costs easily led to larger networks. The new connectivity allowed myriad of applications such as electronic mail, word processing, database management, messaging, shared file and printer access, lower cable and printer costs, simplified software updates, personal graphics, locally controlled security, mainframe access, and single-cable plant operation.

The disadvantages were equally complemented by advantages. For example, a new cabling was employed for LANs, and this new cable had to be run throughout the building. The initial cable costs were high, but once this cable was installed, a company seldom has to run any more cable. This new cable, coupled with LAN hardware and software, could handle any type of device (at the time). The only other cable costs are the short cable runs for the terminals to attach to the network device or the personal computer LAN cable to the network cable. On small and medium-sized networks, these cables can be installed by the individual users themselves, cutting down the cost of installation and maintenance.

Late 1980s (WANs)

Throughout the 1980s, LANs grew dramatically. LANs were no longer used solely to provide host-to-terminal connectivity but to implement distributed processing as well. This elevated networking to a new level—that of the peer-to-peer computing. These concepts proved as popular as they were powerful. Soon the number of installed LANs grew into

Figure 1.4 Downsizing.

millions. They grew large enough that organizations again had to start thinking in new directions, looking for a better way to interconnect LANs, both within a building or campus or over a wide area.

To address these concerns, the vendors came up with interconnect devices that were functionally similar to the front-end processors (FEPs) that LANs replaced. Originally, bridges were used to connect local area segments, improving LAN performance. Later, like routers and gateways, the bridges became part of the internetwork between local and wide area networks. On one side, they provided LAN connections, and on the other side they provided connections to the WAN by way of T1 or other digital lines. In essence, a unique networking fabric was created using new types of internetworking devices—mostly bridges and routers—that could build large and complex internets for both local distribution and wide area connections.

Standardization of internetworking protocols (architectures) was now taking shape. The ISO reference model (a.k.a. the OSI model) was now defined. However, in the meantime, the TCP/IP suite achieved widespread deployment. The computer vendors continued to offer their proprietary networks, gradually supporting the new X.25 service as links under their own protocols—thus the WANs started to become popular means to interconnect LANs with other LANs over a wide area.

1990s (Internetworking LANs and WANs)

The 1990s are turning out to be an era of complex internetworks, a mismatch of media as well as protocol technologies, the need to integrate these technologies into global networks, and to manage these networks effectively and efficiently. What creates this need is the mismatch of LAN-WAN technology and the complexity it creates. LANs—connectionless services—that carry traffic in frames, are appreciated for their bandwidth-on-demand capabilities as well as their high speed. WANs, on the other hand, provide, in large part, connection-oriented services but at very low speeds.

To handle traffic, the WAN opens a circuit—usually a point-to-point line like the telephone—and sends the data over it. Even though the WAN establishes a circuit that can be used for data transmission, the WAN contains no inherent routing capabilities. The data that must be sent to multiple destinations travel to each different destination by way of a different circuit. Consequently, the routing or switching function resides in the bridges and routers that connect the LAN to the WAN. This is the source of the problem in scalability and complexity that are inherent in today's WANs.

Because the switching function of today's WANs is in the bridges and routers, WAN routing must be carefully managed. Most businesses use LANs to support office functions and business-specific applications. Whatever the justification for linking dissimilar networks, it is becoming more popular and so are the devices that are designed to do the job. The connection of neighboring LANs spans to widely dispersed workgroups and finally the entire enterprise, creating a *complex internetwork*.

Initially, these internetworks were arranged in tiers (Figure 1.5), using topology that involved cascading bridges. But this imposed severe performance penalties because the

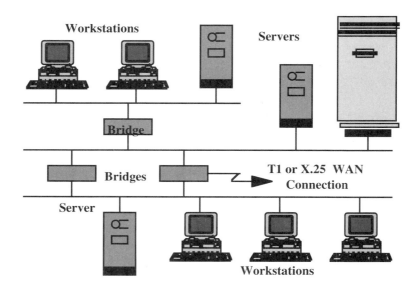

Figure 1.5 An internetwork.

arrangement forced too much traffic to traverse several bridges. The following traffic trends can now be observed:

- The percentage of the data traffic representing LAN interconnection is growing exponentially.
- Increasingly, the intersite traffic is being transmitted to speeds greater than 19.2 Kb /sec.
- Corporate networking requirements are changing from supporting a centralized mainframe with a large population of "dumb" teleprocessing terminals to interconnecting many dispersed LANs supporting PCs.
- Major interconnection services and technologies, such as frame relay, switched multimegabit data services (SMDS), fiber distributed digital interface, 100Mb/sec Ethernet, and T1, T3, are forcing vendors, enterprises, and users to take a new look for building internetworks.
- The need to build and manage hybrid internetworks (Figure 1.6).
- Outsourcing management and control of the data processing and data communication functions to a third party, for minimizing user's investment and reducing financial risks, and for protecting against technological obsolescence.
- Decentralization over wider geographic areas to capture less expensive work forces, relying on increased automation, data communications, and overall more efficient exploitation of the corporate data to reduce costs.
- Downsizing to become more competitive in the global market.

Consistent with the preceding discussions, the contemporary corporate networking environments may be grouped as follows:

- Integrated corporate voice/data network.
- Data network with centralized database accessed over a dedicated backbone; a fraction of remote LANs share peripherals (mostly printers). Voice has migrated to the public network.
- Data network with distributed data processing using dedicated backbone. A high degree of LAN-LAN traffic is present—atypical of today's enterprise networking.
- Hybrid private/public networks with support for voice, video, and graphics.

1990s (The Client/Server Revolution)

The 1980s, with the accompanying explosion of computer and communications technologies, saw similar focus directed at

- Software engineering—an outgrowth of structured techniques.
- Departmental computing—basically taking minicomputers whose predecessors had been around for years, and putting organizational business applications on them instead of just engineering or scientific functions; the minicomputers were often accompanied by personal computers and LANs.

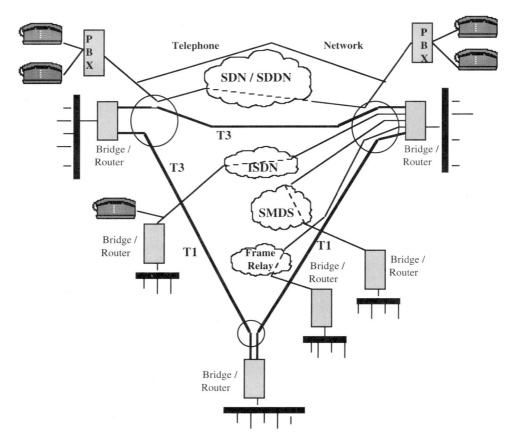

Figure 1.6 A hybrid network.

- Downsizing—in terms of equipment and staff.
- Others such as object-oriented technologies.

As prevalent as "open systems" and "enterprise computing" have become in terms of corporate strategies, most IS professionals would agree that the undisputed champion is the buzzword *client/server computing*. It is difficult to find a product—hardware, systems software, application software, peripheral, communications, or any other—that does not claim support for, implementation of, or other goodness related to client/server computing.

The term *client/server* has multiple meanings and is sometimes used interchangeably with the term *distributed processing*. One definition of client/server computing involves client computers (capable of processing data and running applications) relying on a server computer for shared data and peripherals. In these environments, the server machines are generally powerful PCs set aside to perform the task of a server. Therefore, the personal computer revolution of the 1980s brought the realization of client/server computing.

The architectural basis of client/server computing is consistent across a variety of communicating platforms, whether it be a local area network, a wide area network, shared memory, named pipes, or some other form. In this manner, the same client/server applications revolutionized the concept from single-machine to enterprisewide scenarios.

The *server* provides logically centralized services to one or many *clients* either in the same physical machine or remotely connected in a LAN or a WAN environment. Just as enterprise computing encompasses numerous underlying technologies, client/server computing is based on the following aspects, as a result of the growth of the personal computers:

* Desktop systems (personal computers and workstations).
* Local area networks.
* Wide area networks.
* Communications interoperability.
* Graphical user interface (GUI).
* Database management systems (DBMSs).

Most client/server implementations are based on LAN technologies. The ability to connect numerous desktop systems not only with one another but also with other midrange or mainframe systems has brought a new focus to the typical MIS department. Traditionally, as we discussed earlier, management information systems (MIS) has been *data center oriented* in a centralized fashion. The advent of client/server computing has created a *user-centered* environment in which users *demand* increased flexibility in their hardware and software components. The required flexibility, however, has increased the need for connectivity and cooperability, which is usually done over a LAN environment. Therefore, without the advent of LAN, client/server computing would not have caused such a stir. LAN operating systems typically include support for fundamental client/server operations such as making connections and managing the protocols.

One of the first areas in client/server computing that saw growth in the 1990s was database management. Another most important aspect of client/server is the *user interfaces*. The user interfaces are derived from two aspects: the proliferation of graphical paradigm (GUIs) and portability.

The technical results of personal computer technology are obvious: graphical user interface for ease of use, virtually unlimited access to computer power on individual desks, and a new way of thinking about computers and the applications that run on them. Now the computers are defined by the ways in which they are used, and the client/server concept has opened up a world of new computer users.

Client/server concept is primarily about the server (Figure 1.7):

* Distribution of data.
* Distribution of processing.
* Graphical user interface.

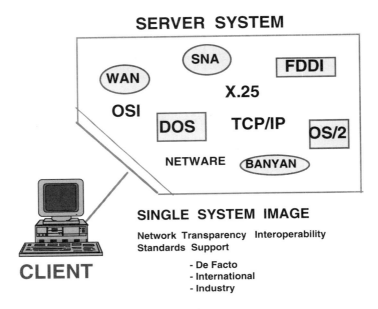

Figure 1.7 The server.

The *server* allows data to be distributed across many computers and other servers so that self-managed terms and empowered employees can perform tasks. The server also allows processing to be distributed out to the teams so that they can customize applications to meet their particular needs. On the other hand, the *client* serves an important function by providing graphical user interface. Since the client/server has brought the computer resources to the desktop, the users as well as programmers have become more productive and efficient. However, the network management is getting more and more complex since the administrators now must manage hundreds of clients and servers. Figure 1.8 shows four different quadrants, depicting the evolution of computing that has led to the concepts of enterprise client/server computing.

Today's corporations comprise specialized workgroups, and a variety of networks may be in place to meet their differing needs. The interoperability of these workgroups is often limited by proprietary computer communication architectures that favor different types of LANs (Figure 1.8).

Another use of the term client/server that may confuse the issue is client/server database applications. These applications are housed and processed at the server, while the client machines only send queries to the server through an interface program. In a client/server database scenario the server processes the query using a central application. This would be central processing, wouldn't it? You may hear the term SQL database (Structured Query Language) used to name a version of this type of database. But the important distinction is where the processing occurs.

CLIENT / SERVER COMPUTING

Requirements:

- **Personal Productivity**
- **Workgroup Productivity**
- **Organizational Efficiency**
- **Enterprise wide Efficiency**

Usage:

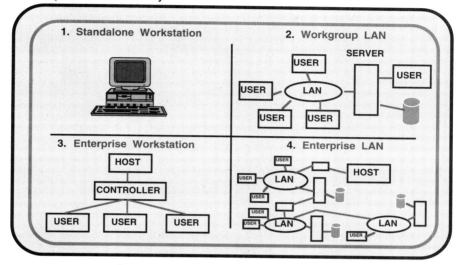

Figure 1.8 Client/server computing.

TECHNOLOGY TRENDS

The new era in information management will focus on connectivity, with increasing emphasis on making sure that the hardware and software resources work, but work together as a unified whole.

To meet the needs of the new *internetworking environments*, many vendors have introduced an array of new services, including ISDN (integrated services digital network), high-speed switched technologies, frame relay, and SMDS. To support the enterprise requirements, in the short run, communication architectures in general, and backbones in particular, must include

- High-bandwidth switching.
- Low network delay.
- Efficient transmission of bursty data.
- Integrated digital data–voice support.
- Support of LANs over multiplexed access.
- Ability to achieve real-time alternate routing.

- Support of mobile and work-at-home users.
- Compatibility among vendors and carriers offerings.
- Comprehensive troubleshooting techniques and devices.
- Comprehensive network management and control.
- Ability to support full-motion video, imaging, and multimedia.
- Support of interenterprise communication.

The industry is responding to the trends of downsizing computer operations. This has increased the importance of LANs, WANs, internetworking, faster and reliable media speeds, and issues related to telecommunications. The processing power of PCs and intelligent workstations is increasing, and complex graphics, full-motion video, teleconferencing, and CAD/CAM–based applications are becoming common usage for network facilities. While long-haul service providers (T1, T3, SMDS, etc.) are trying to consolidate their positions by offering LAN interface and interconnectivity equipment, the industry is still trying to settle issues relating to certification and acceptance.

Many vendors are building (and, in fact, integrating) some levels of standards compliance into their product offerings.

Bridges, routers, and hubs continue to dominate the LAN industry. As the internetworking market continues to gain momentum, the technology behind the products continues to evolve. Multiprotocol support, more and faster WAN interfaces, and the integration of internetworking capabilities in intelligent wiring hubs continue to dominate research community's attention.

TCP/IP is currently the dominant protocol for LANs, while OSI continues to lag in products and user interest. However, today's routers and bridges/routers must support a variety of protocols that include not only TCP/IP and OSI but also IBM's SNA, DEC's DECnet, Novell's IPX/SPX, and Apple's AppleTalk.

Thus in the late 1990s, organizations are dramatically expanding the team concept. No longer satisfied with effective 10- or even 20-person teams, they are out to incorporate everybody, even people outside the enterprise, therefore, a need for internetworking the global landscape. Network management professionals will be the key players in IS departments of the late 1990s.

By rightsizing information systems to client/server–based platforms, corporate engineers at both small and large companies will dramatically improve access to information, increase productivity, and most importantly, gain strategic advantage.

ORGANIZATION OF THIS TEXT

Broadly speaking, this book is organized into four major sections: basics, technologies, internetworking solutions, and network analysis and management. To increase awareness of the covered subjects, a set of review exercises is provided at the conclusion of each chapter.

- *Basics:* Part 1 lays the foundation for internetworking, at a very high level, starting with a discussion of the objectives and the computer revolution, leading to future technology trends. The chapters in this part discuss the history of computer technologies and internetworking basics.

- *Technologies:* Part 2 analyzes the many issues that face the network managers, discusses the existing standards and protocols that have invaded the internetworking arena, explores the network technologies that are the building blocks of a network, defines the many protocols that are required to design and operate a network, and identifies the many internetworking tools required for interconnecting disparate/dissimilar networks into viable enterprise internetworks.

- *Internetworking solutions:* Part 3 builds upon the technologies discussed in previous chapters by the many applications that are required in an effective global network, explores the connectivity and topologies of various vendor specific offerings, and finally the solutions to integrate these disparate protocols and services with emphasis on
  - Integration of the PCs into the enterprise networks.
  - Integration of UNIX with different operating systems, such as DOS, Windows, OS/2, and Novell NetWare.
  - Integration of UNIX with X-Windows.
  - Internetworking with Mac.
  - Mainframe UNIX interoperability.
  - Integration with legacy systems.

- *Network analysis and management:* Part 4 focuses on analysis and tools for troubleshooting internetworks and management of these networks with practical examples.

The book concludes with a summary of the technologies, implementations, problems, and strategies, followed by comprehensive appendixes as follows:

- Appendix 1: Technical notes, in detail, for quick review of some of the major technologies utilized in internetworking.
- Appendix 2: Answers to exercises chapter by chapter.
- Appendix 3: A comprehensive glossary of terms used as well as commonly encountered in an internetworking environment.
- Bibliography and index for references.

SUMMARY

The development of the computer, like other calculating devices, spanned most of the twentieth century. During the 1960s and 1970s, the computer technology grew by leaps and bounds, leading the way toward their almost universal application in major enterprises today.

In the 1980s, LAN became the buzzword of every programmer and enterprise. Local area networking permits information and peripherals to be shared efficiently and economically. That is what networking is all about—*sharing*. Centralized computing used to be the thing for the MIS departments. Networking and network theory are slowly abolishing this philosophy.

Centralized computing is on the decline, but that *does not mean* that mainframes are also on the decline. Mainframes and LANs coexist peacefully. The original method or purpose of the mainframe is not replaced, only the method of connectivity has been replaced. A terminal was connected to the mainframe and applications were run on the mainframe, with input-output data being displayed on the user's terminal.

With LANs and personal computers, the interface connection between the user and the host was replaced. Users still access the mainframe and are able to run the same applications as if they were directly connected to the mainframe with a terminal. Networks simply replace the terminal cable. But LANs offer much more than the simple terminal-host access. Networks, personal computers, and the software that runs them operate efficiently and are cost effective. The user will have the best of both worlds by integrating the centralized computer system with the network computing system.

In the 1990s, integrated environments have developed. The corporate mainframes still exist, but they are complemented by LANs. The mainframe, in many circumstances, is taking a different role, the role of a file server or database server or a compute server or simply a repository of data needed by the LAN. Some corporations are replacing their mainframes with a LAN (a process known as *downsizing*). LANs are seen as having tremendous power rivaling that of a mainframe, being perceived as more flexible and much less expensive.

In the late 1990s, there are numerous options available, making choices for the corporate network planner more challenging. The availability of many varieties of services can be disadvantageous to the user who is willing to use multiple technologies to optimize various options of the network. This approach can result in more cost-effective transmission and optimized response time. The downside of this approach is the need for the enterprise to acquire expertise in many new technologies, deal with many network and equipment vendors, and literally stalk the unstoppable wave of technological progress, which now appears to have a life cycle of fewer than two years.

Networks are being developed both to connect existing machines and to take advantage of the low-cost, high-performance microprocessors the semiconductor industry is churning out. Most wide area networks have a collection of hosts communicating via subnets. The subnets may utilize multiple point-to-point lines or a single broadcast channel or a satellite. The local area networks connect the hosts directly with a coaxial or fiber optic or twisted pair cables or even other subnets in a wide area network (*internetworked*). But the networks as well as the internetworking solutions are always designed as a series of protocol layers, with each layer responsible for some aspect of the network's operation.

You, as an internetwork user, may find yourself traversing uncharted waters with testing just announced equipment, just announced network services, integrating network management for new services into the existing network management system, and exploring perhaps new, unconventional and untested migration paths.

On the other hand, you may prefer to choose a more conservative approach. You may select a single technology across the corporate network, realizing that it may not be totally optimal for every facet of that network. Such an approach has the advantage of minimizing the required level of multi-technology expertise, allowing equipment and unit integration and paced migration paths. By not selecting the latest technology, you allow the other corporations to work out bugs, pitfalls, and downsides of the new technologies.

EXERCISES

1. Before the 1980s, which of the following might have been a primary computing resource for a typical company?
   a. Dumb terminal
   b. A personal computer
   c. An IBM mainframe
   d. A cluster controller
   e. A front-end processor
2. The trend toward decentralization has meant?
   a. Use of many different devices
   b. Few users access the host
   c. Computing power has been widespread to different locations
3. Which of the following are benefits of the personal computer?
   a. Independent computing
   b. Terminal emulation
   c. Downloading host files
4. What is an internetwork?
5. What is a hybrid internetwork?
6. Describe major features of the components of a client/server system.

2

INTERNETWORKING BASIC CONCEPTS

Introduction
Connectivity Issues
Connectivity Goals
Critical Success Factors
Environments
Hardware Platforms
Operating Systems
Clients and Servers
Communication Protocols
Media
Networks
Network Operating Systems

Prevalent Networks
Departmental/Workgroup Networks
Campus Networks
Metropolitan Networks
Enterprise Networks
Hybrid Networks
Global Networks
Role of Standards
De Jure Standards
De Facto Standards
Summary
Exercises

INTRODUCTION

The internetwork is the infrastructure between multiple computer systems. It provides a stable platform for the enterprise to access critical data across all systems. Local area networks (LANs) are data communications that enable a number of independent pieces of equipment to collaborate by intercommunication at high rates of data transmission over a relatively limited geographic area. Wide area networks (WANs) allow widely separated local area networks and computers to be interconnected via public or private networks, on a global scale. Usually WANs operate at slower speeds than LANs.

We have discovered that a number of different network and communications technologies are important to enterprise network computing. Wide area networks, local area networks, layered protocols, routers, gateways, bridges, and standards are some of the technologies that comprise a knowledge base for internetworking. In today's environment, without networks and communications facilities, enterprise computing would not be possible. Therefore, the robustness of the communications facilities throughout all corners of the enterprise bears a direct relationship to the ability to create an enterprise computing environment.

In this section, we will discuss, at a high level, some of the fundamental technologies, processes, devices, and protocols that are critical building blocks of *an enterprise internetwork.*

Connectivity Issues

Networking solutions in use today were generally not selected for their ability to be internetworked. In many cases, there was no mandate to preserve every system or data compatibility among workgroups or discrete systems. As a result, there is no homogeneity base for internetworks. There is no single internetworking strategy which will suit all enterprises. However, we do know that there are many hardware platforms and their operating systems, communications architectures, networking protocols, and even transmission media. These disparities not only create a dilemma for selection alternatives, but also create connectivity and an interoperability nightmare.

Bringing together multiple architectures can be complicated. Many intervendor standards are emerging who have not extensively tried or tested the interoperability. An application that spans multiple vendor platforms may lead to vendors pointing toward each other as the source of the problem.

The enterprise may need to spend more time and effort whether a product is compatible with the existing network or even fits in it at all. Unfortunately, only a few mature internetworking tools and applications are available to run on multiple platforms in a multivendor cooperative processing environment.

To understand the intricacies of internetworking and make a viable internetwork, an enterprise must address at least the following issues:

- Multivendor and multiplatform coexistence.
- Interconnecting architectures and protocols.
- Transmission media and emerging technologies.
- Local and remote internetworking.
- Internetworking management.

Connectivity Goals

A computer network is the connection of independent computers for the purpose of exchanging data. The goal of network protocols is to hide the technological differences between networks, making internetworking independent of the underlying hardware and operating systems. A network should encompass one or more of the following areas of activity:

- *Data sharing* by providing access to spatially separated data items.

- *Load sharing* by allowing relief of currently overloaded computers by transfer of tasks to other lightly loaded computers.
- *Performance sharing* by connecting several computers for processing of complex problems (application distribution or client/server processing) as an expansion of the multiprocessor principle.
- *Availability sharing* by increasing the reliability of the computer system.
- *Peripheral sharing* also allows these companies to spread the cost of expensive peripherals, such as printers, modem pools, optical storage, and so on, over a wider area.

Critical Success Factors

Each generation of hardware and software improves our ability to apply information technology to a modern corporations' goals and objectives. These include

- Protocols.
- Hardware and operating systems.
- Networks.

Protocols provide a framework for developing applications and ensuring that they communicate with each other promptly and efficiently. Commonly employed protocols include SNA, DECnet, TCP/IP, OSI, NetWare, and AppleTalk.

The constant move toward more powerful, low-cost *hardware* has been and will continue to be the driving force behind distributed systems. The increased power of microprocessor-based workstations has also made it possible to manage the overhead required by network computing and cooperative processing.

By contrast, the *operating systems* have remained remarkably similar. Many widespread operating systems such as MVS, UNIX, and MS-DOS have been in existence for 10 or more years. Unlike hardware, they do not seem to be swept aside by a newer, better model every few years. Currently, the big question about operating systems is whether UNIX or OS/2 or MS-DOS or NetWare is the best or even which vendor's version is the best. Further yet, the debate is still ensuing for server operating systems, whether NetWare or NT Advanced Server or OS/2 or UNIX are suited for the type of applications (file/print or database or e-mail or communication server or notes, etc.) the enterprise needs to pursue.

For internetworking, it is questionable whether UNIX or OS/2 is optimal, really matters? As hardware continues to cost less, financial decisions could become more sensitive to price instead of features. As common user interfaces spread and workgroup computing makes interoperability more important, it should not matter as much which operating system controls the hardware. Instead, focus shifts to managing the complex network that ties computers together.

The two basic types of *networks*, which are the building blocks of any internetwork are local area network and the wide area network. LANs provide communication and data transfer among a local workgroup members, while WANs basically connect LANs enterprisewide. LANs and WANs play a part in facilitating cooperative processing, transferring mail, client/server database applications, and resource sharing. Here, too, the debate is which protocol or standard is suitable for e-mail, database, or even remote application execution.

Enterprise computing is an ongoing process and the internetworking is still evolving. To make it a viable enterprisewide phenomenon, some of the following steps may be followed:

- *Identify* enabling hardware/software/networking technologies.
- *Reengineer* existing business processes.
- *Choose* an architecture and stick to it.

ENVIRONMENTS

Hardware Platforms

The computing environment has traditionally been categorized by the computer system being used. The three initial environments were *mainframe, minicomputer,* and *microcomputer*. That viewpoint is now fading as it becomes more and more apparent that integrating various types of computer systems can help meet those needs. In the 1990s, integrated environments are developing. The corporate mainframe still exists, but it is complemented by a LAN. The mainframe may at times take on a different role; for example, it could be a part of the LAN by functioning as a repository of data needed by the LAN. Some enterprises are actually replacing their mainframes or minicomputers with a LAN. LANs are now seen as having tremendous power rivaling that of a mainframe, as more flexible and less expensive alternatives.

Mainframes. The mainframe, the oldest of the computing environments, has traditionally been the workhorse that performed all the data processing for a group or a corporation. The first true business mainframe was IBM 360 and was considered the most sophisticated computer in its time (1960s). It was also the computer capable of both scientific and business computing. This was later followed by an IBM 370.

The Systems 360 and 370 were pioneers in data processing and have gone through numerous upgrades and improvements. The 43xx series became the most popular followed by 3080 and 3090 series. The System 3080 is still widely used and is based on the 360 architecture, while the 3090 is based on the 370 architecture.

These mainframes were installed in their own air-conditioned rooms, ensuring a constant environment and preventing overheating (the same problem with some modern microcomputers).

The disk drives—commonly known as *direct access storage devices* (DASDs)—are quite large and have enormous storage capacity. The capacity and reliability of the DASD is still an attraction for the new brand of PC or PC-LAN users to exploit the mainframe as a file server or a repository.

With the latest model 3090 operating under MVS/ESA operating system, more than 1000 nodes can connect to a computer system. A network is established to allow the central processing unit (CPU) to accommodate that many nodes. However, these nodes are *dumb terminals* or PCs emulating dumb terminals. A dumb terminal is essentially an input and display device, with all the processing being handled by the mainframe CPU.

In addition to CPUs and DASDs, other devices, such as front-end-processors, 3274 controllers, modems, multiplexers, and so on, must be used to create a mainframe network. Designing, implementing, and maintaining such a network is extremely complex.

COBOL was the programming language most commonly used on mainframes. The mainframe's original mode of operation was batch processing, in which the program executed using the appropriate data files with no intervention by the user or operator. Interactive programming was needed when a user wanted to inquire about a certain part. COBOL was not up to this task, and the utilities provided by the operating system did not support the generation of screens and other tasks needed for interactive sessions. This brought about the use of a customer information control system (CICS), a system that allows interactive screens with COBOL programs. While CICS and COBOL are still a strong combination today, more and more mainframes are using fourth-generation languages.

It is suffice to say that the PC LANs generally operate very differently from traditional mainframe terminal connections.

Minicomputers.   It is often difficult to say what makes up a mainframe system and what makes up a minicomputer system because they share many of the same features and functions. It is hoped that the major distinguishing feature is the cost.

The technology of IBM minicomputer started with System 34. Many other such computers were introduced by IBM, Digital Equipment Corporation, Data General Corporation, Xerox Data Systems, and a host of others. As an example, System 34 and System 36 used an operating system known as System Support Program (SSP). COBOL and RPG II were the primary programming languages supported.

These minicomputers did not have the power of the mainframe. They functioned as departmental computers in many large corporations and formed the central data processing systems of smaller corporations. One of the primary advantages of the minicomputer was the ease of interactive programming and ease of use, maintenance, and implementation. Like a mainframe, the minicomputer used dumb terminals or PCs that emulated dumb terminals.

Microcomputers and Workstations.   The PC entered the scene in early 1980s and changed the way we did computing.

Workstations are part of a team of computing resources probably destined to support many of the applications of the future. Workstation computing is a name given to the practice of supporting workers with local processing and storage resources built on a computer platform with a high-performance graphics subsystem capable of rendering application-generated graphics and supporting a sophisticated graphical user interface (GUI). The system should also have a multitasking operating system with software support for such an interface.

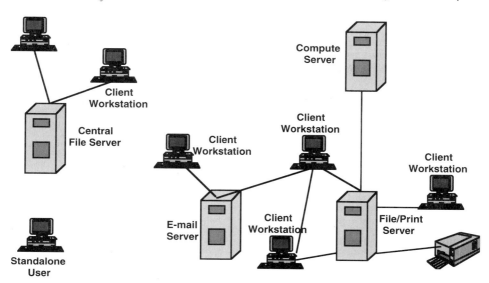

Figure 2.1 Workstation/server roles.

Because distributed computing, networking is so important today, and the value of the workstation in large part depends on its flexibility in playing the various computing roles defined within both business and technical/research environments. Figure 2.1 displays a network in which the most significant of those roles are illustrated.

These are the personal computers like the IBM AT, XT, PS/2, Apple Macintosh, or engineering workstations from SUN Microsystems, but with varying degrees of capabilities (CPU speeds, storage, networking capabilities, etc.). All the computations, calculations, and actual execution of application programs take place at the workstation, which may, for example, receive requests from clients and data from a file server.

Operating Systems

The operating system is software that controls execution of programs in a computer or a computer system. An operating system may provide services such as resource allocation, scheduling, input/output control, and data management. Many operating systems are being utilized since the 1980s, and there are new ones coming on the horizon, such as Windows NT or Advanced NT Server or newer NetWare versions.

Clients and Servers

Client/server computing is the most prevalent in today's environment. On any LAN, there are always two entities: *the client* (the source station, the station that makes requests) and *the server* (the destination station, the station that responds to those requests), as shown in

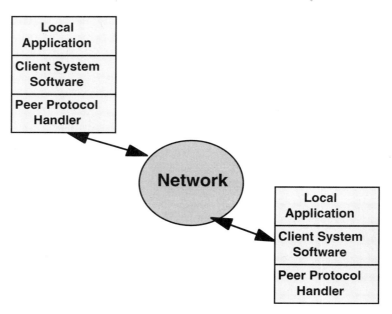

Figure 2.2 Client/server system relationship.

Figure 2.2. This concept originated in the design of operating systems and was implemented with the experimental Ethernet in 1973. In the 1980s, the concept was enhanced again with the introduction of the personal computers and file servers.

Before LANs, terminals were directly connected to the minicomputer or mainframe and all commands were processed directly between the terminal and its host processor. Since the computer hardware was moved from a *centralized* location, the computer room, out to where the users were located, a design was needed to allow centralized computing on a decentralized scale. The problem arose, how do you allow the commands—which were once centralized and that integrated the user with the mainframe—out to the desktop? That need created the concepts of client/server computing as we know it today.

The functions of client/server computing are the same today as they were in 1973. The client makes the request and the server responds to the request. A server may also be a client since it can also make requests to other servers, including to the client (which will act as a server in that context). Client/server computing also allows to share peripherals like hard drives and printers. We also term this arrangement as peer to peer (Figure 2.3).

First-Generation Client/Server Model. When LANs were first conceived, most hosts were directly connected to terminals. Few hosts had the capacity for direct connection to a LAN, but this is done through a device known as a terminal server. The client, a terminal server with a terminal attached to it, makes a request of the server, usually another terminal server attached to a host. A request would be initiated from the client to the terminal server to establish a connection. Once the connection was established, data would flow

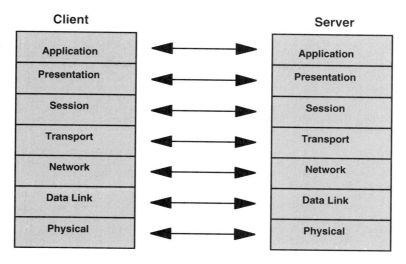

Figure 2.3 Client/server peer to peer model.

on the session that was set up, and the server would respond to the requests via its terminal server. This was a simple client/server relationship.

Second-Generation Client/Server Model. The 1980s brought personal computer on the scene and the client/server relationship expanded. Since the personal computer had more intelligence, the client needs became more complex. The applications that originally ran on a personal computer were now stored on a server PC station, called a file server, located somewhere on the network. This file server would service user requests, usually file or print, from remote PCs.

A user will still initiate a connection, but this time it was from the local PC to the file server PC on the network. The user will then request the application program from the server to be downloaded to the client PC and run it locally just as if the application were stored on the local PC. The user could also save data on the server's disk drive. The file servers may also contain the software to allow the direct attachment of a printer. Using print queues, multiple users could redirect their local printer ports to the file server and print their data on the file server's printer.

The file server could accept multiple connections from any stations that were on the network. The same application software program could be executed from these remote stations. The result would be one copy of software on the server PC and many users requiring access to it. This is how most PC LAN operating systems work today.

Third-Generation Client/Server Model. Today, with database engines becoming as powerful as those on the mini or mainframe computers, the client/server model has expanded again to allow applications not to be downloaded to the PC but to be distributed between the client and the server. This means that part of the application runs on the server and the other part on the client PC.

The best example of this type of computing is an application known as SQL server from Microsoft. The SQL server is run on the file server and is known as the *back end*. A client starts an application program on a PC. The application program can initiate SQL commands that would be transmitted on the network requesting data records from the server. In this case, the whole database file is *not* downloaded to the client PC. The client PC simply makes a request for whatever record or records are currently needed. This concept of distributed computing allows multiple client stations on the network to request the same records from the same file on the server.

All three methods/models are still practiced and can work on the same LAN. Just as enterprise computing encompasses numerous underlying technologies, client/server computing is based on the following hardware and software aspects:

- Desktop systems (personal computers and workstations).
- Local area networks.
- Wide area networks.
- Communications interoperability.
- Database management systems.

Most client/server implementations are based on LAN technologies. The ability to connect numerous desktop systems not only with one another but also with midrange and even mainframe systems has brought a new focus to the typical IS environment. Traditionally, IS has been "data center oriented" in that the primary decisions about technologies were made in a centralized fashion (Figure 2.4).

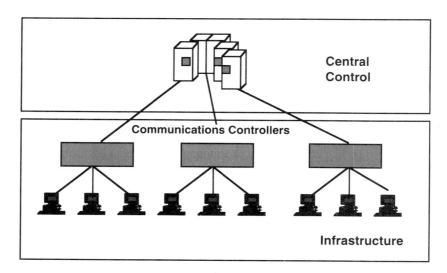

Figure 2.4 (Traditional) enterprise network model.

The advent of the client/server computing created a "user-centered" or "network centric" environment (Figure 2.5) in which users demand increased flexibility in their hardware and software components. The required flexibility, however, has increased the need for connectivity and cooperability, and this is usually started over a LAN environment. LAN operating systems typically include support for fundamental client/server operations, such as making a connection and managing lower-level protocols.

Among the many types of *dedicated servers* that these configurations include are fax, print, file, disk, backup/archive, compute, database, notes, e-mail, communication, terminal, and many other application servers.

- *Disk servers* make it appear as though disks are locally attached to a user system, but they are actually shared devices on a server. The benefit is higher-speed, higher-capacity disks that offer better performance at a lower overall cost than multiple local disks.
- *File servers* also have hard disks but offer more functionality than a disk server and could include other types of storage media and services. The file server has more knowledge about the data format, so files can be stored on a common server and, in some instances, shared among different types of computer systems. In addition, file servers can provide back up, archival, and disaster recovery for critical data.
- *Database servers* store data that can be specified and retrieved. The client application can manipulate the data and store the results back in the database. The database servers allow an enterprise to share the same data and apply activity. In addition, application processing can be performed by the database server.

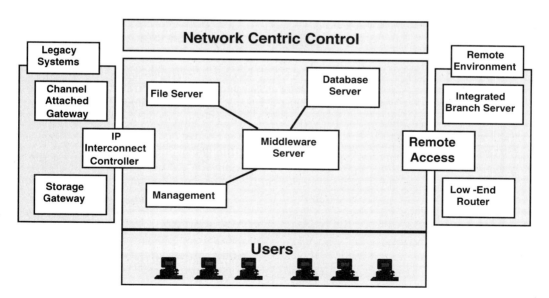

Figure 2.5 Network centric enterprise network model.

- *Application servers* are simply more manageable on a centralized server, and still, other applications could benefit from being broken into segments, with each segment run on a different server. It is also possible to dedicate a server to a single application. A Hyper Text Transfer Protocol (HTTP) server for the World Wide Web, a notes server for internal record keeping, or a File Transfer Protocol (FTP) site are some of the application server examples.

- *Communication servers* act as the interface between the client and various types of networks. Communication servers manage communication between the outside world and the inside LAN or WAN, such as Novell's Netware Connect product for model pooling or Microsoft's RAS server that allows users to connect from remote sites to the network. Users do not have to know the details of how to network because the server takes care of the translations (e.g., LAN to WAN). Communication servers vary by the types of LANs supported (Ethernet, ARCnet, or token ring), the types of transport protocols supported (XNS, Novell's IPX, or TCP/IP), their support for third-party terminal emulators, and the number of ports supported.

- *Terminal servers* enable terminals to be logically connected to any computer on the network, regardless of whether it is located on a LAN or a WAN.

- *Print servers* make high-quality, high-speed, and relatively expensive printers available to everyone on the network.

Communication Protocols

A communication protocol may be defined as a *public, formal specification of rules and guidelines in which two or more components of an information system communicate to accomplish a goal.* There are some characteristics applicable to most communications protocols. First, the protocol must encompass the exchange of both data and control information. Second, multiple layers of protocols are typically present in any substantial information system environment, particularly those that can be considered as enterprises.

Based on the preceding discussion, it may appear that a communication protocol must perform a great many functions. This required functionality is magnified when a network becomes more sophisticated than two nodes communicating with one another in a point-to-point manner. The typical internetworking computing environment contains multiple wide area and local area networks communicating with one another, routing messages to other destinations, controlling devices, and other tasks.

Because of this real-world complexity, most protocols are formed in a *layered* fashion. IBM's System Network Architecture (SNA), Digital Equipment Corporation's DECnet, the U.S. Department of Defense protocol suite built around TCP/IP, and the OSI Reference Model all have multiple layers (typically seven). This layered model of protocols assigns certain roles to each layer, and information must be passed up and down the layers at any given site.

Figure 2.6 illustrates a simple layered protocol stack of three layers. The topmost level is used for application-to-application data sharing. The middle layer is used to route messages across logical networks. The lowest level is used to maintain link-level communications.

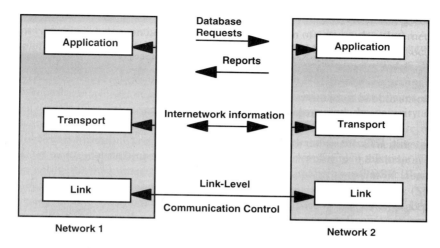

Figure 2.6 A simple layered protocol stack.

If the protocol rules and guidelines are the same in both systems, that is, they are both using the same architecture, the communication is much simpler and no conversions may be required. However, real-life protocols with multiple layers may perform different tasks at different levels, especially if the two systems have differing architectures, for example, SNA and DECnet. This is a reason that interprotocol communication tends to be difficult since there is no guarantee that the network-level protocol within DECnet and the network-level protocol within the SNA would perform the same task.

In the following sections we will study some of these protocols and their differences. We will also explore the means and strategies how to perform internetworking in spite of the differences in protocol definitions.

Media

To provide connectivity between two systems or networks, there has to be a physical link over which the signals can be transmitted between one another. This physical connection is the media over which the signals can travel back and forth. This media can be physical wiring, microwave, optical fiber, radio, or a satellite signal. As an introduction, we will briefly describe some of the physical media (cabling) commonly used to connect LANs and WANs in an internetwork. The cabling used in network transmissions falls into four categories:

- *Unshielded twisted-pair* cable *(UTP)* consists of two insulated, braided copper wires. This is the type of wiring used most commonly for telephone systems. UTP is used in most types of networks since it is inexpensive and easy to install and connect, and buildings are already wired for telephone. However, it is prone to electrical noise and interference, it has lower data transmission rates, and the distances between signal boosts are shorter.

- *Shielded twisted-pair* cable differs from UTP in that it uses a much higher-quality protective jacket for greater insulation. Thus it has longer signal transmission and is less prone to electrical interference from outside because of better protective covering. However, it is more expensive.

- *Coaxial* cable can carry data in excess of 350 Mbps. It has one central wire, and the main conductor is surrounded by an insulating material. Over this insulating material is a stranded shield. Coaxial cable can transmit voice, video, and data. It is usually easy to install. It can also run for longer distances than the twisted pair. But it is more expensive than the twisted pair cables.

- *Fiber optic* cable carries data in the form of modulated light beams. These are used for very-high-speed, high-capacity data communication, enabling data transfer rates exceeding 1 trillion bps. A network that exclusively uses fiber optic cables is known as fiber distributed data interface (FDDI). In addition to high transmission rates, the fiber optics are less sensitive to outside interference, carry data signals for longer distances, and provide better security since these cannot be tapped. However, the fiber optic cable is expensive and requires more skill to install and connect to devices.

Networks

Networks are created by connecting devices that perform data generation, storage, and processing functions. Networks comprise four major building blocks:

- *Nodes:* Devices connected to the network that need to communicate.
- *Topologies:* The physical connection and layout of the network that allows communication.
- *Protocols:* The rules and language used by the devices to communicate.
- *Data or information:* That which is being shared and used on the network.

Connecting Devices.   The major devices used in a network are

- *Terminals* provide the interface between people and the network. IBM 3270-family terminals, ASCII terminals, and personal computers emulating terminals are the most popular types of terminals. Most personal computers are ASCII devices and do not use IBM EBCDIC standards.
- *Protocol converters* are used to translate, for example, between terminal's ASCII coding to IBM's EBCDIC coding.
- *Modems* connect a terminal to a network using public telephone lines instead of being hard wired to a network or mainframe.

- *Physical interfaces* such as RS-232, V.35, and RS-449 are used to connect modems to clusters or communication controllers.

- *Communications controllers* improve performance of a host computer by handling communications functions of the hosts and terminals.

- *Cluster controllers* control a cluster of 8 to 32 terminals or printers. A cluster controller is connected to a host using a channel or can be linked to a communications controller.

- *Front-end processors (FEPS)* are placed between a host computer and other communications controllers or cluster controllers.

- *Concentrators* control a number of cluster controllers, terminals, and *remote job entry (RJE)* devices.

- *Digital switches* are occasionally used as a communications controller and have ports to provide data communication.

- *Multiplexers* combine the data traffic from communications controllers, digitized voice traffic from PBXs, and digitized video traffic from Codecs into high-bandwidth traffic such as 1.544 Mb/sec (DS-1) or 435 Mb/sec (DS-3). These DS-1 or DS-3 facilities are interconnected to provide a backbone network.

Figure 2.7 illustrates the functions of these devices in a hypothetical network of an airline based in Dallas. An FEP buffers the host at Dallas for communications between Chicago and other cities. A concentrator at Chicago combines traffic from the cluster controller in Chicago, the cluster controller in St. Louis, and the RJE devices in Chicago. By combining this traffic, higher-bandwidth circuits can be used between Dallas and Chicago, and this results in network efficiency for the company. The cluster controller in Chicago manages the terminals and printers at the airport gates, while the RJE device in Chicago office can print out checks and tickets in a batch mode. The cluster controller and RJE device are connected to the concentrator in Chicago using digital private line service, such as T1.

The airline has a small hub at St. Louis, and the terminals and printers at this hub are connected to a local cluster controller. The traffic from St. Louis is sent to the concentrator in Chicago via modems and public telephone lines.

As shown in Figure 2.7, the Dallas airport has its terminals and printers connected by a token ring LAN. This LAN is connected to the Dallas host via a gateway and a private data network. Since the gates at Dallas airport are connected using a LAN (bandwidth of 15 Mb/sec), customer service agents at the gates can communicate electronically among themselves and transfer files quickly. If a printer at one gate is down, it is easy for an agent to use the printer at another nearby gate. Such functions would take more time to perform in the cluster controller network at Chicago because the terminals there are connected to the cluster controller using low-bandwidth circuits (9600 bps). The FEP in Dallas and the concentrator in Chicago are connected via public or private line services.

Network Technologies. Local area networks connect devices located within a short distance of one another. LANs carry a significant amount of data traffic. During the last

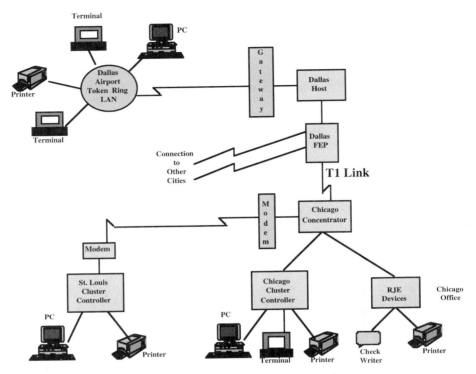

Figure 2.7 A typical small airline network.

decade, demand for LANs has grown tremendously. LANs are beginning to threaten the dominance of mainframe installations at companies because downsizing applications from the mainframes to smaller personal computers hold the promise of lower costs, better response time, more local control, and greater flexibility. A LAN requires use of one of the major LAN interface cards such as Ethernet, token ring, ARCnet, Starlan, and/or fiber distributed data interface in the terminals. Special equipment and software must be used to interconnect these terminals. Because of the expense, LANs, which can operate at speeds of 15 Mb/sec or higher, are typically owned by large organizations.

Wide area networks connect devices located at distant locations. WANs are leased from "common carriers" such as AT&T, MCI, or US Sprint, and customers can either use the public networks or leased circuit-switched or packet-switched networks. AT&T's ACCUNET Spectrum of Digital Services (fractional T1 services) offers intermediate transmission speeds of 9.6, 56, 128, 256, 384, 512, and 768 Kbs to customers. Popular circuit-switched circuits are digital data services (DDS, 56 Kb/sec), T1 (terrestrial 1.5

Mb/sec) service, and T3 (terrestrial 45 Mb/sec) service. T3 services are commonly used by customers to connect the headquarters location to the data center of large organizations. A customer must install special interface devices to connect with the "common carrier" at the originating and terminating locations. Customers typically use circuit-switched networks to integrate their data, voice, and video transmissions onto a single backbone network.

You can also lease packet-switched networks from companies such as Tymnet, Telenet, and AT&T. These networks use packet assemblers/dissemblers (PADs) to connect the customer's equipment to the network. The packet transfer can be performed by using virtual-circuit or datagram services. In a datagram, the route is determined at each intermediate node. In a virtual circuit, the route for a packet is fixed. Virtual circuits are more reliable, but they waste bandwidth.

The common carriers have agreements with other telephone companies around the globe and can help the multinational companies set up global networks. By using *global internetworking* effectively, a company can reduce the charges for data services drastically. For example, an end user on BITNET can send mail and files to other end users globally at an inexpensive rate.

Many end users still use a modem and voice lines for sending and receiving traffic to remote computers. Services such as Prodigy use this feature to let customers access geographically distributed databases by dialing a local phone number at a reasonable monthly rate.

Network Architectures/Protocols. There are many different architectures for connecting LANs and WANs. The major and most internetworked architectures are

* Systems Network Architecture (SNA).
* Transmission Control Protocol/Internet Protocol (TCP/IP).
* Architectures built on the framework of the OSI Model.
* Digital Network Architecture (DNA).

Many of these architectures are proprietary and require devices from that vendor or plug-compatible vendors to operate the network. Overviews of several of these LAN and WAN architectures are covered in this section.

Systems Network Architecture (SNA) is IBM's proprietary architecture for designing and implementing interconnected networks. Using SNA is complex and requires trained technical personnel. However, the advantage to end users is that if their network is SNA based and their terminals are SNA compatible, they can plug in their terminals and access distributed databases and information systems quickly. The SNA network is managed by using software named telecommunications access method (TCAM), residing on the main processor. There are a number of versions of this software, but the most popular today is the virtual telecommunications access method (VTAM).

A network control program (NCP) defines the topology of remote terminals to the telecommunications access method software. An application subsystem runs on the main processor and is used to execute specific user-defined applications, such as systems used in airline reservations, bank teller terminals, and supermarket checkout counters.

A single domain network can have as many as 255 subarea networks. In large networks, many domains are connected using to form a company's interconnected network. Each piece of equipment is assigned a unique address in each subarea, and these addresses are used for effective communication among the terminals and application subsystems. The data traffic generated by an application subsystem is converted to physical bits using protocols in seven layers (Figure 2.8) of the SNA. This allows data to be transported automatically with few errors and with high level of security.

When the originating node sends a message to the destination node, the layers add overhead to the actual data and send to the destination node using many gateway nodes. The overhead or header information in bottom three layers is stripped by gateway nodes and new ones are substituted. The destination node receives the actual and overhead data. It strips the overhead data to retrieve the actual data. The seven layers are designed in such a way that the equipment and software in the originating node, the gateways, and the destination node can be modified or changed without the end user being aware of these changes.

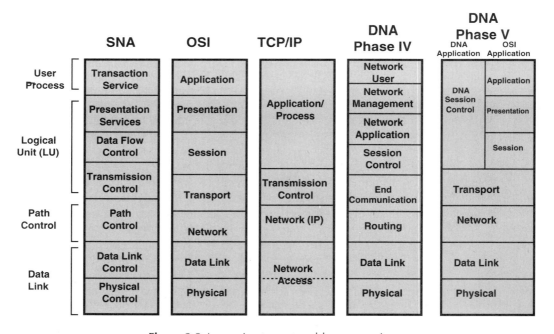

Figure 2.8 Approximate protocol layer mappings.

The seven layers of SNA are similar to OSI layers, although the details of the SNA protocols are proprietary. As shown in Figure 2.8, part of the transport and network layers of OSI generally match the path control layer of SNA.

Advanced peer-to-peer networking (APPN) is an enhancement to the basic SNA. APPN enables computers to communicate dynamically with each other as equals, without the centralized control currently required. With APPN, network directories can be built based on local names in subareas. Also, APPN end nodes can dynamically build local directories and obtain the optimum routing information.

Despite the proprietary nature of SNA, many large enterprises depend on SNA as their networking architecture. This strongly suggests that internetworking solutions will always require to support SNA architectures for long times to come. For that reason, Digital Equipment Corporation, Amdahl, NCR, Hewlett-Packard, Harris, Wang, Data General, and many other third-party vendors market equipment and software that interfaces with SNA.

Open systems interconnection (OSI) is a set of standard protocols proposed by the International Standards Organization (ISO) in 1977. Implementation of these standards is expected to provide better connectivity, transfer of data, and interoperability of networks. The OSI architecture has been accepted conceptually by most vendors and is eventually expected to provide open interfaces between different vendor's devices. However, because such open interfaces will make much of the current internetworking hardware and software obsolete, the new devices and software required to implement OSI are slow to materialize. Customers who use multiple vendors' networks are pushing the vendors to conform to the OSI architectures.

The OSI architecture uses seven hierarchically separate layers to communicate between two end users. Figure 2.8 shows the seven layers of OSI and compares these layers with other similar architectures. The application layer is the top layer and is used to generate data according to specific applications, such as electronic mail, airline reservations, or banking by phone. The six layers below the application layer are for sending the data to another host or workstation so that the message is retrieved without mistakes or errors. The hierarchical layers facilitate changes in protocols, hardware, or software at any layer without the other layers being affected. Thus, changes are confined to a single layer.

Transmission Control Protocol/Internet Protocol (TCP/IP) was developed in the 1970s by the Department of Defense's (DOD) Defense Advanced Research projects Agency (DARPA). These protocols help connect networks such as MILNET, NFSNET, CSNET, and BITNET.

TCP/IP is more flexible than SNA, since TCP/IP was designed to connect the diverse networks of multiple agencies, libraries, universities, defense agencies, and private corporations. Many businesses use TCP/IP protocols in their networks since OSI standards are slow to be implemented. Vendors are marketing networking products based on TCP/IP protocols. Digital Equipment Corporation has added TCP/IP transport support to its networking products under DECNet Phase V (Figure 2.8), the Advantage-Networks. TCP/IP already enables desktop devices running MS-DOS, UNIX, OS/2, and larger proprietary systems to exchange files without difficulty. In addition, many LAN vendors, such as Novell and Woolongong, use TCP/IP architecture in the design of their products.

The *Internet Protocol (IP)* resides on hosts and gateways and relays data from the source host to the destination host. The Transmission Control Protocol resides only on the hosts and assures reliable data delivery. TCP provides a virtual circuit between the two hosts. This means that the route between two hosts is checked and assured to be available before transmission takes place. This provides better use of the host and gateway nodes. Higher-level layers are also supported to provide support to transfer files, send mail, emulate terminals, and manage networks. Some of these application protocols are

- File transfer among dissimilar hosts using File Transfer Protocol (FTP).
- Electronic mail among hosts using Simple Mail Transfer Protocol (SMTP).
- Terminal emulation of a distant host using TELNET protocol.
- Network management using Simple Network Management Protocol (SNMP).

Digital Network Architecture (*DNA*, Phase V) has integrated ISO standards into the architecture. It is designed to support large networks internetworking with dissimilar systems. The lowest four layers conform exactly to the OSI model. Above the transport layer, the user can choose between Digital's proprietary protocols and the ISO standard protocols for the upper three layers of the ISO model.

Novell's NetWare (Novell LAN Workplace) is one of the most popular network operating systems. Novell has many different versions of this product, thereby satisfying the needs of smaller users with four to eight workstations, medium-sized users with up to 100 workstations, and large users with up to 250 users. In addition, NetWare VMS can enable Digital's VAX computers to be a server on a LAN.

NetWare's layers can handle many of the popular protocols. At the physical and data link layers, Ethernet, IEEE 802.3, and ARCNET are supported. At the session layer, the Network Basic Input Output/System (NetBIOS) is available. Proprietary protocols are used in the other layers.

Novell accomplishes connectivity (*LAN Workplace*), based on these protocols, with many other proprietary and open architectures. Internetworking among different computers' operating systems is made possible by incorporating the TCP/IP protocols onto the host's operating systems and hardware platforms. Novell's LAN Workplace supports MS-DOS, OS/2, Macintosh, UNIX, and Xenix operating systems, thereby providing interconnectivity (Figure 2.9) among different computers.

IBM PC-LAN: IBM uses PC-LAN (based on NetBIOS for session layer connectivity) and OS/2 LAN server for internetworking. Of course, IBM was responsible for developing and promoting token ring networks, which are used in most LANs and internetworks today. The PC-LAN software uses PC-LAN protocols, NetBIOS drivers, PC-LAN support programs, and token ring hardware. PC-LAN protocols encompass the application and presentation layers of OSI. NetBIOS, the Network Basic Input/Output System, is a session layer interface developed as a ROM chip or as software. PC-LAN support pro-

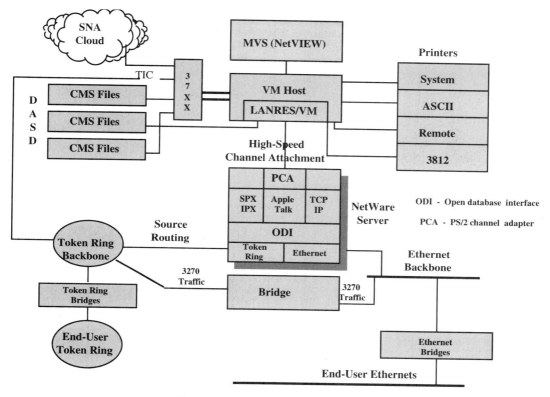

Figure 2.9 NetWare centric universe.

grams provide transport, network, and data link layer functions. The token ring hardware provides the physical layers.

AppleTalk: AppleTalk is a network operating system that is easy to use and is supported automatically in every Macintosh computer. AppleTalk uses both open and proprietary protocols to communicate among the seven layers of the OSI model. It is a popular architecture, with million of nodes installed on thousands of networks.

Xerox Network System (XNS): XNS is a network architecture developed by Xerox Corporation in the 1970s for integrating their computer and office products. These protocols are primarily used for printing and filing applications. XNS is similar in structure to the TCP/IP protocol suite.

Hierarchical systems, like SNA, are intended for applications where one or more mainframe computers dominate the resulting information system and its users. In such systems other elements are clearly subordinate to the large computers. In various ways, network architectures underlying these systems are designed to create and reinforce this relationship. Many networking applications prove to be ill-served by this model.

XNS is a distributed, not a hierarchical, network architecture. XNS achieves a distributed architecture by placing an appropriate amount of computing power in each workstation to enable users to do their primary tasks by relying on local resources. To tie together workstations and servers in a local area network, XNS relies on Ethernet

Banyan Systems' VINES: VINES is a network operating system designed for internetworking with LANs and WANs. VINES software integrates any number of users, sites, systems, and applications into a single, manageable network. VINES provides a number of services to facilitate an office network. These include directory, management, communication, security, and time services.

The *VINES* network operating systems support many clients, including PC-DOS, Windows, OS/2, and Macintosh and their native interfaces. The software allows all these clients to communicate with each other and share files. For Macintosh, VINES supports AppleTalk protocols over LocalTalk, token ring, and Ethernet.

VINES provides a number of server-to-server connectivity options. These include server-to-server LAN, WAN, X.25, TCP/IP, and SNA. No bridges or routers are required to support this broad spectrum of interserver connectivity. VINES uses a dynamic routing algorithm to help ensure network integrity and reliability. This algorithm allows VINES systems software to automatically redirect interserver traffic through an alternate route when a server is removed from service or a communication link fails.

VINES has also implemented gateways for 3270 and provides simultaneous access to an IBM SNA mainframe from a variety of PCs (running DOS, Windows, or Apple Macintosh). The gateway software supports SDLC and token ring connections. VINES provides extended support for HDLC, SDLC, X.25, and X.29. The VINES network server also allows DOS and UNIX share files through TCP/IP and NFS. It also provides connectivity to UNIX platforms such as DEC, Hewlett-Packard, IBM, NCR, and Sun.

AT&T's StarLAN: AT&T originally developed StarLAN to satisfy the need for a low-cost, easy-to-install LAN that offers more configuration flexibility than the token ring. This topology is familiar in the office environment, where each telephone is ultimately tied into the *private branch exchange (PBX)*.

Interconnecting Devices and Networks. The architectures described above for WANs and LANs are used to interconnect devices to create internetworks among enterprises. However, special devices must be installed so that these architectures can work together.

End users desire transparent communication so that they can communicate with any device in the network. However, terminals and/or personal computers at end users' sites are frequently incompatible. Therefore, special devices and software are needed to convert the information from one LAN to another, and from LAN to WAN. These incompatibilities may be in the form of operating systems, network operating systems, or simply applications. This makes the task of achieving transparency extremely difficult.

For example, consider an end user creating a document using WordPerfect version 5.1 on an IBM PS/2 Model 80. The user mails the document to three other people via a network modem and phone lines. No special devices were installed to convert the document at the originating or receiving ends. One receiver uses WordPerfect 4.0 in an IBM 8080-compatible computer, another uses a word processor on a UNIX-based Sun SPARC workstation, and a third uses a Macintosh computer. When the transfer is attempted, the mail will not look the same at the receiving end. The text may be garbled, and the error messages and control characters will appear.

Problems like this are caused primarily due to incompatibilities in the software, hardware, architectures, and operating environments. The problems are compounded when using application software such as WordPerfect or MS-Word, which puts control characters into the document. In fact, a document created with different versions of the particular software will format differently even if it were running in the same computer running the same operating system. Even if special devices were installed to prevent this problem, similar garbled messages will appear when the user chooses a different word processor. Thus, many end users have difficulty sending or receiving files/mail electronically across disparate systems.

For hardware solutions, such problems can be minimized by using special devices and software to connect LANs to LANs and LANs to WANs. Five common types of interconnecting devices are

- *Repeaters* are used frequently by common carriers to regenerate the signals during long distance transmission. Figure 2.10 shows two repeaters that generate the signals in the T1 network between a common carrier's offices in San Francisco and Los Angeles. These repeaters work at the physical layer level and are responsible for regenerating the binary 0's and 1's.

- *Bridges* connect nearly similar networks at a data link layer level. The bridge shown in Figure 2.11 connects to an Ethernet LAN in building B. The bridge reads all frames generated by LAN A and retransmits those addressed to LAN B. It performs similar functions for transmission from LAN B to LAN A.

- *Routers* operate at the network layer and can serve a networkwide connectivity function. Routers are protocol dependent and have intelligence to discover the route of a device connected to a different kind of LAN. There are a variety of routers available in the market. Some routers can facilitate communication among workstations in networks that use TCP/IP, DECnet, XNS, IPX, and AppleTalk protocols. Using an X.25 protocol port, a router can also communicate with a T1 network. Some other routers support IBM physical unit 4 (PU4) routing, which may result in eliminating the need for expensive front-end processors. Such routers in the network have the potential to allow a workstation to communicate with another workstation that must be accessed using different LANs and WANs. Figure 2.12 shows how routers connect Ethernet LANs and token ring LANs to a FDDI-based network. The router also provides connection to an overseas plant using a digital data services network (DDSN).

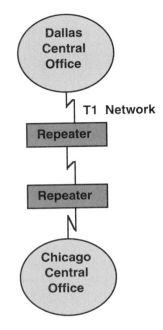

Figure 2.10 Repeaters.

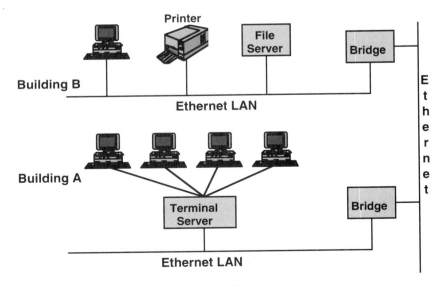

Figure 2.11 Use of bridges.

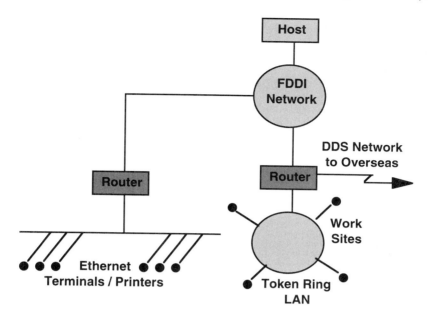

Figure 2.12 Use of routers.

- *Brouters* are a hybrid of bridges and routers. Brouters have the processing speed of a bridge and the internetworking capabilities of a router. An advantage of brouters is that these devices are not dependent on higher-layer protocols and thus provide a safeguard against quick obsolescence.

- *Gateways* operate at all layers of the protocol and protocol conversion may be required at each of these layers. The SNA/DNA gateways allow users of the DNA network to retrieve and transmit information to users in an SNA network. This gateway works at the level of the OSI transport layer and uses complex algorithms.

  For example, the Novell/Banyan gateways facilitate communication between Novell's NetWare and Banyan's VINES LAN networks. Such a connection allows a small work-group using NetWare to access a remote database using the VINES WAN connection. There are other gateways that provide communication capability between AppleTalk and Ethernet gateways.

Figure 2.13 shows how gateways can be used to connect TCP/IP, SNA, and Novell NetWare LAN networks. The hardware and software used by the gateways is different since they are connecting different types of networks on the other side of the gateway.

By using different types of interconnecting devices, we can minimize some of the problems encountered by dissimilar network technologies, protocols, hardware, applications, and operating systems. LAN-to-LAN connection can be made by bridges, routers, brouters, or gateways, while LAN-to-WAN connection requires routers, brouters, or gateways.

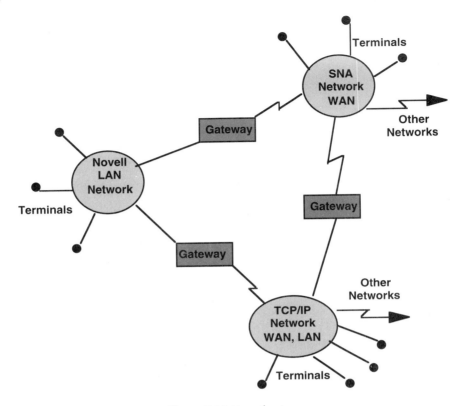

Figure 2.13 Use of gateways.

Network Operating Systems

The network operating system (NOS) is the software that resides on the server. It controls virtually all the activity on the network, much like the operating system of the host mainframe. It also manages access to the data (in case of a file server) on the hard disk and handles data security for the server's storage devices and network access to the users. The network operating system provides true multiuser capabilities and is probably the most important part of the network.

There are a number of network operating systems in the market. Each one of these operating systems has different functions and capabilities. A brief description of major NOSs is provided in the following sections, since you will be dealing with most of these in any given internetworking situation.

Microsoft's LAN Manager. In its early incarnation, LAN Manager required the OS/2 operating system on its file server. Since that time, Microsoft has licensed LAN Manager to other vendors, including NCS, DEC, Hewlett-Packard, SCO, and others. Because these companies have developed their own versions, the product no longer depends on OS/2 operating environment. Presently, LAN Manager is more operating system independent since it can run on VMS, OS/2, Windows NT, and UNIX. All LAN Manager implementations offer a combination of using multitasking operating system capabilities and network-optimized system code. Microsoft LAN Manager's open architecture supports thousands of applications written for MS-DOS and the NetBIOS protocols.

LAN Manager also supports Macintosh clients with a Services for Macintosh program. This option ties Macintosh workstations to the LAN manager network. Macintosh and PC users can share files and printers using their workstations' own standard interfaces.

The Microsoft LAN Manager for UNIX systems extends the client/server computing into multivendor environments, allowing machines based on UNIX and other operating systems such as DEC's VMS to act as servers for PC client applications running under Windows, Windows NT, MS-DOS, and OS/2. LAN Manager for UNIX systems allows the users to share applications, data, and resources from OS/2, UNIX, and VMS servers. With the topology and transport independence, LAN Manager for UNIX Systems gives the user a choice to choose Ethernet or token ring, TCP/IP, NetBEUI, or OSI, within a single system.

LAN Manager is a key component of DEC's Pathworks, allowing PC users to connect to VAX, OS/2, VMS, and Ultrix servers.

Existing Novell NetWare systems have added LAN manager servers without losing functionality or undergoing an immediate, all-or-nothing migration. Consequently, Windows and MS-DOS users can access files between LAN Manager and NetWare servers simultaneously.

IBM's LAN Server. IBM's LAN Server operates under OS/2 and is similar to Microsoft's LAN manager. This network operating system allows for requester-server relationships and provides for distributed databases on the network.

Banyan VINES. VINES is designed to simplify the use and management of distributed networks. The services it includes are

- Directory.
- Communications.
- Management.
- Security.
- Time.

These services are incorporated across a distributed environment to create a single, logical system. VINES supports many clients, including PC-DOS, Windows, OS/2, Novell's NetWare, and Macintosh and their native interfaces. VINES network server allows PC and UNIX users to share files and printers through standard UNIX protocols, including TCP/IP and NFS. VINES also provides connectivity to UNIX on DEC, Hewlett-Packard, IBM, NCR, and Sun platforms.

LANtastic. LANtastic is a DOS-based, peer-to-peer network versus a client/server network operating system. It supports as a peer-to-peer, from 10 to 25 PCs and operates on an 802.3 Ethernet LAN or an Artisoft's proprietary system. This network operating system implements a number of variations, including support for Windows, NetWare, and Macintosh.

Novell's NetWare. Novell NetWare is a dominant force in local area networking. The NetWare software is optimized for managing, sharing, translating, and synchronizing information through network computing. The NetWare operating system defines the capabilities of a network server and manages the sharing of communication services, file/print services, database services, and messaging services. Unlike other network operating systems discussed, NetWare does not run on any other operating system on the server, and the operating system is built into the NetWare, making NetWare more integrated and somewhat seamless.

NetWare has integrated several protocol standards, including Apple's AppleTalk File Protocol (AFP), Sun's Microsystems' UNIX-based network file system (NFS), and open standards such as TCP/IP and OSI. Such protocols are the key to seamless, high-speed communications among dissimilar hardware/software platforms.

Novell's Integrated Computer Architecture (NICA) represents Novell's approach to integrating applications and services in a distributed, multivendor environments, allowing products and applications from diverse architectures to be integrated. NICA works in concert with network applications, including IBM's System Application Architecture (SAA), Hewlett-Packard's New Wave Office, and DEC's Network Application Support (NAS).

Regardless of the server and client operating system used, NetWare uses interprocess communications protocols (IPCs) to establish a network link between the client and the server. NetWare supports multiple-IPC mechanisms, including Novell's IPX/SPX, IBM's NetBIOS and Advanced Program-to-Program Communications (APPC), Microsoft's Named Pipes, AT&T's Transport Level Interface (TLI), and BSD Sockets.

NetWare allows Macintosh, OS/2, and UNIX workstations access to NetWare file and print services, including support for NetWare DOS Open Data Link Interface (ODI) client drivers supporting multiple protocols such as IPX and TCP/IP.

PREVALENT NETWORKS

An internetwork environment is only as good as the network and communications platform on which it resides. Communication technologies as they relate to internetworking can be divided into six distinct categories, each with its own special solution space in terms of media, protocols, topologies, and other aspects. These categories include departmental/workgroup networks, campus networks, metropolitan networks, enterprise networks, hybrid networks, and global networks.

Departmental/Workgroup Networks

Single-building LANs are often the first experimentation point for organizations as they explore new communications technologies. The logical starting point for new LAN topologies, new protocol/media combinations (for example, running FDDI over twisted-pair wiring, which is discussed in later chapters), and new network management schemes is a *departmental* or *workgroup* LAN with the connection points relatively (physically) close to one another. These can also be termed as intrabuilding local area networks.

LANs create a foundation for workgroup computing because they link the computer systems serving local workers who are likely to interact on a close and continuous basis. A workgroup LAN is essentially a distributed departmental computer, and the role of the LAN is expanding.

Campus Networks

Once these intrabuilding communications have been mastered, many organizations with *campus environments* (multiple buildings relatively close to one another) begin to link building-level LANs through technologies such as fiber optics. As technologies are introduced to overcome physical distance limitations of LANs and interoperability issues, this is often the first introduction to inter-LAN connectivity and "extended" LAN environments.

Metropolitan Networks

Metropolitan area networks or MANs do not come to mind when thinking of communications as LANs and WANs. But a metropolitan area network is becoming an important stretch of the road to implementing an enterprise internetwork. An outgrowth of the campus-level environment, MANs come into play when an organization has offices scattered around some central business district within a city, but not necessarily in close proximity as in a campus environment.

Enterprise Networks

Technically, wide area networks form the highest step toward enterprise networking. They are, however, a new concept to many companies just beginning national or global operations and cannot exclusively be considered an aspect of large, multinational corporations anymore. Even for those organizations that have had WANs for years, a burst of new technologies and capabilities has forced at least reevaluation if not implementation of many WAN environments. WAN environments traditionally have been well planned and centrally laid out, with controlled growth patterns. But the explosion of LANs and the need to incorporate those environments into wide area networks has added a great deal of complexity to the enterprise networks using WANs.

Since the early 1990s, the connectivity achieved by LANs is certainly admirable, but the major benefits of that trend were reaped primarily by small businesses or departmental environments of large corporations and governmental organizations. The tremendous growth in areas such as bandwidth and throughput have been achieved within the LAN environments. Inter-LAN activity, especially over large geographical distances, has traditionally lagged behind.

The first efforts in inter-LAN connectivity began at the same departmental or division level that the LAN technology was first introduced and was oriented toward meeting needs of a specific department rather than an enterprise as a whole. Initial connectivity efforts were oriented toward both inter-LAN and LAN-to-WAN environments, based on *local bridges, remote bridges,* and *hybrid bridges/routers* (details provided in later sections of this book). This philosophy has evolved along with technology to focus more on "enterprise-level" issues such as network management and overall network performance.

Much of the growth of LANs and departmental connectivity has also resulted from the changing role of MIS. As inter-LAN and LAN-to-WAN communications evolved, the concept of the *enterprise network* took hold.

Hybrid Networks

LAN environments typically have somewhat "bursty" traffic patterns—long periods of low or no traffic with short periods of high-level activity. The need for these occasional high volumes of data to be sent in a timely fashion from the LAN environment to some other portion of the enterprise (most likely another LAN) will cause problems unless substantial overcapacity is designed into the network. Designing a hybrid network for the enterprise is, of course, much more difficult than having a single WAN architecture. Some of the factors include

- The *network topology*—using a public switched network as either the network backbone or an alternative routing mechanism.
- *Traffic profiles* of all interlocation communications circuits, optimized to avoid both over-capacity and burst traffic delays.
- *Performance* varies between circuit-switched and packet-switched environments. Circuit-switched channels have a fixed end-to-end delays with a delayed with a guaranteed throughput, while packet-switched environments have variable delays due to the various packet processing and routing requirements.
- *Network integration* occurs at several different levels—the physical level, link level, and so on.

Global Networks

LANs and WANs differ in more than just the geographical scope that they cover, but also in characteristics such as bandwidth and traffic patterns. Some leading network practitioners see the LAN concept not only integrating with WANs in a typical enterprise but also expanding in its own right, creating global networks that are similar in profile to LANs but cover the scope of a WAN. The following characteristics will apply to emerging large-scale networks:

- An increasing emphasis on the transmission of video and data in addition to voice.
- Megabit per second transmission as opposed to kilobit per second transmissions.
- RISC-based bridges and routers that promise to help increase network throughput.
- Global addressing using the international standard directory services networks.
- Advances in network operating systems, focusing not only on LAN technology but also on large-area considerations.

ROLE OF STANDARDS

Business activity in the 1990s is characterized by three principal guiding forces:

- *Quality:* A critical success factor in the ability to gather, access, and process accurate information, in designing, selling, and supporting any product or service.
- *Time to market:* Information systems built from highly modular systems enable organizations to readily absorb new and more effective technologies, allowing companies to quickly adapt to changing competitive pressures.
- *Value:* By maximizing the return derived from staff expertise, end-user experience, existing systems, and supplier competition.

In the previous sections, we have seen that there are a plethora of operating systems, network operating systems, networking media, network types, protocols and architectures, complicated by the variations of offerings from a jungle of vendors. In addition, there are hundreds of different solutions offered by hundreds of technologists, creating a mine field for an unsuspecting user.

While many people consider "standards" to be part of a strategic long term imperative, they can have a direct impact on the short term success as well. Standards provide

- Reduced vendor dependence.
- Broadened product acquisition opportunities.
- Lower learning curves for new systems.
- Eased integration of multiple systems.
- Optimized support.

There are two major types of standards:

De Jure Standards

These type of standards are established by a formal and independent standards body with a legal status sanctioned by a national government or a federation of national governments, such as CCITT or ISO. Often, such a standard is not associated with a specific vendor or a product. Unfortunately, it often trails leading edge technology due to the excessive time required to formally codify it (Figure 2.14), for example, the OSI Reference Model.

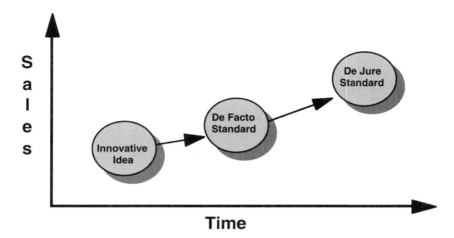

Figure 2.14 De jure standards development cycle.

De Facto Standards

These are also market-driven standards, usually based on specific products. The product is nearly always supplied by a single vendor with monopolistic objectives, for example, MS-DOS and Windows, SNA, DECnet, AppleTalk, and so on. Some standards are also market driven if multiple vendors supply the product and advance the technology, for example, UNIX, TCP/IP, and X-Windows.

In the simplest case (Figure 2.14), an innovative product is developed, sells well, and becomes accepted in the marketplace before competitive products can achieve significant sales. Eventually, when market penetration is high, or when competing technologies appear on the scene, a public body may review the technology and approve it as a standard, for example, Xerox's Ethernet and IEEE 802.3.

SUMMARY

In the past, mainframes performed most of the large business applications, while desktop computers served private, special applications for individuals. Now you view your enterprise computer resources as mainframes, minicomputers, and desktop computers (clients and servers), all interconnected and interworking with each other via networks. Networks allow computing devices to communicate with each other.

Networks within an organization were formerly the sole responsibility of individual departments. Each department manager funded and owned their own respective network. The industry no longer tolerates such an approach with today's enterprise. Emphasis on enterprise networking has accelerated, because of the requirement for interdepartmental networking, competitive pressures, and constantly changing technologies.

CLIENT / SERVER COMPUTING

Requirements:

- Personal Productivity
- Workgroup Productivity
- Organizational Efficiency
- Enterprisewide Efficiency

Usage:

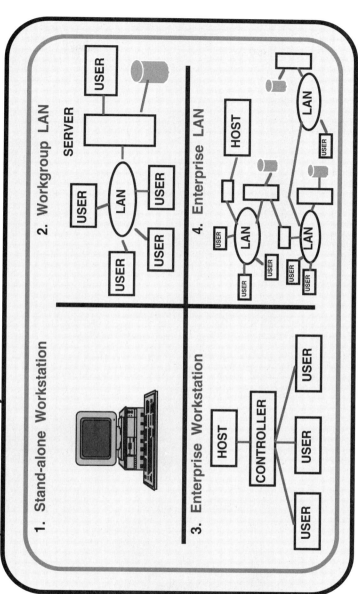

Figure 2.15 Client/server computing.

Client/server technology makes an efficient utilization of network resources (Figure 2.15). Servers make it possible for terminals to share resources and use data and applications in different networks, mainframes, minicomputers, and workstations of varying strengths and architectures. Users of LAN-based personal computers, workstations, minicomputers, and even mainframes reap the benefits of processing integration as well as system integration. Figure 2.15 depicts the evolution of internetworking starting in quadrant 1, progressing toward quadrants 3, 2, and 4 respectively.

The introduction of standards for networks has significantly lowered the cost of internetworking products from different vendors. The heterogeneity of hardware, operating systems, networking protocols, administrative services, and physical media, make most choices difficult. The industry is busily working to improve the interoperability among the disparate systems. When selecting a set of technologies for your network, you must understand all the pieces of the puzzle.

In this section, we briefly discussed most of the important components of an internetwork. In the following sections, we will build upon these principles and explore how these can be utilized in building your networks.

EXERCISES

1. Why is internetworking so complex?
2. What are the four building blocks of networking?
3. Describe some of the internetworking devices.
4. Name some of the prevalent network operating systems.
5. Name some of the prevalent networks.

Figure 2.16 Why Not?

3

STANDARDS AND PROTOCOLS

Introduction
Issues
    Operating Systems
    Application Software
    Mixing Protocols and Networks
    Internetworking and Need for
    Standardization

    The Need for Security
Standards
    De Jure Standards
    De Facto Standards
Summary
Exercises

INTRODUCTION

The computer industry has been driven by its technology rather than the market requirements. Marketing strategies of computer vendors are based on the principle of selling their own technology, specialized on their system, to gain competitive edge. As a consequence, there are a lot of technologically superb products in the computer marketplace, but a lot of users cannot take full advantage of them.

Until the advent of the microprocessors and the PC revolution that followed, computer manufacturers had managed quite successfully to lock their customers into a single supplier purchasing policy by providing systems that would only run applications specifically developed for them. Once the applications were developed, it was often impossible for the users to switch hardware systems suppliers without having to throw away huge investments in software, hardware, and people. Besides the obvious risk of noncompetitive pricing, the *proprietary systems* approach has led to increased costs and inefficiencies both in development and maintenance for both hardware and software.

Computer technology has historically been a closed business with different vendors' systems unable to talk to each other. Islands of automation have sprung up all over user organizations.

To share information, a user might walk from one machine to the next with a diskette or magnetic tape or run complex protocol gateways between computers that are not compatible. All this inconvenience and lack of simplified communication was quite prevalent before the *age of open systems* or simple *standardization.*

To understand the forces that are operating in the computer industry as a whole and to see what standardization there is, in this section, we will examine the issues and the existing standards which affect the outcome of enterprise networking and internetworking.

ISSUES

Many standards exist, including a few that computer manufacturers have created on their own. Because only one manufacturer can use them, they are not standards in the true sense of the word. Products from other manufacturers may have to communicate with equipment produced using these proprietary standards, and this is where most of the problems arise, primarily because of incompatible protocols and standards.

Now that desktop workstations and mainframes have a critical role to play in the information technology strategies, the question to address is how they can best work together. The issues of communication between diverse processors and peripherals, over large geographical areas, around the client/server architecture must be addressed. It became clear in the early 1970s that computing was entering a new era. The Department of Defense (DOD) designed the network control program (NCP) set of protocols—the precursor of today's Transmission Control Protocol/Internet Protocol (TCP/IP) family—for connecting different computers and peripheral in a network. That interconnection was called the ARPANET network, which today has grown into Internet.

Since networking days, an *open systems* revolution has been under way. The mission has been to enable computer equipment and software to speak a common language, to break down the barriers to sharing and obtaining information. In essence, open systems are those computers, software, and networking technologies that permit applications to run across different platforms and systems to communicate. This is quite a departure from the days when the mainframe was the company brain trust. Information is now branching out to the desktop, becoming distributed rather than centralized. End users are empowered as never before—running applications, tapping into corporate databases, sending electronic mail, and even swapping data with users outside the corporate environment.

Operating Systems

Unfortunately, there is no more order in the field of operating systems today than there was a decade ago. UNIX still leads the field as far as open, multiuser operating systems are concerned, and the GUI associated with UNIX is X Windows. Vendor alliances are still producing newer and different versions, which may continue to haunt us in times to come.

When considering different operating systems within a distributed systems environment, the focus of concern is not only on portability but also on the operating system heterogeneity. Unless all operating systems converge on a standard or the POSIX standard—which surely will not happen in the near term—portability of programs across operating systems will continue to be a point of constant contention. And, instead, the users will continue to focus on the interoperability of clients and servers regardless of the operating system used on each.

Free internetworking of unlike operating systems is far more difficult if generalized solution is the goal. Where multiple operating systems must be supported, internetworking may stay limited to transfer of simple data, file, e-mail, and database queries.

The inevitable conclusion in the face of so much contention is that there are no real standards at all. Decisions involving investment in operating systems can only be based on calculations involving the cost of replacing software, converting data, and retraining users. Wherever possible, migration to UNIX has been the easiest path and, in some cases, migration for the sake of migration. Even then, which version of UNIX remains a difficult question, but the differences between OSF/1 and SVR4 are of less significance than the differences between MS-DOS and UNIX or between MVS and VMS.

Application Software

As networks become more pervasive and organizations become more thoroughly connected, the need for different applications to share common data or even common computing resources grow in importance. Cross-platform application development has become an integral part of any cooperative or distributed processing environment.

One major issue in the development across various types of systems is how to develop applications that will run identically—or nearly so—on several different platforms. Now that a large number of commercial developers support many different popular platforms (e.g., DOS, Windows, Macintosh, and UNIX), their cross-platform application development tools and tactics have become corporate assets. The ability to deliver applications for many different platforms in a timely manner gives a company a major competitive edge.

Mixing Protocols and Networks

Bringing together multiple architectures can be complicated. Intervendor standards are emerging, but are not very mature, and have not been extensively tried and tested. Coordinating vendor support for the network may prove difficult, if not impossible—a problem with an application that spans multivendor platforms may lead to vendors pointing at each other. Products may lose some of their features and functionality when they need to conform to a nonnative architecture. Only a few mature network management tools and applications are available to run on multiple platforms in a multivendor cooperative processing environment.

Charles Darwin, in his *Origin of Species*, describes how various isolated tropical species evolve along different paths as a result of mutation and natural selection. A bird may develop a special beak just to dine on the nectar of some tropical fruit. While divergence abounds in the animal and vegetation kingdoms, this is less common in the computer industry, but it is there. As time passes in one area, creative ideas developed in another may be gracefully added to competing products.

Novell now claims a universal directory service inspired by the Banyan VINES' more limited domain name system of TCP/IP. In a similar vein, Windows NT has covered all the bases by bundling network support for TCP/IP, IPX/SPX, AppleTalk, and the native Network Basic Extended User interface (NetBEUI) stack traditionally used by Microsoft and IBM LAN Managers. Of course, the goal is today's enterprise solution, even at the cost of mix and match.

Internetworking and Need for Standardization

To understand the complexities of the computer industry and the forces that are pushing toward increased compatibility and standardization, we need to study the elements that drive the future of the computer industry. These elements include software and hardware portability, scalability, and interoperability.

The *software development* process is now so complex that it is common for an announced product to be delayed for months. Increased sophistication of user expectations, coupled with rapidly evolving technologies, means that software products are taking longer to develop and are lasting a shorter time in the marketplace. Even it is done today, any software developer can ill afford to target software products exclusively to proprietary environments. Few computer manufacturers can offer any guarantees.

As an example, Oracle has ported its products to almost every popular and proprietary operating system. But the cost has been high, and it normally takes months to port the products. The cost of producing a different software version for each proprietary system and the meager sales volumes for that particular version is making software development exorbitantly expensive.

On the other hand, many of the problems experienced by software developers could be dramatically reduced if the computer industry were to move to the supply of standard hardware systems, supported by a majority of the manufacturers.

Hardware manufacturers have made a considerable investment in their own technologies over the years. Managing the migration from proprietary to a standardized set is proving very difficult for both the vendor and the customer. As technology becomes more sophisticated, many vendors have a hard time maintaining their proprietary niche. Both suppliers and their customers need a competitive edge and will need to move to standard technologies.

Today, *data are distributed* throughout organizations on systems of varying functionality, from personal computers through departmental systems to the corporate mainframe. Many enterprises face the problem of bringing these together into one cohesive information system that can be managed efficiently and effectively. That requires interconnecting all the disparate islands of data, hardware, networking architectures, and software systems. To reduce this complexity and management of emerging networking configurations, the industry needs to agree on a set of standards for communication between devices and systems.

LANs in use today are generally not selected for their ability to be *internetworked*, and in many cases, there is no mandate to preserve every system or data compatibility among various workgroups. As a result, there is no homogeneous base of LANs to internetwork. A part of the problem is that internetworking brings into collision two very different business imperatives: local productivity and central management. The companies have invested billions in desktop systems, software, LANs, mainframes, and internetworking hardware. They must preserve this investment.

Portability, Scalability, Interoperability. Applications developed for a particular hardware platform have not been easily moved to execute on a different platform. Incompatibilities between computer systems lead to a dramatically chaotic situation.

In today's environment, few departments, subsidiaries, or companies work independently or in isolation. The production lines must be integrated with information and data not only within the organizations but also with suppliers. What complicates the problem is the heterogeneity of the hardware, operating systems, and applications. Such mixed networks have created plethora of problems for such integration. These problems can only be solved by standardization in the following areas:

- *Application portability* is possible at a basic level by relying on systems using the same central processor. It is possible to install a complete corporate network consisting entirely of machines based on one type of processor. Assuming equally compatible operating systems, this would guarantee portability across equivalent machines and *scalability* up the lower range.

  In cases where there is a single hardware architecture, application portability is a relatively simple matter. A more complex issue is to achieve some degree of compatibility across hardware architectures. Complete binary compatibility between different architectures is impossible because of differences in instruction sets, registers, and so on.

- *Scalability* is the ability for the same application package to run with acceptable performance on computers of varying sizes, from the personal to the mainframe. Some are trying with varying degrees of success, for example, Oracle porting its databases on essentially every size platform. But the performance and functionality suffers in most cases; thus the systems must be retuned.

- *Interoperability* is the need to communicate in order to provide accurate and reliable transmission of data (in case of internetworking) without affecting the applications that are running in separate computers. As the need for better use of corporate information and data becomes increasingly widespread, more and more of these computers will be interconnected. The need for interoperability becomes more intense as it becomes necessary to combine technologies for providing interconnection for distributed and shared software and data. As the applications become "network centric" or "network intrinsic," to achieve interoperability, the application environment and the communication technologies must be evaluated together.

Network Management, Monitoring, and Troubleshooting. Managers face the nightmare of managing a web of computers and networks. Managing one vendor's product can be complex enough, but keeping tabs on different vendors' products with the limited network management tools available today is a daunting task.

Standard communications for multivendor, unlike systems solves some problems, but also creates new ones. The biggest of these problems is the management of a network of unlike systems. To deal with this problem, the existing network management protocols will have to be extended to maintain central repository of information on current activities of each layer of each system on the network.

The Need for Security

The current shift to distributed environment poses a few additional risks. Data have become more vulnerable since it is readily available and is more prone to unauthorized access or tampering. Therefore, it is necessary to strike a balance between making data accessible and preventing misuses of it.

Security is of grave concern to both commercial and government users of computers. Both groups have a need to conceal their confidential data from within as well as outside the organizations. Where information is held only on paper, locks and security procedures have prevented physical access or at least make it evident when a breach has occurred. Information systems have complicated the issue since it is now possible to display, examine, destroy, or corrupt sensitive data without leaving any clues.

In contrast, the computer systems can not only monitor, keep audit trails, and control access to such documents or materials, but this monitoring is an expensive proposition. Secure systems are expensive to develop (i.e., testing, certification, and implementation of the special software and procedures) and require skilled administration. Secure systems also need additional computer resources, causing performance hits for normal operations.

Security issues have been discussed ever since the dawn of computers. But we still have to reach a consensus as to how to accomplish it. The formal science of making systems secure is still very young. But the commercial pressures are beginning to move the technology forward. As in many other fields, development efforts are concentrating on new technologies. But there are more proprietary systems taking part in the networks. So we must devise means to make those secure also, since in internetworking, no single system is an isolated island.

STANDARDS

Protocols regulate what is known as the *data format*, or the manner in which data are exchanged between layers. An architecture combines the existing standards and protocols needed to create a functioning network. The network defined by the combination of standards and protocols is termed as *network architecture*. A network architecture is, therefore, also a standard. It defines the rules of a network and how its components can interact with each other.

The goal of a network is to incorporate the many hardware and software components into a useful, functioning system. Unfortunately, this task is not as simple as it sounds. In an effort to bring hardware and software together, architectures and standards are continually being developed. Various standards organizations are attempting to lay a foundation on which to build internetworking components as well as data communications as a whole.

Different devices from different manufacturers form the basic components of an internetwork, so these are able to communicate with one another and interoperate. The computer industry is being encouraged to develop products that adhere to these emerging architectures and standards. There are two primary mechanisms that bring standards to market: *de jure* or public and *de facto*.

De Jure Standards

De jure standards, also known as public standards, exist because they are produced by a legal body with legal status, to produce standards, usually by consensus. Due to the combinations of interests involved in reaching a consensus, de jure standards invariably take longer to come into fruition than the industry-driven de facto standards. As we will learn, that even though OSI is a well-defined model, all the layer protocols have not been fully described *yet*.

ISO: Open Systems Interconnect Model and Protocols. Although OSI was designed with TCP/IP in mind, the two have dramatically different philosophies and roots. OSI is a seven-layer model, a prepared set of standard protocols developed by the IEEE's international standards organization (Figure 3.1).

Layer 1 is the *physical layer*, where the actual physical connection takes place. The physical layer determines how bit streams are sent across the physical transmission medium.

Layer 2 is the *data link layer*, where data are sent next. Layer 2 prepares the data to be sent over the physical medium.

Layer 3, the *network layer*, is where the data's trip is mapped out.

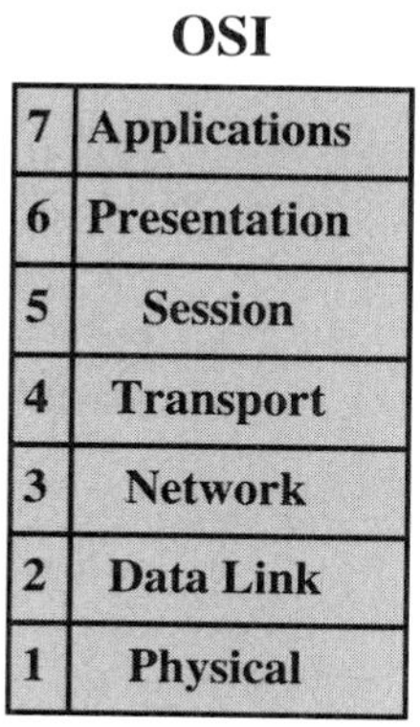

OSI

7	Applications
6	Presentation
5	Session
4	Transport
3	Network
2	Data Link
1	Physical

Figure 3.1 The OSI protocol suite.

The data travel to layer 4, the *transport layer*, which is similar to TCP/IP's TCP layer. Transport layer makes sure that data flowing between systems is sent intact and to the right place.

Layer 5, the *session layer*, sets up and synchronizes a session between applications. It also closes communication when it is complete.

Layer 6, the *presentation layer*, serves as a translator. It converts the data into a common format that both the sending and the receiving stations can understand.

At the top is the layer 7, the *application layer*. Several application protocols serve as the common ground between the network and the computer applications. The applications include e-mail (X.400), file transfer (FTAM), terminal emulation (VT), and directory services (X.500).

IEEE: 802.3, 802.4, 802.5, POSIX. Working in cooperation with IEEE, ISO has produced standards for various OSI layers. Some of these are being widely adopted. At the lower levels, ISO has adopted local area network (LAN) standards developed by IEEE. These include Ethernet (802.3), token ring (802.5), token bus (802.4), and POSIX technologies. The LAN standards are named after the IEEE's # 802 committee.

Ethernet (802.3): The original *Ethernet* technology (Figure 3.2), which was developed by the Xerox Corporation, used coaxial cable and transmitted the data at 10 Mbps and could only support up to 1024 nodes on a number of sections, each not exceeding 500 meters. The technologies now exist for 100 Mbps since the demand is increasing for higher bandwidth. Ethernet is based on carrier sense multiple access/collision detect (CSMA /CD) technology. Each system needing access to the network checks if the access is available. If yes, the system may transmit. If another system transmits at the same time, the two messages collide. If the collision is detected, both systems wait for a randomly generated time interval and try again.

IEEE 802.3 standard is a variation of the Xerox Ethernet technology. It can run over a variety of media, including twisted-pair wiring (as in telephone), coaxial, and fiber optic cables. The CSMA/CD standard specifies a multifunctional model that governs how data are transmitted and received. The data unit is received by the media access control (MAC) sublayer from the logical link control (LLC) sublayer. The data encapsulation/decapsulation and media access management functions are performed by the MAC sublayer itself,

Figure 3.2 An Ethernet LAN.

while the data encoding/decoding function is performed by the physical layer that operates below the MAC sublayer.

Data encapsulation is performed at the sending station. This process entails adding information to the beginning and end of the data unit to be transmitted. The added information is used to perform the following tasks:

- Synchronize the receiving station with the signal.
- Indicate the start and end of the frame.
- Identify the addresses of sending and receiving stations.
- Detect transmission errors.

The data encapsulation function constructs a transmission frame in the proper format. The destination address, source address, type, and other information is passed to the data link layer by the client layer in the form of a packet. When a frame is received, the data are decapsulated by the receiving station, which matches its own address, performs error checking, and removes the control information.

Token Ring (802.5): Token ring is an alternate LAN technology and was designed by IBM as a general-purpose LAN. Operating at 4 or 16 Mbps, the ring is essentially a closed loop (Figure 3.3). A set of bytes called the *token* is circulated around the ring, giving each station in sequence a chance to put information on the network. Any station may seize the station and replace it with an information frame. A token-holding timer controls the maximum amount of time a station can occupy the network before passing the token. At the completion of the information transfer, the station reinserts the token on the ring.

Because each station acts as a repeater and the data packets and the token are regenerated at their original signal strength, such networks are limited by distance or speed based on the length of each run that depends on the number of wiring closets, MAUs, and drops. Only the addressee retains the message, and only the station that put the message on the ring can remove it. The ring topology offers several advantages:

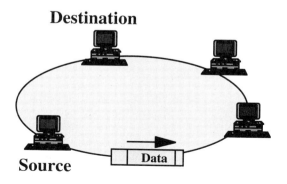

Figure 3.3 Token ring transmission.

- A higher throughput rate is possible, since there is no contention scheme.
- There are no routing problems since all messages are flowing in the same direction.
- Higher-priority traffic takes precedence over lower-priority traffic.
- The cost of expansion is proportional to the number of nodes.

Token Bus (802.4): Token bus or IEEE 802.4 standard connects nodes in a unidirectional closed path. Each node regenerates signals as it reaches its station. Using the ring network, tokens are initiated from the sender to the receiver and regenerated throughout the network until the token reaches the destination station. The destination station makes a copy of the information into its storage and continues passing the data around the ring. When the token combined with information reaches the sender, it is removed and the token freed. Any station which detects the freed token may begin transmission, but it is limited to a maximum period of token retention. The asynchronous priority level makes token ring appealing for many applications.

Token Bus is a technology designed for harsh environments where a guaranteed response time is required, and is therefore specified for manufacturing applications in the OSI standards. It transmits at 10 Mbps on broadband cables and uses a token system to control access to the network.

POSIX (Portable Operating System based on UNIX): Portable operating system based on UNIX (POSIX) is a derivative of OSI and UNIX. The POSIX communications architecture embeds three new interfaces among the applications program and the computer operating systems and hardware. The first is specific to an organization that uses or designs the software; the second relates to industrywide standard software components; and the third, to open systems standard interfaces, is designed to work with the previous two or directly with the applications program.

POSIX offers two types of standard interfaces: the application programming interface (API) and the external environment interface (EEI). The APIs are procedure calls made to the computer in which the application is running to ensure source code portability. The EEI, in contrast, is concerned with interoperability between the computer and the entities with which it exchanges information. Together, they support communication service for applications programs running on networked computers. These services include name space and directory, file transfer, network file access, remote procedure calls, and protocol independent network and data access. Some of the other standards for POSIX are shell and utilities, user portability extensions, transparent file access, Windows-based user, and X.400 message handling interface.

CCITT: X.400 (E-Mail), X.500 (Directory Services), X.25, ISDN. *E-mail (X.400):* X.400 standard is the CCITT recommendation for international electronic mail messaging. The ISO work on message-oriented text interchange systems (MOTIS) is based on the X.400 standard. X.400 is a store-and-forward application, in which messages are sent to a mailbox for collection by a named user, who can access the mailbox from a range of terminals. The essential components of an X.400 system are (Figure 3.4) the following:

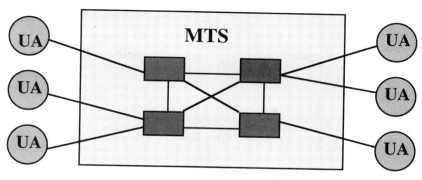

Figure 3.4 An X.400 MHS system.

- The user agent (UA) provides a connection or interface between the network user and the X.400 message handling system (MHS), allowing the user to send and retrieve messages.

- The message transfer system (MTS) operates in support of the network users and determines the screen display the network user will see. The user agent interacts with the MTS.

- The message transfer agent (MTA) consists of the messages sent by the users. Commands and instructions are also provided which create store-and-forward functionality. This function stores messages until a requested delivery time and date, or it may have to convert the message into a form the recipient can understand.

Directory Services (X.500): An enterprise full of objects—including thousands of users—must have some sort of directory service that enables applications and users to find the address of other objects. The X.500 standards can be used within X.400 networks to provide such directory services. The X.500 directory management services allow the users of, or applications running on, OSI networks to obtain information relating to other users or applications on the same or other OSI networks anywhere in the world.

The functional model of an X.500 Directory Service is shown in Figure 3.5. In this model, the directory consists of a number of directory service agents (DSAs), which communicate with directory user agents (DUAs) via a directory access protocol (DAP). This schema looks similar to X.400 because they both have the same architectural foundation. In the ISO/OSI world, X.500 resides at the application layer.

Packet Switching (X.25): ISO adopted the wide area networks from CCITT and are based on packet-switching technology, carried over a variety of line types, and typified by the CCITT's X.25 standard. In recent years, X.25 has become increasingly popular as a means of building wide area networks.

X.25 is a CCITT recommendation for packet switching over a wide area network. It defines the network up to layer of the OSI seven-layer model. It specifies the protocol used

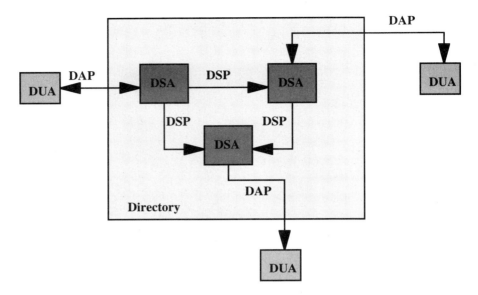

Figure 3.5 The directory services (X.500) functional model.

by "packet terminals" connecting to a packet network, that is, the connection between the terminal or host itself and the packet node or switch. Protocols used for connection between the many nodes on a packet-switched network are often proprietary, or through gateways.

Packet-switched networks carry data in units with a fixed maximum size, called packets. Large packets are broken up into acceptable sizes and are reassembled at the destination, and are transparent to the user. Packets are assembled/disassembled either by the end system itself or by a device called a PAD (packet assembler/disassembler) (Figure 3.6). PADs are used to assemble data into packets which are submitted to the network and to disassemble incoming messages. PADs also buffer messages by storing them, as necessary, to cope with the differences between the transmission speed of the network and that of the system.

X.25 links may be used for user-to-user communications through a public packet data network or for micro-to-mainframe communications. Instead of using dedicated ports to access the mainframe, a single logical connection is provided under X.25 to allow many minicomputers to share the same data stream on a nonblocking basis. X.25 can carry very heavy traffic loads very efficiently. X.25 protocol also provides a certain amount of error correction to ensure data integrity.

Integrated Service Data Networks (ISDN): The ISDN standard is designed to enable the transfer of very large amounts of data quickly to anywhere on a worldwide network. ISDN accommodates a wide range of services over the same line, including voice, data, videotext, fax, and video telephony. Since ISDN is basically a redesign of the telephone system, CCITT has been taking the lead in its development. The key service for ISDN continues to be voiced with many enhanced features, such as display of caller's telephone, name, and address or even caller's database record, on a display while ringing.

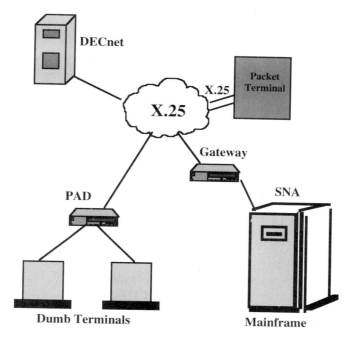

Figure 3.6 X.25 packet-switching network.

ISDN data transmission services allow users to connect their ISDN terminals or computers to any other one on the network. Videotext is becoming a popular service with ISDN, which is interactive access to a remote database by a person at a terminal. Teltex and facsimile are also becoming of common use.

ANSI: FDDI, SQL. *FDDI:* Fiber distributed data interface is a 100 Mbps data rate local area network standard. The topology is a point-to-point connection of links connected in a logical link. There are two such counterrotating rings with one ring configured as a backup (Figure 3.7). Each station connects to both rings, where each station is daisy chained to the previous node. For example, there can be 500 such stations on the network with a maximum ring size of 200 km. The maximum distance between each node is 2 km. The rule for forming an FDDI network is simple—no greater than two logical paths.

The set of dual rings is referred to as the trunk ring. The dual rings are counterrotating. This allows for easy reconfiguration in the case of a single fault (Figure 3.8). Typically, one ring is used for data transfer and is called the primary ring. The second ring, used as a backup, is used only in case of a fault and is known as the secondary ring.

According to the Open Systems Interconnection Reference Model, FDDI specifies layer 1 (the physical layer) and part of layer 2 (the data link layer). The data link layer is responsible for maintaining the integrity of information exchanged between two points. In a LAN environment, because most LANs are shared media networks, the layer 2 is subdi-

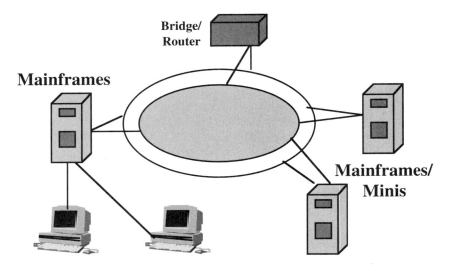

Figure 3.7 FDDI dual-ring trees.

vided into two sublayers: logical link control and media access control. The LLC is the same for different subnetworks. Examples of subnetworks are IEEE 802.3 (CSMA/CD), very similar to Ethernet, IEEE 802.5 (token ring), and ANSI FDDI among others. Different LAN subnetworks have different mechanisms for accessing the shared media. The access mechanisms are specified in the media access control specification of the LANs. The layer 1 FDDI specification consists of two parts: physical media dependent (PMD) and PHY. The PHY is independent of the media which can be multimode fiber, single-mode fiber, shielded twisted pair, and so on.

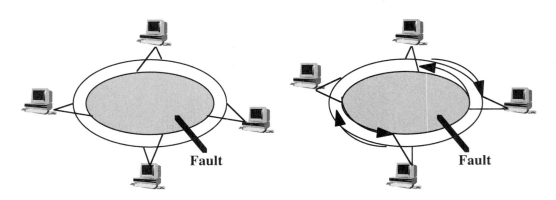

Figure 3.8 FDDI cable fault and reconfiguration.

- PMD defines the type of media interconnection and its characteristics such as transmitter power, frequencies, receiver sensitivities, and so on. It also specifies the maximum repeaterless distance between two nodes. The first media targeted for FDDI was fiber. It was used to accommodate internodal distances greater than a few kilometers, allowing FDDI to be used between campuses and/or buildings and make use of the existing fiber in the public domain. The internodal distances can be extended to 40 km by the use of an alternate media such as single mode fiber (SMF), but it requires the use of powerful transmitters. The function of the PHY is to synchronize the clock with the incoming signal provided by the PMD, encode and decode data and control symbols, and interface with the higher layers and initialization of the medium (fiber, copper). The FDDI PHY bears more similarity to token ring than Ethernet.
- The FDDI MAC specifies a class of control frames that are used to execute low-level (MAC-level) protocols such as ring initialization and fault isolation.

Most of the popular networks today are shared media LANs, including FDDI. It was developed to serve as an integrated voice/video/data network. FDDI specifications have been developed by American National Standards Institute (ANSI).

SQL: Structured Query Language is a standard relational database access language that facilitates data extraction from client stations (Figure 3.9), regardless of where the required data are located on the network, what database or operating system maintains them, or on what type or vendor computer they are stored on. SQL is well suited for this

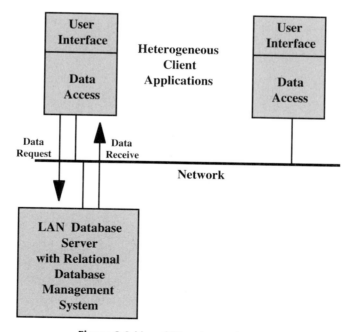

Figure 3.9 How SQL extracts data.

purpose, since it provides a concise, nonprocedural method of requesting data. Basically, SQL is a specialized programming language in which data are represented as a relational model—where data are held in two-dimensional tables with a simple row and column structure.

Using SQL as the data access method for client/server applications offers a number of benefits:

- Application programming is simplified for data requests.
- The language is somewhat portable for applications running on different platforms.
- Network traffic is reduced, since only the data request and the requested data are sent over the network.
- Different applications, through standardizing on SQL, can access data stored in the same format—the tables or views maintained by the server.
- SQL makes the task of accessing distributed database servers possible, since the same database access language is used.

With the emergence of an American National Standards Institute standard for SQL, more and more vendors support SQL for their database engines. Because SQL is considered unwieldy in its raw form, software vendors had to overlay it with more user-friendly interface to shield users from having to learn another command syntax. SQL operates in the background, enabling the user to extract data from anywhere on the network.

De Facto Standards

De facto standards do not have to observe the consensus diplomacy in their production. In fact, many de facto standards are not the result of consensus but a conscious effort to produce a standard, many times from practical implementations (e.g., SNA, DNA). Instead, they originate innovative ideas or attractive products which come to be accepted as standards in the course of time, for example, TCP/IP. A majority of the technologies in use today are the result of de facto standardization process.

Transmission Control Protocol /Internet Protocol Suite (TCP/IP). The TCP/IP four-layer protocol stack began as an experimental approach to connecting networks, and was created by the Internet user community in the 1970s to replace the original DOD NCP. The Internet community continues to nurture and augment the protocols today. Much of TCP/IP success is rooted in the Internet community's heritage.

The TCP/IP technology is maturing, and vendors can more easily implement it. During the past decade, TCP/IP has come out of the campus lab and into the corporate data center. Commercial users are finding it a quick and readily available way to solve their interoperability problems. TCP/IP has become the "glue" of choice for communicating among dissimilar operating systems. TCP/IP is the most prevalent networking architecture in use today and its implementation is growing.

TCP/IP follows a layered approach to networking (Figure 3.10). Layer 1 is the *network access* layer, equivalent to both physical and data link layers of the OSI model, which

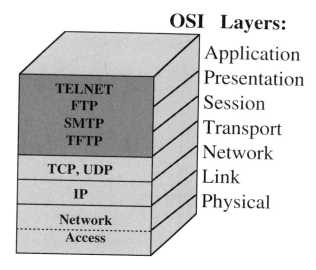

Figure 3.10 TCP/IP architectural layers.

sends data between two processors in the same network. Layer 2 is the *Internet Protocol* layer (IP), which routes data among more than one network. These three layers are also referred to as "lower layers" and essentially perform the networking functions. These layers are equivalent to other networking architectures, such as SNA, OSI, and DECnet.

Layer 3, considered the reliability layer, is the Transmission Control Protocol layer (TCP), in charge of sending the data in sequence and without errors. This layer also includes another protocol, known as User Datagram Protocol (UDP), which allows users to send messages without connection establishment and without any guarantee of delivery or sequencing. Layer 3 is also termed as "transport" layer.

The upper layers are termed as "applications" or "process" layers, which provide the services for three types of applications—electronic mail (SMTP), file transfer (FTP and TFTP), and terminal emulation (TELNET). Other TCP/IP protocols, in addition to the four-layer model, include the Simple Network Management Protocol (SNMP), developed to manage multiple vendors' products and is considered the de facto standard for managing different devices.

Transmission Control Protocol (TCP).   TCP is the primary protocol used in the Internet Protocol suite for reliable transmission of data from one host to another. TCP is a level 4 (of the OSI model) or transport-level protocol (Figure 3.11). TCP is used by TELNET, FTP, e-mail, and other applications.

TCP provides a reliable data delivery service with detection of, and recovery from, lost, duplicated, or corrupted packets. TCP is designed to work with networks which provide a minimal level of service. Two hosts communicate via TCP by setting up a connection (virtual circuit) between them. Establishing a connection results in each host setting

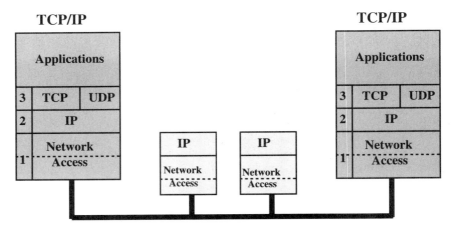

Figure 3.11 Transmission control protocol.

aside a small amount of memory to save information about the connection, such as how much data have been received, what data have been acknowledged, and other information. Briefly, the main attributes of TCP are

- Provides a fully duplex bidirectional virtual circuit.
- As seen by the user, data are transmitted as a data stream (not in blocks).
- Reliable data transmission using
  - Sequence numbers.
  - Checksums.
  - Acknowledgments.
  - Segment retransmission after acknowledgment time-out.
- Sliding window principle for greater efficiency.
- Urgent data and push button.
- Transport-user addressing using 16-bit port number.
- Graceful connection shutdown.

The functionality of TCP is not very different from other complicated transport protocols, such as ISO-TP4. TCP defines procedures for breaking up the data stream into *datagrams* for transmission and ensuring the datagrams arrive at the proper locations without errors. When it receives datagrams, the protocol defines how to reassemble them into the proper order to reconstruct the original stream. If datagrams arrive out of order, the protocol stores them and waits for the missing ones to arrive. To accomplish its task, TCP breaks down the messages or data stream into a manageable size and adds a header to form a datagram. The header consists of (Figure 3.12)

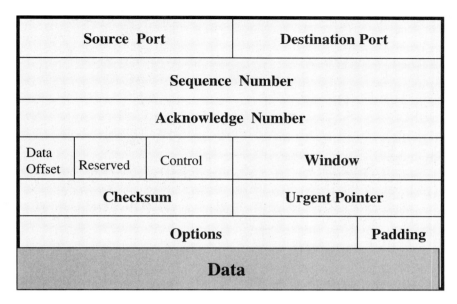

Figure 3.12 TCP header.

- 16-bit *source* and *destination addresses*, corresponding to the calling and called TCP applications.
- 32-bit *sequence number*, a unique datagram number to reassemble the datagrams by the receiving application to form the original sequence.
- 32-bit *acknowledgment number* indicating the identifier or the sequence number of the next expected byte.
- 4-bit *offset* field, indicating the number of 32-bit words in the TCP header since the header size may vary from datagram to datagram.
- 6-bit *reserved* field.
- 6-bit *flags* field, indicating the initiation or termination of a TCP session, resets a TCP session, or indicates the desired service.
- 16-bit *window* field, indicating the number of 8-bit bytes that the host is prepared to receive on a TCP connection.
- 16-bit *checksum* field to determine whether the received datagram has been corrupted in any way during the transmission.
- 16-bit *urgent pointer*, indicating the location in the TCP byte stream where urgent data end.
- 0 or more 32-bit words *options* field, used by TCP software at one host to communicate with TCP software at the other end of the connection. It passes such information as maximum TCP segment size.

The TCP provides robust service by guaranteeing the delivery of data in the order that the packets were sent. TCP uses a positive acknowledgment with a transmit protocol. When a data packet is sent, the sending TCP initiates a timer. If an acknowledgment is not received before the timer expires, the packet is assumed to be lost and it is automatically retransmitted. Consequently, applications can process data sequentially as a stream of bytes. In addition, the TCP is able to respond to congestion on the network by adjusting the timer. As the delay increases, so does the time-out factor, which enables the TCP to reduce the transmission rate. The ability to respond dynamically to network or host congestion without flooding the network with traffic handling messages improves performance.

Internet Protocol (IP). IP is the network layer protocol of the TCP/IP suite (Figure 3.13). IP provides the addressing and fragmentation functions needed to allow routers to forward packets across a multi-LAN network, often referred to as "internetwork." IP is very similar to the level 2 routing between DECnet and forms the basis for the connectionless service of the OSI reference model.

IPs deliver data between different networks by connecting groups of autonomous systems, consisting of subnetworks connected with gateways (Figure 3.13). Thus, the Internet is composed of a series of autonomous systems, each of which is a centrally administered network on a series of subnetworks such as an Ethernet LAN, X.25 packet, or ISDN network. Each autonomous system offers gateways that are used to connect to

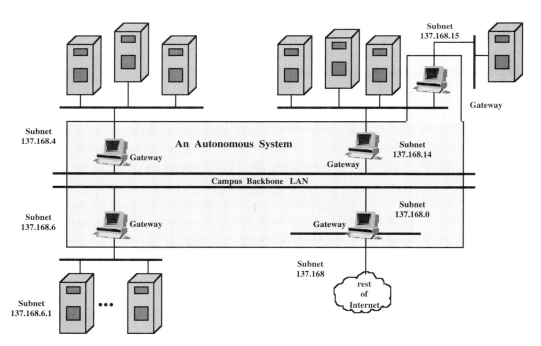

Figure 3.13 LAN subnetworks.

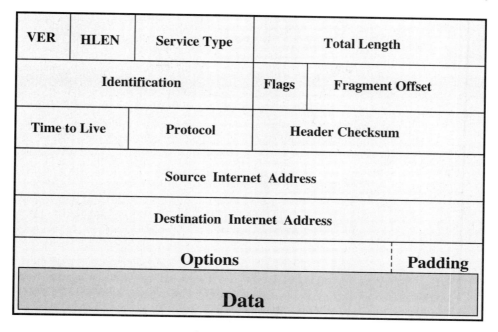

Figure 3.14 IP header.

other autonomous systems. The gateways are the glue that holds all of these different networks together. The IPs define how subnetworks are connected and how the internetworking devices work.

IP also defines how packets are routed from one subnet to another. Each node in the system has a unique IP address (Figure 3.14). The IP adds its own header and checksum to make sure the datagram is properly *routed*. If a particular node has more than one path, the most economical could be selected. If the data packet is too large for the destination node to accept, it is segmented into smaller packets. This is especially important when transferring data from LANs to WANs, since maximum packet size for token ring LANs is 4500 bytes whereas that for X.25 packet is only 128 bytes.

IP provides the "best effort" packet delivery service; that is, it attempts to deliver every packet, but has no provision for retransmitting lost or damaged packets. IP leaves such error correction, if required, to higher-level protocols, such as TCP. This, the trade-off between performance and reliability can be made by the application designer, who can choose a transport-level service meeting the needs of a particular application.

IP's addresses, also called Internet addresses, are composed of two parts: the network identifier (Net ID) or network numbering and the host identifier (host ID) or host address. The network identifier is assigned by a central authority; it specifies the addresses of each network, or related group of networks. Each network ID must be unique across the entire Internet. The host identifier specifies a particular host (station, node) within a given network. Host IDs are assigned by the local network administrator. Host IDs need only be unique within their own network, since each network will have a different network ID.

User Datagram Protocol (UDP). User datagram protocol (UDP) is a connectionless transport protocol. Unlike TCP, UDP is a very simple protocol (Figure 3.15). Its attributes are

- Connectionless.
- Addressing via port numbers.
- Data checksums.
- Very simple.
- "Best effort" forwarding.

The UDP accepts data from the Internet modules that form the IP and forwards them to different processes on the system. UDP supports the network service by serving as a multiplexer for several application programs. In a UDP implementation, there is no assurance that data will arrive at the destination or that individual packets of data will not travel by different routes and arrive out of sequence. Because of this limitation, UDP data must be self-describing since the user must interpret the message and determine what to do with it.

Internet Control Message Protocol (ICMP). Errors occur from time to time in all networks and nodes and must be notified to the senders and receivers of data. The ICMP is used by the IP to transmit IP errors and control messages. ICMP is a component part of every IP implementation and in its role as a transport protocol its only tasks are to transport error and diagnostic data for IP.

ICMP messages are exchanged between different IP modules. One such message is the *echo request*, which is used to test whether it is reachable, and is known as *pinging*. The echo request message also tracks the response time so that average delay time on a line can be determined for comparison with the delay threshold of the application. For example, a host-based application may time out if the delay is too long.

Another common message is "unreachable destination" sent by gateways when they receive a packet they are unable to forward. If the source TCP indicates that packet fragmentation is not allowed, the gateway might also send back this message that it cannot forward without fragmenting the data. This type of message can also be sent if the source-

Source Port Number	Destination Port Number
Length	**Checksum**

Figure 3.15 UDP header.

specified route failed, rendering the target network or host unreachable. There are a number of other message types also.

Simple Mail Transfer Protocol. The *Simple Mail Transfer Protocol (SMTP)* is the Internet Protocol for electronic mail (Figure 3.16). SMTP is a set of standard commands for exchanging mail messages among systems, without regard to the type of user interface or the functionality that is available locally. Although not as sophisticated as X.400, TCP/IP's SMTP specifies how the sending and receiving applications must interact, as well as how control messages should be formatted and exchanged to transfer mail.

SMTP sessions consist of a series of commands, starting with both ends exchanging "handshake" messages to identify themselves. This is followed by a series of commands that indicate that a message is to be sent and receipts are needed and by data commands that actually transfer the data. A single message may be sent to multiple recipients by separating the data message from the address field. This also helps in verifying that there is at least one recipient addressed.

Every message SMTP receives is modified by adding a time stamp and a reverse path indicator. Therefore, every mail message usually consists of a fairly long header with information from each node that handled the message.

TELNET Protocol. The *TELNET (virtual terminal)* protocol defines a *network-independent* virtual terminal through which a user can log in to remote TCP/IP hosts on which the user has an account. The TELNET protocol enables remote terminals to access different hosts by fooling an operating system into thinking that a remote terminal is locally connected.

Most virtual terminals operate in the full-duplex mode. However, there is half-duplex option to accommodate IBM hosts. In this case, a turnaround signal switches the

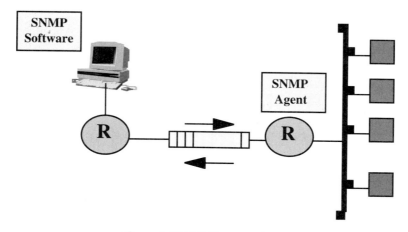

Figure 3.16 SNMP transaction.

sending of data to the other side of the connection. The client and server processes of the TELNET Protocol maintain a logical session with each other. The user TELNET program acts strictly as a pass through entity to allow the exchange of data between the client and server processes. The only exception is for an initial resolution of the protocol-specific transports and establishment of a connection to the TCP/IP server. Both user and server components are available, depending on the role and power of a particular computer. DOS-based PCs usually implement only the user side because of the single-tasking nature of DOS. In contrast, UNIX-based systems can implement both the user and the server components.

File Transfer Protocol. The *File Transfer Protocol (FTP)* is used for bulk transfer of data from one remote device to another. FTP uses Telnet and TCP to implement this protocol. Data in the FTP environment consists of a stream of data, allowing only the entire files to be transferred. FTP can transfer *two types* of data, binary as well as text. A compressed data mode is also available to strip away unnecessary data repetitions.

Sending a file to a user on another TCP/IP network requires a valid user identification and password for a host on that network. This inconvenience can be avoided by using SMTP, which allows mail to be sent to anyone on the network. Since SMTP can only transfer text, the nontext files must be converted to text before transmission and then converted back to their original form by the receiver.

In contrast, X.400 standard allows the user to send text, graphics, telex, facsimile, video, and even voice. In addition, OSI FTAM is also more functional than FTP. FTAM can transfer part of a file instead of the entire file. As an alternative, TCP/IP supports NFS, which can also transfer partial files.

Trivial File Transfer Protocol. The *Trivial File Transfer Protocol (TFTP)* is a file transfer protocol with a minimal function. Like FTP, TFTP also supports text and binary files transmission modes. TFTP uses a connectionless protocol, for sending datagrams via UDP, whereas FTP is connection oriented. Being connectionless, TFTP must be responsible for transmission reliability via algorithms such as time monitoring and package retransmission.

For lack of function and reliability, TFTP is minimally used in loading server programs and fonts in X Window terminals, bootstrapping diskless workstations, and transferring system programs into main memory. Because of its limited functionality, TFTP is a very simple protocol to implement or maintain.

System Network Management Protocol (SNPMP). The *SNMP* is a protocol defined to aid in managing a network. It provides a means for applications on a network management system (NMS) to get information from another node on the network (Figure 3.16). The information obtained is typically system identification data or counters indicating error rates or performance measures in the node being queried.

SNMP is a transaction (sometimes called query/response) protocol which runs over the UDP transport-level protocol. The management application begins a transaction by sending a packet indicating what action it is requesting either GET data or SET a variable in the remote node to some value. The packet will also include the list of objects (management data variables) requested. The node to which the request is directed will examine the packet and retrieve the requested data. The node will then send back a response packet to the NMS.

Management applications can use SNMP, together with the list of objects which can be obtained, to automatically retrieve and display, save, or analyze data for the network administrator.

Systems Network Architecture. The *Systems Network Architecture (SNA)* is a set of IBM proprietary communications products having a similar layered architecture as OSI (Figure 3.17). SNA is the most dominant architecture today and is supported by all major vendors.

Digital Equipment Network Architecture. The *DNA* is the architecture for networking and *DECnet* is an implementation of that architecture. Digital also uses a layered approach to networking (Figure 3.17), similar to the OSI model. Each layer is expressed by a concept, implemented by one or more protocols. Some layers, such as routing, have only one protocol that implements them; others, such as network application and data link, have several protocols. In DNA today, there are two DNA versions in use:

- DNA Phase IV implementations consist of proprietary protocols.

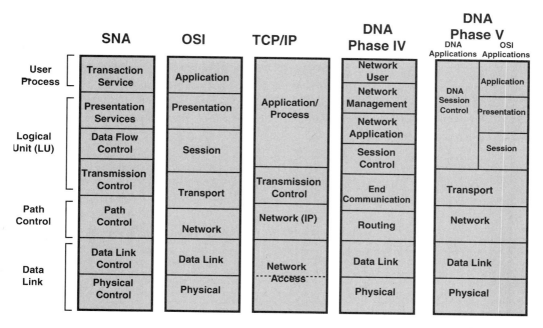

Figure 3.17 Approximate protocol layer mappings.

• Advantage networks, known as DECnet Phase V or DECnet/OSI, is an implementation that is compliant with the ISO's Open Systems Interconnections model.

The Digital proprietary protocol stacks are

• DECnet, a host-to-host communication network, is designed for one host talking to another host. This allows a peer-to-peer network, in which all nodes are equal.
• LAT, local area transport protocol, is a terminal-to-host or terminal T/O network and allows the terminals or printers to communicate with hosts over Ethernet. LAT architecture is able to bypass the session, transport, and routing layers to make direct use of the Ethernet. This protocol multiplexes user data and offloads terminal services management function from the host.
• MOP, maintenance operations protocol, is a maintenance protocol and allows a network processor or host to request and accept down-line load service from a host. It is also used for dumps and diagnostics.
• LAST, local area system transport or LASTport, is a personal computer network service protocol designed for PC LAN environment and can be significantly faster than DECnet. LAST trades the peer connectivity and multiple data link functionality of DECnet for raw performance. Originally used only for virtual disks, DEC now uses it for file and print services also. PATHWORKS for DOS uses LASTport to access CD-ROM drives via Microsoft's interface.
• PATHWORKS implements DECnet, LASTport, LAT, and MOP on the MS-DOS platforms. Variations of this client use Novell's IPX, NetBEUI, or TCP/IP.

X/Open Standards: CAE, TLI/XTI. *CAE: Common applications environment* is being supplied on computers by X/Open and other manufacturers. The goal of CAE is to provide application software portability by defining the following requirements:

• A common user interface.
• A common programmer interface.
• A common connectivity model.

The CAE is designed to provide a support system for the development and running of application software. It is designed to enable levels of portability, interconnection, and interoperability across machines (Figure 3.18). To satisfy the above requirements, X/Open has defined a number of standards to cover the following areas for application portability:

• *Interfaces to the operating systems* are based on the UNIX operating system but have been modified extensively to support the IEEE POSIX standards. The provisions have been made that these systems provide the ability to cope with a variety of natural languages and conventions.
• *Data management* interfaces for the creation and management of files and for access to relational database systems. For access to relational database systems, an extended sub-

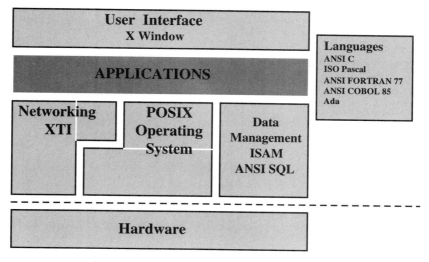

Figure 3.18 Common application environment.

set of the standard ANSI SQL has been defined. This supports embedded SQL calls within C or COBOL source programs.

- *Programming language "C"* is fundamental to standards work on the operating system interface and has been defined as the base language for CAE operating system interface. The CAE definition has been extended to include ANSI FORTRAN-77, ISO Pascal, and ANSI COBOL 85.
- *Window management* includes a user interface common to the X Windows networked window management system.
- *Networking* and *internetworking* interfaces are being developed to respond to the growing importance of networking an internetworking more aggressively.
- The *security of operating systems* is an important element in many commercial data processing environments. CAE offers security features that are consistent with emerging standards.

TLI/XTI: The transport level interface (TLI) follows the ISO transport service definition. *X/Open transport interface (XTI)* denotes an improved form developed by X/Open in which the interface to TLI are barely altered. TLI allows processes on the same or different systems to communicate (as with sockets). TLI provides interface between the user process and the transport provider or transport endpoint. TLI imposes no restrictions on structure of a transport address.

TLI/XTI was conceived as a generic interface to arbitrary transport protocols and is also able to serve TCP/IP. TLI has a synchronous and an asynchronous mode of operation. The application may either wait for an event to occur or be informed of an event by a signal. Only an asynchronous interface is specified for XTI.

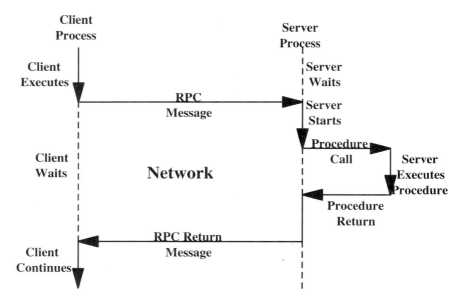

Figure 3.19 Execution of an RPC.

Remote Procedure Call. The *Remote procedure call (RPC)* is a session layer protocol (Figure 3.19) and is an implementation of a client/server model. It was especially developed for network file system (NFS), but is used in many networked applications. RPC forms the basis for message exchange in all NFS applications. RPC may be used in design and development of network services, which are used in a similar way to subroutine calls or procedures in high-level programming languages. This mode of working eases the programmer's tasks in the design and implementation of distributed programs.

Since the RPC protocol is independent of the nature of the message transport, an RPC program may be executed over both TCP and UDP. Some servers offer their services over both protocols and the choice to the client. As a rule, RPC is used with UDP, since the majority of RPC-based applications are transaction oriented. When UDP is used, the maximum size of the data section of an RPC packet is restricted since UDP packets cannot be arbitrarily large. It is normal to send data sets of up to 8 Kbytes over UDP. In contrast, there is no theoretical upper limit for TCP; therefore, if large data packets are to be sent, TCP is used.

The execution of an RPC consists of the following steps (Figure 3.19):

- Activation by the *client* and the request parameters are packed into a data packet.
- Sending of the request and unpacking of the parameters in the *server* program.
- Execution of the request (the *procedure*) in the server.
- Packing and returning of the results to the *client*.
- Unpacking of the results by the *client* and continuation of the normal program execution.

Distributed Computing Environment. The *Distributed computing environment* (DCE), by Open Software Foundation (OSF), is a set of services designed to support the development and use of distributed applications. The availability of a uniform set of services, distributed across a network of computers, enables applications to effectively utilize the available computing resources. DCE is written in standard C language and uses standard interfaces, such as those specified by IEEE POSIX.

Architecturally, DCE lies between the operating system and network services on the one hand and the distributed applications it supports on the other (Figure 3.20). DCE is based on the client/server model of distributed computing and provides a variety of services: fundamental distributed services and data sharing services.

Fundamental distributed services represent the tools for application software developers to create the end-user services needed for distributed computing. They are

- Remote procedure call, for supporting distributed application execution across multiple systems.
- Naming service or directory service via X.500 standards, allowing objects to be identified by human-readable names and location independence.

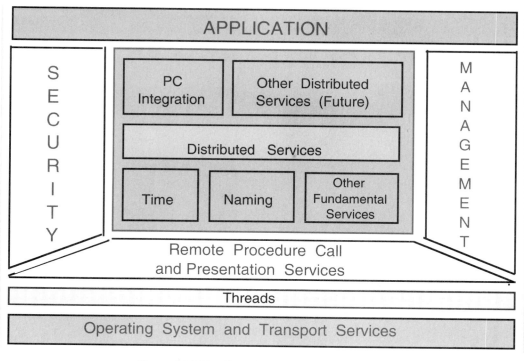

Figure 3.20 Distributed computing environment.

- Time services, by providing precise, fault-tolerant clock synchronization for computers connected in local area networks and wide area networks in a distributed environment.
- Threads, allowing developers to exploit the inherent parallelism in a distributed computing environment for the development of high-performance multithreaded distributed applications.
- Security, providing comprehensive security support via authentication, authorization checking, data integrity by using cryptographic data checksums, and data privacy by encrypting/decrypting data as they are transferred across a network.

Data sharing services provide end users with capabilities built upon the fundamental distributed services. They are

- Distributed file service, making it easy to work with remote files.
- Diskless support service, by allowing diskless computers to use one or more DFS servers for secondary storage.

Each component of DCE provides tools for administrative support. The OSF distributed management environment (DME) is an emerging solution that will address the issues of network and system administration of distributed systems.

File Systems. *Network File System (NFS):* NFS was developed and brought to the market by SUN Microsystems, Inc. NFS allows programs read and write access to files on NFS server computers. This access is transparent to the programs, which need no alteration, special preparation, or additional parameters before operating over NFS. The files on the NFS server are made accessible in that the NFS client computer mounts individual file systems from file systems of the NFS server into its own file system. The allocation of these access capabilities is not usually made in response to a request from the program desiring the access but must be granted to the local system before the access is made.

NFS implementations over UNIX systems with local fixed disks can usually operate symmetrically; thus a processor may be a client and a server at the same time. Two computers may share their files.

NFS is based on a protocol layering which largely corresponds to the layering defined in the OSI model (Figure 3.21). Being modeled on OSI, NFS is theoretically protocol independent. Every layer of the protocol hierarchy may be exchanged for a functionally identical variant with no negative consequences for the rest of the system.

NFS allows an arbitrary collection of clients and servers to share a common file system. Each NFS server exports its directories for access by remote clients. Clients access exported directories by *mounting* them—the mounted directory becomes part of the client's directory hierarchy. The shared files are in the directory hierarchy of multiple machines and can be read/written the usual way.

NFS provides transparent remote access to shared files across networks. Since clients and servers may run on different machines with different operating systems, NFS defines the interface between clients and servers. For this purpose, NFS defines two client/server protocols:

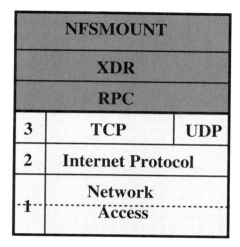

Figure 3.21 NFS protocol layers.

- *Mount protocol:* A client sends a pathname and receives a file handle from the server. This file handle identifies the file system, the disk, and the i-node number of the directory to be mounted. Subsequent calls use this file handle.
- *NFS protocol:* This protocol supports most UNIX file system calls, except for open and close—it is not necessary to open a file before reading it, nor to close it when done. To read a file, a client sends a server a (self-contained) message containing the file handle, the relative path from the mounted directory, the offset to start reading, and the number of bytes to be read. The server does not need to remember anything about open connections.

   Distributed File System (DFS): DFS is a collection of file systems hosted by multiple independent networked computers—the DFS file servers. DFS server systems may be heterogeneous computers running different operating systems. DFS manages and provides access to file system object, such as directories and files, on computers located anywhere in the distributed environment—the DFS clients. The DFS clients may also be heterogeneous computers running different operating systems.

   DFS addresses location transparency, uniform naming, performance, security, high availability, file consistency control, and NFS interoperability. It is scalable and can support both small groups and large groups across wide area networks. DFS files can be distributed across the entire DCE environment. Remote files appear and behave like local files and the distribution is transparent to the users.

   DFS is organized on the usual client/server pattern. Distributed file systems operate by allowing a user connected to a network to access and modify data stored in files on another computer. The computer on which the user is working is the *client.* The computer on which the data are stored is the *server.* When a user accesses the data on the server, a copy is *cached* on the client computer. Now the client can use and/or modify this data and write back the modified data on the server. The problems arise when multiple users access the same data simultaneously.

By allowing the file server to keep track of which clients have cached the data, DFS ensures that users are always working with the most current copy. Therefore, DFS uses a *set of tokens* to keep track of the cached information. If a client wishes to modify and write back the data, it must first request a *write token* from the server. This way, the server can notify other clients who cached that data that their copy is no longer up to date and revokes their write token privileges. Those clients must return those tokens to the server and throw away the old copies. This provides "data consistency" not available on other "stateless" file systems.

DFS uses Kerberos authentication and provides authorization through the use of access control lists. In addition, DFS allows its databases and files to be replicated, which provides for reliability and availability. DFS supports major versions of UNIX and is portable to non-UNIX DCE platforms. DFS is integrated with other DCE components, using services of the RPC facility, directory services, and Kerberos security services. DFS conforms to POSIX for file system semantics and access control security standards. It interoperates with network file system (NFS) clients through the use of protocol gateways.

NetBIOS. *Network Basic Input-Output Operating System (NetBIOS)* was designed for a group of personal computers (originally for IBM PC LAN Manager) to provide both connection-oriented and connectionless services. NetBIOS is a transport-layer programming interface that allows communication between two computers. At the NetBIOS level, there is no distinction between the manager and the client. The communication is done either by sending messages, "datagrams," which have no guarantee for delivery, or by establishing a session called a virtual circuit which guarantees delivery of data packets.

The current specifications of NetBIOS provide expanded network commands for locating names on the network and recording command execution. NetBIOS API for UNIX makes it easier to develop network applications and provides an effective way to achieve interoperability among DOS, OS/2, and UNIX. Since these operating systems can run on Intel processor in the PC family, they can all share resources with each other.

AppleTalk. *AppleTalk* is Apple's networking protocol, used primarily with Macintosh computers. AppleTalk provides simple device-to-device communication, printer sharing, and electronic mail. AppleTalk networks also include non-Apple devices, such as IBM-compatible computers and UNIX-based computers. Many gateways provide dial-up access to AppleTalk networks and interconnection with Ethernet networks.

The protocols defined by AppleTalk reflect the OSI model. At the data link layer, Apple uses the AppleTalk Link Access Protocol (ALAP), which allows devices on the network to transmit and receive frames. AppleTalk uses the Datagram Delivery Protocol (DDP) at the network level. This protocol provides for the delivery of datagrams, either within a network or across networks. The delivery is on a best effort basis, with error recovery left to higher layers.

The transport layer has three protocols: the Routing Table Management Protocol (RTMP), which creates and maintains the routing tables; the Name Binding Protocol (NBP), which provides naming service; and the AppleTalk Transaction Protocol (ATP), which provides reliable, guaranteed delivery of packets from source to destination. AppleTalk implements a number of protocols at the session and presentation layers.

IPX/SPX. Novell uses a version of Xerox Network System (XNS), which comprises a number of protocols, but two are used most frequently: *Internet Packet Exchange (IPX)* and *Sequence Packet Exchange (SPX)*. SPX is used when a message or request is guaranteed to arrive. This protocol establishes a connection, or virtual circuit, between the sender and the receiver. Messages that flow across the connection are assigned sequence numbers that the receiver uses to check for missing, out-of-sequence, or duplicate messages. The receiver returns an acknowledgment. If a message is not acknowledged, it is retransmitted.

IPX is a simpler protocol that does not involve sequence numbers. If a response is not received, the message is retransmitted. While IPX lacks the reliability of SPX, it does not have the overhead.

These protocols have gained considerable acceptance in the market, especially the way Novell implements these protocols and provides interconnectivity among dissimilar operating systems in the LAN environments.

SUMMARY

Standardization can increase the choice of products, reduce the potential obsolescence of a customer's devices, and reduce the need for relays to interconnect networks. However, most devices, networks, and architectures in use today are proprietary, limiting the end user's choice of interconnecting devices.

Standards encourage efficiency, but too many standards exist for each layer, some of them causing incompatibilities. The primary concern of any network connection is successful and meaningful communications. Therefore, the users should select the protocols that not only support existing environments but also provide the flexibility to adapt to future network connections, configurations, and applications. By choosing protocols that are standardized at each individual OSI layer, users can increase their chances for success in implementing future networking solutions.

The majority of large corporate users are moving toward OSI networking protocols at a much slower pace than anticipated. Instead, most enterprises continue to use proprietary networking protocols such as DECnet or SNA while slowly incorporating open systems. The reason for popularity of the proprietary networking protocols is that they are optimized at what they do and provide crucial guarantee of interoperability among a vendor's product line. SNA and DECnet are still richer in functionality and control than open protocols like TCP/IP and OSI. Until there is a universal consensus on OSI with increased functionality, the proprietary protocols as well as X.25 and TCP/IP will continue to be used in multivendor internetworks.

We have discussed a large number of standards and protocols, both public (de jure) and proprietary (de facto). Most of them utilize a layered approach and have the following common characteristics:

- Based on a seven-layer hierarchical model.
- Provide two types of services: connectionless and connection oriented.
- Provide reliable and unreliable delivery of services.
- Provide mechanisms to connect via gateways, routers, or bridges, with incompatible protocols.
- Use the lower three layers of the OSI model as a basis for connectivity and communications.
- Slowly moving toward conformance with OSI protocol philosophies.

In the following sections, we will expand on these protocols and their implementations.

EXERCISES

1. Describe the differences between de jure and de facto standards, with examples.
2. Why do we need standards?
3. What is the major difference between DFS and NFS?
4. What is the most popular networking architecture and why?
5. What is common among DNA, SNA, OSI, and TCP/IP?

4

NETWORK BUILDING BLOCKS

Introduction
Network Communications
    Local Area Networks
    Metropolitan Area Networks
    Fiber Distributed Digital Networks
    Wide Area Networks
    High-Speed WAN Links
    Broadband LANs
    Voice and Digital Network Services
LAN Architecture
    Logical Link Control Sublayer
    Medium Access Control Sublayer
Switching Techniques
    Baseband LANs
    Broadband LANs
    Switch Based LANs
    Hybrid LANs
LAN Topologies
    Bus, Ring, Star, Tree, Hybrid
LAN Components
    User Devices
    Internetworking Tools: Repeaters, Bridges,

    Routers, Brouters, Gateways
    Network Interface Cards
Transport Media Considerations
    Unshielded
    Shielded
    Coaxial
    Fiber Optics
    Wireless
Ethernet Technology
    Ethernet Concepts
    Ethernet Cabling
    Technical Overview
Token Ring Technology
    Token Ring Concepts
    Token Ring Standards: IEEE 802.5
    Token Ring Access Control
Token Bus (IEEE 802.4)
AppleTalk/LocalTalk
    Architecture
    Topologies
Summary
Exercises

INTRODUCTION

The merging of computers and communications has had a profound influence on the way computer systems are organized. The "data center" concept, where one or more large computers are housed in a room or "glass house" and the users bring their work for processing, is rapidly losing ground to the concept of bringing computer power to the user. The old model of a single computer serving all the organization's computational needs is being replaced by one in which a large number of separate but interconnected computers do the same job. These computers are termed as computer networks.

There is considerable debate as to what constitutes networks. Should these be centralized where all users connect to a pool of interconnected computers or should these be distributed across the enterprise and then interconnected over communication lines? There is considerable confusion about the distribution concepts. Many enterprises already have a substantial number of computers in operation, often located far apart.

Unfortunately, most networks are independent entities, established to serve the needs of a single group. The users choose a hardware technology appropriate to their communication problems. It seems impossible to build a universal network from a single hardware technology because no single network suffices for users. Some enterprises need a high-speed network to connect their computers, but as we will learn, such networks cannot be expanded to span large distances. Others, however, settle for slower speed network that connect computers thousands of miles apart.

In recent times, technologies have emerged that make it possible to interconnect many disparate physical networks and make them function as a coordinate unit. The new technology is called *internetworking* or *internetting*. Internetworking accommodates multiple, diverse underlying hardware and software technologies by adding both physical connections and a set of conventions, *protocols*. Internetworking hides the details of the network hardware and permits computers to communicate independent of their physical network connections. With the emphasis on bringing the computing power to the user and the proliferation of cost-effective microprocessors, local area network technologies are gaining wider acceptance.

In this chapter, we will lay a foundation for such technologies that are the fundamental building blocks of network communication. We will explore the basic concepts of communications, implementation trade-offs, the protocol standards, the physical media, and the underlying technologies. With the emphasis on bringing the computing power to the user and the proliferation of cost-effective microprocessors, local area network technologies are gaining wider acceptance.

NETWORK COMMUNICATIONS

Whether the computer networks provide connections between one computer and another or between terminals and computers, there are three techniques for sending that information to that partner: *circuit-switched, message-switched,* and *packet-switched.*

- *Circuit-switched networks* operate by forming a dedicated connection between the two partners. The telephone system uses the circuit-switching technology, where a telephone call establishes a circuit from the originating phone through the local switching office, across trunk lines, to a remote switching office, and finally to the individual telephone. This route is reserved for the entire duration of the connection and is used exclusively for communication between the partners.

While a circuit is in place, it encodes the periodic microphone samples digitally and transmits them across the circuit to the receiver. The sender is guaranteed that the samples can be delivered and reproduced to provide a data path of 64 Kbits/sec, the rate needed to send digitized voice. The advantage of circuit switching lies in its guaranteed capacity; that is, once a circuit is established, no other network activity will decrease the capacity of the circuit. The primary characteristics of this process are as follows:

- Once the connection is made, there are no delays in the transmission other than signal delays.
- Connection establishment and breaking is costly in terms of time.
- Even a relatively small number of connections exploits the network fully.
- Experience has shown that poor use of cabling capacity wastes two-thirds of the circuit connect time.

- *Message-switched networks* use the store-and-forward principle via several intermediate nodes. Each intermediate node stores the information as a whole. The information carries the data specifying the source, target, and the route. The characteristics of this process are

  - Considerable use in the maximum usage of the transmission channels.
  - Varied transmission delays, depending on the load of the network.
  - Flexibility in the case of a physical connection failure by means of rerouting.
  - No explicit establishment and breaking of connections is necessary, with the exception of a virtual connection between the source and the target.
  - Avoid dedicated network capacity with a wide variation in activity.
  - Different information volumes means that short pieces of information are held up by longer pieces of information already in transit.
  - Large, flexible buffers are necessary all along the route, for storing information.

- *Packet-switched networks*, usually used to connect computers, take a different approach. As far as the network is concerned, all information transmitted across the network is approximately equal and relatively short. The traffic on the network divided into smaller manageable pieces, called *packets*, are multiplexed into high-capacity intermachine connections. The transmitting station must split longer pieces of information into packets, and the receiving station must reconstruct the correct information from the incoming packets.

A packet, which usually contains only a few hundred bytes of data, carries identification that enables computers on the network to forward the packet to its right destination. In packet-switched networks, multiple communications can proceed concurrently with intermediate node connections being shared by all pairs of machines that are communicating. However, the circuits could get overloaded, and the users must wait before sending additional packets. The primary characteristics of the packet-switched networks are the following:

- Piecemeal information must be reconstructed in the right order by the receiving station. To avoid lost or duplicated packages, special measures are required by using appropriate protocols.

- Buffers in the receiving station may become filled with incomplete information, leading to a reassembly deadlock.
- Require considerable smaller buffers than with message switching.

A packet needs to hold more than just user data. It must also carry

- Information about the packet's source and target.
- The length of the data.
- Packet sequence number, sued for reconstruction.
- Flags to indicate the beginning and end of the packet.
- Error check bits derived from a cyclic redundancy check used as a basis for checking by the receiver.

Despite the potential drawbacks of not being able to guarantee network capacity, packet-switched networks have become extremely popular. The motivations for adopting packet switching are cost and performance, because multiple machines can share a network and fewer interconnections are required, lowering the cost. Therefore, packet-switching networks have become commonplace, especially in LANs.

Packet-switched networks that span large geographical distances are implemented differently from those that are local. Based on their intended use, the packet-switched technologies are often divided into three broad categories: wide area networks (WANs), metropolitan area networks (MANs), and local area networks (LANs).

WAN technologies allow endpoints to be arbitrarily far apart and are intended for use over large distances. WANs usually operate at slower speeds than other technologies and have much greater delay between connections. MANs span intermediate geographic areas and operate at medium to high speeds. MANs introduce less delay than WANs, but they cannot span as large a distance. LAN technologies provide the highest-speed connections but sacrifice the ability to span large distances.

Speed and distance seem to provide the major criteria. Technologies that provide higher-speed communications operate over shorter distances, whereas the opposite is true for lower-speed transmissions. LAN technologies usually contain a network interface device that connects the machine directly to the network medium, such as passive copper wire or coaxial cable.

In MAN technologies, a network contains active switching elements that introduce short delays as they route data to its destination.

In WAN technologies, a network usually consists of a series of complex packet switches interconnected by communication lines. The size of the network can be extended by adding a new switch and another communication line. Attaching a computer to a WAN means connecting it to one of the packet switches. As we have learned, the switches introduce significant delays when routing traffic. Therefore, the larger the WAN becomes, the longer it takes to route traffic across.

One of the goals of network protocol design is to hide the technological differences between networks, making interconnection independent of the underlying hardware and transparent to the user. The following sections present network protocols and technologies that are the building blocks of network communications.

Local Area Networks

Because of the technology's emphasis on batch processing, data communications in the early generations of computers were minimal. Increased reliance on distributed processing and experience with wide area networks, helped accelerate network technologies such as LANs. LANs have become the building blocks of network communications.

Traditionally, a computer environment was defined by the type of computer system that the enterprise utilized. However, it is becoming more and more apparent that integrating various types of computer systems can help meet the growing computing needs of an enterprise. Integrated environments are now the mainstay of computing. The corporate mainframe still exists, but it is complemented by a LAN. The mainframe, in fact, is taking a different role, such as a node on the LAN by functioning as a repository of data needed by the LAN. The mainframe may be used as a "file server," a "database server," or simply as a "compute server." Of course, some enterprises are also replacing their mainframes with a LAN (downsizing). Overall, LANs exert a considerable influence in the total computing strategy of an enterprise since they are more flexible and tend to be less expensive.

LANs can carry data, voice, and video simultaneously over limited distances but at a much higher rate than traditional wide area networks. All LANs share four common characteristics:

- Limited geographic coverage, usually within a building or a floor of a building.
- Large volumes of data traffic.
- High-bandwidth or high-speed data transfer rates.
- Support for distributed data processing, sharing resources.

Microprocessors are becoming standard fixtures in office and manufacturing environments as enterprises apply information-based technologies to strengthen their competitive edge. Like any commodity, information is valuable only when applied or exchanged appropriately. As communication technology advances, we are faced with an increasing number of alternatives to utilize these devices. Sophisticated solutions need to be devised to ensure open connectivity options, keep costs down, compete effectively in the marketplace, and maintain efficient operations. LANs have come to provide some of these solutions.

By definition, LAN is any electronic communication system that transports information within a given geographic area (usually of limited scope). The area may be an office, a department, a building, a university campus, or even a city. LANs are designed to be economical to implement and reduce costs since a number of users of a microprocessor can share resources and data. LANs usually reduce costs because they allow sharing of their use, equipment, and cabling.

LANs may be configured according to the following methods of operation:

- On a *peer-to-peer* basis, each microprocessor can share some, all, or none of its resources with the other computers on the network.

- With *resource sharing*, one or more centralized servers send and receive files and contain the resources the microprocessors use. The microprocessors perform all the computational processing.
- *Client/server* computing splits an application into client (microprocessor or workstation) and server components. The client interfaces (front end) with and accepts input from the user, prepares it for the server, and issues a request to the server. On the other side (back end), the server receives requests from the clients, processes those requests, and provides the requested service to the client. The client presents these data or results of the requested operations to the user through its own interface. Such an interface frees the user from learning how and where the client interfaces with a server on the network. This process distributes the work on many machines (which may perform specialized service), and the process is transparent to the user.

LANs can be grouped according to the following criteria:

- Architecture.
- Topology.
- LAN components, user devices, and internetworking tools.
- Transport media.
- Encoding technologies (Ethernet, token ring, token bus, AppleTalk).

Metropolitan Area Networks

MAN is any of the several physical network technologies that operate at high speeds over distances sufficient for a metropolitan area. The IEEE 802.6 standard operates on a shared medium with a dual-bus protocol. To support services (overcome the distance limitations of a conventional LAN) across a metropolitan area, the dual-bus subnetwork may range from a few kilometers to more than 50 kilometers in diameter. The subnetwork can be implemented to operate at a variety of speeds greater than 1 M bits/sec, in the range of 34 to 150 Mbps.

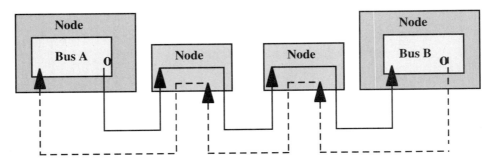

Figure 4.1 Open-bus topology (MAN).

The subnetwork can work in two topologies: open bus or looped bus. In the open-bus topology (Figure 4.1), the bus generates empty slots to be used on the bus, whereas in looped-bus topology (Figure 4.2), the two heads of buses are located at the same node. However, the two topologies provide equivalent service. The dual bus provides a range of services including connectionless data transfer and connection-oriented data transfer.

A MAN can be utilized as a backbone where a number of local LANs can be connected to the backbone with routers and bridges.

Fiber Distributed Digital Networks

The fiber distributed data interface (FDDI) network is a high-speed, fiber optic network standard, supporting speeds of up to and beyond 100 Mbps. As with token ring, this network uses token passing, but it has its own framing and access protocols that differ from 802.5 token ring standard. The FDDI ring can be configured to have a circumference of several hundred kilometers.

FDDI supports elaborate algorithms for detecting and bypassing faulty devices. For redundancy, the architecture includes a dual-ring topology where two separate optic fiber cables are used. If a segment of one ring fails, the two rings are automatically wrapped into a single ring.

FDDI is often used as a higher-bandwidth backbone network that interconnects several Ethernets or 802.5 token rings. Because of its large ring size, FDDI is often employed in MANs.

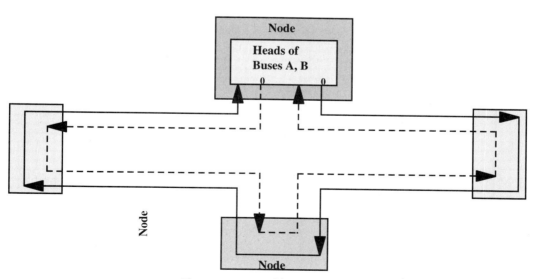

Figure 4.2 Looped-bus topology.

Wide Area Networks

WAN is any physical network topology that spans large geographic distances. WANs usually operate at slower speeds and have significantly higher delays than networks that operate over shorter distances. WAN technologies are sometimes called long-haul networks since they span intercity and continental geographical areas.

WANs generally use point-to-point links. These links are interconnected by routers, with possibly redundant data paths between the routing nodes. Hosts are rarely directly connected to WANs. Rather, the host system is usually connected to a LAN, which in turn is connected to a WAN using a router with connectivity to both the LAN and the WAN (Figure 4.3).

X.25 is a CCITT standard protocol for transport-level network service. Originally designed to connect terminals to computers, X.25 provides a reliable, stream transmission service that can support remote login. X.25 has become increasingly popular as a means of building wide area TCP/IP networks.

When used to transport TCP/IP traffic, the underlying X.25 network merely provides a path over which Internet traffic can be transferred. To send such traffic, you can make an X.25 connection and send TCP/IP packets as if they are data. The X.25 system carries the packets along its connection and delivers to another X.25 endpoint, where they must be picked up and forwarded to the ultimate destination.

High-Speed WAN Links

To achieve high throughput rates, internetworking vendors have turned to high speed WAN technologies such as frame relay, T1 and T3, switched multimegabit data service (SMDS), and asynchronous transfer mode (ATM). Of these, frame relay has emerged as the most popular option.

SMDS is a connectionless, high-speed, public packet-switched data service. SMDS operates at speeds from 1.544 Mbp/sec to more than 155 Mbp/sec.

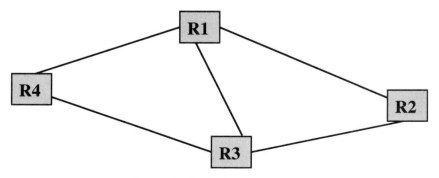

Figure 4.3 Typical WAN topology.

ATM is a transport protocol that operates roughly at the equivalent of the MAC sublayer of the data link layer, allowing it to operate above a variety of physical layer protocols. ATM combines features of multiplexer and LAN backbones, making it able to support LAN, data, voice, and video signals concurrently. ATM can provide dedicated data paths for real-time signals and flexible, configurable bandwidth paths for nonreal-time signals. ATM has been identified as the universal transfer mode for all broadband ISDN services.

T1/T3 Links. High-speed WAN links are sometimes classified as *T1* or *T3* links. The framing used on the higher-speed links is called *T-carrier*. Typical network speeds for such links are 1.44 Mb/sec for T1 and 44.736 Mb/sec for T3 channels. Ethernet and token ring LANs can be connected to each other with high-speed point-to-point links using bridges that transmit the Ethernet and token ring frames over such T1 or T3 connections. To a host on either Ethernet, the two appear as a single network.

Frame Relay. Technologies such as *frame relay* are common carrier replacements for dedicated point-to-point links. Frame relay is packet mode service that strips much of the overhead (such as error correction), but differs from a packet in its length and it also contains both header and trailer control information. A frame can be bit or character oriented. Frame relay uses a separate transmission channel for control characters or header/trailer information, while packet switching uses the same channel for both control and user-defined data streams. Frame relaying is performed by setting up a virtual circuit between the source and the destination.

Frame relay is a connectionless service that provides flow and error control in addition to other standard services. Frame relay is especially suited for bursty traffic, because it offers better routing and error detection capabilities. Frame relay is becoming more common for connecting disparate LANs over wide area links. A frame relay network consists of a set of interconnected switches that are shared by many users. Each site is connected to a frame relay network using a single dedicated circuit. Using a frame relay, you can build a virtual network that appears to have many connections to the network, but in fact has only one.

Broadband LANs

Broadband LANs (IEEE 802.7) differ from the baseband counterparts since they use coaxial or fiber optic cable to carry *multiple channels of data*. A single cable can carry five or six separate communication channels. A broadband network is analogous to cable TV, where one cable connects the house to the cable television service with multiple-channel reception. A broadband network uses 75-ohm coax wire to carry data. Unlike Ethernet or token ring, broadband cabling uses purely analog signaling technology.

Broadband networks can be configured to behave like Ethernet and can even use Ethernet framing, thereby connecting widely separated sites into a very large Ethernet. For data communication, it is likely they will be replaced in favor of FDDI systems.

A broadband network is ideal in a university or hospital like environment because they provide flexibility to carry data, video, and audio transmissions simultaneously within one cable.

Broadband networks use analog transmission methods, which allow the cable to handle information at direct frequency levels. Each frequency forms a separate, autonomous communication channel (Figure 4.4). Frequency levels are basically determined by the number of cycles per second: a frequency between 100 and 300 Hz or cycles per second forms one channel. The frequency between 400 and 700 Hz forms another channel. The number of channels a cable can accommodate depends on how many cycles per second a cable can handle. The higher the frequency, the greater the number of data channels permitted.

Voice and Digital Network Services

Integrated Services Digital Network (ISDN) protocol is designed to enable the transfer of very large amounts of data on a worldwide network. ISDN accommodates a wide range of services over the same line, including data, teletext, videotext, fax, and voice. For home use, the largest demand is for service for television and to access remote databases.

For a long time, telephone has been the primary international communication media, which is proving inadequate for modern communication needs. The primary drawback is that the telephone was designed to carry analog voice signals only. However, today, we

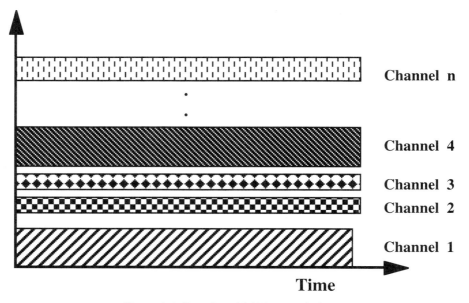

Figure 4.4. Broadband LAN transmission.

must make provisions to transmit data, voice, video, fax, teletext, and so on either simultaneously or in an integrated mode. Since ISDN is based on the existing telephone system, the key service will continue to be *voice*.

ISDN data transmission protocols allow users to connect their computer or ISDN terminals to any other in the world. At present, such connections are difficult if not impossible due to incompatible telephone systems.

ISDN technology has instigated a host of new functions/services that are becoming widespread. One such service is *videotext*. Videotext is interactive access to a remote database by a person at a terminal. With such a facility, you are able to access telephone books on-line without any intervention from the operator, at enormous savings. *Teletext* is another popular application for electronic mail for home or office. It is cheaper to transmit data/mail electronically than physically (mostly paper). *Facsimile* is also becoming increasingly popular to accomplish this task. There is also a need to archive, edit, forward, and broadcast facsimile images.

In contrast to some implementations of OSI, ISDN uses a completely different type of connectors, unrelated to the 25-, 27-, and 9-pin D connectors used for RS-232-C and RS-449. In addition, ISDN bit pipe supports multiple channels interleaved by time division multiplexing. It is also important to note that there is no error checking, no checksum, no redundancy, no acknowledgment, and no retransmission. If errors occur, they must be handled by higher layers in the OSI model. All the ISDN does is provide the user with raw physical bit streams. Integration of OSI and ISDN technologies allows to link both *local* and *wide area networks* and as the underlying network technology for OSI applications, especially voice and video.

LAN ARCHITECTURE

The ISO model is an architectural model based on modularity. The model is not specific to hardware or software, but it defines seven layers and functions at each layer. Local area networking software (protocol suites) of Xerox Network Systems (XNS), Transport Control Protocol (TCP), Internet Protocol (IP), NetBIOS, and hardware protocols such as Ethernet, token ring, token bus, and a multitude of other protocols were designed using this model.

The physical layer defines the methods used to transmit and receive data on the network. It consists of wiring, devices that are used to connect a stations network interface controller to the wiring, and the signaling involved to transmit and receive data on the network.

The data link layer synchronizes transmission and handles packet error control and recovery so that information can be transmitted over the physical layer. The media access control sublayer (MAC) frame formatting and cyclic redundancy check (CRC) are accomplished at this layer. This layer defines the network access methods utilized by most LANs, such as Ethernet, token ring, and token bus. IEEE has defined a number of LAN standards that fit into the Data Link layer. IEEE has defined 10 different standards under the 802⁻ committee. They are

- IEEE 802.1: Provides for higher-layer interface and management functions.
- IEEE 802.2: Logical link control (LLC) is primarily concerned with establishing, maintaining, and terminating a logical link between communicating stations.
- IEEE 802.3: Carrier-sense multiple access with collision detection standard (CSMA/CD) based on bus topology with a decentralized control structure.
- IEEE 802.4: Token bus standard based on token-passing technology over a bus technology.
- IEEE 802.5: Token ring standard based on the token-passing access method, but with ring technology.
- IEEE 802.6: Metropolitan area network standard capable of providing high-speed switched connection over distances of at least 50 km.
- IEEE 802.7: Broadband networks definition.
- IEEE 802.8: Fiber distributed data interface standard.
- IEEE 802.9: Integrated services distributed network standard for integrated voice and data applications.
- IEEE 802.10: Standards for interoperable LAN security (SILS).

IEEE divided the data link layer into two sublayers: the upper logical link control (LLC) and the lower media access control (MAC). The physical layer is subdivided into physical signal generation (PLS), the access unit interface (AUI), and the media access unit (MAU). It is the combination of these two layers where LAN standards (specifically, IEEE 802) have been defined (Figure 4.5).

Logical Link Control Sublayer

The *logical link control sublayer (LLC)* is designed to support a common set of services to the network layer above. It resides at the upper part of layer 2 and is concerned with establishing, maintaining, and terminating logical links between communicating stations. The LLC supports three types of operations:

- *Type 1: Unacknowledged connectionless* (also called datagram) service, where peer entities transmit data to each other without connection establishment. This service does not provide a dedicated logical connection between the receiving and sending units. Individual or group addresses may be used. The data transfer can be point to point, multicast, or broadcast. This type does not provide for flow control or error recovery mechanisms. If needed, the connection-oriented service is provided by the layer above.
- *Type 2: Connection-oriented* operation, which permits peer entities to establish, use, reset, and terminate connection services at the data link layer. It provides for flow control at the network and data link layer boundaries and error recovery. The logical connection may be set up before the transmission sequence, maintained during this sequence, and terminated at the end of it. Data transfer service provides sequencing, flow control, and error recovery at the data link layer. It also provides for acknowledged

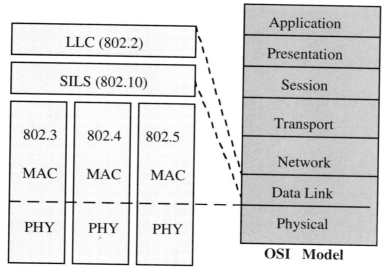

LLC Logical Link Control
SILS - Standard for Interoperable LAN Security
MAC - Media Access Control
PHY - Physical Layer

Figure 4.5 Data link layer and LAN standards.

connection reset, connection termination, packet sequence checking, and flow control across the network layer interface.

- *Type 3: Acknowledged connectionless* services are of independent but related types. The first type is a guaranteed delivery service. This means that the datagram service described in Type 1 is used, but the receiving station acknowledges receipt. The second service offered is a poll with a guaranteed response, which allows previously prepared packets to be exchanged among users.

Media Access Control Sublayer

The *media access control (MAC)* sublayer allows the network to share a single transmission facility. It provides the logic necessary to access the network for frame transmission and reception. Media access control capabilities can be grouped by function, into data link activities and media management activities. The data link activities include both data encapsulation for transmission and data decapsulation for receiving. The media management activities consist of both transmit and receive media access functions.

After a logical link control service is invoked from the upper layers by a service access point, the protocol unit passes to the media access control. The sublayer performs several functions to ensure that network management takes place during operation and that recovery occurs in the event of a network failure. The media access control sublayer passes the protocol data unit to the physical layer to enter the bits on the physical medium that connects the nodes of the network.

The IEEE 802.3 CSMA/CD recommendation covers the MAC sublayer frame format. On receiving a request for transmission, the transmit data encapsulation component constructs a protocol data unit frame using logical link control data. When the medium becomes clear, the transmission begins and the LLC is informed. Similarly, IEEE 802.4 and IEEE 802.5 standards define frame layout standards for the MAC sublayer and how the transmissions are carried out. For a fiber distributed data interface, the media access control format is a derivative of the IEEE 802.5 token passing ring and specifies a physical interface supporting optical fiber cables at a data rate of 100 Mbps.

The media access control frame structure is flexible to accommodate baseband and broadband implementations. For baseband implementations, the IEEE 802.3 standard uses 10 Mbits/second channel over 500 meter segments for coax cable and 1 km segments for fiber optic cable. The following media-dependent physical layer standards are incorporated into IEEE 802.3:

- 10BASE5: 10 Mbps baseband system using coaxial cable.
- 10BASE2: 10 Mbps baseband system using smaller diameter coaxial cable.
- 10BROAD36: 10 Mbps broadband system using coaxial cable with a maximum segment length of 3600 meters.
- 1BASE5: 2 Mbps broadband system using twisted-pair cable.
- 10BASET: 10 Mbps baseband system using twisted-pair cable.

SWITCHING TECHNIQUES

There are many ways to view LAN technologies and to categorize LANs. One of the more common ways is to group them by transmission and switching techniques. LANs fall into four such categories: *baseband, broadband, switch based,* and *hybrid* LANs.

Baseband LANs

The majority of the LANs are baseband. A baseband LAN uses a single transmission medium and a single transmission channel. Because of this, baseband LANs are usually restrictive in terms of the distance and the number of nodes the network can support. Baseband LANs use digital transmission techniques that enhance transmission reliability. Baseband networks, therefore, are less expensive.

Broadband LANs

Such LANs employ many of the technologies used by the cable television industry. These LANs use coaxial or fiber optic cable to carry multiple channels of data. A single cable can carry five or six separate communication channels. Broadband networks use analog transmission methods that allow the cable to handle information at different frequency levels. Broadband LANs have fewer limitations on the number of workstations, transmission distance, and information capacity than baseband LANs. More devices can communicate at once and can be used to transmit different format (e.g., video and data) simultaneously. Because such LANs are more complex, these are more expensive to install and maintain.

A broadband network is ideal in an environment like a university or hospital because it provides data, video, and audio transmissions, and only one cable is enough to network the entire facility.

The broadband networks require more work to allow all these different channels to exist. Items like tuning make them less of a plug-and-play environment.

Switch-Based LANs

Switches of different types, for example PBXs, can also be used as LANs. These are the most commonly used by telephone companies. Traditionally, the telephone wires are used to carry voice. Because every office employee requires a telephone an extra pair of wires are usually installed to carry data as well. The advantage of switch-based LANs is their ability to provide both circuit and packet switching on a single network. Neither baseband nor broadband LANs are well suited for circuit switching.

Hybrid LANs

There are several other LAN types which may combine the features of baseband as well as broadband. One such hybrid is a combined voice and data version of FDDI, a high-speed fiber network standard. FDDI is basically a baseband system because all devices share a single medium. However, because of its 100 Mb/sec bandwidth and its integration of voice and data, FDDI is not considered a baseband network.

LAN TOPOLOGIES

In a network, topology refers to the ways end points or stations or nodes are interconnected. The topology is determined by the layout of the communications links, switching elements, and data paths between any pair of stations. In practice, the choice of a particular topology is governed by reliability, cost, expandability, and performance. In order to achieve this goal, a specific topology must meet at least the following criteria:

- Provide the best possible end-user response time and throughput with efficiency.
- Support the least expensive transmission medium.
- Route traffic across the network's least cost path.
- Easy and inexpensive to install, maintain, and upgrade.
- Ensure proper receipt of all message traffic.
- Minimize the length of the channel.

Every topology cannot meet all the requirements. However, we can build our networks and select a particular topology to meet major objectives in a given environment. We will examine five of the most common topologies employed in business networks: bus, ring, star, tree, and hybrid.

Bus Topology

This is a popular topology since the traffic flow is relatively simple. As shown in Figure 4.6, several nodes are attached to a common cable (transmission line) through which they can communicate with each other directly. This cable is known as trunk line, bus, or network segment. Stations are connected passively so that failure in a local station does not bring down the entire network. Each end of the cable is terminated. Therefore, when network traffic reaches the end of the cable, it is removed from the network and is not allowed to bounce back. Ethernet and LocalTalk are commonly used protocols in bus, linear bus, or tree topologies.

The topology can be implemented as a unidirectional or bidirectional system. In a bidirectional system (e.g., Ethernet), the signal travels in both directions and past the nodes on the cable. The unidirectional system consists of two interconnected one-way channels. Nodes are connected to both channels by passive taps. The tap on the forward portion of the cable is used to transmit the message, and the tap on the reverse portion is used for message reception.

The bus topology has the following advantages:

- It requires short cable length and simple wiring.
- The workstations on the cable act as concentrators or hubs. If one node goes down, it does not affect the rest of the network.
- It is easier to add nodes for network expansion.

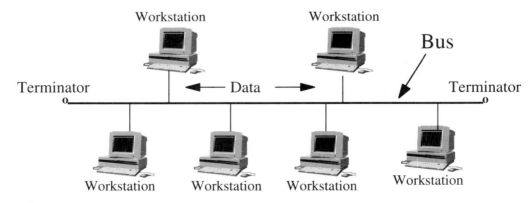

Figure 4.6 Bus topology.

Because of limited points of concentration, it is difficult to diagnose and isolate faults in this topology.

Ring Topology

The ring topology connects several workstations on a single transmission medium, forming a ring. The wiring has no terminated ends because it forms a complete circle. Each node on the cable acts as a repeater, boosting the signal between workstations. Data travels around the ring in only one direction and passes through each node (Figure 4.7). Each workstation is attached via an active tap, which means that the message is examined before it proceeds along the path. A simple access scheme consists of passing the right access sequentially from station to station.

One of the advantages of ring topology is that less cable is needed, reducing cabling costs. There is no central hub, concentrator, or wiring center since the nodes provide this function. On the other hand, since the data are passed through each node (in a store and forward fashion), the failure of one node will bring down the entire network. Modifications to the wiring (adding or deleting stations) are more difficult because the entire network must be brought down. In addition, diagnostics are harder to perform.

Some ring topologies, like IBM's token ring, do come back to a MAU, and the ring is completed within the MAU or MAUs as the MAUs are connected. This prevents one station from bringing the network down. Among the currently used implementations of

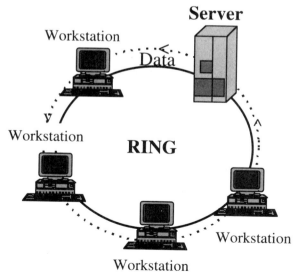

Figure 4.7 Ring topology.

ring topology only FDDI truly depends on each station to function as an active tap and capable of bringing the network down in case of failure.

Most commonly used protocols in ring topologies are token ring and FDDI.

Star Topology

This is the simplest of all topologies to implement. The star network has a central hub to which all the workstations or nodes and the server are attached (Figure 4.8). All network traffic passes through this hub. The stations do not need to make decisions since all messages are routed through the hub.

The advantages include the following: cables are easy to layout and modify, workstations can be added or deleted without affecting the entire network, and centralized control helps in identifying faulty cabling or defective communication lines. Conversely, one node per cable requires an abundance of cabling, increasing the cost of setting up the network, and if the hub fails, the entire network goes down. Arcnet is the most common protocol used in star topologies.

Tree Topology

The tree topology is a generalization of the bus topology (Figure 4.9). One linear bus (the root) may initially be connected to a hub, which splits that bus into two or more linear buses. This splitting can continue, giving this topology the appearance and attributes of a star. The advantages of a tree topology are that it is easy to extend and simplify fault isolation. However, the entire structure depends on the root, and if the primary bus fails, the entire network fails.

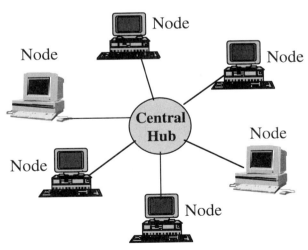

Figure 4.8 Star topology.

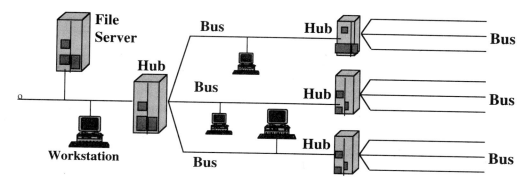

Figure 4.9. Tree or distributed star topology.

Many of the newer linear bus configurations contain concentrators that concentrate the "root" or "trunk" of the bus. This eliminates the risk of primary bus failings.

Hybrid Topology

Today, there is no specific topology to any one LAN, and topologies are commonly intermixed. There are instances where token ring and Ethernet are found at the same site. Such topologies are termed as hybrid topologies.

LAN COMPONENTS

The components required to operate a LAN can be grouped into two categories: hardware and software. The hardware includes

- User devices such as workstations and servers.
- Interconnecting tools such as repeaters, bridges, routers, brouters, gateways, hubs, and concentrators.
- Connecting components or cabling.
- Network interface cards (NICs).

The software includes

- The network operating system, for example, LAN Manager, NetWare, Banyan VINES.
- The operating system for the processor, for example, DOS, UNIX, OS/2, OSF/1.
- The workstation network shell, requester, or redirector.

User Devices

A networked computer that is not used directly by users but that provides some sort of service, such as large disk space or supercomputer or sophisticated database engine, is called a server. Servers are usually high-speed, high-capacity PCs, workstations, mini or mainframe computers. The functions of the servers vary depending upon the enterprise or departmental requirements. These can function as file servers, database servers, computer servers, or a combination of any of these. It is essential to understand that specialized servers are much more efficient and cost effective than a generalized server. However, a generalized server may be all the small enterprise needs. In a network, in addition to the specific function, these servers also perform network traffic management and security functions for the network.

File servers are most prevalent on LANs and function as central repositories of data and/or application programs for the network. They perform information retrieval. File servers usually have large-capacity storage devices attached to them. The network software provides users on a LAN access to these devices. Depending on the requirements, several file servers may be used in a system.

Workstations are usually the personal computers. In a LAN, all the number crunching, computations, calculations, and actual execution of application programs occur at the workstation, which receives shared data from the server. In addition, the workstations are the sites of active communication. Of course, the workstations can also communicate with each other.

Internetworking Tools

No technology provides more flexibility than internetworking tools. The ability to interconnect LANs and WANs in a mix and match fashion allows small LANs to be tailored to individual needs and still remain part of the overall network. When one LAN is overloaded and has reached its upper limits, a second one can be installed and the two can be connected via internetworking devices. Internetworking devices can usually be categorized as repeaters, bridges, routers, brouters, and gateways (Figure 4.10).

Repeaters are the simplest component used in LAN interconnectivity. A repeater is not used to interconnect different networks; rather, it connects segments of the same network to form an extended network. Its purpose is to receive the signal and regenerate or strengthen that signal.

Bridges interconnect local or remote networks at the media access control sublayer. Bridges are used to provide connections between two LANs of the same type and to overcome distance limitations. Bridges are transparent to high-level protocols such as TCP/IP or OSI. Bridges isolate traffic to one or the other segments they connect. Their main purpose is to partition the traffic on each interconnected segment. Bridges forward traffic addressed only to other subnetworks, increasing the effective throughput of the entire network. Local bridges may connect similar networks such as Ethernet to Ethernet, token ring to token ring. Remote bridges use data communications links such as T1 line to join physically isolated networks.

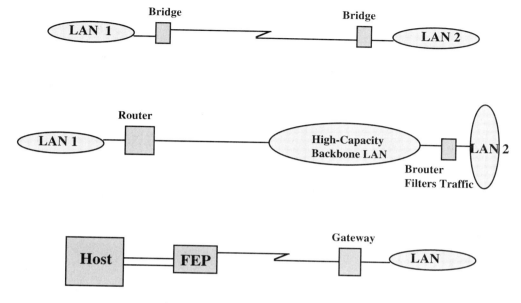

Figure 4.10 Internetworking devices.

Routers are used to link LANs to route messages through intermediate nodes. The routers perform network layer functions of the ISO model and link networks that share the same network layer. Routers create logical subnetworks, allowing large interconnected networks to be organized into domains. Routers can connect LANs of either the same or different type. For example, routers may interconnect token ring and Ethernet networks over a X.25 network.

Brouters combine bridges and routers into one device. Each handles different functions that directly correspond to the ISO layer at which the internetworking function is performed.

Gateways are the most complex of the internetwork products. They interconnect networks that have totally different communications architectures. Unlike the other interconnection technologies, gateways usually interconnect LANs with non-LAN technologies. As such, they perform application (level 7) services. Because of these incompatibilities, the gateways must provide complete conversion from one protocol stack to the other without altering the data that needs to be transmitted. Gateways offer the greatest degree of flexibility in network interconnectivity.

Network Interface Cards

NICs allow the node to communicate with the network's cabling. There are two types of NICs: PC Adapter, which is designed to be used with any computer that has the industry standard architecture (ISA) bus, and another specifically designed for other computers such as IBM Micro Channel Architecture (MCA) bus for PS/2 models. The NICs for token rings as well as Ethernet have the same functions.

The NIC is inserted into one of the expansion slots on the workstation. Each workstation and server on the network have a NIC for attaching the cable. The NIC forms the data packets and transmits those to the network cabling. The NIC also receives data packets from the network cabling and translates them into bytes that the workstation's CPU can understand. Some NICs even have their own microprocessor which allows them to process data without using the PC's CPU.

TRANSPORT MEDIA CONSIDERATIONS

Transmission medium is the physical path between the transmitter and the receiver. The transmission medium establishes the physical connection between stations. The transmission media are evaluated using the following criteria:

- Physical description—twisted pair, coaxial, or optic fiber.
- Transmission characteristics—analog or digital, capacity, frequency range.
- Scope—maximum distance between points in the network.
- Connectivity—point-to-point or multipoint.
- Noise immunity—data protection.
- Cost—cost of components, installation, and maintenance.

Cabling is the network's transmission medium, which carries data packets within the network. The most widely used physical media or cabling falls into three basic categories:

- Twisted-pair.
- Coaxial.
- Fiber-optic.

Twisted-Pair Cabling

Twisted-pair cables are typically composed of 24-gauge wire. These are used for point-to-point connectivity for devices such as terminals for their low costs. The majority of the telephone cabling today is of the twisted-pair type. In addition to their low cost, they are easy to install and maintain. On the other hand the twisted-pair wiring is susceptible to noise with limited data rate and cabling distances. There are two varieties of twisted-pair cables: unshielded twisted pair and shielded twisted pair.

Unshielded Twisted-Pair Cable.   An unshielded twisted-pair (UTP) cable is composed of two insulated, braided copper wires. The wiring used for most telephone systems is UTP. The UTP is very popular because many buildings (houses and offices) are already wired with twisted-pair telephones. Generally the use of telephone wiring for data communica-

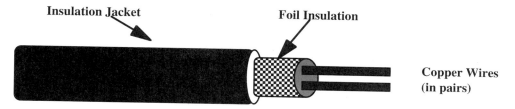

Insulation Jacket   **Foil Insulation**

**Copper Wires
(in pairs)**

Figure 4.11 Shielded twisted-pair wire.

tion has been limited to low-speed point-to-point links between individual computer systems. Popular standards such as the RS-232 interface allow connection to a wide variety of devices.

Shielded Twisted-Pair Cable. Shielded twisted-pair cables use a much higher-quality protective jacket for greater insulation (Figure 4.11). This has a higher bandwidth (longer signal transmission range) than the UTP and is less prone to electrical interference for better noise immunity. However, the improvement in performance is accompanied by higher cost, but the trade-off is not severe, and the increase in performance is noticeable.

Coaxial Cables

Coaxial cable can carry network data in excess of 350 Mbits/second. It has one central copper wire (Figure 4.12), and the main conductor is well insulated. Over this insulating material is a stranded shield, which is a secondary conductor and acts as a ground. All these are surrounded by another protective jacket. The copper wire conductor is the medium over which the data travels.

Coaxial cable is available in different varieties, thicknesses, and impedances. It can be well shielded or poorly shielded. It can be thin and flexible or thick and rigid. It can support both baseband and broadband LANs. It can run unboosted for longer distances

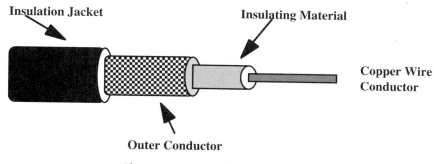

Insulation Jacket   **Insulating Material**

**Copper Wire
Conductor**

Outer Conductor

Figure 4.12 Coaxial cable.

than twisted-pair cables. It can transmit voice, video, and data, and it is easy to install. On the other hand, thick coaxial cable may be too rigid to install, is more expensive to purchase, and is more expensive to install.

Fiber Optic Cables

This type of cable can carry data in the form of modulated light beams, transmitted over the fiber by a light source, which is then detected and converted back into electrical signals by photoelectric diodes. The fiber can be either glass or plastic (Figure 4.13). Fiber optics are used for very-high-speed, high-capacity data communications. They enable data transfer in excess of 1 trillion bits/second. Fiber distributed data interface technology uses fiber optic cables exclusively.

Fiber optic is currently at the top of the media hierarchy and has made significant inroads into the LAN market. Although optical fiber is most commonly used for point-to-point connections, a wide variety of fiber optic cable types are currently being used for fiber optic LANs.

Fiber optic offers numerous advantages over other media types, such as high data transfer, low susceptibility to noise or electrical interference, longer distances, better security, and coverage of larger areas. On the other hand, the cable is expensive, is more costly to install, and requires greater skill to install and connect devices.

Wireless (Satellite, Microwave)

Wireless systems are commonly used for broadcast services. Broadcast systems offer several advantages over copper wire and fiber optic lines and can be divided into two main types: satellite and microwave.

Satellite. *Satellite* systems use geostationary satellites that are positioned 22,300 miles above the earth and maintain the same relative position over the face of the earth. Because of its orbiting distance relative to the earth, a satellite can be viewed from approximately

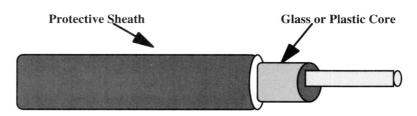

Protective Sheath   **Glass or Plastic Core**

Figure 4.13. Fiber optic cable.

one-third of the earth. Commercial satellites are in communication with earth stations that are equipped with large dish antennas. The earth stations act as transmitter/receiver entities with the ability to transmit and receive signals from the satellite. The popular protocols used for satellite relays include X.25, frame relay, or other standards like TCP/IP and their corresponding transmission protocols.

A satellite is a type of microwave relay station using an uplink frequency band to receive signals from an earth station, amplify them, and repeat (bounce) them to another earth station using a downlink frequency. Satellite systems are being used in television program distribution, long-distance telephone networks, private networks, and mobile systems. A popular use involves the use of satellite systems by long-haul transport companies to keep track of their fleet vehicles when they are on the road.

Signal transmission delays, possible security breaches, cost, and performance distortion in bad weather are some of the factors that must be considered in selecting satellite transmission media.

Microwave Radio Transmission. *Microwave* radio transmissions occur in 4 to 28 gigahertz (GHZ) bands. Microwave signals travel in straight lines at the frequency range within which they operate. To enable transmission, the transmitters and receivers are placed in a straight line, usually on top of buildings or towers about 20 to 30 miles apart. Microwave systems are practical where bypass services are required over local phone company lines. Microwave radio transmission systems are used by common carrier service providers for long-distance communications transmission.

Like satellite, microwave has some disadvantages, including service interruption in poor weather, transmission delays, and possible unauthorized tapping.

ETHERNET TECHNOLOGY

Ethernet is a LAN technology which was developed by the XEROX company in the early 1970s. The version used today was essentially standardized in 1982 by XEROX, Digital Equipment Corporation, and Intel. Ethernet is one of the most widely used technologies for local area networks. At the beginning of the 1980s, a more or less identical version was defined to be an international standard designated IEEE 802.3. In fact, as defined today, Ethernet does follow the specifications of IEEE 802.3; however, older installations may not be entirely 802.3 compliant. There are other related IEEE 802 standards described in this chapter.

Ethernet Concepts

Ethernet follows the IEEE 802.3 standard, using the carrier sense multiple access with collision detect (CSMA/CD) method of network access or protocol. It constitutes the lower two layers of the ISO model. It functions at a transfer speed of 10 Mbits/sec. With this transfer speed and the CSMA/CD access method, Ethernet is an excellent choice for networks that have occasional bursts of heavy traffic. Because of its low cost (existing cabling like the shielded and unshielded twisted pair), wide availability, and technical maturity, Ethernet is by far the most popular medium for LANs.

Ethernet is a multiaccess, packet-switched communications system for carrying digital data among locally distributed computer systems. Ethernet is a bus system with a random access mechanism for the commonly used medium, which is implemented with coaxial cable. CSMA/CD is used for the transmission protocol. An adaptive delay interval is used in the case of collisions. The adaptive method is a modified binary exponential backoff. The modification consists of the interval remaining constant after the 10th attempt to send one and the same packet, and after the 15th collision the transmission is broken off with an appropriate message to the higher levels of the transmission protocol. Although the CSMA/CD procedure can be used for almost all bidirectional media, the basic Ethernet uses a coaxial cable. However, today some systems even use fiber optic cables.

The Ethernet system has several basic components: the station, the controller, the transmission system, and the interface. The *station* is usually a microprocessor that makes use of the communications capability of the network. Each station has an interface between the station's operating system and the Ethernet controller. The *controller* is usually connected to the system bus and can thus be addressed by the station. The controller's functions include algorithms necessary to access the channel, agreements about time-outs, coding and decoding, serial-to-parallel translation, address identification, error detection, intermediate storage, and CSMA/CD and packet formation.

The *transmission system* contains all the components necessary to establish a communication route between controllers. It contains transmission medium, appropriate send and receive units, and perhaps repeaters to enlarge the network. The *interface* represents the connection between the controllers and the transmission system. Since the controller performs a majority of the communication functions, the interface is a relatively simple device. It also contains the data routes to and from the transmission system. It must also be able to transmit status reports and control information.

Ethernet Cabling

Ethernet supports a variety of cabling types. Different cabling types can be intermixed by using the appropriate interconnection hardware since the fundamental access media protocol remains the same.

Thickwire or *10BASE5* is used more often for backbone cabling between building floors or within a computer room. The maximum length of a single thickwire cable segment is 500 meters.

Thinwire or *10BASE2* is much thinner and cheaper, with a maximum cable run of about 300 meters. Other than the distance limitations, the specifications are identical to thickwire Ethernet cable. Because of its low cost, thinwire Ethernet cable is commonly used in small networks.

Twisted-pair or *10BASET* is a very popular Ethernet medium. It is used to transmit and receive the Ethernet signal from each transceiver. Each twisted-pair wire is connected to an active hub that repeats the signal between each wire. Maximum wire runs from the active hub are 100 meters. This can be used to wire entire office floors and even whole

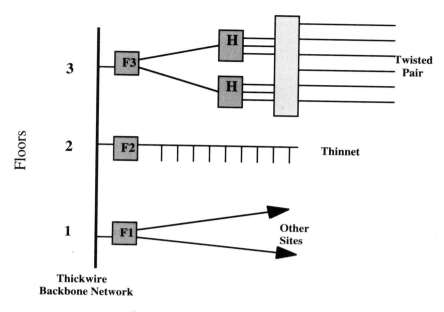

Figure 4.14 Building wiring layout.

buildings. It is much cheaper than either the thickwire or the thinwire, and its installation is no more difficult than the regular telephone wiring.

It is quite common to see all three types of Ethernet wiring in a single installation (Figure 4.14).

Technical Overview

Stations must be able to send and receive packets over the common coaxial cable system using the agreed format and interpacket gap. Each packet should be seen as a series of 8-bit bytes. The least significant bit of each byte is transferred first. The addressing uses a 48-bit address which is fixed in the hardware of every Ethernet controller, which has a unique address. The structure of the Ethernet packet is shown in Figures 4.15 and 4.16.

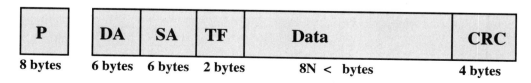

Figure 4.15 Ethernet frame.

Packet Start

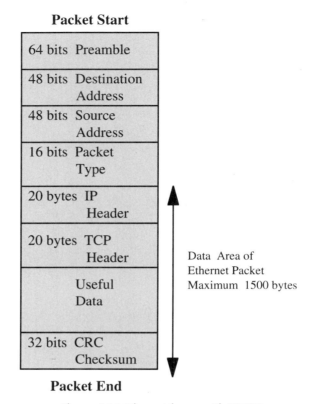

Packet End

Figure 4.16 Ethernet frame with TCP/IP.

A packet is a unit of information which not only contains user data but also the header information. This header information is the control information that is applied to the data in the formation of a packet. Each respective layer (network, transport, and session) that is implemented on the network station will apply its header information into the packet. This information is used by the receiving station to take action.

Maximum packet size is 1526 bytes, of which 1500 are data. *Minimum packet size* is 72 bytes, of which 46 are data. The *preamble (P)* to an Ethernet packet is a special bit pattern which serves to synchronize the receiving station. This is followed by

- *Destination address (DA)* of the station to which the packet is sent (IP address in case of the TCP/IP protocol) is an 6-byte field.
- *Source address (SA),* which contains a 6-byte address of the sending station.
- *Type field (TF),* which contains the 2-byte type identifier of the packet for interpretation by higher-level protocols, for aiding in interpretation of the data.
- *Data field (data),* which contains a whole number of data bytes in the region 8N < 1500. The minimum ensures that correct packets and collision fragments can be distin-

guished. Each bit sequence shorter than the maximum packet length is identified as a collision fragment.

- *Cyclical redundancy check (CRC),* which is a 4-byte field containing a cyclic redundancy checksum produced by a polynomial.

Each station reads the packets on the bus cable and compares the destination address with its own. If the two are the same, the station is the destination and it receives the packet completely. Because of this property, all stations in the network read each packet.

Theory of Operation. Ethernet electrically is a bus and works like a telephone party line. The Ethernet access method basically performs three functions: transmitting and receiving data packets, decoding the data packets for transmission or reception, and detecting errors within the data packet or on the network. A station wishing to transmit checks whether the cable is busy (using carrier sense) and defers transmission of the packet until the cable is quiet (no signal activity on the cable). When the cable is quiet, the deferring station immediately begins to transmit.

When a station is ready to send a frame, the transceiver checks to see if any other host is transmitting. If not, the transceiver sends the frame (Figure 4.17), while monitoring the signal on the cable if any other host started to send at the same time.

If another station is also transmitting, a collision results. A collision is not a disastrous event. Rather, it garbles the signal on the cable, just like two people talking on a sin-

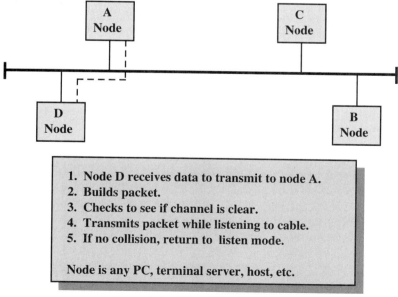

Figure **4.17** CSMA/CD algorithm.

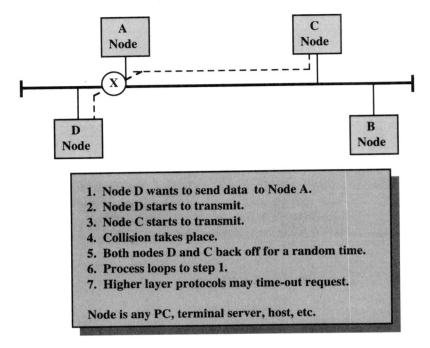

Figure 4.18 CSMA/CD with collision algorithm.

gleplex telephone line simultaneously. When a collision is detected, the transceiver notifies the network interface, which invokes the backoff algorithm (Figure 4.18).

Collisions. On Ethernet networks, a collision occurs when two stations transmit at the same time (Figures 4.17 and 4.18). In a correctly working system, collisions occur only within a short time interval following the start of transmission, since after this interval all stations will detect carrier and defer transmission. This time interval, the collision window or the collision interval, as mentioned earlier, is a function of the end-to-end propagation delay. If no collision occurs during this time interval, a station is said to have acquired the cable and continues to transmit the packet until completion. Once a packet is transmitted, the Ethernet controller assumes that the packet made it without error. No acknowledgment is sent from the recipient of the packet to the sender to indicate the status of the frame. It is up to the higher-level protocols to ensure the packet reliability.

If a station detects collision, the transmission of the rest of the packet is immediately aborted. A collision is detected when the signal level on the cable is equal to or exceeds the combined signal level of two stations transmitting. To ensure that all stations up to the collision have properly detected it, any station that detects a collision invokes a jam signal that, appropriately, jams the cable network. Each station then invokes its respective backoff algorithm and attempts to transmit the packet at a later time. The receiver function of

Ethernet is again activated when the controller sees the cable become active. The process of collision detection, backoff, and retry takes only a few microseconds and is transparent to the host system.

One might think that collisions occur frequently and may degrade network performance. Most Ethernets run with long-term average traffic loads of less than 10% of the available bandwidth. Therefore, on a well-configured Ethernet, collisions should be fewer than 1% of total frames transmitted.

TOKEN RING TECHNOLOGY

Token ring is another popular approach to local area networking. These networks have become synonymous with IBM, the driving force behind their development at the Zurich Research Laboratory. IBM unveiled the token ring network in 1985.

Token Ring Concepts

The token ring is a series of point-to-point links closed up to form a logical ring that connects the stations (Figure 4.19). Each station is connected to the ring by a repeater, which is an active device that regenerates all the data flowing on the ring regardless of whether it is in the transmit or receive mode. When a station receives an idle token and has no data to transmit, the token is passed to the next station on the ring. If the station does have data to transmit, the idle token is modified and the information is sent on the network. The destination station then copies the information and passes on the token. All other stations simply regenerate and pass the signal. When the message returns to the originating station, it is removed from the ring, and the token is modified to indicate an idle state and forwarded to the next station on the ring.

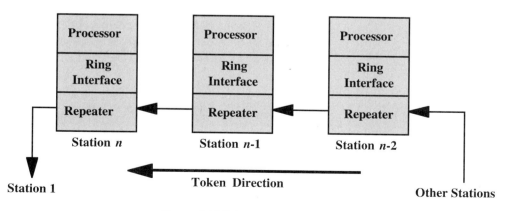

Figure 4.19 Token ring operation.

Token Ring Standards: IEEE 802.5

The token ring architecture is based on the IEEE 802.5 standard. The token ring network uses

- Token passing for access method.
- Shielded and unshielded twisted pairs.
- Baseband transmission.
- Star-wired ring technology.
- Transfer rates of 4 Mbps and 16 Mbps.

The token is passed from node to node until a request to transmit data is made. The token, a predetermined formation of bits, permits a node to access the cable. The topology is a star-wired ring, with the ring formed by the hub. Data flows on the ring only in one direction. The two major versions of token ring have transfer rates of 4 and 16 Mbit/sec, and both use baseband transmission. Both versions use either unshielded or shielded twisted pair. The shielded twisted pair gives better signal reliability and extended signals distances.

A token ring is composed of a number of stations serially connected by a medium. Information is transferred along the ring serially from one node to another. Each station regenerates and repeats each bit and serves as the means for attaching one or more devices to the ring (Figure 4.20). A station gains transmission access by capturing a token passing on the medium. There are four components that make up the token ring network:

- A network interface card (NIC).
- A multistation access unit (MAU).
- A cabling system.
- Network connectors.

The multistation access unit is the hub of the token ring network. It can connect up to 8 nodes. For additional nodes, more MAUs can be added with gross total of up to 72 nodes. The MAUs form the ring portion of the network and the nodes create a star. When the maximum number of nodes on a token ring network has been reached, another network must be established. The MAUs may be in the same physical area or can be separated, but they must be connected to form a ring. The maximum cabling distance from the MAU to the node is from 150 to 500 feet, depending upon the implementation and cable types. Many different types of cabling can be used, including the preexisting telephone wiring.

The IEEE 802.5 standard defines a set of services to be provided by the MAC sublayer of a token ring network. It includes frame transmission, token transmission, stripping, frame reception, priority operation, beaconing, and neighbor notification.

Frame Transmission: When a station receives a transmit request from a higher layer, the MAC layer prefixes the higher-layer protocol data unit with the proper header and puts it in the transmission queue. The station then waits for a "free token" in the ring. It copies

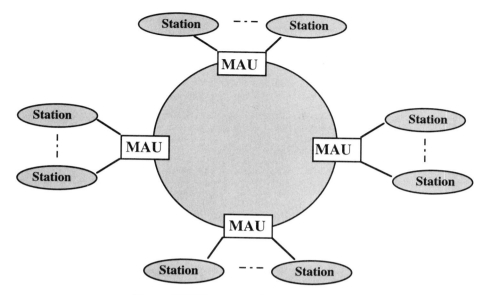

Figure 4.20 Token ring physical structure.

the token's starting delimiter and access control, places them at the front of the data frame, and initiates transmission. The station continues to transmit until it has nothing more to transmit or the token holding timer has expired. After it receives the access control field of the last frame, it places a free token in the ring and inserts the end delimiter byte to the token.

Token Transmission: At the end of transmission token-holding time, the station checks to verify that its address has been returned in the source address field and sets appropriate flags.

Stripping: This function removes all the transmitted frames from the ring.

Frame Reception: While repeating the incoming signal stream, the stations check it for frames they should copy or not. If it indicates a media access control frame, the control bits are interpreted by all stations on the ring.

Priority Operation: IEEE 802.5 supports a three-component priority scheme.

For proper token ring operation, hard failure must be detected and isolated. Failure can occur at the station reporting the failure (the *beaconing station*) or on the intervening ring medium.

The monitor station plays an active role in maintaining the integrity and stability of the network.

The IEEE 802.5 specifies a baseband, shielded twisted-pair cable attachment to the trunk cable of the token ring (Figure 4.21). The communications medium consists of a set of trunk coupling units interconnected sequentially by the trunk cable links. The standard also defines a system with alternative data rates of 1 Mbps or 4 Mbps with a maximum capacity about 250 stations per ring.

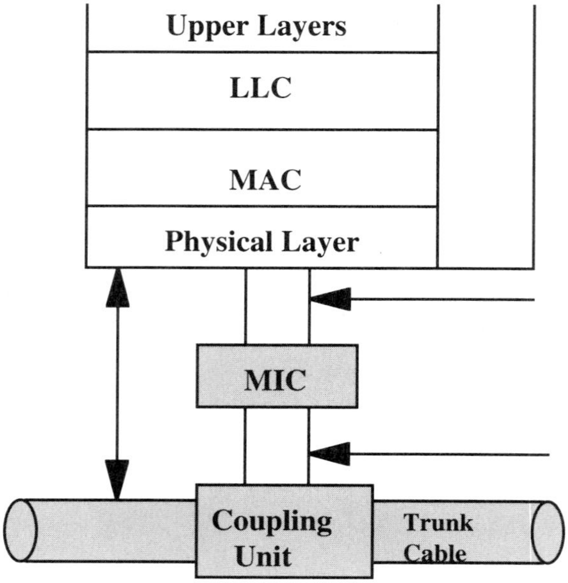

Figure 4.21 Token connection scheme.

Token Ring Access Control (Token Passing)

Token passing is an access method where a node can only transmit on the network when it has the token (Figure 4.22). The high-speed fiber optic networks also use token passing. Station entry into the ring is controlled by the station itself. The insertion and ring bypass mechanisms reside in the trunk coupling unit, which the media interface cable controls.

TOKEN BUS (IEEE 802.4)

Token-passing bus protocol or IEEE 802.4 is designed to operate with both broadband and carrier-band signaling. The standard describes electrical signaling methods, frame format, access methods, contention resolution, and the media access control to logical link control layer. Although the 802.4 standard uses a bus topology (Figure 4.23), it forms a logical ring during typical operation. Right-of-access to the communication medium is indicated by a token passed along the network from node to node. To be a part of the token bus network, a node must know three addresses: the predecessor's address, the next station address, and its transmit address.

The operation of a token bus is similar to that of the token ring, but the stations are physically connected in a bus configuration. The network operates as a logical ring with tokens being passed between stations in a predetermined sequence. The sequence of stations does not necessarily follow the order of attachment. Passive stations may appear at any single point in the sequence, have multiple appearances, or be omitted altogether.

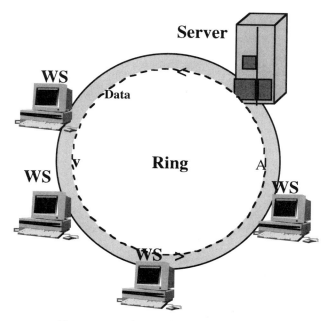

Figure 4.22 Token-passing scheme.

Because they are connected in a bus topology, the token bus is a passive broadcast network.

Individual network nodes do not regenerate the received signals from the network. This improves network reliability since no single node failure stops all signal flow, but signal quality can degrade in the absence of signal regeneration. Because of the broadcast nature of the network and if a node is still attached to the bus, it receives all signals transmitted on the bus. The token, which grants permission to use the transmission media, will never be routed to the node.

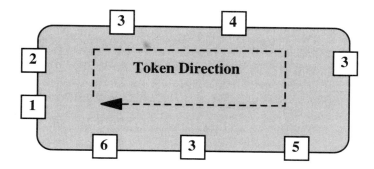

Figure 4.23 Token bus configuration.

To reduce overhead associated with the token, the bit pattern can be turned to idle channel condition. When idle condition is recognized, the next station in the sequence seizes the channel and begins to transmit. Each station constantly monitors the channel for idle channel status.

APPLETALK/LOCALTALK

The popularity of the Macintosh, especially its user interface, has given rise to Apple's networking protocol, generally referred to as AppleTalk. LocalTalk is Apple's networking hardware; AppleShare is the network operating software. At one time, the Macintosh was used as a special-purpose computer, usually for desktop publishing applications. However, recently, the Macintosh and other Apple computers have made tremendous strides within the *Fortune* 500 companies and support a wide range of network hardware and applications.

Like the Macintosh, the AppleTalk is relatively easy to use since the AppleTalk protocols are included in the hardware and its operating system, providing basic networking capability in each unit. AppleShare allows a Macintosh to function as a file server on the network. The protocols are also built in Apple's peripherals, such as laser printers, allowing you to build an AppleTalk network with a shared printer capability simply by connecting the device. From its inception, AppleTalk has been able to share peripherals and files on a Macintosh-based network. Network installation and reconfiguration are easy and inexpensive, with very little system administration requirements.

Gateways provide dial-up access to AppleTalk networks and interconnection with Ethernet LANs.

AppleTalk Architecture

The AppleTalk protocols reflect the *ISO model* similarities. The AppleTalk *physical layer* consists of the interface for the AppleTalk hardware. If Ethernet or token ring are used, the interface is for the respective architecture's hardware since AppleTalk supports both Ethernet and token ring.

AppleTalk Link Access Protocol. Apple uses the AppleTalk Link Access Protocol (ALAP) at the *data link layer*. This protocol allows devices on the network to receive and transmit frames. The ALAP protocol specifies addressing, data encapsulation, media access management, and frame transmission dialogs.

Datagram Delivery Protocol. At the *network layer level*, Apple uses Datagram Delivery Protocol (DDP). This provides the delivery of packets (datagrams) both within the local network and outside this network. DDP is a very simple protocol with error recovery being provided by the upper layers. DDP also facilitates AppleTalk to internetwork using bridges and routers. A key function of the DDP is routing datagrams within the Internet. If a datagram is sent to a destination on the same network as the source node, it is transmitted directly using ALAP.

If the transmission is sent to a node on a network other than the source node, it is transmitted to a router node on the local network. This router checks its tables and determines where the datagram should be forwarded, either to another router or another network or to the destination node. The DDP has access to the Routing Table Management Protocol (RTMP) in the *transport layer*. The RTMP creates and maintains the routing tables.

AppleTalk uses the concept of "socket clients" to allow multiple communicating processes within a single node. A socket client uses a logical entity to send and receive datagrams on the Internet. Each socket is 8-bit in length and can be accommodated within the 16-bit Internet address.

Routing Table Management Protocol. As mentioned earlier, the RTMP creates and maintains the routing tables. For each destination network number, the routing table indicates the next node and the number of hops needed to reach that destination network. AppleTalk uses its own naming service protocol, Name Binding Protocol (NBP). Names can be assigned to socket clients and services available on the Internet. The NBP is responsible for resolving names and addresses with the Internet addresses.

The AppleTalk Transmission Protocol (ATP) provides reliable and guaranteed packet delivery. If a response is not received within a specified time, the datagram is retransmitted. This ensures delivery, but may cause duplication. The ATP is based on a transaction model, consisting of a request and its response type of dialog.

Stream Protocol. AppleTalk uses the *session layer* protocols to establish a communication session. Apple has defined four separate protocols to handle these functions. The Stream Protocol (SP) packages the data into the datagrams of correct sizes, maintains the correct sequencing of these datagrams, and establishes breakpoints during the session to ensure efficient communication. The Data Stream Protocol (DSP) establishes and maintains a full-duplex communication session between nodes, detects and eliminates duplicate datagrams, and requests retransmissions to ensure error-free delivery.

The Zone Information Protocol (ZIP) helps subdivide the network into zones, helps NBP (Name Binding Protocol) identify the networks, and maintains the information to allow the routers & bridges to establish a delivery path for transmissions. The Printer Access Protocol (PAP) services the devices such as printers, and tape backups when a network is to communicate with such devices.

AppleTalk Filing Protocol. AppleTalk uses two protocols to define the presentation services and the syntax usage. The AppleTalk Filing Protocol (AFP) primarily provides the interface for file-server functions with the AppleShare and NetWare operating systems. The AFP provides the network's hierarchical structure for volumes, folders, and files. AppleTalk workstations can access both local and remote files using AFP. The PostScript Protocol (PSP) provides an interface between network workstations and the PostScript devices, such as Apple's LaserWriter.

AppleTalk Topologies

The AppleTalk network uses a bus or tree topology, usually with twisted-pair cabling. Many AppleTalk networks are also using unshielded twisted-pair cabling, known as phone net. AppleTalk uses the CSMA/CD access method. The maximum length is limited to 300 meters; however, networks can be interconnected using bridges and routers.

SUMMARY

Network configurations or topologies are the way computers are physically connected together to form a network. The alternative to providing interconnection, with application-level programs is a system based on network-level interconnection which, in turn, delivers data from their original source to their ultimate destination in real time. In particular, we desire a communication system that is not constrained by the boundaries of the physical networks. We must remember the following two observations while designing networks:

- No single network can serve all users.
- Users desire universal connection.

We have learned that local area networks provide the highest-speed communication but are limited in geographic span. Wide area networks span large distances but cannot supply high-speed connections. We have also noticed that there are many emerging technologies that only provide a specialized utility for specialized environments. At the same time, there are many similarities like the transport media or the mechanism or topologies that lie underneath.

We touched upon various communication structures like LANs, WANs, MANs, high-speed links, and broadband and voice integrated network services. We also discussed architectures and protocols as to how the data are carried on these structures. However, it was only an introduction for which the details will be provided in the ensuing sections.

The primary purpose of this section was to help you build an understanding of the various building blocks of the network technologies.

EXERCISES

1. Explain different configurations of LAN topologies.
2. Why is "bus" topology more common?
3. Define each of the following:
    a. Gateway
    b. Bridge
    c. Repeater

    d. Router

    4. DECnet and SNA are examples of PC LANs? True or false?

5. Which of the following devices can be found in modern PC LANs?

    a. Mainframe

    b. Minicomputer

    c. Engineering workstation

    d. PC/microprocessor

6. Match each of the following terms to its best description.

    a. Downsizing

    b. Internetworking

    c. Peer-to-peer

    d. Client/server

    __ Communication between equipment from different manufacturers.

    __ LAN architecture which stores files on a centralized server.

    __ LAN architecture in which workstations are also used as servers.

    __ Type of application.

    __ Substitution of microcomputer processing for mainframe.

7. Write in Ethernet's characteristics in the blanks below.

    _____ Standard

    _____ Data rate

    _____ Access method

8. Write in token ring's characteristics in the blanks below.

    _____ Standard

    _____ Data rate

    _____ Access method

9. Number the following CSMA/CD events in the proper order.

    ____ Retransmit

    ____ Hear collision

    ____ Wait specified time and listen

    ____ Listen for transmission on LAN (this is # 1)

    ____ Transmit

10. TCP/IP is described by which of the following? (circle all that apply)

    a. An example of communication protocols

    b. A protocol suite

    c. Contains Transmission and Internet protocols

    d. An implementation of the OSI model

    e. Allows dissimilar equipment to communicate

5

INTERNETWORKING PROTOCOLS—I

Introduction
OSI Protocols
  The OSI Reference Model
  The Layers
  Interprocess Communications
  Services
  Standards for the OSI Layers
  OSI Application Layer Protocols
  Network Management Protocols
  Summary
Integrated Services Digital Network
OSI and ISDN

OSI and X/Open Standards
TCP and IP Protocols
  Introduction
  Layering in the Internet Protocol Suite
  The Internet Protocol
  The Transmission Control Protocol
  User Datagram Protocol
  TCP/IP Application Protocols
  Troubleshooting TCP/IP: ICMP
Protocol Dependencies
Summary
Exercises

INTRODUCTION

Internetworking is the connection of two or more distinct networks. In today's complex and heterogeneous business environments, users need to communicate and exchange data. Computer applications communicate with each other by a set of rules, called *protocols*. These protocols govern the exchange of messages between these applications in order to make this exchange efficient and meaningful.

"Roger" and "Over" in radio traffic is an example of a protocol, where both communicating partners acknowledge that they have understood the message by signaling with "Roger" and signal a change in direction of speech with "Over." Data exchange between applications or data processing systems naturally involves a similar exchange.

Because of the complexity of business requirements and communication between data processing systems, a single protocol may not suffice. Therefore, it is usual to apply several data communication protocols simultaneously which cooperate and provide different functions (services) to the user.

In the 1970s, major computer manufacturers developed and marketed proprietary networking products to allow communications between their own computers. As the applications became more complex and users started to move to multivendor purchasing strategies, it became increasingly important to develop standard communication technologies to interconnect machines, independent of the manufacturer.

The ISO (International Standards Organization) standard for Open Systems Interconnection (OSI) is such a standard and underlies all the developments in networking of the last decade. The process of communication between two systems can be visualized as made up of several separate tasks. These tasks can be thought of as separate modules, operating in hierarchies with the two systems. The modules can be visualized as a series of layers, through which messages must pass. In the ISO approach, the communications task was divided into seven layers. The resulting scheme is called the *seven-layer model*.

In this chapter, we will discuss standards for interconnection, examining internationally approved (de jure) OSI standards and the de facto TCP/IP standards in detail. Since all the traffic carried on communications networks also includes voice, telex, facsimile, and even video, we will examine the widespread introduction of integrated service digital network (ISDN) connections, by telephone companies. Therefore, we will also discuss the relationships between OSI, ISDN, and other such standards.

OSI PROTOCOLS

Originally released in 1978, the OSI model describes a network architecture that connects dissimilar devices. The original standard applied to open systems, which are open to each other because they use the same communications protocols or standards. The OSI is concerned with the interconnection between systems—the way they exchange information—rather than the internal functions of particular systems.

The OSI Reference Model

In 1984, a revised version of the OSI model was released and this has since become an international (de jure) standard. Many computer manufacturers have modified their layer network architectures to comply with the layers of the OSI. This seven-layered model is also referred to as the *ISO OSI Reference Model*. The principles that were applied to arrive at the seven layers are as follows:

- Each layer should perform a well-defined function.
- A layer should be created where a different level of abstraction is needed.
- The function of each layer should be chosen with an eye toward defining internationally standardized protocols.
- The layer boundaries should be chosen to minimize the information flow across the interfaces.

• The number of layers should be large enough that distinct functions need not be thrown together in the same layer out of necessity and small enough that the architecture does not become unwieldy.

Each layer of the OSI Reference Model (Figure 5.1) performs a particular, self-contained function. Layering ensures modularity, theoretically allowing a user to substitute one OSI protocol for another at a given layer, without disrupting the protocols/functions above/below that layer. The effect of this is to distribute the work across the layers, which operate in a peer-to-peer fashion. Peer layers are equally ranked layers that communicate with one another by means of peer protocols.

The Layers

Figure 5.1. demonstrates the OSI model layered structure with seven functional levels.

• The *physical layer* is indirectly connected to the physical medium (usually by wires) between the systems. This layer controls, among other things, the exchange of individual information bits (relating to transmission rate, bit coding, connection, etc.) over a

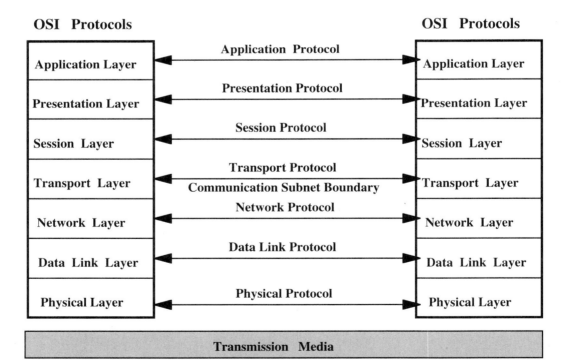

Figure 5.1 The OSI reference model.

transmission medium that lies below the physical layer. The design issues here largely deal with mechanical, electrical, and procedural interfaces.

Examples of the media include fiber optic cable, coaxial cable (thick, thin, and CATV cable), shielded twisted-pair (STP) wire, and unshielded twisted-pair (UTP) wire used for inside telephone wiring as well as local area network (LAN) connections. Of these technologies, UTP is the least expensive, particularly when using the existing telephone wire for data communications. However, STP and coax are less susceptible to interference than the UTP and can thus bear heavier traffic and higher data speeds.

Fiber optic cable, the most expensive solution, supports the highest data rates with the least amount of signal degradation. The standards for fiber optic networks, fiber distributed data interface (FDDI), transcends layers 1 and 2.

Computers (minicomputers, workstations, and/or PCs) are often connected over local area networks using thick or thin coax or 10BASET UTP. In some organizations, multiple lower-speed LANs may be interconnected by a higher-speed backbone LAN. Backbone LANs are typically coaxial or fiber optic cables.

- The *data link layer* specifies *how* the data are transmitted on one physical link (e.g., between a client and a server). It controls the flow of data and the correction and detection of errors. In local area networks, this includes control of the access to the medium, dictating which system can use the network. The task of this layer is to ensure the reliable transmission of information units (packets or blocks) and to address stations connected to the transmission medium. In other words, this layer provides reliable data transmission from one node to another and shields the higher layers from concern for the physical transmission medium. It is responsible for error-free transmission of frames of data.

The data link layer is divided into two sublayers: the media access control (MAC) and the logical link control (LLC). As shown in Figure 5.2, the lower layer, MAC, provides shared access to the physical layer of the network, while the upper sublayer, LLC, provides a data link service to higher levels of the OSI protocols.

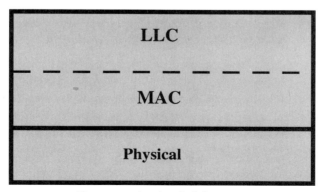

Figure 5.2 The data link layer.

The most popular layer 2 standard in internetworking environment is IEEE 802.3/Ethernet. The other major data link layer technology is 802.5/token ring. Token ring is more robust and more expensive than Ethernet. Therefore, Ethernet is more prevalent in LAN environments.

FDDI standards at the data link layer include FDDI media control access and logical link control.

Frame relay is another layer 2 standard which is fast and inexpensive for LAN interconnection over the wide area. Frame relay is a packet-switching technology similar to X.25, but without the overhead incurred by intermediate node error correction.

- The *network layer* routes and delivers data from one network node to another. It controls routing, flow control, and sequencing functions. It establishes, maintains, and terminates the network connection between two users and transfers data along that connection. It also does fragmentation and reassembly. Only one network connection can exist between two nodes. This activity includes handing off messages from one segment to another without the need to know the final destination. If there is no direct connection between the two systems that wish to communicate, the network layer finds what intermediate system can relay the messages to their destination.

When a message (packet or block) has to travel from one network to another, many problems can arise: the addressing scheme may be different for each network, or the packet may not be accepted because it is too large or the protocols may differ. Therefore, it is up to the network layer to overcome such problems to allow heterogeneous networks to be interconnected.

The most widely used protocols are the Internet Protocol (IP) and the X.25 packet switch interface. IP, the "lower half" of TCP/IP, is designed to interconnect LANs over a variety of layer 2 protocols, such as 802.3/Ethernet, 802.5/token ring, RS 232-C, and the X.25. In interconnected networks, IP is often used to overcome Ethernet's distance limitations (about one kilometer) by supporting communications over network bridges and routers. X.25 is often used in conjunction with IP to support wide area data networking (7 to 7000 kilometers).

- The *transport layer* transports messages between communications partners and usually controls the data flow and ensures that the data are not corrupted. It is the join between the upper and lower parts of the model. It provides and monitors the quality of service and error rate. It provides data transfer between two users at an agreed-upon level of quality. When a connection is established between two nodes, this layer selects a particular class of service. That class monitors transmissions to ensure that the appropriate level of quality is maintained and notifies users when transmission quality falls below that level.

The basic function of this layer is to accept data from the session layer (above), split it into smaller units if necessary, pass these to the network layer, and ensure that all the pieces arrive correctly at the other end. Under normal conditions, the transport layer creates a distinct network connection for each transport connection required by the session layer. If the transport connection requires a high throughput, the transport layer might create multiple network connections, dividing the data among the network connections to improve throughput. On the other hand, it may multiplex several transport connections into the same network connection, to reduce cost. In either case, the transport layer actions are transparent to the session layer.

The transport layer is true source-to-destination or end-to-end protocol. It must recognize both the addresses of the sender and the receiver. In the lower layers, the protocols are only between each machine and its immediate neighbors, not the ultimate source and destinations.

• The *session layer* provides the services necessary to organize and synchronize the dialog that occurs between users and to manage the data exchange. It negotiates "conversation" between the systems. This layer primarily controls when users can send or receive data. A session might be used to allow a user to log into a remote timesharing system or to transfer a file between two machines.

One of the services of the session layer is to manage dialog control. Sessions can allow traffic to go in both directions at the same time or only in one direction at a time, that is, two railroad tracks versus one. A related service of the session layer is *token management*. For some protocols, it is essential that both sides do not attempt the same operation simultaneously. To manage this problem, the session layer provides tokens to be exchanged. Only the side holding the token may perform the critical operation.

This layer initiates and ends communications between processes (i.e., a logical session).

• The *presentation layer* is responsible for presenting information to the network users in a meaningful way. The presentation layers on the two systems agree on a common representation of the data being exchanged. This may include character-code translation, conversion between ASCII and EBCDIC character sets, or data compression and expansion (encryption/decryption). In particular, unlike all lower layers, the presentation layer is concerned with the syntax and semantics of the information transmitted.

Most applications do not exchange random binary bit strings. They exchange information such as people names, dates, amounts of money, and invoices. These items are represented as character strings, integers, floating point numbers, and data structures. Different computers (hardware architectures) have different codes for representing character strings, integers, and so on. The job of managing these data disparities is handled by the presentation layer.

• The *application layer* provides common application services and allows application processes access the system interconnection facilities to exchange information, including services to establish and terminate connections between users. It is also used to monitor and manage the systems being interconnected and the various resources they employ.

This layer contains a variety of protocols that are commonly needed. Users can take advantage of the powerful utilities and applications to help them connect disparate systems, including proprietary systems. Many of the protocols are built into the applications and utilities.

Interprocess Communications

Figure 5.3. shows a schematic of a set of applications operating on each seven-layer stack, connected together through the physical, transmission media. A connection is the link

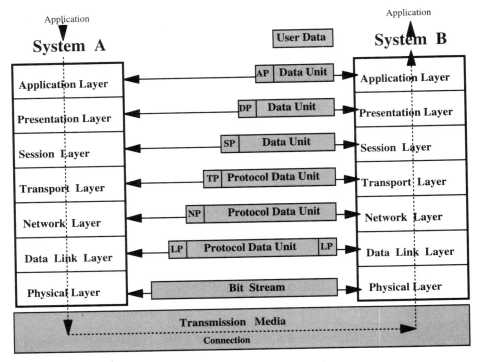

Figure 5.3 Interprocess communication.

between the service access points of the two communicating peer entities. Logically, the connection appears to behave as if each peer layer service were connected together. In fact, the layers underneath are providing services to establish and support the processes.

Communications activity under the OSI model occurs in phases. A connect phase establishes the connection. Once the connection is established, the data transfer phase allows user information to be transferred from one user to another. When the exchange is completed, a clearing phase takes down the logical connection.

When an application on system A needs to transfer data to an application on system B, it travels from the top layer to the bottom layer to the transmission media. Each successive layer adds its protocol-specific information to the user data as it travels downward. At the bottom layer (the physical layer), the entire packet is converted to "bit stream" for transmission to system B. At system B, the information travels from bottom to top layer. Successively, the protocol information is stripped as it hands over the packet to the layer above until only the user data reaches the recipient application.

Services

The primary function of each OSI layer is to provide services to the layer above. We will examine these services in some detail. In data communications, we distinguish between two different types of services (protocols), connection-oriented and connectionless. In the *connection-oriented service*, a connection with the communication partner is established (generated) before any data are exchanged, while in *connectionless service*, only individual messages are sent. These services can usually be distinguished by the volume of their reliability functions. A connection-oriented protocol with many reliability functions usually has higher computational processing requirements than a connectionless protocol. These two services are as follows:

- The execution of message exchange in Connection-oriented service is similar to a telephone conversation. To talk to someone, you pick up the phone, dial the number, talk, and then hang up. Similarly, to use such a service, the user first establishes a connection, uses the connection, and then terminates the connection. The data exchange begins only after the call partners have been introduced to each other and several formal exchanges have taken place. The connection is broken off only when both parties have agreed that the exchanged data are intelligible. From a UNIX programmer's point of view, such services behave like a bidirectional pipe, the sender pushes objects in at one end and the receiver takes them out in the same order at the other end.

  Usually a reliable service is implemented by having the receiver acknowledge the receipt message. However, the acknowledgment process adds overhead and delays. Such delays may or may not be acceptable, depending upon the degree of reliability desired.

  A typical application in which a reliable connection-oriented service is essential is "file transfer" to maintain data and file integrity. The user wants to be sure that all pieces of the file arrive correctly and in the same order.

- The *connectionless service*, in contrast, is modeled after the postal system, similar to telegrams. Each message (telegram) carries the full destination address, and each one is routed through the system independent of all the others. It is quite possible that the second message may arrive at its destination before the first one. Unreliable connectionless service is often called *datagram service*, which, like a telegram, does not send acknowledgment to the sender. However, in some situations, the acknowledgment may be essential but not immediate. In such cases the *acknowledged datagram service* can be provided. It is like sending a registered letter with return receipt requested. This provides the intended reliability of receipt of service.

For some applications, delays caused by acknowledgments are unacceptable. Digitized voice traffic is such an application. It is preferable for telephone users to hear a bit of noise on the line than to introduce a delay to wait for acknowledgments, causing an added cost to the conversation. Database queries can be considered connectionless services.

Because of their stateless nature, connectionless protocols cannot provide such reliability as flow control or retransmission of packets. If a more reliable service is required, using connectionless protocols, the quality of service has to be augmented by a higher-ranking protocol layer.

Standards for the OSI Layers

ISO has produced and is producing standards for the various OSI layers. Some of these have been widely adopted. To complete such standards, ISO has been working closely with a number of international standard making bodies like CCITT, IEEE, ECMA, and others.

For lower layers, ISO has adopted local area network standards developed by IEEE. These standards include Ethernet, token ring, FDDI, and token bus technologies. These are commonly referred to as 802 standards after the IEEE 802 committee. ISO also adopted some of the wide area network (WAN) standards, known as X.25, developed by CCITT. These are based on packet-switching technology, carried over a variety of line types. These were discussed in more detail in Chapter 4.

Standards for Layer 4 (transport) define five levels of service, defined as Classes 0 through 4:

- Class 0 is a basic service with minimum functions.
- Class 1 includes "recovery" service after the link is lost.
- Class 2 includes multiplexing.
- Class 3 includes functions of Class 1 and 2.
- Class 4 is specifically designed to operate over connectionless services, without having a specific data link connection.

In addition to the published session and presentation layer standards, there is a related standard, Abstract Syntax Notation 1 (ASN.1), to assist presentation and application layers to agree on a syntax in which to communicate. This standard defines the encoding of data structures to a bit stream for transmission. This addresses the problem of representing, encoding, transmitting, and decoding data structures that is flexible enough to be useful in a wide variety of applications, yet standard enough for everyone to agree upon.

At the application layer, a different standard is needed for each type of application task. The most important standards are as follows and are discussed in the next section.

- Terminal emulation/virtual terminal/remote login (VT).
- File transfer, access, and management (FTAM.)
- Message handling service (MOTIS/MHS: X.400).
- Network management (SNMP or CMIP/CMIS).
- Directory services (X.500).
- Remote database access (RDA)
- Association control service element (ACSE).
- Commitment, concurrency, and recovery (CCR).
- Office document architecture (ODA).

OSI Application Layer Protocols

• *Terminal emulation/virtual terminal/remote logins (VT)* are widely used protocols. Terminals operate in three modes: scroll, page, and form modes. Form mode terminals are the most sophisticated with built-in microprocessors. The scroll mode terminals are the simplest, with no intelligence or built-in microprocessors for local editing capability. Page mode terminals are typically CRT terminals that can display 25 lines of 80 characters each and were very prevalent prior to proliferation of the microprocessors. Nearly all terminals accept *escape sequences*, for cursor motion, entering and leaving reverse video mode, inserting and deleting characters and line, and so on.

Each manufacturer has its own escape sequences, incompatible with those of every other manufacturer. The problem is further compounded by the incompatibilities of the input from the keyboard. As a result, it is difficult for anyone to write a screen editor that works with an "ideal" keyboard and display. The OSI has defined a *virtual terminal* protocol to solve this dilemma. In OSI, virtual terminal protocol defines an abstract data structure that represents the abstract state of the real terminal. This data structure can be manipulated by the computer and the keyboard. The computer can query the abstract data structure to find about keyboard input and can change the abstract data structure to cause output to appear on the screen.

In *scroll mode terminals*, when a key on the keyboard is hit, it is sent over the line to the processor. When a character comes in over the line, it is just displayed. As new lines are displayed, the old ones just scroll upward. Most hard copy and CRT terminals fall into this category. Because scroll mode terminals do not have intelligence, they cannot communicate with the network using any network protocols. To connect these to the network, a "black box" is placed between the terminal and the network. Thus the "black box" (RS232, in some cases) speaks to the terminal and the network protocol.

Page mode terminals have the same fundamental problems as the scroll mode terminals. However, the computer, in this case, can move the cursor around the screen to modify selected areas of the display. One widely used solution is to define a virtual terminal consisting of commands that most page mode terminals have. When an editor starts, it inquires about the terminal type, and then reads in the entry for this terminal type from a database. This entry supplies the escape sequences required for each virtual command. As long as the software issues the virtual commands recognized in the database, it will run on any terminal having that capability.

The microprocessors in the *form mode terminals* allow local editing, macros, and other processing capabilities. In applications, such as banking and airline reservations, the computer can download a form to the terminal containing some information and the remaining to be filled in by the keyboard input. When a form has been filled in, the microprocessor can run a syntax check on it. If correct, the modified information can be uploaded across the network back to the source computer. There are a number of models that can be utilized to resolve different solutions, based on the terminals as well as the application requirements.

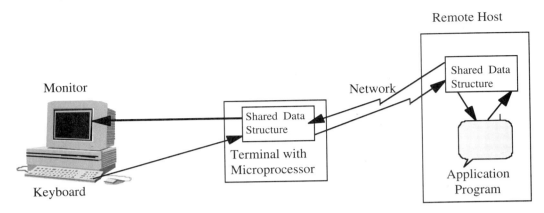

Figure 5.4 Form mode virtual terminal.

Figure 5.4. describes how a user at the keyboard interfaces with a microprocessor, which in turn accesses the remote host. This model of the virtual terminal software maintains an abstract representation of the display image internally. This representation can be read and updated by both the terminal and the application program running in a remote host.

The virtual terminal software is responsible for keeping the screen image updated whenever its abstract representation is modified. The user at the terminal can modify the microprocessor copy of the data structure via the keyboard. These changes are displayed on the screen. Simultaneously, the microprocessor sends virtual terminal commands to the remote host over the network using the virtual terminal protocol. This causes the remote copy of the data structure to be updated to match the local one. The modified structure can then be read by the application program.

The process described is performed synchronously. The asynchronous variant is a lot more complex since two copies must be maintained, one for input and the other for output.

• *File transfer, access, and management (FTAM)* protocol allows transfer and remote access of files. These are the most common applications in any interconnected computer systems. In an enterprise, there is always a need to share the same file.

File handling is one of the primary services in any distributed network systems. One approach is to have a machine where an original of each file is held and have copies transferred as needed. Another approach is to have each file "live" on the machine where it is created. Access to a file located on a remote computer that has its local users is hardly different from accessing a file on a dedicated *file server* that has no local users. In either case, a comprehensive file transfer mechanism (protocol) is needed to manage and maintain that data.

The way in which files are handled varies between systems from different manufacturers. The FTAM standard (Figure 5.5) solves this problem by allowing transfer of whole

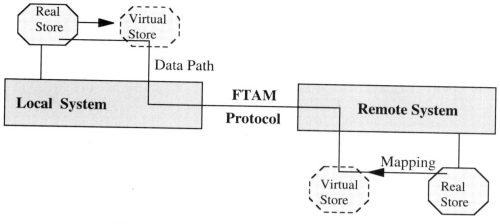

Figure 5.5 FTAM protocols: Transfer of remote files.

or parts of files, from one system to another. The standard guarantees that either a correct copy of the file or a message indicating failure is sent. If there are problems, the transfer restarts automatically, until a correct copy is received.

FTAM can be used to access a file on a local or remote machine. Some current FTAM implementations do not utilize the full ISO standard. However, the usage is gaining wider acceptance.

- X.400 standard is the CCITT recommendation for electronic mail messaging. X.400 is a store and forward application, in which messages are sent to a named user mailbox. This user can access the mailbox from a range of terminals.

One of the X.400 protocols is Message Handling Service (MHS) which allows exchange of messages or electronic mail. These protocols are concerned with all aspects of electronic mail system starting with the time the originator decides to write a message and ending with the time the recipient finally throws it in the garbage can.

Another protocol is Message Oriented Text Interchange System (MOTIS). MOTIS builds upon the X.400 for message text interchange.

X.400 is concerned with all aspects of the electronic mail system, starting with the originator writing the message and ending with the recipient when he discards the received message. There are six basic steps in an electronic message sequence. These are

- *Composition*, which refers to the process of creating messages and answers to messages.
- *Transfer*, which refers to moving messages from the originator to the recipient.
- *Reporting*, which informs the originator what happened to the message.
- *Conversion*, which is necessary to display the message on the recipients display device.

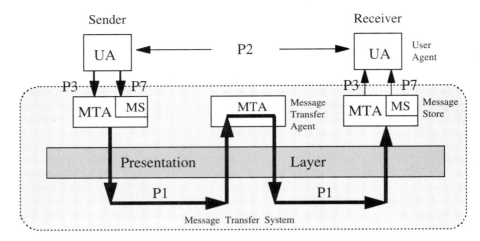

Figure 5.6 X.400 electronic mail system.

- *Display*, which pertains to the form of the displayed message on the recipient's display device.
- *Disposition*, which is the final step as to what the recipient does with the message, that is, throwing it or archiving it for later usage.

Figure 5.6 describes a typical X.400 mail system, known as message transfer system (MTS). The user agent (UA) is a program that provides the "user" interface to the mail system, like a mailbox. It allows users to create, send, and receive mail. The message transfer agent (MTA) accepts mail from user agents and routes it through the network, like the post office. Typically, the user agent resides on PC, whereas the MTA resides on a server/host computer.

If the UA and MTA run on two separate machines, the dialog between the entities that handle the message had to be standardized. Therefore, X.400 (MOTIS) defines these interfaces as

- P1 being the protocol between the MTAs.
- P2 being the protocol between the UAs and is also known as Interpersonal Messaging (IPM).
- P3 is the interaction protocol between the UA and the MTA.
- P7 is the interaction between the UA and the MS.

The essential components of an X.400 system are shown in Figure 5.7, specifically the user agent and the message transfer agent. The UA provides services to the user, that is, sending messages in correct format and retrieving and replying to messages. The MTA carries messages from one UA to another.

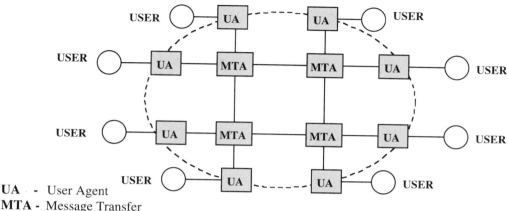

UA - User Agent
MTA - Message Transfer
        Agent

Figure 5.7 Message handling with X.400.

- *Network Management (SNMP* or *CMIP/CMIS)* protocols specify rules and policies needed to manage the networks (refer to the section on network management protocols).

- *Directory Services (X.500)* protocols specify naming services for addressing mail, files, or systems. This is similar to a telephone book that maps "entities" to attributes (addresses). It can be classified into "White Pages" for addresses and "Yellow Pages" for services.

The basic idea of the OSI directory is to allow users to look up names based on attributes. To facilitate look-up as well as accommodate the conventions of different countries, the directory service is based on a hierarchical scheme, as described in Figure 5.8. In this example, the country represents the highest hierarchy and down to the individual. To look up an entry, a user supplies the attributes like C = UK, ORG = ICL, NAME = Jack, or other. The structure is hierarchical and can be represented by a number of levels.

The directory management functions on networks allow users or applications to obtain information relating to other users or applications on the same or other OSI networks.

- *Remote database access (RDA)* protocols specify database access on remote systems.

- *Association control service element (ACSE)* provides the user process to establish and release association with peers. It also establishes one-to-one relationship with the presentation layers.

- *Commitment, concurrency, and recovery (CCR)* provides atomic actions between applications.

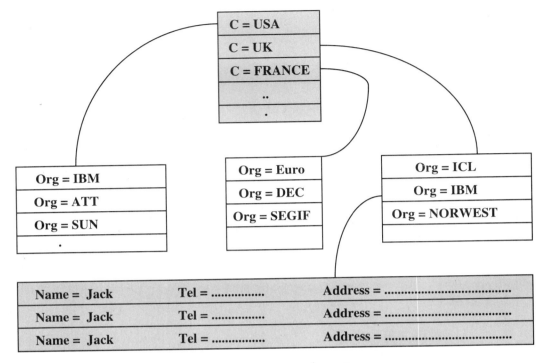

Figure 5.8 A directory hierarchy.

- *Office document architecture (ODA)* is designed for dealing with objects like text, video, and image.

Network Management Protocols

Interest in OSI network management protocols has increased dramatically over the past several years. Progress on standards for OSI management is one of the main reasons for this growing interest. The basic reference model defines OSI systems management in terms of management applications that communicate with one another through application protocols. These management applications provide the following capabilities:

- Mechanism for monitoring, controlling, and coordinating all managed objects within an enterprise.
- The ability to manage objects related to single or multiple layers.
- A framework for connecting open systems that allows suppliers to construct unique systems.

The OSI network management protocols are defined via common management information services (CMISs) and common management information protocols (CMIPs).

CMIS allows OSI systems to exchange information between application management processes. The type of information that these services manage are

- *Fault management* facilities, which permit the detection, isolation, and correction of abnormal operations. Faults manifests themselves as errors, and error detection provides the mechanism for recognizing faults. The facilities provide for maintaining and examining error logs, accepting and acting on error detection notifications, tracing faults, and carrying out a sequence of diagnostic tests, and correcting faults.
- *Performance management* facilities, which evaluate the behavior of OSI resources and the effectiveness of communications activities. The facilities provide for gathering statistical data for planning and analysis.
- *Configuration management* facilities, which control, identify, and connect data from interconnected devices. These provide for setting parameters, initializing and closing resources, and reconfiguration of resources.
- *Security management* facilities, which protect OSI resources. Such facilities provide for authorization, access control, encryption and key management, authentication, and the maintenance and examination of security logs. An implementation may also require to maintain audit trails for fault management.
- *Accounting management* facilities, which make it possible to set charges and identify costs for system resource usage.

The OSI network management software resides in the management node, known as system manager, as well as on the managed node or device known as the management agent (see Figure 5.9.). CMIS allows OSI systems to exchange information between these processes via a series of commands. A "request" is sent by the management system (sys-

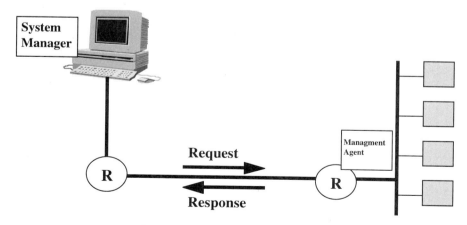

Figure 5.9 System management process.

tem manager) to a management agent (which may reside in a router, workstation, or any such device), and the agent sends a response back to the manager for action.

The structure of management information refers to the logical structure of OSI management information. This information is organized in terms of managed objects, their attributes, the operations that may be performed upon them, and the notifications they must issue. The set of managed objects in a system, together with its attributes, constitutes that system's management information base (MIB). The operation commands used in the management processes are the following:

- *Get* service is a query packet (request) to get information from the managed node or agent. This information may be status or statistical data, such as error rate.
- *Set* service is used by the manager to request modifications of parameter values or reconfigure the network.
- *Event* service is used to report (response) an event by the managed device.

There are some additional commands *(Create, Delete)* that are used for "confirmed service" responses. The common management information protocols are the protocols that provide CMIS.

They permit a communication network system to be uniformly managed.

OSI Summary

The OSI Reference model provides the network manager with a powerful tool for planning, designing, and implementing communication networks. The OSI protocols provide a framework for controlling the proliferation of incompatible network architectures in heterogeneous environments. The OSI model, however, is only a reference and not a specific solution. The value lies in understanding the actual standards that interconnect and access the required functional entities.

INTEGRATED SERVICES DIGITAL NETWORK

Integrated Services Digital Network (ISDN) protocols are complementary to the OSI standards. This protocol is designed to enable the transfer of very large amounts of data on a worldwide network. ISDN accommodates a wide range of services over the same line, including data, teletext, vidotext, fax, and voice. For home use, the largest demand for service is for television and to access remote databases.

For a long time, telephone has been the primary international communication media, which is proving inadequate for modern communication needs. The primary drawback was that the telephone was designed to carry analog voice signals only. However, today, we must make provisions to transmit data, voice, video, fax, teletext, and so on, either simultaneously or in an integrated mode. Since ISDN is based on the existing telephone system, the key service continues to be *voice*.

We can safely assume that the first area of ISDN enhancements is telephone services. One of the telephone features we are witnessing today is the display of caller's telephone number, name, and address. A more sophisticated version will allow the telephone to be connected to a computer so that the caller's database record can be displayed on the screen. Some of the other advanced services include call transfer and forwarding, multiparty conference calls, messaging when the telephone is busy, automatic wake-up calls, and so on.

ISDN data transmission protocols allow users to connect their computer or ISDN terminals to any other in the world. At present, such connections are difficult if not impossible due to incompatible telephone systems.

ISDN technology has instigated a host of new functions/services that are becoming widespread. One such service is *videotext*. Videotext is interactive access to a remote database by a person at a terminal. With such a facility, you are able to access telephone books on-line without any intervention from the operator, at enormous savings. Telephone service is only a small application of videotext. One of the extensions of such a service is the Yellow Pages. You could type the product name and get a list of businesses that supply the product. This can be further extended to include airlines, hotels, theaters, restaurant reservations, bank-by-terminal, and so on.

Teletext is another popular application for electronic mail for home or office. We have witnessed that it is cheaper to transmit data/mail electronically than physically (mostly paper). If we convert the telephone into a terminal/workstation not only for videotext but also for composing, editing, archiving, printing, sending, and receiving electronic mail, it will reduce a considerable load on the postal as well transport systems.

Businesses need to send contracts, signatures, blueprints, charts, illustrations, or other graphic materials to distant places and instantly. *Facsimile* is becoming increasingly popular to accomplish this task. There is also a need to archive, edit, forward, and broadcast facsimile images. However the problem still remains that the scanned images/documents/graphics require high degree of storage and bandwidth for transmission.

Some such services are already available but they are poorly integrated and have not gained universal acceptance. The goal for ISDN remains to integrate all the services described above and make them as commonplace as the telephone is today.

OSI AND ISDN

ISDN is layered similar to ISO model; however, many ISDN protocols are unrelated to OSI protocols in the same layer. Like OSI, the ISDN physical layer deals with the electrical, mechanical, and functional aspects of the interface (see Figure 5.10). Conversely, ISDN is more concerned with the carrier's and customer's equipment. Therefore, CCITT is concentrating more on defining the interfaces for peer protocols in lower layers, than protocols.

ISDN is a massive attempt to enhance the analog telephone system with a digital one, which is more suitable for voice, video, and text. In terms of the OSI model, ISDN has defined a physical layer bit stream from homes and offices into which layers 2 through

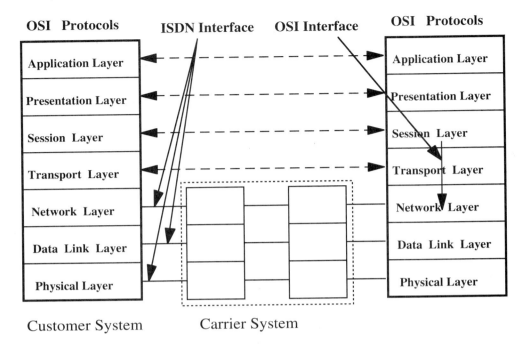

OSI Protocols   **ISDN Interface**   **OSI Interface**   **OSI Protocols**

Customer System   Carrier System

Figure 5.10 OSI and ISDN interfaces.

7 can be built. Standardization of these interfaces will lead to a mass production, economies of scale, and inexpensive VLSI ISDN chips.

In contrast to OSI, ISDN uses a completely different type of connectors, unrelated to the 25-, 27-, and 9-pin D connectors used for RS-232-C and RS-449. In addition, ISDN bit pipe supports multiple channels interleaved by time division multiplexing. It is also important to note that there is no error checking, no checksum, no redundancy, no acknowledgment, and no retransmission. If errors occur, they must be handled by higher layers in the OSI model. All the ISDN does is provide the user with raw physical bit streams.

The ISDN bit stream can be used to support either circuit switching or packet switching. In a circuit-switching scenario, the ISDN customer calls the destination and uses a 64 Kbps channel as a physical layer connection for transmitting digitized voice or data. In the packet-switching scenario, the ISDN customer places a local call to a nearby interface message processor (IMP). The IMP, in turn, transmits them to the final destination via a traditional packet-switching network. When used to access a packet-switching network, the ISDN line is analogous to a link in ARPANET.

Integration of OSI and ISDN technologies is important. This allows a link to both local and wide area networks, as the underlying network technology for OSI applications, especially voice and video.

OSI AND X/OPEN STANDARDS

X/Open is an organization committed to bringing structure and discipline to the overall arena of open-systems standards, through practical implementations. One of the goals of open systems is to provide application software portability by defining common interfaces for users, programmers, and communications. Common application environment (CAE) is designed to provide a complete support system for the development and running of application software. It is designed to enable high levels of portability, interconnection, and interoperability across machines.

CAE has defined interfaces to the many services required by a sophisticated application, consisting of the following:

* A common interface to the user.
* A common syntax for major programming languages, that is, ISO Pascal, ANSI FORTRAN 77, ANSI C, ANSI COBOL 85, and Ada.
* An interface to the operating system.
* An interface to data management services.
* Common standards to facilitate transfer of source code between heterogeneous systems.
* An interface to multivendor networking.
* Security features.
* Window management.

To accommodate the wide variety of applications needed, there are many options within the OSI standards. Different systems may select different sets of options from within the OSI standard, introducing incompatibilities between implementations. To deal with such situations, X/Open advises application developers to build applications either using only the mandatory functions or most commonly used functions in the industry.

The OSI model has a considerable lead on communication and networking. Therefore, X/Open is addressing networking and internetworking and needs to merge its work with that of ISO. Consequently, the X/Open transport interface (XTI) has defined a programming interface to the OSI transport (layer 4) services. This interface is completely independent of underlying protocols and can be used with OSI, TCP/IP, or other such protocols. Figure 5.11 describes relationships between the OSI layers and the standards developed through X/Open.

TCP AND IP PROTOCOLS

TCP/IP are a set of communications protocols developed by the Department of Defense—ARPANET.

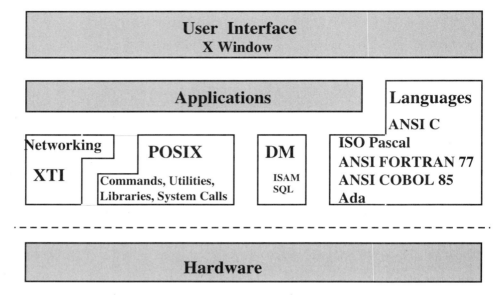

Figure 5.11 X/Open's common application environment.

TCP/IP Architecture

Like OSI, TCP/IP protocols are also grouped into layers. As we can see, the OSI and TCP/IP architectural models share the same structural elements (Figure 5.12). Layers 1–4 are more or less equivalent for both OSI and TCP/IP. However, the differences between OSI and TCP/IP architectures relate primarily to the philosophy in the layers above the transport level. The OSI model has two additional layers, the session layer and the presentation layer. In TCP/IP, the functions of these two layers are viewed as part of the application layer.

The top layer, the applications layer, provides application services to users and programs. The transport layer handles data consistency functions. The transport layer is supported by two protocols, TCP and UDP. The TCP provides a reliable delivery, whereas the UDP does not ensure delivery. Most TCP/IP applications like TELNET and FTP use TCP, while others like voice and video use UDP, since fast delivery is more important than reliability.

The internet layer is the key layer. It has one protocol: IP. IP provides many of the same functions as the network layer, such as addressing and routing. IP provides a common address space across multiple lower-layer network protocols.

The network layer contains whatever IP will run over, such as Ethernet, token ring, FDDI, and so on. A network layer routes packets across a network. The physical, the link, and the network layers in TCP/IP are combined to form a subnetwork layer.

The requirement for universal connectivity is supported by the Internet Protocol (the network layer). Another protocol, Internet Control Message Protocol (ICMP), a component of every IP implementation, transports error and diagnostic information for IP. In

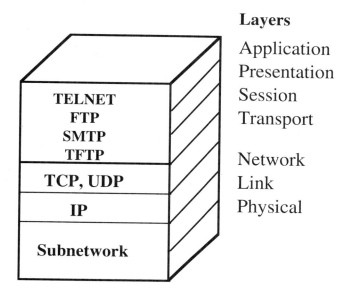

Figure 5.12 TCP/IP protocol layers.

addition to the Transmission Control Protocol (TCP) at the transport level, the User Datagram Protocol (UDP) is also utilized by a host of networking solutions.

History and Evolution of the Internet

The Internet project grew out of the research funded by the Advanced Research Project Agency Network (ARPANET), in 1969. The ARPANET led to the development of protocols that work on several separate interconnected networks. These networks, today, provide communication services for commercial as well as defense industry. For example, the Military Network (MILNET) was split from ARPANET to provide a separate military network facility.

National Science Foundation funded the NSFNET to provide networking services to academic and industrial research groups. The Internet backbone of the NFSNET is actually being used to replace sections of the ARPANET to upgrade to T1, T3, and more advanced technologies. NSFNET has become an important national data network in the United States. There are similar networks that are prevalent in other parts of the world, all based on the Internet protocols.

Because of the maturity and nonproprietary nature of these protocols, the TCP/IP is widely used as a networking platform. The TCP/IP protocols have been embraced by the industry as a standard connecting many heterogeneous computing environments. The TCP/IP protocol has become a de facto standard for business and industry. Even the University of California, Berkeley, programmed TCP/IP as an integral part of the BSD version of UNIX operating system. Most of the TCP/IP implementations available today contain, in some form, either the modifications or the whole code of 4.3BSD as released in 1988. Support of these protocols by companies such as Digital Equipment Corporation, Amdahl Corporation, Data General Corporation, Sun Microsystems, Inc., and Hewlett-Packard Co. has enhanced their commercial status.

In 1973, it became clear that the protocols as defined by the ARPANET were inadequate. Consequently, a project was initiated to enhance this architecture to meet the following goals:

- Standardized application protocols.
- Universal connectivity throughout the network.
- Independence from the underlying network technology and from the architecture of the host operating system or the hardware, in effect, promoting heterogeneity.
- End-to-end acknowledgments.

The existing TCP/IP model has successfully incorporated these goals by providing a common set of application programs, nodes as packet-switching computers, transport protocols for connectivity, and dynamic routing.

The evolution of TCP/IP protocols has been their integration with communications specifications from a variety of underlying network interfaces. Specifications of these network interfaces are often derived from standard set by committees like CCITT and IEEE.

Layering in the Internet Protocol Suite

Although the protocol family is often called TCP/IP, there are more than one embedded protocols as described in Figure 5.13. Regardless of the layering scheme or the functions of the layers, the architecture requires that layering at the destination receives exactly the same object sent by layer n at the source. The TCP/IP suite includes six major protocols that are most commonly used for internetworking. These are

- *TCP (Transmission Control Protocol)* is a connection-oriented protocol that provides a reliable, full-duplex, end-to-end byte stream for a user process. Most Internet applications requiring data integrity and reliability, use TCP. Since TCP uses IP, the entire protocol suite is called TCP/IP.
- *UDP (User Datagram Protocol)* is a connectionless protocol for user processing. Unlike TCP, UDP does not provide a reliable transport. There is no guarantee that UDP datagrams either ever reach their destination or are in the same order as sent.
- *ICMP (Internet Control Message Protocol)* handles errors and control information between gateways. ICMP messages are transmitted using IP datagrams. These messages are generated and processed by the TCP/IP application software.
- *IP (Internet Protocol)* provides packet delivery for TCP, UDP, and ICMP. User processes are normally not involved with the IP layer or the IP protocols.

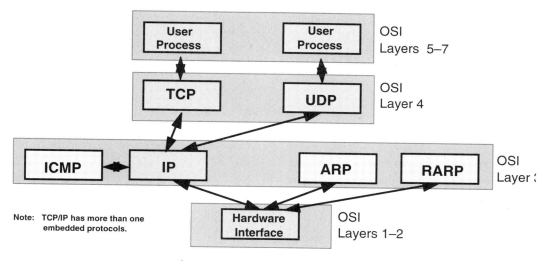

Figure 5.13 Internet protocol layering.

- *ARP (Address Resolution Protocol)* maps an Internet address onto a hardware address. This protocol is not used on all networks. This protocol is primarily used for dynamic conversion of Ethernet (48-bit) addresses into IP (32-bit) addresses.
- *RARP (Reverse Address Resolution Protocol)* maps a hardware address onto an Internet address.

The Internet Protocol

The Internet Protocol (IP) is the foundation of the TCP/IP architecture. The main functions of the IP are addressing of the computers and the fragmentation of packets. It contains no functions for end-to-end data reliability or for flow control.

Internet Architecture. The Internet Protocol is a connectionless protocol and is designed for use in interconnected systems of packet-switched computer communication networks. IP provides for transmitting blocks of data called *datagrams* from sources to destinations. IP also provides for fragmentation and reassembly for long datagrams, if necessary, for transmission through "small-packet" networks. Unlike TCP, there is no mechanism for end-to-end reliability, flow control, or sequencing. The IP protocol implements two basic functions:

- Addressing.
- Fragmentation/reassembly.

IP treats each Internet datagram as an independent entity unrelated to any other Internet diagram. Maximum length of a datagram is up to 65,535 octets. All hosts implementing TCP/IP protocols must be prepared to accept datagrams of up to 576 octets, whether they arrive whole or in fragments. As we will discover in the IP header in Figure 5.14, IP uses four key mechanisms in providing its service:

- Type of service—quality of the service desired.
- Time to live—upper bound on the lifetime of an Internet diagram.
- Options—control functions needed or useful in some situations, for example, time-stamps, security, special routing.
- Header checksum—error detection.

The IP Header.   A typical *IP header* is described in Figure 5.14. The fields included have the following significance:

The 4-bit *version number* contains the current version: 4.

HLEN specifies the length of the IP header in 32-bit words. The shortest IP header contains five words. The length of this field is increased by the addition of optional fields.

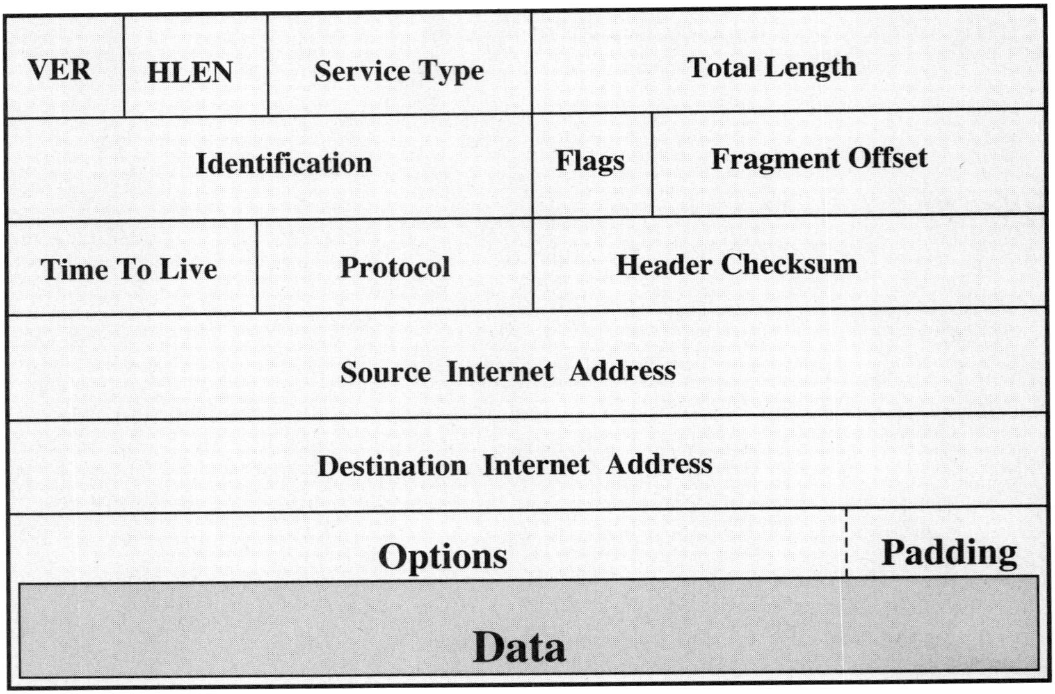

VER	HLEN	Service Type	Total Length	
Identification			Flags	Fragment Offset
Time To Live		Protocol	Header Checksum	
Source Internet Address				
Destination Internet Address				
Options				Padding
Data				

Figure 5.14 IP header.

Service type represents the quality of service desired for the datagram. It is an 8-bit field with options such as precedence, normal or low delay, normal or high throughput, and normal or high reliability and can be specified by turning the appropriate bits off and on. In practice, a value of 0 is almost always used, since no UNIX IP implementation evaluates entries in this field.

Total length is a 16-bit field and is used to specify the length of the datagram (header and data of the packet) in octets. Therefore, the maximum length is 65,535 bytes. This entry is used to establish the data length and is passed to the transport protocol in the "pseudoheader."

Identification refers to 16-bit unique identifier created by the sending host. This field is used in the reassembly of fragments to identify all the pieces of a fragment chain.

The 2-bit *flags* are control bits indicating whether to fragment the datagram if other fragments exist.

If the flag bit is on, indicating fragmentation, the 13-bit *fragment offset* specifies the position of the fragment (in units of 8 bytes) in the original datagram, relative to the beginning of the whole message. The receiving host can use this entry to reassemble the original packet correctly.

The *time to live* counter specifies, in seconds, how long the packet may remain in the network before it must be discarded. The rules dictate that every node must decrease this field by at least 1 even if the processing time is less than one second. Therefore, the time to live is usually equal to the maximum number of nodes that the packet must pass through. If this field contains 0, the packet must be discarded by the current processor.

This field contains the ID of the *transport protocol* to which the packet has to be handed over. The Ids could be 6 for TCP, 1 for ICMP, or 17 for UDP.

Header checksum is a 16-bit field for error detection for the protocol header fields. For efficiency, user data in the IP packet is not checked.

Source and destination addresses are the 32-bit IP addresses of the sending and destination nodes, respectively.

For special tasks, such as security and network management, different options can be specified in a 16-bit field.

The IP protocol header is always a multiple of 4 (based on header length field). *Padding* characters must be inserted, if necessary.

The Transmission Control Protocol

TCP Architecture. The Transmission Control Protocol is a protocol of the layer 4 or the transport layer. The main task of this layer is the reliable transmission of data through the network. A TCP connection is much like a UNIX pipe with added support for a reliable bidirectional byte stream. This means that two processes using TCP do not differentiate the packet boundaries rather see only a continuous sequence of bytes. This sequence of data can be read or written as a single byte or a group of bytes at a time. The primary services provided by TCP are

- Multiplexing: multiple port support.

- Connection establishment, data transfer, and graceful termination.
- Full duplex.
- Reliable data transmission using: sequence numbers, checksums, acknowledgments, and segment retransmission after acknowledgment time-out.
- Ordered data delivery.
- Urgent ("out-of-band") data and push function. Such data must be sent as soon as possible. TCP uses "urgent" flag and pointer to tell the destination TCP about such data.
- Flow control.
- Error checking.
- Reporting service failures.
- Data stream push option.

The TCP Header. *TCP* is a fairly complicated protocol because (1) it ensures the end-to-end reliability and in-order sequencing byte stream, and (2) it tries to optimize available network bandwidth by monitoring and managing the flow of data from the sender to the receiver. TCP processes a stream of data from a host process and divides the data into messages that are sent to the other end of the connection. The remote TCP collects these messages, recreates the original byte stream, and passes it to the remote process. A typical *TCP Header (Packet Format)* is described in Figure 5.15. The fields included have the following significance:

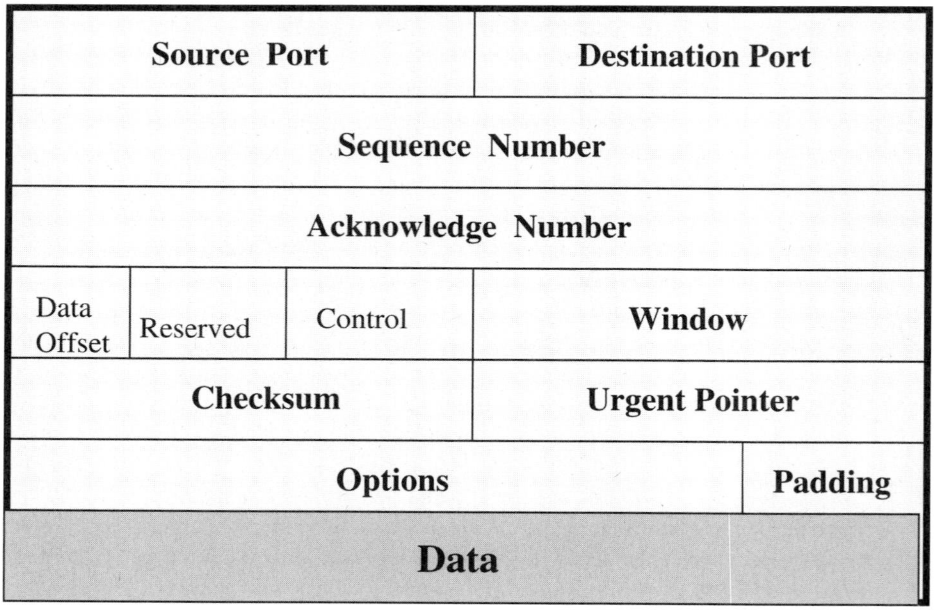

Source Port		Destination Port	
Sequence Number			
Acknowledge Number			
Data Offset	Reserved	Control	Window
Checksum		Urgent Pointer	
Options			Padding
Data			

Figure 5.15 TCP header.

The 16-bit *source and destination port numbers* denote the endpoints of a virtual circuit.

The 32-bit sequence and acknowledgment numbers give the position of the data within the data stream exchanged during the connection. The sequence number refers to the send direction and the acknowledgment number applies to the number of bytes received by the other end. *Port numbers* are used for addressing at the transport level.

The *data offset* entry contains the length of the TCP protocol header in 32-bit words to determine the start of the data.

The *control* flags are used to trigger actions in TCP.

Window size contains the number of bytes that the recipient is able to receive in its data buffers for this connection *(receive window)*.

The *checksum* is applied to the protocol header, the data, and the pseudoheader.

Together with the sequence number, the *urgent pointer* points to a data byte. This data byte is the end of a message section where the following data are identified as being important.

TCP only has three *options*: end-of-option list, no operation, and maximum segment size.

TCP Scenarios. To understand the TCP communications, we will examine three commonly employed scenarios: connection establishment, data exchange, and connection shutdown.

Figure 5.16 shows a *connection establishment. Three-way handshake* is displayed, in which each party, activated by the SYN flag, must acknowledge the other party's sequence number by increasing it by 1. The sequence number (SEQ = 75) of TCP A is

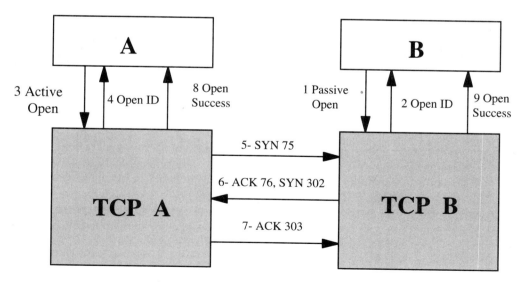

Figure 5.16 TCP connection establishment.

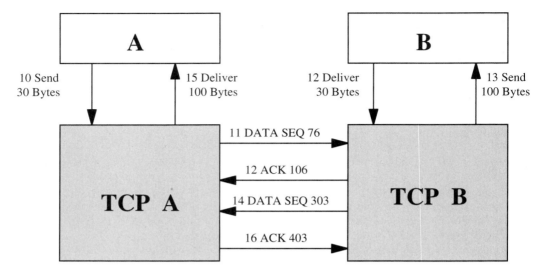

Figure 5.17 TCP data exchange.

found in the response of TCP B in the acknowledgment field (ACK = 76), and vice versa. The ACK flag indicates that the value in the acknowledgment field is valid.

Figure 5.17 shows a *data transfer* which is taking place in both directions simultaneously. Note that the destination always acknowledges by entering the sequence number in the SEQ field (SEQ = 76) increased by the number of data bytes received (DATA = 30) in the ACK field (ACK = 106). Data are sent in the opposite direction together with the acknowledgment and are acknowledged in the same way.

Figure 5.18 shows how the connection is shut down on one side when TCP A sends a FIN flag. TCP B acknowledges the FIN flag by increasing the sequence number (SEQ = 106) in the response segment by 1 (ACK = 107). This acknowledges the receipt of all data sent by TCP A up to that time. After that, no more data should be sent by TCP A. However, TCP B may continue to send until it itself sends a FIN flag, for example, TCP B sends 150 bytes with a sequence number (SEQ = 403), where TCP A acknowledges with (ACK = 554) and terminates the session.

In summary, the primary purpose of the TCP is to provide reliable, securable end-to-end connection service between pairs of processes in hosts attached to (possibly distinct) interconnected communication networks (using dissimilar computer operating systems).

TCP is designed to fit into a layered hierarchy of protocols that support multinetwork applications. TCP is assumed to be a module in an operating system (users can access TCP as they would access the file system).

TCP assumes that the underlying layer (Internet protocol) is unreliable; therefore, TCP must provide

- Reliability.

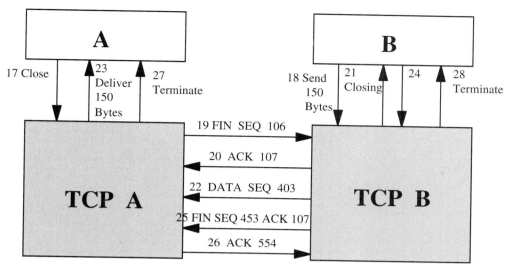

Figure 5.18 TCP connection close.

- Basic data transfer.
- Flow control.
- Multiplexing.
- Connections.
- Security.

The User Datagram Protocol

UDP is defined to make available a datagram mode of packet-switched computer communication in an interconnected network environment. UDP allows application programs to send messages to other programs with a minimum of protocol mechanism or overhead. UDP assumes the Internet Protocol as the underlying protocol. Unlike TCP, delivery and duplication protection are not guaranteed.

Figure 5.19 describes the UDP header with four fields. The source and destination port numbers, as in TCP, are the reference to the transport protocol users. Length is the whole datagram, including the protocol header. The Internet checksum involves the data, the protocol header, and the pseudoheader (a 12-byte structure containing source and destination IP port numbers, protocol, and the length of the datagram).

Over and above the work performed by IP, UDP provides only a port number and a data checksum (see Figure 5.19). Unlike TCP, there are no transport acknowledgments or other reliability measures. However, lack of these additions (overhead) makes UDP particularly efficient and thus suitable for high speed applications (e.g., network file system), which are only suitable for installation on fast, reliable transmission media, such as local area networks. UDP is an unreliable protocol. Messages can be lost or arrive out of

Source Port Number	Destination Port Number
Length	Checksum
Data	

Figure 5.19 UDP header.

sequence, and it becomes the job of the application using UDP to handle these situations. Ninety-nine percent of the messages do get delivered. Therefore, UDP works quite well, except in mission-critical application areas, and is more efficient than TCP.

TCP/IP Application Protocols

The higher protocol layers of the TCP/IP stack is termed as the application layer. Four distinct protocols have been defined which are more prevalent with the applications and users of TCP/IP. These are TELNET, File Transfer Protocol (FTP), Simple Mail Transfer Protocol (SMTP), and Trivial File Transfer Protocol (TFTP). These are shown in Figure 5.12.

TELNET is a simple remote terminal protocol. Sometimes known as *remote login*, TELNET allows a user at one site to establish a connection via TCP to a computer at another site. Keystrokes pass from one system to another over the connection. Most UNIX processors currently incorporate the *rlogin* command, which offers almost the same functionality as *telnet*.

Virtual terminal programs translate terminal-specific characteristics into a generic format that can be understood by a potentially unlimited number of terminal types. TELNET was developed to enable Internet users the ability to communicate with anyone on the network, regardless of terminal type.

TELNET implementations at both the sending terminal (client) and the receiving terminal (server) translate local terminal types into standard TELNET network representation. To communicate, each end requires only what is known locally.

The TELNET architecture (equivalent to the virtual terminal protocol under OSI) defines a network virtual terminal (NVT), provides for negotiation about terminal functions, and operates symmetrically using peer techniques. The NVT consists of a virtual keyboard that generates only specific characters and a virtual printer that can only display specific characters.

TELNET uses TCP to communicate with TELNET server at another node. Once a connection has been opened, TELNET enters input mode for sending text to remote node. To allow interoperability, data and command are transmitted in NVT format.

FTP is a reliable end-to-end file transfer protocol. It provides a set of functions supporting file transfer from one machine to another. FTP also offers facilities for interactive access, format specification, and authentication control.

FTP is a TCP application that transfers files between different types of computers and operating systems (UNIX as well as non-UNIX). It supports three basic file transfer modes which specify file type (record or nonrecord structure), data type (EBCDIC or ASCII), and transmission method.

Most FTP implementations provide for interactive use. FTP is often used directly by programs. FTP uses separate connections for control and data. The data connection is used only for transferring the file, but the control connection remains open until the client closes it.

Among the services FTP provides are login, authorization, directory, copy and file conversion, and third-party transfers.

TFTP uses unreliable datagram service and uses time-outs and retransmissions since most errors terminate the file transfer. TFTP requires less memory, but is less robust than FTP. Therefore, we can see that TFTP can have no advantages as far as regular file transfers are concerned. TFTP is currently used in loading server programs and fonts in X Window terminals and in bootstrapping diskless workstations.

SMTP is the standard TCP/IP application protocol for transporting mail between systems that have full TCP/IP support. The objective of SMTP is to transfer mail reliably and efficiently. SMTP is independent of the particular transmission subsystem and requires only a reliable ordered data stream channel. SMTP focuses on mail delivery across networks, not on the mail interface. SMTP uses TCP as its underlying transport protocol, thus ensuring reliable message delivery.

SMTP travels over TCP/IP to any remote SMTP receiver and supports e-mail exchange between users on the same host or between hosts over a network. SMTP sets up the connection, transfers the message, and terminates the TCP connection. The new Multipurpose Internet Mail Extensions (MIME) protocol extends SMTP to send multimedia messages that can combine text, video, and voice.

In UNIX systems, SMTP is implemented by the program *sendmail. Sendmail* functions as both a client and a server for SMTP. Sendmail uses a store-and-forward mechanism. *Sendmail* is activated only to forward the message. If the forwarding is not immediately possible, the message is put in an output queue. After subsequent efforts, from time to time, the message is forwarded to its destination.

Troubleshooting TCP/IP: ICMP

Errors occur from time to time in all networks and nodes. These must be notified to those responsible for the system. Such notification is the responsibility of the Internet Control Message Protocol (ICMP). ICMP is a component part of every IP implementation. Its primary task is to transport error and diagnostic data for the IP. ICMP messages are initiated and processed internally by both IP and TCP/UDP. The ICMP protocol intercepts network problems and reports the following categories of errors:

The user program is sent an error message when the *destination is unreachable* due to a number of problems such as

- Network, host, protocol, or port are unobtainable.
- Fragmentation is required but the flag was set.
- Source routing option is unsuccessful.

If a gateway does not have the capacity to buffer a message, the transmitting host must reduce the rate at which subsequent messages are sent.

A *redirect* is sent when a gateway recognizes that the sender of an IP packet could send it directly to the next gateway, reducing the time delays or overhead.

The *echo request* and *echo reply* are used to verify operational readiness or measurement of elapsed time.

Time exceeded message is sent to a sender whose IP datagram had to be discarded on expiration of its TTL or for whose message the fragment reassembly timer has terminated.

Due to faulty entries for *parameters*, the packet may have to be discarded and the sender must be notified.

PROTOCOL DEPENDENCIES

While it is not imperative to know all protocols, it is important to understand which protocols do exist and when they can be used. It is also important to know which protocols have built-in dependencies upon each other.

Figure 5.20 depicts dependencies among the major TCP/IP protocols discussed earlier. The protocols are shown for dependency purposes since not all machines or network technologies use them. The bottom layer represents the hardware protocols such as logical link and media access. The layer above depicts ARP and RARP. ARP is normally used with Ethernet topologies, whereas RARP is rarely used except with diskless workstations.

The next layer above is the IP layer which includes ICMP (error and control message protocol). On top of that layer lies the transport protocols, TCP and UDP. The most complex dependencies are among the various application protocols, in the application layer.

SUMMARY

Internetworking has become an integral part of enterprisewide open computing strategies. Over the past few years, technology has emerged to make connectivity much easier than ever before. OSI and TCP/IP protocols have greatly enhanced connectivity between dissimilar operating systems and hardware platforms.

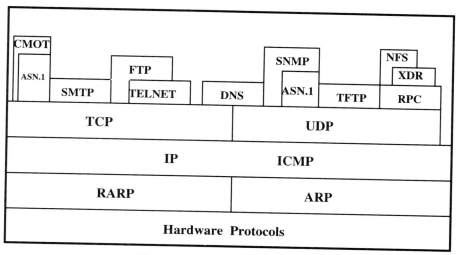

Figure 5.20 TCP/IP dependencies.

The idea of layering is fundamental in protocol design. In a layered model, each layer handles one part of the communication problem and usually corresponds to one protocol. In Figure 5.21, we depict the four-layer Internet model as well as the ISO layer reference model. In both cases, the layering only provides a conceptual framework. The real networking definitions are provided by the protocols within these layers. It is these protocols which spell out the differences, especially above layer 4 in either architecture.

OSI	TCP/IP
Application	Application
Presentation	(Process)
Session	
Transport	Transmission Control
Network	Network (IP)
Data Link	Data Link
Physical	Physical

Figure 5.21 Approximate protocol layer mappings.

Much of the rich functionality associated with the TCP/IP protocol suite results from a variety of high-level services supplied by application programs. The high-level protocols, these programs use, are built on the basic services: unreliable datagram delivery or reliable stream transport. The highest-level protocols provide user services like file and mail transfer and remote login (virtual terminal). The Internet provides universal connectivity and simplifies the application protocols.

One particular design feature of TCP/IP is its ability to operate over a variety of underlying network technologies. Currently, there are large TCP/IP networks that run over T1 links, X.25 public data networks, local area networks (e.g., token ring, Ethernet), satellite networks, and packet radio networks, making TCP/IP the de facto standard for multivendor, multioperating system computer networking.

TCP/IP and OSI are common denominators between the disparate operating systems and computers, and thus are likely to continue to be the major communications backbones for diverse systems.

EXERCISES

1. Describe fundamental differences between the TCP and UDP protocols.
2. The length of the Internet (IP) address can be described by which of the following:
    a. 32 bits
    b. 32 bytes
    c. 4 bytes
    d. 4 octets
3. How does OSI stack differ from TCP/IP stack?
4. Commands or packets used by SNMP are
    TRAP
    MIB
    SET
    GET
5. IP can detect errors in a packet and conduct retransmission if necessary. True or false?
6. Where does IP fit in relation to a seven-layer model?
7. File transfer is always initiated by a user. True or false?
8. Describe differences between connection-oriented and connectionless protocols.
9. TCP protocol does which of the following:
    a. Protects the destination from being overwhelmed with data
    b. Ensures that messages are reliably received at the destination
    c. Provides numbers indicating the correct sequence of routers to use
10. How does a local area network, like the Ethernet, fit the ISO layering model?

6

INTERNETWORKING PROTOCOLS—II

Introduction
Systems Network Architecture
Seven-Layer Structure
Architecture Overview
APPC Overview and Configurations
SNA Peer-to-Peer Networking
SNA-X.25 Integration
Convergence with OSI
Other Protocols
DECnet
NetBIOS/NetBEUI
IPX/SPX
XNS

Internetworking with WANs
Switching Systems
Frame Relay Systems
Broadcast Systems
X.25 Networks
Frame Relay
Switched Multimegabit Data Service
Point-to-Point Protocol
Digital Data Service
Fiber Distribution Data Interface
Asynchronous Transfer Mode
Internetworking Examples
Summary
Exercises

INTRODUCTION

Network protocols are just one of many kinds of architectures. The user wants services, such as printing, computation, remote access to data or systems, messaging, or any of the other myriad services available in a modern computer network.

A computer network is a complex system. The task of the architecture is to hide this complexity and provide the user transparent access to network services. This transparent access to network services is accomplished by dividing the tasks of the network into a series of layers. Each layer accomplishes a specific set of tasks, which are then offered as a service to the user of that layer. How these tasks are accomplished are hidden from the user.

As we discussed in previous sections, the ISO Reference Model is the most widely accepted layered architecture for a computer network. Each layer communicates with its peer on another node using a protocol. Each layer presents a rigorously defined set of services to the layer on top of it.

The abstract concepts in the ISO Reference Model have been implemented into a number of specific architectures. Some of the architectures are general-purpose architectures meant to address a variety of needs. IBM's System Network Architecture (SNA) or DEC's Digital Network Architecture (DNA) are two examples of general-purpose architectures. On the other hand, some architectures are specialized; for example, DEC's Local Area Transport Protocol (LAT) deals only with how terminal servers talk to hosts on an Ethernet.

The purpose of this section is to illustrate the different architectures and their different functions, and to show how the architectures are implemented in various physical media, on different hardware platforms, and in different software packages. This section begins by discussing SNA, DECnet, NetBIOS, NetWare, XNS, and X.25 architectures, followed by a discussion on how these architectures coexist in the heterogeneous world of internetworking.

SYSTEMS NETWORK ARCHITECTURE

IBM mainframe is a staple of business. It contains everything from corporate history in the form of customer databases to personal e-mail. The proliferation of PCs, and subsequently LANs, happened because users wanted more control over their computing environment. LANs arose to solve the problem. But in some cases, there is no substitute for the mainframe environment. The raw power and storage capacity of the mainframe are the key strategic reasons for its role in the enterprise.

When IBM introduced Systems Network Architecture in 1974, mainframes dominated computer environments. The arrangement required the lower-level systems on the network to communicate with each other through the mainframe rather than directly with each other. The popularity of personal computers in the 1980s changed the structure of corporate computing. Computing resources were no longer centralized; rather they were now distributed throughout an enterprise. The growth of PC-based networks further strengthened this distributed environment.

In 1982, in response to the proliferation of PC networks, IBM added LU 6.2 (Logical Unit 6.2) to SNA, for connecting the mainframe to the PC environments. LU 6.2 makes all computers, including mainframes, peer on an SNA network. With LU 6.2, the mainframe no longer plays dictator to its "slave" counterparts on the network. Instead of forcing devices connected to SNA to act as dumb terminals (e.g., 3270s) incapable of handling processing, it permits cooperative processing.

Seven-Layer Structure

SNA, with IBM's market presence behind it, has been a de facto data processing and networking standard for many years. IBM has developed and installed sufficient hardware and software to make SNA the world's most widely installed network topology. As a protocol suite, SNA offers functionality similar to the TCP/IP and OSI protocols. Like these protocols, SNA offers a hierarchical layered approach to communications (it is said that the OSI layering scheme is patterned after SNA), as depicted in Figure 6.1.

From the top down, the SNA's seven layers are end user, transaction and presentation service layers, data flow control, transmission flow control, path control, data link control, and physical layers. Together, they provide services that are more or less synonymous with those of OSI and TCP/IP. However, the layers' functions do not completely correspond with one protocol to another. These layers handle the following tasks:

- The *physical layer* moves data between nodes on a network.
- The *data link layer* uses the synchronous data link control (SDLC) Protocol to pass data across the physical interface.
- The *path control layer* manages routing and traffic control, packing data together to increase throughput.
- The *transmission control layer* initiates, manages, and concludes transport connections or sessions, controlling the data flow rate between layers 3 and 5.
- The *data flow layer* determines which LU can transmit next and helps manage error recovery.

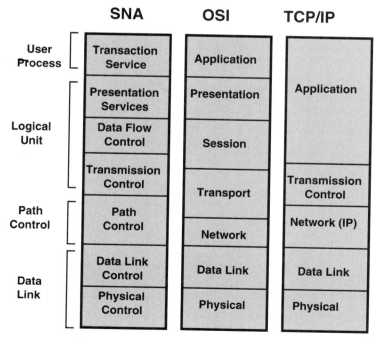

Figure 6.1 Approximate protocol layer mappings.

- The *NAU services layer* handles presentation services to the layer above.
- The *end-user layer* provides the user interface.

The *end user* is either a user at a terminal or an application program (process). An end user interacts with a logical unit, referred to as an LU (layers 4 through 6) to access the network. The type of services provided by the LU to the end user differ for each type of LU. LU types 2, 3, 4, and 7 support communications between processes and terminals, while LU types 1, 6.1, and 6.2 are for communications between two processes.

The logical unit, in turn, interacts with a physical unit, referred to as PU. The PU is the operating system of the SNA node and it controls the data link connections between the node and the network (Figure 6.2).

If we consider the PU as the operating system of the SNA node, then the data link is the device driver. Five types of nodes are currently supported: 1, 2.0, 2.1, 4, and 5. SNA node can be a nonprogrammable device such as a terminal or a printer, since SNA was originally designed to support the networking of nonprogrammable devices, such as 3270 terminals and printers, to IBM mainframes.

Architecture Overview

The primary purpose of SNA is to facilitate communication reliably among programs, device operators, and storage media, which may be located anywhere in the network. The

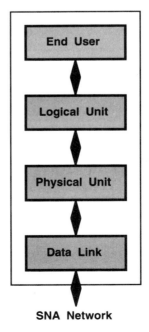

Figure 6.2 SNA node.

SNA defines sets of communication functions that are distributed throughout a network and formats and protocols that relate these functions to one another. SNA network is a system that complies with the systems network architecture. It may be implemented by wide range of hardware and software products made by many vendors. Only the key formats and protocols needed for general communications are defined by SNA.

Logical units and *physical units* are the two primary functional entities in an SNA network. Both are also referred to as network-addressable units (NAUs). PUs are physical systems connected to each other via cabling. Logical units are electronic entities connected by sessions, that make SNA resources like disk files and processing cycles, available for application software. A node on an SNA network can be a physical unit (i.e., hardware) or a logical unit (i.e., a logical session connection). In essence, the LU (e.g., LU 6.2) acts as an interface or protocol boundary between SNA and an end user's application.

The problem that an architect runs into is that of terminology. SNA is not unique in coining its own terms. We will summarize some of the SNA terms :

* *Network-addressable units* are the entities which originate or receive messages, and all these must be assigned unique addresses. NAUs represent the outermost boundaries of SNA, as shown in Figure 6.3. End users, such as host applications or terminal operators, access SNA services via the NAUs that assist them in setting up sessions. Some

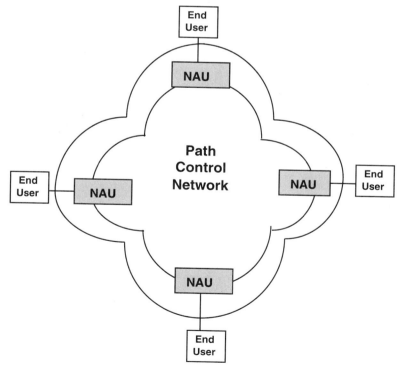

Figure 6.3 SNA node: NAUs and path control network.

NAUs are responsible for managing other NAUs. NAUs reside in SNA nodes, and the nodes are connected with each other via the transport network, which is called the path control network.

This network consists of the path control layer and the layers below it. NAUs are divided into three classes:

- *Logical units* are used by end users to access SNA services. Logical units may be a dumb typewriter terminal to a subsystem such as CICS with PCs and minicomputers in the middle. LUs can be classed as types 0, 1, 2, 3, and 6.2 to allow various degrees of intelligence.

- *Physical units* represent network management and control functions in a node and have no direct interface with the end user. A physical unit represents a distributed control element in a network and manages and controls resources directly attached to it, as shown in Figure 6.4.

  Physical units are divided into five categories, types 1, 2, 2.1, 4, and 5. PU type 5 is represented by the host PU that resides in virtual telecommunications access method (VTAM). PU type 4 is represented by the Network Control Program (NCP) in the front-end processor (FEP). PU types 1, 2, and 2.1 are associated with network stations and terminals. The IBM 3174 cluster controller is a PU type 2. PU type 2.1 is required to support certain LU 6.2 (peer-to-peer) functions.

- The *system services control point* (SSCP) is responsible for the overall management and control of the network and sessions. The SSCP performs its functions in cooperation with the physical units in the network. For example, to activate a line, SSCP sends an activation command to the NCP (PU type 4) and the NCP activates the line. In case

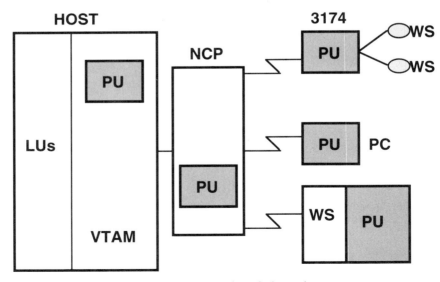

Figure 6.4 SNA network and physical units.

of an application such as NetView, all NetView operator commands for network control and surveillance are forwarded to the SSCP, which actually executes them.

In a multihost network there are multiple SSCPs (one per VTAM). Each SSCP and NCP in an SNA network must be assigned a unique number (address) called its subarea number; thus, the hosts and NCPs are also called subarea nodes. In contrast, all other terminals, clusters, PCs, minicomputers, and so on are called peripheral nodes.

Peripheral nodes do not understand the subarea form of addressing. The peripheral nodes, PUs and LUs, work with their own local addresses.

SNA Sessions. When two NAUs are communicating with each other, they are said to be in session. Setting up a session requires an exchange of handshakes, permissions, and verification that the two NAUs are capable of understanding each other. Figure 6.5 shows a simple network with various types of sessions.

SNA sessions are classified by the types of NAUs involved in the session. *SSCP sessions* are set up at the start of the network. When SSCP activates an NAU, it sets up a session with NAU. Once established, such sessions stay active as long as the network stays up. Some of the activities that occur during activation of a session are route establishment. It must follow this sequence: SSCP-PU session with each NCP on the route to the LU; SSCP-PU session with the peripheral node; and finally SSCP-LU session with the terminal. The session establishment between the host LUs and their SSCP is initiated by the host LU, not by the SSCP.

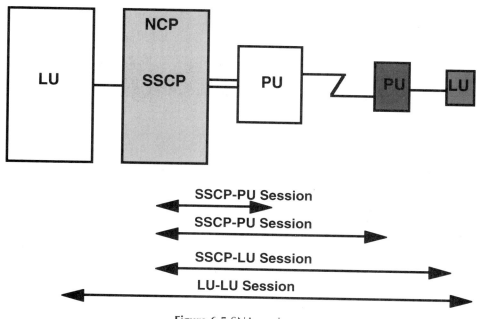

Figure 6.5 SNA sessions.

An *LU-LU session* is a user logon to a host application, such as CICS, IMS, TSO, or JES, and so on. While SSCP sessions represent management and control work, the LU-LU sessions represent application functions. LU-LU session can only be established after a successful SSCP-LU connection, since activation of an LU is completely controlled by the SSCP.

There are two types of LUs: primary and secondary. The primary LUs always reside in the host. A primary LU can support multiple concurrent sessions, whereas the secondary LU can only have one LU-LU session.

In a multihost network, there are multiple SSCPs. To allow for systematic control and management of the network, each SSCP is assigned a "domain." A network with a single host is known as single-domain network.

Physical Control. Physical control ensures that a physical transmission medium is available and transmits or receives data on the medium in a serial (one-bit-at-a-time) manner. This layer defines the electrical and signaling characteristics needed to establish, maintain, and terminate physical connections on which the links in a network are built. Synchronous data link control (SDLC), a data link control protocol, provides logical procedures for controlling the link and recovering from link-level errors. The physical control layer provides specifications for data terminal equipment (DTE) interface.

Data Link Control. The data link control provides protocols for message units transfer across a link and for link-level data flow and error recovery. The data link control supports SDLC, System/390 data channel, CCITT X.25, and token ring protocols. The functions of a link protocol can be divided into four categories as follows:

- *Synchronization* allows a machine on the link to assemble bits received into complete messages. Link protocols, prior to SDLC, were character oriented (basic synchronous communication).
- *Link-level error recovery* allows the link protocol to recover from transient transmission errors. A common scheme for recovering from transmission errors is for the transmitting station to attach a parity or check field to the bit stream being transmitted. The receiving field computes its own check field as it receives the bit pattern and compares it with the check field received with the message. If they do not match, it is assumed that there was an error in transmission since the bits got altered.
- *Controlling multipoint links* are required to uniquely identify each station on the link, with an addressing scheme.
- *Half-duplex management* is provided to ensure proper send and receive states for link stations. This is achieved by designating the front end as the primary and other stations as secondary. A secondary station enters a send state only when explicitly invited (polled). The secondary station goes back to the receive state after it has transmitted all its frames.

SDLC, the synchronous data link control protocol in SNA, can support point-to-point, multipoint, half-duplex, full-duplex, dedicated lines, and switched line configura-

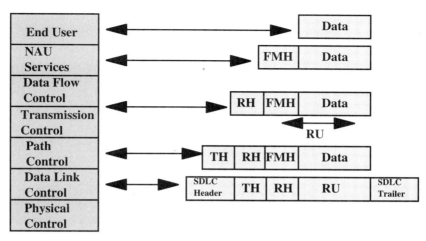

Figure 6.6 SDLC frame structure.

tions. All SNA and user data are enclosed within an SDLC header and trailer, where header and trailer fields contain SDLC control information. Figure 6.6. illustrates the relationship between SDLC control information and data units, known as path information units (PIUs), from higher layers. PIUs are the combination headers from all the upper layers: the transmission header (TH) from path control, the request/response header (RH) from transmission control, and function management header (FMH) supporting NAU services. Figure 6.6 displays the SDLC frame structure. Not all SDLC frames carry PIUs, however.

Path Control. The SNA component that routes and transmits data between network-addressable units is the path control network. The path control is responsible for moving packets around in SNA. It is through this layer that NAUs interface with the transport network in SNA. The functions of this layer include routing of traffic and general management of the transport network. The path control uses data link control elements (link stations) and path control elements to provide its SNA functions. The path control also provides procedures for managing congestion in the transport network and ensures that the PIUs do not exceed the PU buffer in the destination peripheral node. The transmission header (Figure 6.6) carries all path control information.

The transmission header is the path control layer header. It is with the TH we see the relationship between PUs and path control elements. However, not all SNA nodes can support the same level of path control functions.

SNA nodes are divided into subarea and peripheral nodes. Peripheral nodes are those that connect to the peripherals, such as terminals, PCs, and so on. Subarea nodes are of two types: boundary nodes that connect to session partners and intermediate network nodes (INN) that form the backbone network in SNA and are responsible for all routing and for managing network level congestion. Routing and flow control are based on physical topology of the network.

Subarea nodes, that is, hosts and NCPs, are the routing nodes in SNA. The objective of the INN routing is to get a PIU from the source to destination. All information required for routing is contained in the TH part of the header. The subarea number of the destination is used by each node to determine the next node in the message path. Once at the destination, the boundary node delivers the PIU to the appropriate NAU in its subarea. The SNA routing algorithm is basically a pass-the-buck methods. All that a node knows about a route is the next node to which the message is to be passed for a given destination.

APPC Overview and Configurations

LU 6.2 can be considered a subset of SNA. In its most popular form, LU 6.2 is known as advanced program-to-program communications (APPC). The terms LU 6.2 and APPC are synonymous. APPC functions primarily as a resource allocator and controller. APPC ensures that programs have access to network resources when they need them and that network resources are not corrupted, such as when two users attempt to make simultaneous updates to the same file. A version, APPC/PC connects the PCs (especially OS/2) with the mainframe.

LU 6.2 provides a connection-oriented, reliable, half-duplex service. LU 6.2 allows data flow between the user processes only in a single direction. In SNA terminology, the peer-to-peer connection between two processes is called a *conversation*. The peer-to-peer connection between two LUs is called a *session*. A session is usually a long-term connection between the two LUs, while a conversation is often of short duration. Figure 6.7 depicts a peer-to-peer connectivity among various PCs via a token ring backbone.

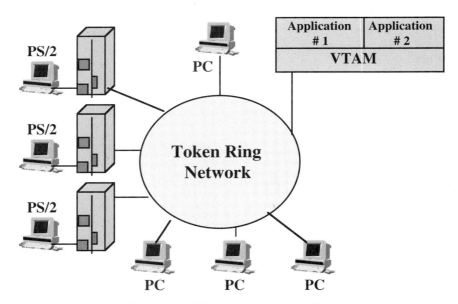

Figure 6.7 SNA peer-to-peer networking.

The interface between a user process and the LU is called *presentation services* in SNA. The interface is defined as a collection of verbs that a transaction program can execute to request a service from the LU. This defines a protocol boundary between the program and LU 6.2. Therefore, the architectural specification for LU 6.2 is merely a set of verbs that a user process or a transaction program can address.

APPC has enhanced SNA support for distributed processing, especially transaction processing. The interface is simplified, focusing on distributed applications, rather than on communication protocols. APPC has a structured programming interface to the communications subsystem for

- Initiating and terminating connections.
- Sending and receiving data.
- Administering the communication path.
- Managing distributed data.

APPC reduces the number of options for interconnection, thereby facilitating peer-to-peer networking.

SNA Peer-to-Peer Networking

APPN is another form of LU 6.2 implementation. It adds network management capabilities to the LU 6.2 peer-to-peer (APPC) communications. APPN is limited to PU type 2.1 nodes and was first implemented for S/38 as the APPC architecture. APPN also includes a routing capability that can dynamically create new routes between nodes on a network.

APPC allows for parallel LU 6.2 sessions between partner applications to support synchronous program-to-program communications as peers. In implementing APPC on AS/400, IBM combined APPC with SNA low-entry networking, SNA Node 2.1 transport layer functions. The functional capabilities of the type 2.1 node are the logical point-to-point connection of APPC/LU 6.2 to the actual physical connection between systems.

In AS/400 communication environment, the capabilities of type 2.1 node are significantly enhanced: APPN distinguishes between a network node (NN) and an end node (EN). Network nodes contain the advanced functions of the control point in their path control layer that allow intermediate routing and distributed network LU address searches to be performed within the type 2.1 nodes. End nodes, on the other hand, provide only a subset of the network node functions and rely on the network node for session requests that involve multiple nodes.

As a result, an APPN network can be configured in such a way that the end users on one token ring local area network (LAN) use end node services, while each LAN contains a network node that acts as a control point. Instead of connecting each end node in one LAN to each end node in another LAN, the connection between corresponding control point is sufficient, facilitating communication between any two users residing in different LANs.

Advanced facilities of AS/400 APPN provide the following major functions:

- Distributed searches of the network locate any remote LU requested by local application.
- Optimum route calculation occurs by implementing network path topology.
- Once the correct and virtual route is determined , configuration can be automatically created and activated by the operating system, including activation of a nonconfigured remote LU.
- The transport assigns transmission priority allocates buffers and system capabilities while the session is being established.

SNA-X.25 Integration

X.25 has become an important wide area network standard for enterprise network applications. CCITT X.25 describes data flow between nodes, but does not describe how to use data. CCITT describes this function in terms of an interface. The interface describes physical layer characteristics such as connectors, voltages, and cables. The interface also describes data link and network layer functions, such as packet framing, error detection, and recovery. This is similar to a point-to-point network specification. In a way, X.25 describes a simple LAN that you use to access a WAN.

SNA and X.25 are the two most common architectures for wide area networks. Even though most SNA networks tend to be self-sufficient, they may have to provide connectivity to X.25 interfaces in the following situations:

- Enterprise communication requirements using public networks such as Tymenet or Telenet where X.25 is the most common interface.
- Connectivity requirement within the enterprise where subnetworks use non-SNA technologies, such as AT&T, DEC, and HP.
- Building multinational networks almost always requires the use of X.25-based public packet networks.

SNA and X.25 are inherently incompatible, and an interface between the two requires a protocol conversion or enveloping. X.25 defines only network access transport protocols. When using X.25, you still require other architecture to provide higher layer functions. It is not possible to switch the lower three layers between X.25 and SNA. We can compare these layer by layer as follows:

- The physical control layer defines the interface to the physical media, including the modem interface. SNA and X.25 can use the same interface.
- The link layer SDLC can be replaced by LAPB (link access protocol, balanced), with some SDLC commands being transported through X.25 network. SDLC control information is also transparent to X.25.
- The packet layer defines maximum packet size, destination address, packet level flow control, and so on. and procedures for establishing end-to-end connections. These pro-

tocols do not replace SNA path control or higher levels. While the packet header must follow the LAPB, the remaining SDLC headers—TH, RH, FMH—must be preserved. Some of the specific differences between X.25 and SNA are the following:

- SNA has no exact equivalent of X.25 packets, packet-level sequencing, flow control, or end-to-end packet-level assurance.
- The LAPB and SDLC have different header structures, so they must be converted.
- X.25 is only a transport, whereas SNA is complete end-to-end architecture.
- SNA and X.25 have different command structures.

There are two complementary strategies for X.25 and SNA interface. These are:

- Network packet switching interface (NPSI) software that runs in a 37xx or a front-end processor and allows SNA hosts to communicate with X.25 DTEs by mapping virtual circuits of X.25 into real circuits. NPSI allows the IBM front-end processor to act like data terminal equipment (DTE). This way, the X.25 network acts as a substitute for data link control and physical layers of SNA. Figure 6.8 shows how X.25 and SNA networks can coexist.

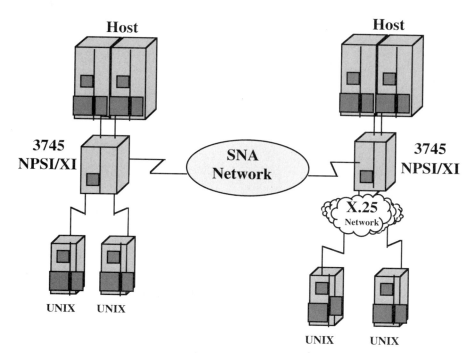

Figure 6.8 SNA—X.25 integration.

- The X.25 interface (XI) allows the SNA network to act as a packet-switching network by mapping X.25 virtual circuits into SNA sessions. The network provides the X.25 interface and thus can connect UNIX machines using TCP/IP. XI enables the IBM front-end processor to act as an X.25 DCE. The data are routed between XI nodes using SNA protocols. XI can eliminate the need for a separate X.25 transport, and X.25 DTEs can be directly connected to the existing SNA networks.

Convergence with OSI

As shown in Figure 6.1, the SNA layers have certain features in common with those of the OSI model, particularly the lower layers. The structure of the OSI model appears to be similar to the structure of the SNA model. They both represent hierarchical architecture, consisting of seven layers. Layers of both models have the same properties—each layer performs a specific function, lower layers provide services to the upper layers, and layers of the same level can communicate with each other as peers. However, the purpose of the OSI model is different from that of the SNA model. The OSI protocols are a means of implementing unified system communications between heterogeneous networks, whereas SNA is the basis of system communications in a homogeneous communications network.

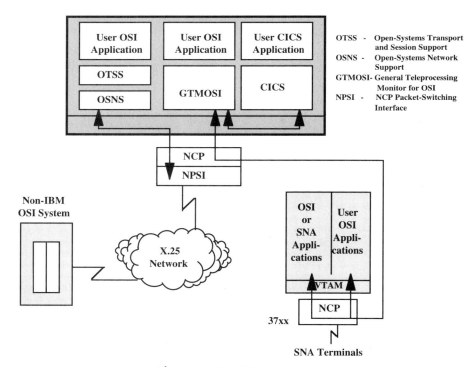

Figure 6.9 SNA-OSI coexistence.

The functions of both SNA and OSI layers are similar, even though there is not a one-to-one correlation between the SNA and OSI layers; specifically,

- The SNA physical control layer and OSI physical layer are functionally equivalent.
- The SNA data link control layer can use SDLC and X.25 interface and SDLC is a subset of High-level Data Link Control (HDLC), which is used for OSI data link layer.
- The SNA path control layer provides functions similar to those defined for OSI transport and session layers.
- The SNA data flow and transmission control layers provide functions similar to those defined by OSI transport and session layers.
- The SNA presentation services and transaction services are also functionally equivalent to OSI presentation layer services.

Even though IBM developed a separate suite of OSI products, there never has been an attempt to integrate the two architectures. As an interim solution, IBM has developed a number of products at different layers to provide an SNA-OSI gateway as shown in Figure 6.9.

OTHER PROTOCOLS

DECnet

There are several DEC architectures. the most general network architecture is the Digital Network Architecture (DNA). DECnet consists of a series of DEC products that conform to the DNA architecture specifications. Figure 6.10 shows the layers of the DNA protocol stack.

Digital Network Architecture. DNA provides the interfaces and protocols that enable users to create their own networks using DEC systems. The family of network products supporting DNA is generally called DECnet. DNA employs a layered architecture. DNA defines six levels: physical link layer, data link layer, routing layer, transport layer, session control layer, and network application layer. DNA has defined three separate protocols, but we will discuss two of the commonly used protocols in the following sections: the Digital Data Communications Message Protocol (DDCMP) and Local Area Transport (LAT) Architecture.

Digital Data Communications Message Protocol is an example of a traditional data link protocol. DDCMP is used to form a point-to-point link between two computers. The physical medium used by DDCMP could be a simple RS-232C cable or a satellite, microwave, or other wide area communications link.

DNA uses a number of subnetwork technologies, including Ethernet and X.25. The routing layer of DNA is responsible for taking packets of data and deciding which data link the packet should travel on. The end-to-end communications of DNA is identical to ISO's transport layer. The session layer validates incoming connection requests, activates the appropriate service for a user, and provides a node name to address mapping service. The session layer also translates those logical names into DECnet addresses.

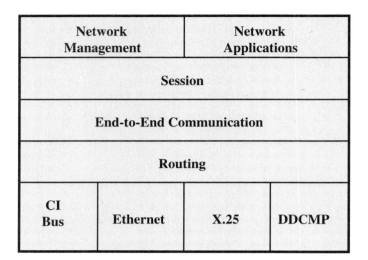

Figure 6.10 Digital Network Architecture.

Services in DNA fall into two categories:

- *Network management services* are a set of protocols used to manage the network. These services use the facilities of the network to exchange data on the current state of nodes, lines, and other network components. A variety of user interfaces are present that displays the status or audit trails of the network activity.
- *Network applications* are the services that the users see. One of those services is the "virtual terminal" service, which allows any user on any node to log into any other node on the network.

Local Area Transport Architecture. Figure 6.11 shows the local area transport architecture (LAT) protocol stack. LAT is used exclusively on Ethernet medium and provides an efficient method of sending terminal traffic to a host. LAT is also able to use a single Ethernet packet to send data to many different users to the same host. LAT establishes a virtual circuit to that host and then puts many slots of data into each packet. LAT has many other features oriented toward terminal applications.

The LAT mechanism provides an efficient method to connect terminals to an Ethernet via a terminal server.

DECnet and SNA Architectures. Although DEC and IBM computers offer different operating alternatives, it is common to find both in the same enterprise. Connecting to SNA environment can use either a dedicated gateway or the services of a general-purpose VAX. As with X.25 connections or DECnet routers, different speeds are available for such connections. It is also fairly common to connect PCs to the SNA environment using DECnet. Three types of gateways can be employed: DECnet/SNA Gateway, DECnet/SNA Gateway for synchronous transport, and the DECnet/SNA gateway for channel transport (CT).

LAT Slot Layer	DNA Transport
LAT Virtual Circuit	DNA Routing
Ethernet	

Figure 6.11 Local area transport protocol stack.

The *DECnet/SNA gateway* provides the software routines to map SNA sessions to DNA logical links and to manage all the SNA protocols. A separate access routine is required to provide the upper layer functionality. The access routines communicate with the gateway over DECnet using Gateway Access Protocol (GAP).

The *DECnet/SNA gateway* for synchronous transport is able to support a greatly increased level of activity. It also provides a direct channel attached connection to a System 370 architecture mainframe at very high data transfer rates. The channel transport gateway connects to the IBM channel using standard bus and tag cables. All three gateways provide the same functionality but have different performance characteristics.

DECnet Phase V or DECnet/OSI. DECnet/OSI is based on OSI protocols. It includes support for all the physical media that are supported in Ethernet environments, X.21 support for switched or leased circuits, and for dynamically established links.

NetBIOS/NetBEUI

NetBIOS/NetBEUI (Network Basics End User Interface) is a key standard for local networks in the IBM microcomputer environment is the Network Basic Input/Output System (NetBIOS). All network operating systems and software applications for PC-DOS, MS-DOS, and OS/2 use or support some form of NetBIOS. NetBIOS's existence has been a major factor in the explosive growth of LANs for personal computers. IBM released its first LAN (the IBM PC network) in 1984. It was similar in concept to Ethernet, but ran at 2 Mb/sec, whereas most Ethernets ran at 10 Mb/sec. When IBM introduced its token ring LAN in 1985, it provided an implementation of NetBIOS for the Token Ring. The third implementation was introduced for PS/2 systems.

NetBIOS is a software interface, not a network protocol. For example, the data packets that are exchanged across the (IBM or Microsoft) PC network differ from those on the token ring network. The interfaces for all IBM implementations of NetBIOS provide a consistent software interface that has become a de facto standard for personal computers. In addition, there are implementations of TCP and UDP as the underlying transport protocols.

Technical Overview. Because NetBIOS specifies an interface only, it cannot guarantee that different network adapters will be able to communicate with each other. NetBIOS does define a consistent interface for applications software (service message block, SMB protocol), which guarantees that different adapters will support the same application. Like most software interfaces, NetBIOS is accessed through a software interrupt. Whenever an application needs a NetBIOS service, it executes a specific software interrupt. The interrupt directs the microprocessor to transfer control to the network adapter's software, which can process the request.

In many PC environments the application that NetBIOS is used for is *file sharing*. In this case, another protocol interface is used above NetBIOS. This interface is called server message block interface protocol. This interface is shown in Figure 6.12. The primary SMB functions are: directory creation, open file, read from file, and line printer access for print files.

NetBIOS provides both a connection-oriented service (virtual circuit) and a connectionless (datagram) service. Four types of services provided by NetBIOS are

- Name services.
- Session services.
- Datagram services.
- General services.

Figure 6.13 shows the relationship of these services to general services. In most implementations, a single box providing some form of datagram delivery (similar to the IP layer in TCP/IP suite) is used. But unlike the IP layer, the NetBIOS user process has no access to any additional services.

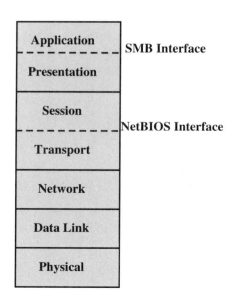

Figure 6.12 Relationship of OSI model to SMB and NetBIOS.

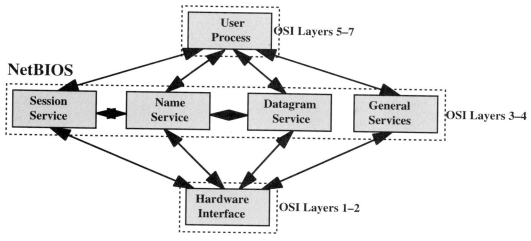

Figure 6.13 NetBIOS services.

Naming Services. Names are used to identify resources in NetBIOS. NetBIOS allows applications software to use "network name" of its own or remote application choosing, which can be simple, logical, and mnemonic. There are two types of names: unique names and group names. A *unique name* must be unique across the network, whereas the *group name* does not have to be unique since all processes that have a given group name belong to the group. Name services occur in three phases:

- The *name registration* function is used to add individual name or a group name to the directory database. Before granting the individual name registration, the adapter makes sure that it is a valid name and is unique on the network. However, for group name registration, it does not have to be unique.
- The *name discovery* function identifies the specific network adapter at which this name exists. Most of the time, name discovery takes place without the knowledge of the application program. When an application establishes a session or transfers a datagram, the application uses only names, which are translated to network addresses by the adapter.
- The *name deletion* function cancels any association between the name and the application, and it allows other applications to use the name.

Session Services. Session services provide connection-oriented communications, like an ordinary telephone. One application program calls to establish a session, and the other answers the call. Session services also have three separate phases: *session establishment*, *data transfer*, and *session termination*.

- *Session establishment* occurs when two application programs start to communicate. One application issues a "LISTEN" command, telling the adapter software that the application is willing to accept a session. The second application issues the "CALL" command to direct the adapter software to actively establish a session.

• *Data transfer* uses "RECEIVE" and "SEND" commands to exchange data between the two applications when the session has been established.

• *Session termination* occurs when a application no longer needs a session by sending "HANG UP" command. Either application involved may issue this command. However, only the adapter can end the session by sending an error code in one of its commands.

Datagram Services. As an alternative to "session services," an application may exchange information with datagrams or in a connectionless mode. Datagrams resemble mailed letters as compared to telephone calls in a session service. When an application sends data in a datagram, it simply gives the data to the adapter software and tells the adapter who to send to. The application does not establish any handshake or session with the other application.

The datagrams can be up to 512 bytes in length. These can be sent to a specific name (a group name or a unique name) or can be broadcast to the entire network. As with other datagram services, such as UDP, the NetBIOS datagrams are connectionless and unreliable. In addition, NetBIOS datagrams support only a limited amount of data: whereas an application can send as much as 131,072 bytes of data with a single CHAIN SEND command, datagrams limit the application to 512 bytes at a time.

An application can use datagrams to send data in three modes:

• To a single remote application, in *point-to-point transfer mode*. This is the simplest way an application can use datagrams to send data to another application, involving one sender and one recipient, or

• To a group of applications, in *group-data transfer mode*, where the recipient's name is a group name instead of a unique name. However, all applications who issue a RECEIVE DATAGRAM command get that data, or

• To all NetBIOS applications, in *broadcast-data transfer mode*, where the data is broadcast over the network and the implied destination is every adapter on the network instead of a destination name. Selected applications may issue the RECEIVE BROADCAST DATAGRAM in order to receive this data.

General Services. The NetBIOS general services manage and configure the network adapter. The most commonly used functions are *reset*, to specify configuration parameters and cancel the previously issued command, and *status*, to obtain status about the local or remote network adapter. The status command can also gather self-test results, traffic and error statistics, resource statistics, and name-status information.

NetBIOS Internetwork Communications. Because of the proprietary nature of this protocol and IBM's push for its use in their token ring network, few vendors have been willing to develop network products that interoperate with the PC network adapter. Since there is a separate interface for token ring, the token ring adapter supports NetBIOS through a software emulation of the NetBIOS interface.

NetBIOS is a session layer interface and does not have a definition at the network layer. In its native form, NetBIOS is not used on an internetwork, but with routers. When implementing NetBIOS with routers, special software must be implemented. However, this can be accomplished with XNS or TCP. Since bridges operate at the data link layer, they do not know about the NetBIOS naming schemes. Therefore, bridging NetBIOS LANs require that registered NetBIOS name must still be unique across all the LANs that the bridges interconnect.

IPX/SPX

Internetwork Packet Exchange (IPX) is Novell's NetWare specific packet-forwarding protocol and Sequential Packet Exchange (SPX) is Novell's implementation of SPP (Sequential Packet Protocol) for its NetWare network operating system. Novell's NetWare operating system relies on communication protocols like IPX/SPX to provide a network computing environment.

Each of these protocols—IPX and SPX—provide a specific service, allowing users to access shared resources. Once a hardware connection has been established between nodes on a network, a transport protocol is needed to provide the next level of network services. All these protocols are integrated in the NetWare operating system.

NetWare servers and bridges can route SPX / IPX and other supported protocol traffic between different LAN architectures. Open Data Link Interface (ODI) is Novell's medium for multiprotocol support. NetWare interoperability encompasses workstations running DOS, OS/2, Windows, Macintosh, and UNIX operating systems. All workstations can access their native files systems on the NetWare server. Figure 6.14 shows a schematic how SPX/IPX coexist with other network protocols like AppleTalk and TCP/IP on top of ODI.

Integration and interoperability have long been Novell's strengths. NetWare has always run on multiple topologies, including Ethernet, token ring, ARCnet, and Omninet. NetWare LAN drivers are available for nearly every network interface card. Figure 6.15 shows how two applications running on DECnet/LAT and IPX/SPX use a TCP/IP gateway for communications.

XNS

XNS or Xerox Network Systems is a network architecture developed by Xerox Corporation in the 1970s for integrating their computer and office products. These protocols are primarily used for printing and filing applications. XNS is similar in structure to the TCP/IP protocol suite.

XNS is a distributed, not a hierarchical network architecture. Hierarchical systems, like SNA, are intended for applications where one or more mainframe computers dominate the resulting information system and its users. In such systems other elements are clearly subordinate to the large computers. In various ways, network architectures under-

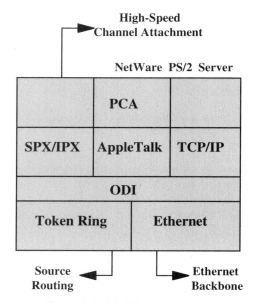

Figure 6.14 NetWare server system.

lying these systems are designed to create and reinforce this relationship. Many networking applications prove to be ill-served by this model.

XNS achieves a distributed architecture by placing an appropriate amount of computing power in each workstation to enable users to do their primary tasks by relying on local resources. To tie together workstations and servers in a local area network, XNS relies on Ethernet.

XNS and the OSI Model. Basic to most network architectures, including XNS, is the concept of layering. Figure 6.16 shows the basic structure of Xerox Network Systems, organized into a series of layers, approximately corresponding to the OSI model layers.

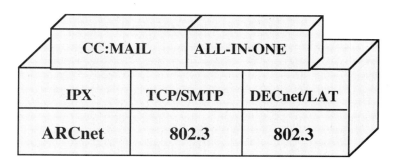

Figure 6.15 DECnet and NetWare with TCP gateway.

OSI Layers	XNS			
Application Layer	**Office Document Architectures**			
	Filing	**Mail**	**Virtual Terminal**	**Printing**
	Application Support: Authentication, Time, Char Code			
Presentation Layer	**Courier**			
Session Layer	**Courier**			
Transport Layer	**Internet Transport Protocols**			
Network Layer	**Internet Datagram protocol**		**X.25**	
Data Link Layer	**Ethernet Data Link Layer**	**Synchronous Point-to-Point**	**HDLC / LAPB**	
Physical Layer	**Ethernet or 802.3**	**RS-232**	**—**	
	Cabling Alternatives			

Figure 6.16 XNS and OSI layers.

Since XNS predates the OSI model, XNS does not have exactly the same number of layers as OSI. Each XNS layer corresponds functionally to one or more of the OSI layers.

At the lowest layer of the XNS architecture, we must consider data transmission between different devices of the network, corresponding to the physical and data link layers of OSI. At the next higher layers, we consider the addressing, routing, and switching decisions that provide for reliable transport through the network. Within XNS, Ethernet provides the OSI physical and data link layers' functionality, XNS's Internet Transport Protocols provide the OSI network layer functions (OSI layer 3), and the Sequenced Packet Protocol provides connection oriented OSI transport layer functions (OSI layer 4).Therefore, XNS operates at layer 3 as well as layer 4 of the ISO model. Figure 6.17 shows the XNS protocol suite.

XNS Internet Architecture. The XNS Internet Architecture offers a number of protocols corresponding to the network and transport layers of the OSI Reference Model. The XNS

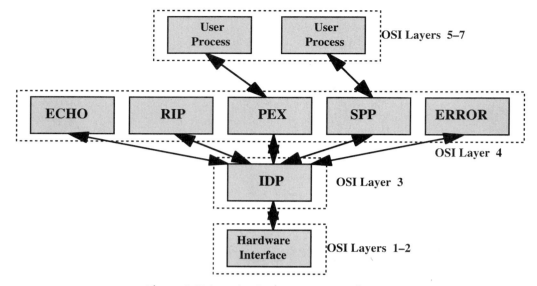

Figure 6.17 Layering in the XNS protocol suite.

Internet Architecture enables Ethernets to be directly interconnected to each other in a variety of ways: directly, via telephone lines, through public data networks, or via long-distance transmission media. The Internet architecture makes use of several protocols that move information from source to destination in an organized and reliable manner. XNS implements six separate protocols at two levels of the ISO model.

At the *network layer*, XNS implements the *Internet Datagram Protocol* (IDP). IDP provides a connectionless and unreliable delivery service, similar to the IP layer in the TCP/IP suite. Every IDP packet contains a 30-byte header, consisting of the following fields:

- *Source XNS address* (32-bit network ID, 48-bit host ID, 16-bit port number).
- *Destination XNS address* (32-bit network ID, 48-bit host ID, 16-bit port number).
- Checksum.
- Length of data.
- Higher-layer packet type (SPP, PEX, ECHO, ERROR, RIP).

IDP packets are not fragmented as Internet IP datagrams might be. Most XNS systems enforce a maximum of 576 bytes for an IDP packet. It can transport up to 546 bytes of data, allowing 30 bytes for the IDP header.

At the *transport layer*, there are five distinct protocols to provide different services:

- *Sequenced packet protocol (SPP)* is the prominent XNS transport layer protocol and is similar to TCP. It provides a connection-oriented reliable, full-duplex service to an application program. However, unlike TCP (which provides only a byte stream interface), XNS presents three different interfaces to a user process. These interfaces are *a byte stream interface*, delivering bytes to the user process in order and preserving message boundaries; a *packet stream interface*, delivering packets in order by reading or writing the entire packets; and a *reliable packet interface*, delivering packets to the user process as they arrive. But these packets may be out of order. However, duplicate packets are removed prior to delivery to the destination. The SPP packet can carry a maximum of 534 bytes, allowing 12 bytes for the SPP header.

- *Packet Exchange Protocol (PEX)* is a datagram-oriented protocol at the transport layer and is similar to the UDP. Although PEX is not a reliable protocol, it does retransmit a request whenever necessary and does not duplicate detection.

- *Error Protocol (ERROR)* is a protocol that can be used by any process to report discovered errors and that it has discarded the packet.

- *Echo Protocol (ECHO)* is a simple protocol that causes a host to echo the packet that it receives.

- *Routing Information Protocol (RIP)* is used to maintain a routing database for use on a host to forward IDP packets to another host.

The main use of the XNS today is to communicate with Xerox hardware.

INTERNETWORKING WITH WANS

Today's enterprise networks consist of LANs of various protocols, supporting multiple media and architectures, connected to wide area networks consisting of a variety of communication systems. These complex networks span cities, countries, and continents and are being influenced by emerging technologies driven by user demands and vendor innovations. Managing these multivendor/multiprotocol/multimedia systems can be a formidable challenge even to the more technological informed network administrator.

Designing a LAN-to-WAN internetworking system and managing it successfully demands in-depth knowledge of these technologies. While it is possible to exercise sufficient control over the LAN segments of the network, the WAN portions are usually leased from service providers that offer a variety of control options.

The industry offers several WAN segment options depending on whether the information is to be packet switched or frame relayed, once it leaves the source LAN segment and reaches the destination LAN node. The information can be transmitted through physical media such as twisted-pair copper wire and fiber optic lines or broadcast over microwave or satellite.

Depending on the transmission technologies used, available WAN options can be categorized as follows:

- Switching systems (circuit or packet switched).
- Frame relay systems.
- Broadcast systems (satellite or microwave).

Switching Systems

Switching systems are physically connected through nodes using one or more media types. Links are established between nodes to enable the signals to pass through them on their way to the addressed node.

Circuit switching systems establish dedicated circuits between the nodes before the data signals are transmitted. The data path is established between the source and the destination nodes before the data are sent. Circuit switching systems send exploratory signals requesting the transmission path to the addressed node. Intermittent nodes examine the request and determine which downstream circuit paths are available for connection. Once all circuits or paths are switched and a source to destination dedicated link is established, the source is ready to transmit the signals. The data signals can be digital, analog, or integrated analog/digital. The circuit is dedicated as long as the connection is required and is disconnected as soon as the transmission is completed.

Packet switching systems are also known as packet data networks (PDNs). Packet switching systems combine the advantages of message and circuit switching. The data are broken into small chunks or packets, consisting of header information and user defined data, and transmitted packet by packet. Different packets can be launched along different network paths and are received at the destination node where they are reassembled to form a complete message.

Packet switching can use two methods to transmit streams of data from source to destination. In the *datagram* approach, each packet is treated as an independent entity and is received and launched on different links; the X.25 interface at the receiving end then strips the headers and reassembles them in proper sequence before delivering them to addressed node. *X.25 packet switching standard* uses this approach (a virtual circuit). The *virtual circuit* approach establishes a logical connection between the source and the destination before packets are transmitted, the network makes sure that a link is established by exploring the available links, giving the appearance that a dedicated link has been established.

Frame Relay Systems

Frame differs from a packet in its length and header. A frame can be a bit or character oriented. Frame relay uses *separate channel* for control characters or header/trailer information, while packet switching uses the same channel for both control and user-defined data streams. Frame relaying is performed by setting up a virtual circuit between the source and the destination. Frame relay is a connection-less service that provides flow and error control in addition to other standard services.

Frame relay is particularly suited for bursty traffic, because it offers better routing and error detection. It can be employed in connecting disparate LANs over wide area links. There are number of different services that Frame Relay technology utilizes:

- Lease Line Services which operate at 56 Kb/sec, primarily from the telephone carriers.
- T1 service offer transmission facilities for both voice or data or integrated voice/data signals with a data transmission capability of 1.544 Mb/sec.

- T3 service with transmission speeds of 44.736 Mb/sec.
- Fractional T1 services enable the user to lease T1 lines but pay only for required bandwidth. These operate at any multiple of 64 Kb/sec up to 768 Kb/sec.

Broadcast Systems

Broadcast systems offer several advantages and some disadvantages over copper wire and fiber optic lines. Broadcast systems can be divided into two main types: satellite and microwave.

Satellite. *Satellite systems* use geostationary satellites that are positioned 22,300 miles over the earth and maintain the same relative position over the face of the earth. The satellites are in communication with the earth stations that are equipped with large dish antennas. The earth stations act as transmitter/receiver entities with the ability to transmit and receive signals from the satellite. A satellite is a kind of microwave relay station.

Satellite systems have been used for television program distribution, long-distance telephone networks, private networks, and mobile systems.

Microwave. *Microwave radio transmissions* are used by common carrier service providers for long-distance communication transmissions. Both analog and digital signals can be carried by microwave.

X.25 Networks

X.25 is probably the best known and most widely used wide area network protocol. It is also most commonly associated with the ISO model. X.25 was established as a recommendation by CCITT. X.25 has been adopted by public data networks throughout Europe and the United States.

Architecturally, in X.25, a network operates like a telephone system. The X.25 network is assumed to consist of complex packet switches that contain the intelligence needed to route packets. Hosts do not attach directly to communication wires of the network.

X.25 is actually a family of protocols that define how a user of the network, known as data terminal equipment (DTE), communicates with the boundary of the network, known as data circuit-terminating equipment (DCE). Once a packet of information is presented to DCE, the X.25 network routes the information to the DCE closest to the destination DTE. Figure 6.18 shows the basic components of an X.25 network.

X.25 Architecture. X.25 is a three-layered network architecture based on CCITT standards and operates at the bottom three layers of the OSI reference model.. The DTE-DCE interface uses the lower three layers, with options available at the physical layer (Figure 6.19).

The *network layer* implements Packet Layer Protocol (PLP). This *connection-oriented* protocol serves as the highest layer in the X.25 model. PLP provides full-duplex data transfer, flow control mechanisms, and negotiation of options in a similar manner that the

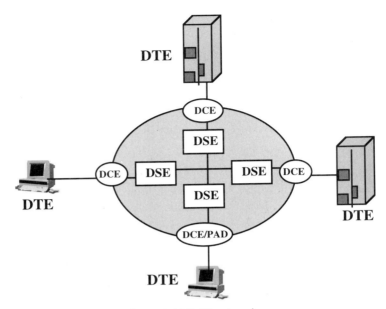

Figure 6.18 X.25 network.

transport layer does in the OSI specifications. Because this interface is a point-to-point connection, *PLP does not perform any routing functions.*

The *data link layer* implements link access procedure balanced (LAPB). Like PLP, LAPB is *connection oriented.* LAPB are a subset of the OSI HDLC data link protocols. Mechanisms ensure data integrity, provide sequenced transmission of packets, and support flow control, error detection, and recovery.

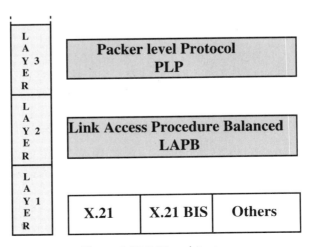

Figure 6.19 X.25 architecture.

The *physical layer* implementations offer a number of optional protocols. In Europe, X.21 is popular. X.21 defines a digital technology. In the United States, X.21 BIS is more popular. X.21 BIS is very similar to the RS-232C standard. CCITT also has defined other options not discussed here.

CCITT recommendation X.25 basically defines the interface between data terminal equipment and data circuit–terminating equipment for terminals operating in the packet mode on public data networks. However, strictly speaking, X.25 is not an interface. In fact, X.25 is a set of three peer protocols as follows (Figure 6.20):

• A peer protocol between physical level entities in the DTE and the DCE.
• A peer protocol between link control level entities in the DTE and the network node.
• A peer protocol between packet-switched network level entities in the DTE and the network node.

Each of these levels functions independently of the other levels, with the exception that failures at a level may affect the operation of the higher levels.

Internally, X.25 network is a complex routing topology. Each message is decomposed into packets at the origin DTE, before it is passed to the network. Packets traverse the network independently from origin to destination. Routing methodologies vary depending on the network. Routing is not defined by X.25. Most networks use dynamic routing. Packets are reassembled into the original message at the destination by the receiving DTE.

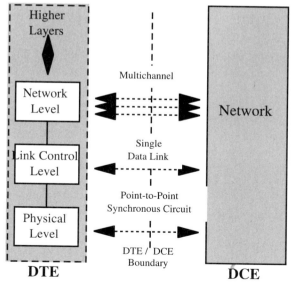

Figure 6.20 Structure of X.25.

X.25 in a LAN Environment. You can implement X.25 without the presence of a network carrier. For example, a proprietary device can simulate a public or private network and instead provide a LAN solution. Such a device must provide only the standard DTE-DCE interface to its user devices. This alternate use of X.25 exists because of the popularity of the DTE-DCE interface. If a computer can connect to a carrier DCE, it can also connect to a LAN-based DCE.

Frame Relay

Frame relay is an emerging technology designed as replacement for dedicated point-to-point links. A frame relay network consists of a set of interconnected switches that are shared by many customers. Each site is connected to the frame relay network using a single dedicated circuit. Thus with frame relay, you can build a virtual network that appears to have many connections but in reality has only one.

Frame relay is designed to eliminate protocol sensitivity and unnecessary overhead to speed up transmission. Error correction and flow control already exist at network and transport layers and therefore, may be relegated to the edges of the network rather than at every node. Although frame relay detects errors, it does not correct them. Incorrect frames are simply discarded. Therefore, when a receiving device detects a missing frame, it can request retransmission from the originating device.

Architecture. Frame relay operates at the first layer and lower half of the second layer of the ISO reference model. On layer 2, frame relay only supports core functions needed to transport frames, specifically,

- Frame delimiting, alignment, and transparency.
- Inspection of the frame to ensure that it consists of an integer number of bytes.
- Frame multiplexing and demultiplexing using the address field.
- Ensuring that the frame is of the right size.
- Detection of transmission errors.

Even though a frame relay network may be configured so that the physical links are always available, getting the data to their proper destination requires that specific paths be taken through the network. Such services require a path to be set up between two or more users. These paths are called *virtual circuits*.

Packet networks support a large number of nodes through the use of virtual circuits referred to as logical channels. Unlike a physical channel, which is a port on a computer, a logical channel is merely a temporary connection that is made between portions of the network. Two primary types of virtual circuits are supported by frame relay protocols: *switched virtual circuits (SVCs)* analogous to dial-up connections and *permanent virtual circuits* analogous to dedicated private lines.

Advantages. Frame relay has emerged as a standard for high-speed packet-switched transmissions. When properly implemented, frame relay can solve the bottleneck problem experienced by users when their LAN traffic hits the wall of currently available wide area transmission options, including conventional X.25 and T1 lines. As a faster method of packet switching, frame relay can transmit information in bursts at T1 rate or T3 rate, and it may become feasible to use frame relay to interconnect LAN backbones that operate up to 100 Mb/sec. under FDDI protocol mechanisms.

Frame relay provides *bandwidth* on demand for supporting the increasing amounts of bursty data that must traverse the corporate backbones. This includes such traffic generators as wide area store-and-forward electronic mail systems and distributed client/server database systems that access only the WAN where there is a need to transmit data or handle requests across the network. Frame relay accommodates such applications by *dynamically* allocating the bandwidth so that burst of data from a LAN could fill the idle time left by other users.

Switched Multimegabit Data Service

SMDS is a high-speed switched data service, providing connectionless transport at speeds of 1.544 Mb/sec (T1 rate) and 44.736 Mb/sec (T3 rate) with potential extensions. SMDS allows an enterprise to

- Interconnect LANs over a wide area, especially through the use of high-speed fiber (FDDI).
- Provide broadband connectivity for enterprise wide networking.
- Provide for growth and flexibility for reconfiguration as needs change.
- Support the performance demands of the high-speed processor technology.
- Reduce costs.

SMDS has several advantages over other alternatives:

- It provides for simplified routing with the ease and versatility of connectionless network versus connection-oriented frame relay network.
- It provides fault tolerance with high survivability and reliability derived from dual-bus ring structure.
- It supports voice traffic for fixed-size packets or slots traveling at extremely high-speed data, voice, and video services.
- It is compatible with emerging broadband networks.

SMDS provides a number of interface options: The *subscriber network interface (SNI)* is used for connection with LANs by means of an encapsulating bridge or a router or directly from the computer. SNI incorporates both a MAC-level LAN connection and its own SMDS Interface Protocol (SIP).

SMDS is designed to take advantage of evolving MAN standards and technology that can be deployed by telephone careers to provide cross-premises communications services. The users should be able to send a packet over dedicated interface at T1 to T3 rate to the nearest switching office for forwarding to the destination. Once at the local exchange, transmissions can be routed between SMDS switches without dedicated leased lines. Higher-speed interfaces operating over optical facilities may provide transmission rates up to 622 Mb/sec.

In addition to higher data throughput and low delay, SMDS provides users with greater flexibility in configuring their LANs. The SMDS reliability can be enhanced by the use of redundant rings, where if the primary ring goes down, a segment of the secondary ring is immediately brought on line.

Point-to-Point Protocol

Low-speed Serial Line IP (SLIP) and PPP links are usually carried over switched telephone circuits that are connected directly to a host or a router via a modem. Switched circuits can support speeds of up to 56 Kb/sec using various signaling and compression techniques. Low-speed IP links are either SLIP or PPP encapsulation method, both of which usually use low-speed (RS-232) serial ports. SLIP or PPP links are very useful for either low bandwidth or intermittent connectivity. They also provide a low-cost entry-level means of connecting to the Internet itself.

Digital Data Service

Digital data service (DDS) was introduced by AT&T in the 1970s for private line communications. It offers a range of speeds from 2.4 Kb/sec to 56 Kb/sec. The appeal of DDS is its higher quality of digital versus analog transmission. Until recently, it was a popular way to interconnect LANs via remote bridges. However, 56 Kb/sec is considered a bottleneck for 10 Mb/sec LANs.

DDS is relatively expensive because of its reliance on "hubs," which increase the distance between endpoints and, consequently, inflate the cost of transmission. DDS is gradually being replaced by services like T1 or fractional T1.

Fiber Distribution Data Interface

FDDI is a high-speed LAN that employs a counterrotating token ring technology. FDDI can be characterized in terms of broadband, capable of voice, video, and data transport through packet switching. It is designed to provide high-bandwidth, general-purpose interconnection between computers and peripherals, including internetworking of LANs and other networks, supporting speeds of up to and beyond 100 Mb /sec.

Operation. FDDI is a token-passing ring network over an optical or copper medium. Like all rings, it consists of a set of stations connected by point-to-point links to form a closed loop. Each station receives signals on its input side and regenerates them for retransmission on the output side. Theoretically, any number of stations can be attached to the network.

FDDI uses two interrogating rings: *primary* ring is used for data traffic and *secondary* ring operates in the opposite direction and is available for fault tolerance. If appropriately configured, stations may transmit simultaneously, thus doubling the bandwidth of the network. FDDI provides an optional bypass switch at each node to overcome a failure anywhere on the node. In the event of a node failure, it is bypassed optically and removed from the network.

With the explosive growth of local area networks in the 1980s, network administrators outgrew traditional LAN protocols. For user-intensive applications, they needed more capacity, communicated over longer distances, and increased data security. Using multimode fiber, FDDI has emerged as a general-purpose LAN backbone for linking traditional LANs. FDDI provides a comprehensive backbone path upon which all LAN protocols—Ethernet, token ring, and so on—can be transported. The typical FDDI application is generally for

- Backbone connectivity between separate LANs in a building or campus.
- A LAN for high-end graphics and CAD/CAM workstations.
- A connection device for host-to-host or backbone-to-backbone applications.

Architecture. The FDDI standards address four functional areas of the FDDI architecture:

- *Physical media dependent (PMD)* protocol specifies the connectors and media characteristics for point-to-point communications between stations on the FDDI network.
- *Physical layer (PHY)* protocol defies data encoding/decoding, clock synchronization, and handshake sequence between the stations.
- *Media access control (MAC)* governs access to the medium, describes the frame format, interprets frame content, generates and repeats frames, issues and captures tokens, controls timers, and interfaces with station management. The FDDI MAC, like the token ring MAC, defines the token and the frame.
- *Station management (SMT)* provides the system management services for the FDDI protocol suite, detailing control requirements for proper operation and interoperability of stations on the FDDI ring. SMT is used to manage connections, configurations, and interfaces. It is also used for fault isolation and recovery, error control, statistics gathering, address administration, and ring partitioning.

FDDI only specifies how a frame is formatted and controlled over the backbone. Since multiple LANs can attach to the backbone, it is necessary to employ devices such as bridges or routers to facilitate internetworking.

Strengths and Weaknesses.

- The FDDI is tailor made and very effective as a high-speed LAN for workstation traffic and as a backbone for transporting LAN traffic.
- FDDI provides a framework for internetworking, that is, communication between different LAN protocols.

- Compared to traditional LAN protocols, FDDI provides greatly increased data capacity and performance by providing 100 Mb/sec transmission speeds.
- It can accommodate large networks upwards of 500 backbone nodes.
- Through its dual-ring architecture, FDDI offers a higher degree of network availability as compared to existing LAN protocols.
- Using a token-passing scheme, network traffic can be dealt with on a deterministic basis.
- FDDI provides a relatively long-distance communication by using fiber optic cables, allowing the rings to have upward of 100 kilometer circumference, with a distance of up to 2 kilometers between stations.
- On the other hand, FDDI can accommodate only LAN traffic and is not capable of transporting real-time signals (voice, host-to-terminal, etc.).
- Being processor intensive, the cost of implementing FDDI can be prohibitive.

Asynchronous Transfer Mode

ATM is a packet-oriented transfer mode. ATM is similar in concept to frame relay. Both take advantage of the digital line's higher reliability and fidelity to provide faster packet switching than X.25. Like frame relay and X.25, it allows multiple logical connections to be multiplexed over a single physical interface. The information flow on each logical connection is organized into fixed-size packets, called cells. ATM does not provide for any link-by-link error or flow control.

ATM is *connection oriented*. The header values are assigned to each section of a connection for complete duration of the connection. Signaling and user information are carried in a separate virtual channel. All services (voice, video, data, etc.) can be transported by ATM, including connectionless service.

ATM technology provides the ability to combine the best features of multiplexing and LAN backbones, creating a universal transfer method that will accommodate all applications. In implementing cell synchronism, ATM can provide the speed, density, flexibility, and reliability. Because of relatively short fixed length cells, low-cost hardware can be quickly implemented for processing ATM data.

ATM has been optimized to accommodate both real-time and nonreal-time data efficiently and cost effectively. ATM is not protocol dependent. Therefore, any kind of packet can be "mapped" into an ATM cell and transported.

INTERNETWORKING EXAMPLES

Designing an efficient internetwork is influenced by several facility-specific issues. This includes

- Types of users.
- Size of the network.
- Geographical distribution of network nodes.

- Enterprise computer hardware.
- Operating systems.
- Existing hardware and software.
- A host of others.

The ability to provide error-free throughput at the required speed to network nodes, cost, reliability, and efficiency are vital to the success of the enterprise. In addition, user demands, mergers and acquisitions, and a host of other priorities require frequent network reconfiguration. Since all these factors vary from enterprise to enterprise, there is no single ideal solution. However, we will discuss a few such solutions to include some of the technologies we have encountered in the preceding sections.

A DECnet Internet

Figure 6.21 displays internetworking of many different network architectures as well as operating environments. It also depicts the use of bridges and routers to interconnect LANs with LANs, LANs with WANs using OSI, TCP/IP, DECnet, and other architectures.

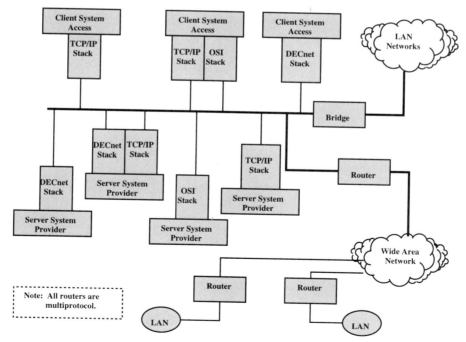

Figure 6.21 A DECnet Internet.

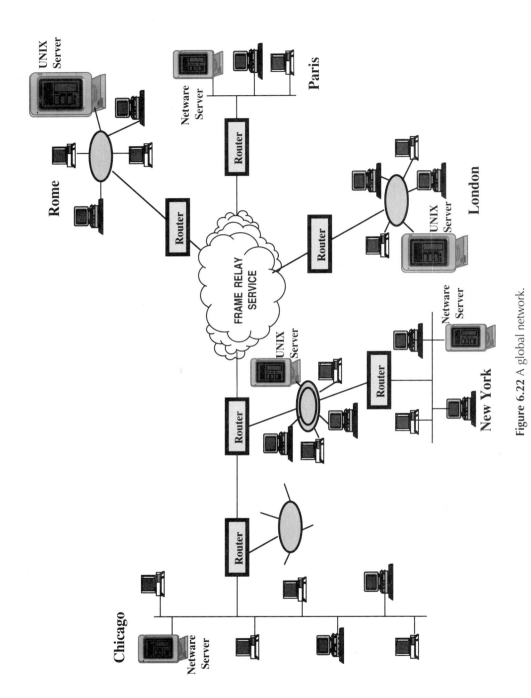

Figure 6.22 A global network.

A Global Network

Figure 6.22 shows a global network utilizing frame relay service with multiprotocol routers interconnecting LANs running UNIX and NetWare operating systems.

SNA Universe with NetWare Server

Figure 6.23 shows that NetWare and SNA resources on token ring and Ethernet are fully integrated. PCs, PS/2s, Macs, and UNIX workstations can take full advantage of NetWare interoperability. The NetWare server is directly connected to the VM host by a PS/2 System /370 channel adapter (PCA) for optimal performance. VM resources can be used by the NetWare workstations for file serving, software and data distribution, and LAN administration. 3270 traffic is routed from Ethernet to token ring so that Ethernet stations can talk directly to the 37xx front-end processor via data link control (DLC) interface. NetWare routes the other protocols and frame types.

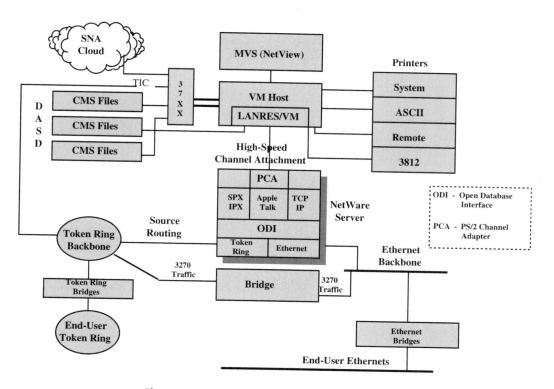

Figure 6.23 SNA universe with NetWare server.

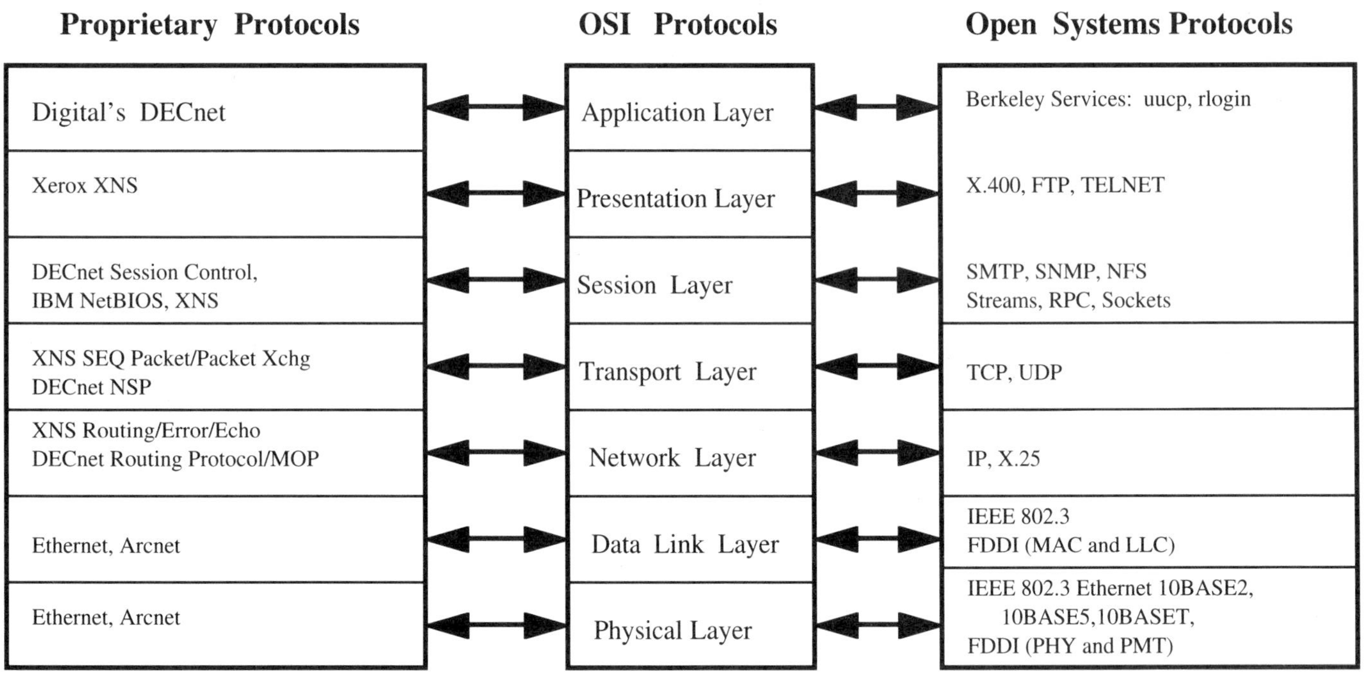

Proprietary Protocols	OSI Protocols	Open Systems Protocols
Digital's DECnet	Application Layer	Berkeley Services: uucp, rlogin
Xerox XNS	Presentation Layer	X.400, FTP, TELNET
DECnet Session Control, IBM NetBIOS, XNS	Session Layer	SMTP, SNMP, NFS Streams, RPC, Sockets
XNS SEQ Packet/Packet Xchg DECnet NSP	Transport Layer	TCP; UDP
XNS Routing/Error/Echo DECnet Routing Protocol/MOP	Network Layer	IP, X.25
Ethernet, Arcnet	Data Link Layer	IEEE 802.3 FDDI (MAC and LLC)
Ethernet, Arcnet	Physical Layer	IEEE 802.3 Ethernet 10BASE2, 10BASE5,10BASET, FDDI (PHY and PMT)

Figure 6.24 OSI model and competing architectures.

SUMMARY

This chapter has described a number of protocols. Even though most of them are used in different environments (LANs, WANs, or telecommunications), the major ones that are prevalent in internetworking are

- SNA.
- X.25.
- IPX/SPX.
- NetBIOS.
- DECnet.

In this chapter the emphasis has been on SNA and X.25 protocols, especially for building wide area networks. Figure 6.24 shows a summary of similarities and differences in some of these architectural implementations.

In the next few chapters, we will explore how different operating systems, protocols, and technologies can be bridged together to provide internetworking solutions.

EXERCISES

1. Explain different NetBIOS services and its relationship to ISO model.
2. Before the 1980s, which of the following might have been an enterprise's primary computing resource?
   a. Dumb terminal.
   b. PC.
   c. Mainframe.
   d. Cluster controller.
   e. Front-end processor.
3. The trend toward decentralization has meant what?
   a. Use of many different devices.
   b. Few users access the host.
   c. Computing power exists at widespread locations.
4. Which of the following illustrate the concept of distributed processing?
   a. User A computes marketing statistics; user B incorporates these in a report.
   b. A mainframe at San Francisco downloads specifications to a workstation in Los Angeles, where they are matched to other data.
   c. A programmer in Chicago enters raw data to a mainframe.
5. Which of the following are benefits of a PC?
   a. Independent computing.

    b. Terminal emulation.

    c. Downloading host files.

6. Which of the following are typical transmission options available in networking?

    a. 56 Kb/sec line.

    b. T1 line.

    c. Fractional T1 line.

    d. LAN.

7. Which of the following is true of X.25 packet switching?

    a. A message will take the most direct route.

    b. It is the cheapest option.

    c. Parts of the message can take different routes and be received correctly.

8. Interoperability means?

    a. Connecting devices together.

    b. Use of any LAN component.

    c. Communication between devices.

9. In the layering scheme what are the most common layers among TCP/IP, OSI, SNA, X.25?

10. What are the three different categories of WAN internetworking systems?

7

INTERNETWORKING TOOLS

Introduction
Network Interconnection
   Internetworking Tools
Repeaters
   Functions
   Benefits
   Limitations
Bridges
   Functions
   Benefits
   Limitations
Network Configurations with Bridges
Routers and Layer 3 Devices
   Functions
   Operations
   Advantages
   Disadvantages
   Brouters with Examples

Multiprotocol Routers
Network Configuration Examples
   with Routers
Gateways
   Functions
   Advantages
   Disadvantages
Network Configuration Examples
   with Gateways
Backbones
Seven-Layer Protocol Conversion
   Protocol Layers
   LAN-LAN Internetworking
   Mainframe and Multiprotocol Network
   Summary
Summary
Exercises

INTRODUCTION

As organizations become more complex, the ability to share files and communicate information, across dissimilar operating systems and networks, becomes necessary to improve efficiency and productivity. The need to connect dissimilar LANs may also result from mergers or acquisitions.

Corporate computing has rapidly evolved into a confusing conglomeration of diverse and often transient system platforms. For the most part, each platform remains dominated by its own native communication protocols. From the network perspective, the multiprotocol environment sometimes seems to be spiraling toward a state of near chaos.

Networks have seen an influx of competing protocols, cooperative protocols, native protocols, and encapsulated protocols. Given the same upper-level interface, protocol stacks may be compatible or incompatible because of similar or dissimilar underlying layers. The proliferation of communication protocols could stifle enterprise interoperability across the corporate networks if it continues out of control.

Interconnectivity is not easily achieved. For computer nodes to communicate over the network, several conditions regarding physical connectivity, transport protocols, and protocol stack must be satisfied. Standardization of network architectures has so far failed to take hold in corporate systems. Divergence remains the rule rather than the exception. The ISO OSI Reference Model has made tremendous inroads by serving as a guideline for the evolution of real-world product architectures. Vendors have implemented many aspects of the OSI model as their products evolved over time. Nevertheless, the product offerings of leading LAN vendors remain primarily proprietary or tied to a particular platform, especially when applied to communication protocols.

In the absence of such standards, the commercial world has devised tools that provide some sort of internetworking among these disparate systems and protocols. In the nonstandard environment, the multiprotocol workstation is flexible and is uniquely positioned for satisfying diverse interoperability requirements. Protocol gateways, routers, bridges, and multiple protocol stacks running on back-end application servers present appealing options.

In this chapter, we will discuss the protocol layers that have achieved interconnectivity. We will also explore various internetworking tools and how they provide interconnectivity between diverse operating systems, transmission media, and communication protocols. Gateways, routers, bridges, and repeaters are some of the tools that facilitate system interconnection and application interoperability. In particular, bridges, routers, and gateways relieve host computers of the processing-intensive tasks of protocol conversion and routing information to appropriate locations. Because these devices can be shared among many users, they contribute substantially to lowering the cost of networking.

NETWORK INTERCONNECTION

Each interconnection device is designed to operate in conjunction with a different layer of the OSI Reference Model (Table 7.1), which provides specific levels of network functions. When properly integrated, bridges, routers, and gateways offer the following advantages:

- Simplified cabling topologies.
- Extended network coverage.
- Improved performance.
- Configuration flexibility.
- Simpler network management.
- Reduced cost of operations.

TABLE 7.1 Tool Capabilities and the OSI Layers

INTERNETWORK TOOL	DESCRIPTION	FUNCTION	LAYER
Gateway	Selects services for application.	Application	7
Gateway	Provides code conversion and data reformatting.	Presentation	6
Gateway	Interaction between processes.	Session	5
Gateway	Provides end-to-end data integrity and reliability.	Transport	4
Router	Routes information.	Network	3
Bridge	Transfers information.	Data link	2
Repeater	Transmits information.	Physical	1

Internetworking Tools

The most basic internetworking device used (with LANs) is a repeater. A repeater regenerates a signal, allowing the electrical signal to traverse a longer distance without becoming distorted. For this reason, a repeater is most often used to interconnect networks that are close together, typically in the same building. The repeater operates at the physical layer of the ISO model and can be used only to link with the same protocols.

Bridges operate at the data link layer of the ISO model and are independent of upper-layer network architectures; that is, bridges only see data link addresses (Figure 7.1). Bridges can only connect networks (especially LANs) that have the same type of operat-

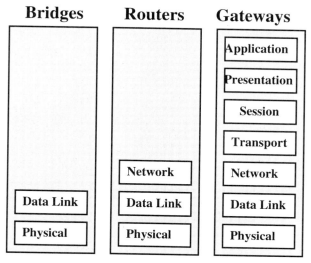

Figure 7.1 Internetworking and ISO model.

ing system. Therefore, the bridge does not have to perform protocol conversions. The bridge only looks at the packet destination address and forwards that data packet destined for an address to another network, beyond the local network. For example, a bridge can interconnect DECnet, TCP/IP, or Xerox Network Services (XNS) networks, but cannot ensure that users on one network can communicate with users on another. Bridges allow LAN-to-LAN connectivity via WAN.

Routers have more intelligence than bridges because they can handle several levels of addressing. They operate at the network layer (Figure 7.1). Routers are dependent on network protocols, such as IP, IPX, SNA, and so on. The routers keep a map of the entire network, including all the devices operating above or below its own protocol level. To forward a data packet, the router refers to its internetwork map, examines the status of the different paths to the destination, and selects the best route to get the packet to its destination. Routers are protocol dependent therefore, they can only be used to link "identical" protocols. The routers are the true "internetworking tool." Routers usually provide value-added functions, such as adaptive routing, traffic filtering, network management, and security.

Gateways operate on the full seven-layer stack of the ISO model (Figure 7.1). Gateways interconnect networks or media with different architectures by processing protocols to allow a device on one type of network to communicate with a device on another type. Gateways act both as conduit over which the computers communicate and as translator among the various protocol layers (including application level protocol conversions). Implementations usually contain compromises in the network architecture functions.

Not all devices fit neatly into these basic categories. Numerous hybrid tools have been developed that include functions traditionally associated with one or another of these categories; that is, a gateway may include some attributes commonly associated with a bridge or a router. At the same time, another device may operate as a gateway and as a bridge under other circumstances.

REPEATERS

Repeaters are hardware devices that operate at the physical layer of the ISO model, repeating all electrical signals from one segment to the other (Figure 7.2). Repeaters extend the geographic coverage of a local area network by interconnecting multiple segments. Repeaters also interconnect segments using different physical media such as thick coaxial, thin coaxial, twisted-pair, or fiber optic cables.

Splitting a segment into two or more segments with a repeater allows a network to continue to grow. A repeater connection counts in the total node limit on each segment. For example, a thin coax segment may have 29 processors and 1 repeater, or a thick wire segment can have 5 repeaters and 95 processors.

Remember that at the physical layer, there is very little intelligence in any of these units. Repeater units do not know about other repeater units on the network.

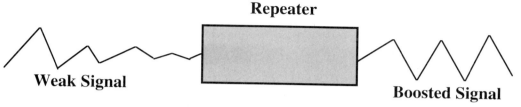

Figure 7.2 Repeater operation.

Functions

Ethernet repeaters are necessary in star topologies. The repeater counts as one node on each segment it connects. A network with only two nodes is of limited use. If the repeater is attached to a backbone, then all computers at the end of the twisted-pair segments can communicate with all the hosts on the backbone.

Repeaters monitor all connected segments for basic characteristics necessary for Ethernet to run correctly. When a break occurs, all segments in an Ethernet may become inoperable. Repeaters limit the effect of these problems to the faulty section of cable by "segmenting" the network, disconnecting the problem segment, and allowing unaffected segments to function normally.

Token ring networks involve three kinds of repeaters: token ring, lobe, and connecting repeater.

- *Token ring repeaters* are used when the network has more than one wiring center. This repeater can be used to regenerate both the main ring path and the backup ring path. When the backup path is boosted, it is assumed that the main path is boosted as well.
- *Lobe repeaters* boost the signal only for one lobe attached to a multistation access or media attachment unit (MAU).
- *Connecting repeaters* boost the signals between hubs, usually doubling the distance between hubs.

There are three basic types of repeater units, and all three may be intermixed through the use of backbone, as shown in Figure 7.3. These are

- Multiport repeater units, used with 10BASE2 wiring only.
- Multiport receiver units, used with 10BASE5 wiring only.
- Wiring concentrator, used with all types of wiring schemes.

Multiport repeater or *transceiver units* may only be used on thin or thick coaxial cables, respectively. These may also be intermixed on a backbone. For example, if you have thick coaxial cable as the backbone, each type of repeater may be connected to it. Transceivers normally connect a single device to the Ethernet. Workstations, terminal

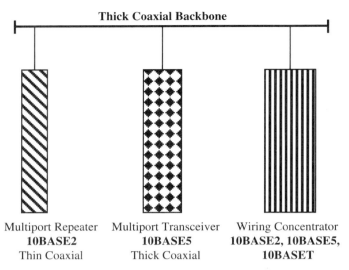

Figure 7.3 Mixing different repeater types.

servers, repeaters, and bridges use them on their ports to connect to various Ethernet media. However, in some instances, it is desired that several devices be connected to the network in a location where only one transceiver tap is possible. Repeaters or concentrators can do this job, but they may not be cost effective if only a few stations need to be installed. In some cases, extra ports on a transceiver can help rather than new network segments.

Wiring concentrators are special repeater units and are most common in use. These are also called wiring hubs. Not only do they extend the cable plant, connect multiple wiring types together, and contain certain errors to their respective cable plants, these wiring concentrators contain the intelligence for network management functions. These management network functions enable a network administrator to query the wiring concentrator to gather statistics from each of the wiring concentrator repeater modules, enable or disable individual wiring ports, and perform many other functions.

Wiring concentrators contain intelligence to know when an error is occurring on the physical part of the network. Therefore, these will not repeat these errors to any other cable plants that they are connected to.

In Ethernet networks, there is an inherent error that will occasionally occur, known as "collision." This error occurs when two stations try to transmit on the same cable plant at the same time. This collision will cause the original packet to become fragmented. The wiring concentrator will detect the collision fragment and will not transmit the fragments to any other cable plants attached to this repeater.

Another feature of the wiring concentrator is fault isolation. If a module in the repeater unit counts too many collisions, an open circuit, or even a short circuit, the repeater module will remove itself from the network. This will not affect any other modules of the repeater unit.

Although the 10BASE2 and 10BASE5 concentrators are still used today, many wiring concentrators have evolved. Some such repeaters are equipped with several features that work to identify and isolate network faults. In an Ethernet network, when a repeater detects network collision, it automatically ceases to repeat signals from a segment that is exhibiting abnormal numbers of collisions.

Benefits

Repeaters extend the cabling distances by strengthening the received signal, as shown in Figure 7.2. Repeaters can also be used to link LANs with the same protocols, at the physical layer.

Limitations

Repeaters, in general, cannot control or route information, and do not have management capabilities. In addition, repeaters are limited to connecting two or three LAN segments. Beyond that, the delay becomes too long, which may cause time-outs in upper layers.

Repeaters attached to thin coax restrict the network size and the length of the medium: 185 meters in length for a segment and a limit of 30 nodes or connections per segment.

Multiport repeaters have very little intelligence and do not provide any type of traffic isolation. However, the wiring concentrators do provide some degree of intelligence for error detection and fault isolation network management functions. Unlike bridges, repeaters do not act like an Ethernet station on the network.

The IEEE 802.3 standards have placed limitations on the repeater configurations. The maximum number of repeaters that can be found in the transmission path between two nodes is four. The maximum number of network segments between two nodes is five. These rules are determined by calculations of maximum cable lengths and repeater delays. Networks that violate these rules may still be functional, but they may experience sporadic failures or frequent problems. Using repeaters simply extends the network to a larger size, and the available bandwidth on the network could become a problem. In this case, switches, bridges, and routers can be used to partition one large network into several smaller segments which operate more efficiently. Placing multiport repeaters and file servers on the backbone may prevent clients from transmitting through the maximum number of repeaters.

BRIDGES

Functions

Unlike a repeater, a bridge connects disparate networks. The bridge functions at the data link layer of the ISO model. Its main purpose is to partition traffic on each interconnected segment. Although all segments interconnected by a bridge form a single logical network, they are electrically isolated from one another. The bridge does more than just generate a signal between disparate networks. It is much more intelligent than a repeater: it can examine a packet header and decide on which of the two networks that packet belongs.

Basic principles for a bridge are learning, filtering, and forwarding. Any combination of these three operations may be turned on or off.

For the *learning algorithm* to function, the bridge listens to all traffic on its attached segments. It then checks the source addresses of all packets received and the destination address. The bridge first checks its routing table to see if the source address is registered. If it is not registered, the bridge adds the address to that table. If the bridge does find the address, it updates the date function. If a predetermined time allotment has transpired, the bridge does have the capability to remove the address from the routing table, thus saving time for address look-up and conserving RAM (Figure 7.4).

The *filter* and *forward algorithm* bridges also check the destination address of every packet received to determine whether it should be forwarded or filtered from the next segment. The bridge first checks its local table to ascertain if the destination address is on the port that the packet was received from. If the address is not there, it checks the address table for the port of the next segment. If the address is found, the bridge forwards the packet on that particular port. If the destination address is not found on the other port again, the bridge assumes that the address is remote and forwards the packet. *Essentially, a bridge's tables are built on the source address only.* The destination address is looked at only to see if the packet should be forwarded.

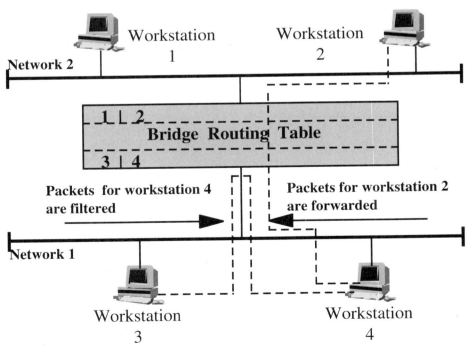

Figure 7.4 Ethernet bridge with routing table.

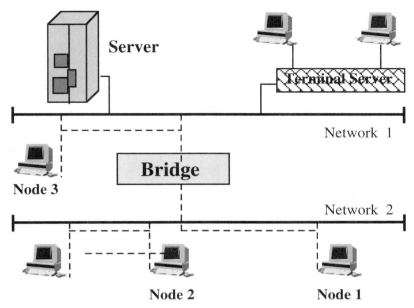

Figure 7.5 Ethernet bridge with filtering and forwarding.

Figure 7.5 helps to illustrate the filtering and forwarding processes. The first time workstation 1 sends a packet on the network, for example, to workstation 2, the bridge forwards the packet to network 1, since it does not yet know where workstation 2 resides. When workstation 2 responds, the bridge then learns that it is on network 2. The next time workstation 1 sends a packet to station 2, the bridge will filter it so that it is not forwarded to the network 1. The next time workstation 1 sends a packet to workstation 2, the bridge will filter it so that it is not forwarded to network 1. Similarly, a transaction between workstations 1 and 3 alerts the bridge to workstation 3's location.

The maximum number of bridges that a packet is allowed to traverse is linear 8 (number of bridges between source and destination). The primary reason for this limit is the delay each bridge introduces to the network time. If the total delay is long enough, the upper-layer protocols of the originating workstation may time out and retransmit the packet again. If the packet was delayed and not lost as a result of a collision, the destination workstation could receive a duplicate packet, causing undetermined problems in the network. If the network were designed optimally, there is no need for a packet to span eight bridges without being separated by a router. The learning and forwarding processes assume that the topology of the network is a tree or there is only one path between two workstations. If parallel paths exist, such problems may occur. To deal with the duplication problem due to parallel paths, some bridges implement intelligent algorithms to detect loops and shut down alternate paths.

The three basic processes for a learning, filtering, and forwarding bridge may be used in any combination. To disable the bridge to learn any new addresses, the learning process may be turned off and individual addresses transmitted manually. The bridge will still forward and filter. On the other hand, for security reasons, the forwarding function may be turned off, preventing any packets from being forwarded.

There are two basic types of bridges—local and remote. Filtering and forwarding are relatively simple when connecting two local networks. However, they become increasingly complex when local or remote bridges interconnect multiple networks.

Local bridges may connect two similar networks such as Ethernet to Ethernet or dissimilar networks such as Ethernet to broadband or Ethernet to token ring. Such bridges take packets from the second network and place them on the first. Every time the packets are swapped, the bridge also generates a signal. Therefore, in addition to connecting two disparate networks, local bridges also act as repeaters. Basically, a bridge receives all the packets of the networks to which it is connected, looking at the source and destination addresses of each packet.

When a bridge is attached to an Ethernet network *(Ethernet bridge)*, it begins by sending broadcasts to the nodes on the local network to respond. It captures the local addresses for those who respond. As packets pass through, the bridge stores addresses of nodes communicating through the bridge, determining which addresses are on LAN A versus LAN B (Figure 7.6). When a bridge receives a packet, it looks at the source address.

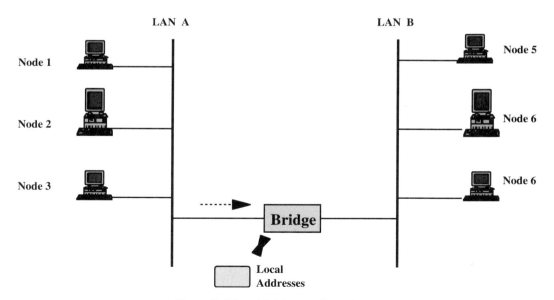

Figure 7.6 Local bridge configuration.

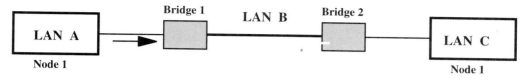

Figure 7.7 Multiple bridge configuration.

If the packet's address is local, the bridge ignores it. If the packet does not have a local address, it is copied into the other connected LAN.

When multiple bridges are used, address information must be supplied for all the available nodes. Therefore, if node 1 on LAN A (Figure 7.7) wants to communicate with node 1 on LAN C, bridge 1 must know to forward the packet to bridge 2. The bridge between LAN B and LAN C then forwards the message to its node 1.

When using multiple bridges, only one path can connect any two networks. If more than one path exists, duplicate messages could be created or messages could arrive out of sequence. Ethernet networks are an exception when a spanning tree bridge is used. On an Ethernet network, a spanning tree bridge takes a parallel path known as backup bridge. If the primary bridge fails, the backup bridge takes over.

Token ring bridges take a different approach for forwarding packets and allowing redundant paths. A station that wishes to communicate with another station, first sends an all-stations discovery packet, hoping to find the destination node on the local ring. If there is no response, the originating node transmits either "all-routes" packet or "single-route" packet. If it is all-routes packet, the token ring bridge will copy it and forward it to the next ring. As the packet crosses the bridges, it collects routing information from each bridge it traverses. Once the destination node receives this packet, it responds via an all-routes broadcast.

In token ring networks, source routing is used by bridges. With source routing, the packet itself contains routing information specifying the networks and bridges through which it will travel. The originating node is responsible for entering that information into the packet for ensuring its delivery to the destination. It also determines the routing paths available. However, source routing adds extra overhead to the network. Source routing uses two distinct techniques:

* In *all-routes broadcast route* determinations, the originating station sends the same dynamic route discovery packet out to all rings. This packet traverses through all the rings via the bridges, collecting routing information while crossing the bridges. When the packet is forwarded through the bridges, each bridge inserts routing information into the packet.

  If more than one route to the destination still exists, then more than one packet reaches the destination. When the destination node receives each packet, it responds by returning all the acquired routing information to the originating station. This response packet follows the original path in reverse. If multiple bridges forwarded the packet, all responses are returned to the originating station. It is up to the originating station to choose the path to the destination station. The originating station chooses a preferred route by the first nonbroadcast packet it receives. The originating station then uses this route for all subsequent communicating packets.

- An alternative to the all-routes broadcast for route determination is *the single-route broadcast*. In this case, a node issues a dynamic route discovery frame to the ring so that only one frame appears on each ring. On receiving the frame, the ring issues a response via all-routes broadcast. The originating station receives multiple copies of the response packet and chooses the preferred route.

  Single-route broadcast for route determination ensures that only one copy of a limited broadcast traverses each network segment. Bridges in the spanning tree are configured for forwarding single-route broadcast frames. This is the preferred method for route determination.

  If a ring network is configured for all-routes broadcast only, these packets would be duplicated for as many bridges as are on the network. This means that all nodes that receive these special packets would be interrupted many times, possibly slowing down the network. In a single-route broadcast network, these nodes would only receive one copy of the frame and be interrupted only that one time.

  Remote bridges connect LANs that are located remotely. Usually there is some sort of telecommunications link between the two bridges. This link may be via satellite or telephone lines, that is, X.25 network, as portrayed in Figure 7.8. A bridge at one end of the bridge sends packets meant for a LAN on the link. A bridge at the other end of the link receives these packets and forwards these to its LAN or vice versa. The only difference between remote bridges and local bridges is that the remote bridges require a telecommunication link between them.

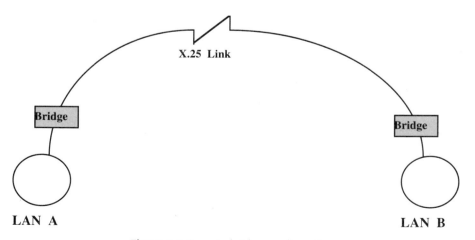

Figure 7.8 Remote bridge configuration.

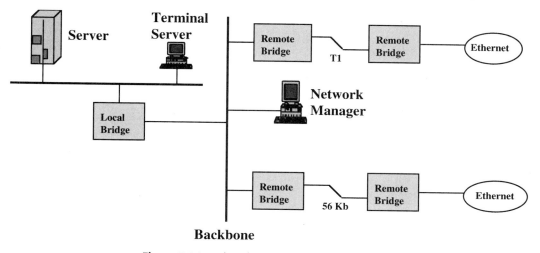

Figure 7.9 Local and remote bridge configuration.

For remote bridges, parallel lines from the same local bridge to a remote bridge do not constitute a loop, so bridges can balance the traffic among multiple lines (Figure 7.9). This allows certain degree of redundancy in the design of the network. When remote bridges participate in spanning tree protocol, all remote links connected to the same remote bridge are considered as one interface.

In cases where performance has degraded due to traffic bottlenecks, bridges can divide the network into segments. Bridges can then control the monitor intersegment traffic, restoring the efficiency of each segment. A high-speed backbone is a reasonable alternative in cases where many segments need to be linked. This also improves performance since intersegment traffic passes over only one intervening segment between source and destination segments. A backbone configuration (Figure 7.10) is extremely efficient in an office tower with many floors. In this example, an Ethernet backbone, a thick coaxial or fiber optic cable, runs the full height of the building and bridges partition the traffic among the floors, maximizing the traffic in each segment.

The *star topology* is the most common when using remote bridges. It allows remote LANs to be interconnected with a minimum number of segments.

For Ethernet (and IEEE 802.3) networks, all bridges follow the spanning tree algorithm. This algorithm is used to close loops in the network caused by the addition of two or more bridges connecting the same two physical networks. As we have learned, the loops in a network can create many problems. Any node may receive the same packet twice or the packets may loop through the network endlessly. Remembering that only one physical node may transmit at a time on Ethernet and bridges must follow this algorithm, two packets would arrive at different times at the node, but duplicated. This duplication requires additional processing time by the receiving node, causing performance hits. The spanning tree algorithm contains a special packet that other bridges use to maintain a configuration, and this is the only packet that a bridge will transmit for management functions.

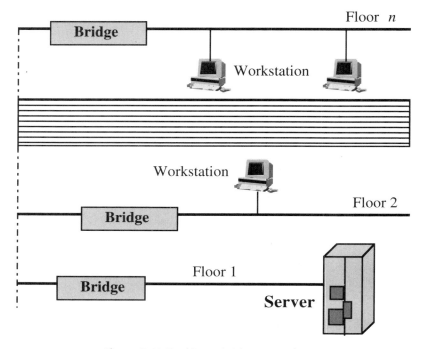

Figure 7.10 Backbone bridge network.

Performance is an important area requiring careful study. A bridge receives all the packets transmitted on each attached network. This means that the bridge must be able to receive and check packets at a rate corresponding to the maximum anticipated usage for each network segment. If the bridge cannot accommodate this traffic load, it has the ability to drop packets, causing the originating station to retransmit them. This results in performance degradation and possibly session disconnects. The modern bridges, normally, partition the load on the different segments so that the amount of intersegment traffic is relatively limited. For performance considerations, the users and their file servers should be on the same network segment. Graphics workstations should be on their own segment separated from the hosts on their own segments.

Benefits

Bridges have much more intelligence than repeaters. They can perform a filtering operation by examining a packet header and decide which of the two networks that packet belongs to. Bridges are fast and usually create less overhead on the network and are less complicated devices. Bridges make simple decisions as to forward or filter according to the destination address.

Bridges are invisible to other stations on the network; that is, bridges only talk to other bridges. Network stations do not need special software to operate with a bridge.

Bridges increase the available throughput of a LAN by physically segmenting network stations to their respective LANs.

Bridges are also protocol independent. Therefore, a bridge does not care what protocol is used on either LAN. The bridge receives the packets and either ignores them or transmits them regardless of the type of protocol, since the bridge is not concerned with translating the packet. Consequently, it treats TCP/IP, SPX/IPX, and other communication protocols equally. But the LANs must use the same communication protocol on either side.

Source routing bridges can also be faster than transparent routing bridges because they only have to read the destination information rather than the entire packet.

Limitations

Bridges do not keep any management data or perform sophisticated network management function, leaving it to the LAN and or the application. Bridges have no facility to fragment or reassemble packets like other devices.

Most vendors' links between the bridges, over a telephone line link, are proprietary. This, inherently, creates compatibility problems if the bridges from different vendors are intermixed, since they all implement protocols differently. There are some emerging standards that may alleviate vendor interoperability problems.

NETWORK CONFIGURATIONS WITH BRIDGES

Example 1: Bridging Token Ring–to–Token Ring LANs.

In this example, two token ring LANs are connected via a bridge (Figure 7.11). The question we need to answer is why use a bridge? Why not combine the two LANs into one since these both employ token ring protocols?

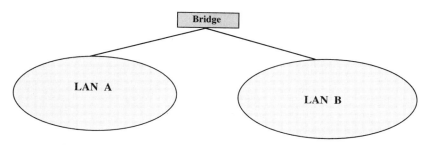

Figure 7.11 Bridging two token ring LANs.

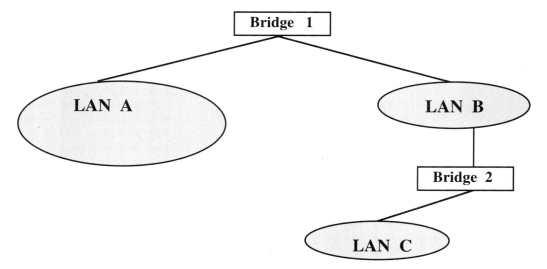

Figure 7.12 Three Ethernet LANs with two bridges.

The bridge joins the two LANs. The users on LANs A and B have developed the need to share each other's data, but they prefer to stay decentralized for many reasons, among them being independence, performance, and management control. By storing the addresses of the local and remote nodes in its address table, the bridge can forward the request from users on LAN A to the users on LAN B.

The user sends a request, the request is passed on to the bridge since it is a remote node, the request is processed, and the information is transmitted back to the requesting node via the bridge. Using the bridge, the network traffic stays the same on both LANs, yet there is communication between the two. This allows not only data sharing, for example, e-mail between the two LAN groups, but it makes maintenance and network management easier.

Example 2: Bridging Three Ethernet LANs

In this example, the requirements as well as the concerns are the same, but it requires two bridges instead of one to connect the three LANs (Figure 7.12). One bridge is installed between LANs A and B, and another bridge is installed between LANs B and C.

The advantages of this arrangement are that each LAN can maintain its own domain and still communicate the other two LANs.

However, since LAN B is sandwiched between LANs A and C, it will experience higher traffic than the others. Therefore, LAN B will experience response and performance problems. In addition, if the connection fails on LAN B, neither LAN B nor LAN C could communicate with LAN A until the connection is reestablished.

ROUTERS AND LAYER 3 DEVICES

The third component of network internetworking is the router. Routers are devices that interconnect multiple networks, primarily running the same high-level protocols. They operate at the network layer of the ISO model, one layer higher than the bridge. Each network protocol has a routing protocol built into it. Through this, the router accesses the addressing information and shares it with other routers and hosts on the network. Routers have more software intelligence than bridges, provide more sophisticated functions, and are well suited for complex environments or large internetworks.

Unlike bridges, routers support active redundant paths (loops) and allow logical separation of network segments. Routers are also better suited for interconnected network segments using different protocols such as token ring and Ethernet. Because routers are protocol specific, more than one router may be needed to support an enterprise. Some multiprotocol routers can route several protocols simultaneously, thereby approaching the function level of gateways.

The routers are used to route messages through intermediate nodes, not nodes on the same LAN. A router is actually an intermediate station or node. Figure 7.13 demonstrates a router connected to two LANs. Node X on LAN 1 wants to send a packet to node Z on LAN 2. It first sends the message to node Y, the router. The router processes the information embedded in the packet's network layer. Based on that information, node Y forwards the packet to LAN 2 addressed to node Z. This way, the router reads the destination information embedded in the packet and forwards the data to the correct node.

Examining Figure 7.14, we can ascertain that with multiple routers, all possible paths between nodes 1 and 6 have been mapped out, but the router sends the packet along the designated route. Since messages are sent to a specific router node, the existence of multiple paths will not cause the message to be duplicated.

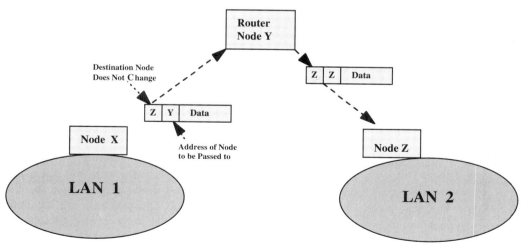

Figure 7.13 A router configuration.

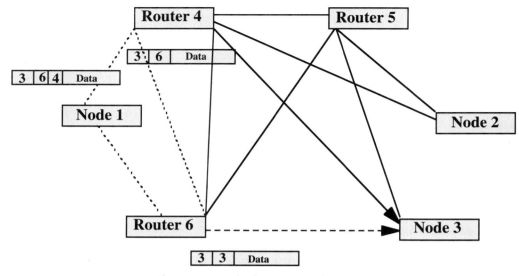

Figure 7.14 Multiple router configuration.

Functions

The primary function of a router is to determine the next node to which a packet is sent. To send packets to their destination, a router must perform several functions. When a packet arrives at the router, it holds the packet in the queue until it is finished handling the previous packet. The router then scans the destination address and searches in the routing table. The routing table lists the various nodes on the network, the paths between these nodes, and how much it costs to transmit over these paths. If a particular node has more than one path, the router selects the one that is most economical. If the packet is too large for the destination node, the router breaks it into a manageable frame size. This is important in WANs, in which telephone lines provide the link between LANs. With smaller packets, there is less chance that the data will be corrupted by noise on the line. There are two types of routing mechanisms:

- *Static routing*, where the network manager must configure the routing table. Once these tables are set, the paths on the network never change. This may be acceptable for a small LAN, but it is not practical for wide area networking. A static router may issue an alarm if and when it recognizes a downed link, but it does not automatically reconfigure the routing table or reroute the packet. As new bridges and/or routers are added to the network, the routing tables in the participating network routers or bridges must be manually updated. It is time consuming and frustrating for the administrator to manually update all the routing tables, if a router breaks and is removed from the network. Once the router becomes operational, in some implementations, the routing tables must be updated again to allow other routers to know that this router is once again operational.

- *Dynamic routing*, automatically reconfigures the routing table and recalculates the least expensive path or with the least traffic. Routers periodically send routing tables to one another to identify the routes available to one another. Whenever a new router is added to the network, all other routers will automatically find this router and update their tables as to the new router's available paths. At the same time, if the routers find a new and better path, the routers will start traversing the new route. Dynamic routing is by far the most advantageous as the administration becomes transparent.

Operations

Networks that allow the use of routers must employ a network number. This, in combination with the physical address of the station on the network, can identify any station on a wide area network. The same is true for a telephone number where the combination of the area code and phone number can address any individual phone in any country. Network stations are grouped into one network ID and a separate (unique) network ID is used for stations on the other side of the router. A special software may be required for a station on a LAN, if the network station employs a router to transmit its data. It is usually embedded in the network operating system (NOS) on that particular station.

When the network layer software receives a packet from its upper layer bound for a station across a router, the NOS looks at the network address of the destination packet and compares it to the local network address. It is just like comparing the telephone area code of the destination with that of the originating station. If the network number is different, the packet is marked as bound for a remote network.

The NOS that resides in a station on a network holds a table of routers that it knows about. The entries in the table contain the physical address of the router, the associated network IDs this router is associated with, and a number called "hop count." The hop count is the number that indicates the originating station as to how many routers the packet must traverse before reaching its final destination. If the router is in the table, the NOS builds a packet and sends it directly to the router that can process this packet via the shortest number of hops.

If the router is not in that table, the NOS transmits a special packet the LAN requesting routing information from the routers on that network. All routers on that network pick up this packet and transmit its routing information back to the original requester, including the hop count information. The requesting station, in turn, uses this information to address its packet to be handled by a router or series of routers to enable the packet to reach its final destination.

Once formatted, the requesting station submits the packet to the router with the destination address. If the network number is directly on the other side of this router, it will forward the packet directly to its destination. If not, it simply transmits the packet to the next router.

If any packet is destined to traverse across a router, the originating station submits the packet with the destination address as router's physical address. It is up to the router to push it across the router toward its final destination. When the packet does reach its final destination, the address is that of the final destination, and the source address is that of the

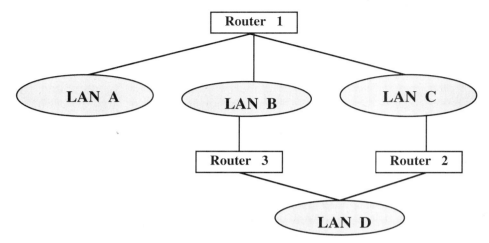

Figure 7.15 Ethernet LANs with redundant LANs.

router. Upon receipt, the destination station submits a packet back to the router and the router or routers will traverse the packet back to the originating station.

For example, in an Ethernet frame (Figure 7.15), the routing information is appended to the data field of the Ethernet frame, and the routers read this information and determine the packet route. In this fashion, requesting stations send their packets to the routers and the routers route the packet to the destination. Essentially, the source and destination stations talk to each other via routers.

Advantages

Routers are *self-configuring* since they know all other routers and optimal routes within the internetworked segment. Routers exchange routing tables with other routers and broadcast information packets to stations on their local segment. Routers automatically allow for redundant (loops) without the use of source routing. In this sense, routers offer some intelligence by responding to an originating station when the destination is unreachable or if there is a better route. Routers allow for load balancing by selecting another path if one channel gets congested.

Routers allow for different size packets on the network. For Ethernet, the largest size is 1518, and there is no maximum length requirement for token ring. However, routers have the capability to fragment the packet into multiple packets and reassemble them at the remote end. If one segment on the network allows for only 1518 bytes and the other segment 512, the routers will automatically fragment the packet and reassemble at the other end. Routers also segment the network into logical subnets (especially for decentralized management environment) by assigning an ID number to each segment. This allows for better network management. Broadcast packets are special packets that all stations will automatically pass to their upper-layer controls, which may also cause "broadcast storms." Routers do not forward broadcast packages, thus eliminating such storms.

Routers do not impose topology constraints and provide sophisticated routing or flow control as well as traffic isolation. But the routers do require full participation of sending and receiving stations. Using a hierarchical addressing scheme, the network managers can divide a large internetwork into smaller and manageable administrative domains.

Because routers selectively forward packets, loops are allowed in the topology. In addition, most routers implement time to live (TTL) for packets. This process, by destroying packets that have traveled too long or through too many routers, prevents defective packets from congesting the network.

Disadvantages

The speed of a router is about two-thirds that of a bridge. But speed is not what routers are primarily used for. Standard routers can only be used to link LANs (networks) that have identical protocols.

Brouters with Examples

A brouter is a special device that allows for routing and bridging in the same box. For example, if a TCP/IP suite is running on some stations, a small workgroup system is running the XNS protocol suite, and some DEC equipment is running the local area transport (LAT) protocol suite for terminal servers, a brouter can be configured to route the TCP/IP and the XNS traffic and bridge all other traffic.

Single-unit bridges and routers (i.e., brouters) are really bridges that include some router capabilities. Depending on the protocol or packet, the data are bridged or routed through the LAN. The brouter is like stuffing multiple routers into one bridge box. Use brouters whenever possible. Both large and small networks will benefit.

MULTIPROTOCOL ROUTERS

Because routers are protocol specific, more than one router may be needed to support all of an organization's internetworking needs. Some multiprotocol routers become necessary. This essentially leads to similar requirements of a gateway.

NETWORK CONFIGURATION EXAMPLES WITH ROUTERS

In this example (Figure 7.15), we notice there are four distinct LANs, fortunately all Ethernet LANs. One of the requirements for connectivity in this example is to provide redundant links in case one of the routers goes down and for performance efficiency.

Since they are using the same protocols, no conversions are required and routers provide a little more intelligence than bridges, we decide to use routers to accomplish this connectivity.

Three routers can connect all four LANs. Router 1 connects LANs A, B, and C. Router 2 connects LANs C and D. Router 3 connects LANs B and D. These connections provide two distinct paths between any two LANs. If any one network cabling fails, it will not halt the interconnection.

GATEWAYS

Communication between computers running different protocols is often handled through gateways. A gateway is an application-specific device that operates at all seven layers of the ISO protocol stack (Figure 7.1). The gateway hardware is a very sophisticated processor. The hardware device maintains separate connections to the networks being combined. The gateway runs software that performs protocol conversion on a layer-by-layer basis as necessary. Gateway is the final component needed for internetworking. It is also the most complex. Gateways offer the greatest degree of flexibility.

There are two primary approaches to implementing gateways. First is the software dependent which requires adding network interface cards (NICs) to personal computers. The other is all-in-one "black boxes" for specific protocols, for example, AppleTalk to Ethernet gateways. Either way, the functionality of one system must be mapped to the capability of the other systems. In addition, many major network operating system providers integrate protocol encapsulation or conversion capabilities into their system software.

One protocol may also be encapsulated into another. For example, AppleTalk protocols are often wrapped in TCP/IP packets in a process called tunneling, which allows MAC users to access TCP/IP services.

Functions

Gateways are used to connect networks that may have entirely different architectures. Since the network facilities and addressing schemes are completely different, the gateway must provide complete conversion from one protocol stack to the other without altering the data that need to be transmitted. To link different networks, for example, Ethernet and AppleTalk, a server is equipped with circuit cards for each network. The circuit then performs the necessary protocol conversion. When a device performs protocol conversions that allow information to be exchanged among different types of networks, it is known as gateway.

Through SNA protocols, an SNA-to-TCP/IP gateway (Figure 7.16) can give access to SNA hosts to the users on a multivendor TCP/IP LAN. A gateway can be connected to the network via a two-port card that plugs into the expansion slots of the gateway server microprocessor. Such configurations allow gateways to perform speed conversion and in

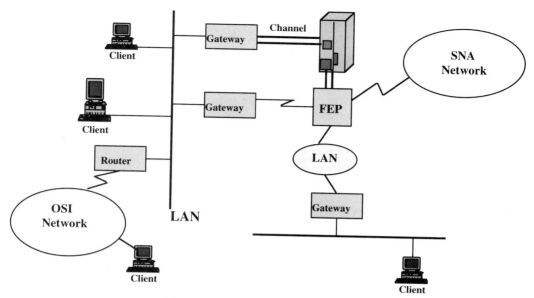

Figure 7.16 OSI-SNA interoperability.

some cases packet assembly and disassembly to provide logical access. Access to the gateway is controlled by assigning specific ports on the microprocessor. Each port may have access rights associated with it. Because no other microprocessor can access the port, security is enforced. However, when security is not an issue, a gateway can provide access to all ports on a contention basis.

Gateway protocols are equipped to perform flow control and respond to congestion indicators. When congestion is detected, the intelligent gateway assigns priority to the information that is to be routed. Intelligent gateways allow diagnostic information to pass through or around congested areas, providing instant reports on each link. If the entire network is congested, the packets can bypass the alternative gateways located on the other side of the network in favor of hopping through a different network. Intelligent gateways maintain security by distinguishing between routine and sensitive information during the routing decision.

The gateways are the means by which application interoperability is realized. The basis for evaluating a particular gateway depends on the functions it offers. The success and health of your enterprise network depends upon the choices you make in selecting the right internetworking tools, especially gateways. You need to consider at least the following criteria in selecting gateways:

- *Scope of the gateway functions:* Can the user access the gateway effectively, regardless of the user's location on the network?

- *User transparency:* Does the user need to understand naming, addressing, command syntax for either network or they are transparent to the user. Most effective solutions are generally those that hide the intricacies of the network from the user.
- *Desired performance:* It is important to understand not only the product's basic performance but how effectively the product can be managed and controlled.
- *Gateway reliability:* The product must be able to provide correct operation over a sustained period of time. Moreover, the product must be highly robust in its operation and still sufficiently flexible to circumvent faults before they do occur.
- *Ability to manage the network's delivery services:* The key areas are configuration, fault, performance, security, and accounting management. It is important that the gateway fit into the overall enterprise network management structure.

Advantages

When a separate server is used as a gateway (Figure 7.17), managers can monitor one gateway, which appears to the host as a single peripheral device, instead of monitoring the traffic of a number of processors on the network, providing a simplified network management. In this case, a separate expensive cluster controller is unnecessary because the gateway replaces it. Because a gateway can connect several microprocessors to a WAN, it can reduce operating costs and streamline the network.

Gateways help reduce the cabling costs and make configuration moves and changes easier. Users can change the physical location of their equipment and retain the same logical address on the network.

Gateways extract detailed information about the data traffic that passes through them. The gateway ensures that the links are handling data reliably, without exceeding user-defined error rate thresholds. Gateways also monitor various protocols being used, ensuring that enough protocol conversion processing power is available for any given application. Gateways gather network statistics which can be specified to produce report and/or archived for future statistical analyses.

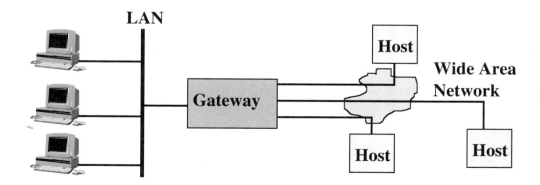

Figure 7.17 LAN-WAN gateway connection.

The network management tools that are available with gateways allow remote configuration of channels, links, and interconnection devices such as bridges and routers. In wide area networks, the gateway balances load levels, bypasses failed links, and finds the most efficient route. In this environment, the ability to detect, isolate, and diagnose problems becomes important.

Intelligent gateways can communicate with each other to determine the best way to route information, considering congestion, priority, performance, (e.g., throughput, error rate, and delay), security, and even cost. Gateways must perform flow control and respond to congestion indicators. When congestion is detected, the intelligent gateway assigns priority to the information to be routed.

A TCP/IP-to-SNA gateway gives users on a multivendor TCP/IP LAN access to IBM hosts through the SNA protocols. Gateways between LANs and X.25 wide area networks connect LAN users to either X.25 hosts or a large database on an X.25 public data network.

Terminal servers also play an important role in supporting multiple protocols and providing some level of application interoperability among differing network protocols. In fact, it is quite possible for a terminal to be accessing a DEC host using the LAT protocol and a UNIX host using TCP/IP simultaneously.

Disadvantages

Because gateways perform protocol conversion at every layer of the ISO model, performance bottlenecks may become a problem. Every new connection, hop, and protocol that is added to the network not only intensifies the problem but also invites new problems, which complicates network management.

An inefficient routing scheme can cause traffic to stay on the primary data link longer than necessary, slowing down the entire network. Simultaneously, the congestion may occur in the gateway itself, particularly when there are too many packets to filter.

NETWORK CONFIGURATION EXAMPLES WITH GATEWAYS

Example 1: OSI-SNA Interoperability

Gateways can provide application-level interoperability between two disparate network protocols, like OSI and SNA, as portrayed in Figure 7.16. The means by which this interoperability is achieved depends on the configurations and priorities. Most gateways operate where the systems are physically connected to both networks. In this case, the connection is made through synchronous circuit connections to a front-end processor and direct channel connection from the gateway to a mainframe and a LAN on the other end. The connection to the OSI network may be implemented via an Ethernet, token ring, or token bus LAN.

The physical connection must satisfy a number of criteria:

- The interconnect bandwidth and the data rate.
- The proximity of the two networks.
- The additional costs of making this connection successful.

Such a gateway can employ two distinct approaches to realize protocol interoperability: encapsulation or full conversion. Encapsulation usually takes place at the client. The overall objective is to provide OSI network–based terminals the ability to appear to the SNA network–based application as real 3270 devices or vice versa. In this manner, the base transport functions within the respective networks carry the encapsulated protocol packets from the client system to the gateway systems, where these packets are converted to their full homogeneous packet version for either network.

In full conversion, a translation of the packet occurs (but not in case of OSI-to-SNA protocols because they are too diverse) for each operation performed. For conversions to be reliable and successful, both the protocols for a particular function must support comparable semantics.

Example 2: LAN-Mainframe Interoperability

A medium-scale enterprise has a number of departments that want the company data available so they can manage their own information needs and the specialized applications. Each employee in the department has a PC. Currently, these are all connected to a mainframe using 3270 emulation mode (as dumb terminals). The mainframe serves as the repository of all the company's data. With the implementation of LANs, the data can be downloaded from the mainframe to the LAN, making it available to multiple users (Figure 7.18).

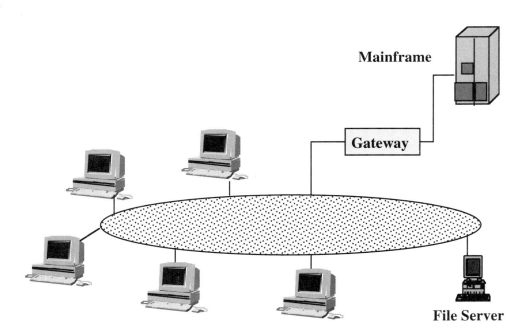

Figure 7.18 Gateway between LAN and mainframe.

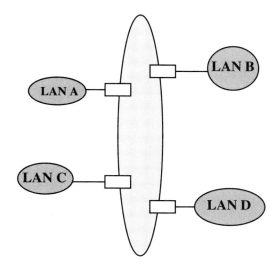

Figure 7.19 A backbone configuration.

The PCs can perform 3270 emulation to maintain the use of the programs or access the data directly on the mainframe. A key component in this example is the gateway that allows the LAN to communicate with the mainframe. Depending on the size of the LAN, a single gateway may support the entire network, as shown. If the LAN is large, more than one gateway may be necessary. Usually, each LAN requires its own separate gateway since the protocols may be different.

For IBM host mainframes, it is preferable to employ token ring LANs, whereas for a DEC host, an Ethernet LAN is desirable.

BACKBONES

Another internetworking method is via the use of backbones (Figure 7.19). Backbone can be used to connect several smaller networks, thus providing less complex environment of a large network. In this algorithm, each LAN can continue to operate should one of the other networks fail. Several smaller LANs are easier to administer than a large LAN. Backbones perform filtering. Therefore, the only traffic that is meant for other networks needs to pass over the backbone.

These access (small LANs) networks may require a bridge, router, or a gateway to attach to the backbone, depending upon the protocols of the backbone and the LANs. A backbone does require a high bandwidth since it should be able to transmit over large distances. Because fiber optics are normally used for these networks, the backbone is often designed as an FDDI network.

As shown in Figure 7.19, one other way to connect four LANs is through a backbone. This is a viable approach if the LANs to be connected are neither large nor sophisticated. The backbone can filter the traffic in such a way to forward only those messages destined for a different LAN.

The use of backbone network removes the problem of communication failure when more than two LANs are bridged. None of the access LANs act as intermediate LAN. However, the backbone must be reliable because the LAN internetworking depends on it. The primary advantage from network management point of view is that it appears to be a large LAN, when in fact it comprises four separate LANs operating in parallel.

SEVEN-LAYER PROTOCOL CONVERSION

The most commonly used protocols today are IPX, NetBIOS, TCP/IP, and SNA. These protocols dictate how information is passed back and forth over the network. IPX is the popular progeny of Xerox's XNS protocol. NetBIOS is used in IBM environments in a peer-to-peer fashion. TCP/IP is a popular protocol in the UNIX environment and has been adopted into many government, research, and business environments. Of course, SNA (e.g., APPC, APPN) has been the most prevalent in the WAN and the IBM world.

Interoperability is a much abused terminology. For most, interoperability could mean nothing more than straightforward plug-and-play compatibility, such as connecting Ethernet cabling with different vendor's products. In this case physical interoperability merely gives users the ability to connect one vendor's computing devices to another over a network.

This is not true interoperability. VAXs, PCs, Sun SPARCs, and MACs can be connected to an Ethernet via network adapter cards. But it does not mean that VAXs running DECnet over Ethernet cabling can communicate with PCs on a Novell NetWare workgroup attached to the same wire. That is far more complex task, involving gateways that convert one protocol to another.

Examining Figure 7.20, we notice that except for layers 1 and 2, where there is some consistency of the standard protocols, there is very little commonality among the various proprietary protocols. Since the actual implementations have evolved over time using vendor-specific protocols, protocol conversions become a necessity to achieve some degree of interoperability.

In terms of the OSI model, Figure 7.20 depicts typical communications protocols and utilities. The most important of these are TCP/IP, which ensure interconnectivity for the LANs at the lower three layers of the OSI model.

Protocol Layers

The physical layer must provide a path for data from one node to reach the other. If a physical connection does not exist, then communication is impossible. Therefore, the transmission media and the internetworking tools are a necessary ingredient in interprotocol conversions. In addition, if the packets or data need to pass through bridges or routers,

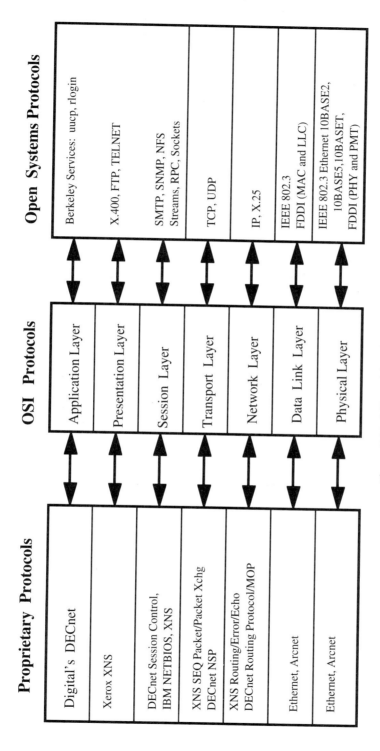

Proprietary Protocols

Digital's DECnet	
Xerox XNS	
DECnet Session Control, IBM NETBIOS, XNS	
XNS SEQ Packet/Packet Xchg DECnet NSP	
XNS Routing/Error/Echo DECnet Routing Protocol/MOP	
Ethernet, Arcnet	
Ethernet, Arcnet	

OSI Protocols

Application Layer
Presentation Layer
Session Layer
Transport Layer
Network Layer
Data Link Layer
Physical Layer

Open Systems Protocols

Berkeley Services: uucp, rlogin
X.400, FTP, TELNET
SMTP, SNMP, NFS Streams, RPC, Sockets
TCP, UDP
IP, X.25
IEEE 802.3 FDDI (MAC and LLC)
IEEE 802.3 Ethernet 10BASE2, 10BASE5,10BASET, FDDI (PHY and PMT)

Figure 7.20 OSI model and open systems.

235

those bridges or routers must support the transport protocol of the packets. For example, if NetBIOS is routing for IBM and Microsoft implementations, connectivity does not exist for NetBIOS traffic unless the router is configured with options to bridge NetBIOS. However, TCP/IP is routable and NetBIOS can be encapulated within it via a gateway.

Application layer communication software can be configured to work with a particular network environment and corresponding transport protocol. The protocol stack on two communicating nodes must be identical, from the session layer to the data link layer frame type.

LAN-LAN Internetworking

The dominant LAN transport protocols in the DOS world are SPX/IPX and NetBIOS. SPX/IPX is most popular in Novell implementations, whereas NetBIOS continues to be widely used by the Microsoft LAN Manager as well as the IBM LAN Server.

From the top-down perspective (Figure 7.21) of the "upper layers," NetBIOS applications largely see the same interface with native NetBIOS or Novell NetBIOS. This is accomplished by making the application, presentation, and upper session layer interfaces the same.

The lower layer interfaces present different set of problems, because Novell's NetBIOS emulation interfaces with IPX at the transport layer, whereas Native NetBIOS interfaces with IEEE 802.2 or NDIS, respectively, at the data link layer. The result is that Novell NetBIOS cannot talk to Native NetBIOS and vice versa because of the differences in the middle layers of each protocol stack. DOS and OS/2 NetWare nodes on token ring have the option of using Native NetBIOS. However, that is not compatible with Ethernet.

Most interoperability approaches, including multiple stacks on the workstation and protocol gateways, have not yielded cross-NetBIOS system integration. On the other hand, Microsoft LAN Manager and IBM LAN Server protocols have evolved separately, the users seem to interoperate in both worlds. Microsoft allows NetBIOS to run on top of TCP/IP for global networks. NetBIOS and SPX/IPX cannot intercommunicate with TCP/IP either. However, Native NetBIOS is not routable and must use bridges. Network designers prefer to build complex, large-scale networks around "routers" rather than bridges since routers exert greater and more intelligent control over the flow of network traffic.

Microsoft introduced "named pipes" that run on NetBIOS. However, these cannot communicate with implementations on Novell NetWare. In theory, dual stacks can be run on back-end servers to relieve the workstations from switching between NetWare and LAN Manager.

UNIX has made significant inroads as a platform for midrange processors as high-end servers. The DOS workstation must use TCP/IP to access these servers.

Novell's and Microsoft's competing protocol architectures are shown in Figure 7.21, in relation to OSI layers 1 through 7. None of the architectures directly intercommunicate. Within each architecture, the different cooperating protocols facilitate communication among LAN nodes. NetWare matches the OSI model somewhat better than the Microsoft architecture. Microsoft's reliance on NetBEUI has proven to be disadvantageous for performance from a global network standpoint.

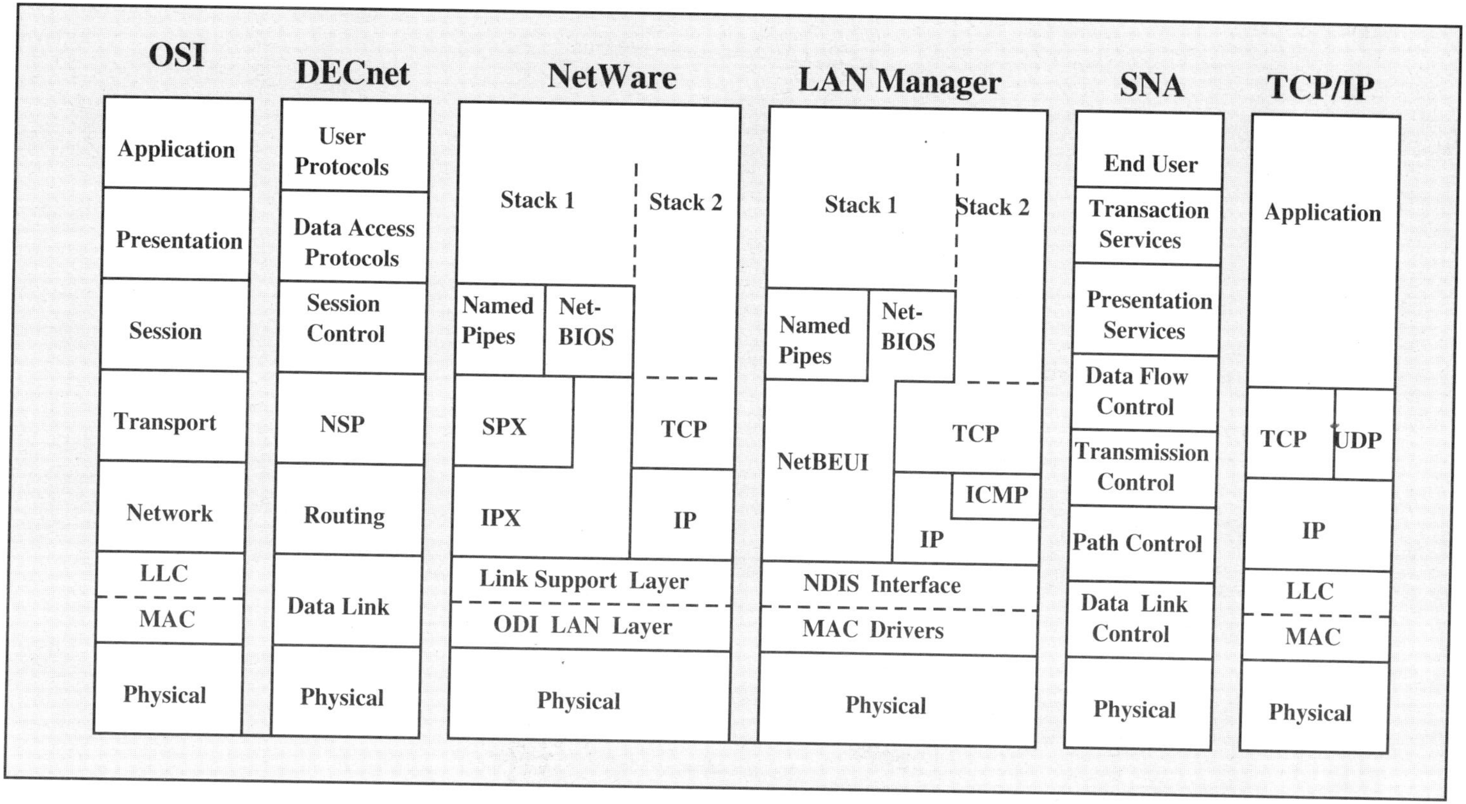

OSI	DECnet	NetWare	LAN Manager	SNA	TCP/IP
Application	User Protocols	Stack 1 / Named Pipes / Net-BIOS — Stack 2	Stack 1 / Named Pipes / Net-BIOS — Stack 2	End User	Application
Presentation	Data Access Protocols			Transaction Services	
Session	Session Control			Presentation Services	
Transport	NSP	SPX / TCP	NetBEUI / TCP / ICMP	Data Flow Control	TCP / UDP
Network	Routing	IPX / IP	IP	Transmission Control	IP
				Path Control	
LLC / MAC	Data Link	Link Support Layer / ODI LAN Layer	NDIS Interface / MAC Drivers	Data Link Control	LLC / MAC
Physical	Physical	Physical	Physical	Physical	Physical

Figure 7.21 Competing protocol architectures.

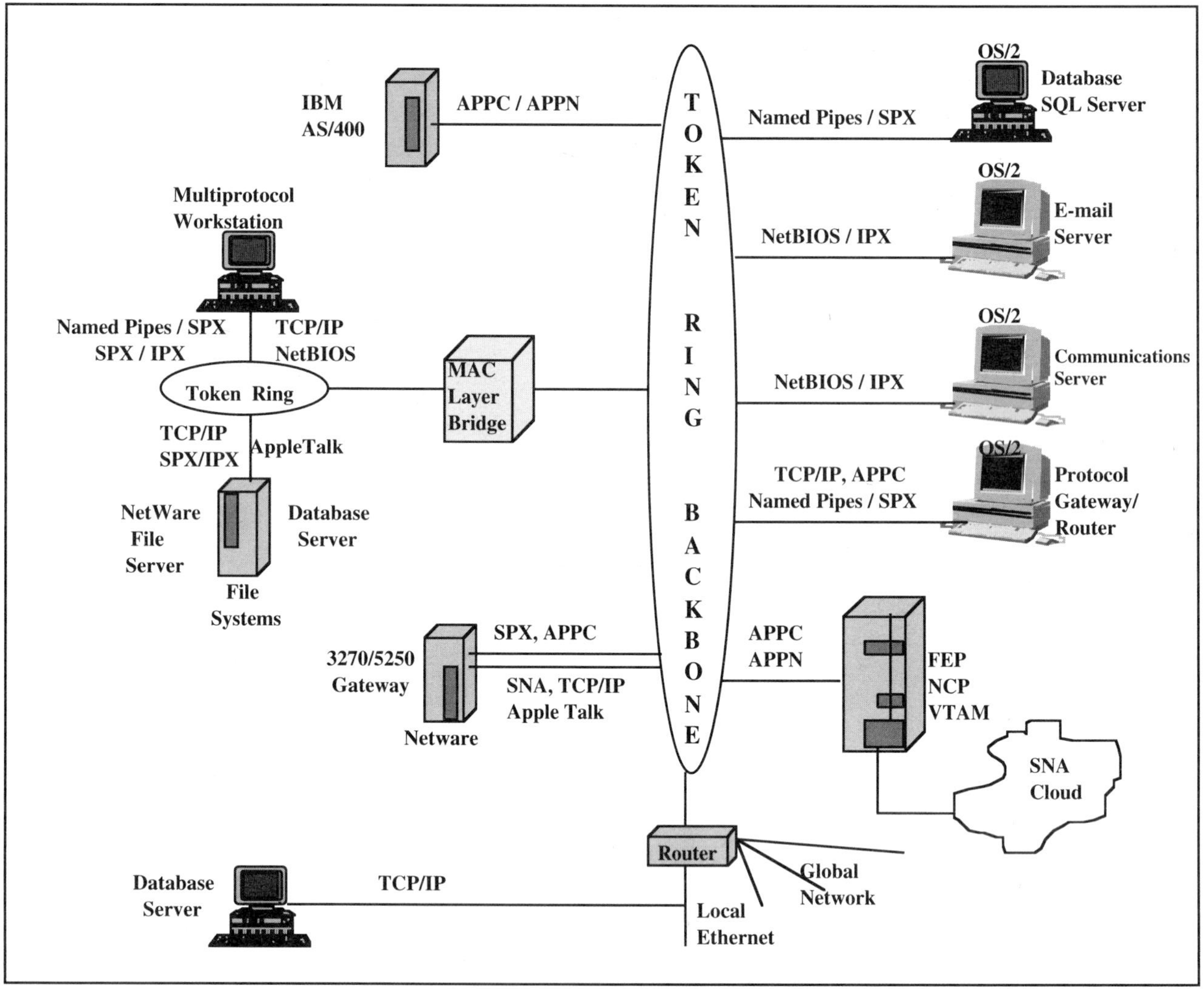

Figure 7.22 Multiprotocol network.

Mainframe and Multiprotocol Network

Despite aggressive downsizing efforts, mainframe protocols still represent the majority of corporate computing. Most mainframe data communication is at least partially LAN based. Large-scale IBM mainframes connect directly to the local network (Figure 7.22) via front-end processors. The FEPs can also be used as a high-powered SNA gateway for enterprise 3270 and Advanced Program-to-Program Communication (APPC) traffic. SNA, still, remains a network separate from the global area network because it is not yet feasible to route the SNA traffic across the routers. TCP/IP encapsulation of SNA is a commonly used technique to facilitate combining the two types of networks.

Since mainframes usually do not speak the protocols of the LAN-based NOSs, a gateway must be deployed to translate between LAN and mainframe protocols. In Figure 7.22, a token ring backbone facilitates the connection between LAN-based networks, SNA networks, and other global networks. Many critical nodes are connected to the single-segment token ring backbone only for this diagram to simplify connectivity solutions, when in reality they would be distributed across multiple segments to avoid total outage in the event of segment or link failures. Users can utilize the database servers via named pipes on SPX for database servers employing NetWare Requester for OS/2, named pipes on NetBIOS for database servers running LAN Manager, and TCP/IP for database servers operating on UNIX platforms. The Novell NetWare gateway emulates a cluster controller, which speaks SNA or APPC to the FEP and SPX to workstations running 3270 emulation.

Workstations on token ring or Ethernet can use the gateway also. On the token ring side, the gateway serves as an alternative to direct communication with the FEP. NetWare can also serve as a 5250 gateway for workstations to access IBM AS/400. DOS, OS/2 , Macintosh, and UNIX workstations can run all IBM host terminal emulation through NetWare.

Summary

This uniformity ensures that the LAN-based platforms can have access to traditional host-based data processing systems over the LAN. The corporate multiprotocol network can accommodate substantial diversity, and a mix of protocols permit a wide range of logical connectivity. In the scenario, PCs running DOS and Windows are dominant within the NetWare architecture. OS/2 is widespread as an application server platform for database, e-mail, communication services, and communication and protocol gateways. Remote mainframe access is available via a 3745 or another FEP gateway to SNA. The router provides clean linkage between token ring, Ethernet, and remote LANs.

SUMMARY

Gateways, bridges, routers, and repeaters provide varying degree of connectivity, efficiency, and economy to the enterprise. The choice of an interconnection device hinges on the topology of the network and the types of applications being run on the network. In addition, such devices help to unify disparate and scattered networks into an enterprise entity.

In *multiprotocol environments*, bridges provide more flexible and mature solutions. They are transparent to high-level communication protocols and accommodate many different applications. For instance, bridges would be a good solution where the users want to interconnect networks supporting a mix of protocols such as TCP/IP, DECnet, SNA, IPX, NetBIOS, and XNS. Bridges also make good sense if the entire network is administered from a central location. In this instance, a bridged network acts as a single logical network, since the network administrator must account for all stations of a bridged internetwork.

In *multivendor, single-protocol* environments, routers are very prevalent. Network complexity will determine whether a bridge or a router is used. In small configurations, bridges are a sensible choice. As complexity increases, so does the need for traffic isolation and control capabilities of routers. A combination of bridges and routers, however, can solve particularly complex internetworking problems. In a decentralized environment, the use of routers allows more flexibility. A network interconnected by routers allows each segment to be logically independent. Interconnected networks that have many distant sites or that are relatively large may require several management administrators.

Bridges and routers offer equal capabilities in the areas of network statistics and monitoring. Both can provide automatic audit trail and sophisticated analysis of such information. For ease of installation and maintenance, bridges offer definite advantages over routers. Bridges require little intervention and can make extremely basic routing decisions themselves, whereas routers are more sophisticated devices. Routers can link failures and congested nodes, which is critical for applications that cannot tolerate unnecessary delays or prolonged outages. Bypasses are enhanced by the ability of the routers to share information with each other through the OSI network layer. On the other hand, do not have access to the network layer, and when a bridge gets overloaded, the others will never know it.

Routers were born out of the necessity for dividing networks logically instead of physically. Routers work in a manner similar to bridges, by filtering out network traffic, rather than doing so by packet addresses they filter by specific protocol. An IP router can divide a network into various subnets so that the only traffic destined for particular IP addresses can pass between segments. The price paid for this type of intelligent forwarding and filtering is usually calculated in the speed of the network. Such filtering takes more time than is exercised in a bridge, which only looks at the MAC layer.

Brouters describe devices that have both bridging and routing capability. However, bridges frequently have router-like features such as selective protocol filtering.

A gateway is a device by which application interoperability can be realized between disparate protocols and operating systems. The interoperability between an IBM or SNA network means support of the 3270 data stream (for access from a 3270 terminal to a non-IBM host or from a non-3270 terminal to an IBM host). This also means support for mail exchange or file transfer from one proprietary protocol relative to either OSI or TCP/IP or vendor-specific protocols that perform similar functions. A degree of such interoperability can be achieved via either encapsulation or full conversion. The approach used largely depends on how closely the protocols on one system align with the protocols used on the other system.

Given its natural ability, a multiprotocol terminal server (gateway) can perform conversions between the protocols it knows, like LAT (DEC systems) and TCP/IP (UNIX systems). While terminal server bandwidth is not adequate for large file transfers, it can easily handle host-to-host inquiry/response applications, such as electronic mailbox checking.

Gateway solutions tend to be highly specialized, introduce structural degradation (sometimes gateways act as natural bottlenecks), and must be carefully placed from a logistical point of view. The ultimate solution is a high-speed gateway that translates between all common LAN and mainframe communication protocols. Funneling the majority of LAN traffic through protocol gateways must be carefully designed to avoid performance degradation and centralized points of failure.

EXERCISES

1. What are the various internetworking tools? Give a brief explanation of each.
2. Describe the difference between routers and bridges. When should they each be used.
3. How would a user on an Ethernet LAN communicate with a user connected through SNA?
4. At what layer does a repeater work? Is repeater a hardware or software device? How does it function?
5. Gateways can be either hardware or software. How are they most commonly implemented?
6. Brouters act as two devices: _____and _____.
7. Show a schematic at which layer the following devices work.
   Gateway
   Router
   Bridge
   Repeater
   Brouter

8

APPLICATIONS

Introduction
Issues
    Connecting Components
    Different Operating Systems
    Different Network Operating Systems
    Different LANs
    Media and Transmission Speeds
Application Types
    Stand-alone
    Network Aware
    Network Intrinsic
Applications and Utilities
    Terminal Emulation

    X Windows
    Network Applications
    User Applications
Incompatibility Solutions
    Multiple Platforms
    SQL Compatibility
Applications of LANs and WANs
    Small LANs
    Large LANs
    WANs
    Hubs and Backbones
Summary
Exercises

INTRODUCTION

Developing computer applications used to be a breeze, relatively speaking. Back when computing was synonymous with IBM 360/370 mainframes, MIS organizations and commercial developers did not have to worry about supporting multiple platforms for their software. In fact, most computing environments were homogeneous, and predictable.

Today, the situation has radically changed. Organizations typically employ a smorgasbord of computers, consisting of mainframes, minis, and microcomputers, from many different companies, running many different operating systems. This situation makes developing and supporting mission-critical applications a daunting task. Cross-platform development has become a way of life for MIS departments and commercial developers alike. Too often, it is fraught with setbacks and frustrations.

No longer is it enough to have a standard compiler for each platform. As complex GUIs and distributed processing take the place of character-based PCs and dumb terminals, the problems of supporting heterogeneous environment grows exponentially. The challenge is to acquire a standard set of tools that can deal with multiple platforms, network topologies, and transmission media and let you adapt to rapid changes in technology.

As the Intel/IBM/Novell/Microsoft monolith fragments and more and more migration occurs from "big iron" to the desktop and LAN servers in a network-centric *environment*, confusion is beginning to reign both in the marketplace and inside the organizations of all sizes.

Local area networks which connect devices that are proximate (within the same or nearby building), have grown in number tremendously in the last decade and have threatening the dominance of mainframe installations. Wide area networks are linked together by leasing from common carriers such as AT&T, MCI, or US Sprint and cover a much larger geographic territory. Customers either can use the public networks or lease circuit-switched or packet-switched networks to create WANs.

Various enterprises have gained a competitive advantage by interconnecting devices that perform *data generation, storage*, and *processing functions*. By linking operating system software, computers, and terminals, an organization can create an "internetwork" that allows it to respond more quickly to customer requests. These networks vary in size from local networks to those that span the globe. Such networks includes terminals, protocols converters, remote job entry (RJE) devices, modems, physical interfaces, cluster controllers, communications controllers, and multiplexers.

The task of interconnecting equipment, in a heterogeneous environment, is complex and requires knowledge of multivendor equipment, operating systems, networks, and applications. The options are many, and choosing the right combination of equipment, software, applications, and networks is a difficult decision.

This chapter provides an overview of the issues, applications and utilities, relating to multioperating systems, network topologies, hardware platforms, data formats, and media speeds, that affect enterprises' ability to successfully utilize its resources (applications and data).

ISSUES

As networks become more pervasive and organizations become more thoroughly connected, the need for different applications to share common data or even computing resources has grown considerably. Cross-platform development has become an integral part of any cooperative or distributed processing environment. This heterogeneity of platforms, operating systems, and interconnecting architectures has created a dilemma and a chaos for application developers and network systems administrations alike.

A major challenge facing information technology-intensive organizations is being able to interconnect different vendors' "application facilitators," like database management systems (DBMSs), data marts, data warehouses, computers, LANs, WANs, and personal computers (PCs) effectively. Interconnection provides the enterprise with quick access to the vast computing and database reservoirs of that organization and allows them to service their customers in a more timely manner. Such intelligent use of an organization's computing and information resources can provide the enterprise with a competitive edge.

Connecting Components

Internetworking multiple vendors' devices, networks, and architectures is a complex job. MIS and telecommunications manager need to be aware of the major management and technical issues of.

- Performance.
- Standardization.
- LAN-WAN interconnection.
- Security.
- Integrity.
- Internetworking over national boundaries.

Performance decreases when networks are connected together. It is extremely difficult to compute network performance measures on an end-to-end basis. A major difficulty is that the data traffic to a destination may go through many (access providers) local telephone companies, long-distance companies, and foreign companies. Computing an end-to-end performance of all vendor's equipment and networks are to be combined. Depending on the number of circuits between the originating and terminating nodes, the performance computation can be difficult.

The performance measurement units also vary between device and network vendors. Therefore, enterprises must carefully select the networks to be interconnected (if they have a choice) so that the end user's performance objectives can be met.

Standardization can increase the choice of vendors, reduce the potential obsolescence of a customer's devices, and reduce the need for relays to interconnect networks. However, most devices, networks, and architectures in use today are proprietary, limiting the end user's choice of interconnecting devices.

Increased complications are introduced when a foreign telecommunications company is used, since those company's network standards may not conform with the native set.

Bandwidth, rerouting, and *integration* of backbone networks becomes an important issue in *LAN-WAN interconnection.* The bandwidth available in LANs is on the order of megabytes per second, while equivalent bandwidth on long-distance networks costs much more. If a customer leases a backbone network to carry high-bandwidth WAN traffic among major cities, that customer frequently requests automatic rerouting in case of failure of a major facility. Sophisticated software and hardware are required for such functions.

Some type of *security* must be provided for network users. Users on a LAN are often logged on to their personal computers, even though they are not using them all the time. Such open terminals invite hackers with the opportunity to access computer systems using remote logins. In addition, when the traffic is transmitted using long-distance lines shared with other users and if the long-distance vendors do not provide their customers with transmission security, one customer's traffic can be tapped by other customers.

Assuring the *integrity of corporate data* is an important issue. LAN-WAN interconnection gives an end user the ability to access and change the databases remotely. Internetworking makes it possible for an end user to corrupt the data in corporate databases.

The above issues multiply as *different countries* are internetworked. Standards are different in every country, and the equipment from such countries is not compatible. An organization must retain and recruit talented personnel to address such issues.

Different Operating Systems

One major issue in development across various types of systems is how to develop applications that will run identically—or nearly so—on several different platforms. Many large commercial developers have multiplatform strategies by supporting as many different popular platforms (e.g., DOS, Windows, Macintosh, UNIX, and MVS) as their resources permit. For example, Oracle has ported its many products to almost every imaginable platform, but at a considerable cost since they are different.

Cross-platform development is not the exclusive domain of the big-time commercial developers anymore. In-house developers also must support many different standards. The computing infrastructure in most companies consists of a heterogeneous mix of platforms and networks. With end users clamoring for greater access to data repositories from their desktops, many MIS departments confront the task of supporting a variety of platforms in their in-house development efforts.

When developing cross-platform applications, you have to decide how closely you wish to support the native environment of each one. The approach you take depends entirely on the goals of your organization and the needs of its end users. If, for example, it is the goal of your company to supply the same interface to corporate data from every desktop to save on training and software support costs, you will want to create a common interface across platforms. But if seamless integration of in-house and commercial applications on each platform is the stated goal, you will have to tailor in-house development to the needs of the different supported platforms.

Different Network Operating Systems

Network operating systems are what finally make all that hardware function as a network. Originally, network operating systems functioned only to allow sharing of printers and disk files, and only one workstation at a time could access a disk volume. Today's network operating systems allow much more than that, providing the basis for client/server applications, integrating computers of various sizes and types, and allowing the formation of workgroups based on the electronic messaging capabilities of the LAN.

There are two network operating paradigms: dedicated server-based systems and peer-to-peer systems. *Dedicated systems* are centered on a powerful server machine that stores all files and applications or connect to the outside world via a communications server or to the network from remote locations. *Peer-to-peer based systems* allow the workstations to act as servers.

Although there are as many definitions of a network operating system as there are network operating system products, most NOSs have certain features in common. However, all are slightly different in their solutions providing LAN functions. A network operating system can be thought of as an extension of the operating system being used at the processor. The use of the network operating systems has proliferated rapidly over the last few years and some of the most popular network operating systems (Figure 8.1) are

- *Novell's NetWare* is the most popular because it is hardware independent and runs on Ethernet, token ring, ARCNet, Gnet, and other networks. Most commonly, NetWare provides high-performance in a workgroup environment as a file and print server. NetWare also supports database applications to share data, perusing a file, and making changes to a file or record.
- *Banyan's VINES* works with large networks, even those with more than 500 nodes at more than one location. VINES is capable of connecting to many LANs to create virtual networks. VINES also provides a naming service, StreetTalk, which is a global, distributed database that maintains lists of the names and attributes of all users, file storage devices, individual services, and communications devices on the network.

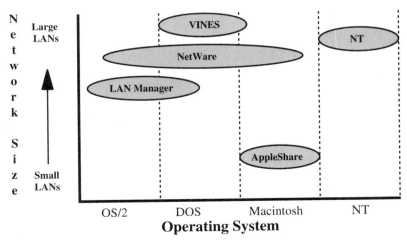

Figure 8.1 Network operating systems.

- *Microsoft's LAN Manager* provides a robust and flexible networking environment. It provides connectivity to most LANs using different technologies.
- *AppleShare*, for the Macintosh environment, is easy to use, manage, and install. It is a low-end product with relatively few security features, but it is very popular with Macintosh users. It supports 20 to 50 users.

A network operating system frequently provides a mail-like utility that allows for basic communication among all the machines on a network. Most network operating systems allow the users to send files. Network security is usually under the control of the network administrator, using services provided by the network operating system. Most network operating systems provide the following services to the users/networks:

- *File Services:* A network operating system allows users to share data and storage devices on the network. The network also provides centralized backup, data integrity, and data security resources.
- *Print Services:* Workstations can share printers and administer printer sharing by building a queue that serves as a storage zone or buffer on the file server.
- *Administration Utilities:* These utilities manage other network services (e.g., file and printer sharing and messaging). The network administrator can use these utilities to optimize network performance.
- *Application Programming Interfaces (APIs):* These are commands that programmers can use to incorporate the services of the network operating system into their program. For example, Named Pipes is a set of calls that allows a programmer to open a pipe, or a channel, from one program to another, for carrying a message or data between the programs.
- *Third-Party Products:* Such products are usually added on to the network operating systems to complement its native functions. They provide automated data backup and communication between separate similar or dissimilar operating systems using different types of computers on the network.

In selecting a network operating system, users need to consider which system features are the most important. Most NOSs make data and print sharing transparent to the user. However, some incompatible applications cannot function on internetworked computers. Some of the older applications, for example, perform disk operations by going straight to the drive, bypassing the operating system.

No longer are computers the only resource and networks simply the tool to connect those resources, networks have become an integral resource. Network operating systems have played a large role in bringing this about. As network operating systems grow, add more functionality, and become complex, they will become a hub of the networking environment. Therefore, we have to be cognizant of the incompatibilities they could introduce in the networking environment and cause added pain.

Different LANs

In the past, IBM equipment and PCs or PS/2s that needed to communicate with IBM equipment were connected via token ring LAN, and Digital Equipment and Digital-oriented PCs went on the Ethernet LAN. However, with the increasing need for systems of all sizes and shapes to share common LANs, these artificial boundaries have eroded. The unmanageability of running separate LANs for a particular vendor's equipment has taken its toll on the minds and budgets of the enterprise networking managers. In addition, the rising needs for cooperative processing between dissimilar systems and the maturity of the de facto integration products like Novell NetWare, TCP/IP, and OSF DCE have produced pressure on LAN integration.

Different vendors responded by adding support for token ring, Novell NetWare, and/or Ethernet. This resulted in giving more flexibility to the user, e.g., TCP/IP and Novell NetWare running over a variety of LAN types, which is certainly remarkable change for massive and lumbering proprietary architectures like DECnet and SNA. But this flexibility has created some new issues:

- Which is easier to troubleshoot?
- Which is easier to install?
- Which is best for IBM or DEC connections?
- Which is best for multivendor environment?
- Which supports more stations?
- Which offers better performance?
- Which has a better future?

Such are the issues with LANs that will continue to complicate the user choices as long as the technology continues to change and the competition prevails.

Media and Transmission Speeds

The dramatic increase in desktop computing power and the rise of LANs for distributed computing have fueled the demand for high-speed data transport over public networks. However, bandwidth-hungry applications that require full LAN-LAN connectivity or multimedia must use private lines because the public networks are currently unable to manage high-speed bandwidth. What is needed is a data "superhighway" that could speed transactions. Compared with present telephone system, which is primarily based on voice, emerging applications will require a 1000-fold increase in capacity, bringing the broadband interconnecting trunks into the gigabit range.

Probably, the solution is to be found in the virtually unlimited bandwidth capacity of single-mode optical fiber. Anticipating the need for exponential leaps in bandwidth capacity on the public network, the interexchange carriers and telephone companies have recommended a new family of synchronous optical networks (SONETs). Once SONET becomes widely available, in the short run, businesses will be able to extend their networking to other applications such as videoconferencing and computer imaging. As users interconnect their separate LANs, it is hoped that more and more traffic will also take advantage of SONET for data flow through public and private broadband WANs.

APPLICATION TYPES

In today's environment, few departments, subsidiaries, or enterprises work in isolation. The offices and production lines must be integrated, often in direct electronic communication with other offices, manufacturers, or suppliers. To handle such complicated and cooperative working situations, multiple systems must work in unison, able to communicate, and share data and tasks, with acceptable efficiency and accuracy. To achieve this, communication methods between systems, both new and old, that provide reliable and accurate transmission of data are needed, without affecting the applications that are running in separate servers.

To deal with such issues of distributed and shared software, it becomes imperative to combine the technologies for providing interconnection with the technologies that control the software applications. As companies become flatter, more applications are being distributed, and electronic communication is increasing. Consequently, new applications, which are specifically designed for these shared tasks, are emerging. Replacing a single mainframe by workstations on a LAN does not make new applications possible, even though it may improve local control, performance, and availability. However, availability of a WAN makes many new applications feasible.

When systems were first connected over a network, users wanted them to communicate to move data from one to the other or to enable them to share more expensive peripheral equipment, such as laser printers and fax machines. Now the emphasis has moved to full *interoperability*, *portability*, and *scalability*. The evolution of the application development cycle can be traced as

- *Stand alone applications* (Figure 8.2) were originally designed to exist on a single processor to which several terminals, printers, and storage devices were attached. It was also termed batch processing. Portability or scalability or interoperability was never the issue since the applications all resided on the same system and interpreted on the same

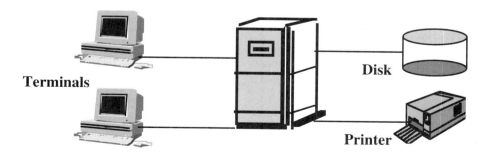

Terminals

Disk

Printer

Figure 8.2 Stand-alone applications.

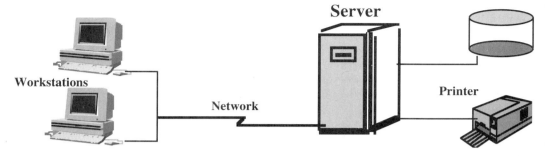

Figure 8.3 Network-aware applications.

hardware, operating system, and architectures. But the problems did surface when these had to be ported to a different machine with different operating system, or architecture, or vendor.

- Over time, applications became *network aware* (Figure 8.3). The application resided and was executed on a single computer, but the terminals or users were also connected via a network, using communication lines or links. Timesharing is a good example of such applications. Here the application sees the network as a device for communication between processors and sharing peripherals.

- Applications today have become more *network centric* or *network intrinsic* (Figure 8.4), in the sense that they are distributed over different processors (such as client/server arrangements). Such applications need the presence, functionality, and interoperability of other processors on the network in order to share the computing resources and/or computation.

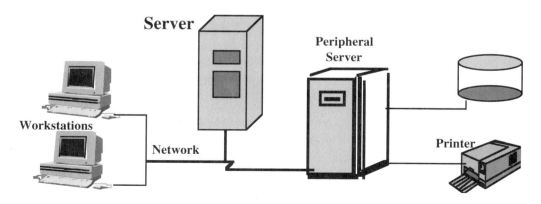

Figure 8.4 Network-intrinsic applications.

Network-intrinsic applications have become the norm in the internetworking environment. Although relatively few comprehensive software packages or applications exist yet, but it is anticipated that many new applications are on the horizon.

APPLICATIONS AND UTILITIES

Replacing a single mainframe by workstations on a LAN does not make new applications possible, although it may improve the reliability and performance. In contrast, the availability of WANs makes many new applications feasible. Some of these new applications may have important effects on enterprises as a whole. Most applications use networking for economic reasons: calling up a distant computer via a network rather than connecting to it directly.

Ultimately, the intended purpose of networking is to support an automated applications process. The nature of this process can range from scientific to manufacturing to business. The potential uses of networking in office applications are limitless. Some of the office applications are electronic mail, file transfer and exchange, database access and administration, data warehousing multi-dimensional analysis, on-line analytical processing, desktop publishing, and execution of distributed applications.

In addition, data communications is fast becoming an integral part of today's computer-aided design (CAD) and manufacturing systems (CAM). This application is nowhere more evident than in the manufacturing automation protocol (MAP) arena.

Of course, in support of the office and manufacturing network applications are the generic support utilities/applications, such as network management, terminal emulation, X windows, and security management.

Terminal Emulation

One of the most common areas of incompatibility between computer systems is due to proprietary terminals with unique control and dialog structures that can only be used with certain types of processors. Two protocols have been defined to isolate applications from such differences in terminal characteristics:

- The *OSI Virtual Terminal Protocol (VTP)* is a service that allows host systems to communicate with terminals and terminal controllers in a standard way over an OSI network. It assumes that the terminal has certain amount of intelligence available in the terminal controller. On a multivendor network, systems connected to the network may be accessed by any one of a number of terminals connected to the network. With the move to open systems and subsequently multivendors, a large number of incompatible terminals, each with characteristics that are proprietary to its own manufacturer, may be connected to a single system. Software running on the network system must be able to recognize and deal with this collection of different terminals and terminal controllers.
- *TELNET,* also known as remote login or virtual terminal, is intended to provide access, in the form of a terminal session, from one computer to another. TELNET is a simple

remote terminal protocol. It gives the appearance that the user's terminal is attached directly to a remote machine. TELNET uses TCP to communicate with the TELNET server at another node. The protocol is concerned with setting up and manipulating two simplex data streams, one in each direction. As keys are hit on a terminal, a stream of 8-bit bytes is transmitted over the line. The terminal process is converted to the network standard ASCII. The client and server processes of the TELNET protocol maintain a logical session with each other.

TELNET is very valuable, especially for terminal activities that are less interactive such as checking e-mail, starting jobs on remote hosts, and viewing output. Options to the protocol are available for items such as remote echo of characters, binary transmission of characters, and character-at-a-time transmission. Other terminal options are available to emulate commonly used terminals such as VT100 and IBM 3270.

X Windows

The X Window system, called X for short, is a network-based graphics window system that was developed at MIT. X is typically run on a workstation with a large screen or on a special graphics terminal known as an X terminal. It can also run on PCs and many larger systems. X allows you to work with multiple programs (windows) simultaneously, each in a separate *window*.

The operations performed within a window can vary greatly, depending upon the type of program running it. Certain windows accept input from the user—functioning as terminals to create graphics or control a database. Other windows simply display information, such as time of day or a picture of the characters in a particular font. The windows you will use most frequently are *terminal emulators*, windows that function as standard terminals, usually called as *x term*.

One of the strengths of the X is that you can run several processes simultaneously in several different windows. It also allows you to run programs on machines connected by a network. You can run a process on a remote machine while displaying the results on your own screen.

It makes sense that networks and window systems should be used together. The window system allows the building of a user interface for applications. If it makes no distinction between local and network connections, the applications automatically provide a user interface to the network. The window system allows users to access the remote computing resources involving only the commands they use for running programs locally.

The protocol basis and concomitant portability of the X Window System is especially important today when it is very common to have several different manufacturer as well as size machines in a single network. Until X, there were no common mechanisms to hide the differences between operating systems and graphics hardware. Implementations exist for machines ranging from Atari personal computers to Cray supercomputers. The system is so hardware and operating system independent that properly written application software can be compiled and run on most systems.

X Window System provides a common graphics language which greatly lessens the effort required to port applications to different machines. Reducing this porting load means more and better applications available for the multivendor platforms. For the user, the X Window System promises to make more applications available on more machines.

Network Applications

The objective of computer networks is to provide a mechanism for access and manipulation of information. This information is typically dispersed across multiple locations, in differing formats, and in a variety of computer systems.

Distributed processing has generated the need for many applications that are unique for the LAN environment. A LAN can send data through the network at much faster rates than can a mainframe or minicomputer. The transfer rate on a LAN ranges from 1 Mbps to 100 Mbps, today. LANs are still being developed that can transfer data at the rate of 1 Gbps (1 billion bits per second). By comparison, the most commonly used speed of a WAN is up to 56 Kbps. However, faster rates for the speed of a WAN data network are being attained by using T1/T3 lines, which are digital service lines capable of data transfer rates from 1.55 Mbps to 45 Mbps. But the T1/T3 media are expensive to use.

The ability to transfer data rapidly within and between the networks has resulted in more efficient use of the network and the data residing on the network. This has facilitated many applications that can now be distributed across the network instead of just being run on a single isolated processor or PC. We will examine a number of applications that have become commonplace in this environment.

Network Management.   Recently, a lot of emphasis has been placed on network management. The Simple Network Management Protocol (SNMP) was developed to manage TCP/IP networks. SNMP is implemented by each subnetwork. Each has a database of network information called management information base (MIB), which defines the subnetwork. SNMP applications use this information as they perform functions such as sending out requests for information and configuration settings, receiving responses, and receiving alert or trap messages. Messages are sent between SNMP applications via UDP.

Network management applications also provide fault detection. A network fault can mean that communication has ceased or that performance has degraded. Some network management applications are simple and others are sophisticated. The sophisticated packages can inform an operator which particular node is failing; others just provide implications as to the nature of the failure. When a network fails or performs poorly, it is important to solve the problem immediately.

Network Security.   *Kerberos* is a method of distributed network security that is popular today. While it is not officially part of TCP/IP installations, it is rapidly gaining support. Kerberos has also been made a basis for OSF's distributed computing environment (DCE) security. The two key concepts behind Kerberos are authorization and authentication. Authorization gives users access to those resources they are authorized to access. Authentication verifies that a user requesting access to a resource has the authority to access the resource.

To help make it secure, Kerberos does not transfer passwords across the network. Instead, a unique token, which can be used only once to access a particular resource, is generated. Half the token is sent to the resource and the other half to the user. This technique is sometimes referred to as the "broken poker chip."

Electronic Mail. The advent of the personal computer made it possible for an individual to perform data processing at his desk, greatly enhancing individual productivity and the quality of work. However, the users still needed the ability to communicate with one another. The telephone was not always convenient or efficient, and messages were still usually carried by hand (the pink slips or stick-ups).

With computer internetworks, the need to communicate has been met through the use of electronic mail, or *e-mail*. E-mail is a specialized application program that runs on the network and functions much like the postal system. This application program interacts the PCs on a LAN. Each user on the LAN has a directory of addresses or nicknames for e-mail, commonly known as *mailbox*.

The real electronic message is simply information, in the form of a memo or letter or even a file attached to it, that you type as if using a word processor. This electronic letter is then forwarded to the desired person's mailbox. The users check their mailboxes from time to time to see if any messages have been forwarded. Most e-mail applications even notify the addressee when messages are received by displaying or pinging a notice on the workstation screen.

E-mail programs today are very sophisticated and offer many features that would enhance any work environment. For example, e-mail is being used to schedule meetings or conference rooms or even conventions and send memos to people in different buildings or across continents. E-mail is one of the most commonly used applications on the network. But e-mail no longer means that one user simply sends a message to another user. Today, e-mail packages are much more sophisticated, often integrating *calendaring* and *scheduling* features into the application.

- With the *calendaring feature*, the user can record the time and day of meetings without being in danger of scheduling two appointments for the same time. When a user schedules the meeting for a certain time, the calendaring system prompts for the times of the meeting. The user usually keys in the estimated length, and the calendaring system resolves the conflicts between the invitees' schedules or already scheduled meetings. A conflict exists if the time allotment exceeds normal working hours or overlaps another meeting.

  Another useful feature of the calendaring system is that others may have limited viewing access to the user's calendar. The user can assign access privileges on a need-to-know basis, thus preventing unauthorized access to the calendar data. For example, they may only view the time that is already allotted, but they cannot see the reason for the allotment.

- The *scheduling feature* goes hand in hand with the calendaring feature. It is very frustrating and time consuming to get several people together for a meeting or a tele- or video conference. The scheduling features resolve such problems.

The network services and associated applications providing this functionality can be accomplished via e-mail services. Various standards affect the use and development of e-mail. They include the following:

- *Simple Mail Transfer Protocol* (SMTP) is a simple, easy-to-use e-mail system for the Internet. SMTP is a part of the application layers of the TCP/IP suite. SMTP is commonly used to transfer mail between to network stations that are connected remotely.
- Novell's MHS (message handling service) provides gateways to other networks. MHS is 100% compatible with X.400. In addition, MHS contains X.400-like services, including
  - Management of access to user agents.
  - Delivery notification.
  - Message relay and forwarding.
  - Workgroup addressing.
  - Nondelivery alert.
  - Dead letter notification.
- CCITT developed the *X.400* specification (adopted by the ISO in layer 7) as guidelines for a message handling system. E-mail is just one application within a broad spectrum of messaging applications. The X.400 message handling system (MHS) provides both an architecture and a set of communication protocols for interconnecting disparate mail systems, especially in the client/server environments.

  The MHS is made up of three main parts (Figure 8.5): UA, MTA, and MS. The client submitting or receiving messages on behalf of a user is called the user agent (UA). UAs submit or retrieve messages through the message store (MS). Message stores use a message transfer agent (MTA) to forward messages along the backbone. The three parts of the MHS communicate through the use of one or more of the interconnecting protocols, P1 through P7.

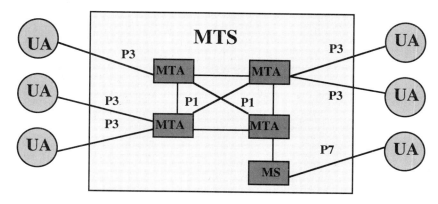

Figure 8.5 An X.400 message handling system.

P7 specifies how the interaction between UA and the MS is conducted. P1 specifies how the MTA should relay messages along the backbone. It contains rules for routing information between two MTAs. These rules govern formatting, or how the information is to be packaged. The data to be sent may be referred to as an envelope. Other fields associated with the envelope are

- A unique message identifier where the message originated.,
- Name of the sender.
- A description of the destination address and the recipient.
- Delivery instructions, if return receipt required.
- A description how the information should be displayed.

P2 specifies how the contents of these messages should be structured and the type of services requested, such as

- Allowing only authorized users to send messages.
- Specifying the type of notification required of the recipient.
- Providing message subject information.

P3 specifies how the clients (UAs) and servers should communicate and provides rules for changing existing parameters for e-mail routing and delivery, including

- The need for a password.
- A need to alter maximum size of the message.
- The need for a test to determine if the message can be delivered.

The clear separation of the message envelope and its contents enable X.400 to be used as a transport mechanism for a multiple of messaging applications, beyond the core e-mail application widely in use today. Different body parts within the X.400 envelope can accommodate different representations of data, such as memos, forms, office documents, telex, fax, graphics, schematics, and voice messages. X.400 is also rapidly being deployed as a transport mechanism for structured business transactions, such as electronic data interchange (EDI) and electronic funds transfer (EFT).

The open-ended address format of X.400 allows for originator/recipient (O/R) addresses to include any type of end user, whether its is a person, an electronic device, or a service. Contrary to the TCP/IP environment, X.400 is in no danger of running out of addresses.

Directory Services. Messaging cannot be designed with only the transport mechanism in mind. It is also necessary to make sure that the location of data and resources are known to users and the network. Mainframe-based mail systems use their own proprietary ways, and the public carrier services have their own subscriber databases. A backbone transport mechanism such as X.400 requires a fully functional directory service. X.500, CCITT's standard for OSI directory service, is structured in a similar way as X.400. The X.500

model provides for a fully scalable information retrieval service applicable not only to X.400 O/R addresses, but also to any network object.

The X.500 logical database is known as the directory information base (DIB) with an internal structure known as the directory information tree (DIT). This logical directory is physically located in a scaleable number of directory service agents (DSAs), as shown in Figure 8.6. X.500 uses a hierarchical directory structure. A user of the directory would access information contained in a DSA through the use of a directory user agent (DUA). When a user wishes to view, modify, or create an entry in the directory, the DUA ensures that the request is correctly formatted. The DUA then accesses one or more DSA servers.

Because the directory can be much larger than is possible to contain within a single DSA, each DSA contains sufficient knowledge to pass a request on to any other DSA that may contain the desired information. The DIB is thus distributed across the network. Information on the DIB is classified as objects, divided into classes. Objects within these classes are stored as entries with a set of attributes, each of which can have one or more values. X.500 associates each attribute with an attribute syntax that makes sure each entry is unique by providing a way of defining the entry's relative position in the DIT hierarchy.

X.500 operates in real time. Any deployment needs to be carefully planned to meet user performance and availability expectations. X.500 has been accepted as an enterprise backbone directory service, in conjunction with existing proprietary directories. X.500 functionality has enabled the development and deployment focus from plain directory protocol implementations to do directory synchronization and integration issues.

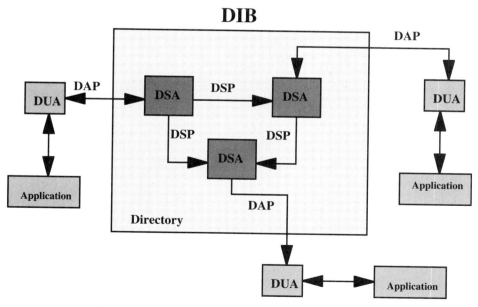

Figure 8.6 A directory services (X.500) functional model.

Directory services provide a look-up function similar to an address or phone directory. Nodes (UAs) on a network have unique addresses. A network directory is a master list of all the nodes on the network. When you add a new node to your network, the system makes a new entry in the directory. When one node must communicate with another node, the system queries the directory.

Directory services applications simplify network administration. With a master directory, you can refer to a remote node with a logical name (i.e., marketing print server) or a nickname (i.e., finance). The master directory translates "marketing print server" into a network address that the network software and hardware understands. Because all or some nodes know how to query the directory, you need only update the directory node instead of every node on the network.

Data Backup/Archival. Data have become the single most valuable asset in a network that changes rapidly. But there is so much of it, spread throughout the network, that it cannot be managed with traditional data administration tools. Workstation networks have enabled the creation of a diverse range of applications capable of processing and generating extremely large amounts of data. Access to massive computing power at the desktop has enabled the creation of distributed applications that once only the largest mainframes could emulate.

As a result, more and more resources are being spent on network storage, but performance, reliability, and data integrity are declining, and user productivity is suffering.

All file servers and most workstations are configured with local disk storage. The demand for more storage has created data management problems that do not exist in the mainframe world. Without adequate tools in the internetworking environment, the data integrity is at risk. Locating data close to the user, and guaranteeing quick access to it, requires a new management approach to network data administration. Ideally, data that must be quickly or frequently accessed by an individual user should be placed on the user's own local storage, while shared data should be placed on a server where it is available to all users. Inactive data should be archived to inexpensive media to free local and shared disk space for more current work, but it must remain on-line, easily available for reference.

To date, there has been very little recognition of the relationship between data storage, backup, and archiving aspects of network data management. Only an integrated approach, that reaches out and manages all aspects of valuable data resources transparently and without human intervention, can ensure virtually continuous smooth operation throughout a network. Some vendors have already started to address these issues to integrated approach for backup and archival of data. Some of such systems offer

- Networkwide hierarchical storage management.
- Networkwide backup and disaster recovery.
- On-line archiving.
- Library management.

File Transfer/Exchange. File transfer is an important network function. You use file transfer to relay the information that the computer stores. Such information can be product documentation, spreadsheets, memos, or graphics. Large files take longer than small ones to transfer across the network. This can result in delays that are not acceptable in today's networking environments. Therefore, we must build applications that allow for parallel file transfer mode.

File transfer and remote file access are two of the most important applications in any network. People who are working together commonly need to share files. One approach is to have a machine where the original of each file is held and have copies transferred to other machines as needed; that is, a server holds all the files, and copies are sent to clients as requested. Another approach is to have each file "live" on the machine where it is created and maintained and have users on other machines ask for copies when they need them. Remote file access is similar to file transfer, except that only pieces of files are read or written rather than entire files.

The techniques used for file transfer and remote file access are similar, since access to a file located on a remote node that has its own users is hardly different from accessing a file on a dedicated *file server* that has no local users. We can simplify it further and assume that files are located on file server machines, with users on client machines who need to transfer these files in whole or in part for reading and/or updating.

The key idea behind the file server concept is that of a *virtual filestore*. The virtual file server provides a standardized interface and a set of standardized operations that the clients can execute. Transfers to and from the virtual filestore use standardized protocols, such as file transfer, access, and management (FTAM), file transfer protocol (FTP), and trivial file transfer protocol (TFTP). By standardizing on a particular virtual filestore, it is possible for application programs to access and transfer remote files without knowing all the details of numerous incompatible file servers.

Every file server has some conceptual model of what a file is. A file server can be characterized by three properties: *file structure*, *file attributes*, and *file operations*.

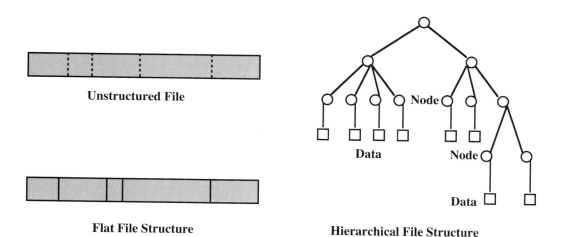

Figure 8.7 File models.

Different servers have different *file structure models* (Figure 8.7). Three models are widely used:

- A file with *unstructured* lump of data nas no substructure. The file server knows nothing of the internal structure of the file; therefore, it can read and/or write *only* the entire file and cannot perform any operations on parts of the file.
- A *flat file* consists of an ordered sequence of records. The records do not need to be of the same size or type. Some or all the records may have labels (keys) associated with them. With these files, it is possible for clients to address specific records, either by their labels or relative positions. This allows the file server to perform operations on individual records such as extending, replacing, or deleting them. A UNIX file can be regarded as a sequence of 1-byte records that are individually addressable by position.
- The most general model of a file is the *hierarchical file*, which is shaped like a tree. Each node of the tree may have a label, a data record, both, or neither. If all the nodes are labeled, a specific node may be addressed by giving its path from the root. The node indices also serve for addressing the entire subtrees.

All files have *attributes* that describe them. Each file must have a name or an identifier, a type, and a size describing how much storage it occupies. Some attributes are created when the file is generated and are frozen, while others can be explicitly changed by user operations, and still others are automatically maintained by the file server(s). Which file attributes are modifiable varies from file server to file server. Some of the file attributes include the following:

- Access control determines who may access the file and how.
- Contents type tells something about the file structure.

File operations can apply to a file as a whole or to its contents. The files operations may be file creation, deletion, selection, opening/closing, reading/updating, reading/changing attributes, locating/reading/inserting/replacing/extending/erasing records, and others.

Network file servers have multiple clients. If two or more clients access the same file at more or less the same time, and each of them issues a request to replace the first record of the file, the file could be corrupted. To avoid this problem, most file servers have implemented *concurrency control* algorithms. The algorithms can take the form of locking mechanisms, known as *shared* or *exclusive locks*. Shared locks are typically used for reading. Exclusive locks are normally used for writing.

Networks often have multiple servers for several reasons:

- To split the workload.
- To allow availability of data even if a server is down.
- To increase reliability by having independent backups of each file.

There are multiple solutions in such situations, such as *replication*. One option is that each user opens accounts with as many file servers as desired and manage the replications. But this creates considerable administrative burden on the user. Another option is to have the file server perform the replication *automatically*. As long as the files are not updated, maintaining multiple copies is easy. The trouble starts when one copy is updated; then the others must be too. There are many a robust techniques for replication, such as *mirroring* and *striping* volumes, or *buffer cache* techniques, which are beyond the scope of this discussion.

There are a number of file transfer protocols and standards. Three of those, nonproprietary protocols, are worth consideration for internetworking:

- The file transfer, access, and management model is the OSI standard and is based on the idea of a virtual filestore that is mapped to a real filestore. FTAM supports only the hierarchical file type, but it is possible to specify constraints that give other types as special cases. In this situation, the structured file can be manipulated as a unit, with no filestore operations. The virtual filestore is connectionless.
- The file transfer protocol is the Internet standard protocol and is used for bulk data transfer from one remote device to another. FTP supports only a stream of data, that is, transfer of the entire files, not selected records within a file. However, FTP can transfer any type of data, binary as well as text.
- Trivial file transfer protocol is also the Internet standard protocol. TFTP uses unreliable datagram service. Like FTP, TFTP also supports a text and binary file transmissions. TFTP is used primarily for downloading of software and configuration files to a diskless workstation.

File Sharing. When every computer in your department or enterprise shared the same architecture and operating system—and was connected by a single-protocol network—cooperation between applications that accessed the same body of data was not too difficult. Today, sharing data over a network is more of a challenge.

File sharing allows a host to act as a file server for a set of clients. From a client point of view, the shared files look like other local disks on the client. However, they are accessed over the network. This setup has the advantage of letting clients access commonly shared files without having to duplicate them locally. It also allows for easier backup of the commonly shared files with the more functional file backup software, commonly available on the server. Several proprietary file sharing systems are available:

- By far the most common is Novell NetWare, which uses an adaptation of the XNS (Xerox Network System) for LAN environment.
- Macintosh uses AppleShare of NFS for Macintosh to UNIX file sharing.
- PC NFS clients enable a PC to share UNIX files as if those files were mounted as a separate file system. Essentially the NFS client translates the filesystem calls into NFS RPC calls and retrieves the files across the network.

Distributed Applications (Using Remote Procedure Call). In recent years, corporate computing has moved from the traditional centralized mainframe toward distributed networks and resource sharing mechanisms. Most of the computing resources sit on people's desks, but other resources are different location locations and must be shared. This has necessitated the evolution of distributed applications. Client/server concepts make efficient use of the network resources. Servers make it possible for users on their desks to share resources and use data and applications on different networks and mainframes.

In the client/server model (Figure 8.8), an application program can be broken into two parts on the network. The front-end portion is run by the clients or the individual users at their desktops and perform such tasks as querying the database, produce a printed report, or enter a new record. These can be executed through Structured Query Language (SQL). The back-end program is resident on a server that is configured to support multiple clients, offering them shared access to numerous application programs as well as other resources such as printers, file storage, database management, communications, and other capabilities.

One of the better known tools for producing distributed applications is the *remote procedure call*. RPCs are conceptually simple. All programs make procedure calls. In a majority of the cases, these procedures are contained within the calling program or are at least located on the same machine. RPCs are procedures located on different machines. They still take parameters and return results. They simply execute on some other machine that is on the network.

For RPCs to work, you need a common format for the calling application and the called procedure and a naming service that lets the application find the proper remote procedure. Less sophisticated RPCs use early binding. More sophisticated systems use late bindings, where a naming service matches calling applications and called procedures at runtime.

The *distributed computing environment* from the Open Software Foundation (OSF) is built on RPCs. With its sophisticated naming, time, and remote file services, DCE allows you to create globe-spanning distributed applications.

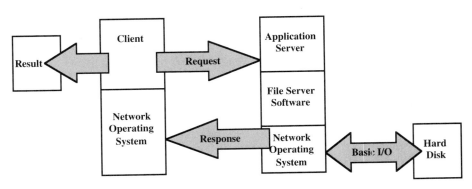

Figure 8.8 The application client/server concepts.

Another innovative solution to building distributed applications over multiple protocol networks is *Pipes*. The Pipes kernel supports a range of operating system and network-transport pairs, such as DOS-IPX, DOS-NetBIOS, NetWare-IPX, NetWare-TCP/IP, OS/2-NetBIOS, SunOS-TCP/IP, AIX, TCP/IP, MVS-LU6.2, and AppleTalk. Written in C, the Pipe's kernel augments each host's native interprocess communication services with a message-oriented peer-networking subsystem. The Pipes application programming interface (API) is common to all supported Pipes platforms. This way, you can build a distributed application for a NetWare LAN without any references to IPX and immediately port it to TCP/IP or NetBIOS LAN. The same distributed application can run in a mixed environment in which DOS-IPX and UNIX-TCP/IP nodes work as peers.

User Applications

Desktop Publishing. One application that is very popular with personal computer users is desktop publishing. Many vendors have their own fonts and structures for these applications. The problem is lack of compatibility among all the equipment types and software utilized by the vendors. Dissimilar operating systems and file formats have led users to integrate their own systems, causing further incompatibilities.

The technical office protocol (TOP) offers one solution to such a dilemma. When used on a high-speed Ethernet network, TOP enables the user to manipulate text and graphics and perform all pre-press functions with ease. The importance of TOP is interoperability between different microprocessor environments (e.g., Macintosh and MS-DOS).

Industrial Applications. The factory of the future is already a partial reality today. With ever-increasing automation, there is a rise in the demands made on systems to transfer data between the steering and controlling elements and the elements controlling automated machine tools, robots, and other production equipment at a logical level and with the utmost reliability. Today, most of the relevant information is handled by humans. This method is neither efficient nor problem free. If, on the other hand, the man-machine communication relationship is implemented by direct networks, it would improve the efficiency and throughput of industrial operations.

Computer-aided design/computer-aided manufacturing (CAD/CAM) are being increasingly utilized on the industry floor. The token bus (802.4) is particularly suited for a factory floor LAN because of its reliability under rugged conditions. The following features become important in such an environment:

- Robust implementation and insensitivity to magnetic or electrical fields.
- Universal basis for communication between very different end devices on the factory floor.
- Provisions for minimum operating capability even in the case of failure of particular components.
- Redundancy to avoid larger and catastrophic failures.
- Decentralized management.

Network Fax. Fax today is incorporated into the office LAN. You can create a document on your workstation that you need to fax. That document can be sent directly to the fax machine as if it were e-mail. If you are using a word processor, you can stay in that application and send the document to the fax machine. On the other hand, if you receive a fax, you will be notified of a pending fax. You can read it on the monitor and even send it to the network printer.

Fax servers can allow users to print files directly to the fax line, eliminating the necessity of getting and walking to the fax machine to push papers into it.

Database. The challenge of the 1990s is to connect disparate computers and operating systems into a unified computing and information sharing network. The fundamental problem is that mainframes, minicomputers, workstations, and PCs run incompatible software. Even when networked together, these computers still cannot cooperate because they cannot share data.

A *distributed database management system* (DBMS) provides transparent data sharing within a network. Transparent data sharing means that data located on any computer in the network are accessed in the same way and with the same ease as if all the data were stored on a single computer. In this way, the distributed DBMSs make a complex network of computers look like a single computer, making the network essentially transparent.

Distributed DBMSs give the organizations the ability to integrate different computers, different operating systems, different networks—even different DBMSs—into a unified computing and data sharing resource. In addition, the distributed DBMSs make it simpler for the applications to be distributed.

Database servers store data that can be specified and retrieved. The client application performs functions on the data and stores the results back in the database, generating reports and invoices or performing other functions. Application functions, such as data manipulation or format translations, are performed by the database server.

Many of the newer client/server applications have taken a different approach than e-mail, viewing the asynchronous flow of data within an organization not as discontinuous messages but as structured exchange of tasks, events, and results. For such applications, moving information from one place to another is not as important as with the ease and speed the users can synthesize that information with the rest of their work at the desktop.

Distributed databases typically use a two-way message store in which master copies of documents, schedules, and so on, reside on a server. The server, in turn, replicates copies of these files, as well as updates as they occur, to the local client machines. Distributed object-oriented databases arbitrate and reconcile complex, evolving information better than traditional file-based, store-and-forward messaging architectures.

INCOMPATIBILITY SOLUTIONS

Software applications are increasingly being written to take advantage of network operating systems. Although older applications were not designed to recognize that additional functions and peripherals may exist, very few of today's applications are incompatible with network operating systems, since they can still work on the workstations in a stand-alone environment.

Multiple Platforms

Integrators looking for ways to deliver networked applications on multiple platforms really need a general-purpose solution. Just as ANSI C adapts to Motorola is 68000, Intel's 80x86, IBM's RS/6000, and Sun's SPARC architectures, and GUI toolkits can work with a Mac, Windows, and Motif, what is needed is a communication layer that handles IPX, NetBIOS, TCP/IP, AppleTalk, LU 6.2, and other protocols.

SQL Compatibility

Cooperative processing in practical terms means common access to a relational database that resides on one or more servers. These servers can be the other workstations, LAN servers, a large minicomputer, or a mainframe. Today, the most popular way to access relational database is via Structured Query Language. SQL is a nonprocedural language used to create and access relational databases. It is supported by all major database engines in one form or another.

With client/server architecture, a number of different applications running on several different (incompatible) platforms can all access a common data repository by sending SQL queries over a network to the database engine. The engine processes the query and returns any resultant data back to the application. By separating front-end applications from the database engine, the client/server scheme allows you to use any application to access the database—even a spreadsheet or a word processor—as long as the application can generate standard SQL queries.

Because SQL is a standard across all types of incompatible platforms (e.g., desktops, minicomputers, and mainframes alike), it has the potential to provide access to large databases from PC-based applications. It is also one of the driving forces behind the downsizing movement, where core corporate applications that formerly ran on mainframes migrate to PC-LAN environments. There are a few obstacles, however. Not all database engines speak the same dialect of SQL, and you must solve the universal connectivity problem before you can implement universal database access. In addition, there are basic security problems that must be solved when you try to integrate networks of PCs with corporate data repository. Despite the obstacles, products such as Microsoft's EXCEL and Lotus 1-2-3 are built with the ability to generate SQL queries, and many companies are providing back-end databases that run PC-based LANs.

SQL connectivity solutions make it possible to share a common database engine, but they are not capable of the more general task of sharing processing among all the computers on the network. In other words, it takes something other than SQL to create network-aware applications. Sharing machine cycles, whether in a peer-to-peer environment or a client/server arrangement, can greatly increase the power and efficiency of a computing environment. An application can take advantage of the computing power of an entire network and access subroutines that reside on any other machine.

APPLICATIONS OF LANS AND WANS

In the context of the development of networks, several application areas have arisen where the use of these systems for high-performance information transfer is especially valuable. Each of these areas has specific characteristics and makes particular demands on the construction of LAN and WAN networks suitable for that area. The areas of application are

- Small LANs, suitable for very localized or departmental networking.
- Large LANs, suitable for more robust connectivity within buildings and campuses.
- WANs that connect the LANs into a global network.
- Hubs and backbones that provide interconnectivity for inter-LANs and between LANs and WANs.

Small LANs

- *ARCnet* is a token-passing protocol and operates only at 2.5 Mbps. It is reliable, economical, and more flexible than Ethernet or token ring LANs.
- *Starlan* topology consists of a central node to which all devices on the network are connected (therefore the application is geographically limited). This topology is familiar in the office environment, where each telephone is ultimately tied into the *private branch exchange (PBX)* .
- *LocalTalk* is Apple's networking hardware and provides very simple device-to-device communication and printer sharing. Network installation and reconfiguration are easy and inexpensive. Gateways can provide connectivity with Ethernet networks.

Large LANs

Ethernet is one of the best known examples of a LAN based on bus topology. The bus topology is contention based, typically operating at a data rate of 10 Mbps. Stations access the network by listening to the network if it is idle. Upon sensing that no traffic is currently on the line, the station is free to transmit. Bus networks are relatively less expensive to install and maintain. Terminals may be added or removed from the network without disrupting service.

Token ring operates at 4 or 16 Mbps in the form of a closed-loop ring. A set of bytes called the *token* is circulated around the ring, giving each station, in sequence, a chance to put information on the network. A token-holding timer controls the maximum amount of time a station can occupy the network before passing the token. At the completion of the information transfer, the station reinserts the token on the ring.

FDDI is a high-speed LAN that employs a counter-rotating token ring technology. FDDI can be characterized in terms of broadband, capable of voice, video, and data transport through packet switching. It is designed to provide high-bandwidth, general-purpose interconnection between computers and peripherals, including the interconnection of LANs and other networks.

100BASE-T, also known as 100 Mbps fast Ethernet offers throughput speeds upto 100 Mbps—and most important, it uses the existing Ethernet technology. Like 10 Mbps Ethernet, 100 Mbps Ethernet can be configured in switched or shared-media implementations and can support half- or full-duplex connections. Full-duplex fast Ethernet switches are capable of increasing the network throughput speeds to 200 Mbit/s. The 100-Mbps specification can run over the existing wiring already in place for 10-Mbps Ethernet. It also runs over fiber optic cabling already installed.

WANs

T1, T3 services are offered at the rates of 1.54 Mbps to 44.736 Mbps, respectively, and typically over fiber facilities. Today, stand-alone bridges, routers, and gateways rule LAN internetworking. While these suffice for connecting into relatively low-speed, simple WANs, it is the T1 and T3 multiplexers that rule the WAN. As T1 hybrids are introduced, the chaotic LAN-to-WAN networks will evolve into more manageable T1 networks. The applications of such networks will dominate

- LAN interconnection.
- High-speed backbone integrating voice, data, video, and image.

X.25 has been the basis for wide area networks for the last 20 plus years, using packet-switching technology on a global basis. However, as we move forward to new technologies, such as ISDN, the role of X.25 may diminish. X.25 is, essentially, an interface between DTE (user of service) and a DCE (provider of service). The mode of operation is packet mode as opposed to circuit mode, where messages are embedded in packets that have distinct beginning and end. The X.25 is dedicated to move "data" only.

ATM is the basis for the transfer of information within broadband network. ATM provides higher-bandwidth, low-delay, packet-like switching, and multiplexing. The viability of ATM as a broadband network is in a state of flux because of a number of reasons, including large investment in narrowband infrastructure.

ISDN is an all-digital communication network that provides a broad range of services. It is a convergence of communications and computers that integrates networks and customer premises equipment. Voice, video, data, facsimile, and record traffic can be transmitted in digital form. The ISDN is essentially a replacement of the analog plant for using standardized access to transmit voice and/or data over a worldwide network (Figure 8.9).

Frame Relay is a connection-oriented, fast-packet data service, conceptually similar to X.25. Unlike X.25, frame relay has only two layers of protocol and relies on higher-layer protocols for end-to-end message assurance.

SMDS is a service specification for a metropolitan area, high-speed data service. SMDS LANs provide a high-throughput and low delay for geographical areas less than 100 km. Any application requiring high-speed data transfer, such as imaging, computer-aided design engineering, publishing, telemedicine, disaster recovery, or financial applications, can benefit from SMDS. SMDS goals are to provide features available in LANs,

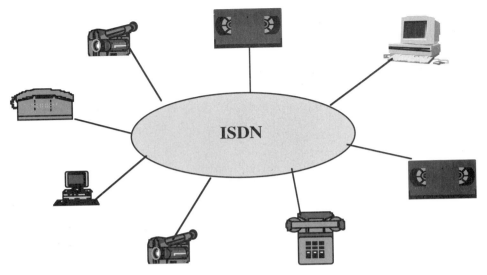

Figure 8.9 ISDN services.

easy integration within existing systems, implement security, and connectionless high-speed packet service.

Hubs and Backbones

Hubs and concentrators are the central elements of LANs based on a star topology, including 10BASE-T Ethernet, 100BASE-T Ethernet, token ring, most Arcnet, and FDDI. In general, when employed in an Arcnet or 10BASE-T Ethernet network, these devices are referred to as hubs. In token ring and FDDI, they are called as MAUs (multistation access units). The hubs are aimed at workgroups whereas high-end concentrators are facility wide devices, capable of connecting many networks—even networks of different types—at a single location. With intelligent hubs, administrators can manage all networks connected to these hubs. Hubs can also regenerate signals and essentially extend LANs allowing topologies that simplify building wiring.

    Backbones are typically used to connect lower-capacity LANs in various locations within a facility. A backbone may also provide for priority routing of certain messages in case of e-mail.

SUMMARY

The network knows no application boundaries. Nearly any application that can run on a stand-alone PC can run on a network. Although some applications, such as database management systems and mainframe gateways, can take better advantage of the benefits LAN has to offer than, for example, word processing can. Many of the benefits distributed applications offer in a networking environment are not that obvious. One succinct advantage is that of downloading, ensuring that all users have the latest version.

Intelligent use of internetworks can result in competitive advantages for companies, governments, and public organizations. The skill to internetwork dissimilar systems has begun to be a valuable job requirement of the future.

The skill and education of information technology workers must be broadened to include an understanding of different vendors' hardware and software. Systems integration skills and the application of the internetworking technologies are more in demand. MIS and telecommunication staffs are expected to be skilled both in technology and management.

By providing a global information highway, network applications finally can deliver on the elusive promise of worker productivity gains through information processing. A knowledgeable worker need no longer be limited to local information sources. Message-based work flow applications are now changing the way organizations operate, and the way they are structured.

EXERCISES

1. Name a few network applications that are prevalent in the enterprise.
2. What is common among most of the network operating systems?
3. Why is SQL becoming a popular means of sharing applications?

9

UNIX INTERNETWORKING

Introduction
Networking with UNIX
  PCs and UNIX Servers
  UNIX Streams
UNIX Facilities
UNIX-to-UNIX Communications
  Terminal Emulation
  X Window System
  Electronic Mail
  File Transfer
  File Sharing
  Remote Procedure Call
UNIX-to-Non-UNIX Communications
  DOS/Windows-to-UNIX Connectivity
  Mac-to-UNIX Connectivity

Mainframe-to-UNIX Connectivity
Desktop-to-UNIX Connectivity with
  Hitachi Data Ssystems' Osiris
VMS-to-UNIX Connectivity
LAN Implementations
  NetWare (Novell)
  LAN Manager (Microsoft)
  VINES (Banyan Systems)
  PathWorks (Digital Equipment)
  OS/2 LAN Manager (IBM)
Internetworking Scenarios
  LAN-LAN Internetworking
  LAN-WAN Internetworking
Summary
Exercises

INTRODUCTION

UNIX has been traditionally viewed as a compute-intensive system best suited for university, government, research, and engineering applications. However, because of rapid changes in business practices and rapid advancements in PC technologies, the very characteristics that once prevented business users from adopting UNIX are now attracting them in droves. Given the explosive development and implementation of network computing, it is not surprising that many users have discovered that UNIX's multitasking and multiprocessing capabilities make it an ideal platform for network applications and distributed processing.

UNIX has become an integral part of enterprisewide open computing strategies. Organizations are finding that UNIX offers price/performance advantages, scalability from PCs to mainframes, and purchasing alternatives from multiple vendors. As organizations include UNIX in their overall strategies, it is essential that they have the facilities to connect UNIX systems with the rest of the organization's computers, so that data and applications may be shared.

While UNIX has built in communications features to connect to other UNIX implementations, connecting UNIX to non-UNIX platforms has traditionally been challenging, to say the least. Over the past few years, however, technology has emerged to make connectivity much easier than ever before. A host of UNIX communications products can now unite different UNIX implementations, as well as integrate UNIX into MS-DOS, Macintosh, VMS, and mainframe environments. In particular, open architectures such as Sun's open network computing (ONC) and OSF's distributed computing environment (DCE) are beginning to replace the limited file transfer and terminal emulation utilities commonly in use today.

Because UNIX has the power to handle complex networking applications and users can now buy PCs capable of supporting a full-UNIX environment, UNIX directly competes with such high-performance PC operating systems as Microsoft's Windows, Windows NT, IBM's OS/2, and Apple Macintosh Systems.

In this section, we will explore UNIX communications with a look at basic UNIX networking, UNIX-to-UNIX and UNIX–to–non-UNIX communications and utilities. We will also discuss connectivity scenarios for integrating UNIX into MS-DOS, X-Windows, Apple Macintosh, Digital VMS, IBM mainframe, and other proprietary environments.

NETWORKING WITH UNIX

Networks play an important role in today's information age. The need to share information and resources makes networks a necessity in almost any computing environment. The speed and capabilities of some networks today are so great that a general user may use the network constantly without even knowing it. Terminals, modems, and serial lines have but all been replaced by diskless workstations and high-speed network connections.

UNIX is a multiuser, multitasking operating system, written in C language. UNIX structure has three fundamental parts: the kernel, the shell and utilities, and the applications. UNIX essentially comprises three facilities (Figure 9.1):

1. *Kernel*, the nucleus of UNIX operations. The kernel is the operating system. The kernel provides services such as file system, memory management, CPU scheduling, and device I/O for programs. Typically, the kernel interacts directly with the underlying hardware, but there are some implementations of UNIX where the UNIX kernel interacts with another operating system that in turn controls the hardware.

2. *Shell or user interface.* A UNIX shell is a program that sits between an interactive user and the kernel. Typical shells are command line interpreters that read commands from a user at a terminal (or from a file) and execute the commands. The UNIX shells are more than command line interpreters—they are programming languages. One or more shells are typically found on a UNIX system:

   • The Bourne shell: */bin/sh*—is found on almost every UNIX system.

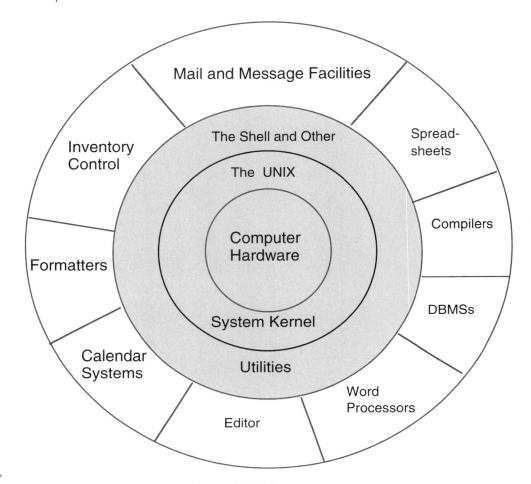

Figure 9.1 UNIX structure.

- The Korn Shell: */bin/ksh*—is a newer replacement for the Bourne shell and contains features not in the Bourne shell, such as command line editing.
- The C shell: */bin/csh*—is usually found on 4.3 BSD (Berkeley Software Distribution) systems.

3. *File system,* the operating system directory. Every UNIX file, directory, or special file has a file name. Every file has many attributes. A directory is a special type of a file that the kernel maintains, since only the kernel can modify directories.

Through the UNIX file system, for example, users can copy, delete, print, rename, display the contents of a file, or check disk space. Although the acronyms used to activate each function may differ, most UNIX facilities correspond to those used in other operating systems.

The UNIX system has been a favorite development bed for networks because of its simplicity, scalability, and interoperability. Today, only a few UNIX systems exist without some network connection. In fact, almost all UNIX systems offer some sort of interconnectivity solutions.

There are many UNIX versions and flavors in use today (Figure 9.2). Three versions are predominant:

* AT&T UNIX System V.
* Berkeley Software Distribution or 4.3 BSD.
* OSF/1.

The Common Open Software Environment (COSE), composed of major software vendors, has the potential to bring unity to the divided UNIX market. COSE is focusing

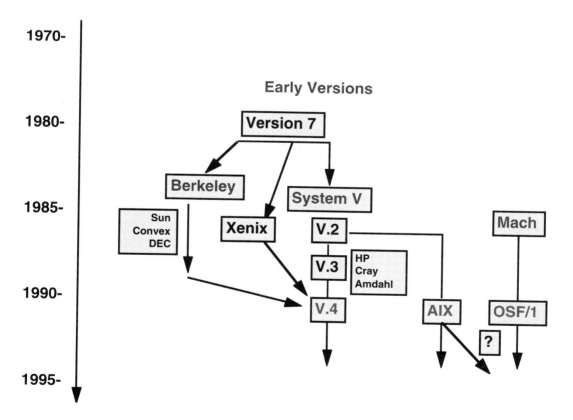

Figure 9.2 Evolution of UNIX.

on the UNIX industry's most pressing issues, including networking, the desktop environment, graphics, multimedia, object technology, and systems management.

PCs and UNIX Servers

UNIX-based servers provide network capabilities that allow PCs connected to the server to communicate directly with the UNIX system as well as with one another. The primary advantage of a UNIX server is that it provides all the benefits of UNIX plus the communications and resource sharing benefits of a PC network. In addition, the UNIX server–based network has more capacity than a PC-based network, supporting many times the number of users than by a non-UNIX networking device.

Since the UNIX operating system provides scalability, a UNIX server (Figure 9.3) can be implemented on any type of system, from a PC to a supercomputer. This hardware flexibility and portability make it a perfect fit for sites that want to scale down their system platforms, such as a mainframe to a workstation or simply use the mainframe as a super file server. There are two major types of UNIX servers:

- *Reduced instruction set computer (RISC) systems*, initially developed by IBM and popularized by Sun Microsystems, were specifically developed to run UNIX using algorithms that scale down the processing requirements. Because of these characteristics,

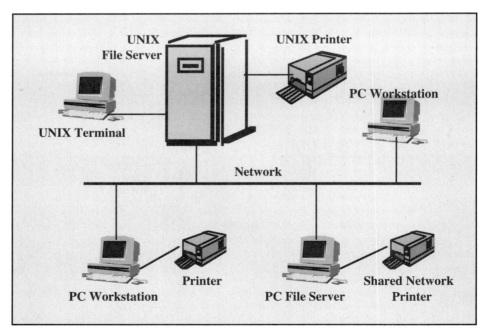

Figure 9.3 UNIX servers.

RISC-based servers outperform PC-based UNIX servers. At the high-end, RISC super-servers employing multiprocessing architectures have even outperformed mainframe systems in various benchmark tests.

- *PC-based servers* use the Intel processors that are typically found in commercial PCs. With the introduction of powerful new PC processing chips such as Intel Pentium, Digital's Alpha, and IBM/Apple PowerPC, and the next generation of even more powerful chips, PC-based UNIX servers may soon rival RISC servers in capacity and performance. In general, network administration is simpler and user training can be more comprehensive if the server type matches the majority of the workstations.

As noted, UNIX server processing can be enhanced through multiprocessing, which can also be asymmetric, with each processor handling a particular type of processing, or it can be symmetric, with processing tasks spread out evenly among the processors. Both PC- and RISC-based systems can be multiprocessors.

In terms of enhanced security, most UNIX systems now offer limited user identification and password checking. In addition, some systems offer security techniques known as "firewalls" that monitor data movement and verify user identification and authorization before allowing data to pass. While security in UNIX systems has improved, it is still one of the operating system's biggest weaknesses.

UNIX Streams

UNIX Streams is a modular component that provides a set of tools for developing UNIX system communications services ranging from complete networking protocol suites to individual device drivers. *Modularity* is one of the most distinctive components of streams. Streams modules reside in the kernel of the UNIX operating system and offer a set of processing functions and associated service interfaces. At the user level, a system programmer can select and interconnect specific modules to provide valid processing sequences. Kernel programming, assembly, and link editing are not required to create interconnection. The benefits of streams modularity include support for

- User-level programs that are independent of underlying protocols and physical communications media.
- Various network architectures and higher-level protocols that are independent of underlying protocols, drivers, and physical communication media.
- Higher-level services that can be created easily by selecting and connecting lower-level services and protocols.
- Enhanced portability of protocol modules to other hardware/software environments resulting from Streams' well-defined structure and interface standards.
- Multitasking for processing interleaved data streams, such as those that occur in IBM SNA, X.25, and Microsoft Windows environments.
- Support for asynchronous operation and user processes to allow Streams' operations to be performed efficiently from the user level.

- Error and trace loggers for debugging and administering modules and drivers.

Streams provides a way for an application to submit messages directly to a transport module. If the transport modules at the network transport layer are developed to accept the same type of messages, the application program can choose the most appropriate transport stack to get the job done. This enables a message to establish links, for example, on both TCP/IP and Novell's SPX transport modules.

Within the UNIX kernel, Streams defines standard interfaces for character I/O, which are also applicable to the kernel and the rest of the UNIX system. The mechanism is simple and open ended, consisting of a set of system calls, kernel resources, and kernel utility routines. This mechanism permits modular, portable development and easy integration of higher-performance network services and their components. Therefore, the network programmers can focus full attention on network applications development without getting bogged down with lower-layer network mechanics.

UNIX FACILITIES

UNIX uses a number of basic facilities to support networking. We will discuss a few in detail that are more commonly used in UNIX communications. These facilities are

- Daemons.
- Files.
- Pseudoterminals.
- Signals.
- Message queues.
- Semaphores.
- Pipes.
- Sockets.
- Streams.
- Transport level interface.

A *daemon* is a process that executes *in the background* (without an associated terminal or login shell). Daemons do useful work but are hidden from the casual observer. Daemons are fired up at boot time or are fired up by other daemons. Functions of daemons are manifold. In networks, daemons are used to connect the actual network with the process using network facilities. For example, *inetd* process listens to the network on one side and user processes on the other.

The line printer has a daemon process that is waiting for a request to print a file on a line printer. In the same way, a remote login program that allows users to login to one system from another on the network would have a daemon process that waits for a request to come across the network for someone to login.

In case of LAN Manager/X, the daemon process is the first process to run. It is responsible for loading and maintaining the server configuration data and remains active until the server is shut down. In addition, the daemon process established a shared memory pool that is used to communicate with all other active processes and especially workers. The daemon is also responsible for initiating and terminating client connections.

Files in UNIX are stream oriented as opposed to message oriented. Files normally live on the disk which may be local or remote. Files can be opened, closed, read, or written. Files can be partially or fully locked.

Pseudoterminals are used by TCP/IP and other network entities. They allow a daemon connected to the network to talk to a user process. Pseudoterminals live in the */dev* directory and are often referred to as *pty*.

Signals are used to send an asynchronous interrupt from one process to another and provide a low overhead interprocess communication. A signal is a notification to a process that an event has occurred. Signals are sometimes called *software interrupts*. There are a number of different signals, and each has a specific meaning. Networking uses the *sigurg* signal with sockets for out-of-band data. User processes can catch, ignore, or take default action on any signal.

Message queues are used to pass data at memory speeds. These pass messages rather than streams. Multiple processes can share a message queue. A process can both read and write messages to the queue. A host can have many message queues.

Semaphores are used to control networking synchronization. The primary use of semaphores is to synchronize the access to shared memory segments. Semaphores give a process access to a resource and prevent all other processes having access to that resource. For multiple resources, semaphore operations are atomic.

Pipes are medium-speed IPC devices. They provide one-way flow of data, but both ends of the pipe must be connected to processes.

Sockets facilitate interconnection between layers and provide an endpoint for communication. Sockets support various communication semantics:

- *STREAM* is a sequenced, two-way communication based on byte streams with out-of-band transmission (similar to pipes).
- *DGRAM* for connectionless datagrams to send unreliable messages of fixed dimension.
- *RAW* provides access to internal network interfaces, under superuser only.

Streams provide a full-duplex connection between a user process and a device driver. Streams were developed at AT&T because the character I/O system was not adequate or efficient enough to support networking. Streams live within the kernel (Figure 9.4).

The *transport level interface (TLI)* allows processes on the same or different systems to communicate (as with sockets). TLI provides an interface between the user process and the transport provider or transport endpoint. TLI is implemented using "streams" (Figure 9.5).

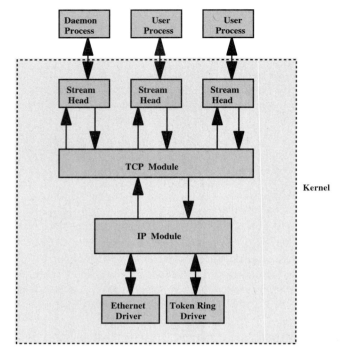

Figure 9.4 Possible streams implementation of TCP/IP.

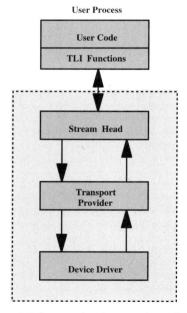

Figure 9.5 Streams implementation of TLI.

UNIX-TO-UNIX COMMUNICATIONS

UNIX users can take advantage of powerful utilities and applications to help them connect disparate UNIX systems as well as connect UNIX with proprietary systems. Many of these utilities are built into UNIX systems, while others are available from third-party vendors. This section examines the major categories of communications utilities and applications typically used in UNIX installations. They include the following:

- Terminal emulation.
- X Windows.
- Electronic mail.
- File transfer.
- File sharing.
- Remote procedure call.
- Network management.

Terminal emulation and application binary interfaces are widely used UNIX technologies. X Windows emerged to support multisession communications. File sharing and remote procedure calls go a step further by supporting distributed computing. Electronic mail may be the most familiar form of communication and continues to grow in popularity. Network management systems are emerging to manage network traffic and applications.

Terminal Emulation

Terminal emulation, virtual terminal, and remote login utilities allow UNIX users access to remote systems. Terminal emulation software allows you to make a connection from your PC serial port to a UNIX host. The connection can be hard-wired cable or remote modem. When the connection has been made, terminal emulation software lets your PC act as if it were a terminal directly connected to the UNIX host.

Remote login (rlogin) allows a remote UNIX user to log in to another remote terminal, giving the user access to remotely located files and applications. Remote login utilities are rather limited, in that they only support one type of operating system. For example, *rlogin*, which is integrated into BSD, is supported almost exclusively by Berkeley UNIX systems.

Similar to remote login is remote command execution, which allows a user at a local terminal to execute commands on a remote UNIX system. BSD includes the *rsh* utility for remote command execution, similar to IBM's remote job entry (RJE).

The *rsh* and *rlogin* commands are confined to UNIX systems on a LAN. For wide area dial-up connections, UNIX provides the call UNIX or *cu* command, which connects a terminal to a remote UNIX system through a modem. Once the connection is established, the user can transfer files between the local and remote systems and use remote applications. However, *cu* is very slow and prone to transmission errors. On the other hand, the

UUCP command includes an automatic dialer for WAN connections plus automatic login to the remote systems.

Terminal emulation is the traditional UNIX solution to connect heterogeneous systems with incompatible terminals, and is still being widely used. Terminal emulation programs allow a UNIX user access to a remote non-UNIX host computer or a PC user access to a remote UNIX host. Terminal emulators translate local terminal-specific characteristics into a format that the foreign system can understand. This gives users access to remotely located applications and files on disparate systems.

Terminal emulation programs support a limited, specific set of proprietary terminal types. For example, a given terminal emulation package may allow a Sun workstation running Sun SOLARIS to appear as an IBM 3270 terminal, to access an IBM mainframe or a VT100 terminal, or to access a digital computer, but it may not support Apple Macintosh emulation; however, this is overcome via the TCP/IP or OSI virtual terminal programs.

Virtual terminal programs translate terminal-specific characteristics into a generic format that can be understood by a potentially unlimited number of terminal types. The most well-known UNIX virtual terminal program is TELNET, which runs over TCP/IP protocols. TELNET implementations at both the sending (client) and receiving (server) terminals translate local terminal types into standard TELNET network representation. To communicate, each end requires only what is known locally.

Terminal emulation and virtual terminals create significant communications overhead, affecting response times and the inability to share application processing and database access or to use data files simultaneously between local and remote systems. The use of the two systems is mutually exclusive; that is, the terminal is either in local or remote mode.

X Window System

X Window system manages graphics over UNIX networks and is used for connectivity for graphics-based UNIX applications. X Windows overcome mutually exclusive system access by allowing a user to simultaneously view both local and remote applications on multiple windows of a terminal screen. X products are usually bundled with one or more terminal emulation programs, such as VT100 and VT200, to support windowing capabilities into non-X Window environments.

Electronic Mail

UNIX operating systems are bundled with e-mail functions to send and receive text messages. E-mail supports short text-based communications between users, as opposed to bulk data transfer. E-mail software, generally, is not well suited for large file transfers, as it lacks error checking and flow control features of large mainframe operating systems. However, it is extremely useful in communicating relatively brief messages. Two forms of e-mail and two forms of information services are available for UNIX systems—SMTP, X.400, Usenet, and Internet.

The *Simple Mail Transfer Protocol (SMTP)* is widely used in thousands of TCP/IP e-mail environments. SMTP travels over TCP/IP to any remote SMTP receiver and supports e-mail exchange between users on the same host or between hosts over a network. SMTP sets up the TCP connection, transfers the message, and terminates the TCP connection.

ISO's emerging *X.400* resembles SMTP, but supports a much richer functionality such as non-ASCII message types.

Usenet is an informal network of UNIX sites. Usenet provides a forum for group discussions to thousands of UNIX users around the world. Usenet runs over UUCP and is available free. Backbone sites, typically universities or research organizations, are responsible for distributing news groups to local sites in their regions. A backbone site may choose to distribute or suppress a particular news group.

The Internet and the world wide web (WWW) is an internetwork consisting of hundreds of thousands of hosts in most countries, making a central hub for global electronic mail interconnection to more than 100 million people. The Internet comprised four networks in the United States: Milnet (U.S. Defense Communication Agency network), NSInet (connecting NASA test centers and laboratories), ESnet (Energy Science network), and NSFnet (National Science Foundation network connecting universities and governmental agencies). Most businesses have established their own networks connected to the Internet and it is still growing.

File Transfer

File transfer programs support bulk data transfer between remote systems, often with added features such as error checking, flow control, and unattended file transfer. However, it does not support cooperative application processing or simultaneous access to a file by multiple computers over a distributed network. Thus a user running a local application must transfer the entire remote file to the local system before the application can use the file. To make the transfer, the user must know details about the device where the file is stored and the file transfer request commands expected by the remote system. UNIX file transfer is usually a slow process.

There are two commonly used file transfer utilities: UNIX-to-UNIX Copy Utility (UUCP) and File Transfer Protocol (FTP).

The first UNIX networking application was UUCP (UNIX-to-UNIX Copy) program, and all its associated commands. UUCP is a batch-oriented system, as opposed to interactive processing, that is typically used between UNIX systems with dial-up telephone lines or systems that are directly connected. Its major uses are for software distribution (file transfer), remote execution, maintenance, administration, and electronic mail. UUCP is still as widely used as UNIX networking application. When the CPU is free, UUCP delivers the file to the remote system.

UUCP consists of several commands: *uucp* requests a file to be sent from one machine to another, *uucico* performs the actual transfer of files, *uux* requests execution on a remote machine, and *uuxqt* actually executes the command. In other words, UUCP is a collection of processes that include both file transfer and remote command execution.

UUCP can be used on standard asynchronous phone lines and modems as well as in LANs and WANs. It is well suited for data transfer over telephone lines. Its major drawback is that it is somehow slow and not suited for exchanging information in both directions simultaneously. UUCP is bundled with virtually all UNIX systems, so the user has a built-in access to this utility and thus the system.

File Transfer Protocol is a TCP/IP application that transfers files between different types of computers and operating systems (UNIX as well as non-UNIX). FTP supports three basic modes which specify file type (record or nonrecord structure), data type (ASCII or EBCDIC), and transmission method. FTP is widely used in TCP/IP environments. FTP is an important vehicle for integrating UNIX into MS-DOS and other non-UNIX environments.

File Sharing

File sharing or *distributed file access* allows the users to interactively access files located in specified directories on remote systems. Distributed file systems shield users from details, such as what device the remote file resides on and what file transfer commands that service expects. The most popular standards for distributed file access in UNIX environments are Sun's Network File System (NFS), the Andrew File System (AFS), and AT&T's Remote File System (RFS). File sharing provides the following advantages:

- Maximum use of system resources afforded by distributing the work load among available systems.
- Transparent user access to all computing resources, making it easier to share information quickly.

Network file system is a multivendor networking tool that runs independent of the underlying operating systems. Developed by Sun Microsystems and then placed in the public domain, NFS supports large and diverse networks, including those consisting of UNIX, MS-DOS, Xenix, Digital's VMS and ULTRIX, and IBM's AIX and VM. NFS integrates an unlimited number of clients. Rather than forcing users to log on to specific servers as is common in non-UNIX LANs, NFS clients directly access the network. Once access to the network is established, clients can choose access to servers.

Basically, the NFS protocol is a library of remote procedures that can be used to connect to remote files on like or unlike computers. The NFS RPC protocol contains several procedures. Each one operates on either a file or a file system object. These procedures can be grouped into several directory operations such as *mkdir* and *rmdir,* linking the UNIX link operations; and file system operations, such as mounting and unmounting a file system.

NFS is highly dependent on two other services also developed by Sun: Remote Procedure Call (RPC) and eXternal Data Representation (XDR). RPC is much like a local procedure call in regard to how it behaves and how it is used. With RPC, a local routine can call and bind to a remote service. In addition, RPC uses another set of procedures called the XDR library. The XDR accounts for inconsistencies in the internal data of various hardware platforms. XDR provides a standard data representation that all computers can understand.

NFS's main limitation is that it is optimized for the LAN environment and currently it is not well suited for file access across wide area networks. On the other hand, Digital's DECnet and Andrew File System contain features that support WAN file access, including the capability to support non-UNIX as well as UNIX systems, and an authentication/directory scheme to control access to distributed files.

Andrew File System is designed to share file access for up to 10,000 workstations and is built upon Sun's Vnode interface as well as an RPC mechanism called Rx. Rx supports a modular authentication scheme and an enhanced RPC interface for interprocess communications.

Remote File System is a UNIX-specific system that provides remote device access. However, RFS is restricted to UNIX implementation only, limiting its usefulness in today's multivendor, multioperating system environments. Like NFS, RFS extends the standard UNIX file system to accommodate distributed file access. In this case, ordinary files are "remote mounted" to a local directory. Once this process is accomplished, remote (networked) files appear to the user just like local files, unless there is a network failure or a physical problem with the remote storage device. RFS is implemented using Streams and remote system calls from the local UNIX kernel.

Remote Procedure Call

The objective of the distributed computing is to maximize the efficiency of applications processing—even if it means breaking up the applications into pieces and using different machines across the network to process each piece. To accomplish this, a remote procedure call mechanism is used in addition to the file sharing systems such as NFS and AFS. Just as file sharing systems make remote files appear as if they were local, RPC makes procedures residing on remote systems appear as if they reside within the locally stored software program.

There are two competing distributed file systems today: Sun's transport-independent (TI) RPC and HP/Apollo's Network Computing System (NCS). Both of these accomplish the same results with some subtle differences. The Open Software Foundation (OSF) has chosen NCS as the core technology for its distributed computing environment. TI RPC, along with NFS, form the backbone of Sun's widely accepted open network computing.

An RPC is a programming instruction that executes a procedure on a remote system. By exploiting a concept of "calling a procedure" and by providing an interface on top of the network transport, the RPC allows developers to write distributed applications and services without being overly aware of the mechanisms of the communications procedure.

The ONC RPC also supports data translations for heterogeneous networking through the use of eXternal Data Representation. ONC RPC also supports connection-oriented and connectionless network transport protocols (TCP and UDP sockets) over LANs and WANs. Since transport independence is important in the heterogeneous environments, TI RPC is implemented on top of the transport layer interface and provides runtime transport independence.

UNIX–TO–NON-UNIX COMMUNICATIONS

In today's demanding business computing environment, the world of UNIX-to-PC connectivity has grown to include full networks based on UNIX file servers and support MS-DOS PCs (Figure 9.6), Macintoshes, and even PCs running powerful new versions of workstation UNIX.

Figure 9.6 illustrates a UNIX–to–non-UNIX connectivity configuration that uses multiple protocol stacks on the host system to accommodate various network operating systems. This approach places the burden of supporting different protocols on the host, which can afford the extra memory and CPU overhead incurred by multiple stacks. Each workstation, on the other hand, needs only one protocol stack.

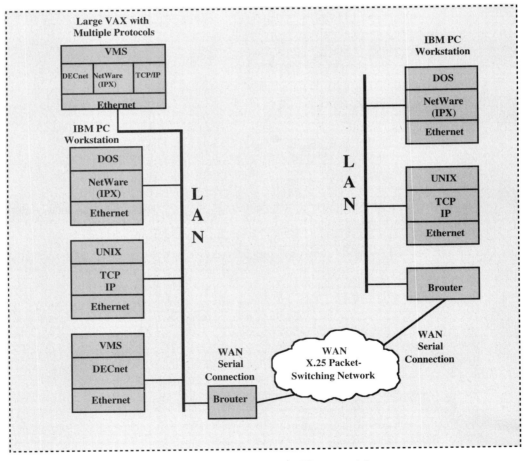

Figure 9.6 UNIX–to–non-UNIX connectivity.

DOS/Windows–to–UNIX Connectivity

A huge number of organizations have made significant investments in Macintoshes and DOS- and Windows-based applications. Many of these organizations are now in the process of integrating their Macintosh and DOS applications with their UNIX systems. With over 80 million DOS- and Windows-based PCs installed worldwide, DOS-to-UNIX connectivity is a matter of necessity.

Non-Networking Solutions. The nonnetworking solutions integrate DOS and UNIX, but do not support the wider functionality of the networking solutions such as peripheral sharing, e-mail, remote job execution, file transfer, or file sharing between different machines.

Existing Applications: Many DOS/Windows-based commercial applications have been ported to UNIX. While these applications give UNIX users the advantage of familiar DOS applications, data are not always very compatible between the UNIX and DOS versions. Examples of successful software applications that have been ported to both UNIX and DOS/Windows include database packages such as dBASE, Informix, and Oracle; spreadsheets such as Lotus 1-2-3; and word processing software such as MS Word and WordPerfect.

Software Emulation: Creating an emulation to run DOS applications on UNIX machines is a relatively simple solution. Using software emulation products, a workstation user can run several DOS applications simultaneously or run UNIX programs under a DOS shell, allowing users unfamiliar with UNIX to operate in a more familiar DOS environment. Users can jump between DOS and UNIX without rebooting.

Application binary interfaces (ABIs) do essentially the same thing as emulation software and allow UNIX users to run Windows applications. SunSoft's new WABI product eliminates the limitations of software emulation's drain on system resources and reduced application performance by translating function calls made by a Windows application into those recognizable by X Windows.

Plug-in Boards Allowing UNIX Machines to Run DOS: This option provides the simplicity of software emulation at improved speeds.

Plug-in Boards Allowing DOS PCs to Run UNIX Workstation Applications: In general, the UNIX RISC application does not run as fast on DOS as it does on UNIX workstations.

Networking Solutions. Implementing a network is a complex way to integrate DOS/Windows and UNIX, however, this is the only way to achieve large-scale resource sharing and communications between systems. There are two major approaches for networking DOS and UNIX:

- Add UNIX file servers to DOS/Windows local area networks.
- Modify PC to communicate in a UNIX-based Ethernet network.

While both approaches achieve similar results, the fundamental architectures are quite different.

UNIX File Server to DOS/Windows LANs: Most PC LANs have a logical star topology, with a central server governing access to all disk drives, printers, and other resources. Communications between PCs must first pass through the server. Novell NetWare and Microsoft LAN Manager are two popular LAN network operating systems supporting this configuration.

Both Novell and Microsoft have developed LAN operating systems that keep the DOS environment intact while allowing DOS users to take advantage of UNIX's e-mail, file sharing, and remote access. While slightly different, each creates a LAN where DOS-based PCs access a UNIX file server. The UNIX machine acts as the server, files appear as an extra disk drive under DOS, and the PCs can use printers or other resources attached to the UNIX server.

Microsoft's LAN Manager for UNIX adds communications protocols to each PC so that it can tie into a UNIX server. One advantage of this approach is that each PC can also talk directly with any other UNIX system without going through the server. In contrast, NetWare for UNIX modifies the UNIX server (host) to support access from DOS-based PCs. Under NetWare for UNIX, PC traffic must go through the server before reaching any other UNIX machines.

Communication with UNIX-Based Networks: In contrast to server-based PC LANs, UNIX-based Ethernet networks are usually peer to peer. Unlike DOS, UNIX is a multitasking system, thus eliminating the dependence on a central server for access to shared resources such as files, printers, and applications.

Individual PCs can tie into UNIX networks using a combination of hardware and software. The hardware includes Ethernet adapter cards that fit into the PC expansion slot, supporting lower-layer connectivity. The networking and network application software may include TCP/IP and related applications (FTP, TELNET, SMTP, and SNMP) plus NFS, or specialized/proprietary terminal emulation software.

DOS/UNIX Networking Software: Once lower-level connectivity is established, networking software and network applications must be used to facilitate e-mail, terminal emulation, file transfer, file sharing, and other communications functions. Terminal emulation provides PC users access to UNIX and initiate program execution, share files, and send e-mail. However, terminal emulation is often awkward and slow, and it does not support distributed processing on file sharing.

TCP/IP software is an increasingly popular alternative to proprietary terminal emulation, supported on virtually all hardware systems today. In addition to providing transport and network layer communications, most TCP/IP packages include FTP for file transfer, SMTP for e-mail, TELNET for virtual terminal emulation, and Simple Network Management Protocol (SNMP) for network management support. Another popular add-on to TCP/IP is an NFS capability to allow file sharing between DOS and UNIX systems.

Mac-to-UNIX Connectivity

Apple has always provided connectivity support for the Macintosh. However, the integration of Mac workgroups into UNIX environments has been relatively slow, primarily due to the closely guarded proprietary nature of the Mac operating system. The availability of Mac-to-UNIX connectivity solutions are beginning to accelerate as Apple expands communications tools to provide Apple services for UNIX engines tailored for IBM, HP, and Sun Microsystems platforms. This allows the workstation users to run Macintosh applications without modification.

Nonnetworking Solutions. Stand-alone integration approaches are used to create the popular Macintosh interface on a UNIX system, as follows:

- *Install both System 7 and A/UX on one Mac:* A/UX is Apple's version of UNIX System V for Mac users. When both operating systems are on the same machine, users can window back and forth between A/UX and System 7 applications.
- *Create software emulation to run Mac applications on UNIX machines:* MacOS software emulators for UNIX are rare, since Apple aggressively maintains exclusive control over MacOS technology. However, new emulators that use a portable implementation of the Mac API, especially for Mac-based Microsoft Word and Excel. This allows Mac System 7 source and binary code applications to run directly on RISC systems.

Networking Solutions. Mac-to-UNIX networking takes the form of connecting Macs to UNIX servers or more commonly, connecting Macs to a UNIX-based Ethernet network, either individually or by hooking on an entire LocalTalk LAN. LocalTalk is the lower layer of the Macintosh LAN, serving the same function as Ethernet. The AppleTalk protocol suite runs over LocalTalk, as does the AppleShare network file server and other communications software. Apple's System 7 operating system includes Macintosh File Sharing, a program that allows any networked Mac to act as a nondedicated server.

- *Run UNIX servers on an AppleTalk LAN:* Some vendors offer software that runs a UNIX host into an AppleShare file server.
- *Connect Macs into Ethernet:* There are two options for tying Mac to a UNIX-based Ethernet network:
  - Connecting each Mac individually is an inexpensive and straightforward solution for connecting later model Macs with expansion slots. An Ethernet adapter card is plugged into the slot; cards support connections to either thin or thick coax or twisted pairs. Additional Mac/UNIX networking software is required, however, to allow file sharing, e-mail, and other basic communications between the Mac and any UNIX machines on the Ethernet network.

    These connections consist of LocalTalk-to-Ethernet bridges and additional software. The bridge typically resides in an external box that sits between the LocalTalk and Ethernet. The additional software translates AppleTalk to TCP/IP or some other protocol. It can also provide a bridging function from AppleTalk data link layer into Ethernet and between Apple filing protocols and NFS. But the users are restricted to AppleTalk speed, with slower response times.

There are a number of popular gateways that provide connectivity between LocalTalk and Ethernet networks, including those for routing messages between LocalTalk, TCP/IP, and DECnet. There are others that route traffic on broadband and fiber optic networks as well as between LocalTalk and Ethernet. The hardware system is capable of running TCP/IP implementations, which include word processing, file transfer, and other applications that provide a Mac interface to UNIX and VAX/VMS systems.

- *Run Mac/UNIX networking software:* Once Macs are on Ethernet, additional software is required to support file sharing and other communications functions. The most widely used implementations of TCP/IP for Mac is Apple's MacTCP. In addition, NFS/Share allows Mac users to access remote NFS filesystems.

Mac connectivity using X Windows is also increasing, allowing users to run Mac applications on a UNIX workstation or X terminal. This is accomplished by installing X server software on the X terminal or the UNIX workstation and X client on the Mac. Users can bring up the Mac applications in an X Window and output on the X terminal. For performance reasons, both the Mac and the X terminal should be on Ethernet network. The major benefit for such an arrangement is that a user does not need both a Mac and a UNIX station on each desk. To provide connectivity in Sun environments, Sun offers an X server software for connectivity with Mac.

Other software allows Mac to run as an X server, which even allows the users to run DECwindows, xterm, FTP file transfers, and other X applications remotely from the Mac.

Mainframe-to-UNIX Connectivity

IBM mainframes continue to be important platforms for UNIX connectivity (Figure 9.7). Mainframes continue to house legacy, mission-critical data, while organizations' rightsizing and downsizing initiatives are moving less critical applications and processing to UNIX or other servers and PC desktops. Therefore, UNIX-to-IBM connectivity is important. There are a wide variety of scenarios available for such connectivity, but connecting UNIX systems to IBM mainframes is proving to be a difficult task.

The primary obstacle in UNIX-to-IBM connectivity is that IBM's Systems Network Architecture (SNA) is essentially different from UNIX's TCP/IP. Beginning with basic topologies, SNA is hierarchical, whereas TCP/IP is peer-to-peer. Most large system installations are running both TCP/IP and SNA, and TCP/IP is beginning to move ahead of SNA as the principal transport protocol in large system shops. IBM's new Advanced Peer-to-Peer Network (APPN) Protocol, is beginning to displace both the traditional SNA and TCP/IP as the primary protocol for large systems.

IBM Solutions. There are a variety of solutions that can provide UNIX-to-IBM connectivity. AIX/6000 provides the server capabilities and connectivity between the LAN environments and the mainframe. AIX operating system includes support for TCP/IP and related protocols, including NFS, YP, and RPC. Some of the solutions are

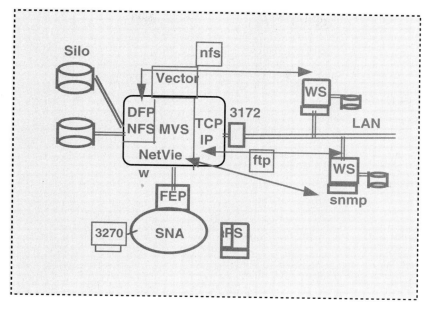

Figure 9.7 An IBM mainframe connectivity.

- Advanced peer-to-peer Networking.
- UNIX-based AIX operating systems to mainframe.
- UNIX-workstation to OSF/1-based Osiris on mainframe.
- AIX 3270 host connection program.
- AIX SNA Services/6000.
- AIX 3278/79 Emulation/6000.
- IBM 3270 emulator for the X window system.

Advanced Peer-to-Peer Networking. APPN is a distributed networking feature that IBM has incorporated into SNA for optimized communications routing between devices. APPN has simplified the process of adding workstations and systems to a network, enabling users to transmit data and messages more quickly. APPN also supports transparent sharing of applications in a distributed computing environment. IBM addresses key network paradigms with APPN as follows:

- Multiprotocol networking, using a wide variety of networking protocols for exchanging information. Some examples are Internet Packet Exchange (IPX), Xerox Services Internet Transport (XNS), AppleTalk, DECnet, and SNA.
- Subnetworking pieces of larger networks, such as bridged token ring local area network connections enabling distributed management functions. Additional subnetworks

include Ethernet LANs and wide area networks using frame relay transport services and eventually ATM.

- Systems management in both a distributed and centralized manner, under the SystemView umbrella, encompassing all management disciplines, such as problem, change, configuration, and performance.
- Multivendor application support and services extending the reach of different applications throughout the network environment and enabling the user to freely access and share information. These diverse application services include
  - Remote procedure call, distributed processing requests over an entire network.
  - Support for OSF's distributed computing environment.
  - Message queuing, suited for critical transaction-based processing applications used in reservation and banking systems.
  - Conversational, used by common programming interface for communications (CPI-C) and transaction processing (TP) for OSI.

Desktop-to-UNIX Connectivity with Hitachi Data Systems' Osiris

Osiris is Hitachi Data Systems' (HDS) UNIX-based operating system (Figure 9.8) patterned after Open Software Foundation's OSF/1. It runs in a logical partition on HDS processors (IBM 370 architecture compatible) under Hitachi's Multiple Logical Processor Feature (MLPF). Running under MLPF, Osiris can coexist with MVS or any virtual partitions on HDS processors. Osiris shares a portion of the HDS processor and the HDS

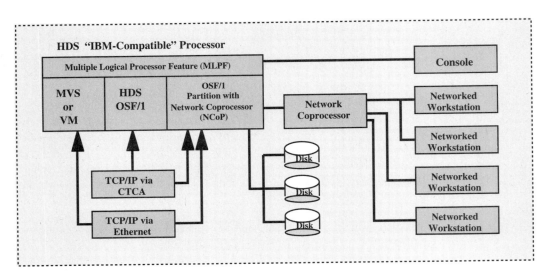

Figure 9.8 HDS's Osiris overview.
Source: Hitachi Data Systems, 1995

direct access storage device (DASD). Interoperability between the operating systems is supplied through Transmission Control Protocol/Internet Protocol and NFS over Ethernet.

Central to Osiris' function as a superserver (Figure 9.9) is the front-end processor known as network coprocessor (NCoP). Channel attached to the mainframe, the network coprocessor, is a physical interface to the network and provides NFS acceleration. The mainframe can support up to four NCoPs attached to each partition.

UNIX communications with LAN clients (Figure 9.10) is accomplished by using TCP/IP and the Network File System. Alternatively, Ethernet (using TCP/IP) may be used to exchange data with other environments such as MVS. Connectivity to LANs other than Ethernet is also being provided via third-party front-end processors and routers.

ISV Solutions. A number of software vendors offer terminal emulation and file transfer products for IBM SNA to non-IBM UNIX communications. Typically, these products allow the UNIX system to emulate an IBM 3270 terminal. Some of these products use the high-level language applications interface (HLLAPI) to accept data input into a UNIX display and to translate it to 3270 format before shipping it to the SNA mainframe. This allows UNIX users to interact with the familiar display rather than attempt to learn the intricacies of IBM PF (program function) keys and other 3270 details.

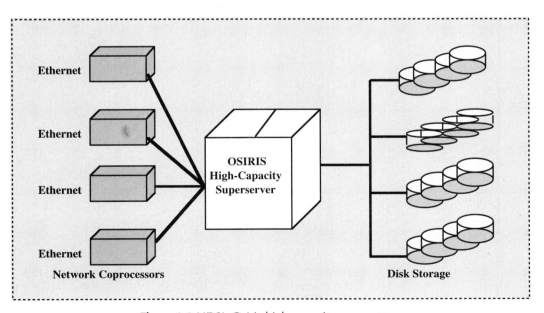

Figure 9.9 HDS's Osiris high-capacity super server.
Source: Hitachi Data Systems, 1995

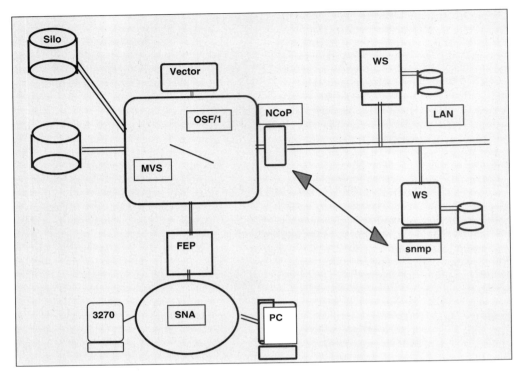

Figure 9.10 HDS's Osiris mainframe connectivity.
Source: Hitachi Data Systems, 1995

VMS-to-UNIX Connectivity

Digital's primary thrust is the new AXP computers (based on DEC OSF/1 and Windows NT), but Digital is still supporting VMS-based VAX systems. Digital's proprietary network architecture, Digital Network Architecture (DNA), connects VAXes and its other hardware systems. DNA includes DECnet services supporting file transfer, e-mail, peripheral sharing, and local area transport (LAT) Protocol for terminal server-to-host communication. Despite the widespread use of DECnet and LAT, the fastest-growing area of DEC-UNIX connectivity includes TCP/IP, NFS, and X technologies.

DECnet on UNIX. Digital's DECnet software allows Digital's OSF/1 and Ultrix systems to communicate with VAX computers. The products use a semitransparent, bidirectional gateway that acts as a bridge between DECnet and TCP/IP based networks. The capabilities supported include remote login, e-mail, file transfer, and limited network management.

Some third-party solutions provide a comprehensive file transfer utilities for bidirectional, single or multiple file manipulation, and e-mail between local and remote systems. Such utilities also shield the users from the differences in the file systems between UNIX and VMS, allowing users and VMS applications to access UNIX files. Other utilities allow both DECnet and LAT to support remote login, file transfer, and e-mail between VAX and UNIX systems. In addition, OpenDNA provides a network management system that displays, handles, configures, monitors, and acknowledges network events. Based on the Motif GUI, it configures DECnet, LAT, and MOP nodes; performs fault control; and analyzes protocols.

Digital Advantage Networks. For enterprises running a variety of UNIX and Digital Equipment computers, Digital's Advantage-Networks products can be used to integrate OSI, TCP/IP, and DECnet networks into a single network. The Advantage-Network products provide X/Open Transport Interface (XTI), Internet, integrated IS-IS routing, and FTAM/FTP and X.400/SMTP gateways between TCP/IP and OSI environments. It also provides UNIX access to SNA environments. Digital's Ultrix and OSF/1 both support TCP/IP.

LAN IMPLEMENTATIONS

PC LANs play a major role in any enterprise's attempt to develop an internetwork. However, this creates technical difficulties in that PCs were not designed to be internetworked. Interconnection of PC LANs is not a simple organizational issue, nor is it a simple technical matter. There are a number of possible configurations for connecting and implementing LANs. This section examines the key considerations and technologies when connecting UNIX with networks that utilize different protocols such as IPX/SPX, TCP/IP, AppleTalk, Banyan VINES, Digital's PathWorks, or others.

NetWare (Novell)

Novell's NetWare is a full fledged operating system. NetWare has integrated several protocols, including AppleTalk File Protocol (AFP), Network File System, TCP/IP, and OSI. As a result, it provides a seamless, high-speed communications among dissimilar systems. NetWare is capable of providing the network services in the user's native environment for other operating systems, including DOS, Macintosh, and OS/2 applications. At the same time, it provides Macintosh, OS/2, VINES, and UNIX workstations access to NetWare file and print services.

NetWare database services allow developers to customize their applications using SQL. NetWare messaging services are supported with gateways for X.400, IBM's PROFS, SNA networks, UNIX systems, DEC's All-in-1 Mail, VMSMail, MCI Mail, fax machines, and others. Communication services support LAN-to-IBM host connectivity, dial-in/dial-out connectivity, and internetworking with Ethernet, token ring, LocalTalk, and other networks.

LAN Manager (Microsoft)

The *Microsoft LAN Manager* was originally designed to run on top of OS/2, but is also available in a UNIX version. The LAN Manager also supports the client/server version of the Windows/NT and looks as if it is a UNIX implementation with hooks to the Windows graphical user interface.

Support for Local Networks. The LAN Manager allows PCs running MS-DOS or OS/2 to use a UNIX system as a file server or host for distributed applications. From the workstation's point of view, a UNIX system installed with LAN Manager provides all the services of and behaves identically to an OS/2 system running OS/2 LAN manager software. Because it runs on UNIX instead of OS/2, access has been provided for additional services, including transparent file access to other network servers accessible only from UNIX and gateway facilities to UNIX services such as printing.

LAN Manager is portable across a wide range of UNIX variants running on the full spectrum of hardware platforms from PCs to large mainframes, including VMS and Windows NT. This implementation allows Windows NT and VMS to act as servers for PC client applications running under Windows, MS-DOS, and OS/2. To provide full portability across many variants of the UNIX operating systems, it has reimplemented mappings of its interface into the underlying network services. Therefore, it provides interfaces to Berkeley Sockets via TCP/IP transport and TLI. For an LAN Manager/X server to communicate with a DOS or OS/2 client, the LAN Manager's interface is closely modeled after the functionality of NetBIOS.

LAN Manager for UNIX (LAN Manager/X) allows users to share applications, data, and resources from OS/2, UNIX, VMS servers, Macintosh, NetWare, NCR, Data General, Groupe Bull, Hewlett-Packard, SCO, and others. It shares common client software, interfaces, performance, security, and administration commands with all these implementations.

With topology and transport independence, LAN Manager/X allows the integration choice of token ring or Ethernet, TCP/IP, NetBEUI, OSI TP4, or other network transport, all within a single system. It can also act as a bridge to the NFS, Remote File System, and Andrew File System.

Support for Wide Area Networks. Microsoft has three products that allow migration to wide area networks:

- Communication server allowing Windows-, DOS-, and OS/2-based clients to communicate with other systems using IBM SNA protocols, including full-screen 3270 emulation.
- Microsoft TCP/IP transport services allowing PC Workstations running Windows, MS-DOS, NT, or OS/2 for seamless interconnectivity with LAN Manager implementation on OS/2, UNIX, VMS platforms, and NetWare.

- LAN Manager Remote Access Service gives remote PC users full access to network features. Users of remote workstations running Windows, MS-DOS, NT, or OS/2 can access LAN Manager using standard modems.

VINES (Banyan Systems)

Banyan VINES is a UNIX-based network operating system intended for large networks where multiple server operation and wide area network integration are of paramount importance. VINES' simple, yet powerful, global naming system, StreetTalk, identifies any network-attached resource. The StreetTalk global naming system provides replication of directories across the network to enhance speed and reliability.

VINES runs on a proprietary version of UNIX and has also ported to SCO UNIX. VINES for SCO UNIX is an enterprise network solution providing connectivity with UNIX and PCs. Banyan's enterprise network runs directly on SCO UNIX operating system, converting the SCO platform into a VINES enterprise network server.

Banyan systems not only allow NetWare networks to communicate with VINES, but also to share VINES' system services, including the highly regarded StreetTalk directory system.

VINES gateway service allows access to any IBM SNA mainframe from a variety of PCs on a VINES network. A single gateway can support PC running DOS, Windows, and Macintosh computers.

For Macintosh, VINES provides transparent access to directory, security, and resource sharing with AppleTalk networks via token ring, Ethernet, and LocalTalk through all supported LAN and wide area network topologies.

Banyan VINES, also a network operating system for personal computers, is competitive with NetWare. Its strength lies in its capacity to work with large networks, even those with more than 500 nodes in more than one location. VINES can transparently connect many LANs to create one virtual network.

PathWorks (Digital Equipment)

For one reason or another, Digital Equipment has always tended to group local interconnection of its LANs into the basic products and architectures of Ethernet and to consider internetworking the interconnection of LANs through wide area network services. Bridges are principally (in Digital's view) high-performance links to be applied within a local environment to connect Ethernet areas or to create FDDI backbone. Digital implements three types of bridges in LANs:

- Local bridging of Ethernet LANs either via private copper or fiber.
- Remote bridging of DECnet LANs of any type.
- Ethernet-to-FDDI bridging, generally conducted locally to create an FDDI backbone for a large Ethernet community.

DECnet LANs are normally centered around one or more VAX systems, which act as routing nodes in DECnet networks. It is also possible to connect DECnet networks through the VMS computers, using either public data networks or leased lines.

Microsoft LAN Manager is a key component of DEC's PathWorks, allowing PC users to connect to a VAX server. PathWorks also supports LAN manager APIs for OS/2, VMS, and UNIX servers.

OS/2 LAN Manager (IBM)

IBM has two implementations of the LAN Manager:

- LAN server operates under OS/2, allows client/server implementations, and provides services for distributed databases on the network. The OS/2 Extended Edition includes the communication manager and the database manager and supports advanced peer-to-peer communications for OS/2. LAN Server is similar to Microsoft's LAN manager and it adheres to IBM's Systems Application Architecture (SAA).
- PC local area network program is designed for small, DOS-based networks. It permits sharing of disk drives and printers as well as sending and receiving of messages and files.

Even though IBM offers these network operating systems, the emphasis has been on supporting Novell's NetWare.

INTERNETWORKING SCENARIOS

Migrating from a single LAN to two or more interconnected LANs and eventually to a complex wide area internetwork is no small undertaking. By definition, a wide area network must be capable of linking various computing platforms over a large geographical area. True interoperability between computing platforms is being achieved today primarily through UNIX implementations of TCP/IP protocols.

TCP/IP has emerged as the primary communications protocol for developing UNIX-based internetworks, because it meets the interoperability criteria. Almost every conceivable combination of computer hardware and operating system has a driver available for TCP/IP and provides a common denominator across many communications services (Figure 9.11).

LAN-LAN Internetworking

For interconnecting a LAN to a LAN, bridges and routers are the most commonly implemented solutions in the LAN world. Internet routers are less often used to interconnect local networks directly, but become an important option when interconnecting remote LANs through a public, packet-switched network. The use of protocol translation gate-

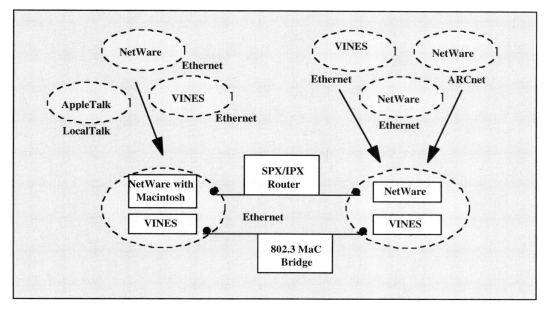

Figure 9.11 An internetworking example.

ways at the application layer are rarely used to interconnect LANs, but are important in the context of providing interoperable solutions between organizations.

Since bridges are protocol independent, they are unaware of the protocols in use. When a packet is received by a bridge, the bridge examines the information in the data link header and forwards the packet or discards it if the destination is located on the same side the packet was received from. For example, the DEC LAT protocol does not have the ability to be routed. To connect multiple DECnet networks, a bridge is required. Figure 9.12 illustrates a UNIX server being accessed by terminals wired to it using RS-232 asynchronous connections. By using "terminal emulation," any MS-DOS PC attached to the LAN can act as a UNIX terminal, accessing the UNIX server at network speeds. A LAN adapter, installed in the UNIX server, allows networked PCs to access the UNIX system as terminals.

Mac bridges or data link layer relays connect separate independent LANs, especially when connecting UNIX-based LANs to non-UNIX–based LANs. The degree of performance transparency in accessing resources across the bridge is primarily a function of contention for the bridge and application resources. Bridges are primarily used to connect compatible or nearly compatible LANs (Figure 9.12).

Connecting a large number of LANs is a significant undertaking. The task is further complicated if the LANs use different types of media (Figure 9.13), access methods, and protocols. In these complex multiprotocol LAN internetworking environments, multiprotocol routers are the preferred approach.

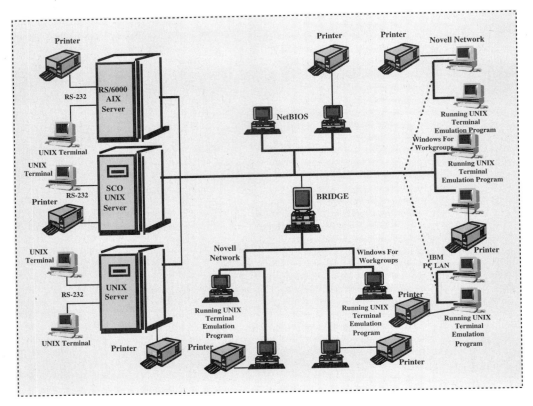

Figure 9.12 A LAN-to-LAN internetwork.

LAN-WAN Internetworking

Just as LANs are effectively linking workstations and departmental PCs, LAN-WAN interconnections extend LAN capabilities to computing resources distributed nationwide or even worldwide. The trend toward LAN-WAN internetworking is accelerating at a phenomenal rate, and new architectures supporting internetworks will continue to proliferate, enabling the majority of all existing LANs to interconnect via WANs.

More commonly, LAN-WAN internetworks interconnect departmental and local site computing beyond their physical boundaries. The goal of internetworking is to gain benefits from centralized control of shared resources while preserving the impedance of decentralized computing. While UNIX provides a basis for any LAN-LAN or LAN-WAN interconnection technology, there are many other diverse technologies that must also be internetworked.

Migrating from a single LAN to two or more interconnected LANs and eventually to a complex wide area internetwork is not a small undertaking. As more organizations begin this migration path, the issues and problems of LAN interconnection, especially

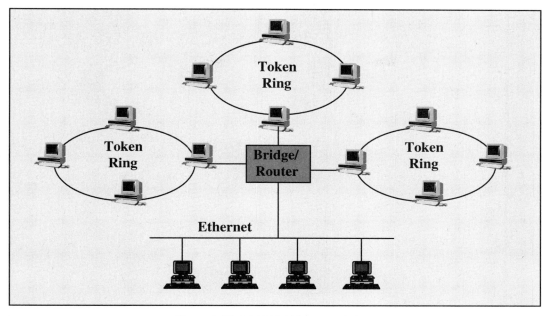

Figure 9.13 A LAN-LAN connectivity.

those associated with protocol compatibility between the linked networks, have become more prevalent. We will discuss a few examples to illustrate the UNIX technologies just described. Figure 9.14 illustrates token ring and Ethernet LANs connected via repeaters, bridges, and routers.

Internetworking with Remote Bridges. LANs can be extended using repeaters. Local LANs can be interconnected with each other using local bridges and/or hubs. However, for a LAN-WAN environment, the remote bridges provide one of the means of connecting while ignoring complexities of the upper protocol layers. Remote bridge pairs offer a viable approach for small organizations seeking LAN interconnection solutions for a limited number of applications. These bridging devices filter all packets addressed to the local LAN and forwards those packets addressed to remote locations on the other LAN. Figure 9.15 illustrates a small-scale, bridged LAN-WAN internetwork.

Internetworking with Routers. Connecting a large number of LANs is a significant undertaking. The task is further complicated if the LANs use different types of media, access methods, and protocols. In these complex multiprotocol LAN internetworking environments, multiprotocol routers, operating at the network layer, are the preferred approach for interconnection protocols used. Routers are more complex than bridges, and the increased complexity of these devices stems from the additional functionality in flow control, hierarchical addressing of each source and destination, packet

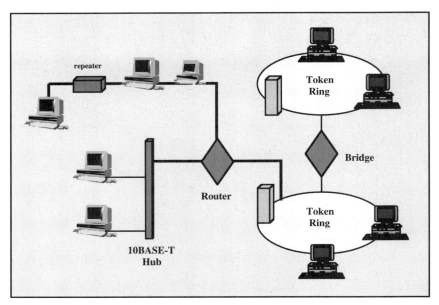

Figure 9.14 Ethernet and token ring internetwork.

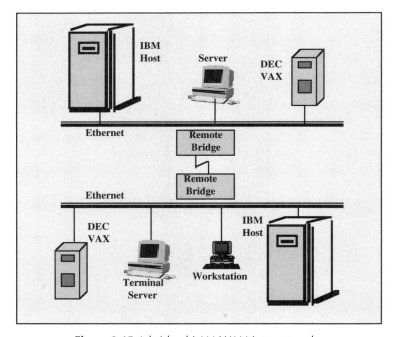

Figure 9.15 A bridged LAN-WAN internetwork.

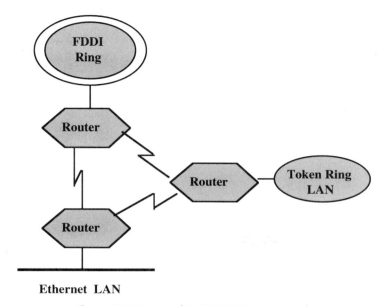

Ethernet LAN

Figure 9.16 A routed LAN-WAN internetwork.

fragmentation/reassembly, and network congestion control. Figure 9.16 illustrates a typical branch office routing configuration for internetworking.

Internetworking with Gateways. Gateways provide several different types of internetwork services such as protocol conversion, virtual terminal service, and file access services. Simple gateways called *protocol converters* provide only basic conversions between various protocols. More robust gateways offer transparent file transfers across different NOS environments. The gateways can translate file structure used in one NOS environment to another network operating system's file structure. For example, a workstation running MS-DOS can transfer files from native Novell IPX to Digital VAX VMS operating system on a DECnet network.

Terminal servers are microprocessor-based devices providing an RS-232 interface to a LAN, allowing to connect display terminals, printers, and plotters to the LAN's network operating system. Figure 9.17 illustrates a terminal server gateway providing IBM terminal service to Digital's VT display terminal users.

Complex Internetworking. Many organizations link hosts and workstations over two or more network operating systems environments. One solution is to load several protocol stacks into host systems to service workstations on the network that are running different network operating systems. Figure 9.6 illustrates a configuration that uses multiple protocol stacks on the host system to accommodate various network operating systems. This approach places the burden of supporting different protocols on the host. This approach is

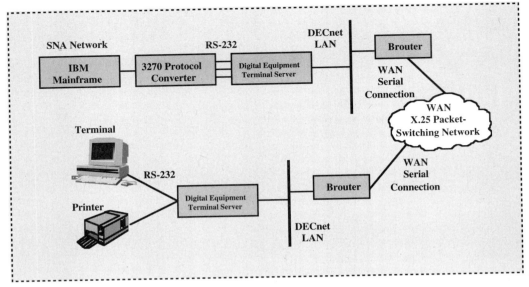

Figure 9.17 Terminal server gateway.

especially important for organizations that must integrate DOS-based workstations with memory constraints.

Another approach to internetworking is to load multiple protocol stacks to workstations that must communicate over several network operating systems. An example is a workstation equipped with a TCP/IP host and a NetWare file server at the same time. Loading multiple protocol stacks to a workstation is most feasible on workstations running UNIX or IBM OS/2.

SUMMARY

There are many challenges in making UNIX work within the enterprise network. Diverse UNIX implementations must not only communicate with each other, they must also communicate with DOS- and Windows-based systems, Macintoshes, differing network operating systems, and proprietary midranges and mainframes. To assist developers in building connectivity solutions, UNIX suppliers have included communications facilities with their UNIX operating systems. In addition, a horde of third-party vendors offer alternative UNIX communications and interoperability solutions.

Over the past few years, the UNIX industry has undergone several major changes that have affected the way UNIX interoperates with non-UNIX systems. For example, Novell NetWare has expanded its interoperability with most non-UNIX platforms; SunSoft is providing a simpler way for DOS Windows to run on UNIX workstations and is beginning to unseat some of the existing DOS-to-UNIX connectivity solutions. The

COSE initiative will also standardize many UNIX technologies, leading the way for an easier coexistence with non-UNIX systems as well as between disparate UNIX versions.

As internetworking among dissimilar operating systems is maturing and non-UNIX platforms are providing some of the UNIX capabilities, UNIX communications needs are also changing. For example, only a few years ago, it was considered a complex task to simply integrate PCs into a UNIX department network and the unconnected islands of departmental or small workgroup islands were a norm. Now the integrated networks and internetworks of PCs, Macs, UNIX workstations, mainframes, and servers of various size supporting thousands of users, are a common place.

Still, the users are struggling to find solutions that can handle extremely diverse environments and coexist with their current installed base. In the UNIX environment, TCP/IP and NFS are common denominators between the disparate operating systems and computer systems. This trend is likely to continue as a major communications backbone for diverse systems for a few more years.

EXERCISES

1. When should the bridges, routers, or gateways be used in internetworking?
2. List some of the utilities and applications of UNIX-to-UNIX communications.
3. Briefly discuss UUCP.
4. List different file sharing techniques supported by UNIX networking.
5. List a few network operating systems that facilitate UNIX–to–Non-UNIX internetworking.

10

INTEGRATING THE DESKTOP

Introduction
Environments
PC-UNIX Connectivity
Options for Integrating PCs
Hardware: Desktop Microprocessors
DataBus: ISA versus MCA versus EISA
Operating Systems: DOS versus UNIX
versus OS/2 versus NT
UNIXs: SCO, AIX, SVR4, OSF/1
Network (LAN) Operating Systems
Graphical User Interfaces
Interaction Between OSs, NOSs, and GUIs
Running TCP/IP on a PC
Desktop Connectivity Basics

Major Functions: TELNET, FTP, SMTP,
TN3270
Application Services: NFS, RPC, X
Window System
Connecting with UNIX
DOS
Microsoft Windows for Workgroups and
Windows NT
OS/2
Novell NetWare
Hewlett-Packard HP-UX
Summary
Exercises

INTRODUCTION

First there was the mainframe and many organizations embraced the paradigm of the centralized host. Later, as economic forces drove organizations to decentralize, it became necessary to connect these isolated hosts. SNA became the predominant architecture for large enterprise networks.

As these organizations embraced SNA as the backbone that would allow broader organized access to the mainframe, another force became predominant. The economics of PCs and LANs became impossible to ignore. With the advent of PCs and workstations, organizations saw an opportunity to economically expand computing throughout their companies. Inevitably, companies saw a need to connect these newly discovered devices so that users with similar needs and applications could share data and communicate with one another and contribute to enhanced programmer productivity. This trend led to the creation of LANs and client/server environments, in which disparate components could participate in a peer-to-peer network.

As computing became more commonplace, applications proliferated and organizations reengineered themselves into small workgroups. SNA became a challenge as the different proprietary operating systems made interconnection difficult. Eventually, TCP/IP emerged as the dominant communications protocol by which integration of the PC and PC LANs into the data center could be achieved. These groups of interconnected LANs with WANs. Finally, IS managers addressed a major stumbling block: interconnection of LANs and WANs in the field with glass house mainframes at the headquarters. TCP/IP proved to be an effective common denominator, connecting geographically dispersed LANs and UNIX-based client/server systems. Without such enterprisewide interconnection, mainframes were becoming nothing more than static repository in an otherwise dynamic environment.

Gateways represent an elegant solution to the problem of enabling mainframes to participate in client/server systems. Many of these solutions are centered on mainframe host applications and distributed programmatic standards supporting extended high-level language application program interface (EHLLAPI) and IBM advanced peer-to-peer communication (APPC) across a range of operating systems, including DOS, UNIX, and Windows. This is the key to achieve independence, seamless integration, universal user interface, and complete scalability.

ENVIRONMENTS

Traditional information processing has relied on central computing resources and central data storage. Both developed as a result of the characteristics of the early computer applications. With computers offering less than 1 million instructions per second (mips) of performance at costs of a million dollars or so, users are not likely to spread them about the organization or use them for anything but critical applications generating information of broad value to business.

The microprocessor technology changed the price/performance ratio for computers and allowed smaller systems to be applied to tasks that were beneficial to local productivity but did not necessarily generate data of broader significance to the company. But once on the desktop, these smaller systems were clearly applicable to more critical needs.

To reconcile the goals of information resources management and productivity support, businesses turned to the linking of PCs with central resources. This allowed applications critical to the business as a whole to be based in part on host-owned data storage facilities, which were under firm professional control. PC integration via communications is now an accepted part of the MIS plan.

Having come to terms with the PCs, Information Technology (IT) management is now facing another desktop challenge. High performance technical workstations based primarily on the UNIX operating system are finding a place in many companies. These systems offer startling cost/performance figures, and in many ways their sophisticated operating systems are more conducive to the development of mission-critical applications.

PC-UNIX Connectivity

In the beginning, users connected PCs to UNIX hosts via serial lines or modems, and by running terminal emulation software on the PC, making the PC appear as a UNIX terminal. One of the primary motivations for PC-UNIX integration was to provide print and file services to the PC user. Terminal emulation enabled the PC user to run UNIX applications in character mode and provided the ability to copy files to and from the UNIX host.

Although thousands of PC users still connect to character-based UNIX applications, with terminal emulation software, and access print and file services with proprietary protocols, the new generation of PC-UNIX products is built on open standards integrating TCP/IP, NFS, and PC X Windows software. These open standards solutions are rapidly gaining widespread acceptance as key interoperability technologies for networking PCs to UNIX-based computer systems.

Emerging in the early 1980s, Ethernet and the TCP/IP protocol suite represented major technological advances in the evolution of PC-UNIX connectivity. Ethernet significantly increased the bandwidth, speed, and functionality of networks from snail-like 2400–9600 bps serial lines to a warp speed of 100 Mbps. The TCP/IP protocol is a standard for networking and has rapidly become a de facto standard for PC-UNIX integration.

Although a variety of other options exist for connecting PCs to UNIX hosts, the TCP/IP protocol is scalable, providing transparent internetwork connectivity (interoperability), and integrates the Sun Microsystems' Network File System (NFS) as a common element.

Perhaps one of the most important software products built upon the Ethernet-TCP/IP platform is Sun Microsystem's Network File System, which has become a de facto standard for PC-UNIX host connectivity. NFS provides file and print services and allows PCs to remotely mount UNIX file systems, so that they appear transparent to the PC user, as if they were another drive on the PC.

The Windows Sockets Application Programming Interface (WinSock API) is recognized as an open standard specification for the development of Microsoft Windows and Windows NT TCP/IP applications. The objective of WinSock is to provide single application programming interface (API) for application developers and a standard interface that all TCP/IP suppliers can support. A major advantage of WinSock is that applications (X Windows display servers, terminal emulators, SQL interfaces, etc.) that are compliant with the API are able to run over any WinSock compliant TCP/IP.

Options for Integrating PCs

There are basically two approaches for integrating PCs into networks: running an open operating system on a PC or providing access via a network. The physical connectivity choices are an asynchronous connection via RS-232, X.25 connectivity, token ring, or Ethernet LANs (Figure 10.1). The integration options are many, but the most common are

- At the low end, the PC can emulate an asynchronous terminal and dial into a UNIX server, for example, VT100.

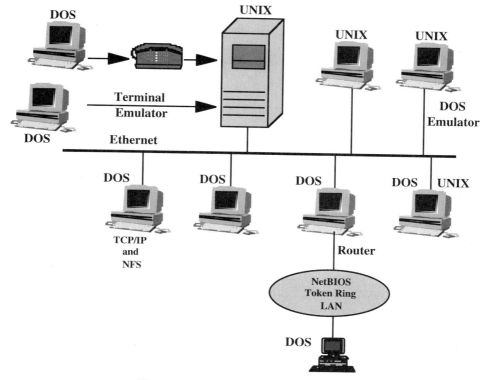

Figure 10.1 Options for integrating PCs.

- Supporting TCP/IP on a PC, which can allow
  - Virtual terminal and login capabilities.
  - Accessing to file and print servers.
  - Using the PC as a file/print server.
  - X Window System.
- Using the PC as an application server.
  - Emulating PC on a multiuser system.
  - Using multiple operating systems on a PC.

LANs: *Token Ring/802.5* is implemented in versions that run at 4 Mbps or 16 Mbps and can operate on shielded or unshielded twisted-pair wire as well as on fiber optic media. The desktops on a token ring LAN can be arranged in a star topology, with a hublike device called a multistation access unit (MAU) at the center of the star (Figure 10.2). Its access method—token passing—makes the physical star arrangement act as if the stations were arranged in a ring, as the token is passed from one workstation to the next in sequence.

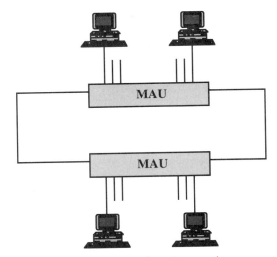

Figure 10.2. A token ring topology.

Ethernet/802.3 is usually implemented as a 10 Mbps bus-based network that can run on two types of coaxial cable, on unshielded twisted-pair telephone wire, or on fiber optic media (Figure 10.3). It uses a random access method carrier sense multiple access with collision detection.

ARCnet (Attached Resource Computer Network) is a 2.5 Mbps network that can run on coaxial cable or unshielded twisted pair. It is most often implemented in a hub-based star configuration and uses token passing to control access. ARCnet is closest to the 802.4 specification and uses token passing on a bus. Because it uses both active and passive hubs, ARCnet is excellent for elaborate wiring configurations. Active hubs relay messages

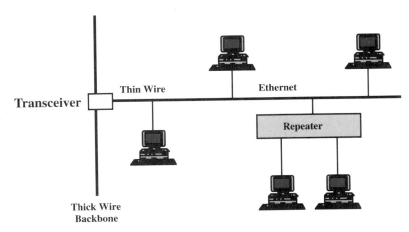

Figure 10.3 An Ethernet topology.

as well as repeat the signals, whereas the passive hubs can only be used to relay signals. The most common ARCnet network has a limit of 255 stations.

FDDI (fiber distributed data interface) is a 100 Mbps network that operates over optical fiber or, for limited distances, shielded or unshielded twisted pair. It is implemented using a dual-ring topology—FDDI concentrators and dual attached workstations require four separate fiber optic connections—with receive and transmit sides of each ring. Dual attachment provides fault tolerance in case of a cable break. Single attached stations can also be implemented, where many stations can be attached to a single concentrator in an economical manner. If a cable breaks in a single attached topology, only that workstation will be disabled since workstations are not directly attached to the main ring. However, single attached stations can be directly attached to the ring also.

FDDI is a frame-based technology that uses variable-length frames to transport information across the network. This allows it to easily map (translate) packets from other technologies, such as Ethernet and token ring. FDDI provides the ability to transport limited levels of isochronous bandwidth to support video and multimedia applications. FDDI can operate over both single-mode and multimode fiber optic cable, spanning between 2 and 20+ kilometers in distance between nodes.

In addition to a high-speed transmission rate, FDDI is designed to provide highly reliable communication. Certain reliability-enhancing techniques have been designed into the FDDI, including the use of wiring concentrators and automatic optical bypass switches, which make it easier to locate faults and bypass nonfunctioning stations. The typical FDDI application is generally used for

- Backbone connectivity between separate LANs in a building or campus.
- A LAN for high-end graphics and CAD/CAM workstations.
- A connection device for host-to-host or backbone-to-backbone applications.

As a foundation technology for ISDN protocol stack, *asynchronous transfer mode (ATM)* is at the center of a new era of WAN technology. This new era promises integrated transmission of voice, video, image, traditional data, and high-quality voice for all over one backbone network. In addition, ATM is being increasingly viewed as a viable protocol to use on the LAN.

The barriers between LAN and WAN are significant. Local area networks are optimized for data transmission and peripheral sharing, whereas wide area networks are primarily suited for telephony. Linking two LANs through the wide area network usually requires a LAN-to-WAN bridge or router that converts the LAN interface (Ethernet, token ring, AppleTalk, etc.) to a WAN-compatible interface (T1, X.25, etc.). This process is inefficient and introduces significant delays in the link. ATM can erase the barriers between local area networks and wide area networks.

ATM is generally considered a campus and wide area technology. With bandwidth initially in the 155 Mbps range, ATM is a one-step solution for building WAN-campus-LAN networks. Other high-speed technologies like Fast Ethernet and 100VG-Any-LAN lead us to believe that, at a minimum, we need 100 Mbps at the desktop. At the top end, we seem to need 100 Mbps, and at the lower-end, we may be able to live with 10 Mbps in

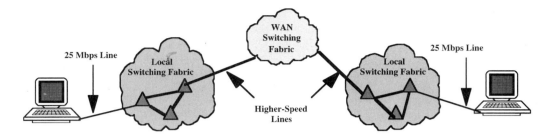

Figure 10.4 Basic ATM connectivity options.

the short run. However, with video-conferencing and other multimedia applications, we need higher speeds. With today's encoding technology, 25 Mbps can run over any twisted-pair wiring topology that 10BASE-T can use. This ability to run over existing wiring is important for any technology (Figure 10.4).

One of the most significant features of ATM from the network interconnection viewpoint is that it may be used to encapsulate any protocol for transmission across any flavor of backbone network. ATM employs a single format for all digital traffic based on fixed-length data units known as cells. Each cell is transported from source to destination through a direct connection over high-speed switched networks (Figure 10.4). ATM is based on the concept of a fixed-length cell, always defined as 53 byte (a 48-byte data cell combined with a 5-byte address header), that optimizes the movement of data through an enterprise. Because the cell's relatively small and uniform size—5-byte header and 48-byte data packets—results in predictable delay characteristics, ATM can guarantee performance for a range of delay-sensitive applications including voice and video.

Implementation of ATM at the desktop varies depending on user requirements and cost/performance parameters. High-end workstations or servers requiring multimedia services are being migrated to ATM first. ATM can provide a high-speed backbone for multiple-legacy LANs connected to an ATM router via a shared media hub. High-end ATM workstations and servers are able to connect directly to an ATM hub. ATM hubs and routers can be interconnected through an ATM switch to ATM and LAN workstations and servers.

Ethernet traffic is switched among the directly connected ports or converted to ATM using LAN emulation and transported over virtual circuits to the ATM switch. A PC on an Ethernet-to-ATM converter can connect to an ATM attached server or to another Ethernet port elsewhere in the network. If the destination is a different type of LAN, the connection would need to be through a router. The PC client connected to a port on an Ethernet-to-ATM converter has a dedicated 10 Mbps of bandwidth and direct access into the campus ATM backbone. ATM's quality of service and the related ability to reserve bandwidth allows various kinds of data to be transported at different priorities. As a result, desktop ATM is uniquely suited to real-time, interactive multimedia. Even while handling delay-sensitive traffic, ATM can at the same time support other bulk data transfers without degrading the quality of the voice and video.

WANs: (X.25, Frame Relay). As networks grow in complexity, and as the expectations of users escalate, a desire to consolidate the network architecture around a limited number of protocols has emerged. In addition to X.25, frame relay (FR) and asynchronous transfer mode represent an evolutionary step to future wide area networks.

X.25 has been a major factor in the area of data communication for almost 25 years. It has been the basis for "wide area networking" using packet technology on a worldwide basis. Most providers of data transport services have implemented it in their networks.

X.25 is an interface between data terminal equipment (DTE) and data circuit-terminating equipment (DCE) for terminals operating in the packet mode and connected to public data networks (PDNs) by dedicated circuits. It addresses the following:

- X.25 describes an interface and specifies a set of services available at that interface and the allowed set of interactions by which these services are requested and received.
- The interface is between a DTE (user of service) and a DCE (provider of service).
- It allows communications to take place between two users (i.e., DTEs) without constraining the nature of that communication.
- The terminal operates in a *packet mode*, as opposed to circuit mode, whereby messages are embedded in packets that have a distinct beginning and end. The packets can be interleaved, thus providing for the sharing of resources among several instances of communication.
- The terminal to be connected is *public* as opposed to *private*.
- The network is dedicated to moving data as opposed to voice or voice and data. Such a network is known as a packet-switched public data network (PSPDN).
- The connection between DTE and DCE is via a dedicated circuit.

Frame relay is a reliable, digital transmission system, based on the tenets of future high-speed networks. While technically capable of operating at speeds of 45 Mbps and beyond, FR is being offered at only 1.544 or 2.048 Mbps in the short run. In addition to being used for LAN interconnection, FR allows disparate protocols to be transported on a common backbone. Frames may be of any length between 262 bytes and 8 KB, with most implementations using 2 KB. Within the network, the frames may be broken down into other packet sizes, such as an ATM 53-byte cell.

FR is an interface much like X.25. It is purely implementation dependent and may or may not be used internally in networks. FR was not designed to work with a particular physical layer protocol and consists mostly of a data link control layer. A virtual link across a network consists of a pair of local addresses representing the ports to the links on each end of the network. All data are passed through the network transparently, as the network never looks inside frames for the purpose of distinguishing between such things as polling procedures and user data. All nonerror frames are transported through the network, whereas the frames in error are discarded and no recovery is attempted at this layer (this feature does cause some problems for protocols such as SNA).

FR can be implemented fairly easily with existing packet-switching technology and can dramatically increase immediate throughput. FR is considered as a natural successor to X.25 because of low protocol overhead. In addition, the lack of packetizing process requires less resources within an SNA node when attaching to an FR network as opposed to an X.25 network. FR provides a method of integrating a number of different protocols into one backbone and thus has become a popular protocol in the WAN environment.

Hardware: Desktop Microprocessors

Microprocessors determine and control the computer's processing characteristics, power, and the types of software programs the computer can process. The system board is the primary circuit board, and the data bus provides the foundation circuitry for the computer and attachment points to which other components can be added. Memory is required by the CPU to carry out its functions. The amount of memory determines what programs and how fast the CPU can process. The output system is made up of the parallel and serial communication ports. These ports are vital to the efficiency and flexibility of the attached devices.

Intel Processors. In the evolution of computers, many different microprocessors have been designed. The Intel microprocessors have become standard CPUs around which IBM and its compatible microcomputers are built. The microprocessors manufactured by Intel are

8086 was introduced in 1978. It featured both a 16-bit microprocessor, a 16-bit external data bus, and a 20-bit memory addressing scheme (capable of addressing one megabyte of memory). At the time, memory was expensive, and few other chips could handle 16 bits. For that reason, the 8086 was put on hold.

8088 was introduced in 1979 for use in the IBM PC. It also had 20-bit addressing and used a 16-bit instruction set and a 8-bit data bus, allowing it to use the available 8-bit support hardware, and was essentially limited to DOS.

80286 was first used in IBM PC AT in 1984. It could use 16 MB of memory and allow multitasking. It was primarily used for DOS, but it also supported a subset of UNIX (XENIX).

80386 was first used by COMPAQ in 1986, followed by IBM. It introduce 32-bit processing data path with expanded addressing and virtual memory. However, most of the PC add-on expansion boards still were 8 or 16 bit and were unable to use its full capabilities. It can run DOS, UNIX, and OS/2 efficiently.

80486 was introduced in 1989 and has been quite prevalent until the introduction of Pentium-grade processors. In one chip, it incorporated a math processor and a cache memory controller.

Pentium processors have increased performance over Intel 486 processors by a wide margin by increasing the number of transistors, increasing the clock speed, and increasing the number of executions per clock cycle. Pentiums are capable of executing two instructions at once. For mission-critical applications, Pentium incorporates functional redundancy checking (FRC) which uses two Pentium chips in tandem, one as a master and the other as a checker.

P6 integrates about 5.5 million transistors on the chip and operates at about 133 MHz. It provides for enhanced data integrity and reliability features and ensures complete binary compatibility with previous generations.

Motorola Processors. Unlike the IBM compatibles, the Macintosh uses a microprocessor built by Motorola.

MC68000 was introduced in 1979 and became the microprocessor of choice for computers and workstations designed for engineering, graphics, multiuser, multitasking, artificial intelligence, and control applications. It has 24-bus internal address bus, 16-bit data bus, and 16 MB direct memory addressing. The Macintoshes were built around this microprocessor. Novell also used this microprocessor in its first NetWare file server.

MC68020 is the first full 32-bit processor with 32-bit internal address bus, 32-bit data bus, and 4 GB direct memory addressing along with a math coprocessor support. Macintoshes again adopted these microprocessors.

MC68030 includes two independent 32-bit address buses and data buses, on-chip data and instruction cache, and multiprocessing capabilities.

PowerPC refers to the RISC processor–based computing platform developed jointly by Motorola, Apple, and IBM. It is based on IBM's POWER (Performance Optimization with Enhanced RISC) processor technology. The most obvious difference between the superscalar PowerPC and its predecessor is the fact that it offers a more scaled-back instruction set. It enables a processor to execute more than one instruction in parallel per clock cycle. The consortium enhanced the POWER architecture to better meet the combined low-cost and high-performance goals of the alliance.

The follow-on PowerPC models also include a full 64-bit processor and the multiprocessing support which is already available on SunSoft's Solaris and Windows NT. The PowerPC's floating point unit is supported directly in the instruction set architecture, resulting in a more tightly integrated system with improved floating point performance— a must for multimedia, graphics, and voice recognition–type applications.

The PowerPC also incorporates the 64-bit address bus. Because they are so advanced, members of the *PowerPC family* are faster than the buses they support. However, an on-chip clock divider provides easy interfacing to standard buses. Those buses include ISA, EISA, and MCA. EISA and MCA run just under 32 MHz, while the processor 601 runs at either 50 or 66 MHz. Other key system components such as 32-bit operating systems with graphical user interfaces, multimedia, high-end graphics, networking, and SCSI-2 disk drives are also handicapped by the slower bus speeds.

Because a system is only as fast as it slowest components, the PowerPC is designed to be bus independent. It supports all industry standard bus designs, including Intel's Peripheral Chip Interconnect (PCI) local bus. Since the local bus connects directly to the processor, it speeds up networking applications, graphics accelerators, and hard disk controllers. Support for PCI enhances the PowerPC support on the desktop.

The PowerPC 601 operates at either 50 or 66 MHz and includes 32 KB on-chip cache. The PowerPC 603 operates at 80 to 85 MHz. The PowerPC 604 is designed for high-performance PCs, workstations, and servers and has graphics-intensive applications.

This model supports symmetric multiprocessing and offers two to three times the performance of the PowerPC 601. The PowerPC 620 is a full 64-bit high-end processor for both uniprocessor and multiprocessor workstations, servers, and supercomputers. The major emphasis is on performance with speeds up to 400 SPECmark range.

Both the *Pentium* and *PowerPCs* are based on superscalar architectures. PowerPCs have three pipelines (integer, floating point, and branch processing units), whereas the Pentiums have two instruction pipelines (arithmetic logic unit, address-generation circuitry, and data-cache interface—the dual pipelines capable of processing only two integer or one floating instruction per clock cycle). PowerPC's larger cache translates into a smaller wait state, which improves overall processor performance. Windows NT is available on both processors, giving users access to a broader selection, especially as high-end servers.

Sun SPARC Workstations. Sun has introduced a number of SPARC workstations and servers with varying CPU speeds, memory, type of data bus, and disk storage. SUN groups these into desktop SPARCS, SPARC workgroup servers, SPARCsystem departmental servers, and SPARC data center servers.

Data Bus ISA versus MCA versus EISA

The system board data bus furnishes the connections needed for moving data around add-on circuit boards, the main system memory, the microprocessor, and other circuitry of the computer. The data bus provides a path for data transfer and one or more paths for controlling the data to be transferred.

The expansion bus of the original IBM PC and the PC/XT represents the simplest design and utilizes the barest minimum of support circuitry. The bus had a 8-bit-wide data path and was tied to the Intel 8086/8088 microprocessors.

Industry standard Architecture (ISA) is the PC-AT 16-bit bus universally acknowledged standard, open hardware architecture, and has been available since 1984.

Micro channel architecture (MCA), introduced in 1987, is a full 32-bit bus architecture and is included in PS/2s. It is not compatible with ISA add-on circuit boards. Micro Channel Architecture is totally incompatible with the earlier PC and AT bus designs. It worked with 80386 class microprocessors and was introduced in IBM PS/2. The MCA bus can handle multiple devices and allows automatic system reconfiguration when expansion boards are added.

Extended industry standard architecture (EISA) is a standard developed by the "gang of nine" in response to IBM's MCA and is compatible with PC-AT add-on boards. Like the MCA bus, it can handle multiple devices, but unlike the MCA bus it is backward compatible with ISA expansion boards.

The Macintoshes are built around the *NuBus* bus. It includes a multiplexed 32-bit addressing.

The *Peripheral Chip Interconnect (PCI)* local bus system is capable of moving 32-bit data at 33 MHz. It takes peripherals on the I/O bus and connects them, together with the CPU and the memory subsystem, to a wider, faster pathway for data. It allows faster transfer of data between the CPU and the peripherals, especially important for servers and graphic-intensive software like Windows and OS/2. Most PCI systems support three to five performance-critical peripherals. These peripherals are either integrated directly into the motherboard or can be added via PCI extension cards, such as multimedia, graphics, disk drives, and LAN cards. PCI also coexists with ISA, EISA, and MCA add-on cards.

SCSI is the *Small Computer System Interface* standard designed for high-end and high-speed data transfers needed for multimedia and graphics applications.

Choice of a bus is not really that critical. DOS, OS/2, and UNIX will work well with any of these buses.

Operating Systems: DOS versus UNIX versus OS/2 versus NT

The function of an *operating system (OS)* is to provide an environment in which applications can run. An OS is a program that is made up of a collection of miniature programs *(functions and system calls)* that provide recurring services to computer users or to other types of software, such as spreadsheets, word processors, graphics, and database management applications. These services include disk and file management, memory management, and device management.

If there were no OSs to provide these services, the user or the application program would have to deal directly with the details of the computer's hardware, file, and memory systems. The most interesting developments in the OS world pertain to the desktops: personal computers and workstations. Since these computers (unlike the mainframes) keep most of the operating system commands and routines on a disk rather than in memory, the operating systems themselves are called *disk operating systems (DOS)*. The most familiar desktop PC, microcomputer, and workstations OSs include

- Microsoft MS-DOS.
- Novell Desktop Systems (DR-DOS).
- IBM OS/2.
- Apple Macintosh System.
- Microsoft (Windows) NT.
- A variety of UNIX implementations for the desktop. These include Apple's A/UX, IBM's AIX, SunSoft's Interactive UNIX, and Solaris, Santa Cruz Operation's SCO, NeXT NeXTstep, and the Open Software Foundation's OSF/1.

As shown in Figure 10.5, the three operating systems differ substantially in features and design. Although well documented and understood, DOS is not an "open system" because Microsoft controls it. But DOS can integrate in many ways with open systems. Multiuser DOS products eliminate some of the basic DOS design deficiencies. However integration issues are similar to DOS.

Features for UNIX may vary, depending on the implementation. UNIX on a PC is the easiest to integrate but requires a powerful PC. SCO (Santa Cruz Operation) UNIX (depicted in the Figure 10.5) is primarily based on AT&T System V.

Feature	MS-DOS	SCO UNIX	OS/2
Multiuser	No	Yes	No
Multitasking	Limited	Process	Process/thread
Semaphores	No	Yes	Yes
Pipes	Limited	Yes	Yes
Shared memory	Yes	Yes	Yes
Sockets	No	Yes	No
386 addressing	Partial	Yes	Yes
Shared libraries	No	Yes	Yes
Main GUI	Windows	Optional	Yes
TCP/IP	With NT	Yes	Optional

Figure 10.5 DOS versus UNIX versus OS/2.

32-Bit Systems and Beyond. Until recently, all PC OSs, including DOS, the Macintosh System, and OS/2, were 16-bit systems. This was due to the limitation of the CPU chips which could only access 16-bit address space. The current technology allows 32-bit capabilities. However, the UNIX systems have had such capability since the 1970s. Microsoft's NT and Digital's Alpha AXP chip are even capable of 64-bit addressing.

Object-Oriented OSs. Like other object-oriented software, object-oriented OS consists of objects and their associated messages. Icons, scroll bars, windows, and even hardware can be designed as objects. But the critical issue with respect to object-oriented OSs is that, by providing a common set of interfaces and messages, any application or service on one platform can communicate with another application or service on another (such as Sun Workstation or IBM AS/400).

Microkernel-Based OSs. A microkernel-based operating system is a system that consists of largely platform-independent code. Such a system can be separated into the nonplatform-specific main part, running on a variety of processors, and a smaller platform-specific *microkernel*. To maximize platform independence, the OS is usually written in C language.

Microkernel OSs are relatively easy to port between platforms, since only the Microkernel needs to be rewritten and/or the system can be run as is, no matter whether it is operating on a PC or a RISC-based workstation.

Pen-Based OSs. Although most of today's portable PCs operate from a keyboard (with a mouse or trackball, as well), there has been an increasing amount of interest in portables that can take handwritten input from some type of a stylus, or pen, or device. At the present time, there are a number of such systems available in the market.

UNIXs: SCO, AIX, SVR4, OSF/1

The origins of UNIX are, for the most part, common knowledge in the computer community. UNIX was created at AT&T Bell Labs in the late 1970s.

The concept of open systems is closely associated with the UNIX operating system, so let's take a brief look at the history of UNIX. Today there are three distinct "flavors" or implementations of the UNIX operating system: System V Release 4 , AIX, and OSF/1, as illustrated in Figure 10.6.

System V Release 4, or *SVR4*, evolved from the original UNIX system developed by AT&T Bell Laboratories. It is now owned by Univel which is part of Novell. SVR4 has subsumed several versions of earlier UNIX implementations, including Berkeley, XENIX, and other UNIX System V releases. SCO UNIX is based on the SVR4 and XENIX derivatives.

IBM has developed several UNIX systems, but has used a common umbrella name for these products: AIX. The various AIX are AIX/ESA for the mainframe, AIX for personal computers (PS/2), and AIX 6000 for RISC systems 6000.

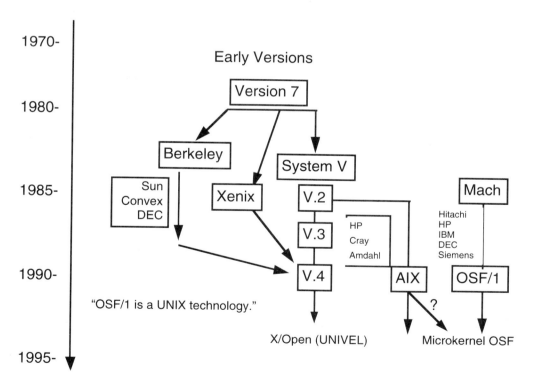

Figure 10.6 History and evolution of UNIX.

OSF/1 has been developed and offered by the Open Software Foundation as a UNIX technology to be productized by the vendor members.

UNIX has been plagued by market fragmentation due to the many versions available. However, the key UNIX players are joining forces to compete against alternative environments, in particular, Windows NT. We're seeing more and more agreements among UNIX providers to ensure standards.

The Common Operating Software Environment (COSE) is one example. It's an initiative by the major UNIX vendors to create a consistent applications environment and user interface across the UNIX variants. OSF has committed to following the COSE guidelines.

In addition, much of the new OSF technology is being incorporated into the other UNIX and non-UNIX offerings. The OSF *microkernel* is a multithreaded, scalable kernel that will take advantage of machines with multiprocessing capabilities, such as parallel, multi-, and cluster processing hardware.

Network (LAN) Operating Systems

Network operating systems (NOSs) are what finally makes all that hardware function as a network. Originally, NOSs functioned to allow sharing of printers and disk files with limited access by a workstation. However, today's NOSs provide the basis for client/server applications, integrating computers of many types and sizes.

A network operating system functions in the same way as an OS, except that it works to control multiple computers and peripherals. Its mission is to make shared resources (such as hard drives, CD-ROMs, servers and server-based applications, or printers) local. An individual computer's operating system takes requests from application programs and translates them—one at a time—into actions performed by its monitor, hard disk, diskette, or printer. The NOS, on the other hand, takes requests for services from many application programs and individual computers at the same time and satisfies them using the network's resources.

Like the OS, the NOS is a collection of functions and system calls. Some of them provide and control simultaneous access to disk drives, printers, and other devices—these normally reside on the shared network computer, or *server.* Others intercept and redirect requests for service from the computers themselves and send these requests to the appropriate server—these normally reside on the individual PC or workstation.

Since the communication servers support TCP/IP, IPX, NetBIOS, and other types of LANs, workstations can be attached to LANs running NetWare, Windows NT, LANtastic, Banyan VINES, LAN Manager, PC LAN, or any other popular network operating system.

There are two main types of NOSs. The most common type is the *client/server* network, in which the individual workstations function as clients and the shared network computers function as servers. The other type of network is the *peer-to-peer* network, which consists entirely of individual PCs that can function either as clients—by making requests for resources from other connected computers—or as servers—by providing resources to other connected computers. Although peer-to-peer networks are making inroads in small businesses and workgroups, they are much too slow and cumbersome to be used to connect an enterprise. In addition, they are not as easy to put together as the client/server arrangements. The most popular peer-to-peer systems can link up to larger client/server networks. The best known client/server NOSs include

- Apple Computer AppleTalk/AppleShare.
- Artisoft LANtastic.
- Banyan VINES.
- Microsoft LAN Manager/IBM OS/2 LAN Server.
- Microsoft Windows for Workgroups.
- Novell NetWare and NetWare Lite.
- Digital's PATHWORKS.

AppleTalk is a set of protocols designed for peer-to-peer "plug-and-play" Macintosh networking. The AppleTalk filing protocol is built into the Macintosh operating system that governs how files are shared over AppleTalk networks. The AppleTalk architecture supports TokenTalk, EtherTalk, and LocalTalk cabling schemes. PC, UNIX, VAX/VMS, and other operating systems can access AppleTalk networks as long as they have AFP-compliant client software and a physical interface to the AppleTalk. The AppleTalk Internet router routes data along the best path, assigns names to zones, shows all network connections, keeps addresses of other routers in the routing table, and routes traffic between LocalTalk, EtherTalk, and TokenTalk.

AppleShare is a distributed network operating system built into Macintosh's operating system. It allows the users to share their hard disk or certain folders with all or selected users on the network. Netware for Macintosh provides connectivity to NetWare servers throughout the internetwork, using AppleShare client software.

Artisoft LANtastic is comprised of a series of software and hardware for entry-level networking environments. When fully featured, LANtastic supports NetBIOS-compatible networking. LANtastic is a peer-to-peer LAN that requires no dedicated server. Any PC on the network can act as a server, workstation, or both. The LANtastic network operating system is designed for DOS-based networks including Microsoft Windows. A variety of network adapters support attachments to most desktop platforms, including IBM PC families, PS/2, and EISA-based Intel microprocessors.

LANtastic is simple and uses a small amount of RAM—less than 40K bytes on a server and less than 12K bytes on a workstation. LANtastic supports

- An electronic/voice facility that is menu driven and allows text and voice messages to be sent and received on the LANtastic network.
- Message saving by recipients.
- A "chat" feature that enables users to verbally chat in real time across the network and to textually chat using pop-up chat windows.
- File and record locking, disk caching, and simultaneous despooling to multiple printers.
- Multiple levels of built-in security.

- Network management using extensive audit trails to monitor access to subdirectories and printers.

LANtastic can run on NetWare with Novell's NetBIOS emulation. LANtastic NOS operates as a Windows application in enhanced or standard modes and supports Windows Object Linking and Embedding (OLE) Protocol, allowing the users to incorporate sound into their spreadsheets, database, word processor, and multimedia extensions.

LANtastic for Macintosh transparently integrates a Macintosh network and PostScript printers into the LANtastic NOS environment. It allows real-time file sharing between the two environments. For PC users, it establishes a dedicated gateway PC where users can access PostScript printers on the Macintosh network and manipulate files transparently.

Banyan VINES is a UNIX-based network operating system (running on a proprietary as well as SCO versions of UNIX) intended for large networks where multiple server operation and wide area network integration are of paramount importance. VINE's StreetTalk global directory and naming service are not only global, but distributed and replicated, offering speed as well as reliability—identical directory databases maintained in various locations on the network. This redundancy greatly enhances the performance of directory search operations on large wide area networks, as well as enhancing the fault tolerance of such networks.

VINES operates in large corporate networks with multiple servers, thousands of nodes, and a broad geographic scope requiring wide area connections. This includes mainframes, VAXs connected by DECnet, and SNA networks. VINES uses LU 6.2 transport protocol and IBM's front-end hardware to transport VINES traffic over SNA wide area facilities. Some VINES versions provide gateway connectivity to DOS, Windows, and Macintosh VINES clients with 3270 terminal and printer emulation.

VINES network server allows PC and UNIX users to share files and printers through standard protocols such as TCP/IP and NFS. In addition, it provides connectivity to UNIX platforms such as DEC, Hewlett-Packard, IBM AIX, NCR, SUN, and NetWare users.

Microsoft LAN Manager supports most desktop implementations such as OS/2, UNIX, VMS, DOS, Macintosh, and Windows NT. It provides a wide variety of application services, such as database management services via a SQL server, high-performance file sharing, printer and peripheral sharing, UNIX connectivity, wide area connectivity, interoperability with Novell networks, management, and administration of networks.

The *Windows for Workgroups LAN Manager* provides users with central management and security, connectivity to multiple platforms, and a platform for client/server computing. Options available with LAN Manager include

- MS-LAN Manager remote access service, allowing the users to connect remote desktops to a LAN Manager network over standard phone lines.
- MS-LAN Manager Services for Macintosh allows Macintosh systems to fully participate in LAN manager network systems.
- MS-LAN Manager Toolkit for visual basic for easy-to-use LAN manager development platform.

IBM offers two network operating systems: the *LAN Server* and the *PC Local area network (PC LAN) program*. The LAN Server operates under OS/2 and provides for distributed databases on the network. LAN Server is similar to Microsoft's LAN Manager. Workstations on the network require either IBM's DOS LAN requester or LAN support program for DOS or OS/2.

The PC LAN is limited in scope and is designed for small DOS-based networks. It permits sharing of disk drives and printers as well as the sending and receiving of messages and files.

Workstations on a token ring, PC network, or Ethernet LAN can use OS/2 LAN Server. OS/2 LAN Server relies on OS/2's inherent multitasking capabilities, print-spooling functions, automatic job routing, support for multiple print priorities, and the ability to use installable print processors as PostScript interpreters and graphics print programs.

OS/2 LAN Manager uses Microsoft's Server Message Block (SMB) Protocol, which provides faster response time and the ability to read and write large blocks of text per transaction. The LAN Server's network management and security functions consist of a three-level hierarchy for establishing user-access privileges. The LAN Server is designed for use on 32-bit servers.

Even though IBM offers these network operating systems, the emphasis is on supporting Novell's NetWare operating system.

As aging IBM 3270 terminals are phased out in most enterprises, they are being replaced by PCs and are being linked to the network via Ethernet over *Novell NetWare* in a majority of the cases. As these DOS-based PCs become functional, it is inevitable that the users will need more functionality than simply 3270 emulation.

Novell offers comprehensive set of communication services that are fully integrated with the NetWare environment, giving access to host resources and wide area networks. It supports any combination of LAN-to-host, LAN-to-LAN, and remote LAN access services. NetWare is a distributed, multitasking local area network operating system. It allows administrators to easily manage large networks. Novell's NetWare Directory Services (NDS), a global, distributed database, maintains information about every resource on the network by providing users with a consistent and cohesive network view. It also provides wide area networking support between distributed NetWare environments.

NetWare supports a wide variety of workstation connectivity giving Macintosh, OS/2, DOS, and UNIX desktops access to NetWare file and print services; database services; messaging services; LAN-to-LAN, LAN-to-host, or remote LAN access communication services; and communication management.

NetWare Lite is a simple, peer-to-peer network operating system for 2 to 25 users who need basic network features and functions. It allows the PC network users to share PC resources such as applications, files, and printers.

NetWare/IP seamlessly integrates into TCP/IP environments, giving the users the option to run over IP or IPX (Internetwork Packet Exchange). This essentially extends DOS and MS Windows or Windows NT clients on TCP/IP networks to continue using the applications and services they need even across internetworks supporting IP-only traffic. NetWare/IP can act as a gateway to support both IPX and IP network protocols simultaneously or convert an IPX network to an IP-only network.

Digital's PATHWORKS includes networking client/server software products that permit users to access basic network utilities. In the PATHWORKS client/server relationship, the client receives system software, application software, mass storage, and printer resources from PATHWORKS servers dispersed throughout the network. PATHWORKS allow desktops, via a common network operating system, to share files, applications, and attached network resources, such as printers, disks, CD-ROM drives, and common electronic mail system.

When users link a PC to the network, the PC's system software and applications operate locally. However, the PC can remotely and transparently access applications and files from virtual drives contained on the server system. Pathworks supports a variety of industry-standard desktops on a peer-to-peer basis.

Some PATHWORKS features are common to all supported server types, whereas some are unique. Common PATHWORKS server features include

- Microsoft LAN Manager file and print services for DOS and OS/2.
- LAN and WAN capabilities.
- Support for a common electronic mail system throughout the network.
- LAN administration via menu-driven facilities.
- High-level security for PC files.
- Broadcast utility that allows the network administrator to transmit a single message to multiple PC users on the LAN.

PATHWORKS products also support a variety of popular networking technologies, including Ethernet, token ring, and Apple's LocalTalk, that can accommodate network transport facilities such as DECnet, TCP/IP, Novell IPX, AppleTalk, and the CCITT X.25-packet switching protocol. They also support industry-standard database services, transaction processing, and other applications. The PATHWORKS support includes

- PATHWORKS for VMS Server.
- PATHWORKS for OpenVMS LAN Manager.
- PATHWORKS for OpenVMS NetWare Server.
- PATHWORKS for DEC OSF/1 AXP.
- PATHWORKS for OpenVMS Macintosh Client.
- PATHWORKS for VMS ULTRIX Server.
- PATHWORKS for OS/2 Server.
- PATHWORKS for VMS SCO UNIX Client/Server.
- PATHWORKS for DOS and Windows Client.
- PATHWORKS for Windows NT Client.
- PATHWORKS for DOS (TCP/IP) Client.
- PATHWORKS for X.25 (DOS).

Graphical User Interfaces

A computer's user interface is the way in which you give commands to your computer. These commands are, of course, processed by the application software, the OS, the NOS, or any combination of the three. There are two types of user interfaces: a *character-based user interface (CUI)* and a *graphical user interface (GUI)*. MS-DOS is an example of a character-based user interface. To communicate with DOS, users type out commands or select items from the menu. On the other hand, MS-Windows is a GUI. It makes use of graphical elements such as icons, windows, menus, and scroll bars to represent a computer's hardware and software components and allows users to interface with and control their computers by directly manipulating these elements.

Except for the Macintosh, most of today's GUIs are layered atop an underlying character-based OS. This is certainly true of Windows (on top of DOS) and the Presentation Manager and Workplace Shell (on top of OS/2). In contrast, the Windows GUI is directly built into NT, much like the Macintosh Finder or desktop. Therefore, in case of the Mac OS or NT, the only way to interact with the OS is through its GUI.

Interaction Between OSs, NOSs, and GUIs

Figure 10.7 illustrates how OSs, NOSs, GUIs, and applications software work together. At the heart of the system is the workstation which may be running one or more OSs. When a user

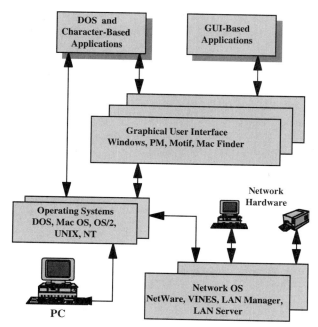

Figure 10.7 Interaction between OSs, NOSs, and GUIs.

wants to perform an action such as moving files between local disks and directories, the user calls through the OS, which then sends a request to the appropriate workstation hardware.

If the user is running a locally installed application, such as a spreadsheet, and wants to redraw the screen display, the request is sent through the application. If there are no GUIs running (e.g., using MS-DOS PC), the application relays the request back down to the OS, on to the hardware, and back to screen. If a GUI like Windows or Presentation Manager is also running, the application relays the request to the GUI, which forwards the request through the OS.

Except for Macintosh Finder, most GUIs can run character-based applications in a character mode, as well as running graphically based applications in the native graphics mode. Windows, for example, can run DOS applications through icons or directly through DOS using the DOS prompt option.

The situation is the same when the individual workstation is connected to a network, except that NOS mediates between the client workstation and the network resources (servers, printers, installed applications, CD-ROMs, etc.). The NOS receives requests for resources from the workstation OS (via the applications) and channels them to the appropriate resource.

RUNNING TCP/IP ON A PC

IBM's original personal computer, equipped with a cassette port, 16 Kbytes of random access memory, and a built-in BASIC interpreter, was a somewhat uninspiring though perfectly serviceable product. The most remarkable feature was its open architecture, which made it capable of supporting a variety of new types of hardware and software.

One of these new products was a networking package described in the *IBM PC Network Technical Reference*. This document contained a description of a programming interface known as NetBIOS. At the same time, several proprietary network products were introduced by other vendors. The NetBIOS specification became so widely used that more than 99% of all the personal computer LANs currently installed support NetBIOS. However, because of the popularity of the Novell products, less than half the personal computer LANs that have NetBIOS actually use it for their own applications. Even those networking products that do use NetBIOS are not interoperable because of differing protocols and hardware media used in their implementations.

At the same time, DARPA was developing a new suite of protocols, the Transmission Control Protocol and Internet Protocol (TCP/IP). These protocols were designed to allow interoperability between dissimilar computer systems. The TCP/IP protocol suite includes a variety of applications and protocols to provide connectivity. These include TELNET and TN3270, a variation of TELNET, which provide virtual terminal access to minicomputers and mainframes; the File Transfer Protocol (FTP) and Trivial File Transfer Protocol (TFTP), which allow remote file transfer; and the Simple Mail Transfer Protocol (SMTP), which transfers mail. In addition, protocols exist for network management, file sharing remote operations, data representation, name resolution, and many other networking tasks.

The TCP/IP protocol suite achieved widespread use when it was installed in most of the educational and scientific environments. Use of the TCP/IP suite of protocols became increasingly widespread as businesses adopted UNIX and its networking applications.

Today, TCP/IP is the protocol suite of choice for heterogeneous LANs and WANs. Virtually every LAN OS supports the TCP/IP protocol stack. While some configurations and installations lend themselves to adding TCP/IP capability directly to the mainframe via TCP/IP for MVS or VM or NCP, others are better served by using TCP/IP for internetworking on the workstations and LANs. The latter approach can significantly simplify the task of providing TCP/IP access to the enterprise data and applications because nothing on the mainframe needs to change.

Therefore, the question of how to integrate the plethora of personal computers and LANs into a coherent network is often the question. In the scenario described in Figure 10.8, each LAN connects to the host via its gateway independently of other LANs. Workstations on either LAN access the gateway via the TCP/IP WAN. The gateway connects to the host via SDLC, SNA coax, non-SNA coax, LLC, X.25/QLLC, bisync, or channel attachment. This solves half the problem. Intelligence is brought to the desktop, giving users multifunction capability, enabling them to both access the mainframe and run local applications. Even though each desktop has its own discrete path to the host and cannot readily share data and resources with other desktops, they can be configured in such a way

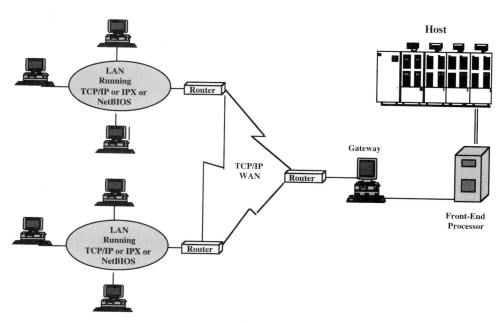

Figure 10.8 TCP/IP connectivity.

to share data and resources. An effective means of interconnecting these LANs is via routers and TCP/IP as illustrated in Figure 10.9.

Desktop Connectivity Basics

Today's desktop systems require access to all the enterprises' computer resources. On the TCP/IP workstations, TN3270 for UNIX, DOS, MS/Windows allows TCP/IP users to have 3270 terminal emulation, 3287 printer support, and API to mainframe. Adding PCs to a TCP/IP network has never been easy. The biggest improvement is the wide acceptance of the Microsoft Windows Socket application programming interface (WinSock).

Connecting desktops to TCP/IP involves four main layers (Figure 10.10): the network interface card (NIC), device drivers (for Ethernet), a TCP/IP protocol stack, and applications. Current Macintosh and PowerPC systems use standardized system components and protocols that make all layers easy to implement. The much more prolific IBM-compatible PCs, on the other hand, generally lack plug-and-play networking components.

To overcome such incompatibilities, a smorgasbord of add-on PC Ethernet hardware network interface cards has arisen that works with the variety of PC peripheral bus architectures.

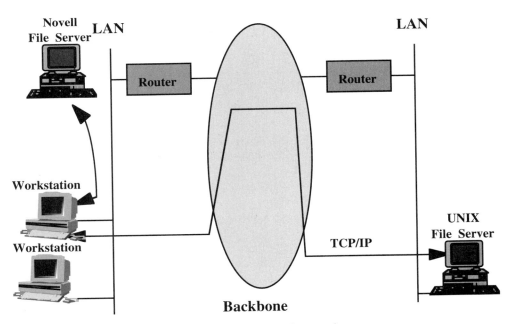

Figure 10.9 Multiprotocol networks.

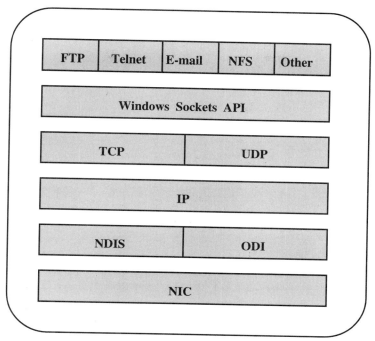

Figure 10.10 Major TCP/IP elements and interfaces.

Network Interface Card. Network interface cards (NICs) are boards that fit in the expansion slots of the popular types of microcomputers and are the only way to connect these machines to networks. There are a number of common characteristics which these NICs share. The most prominent of these are

- Microcomputer bus support.
- Bus size—size of the data path.
- Media type—type of wiring and connectors.

  Both microcomputer bus support and bus size are largely defined by the types of microcomputers in widespread use. Some of the more familiar types are

- An 8-bit bus used for the original IBM PC, PC-XT, and compatibles.
- The ISA 16-bit bus or the 8-bit bus used with the IBM PC-AT which is based on Intel 80286.
- The EISA bus, which is a 32-bit bus designed to support the older PC-AT 16-bit cards as well as new 32-bit cards.

- The MCA cards that support the bus used in the high-end models of IBM PS/2, supporting both 16-bit and 32-bit cards.
- Apple NuBus cards that fit the high-end Macintosh machines. This bus supports both the 16-bit and 32-bit cards.
- A set of new bus architectures such as PCI and SCSI that are beginning to be supported with Pentium class processors.

Media type and the type of connector supplied with the card vary:

- ARCnet runs on both coaxial cable and unshielded.
- Ethernet runs on three types of media—thick and thin coaxial and unshielded twisted-pair cables.
- Token ring runs on shielded and unshielded twisted-pair cables.
- FDDI runs on optic fiber, shielded, and unshielded twisted-pair cables.

Device Driver. A *device driver* is needed for the network interface. Device drivers also come in an assortment of types, including the Microsoft Network Driver Interface Specification (NDIS), the Novell Open Datalink Interface (ODI), and the packet driver specification from 3COM and FTP Software. Some network applications come with their own built-in drivers. ODI and NDIS drivers have multiple sublayers that fit into a single data link layer. The sublayer at the very bottom that talks directly to the NIC is the media access control (MAC) layer. You may have more than one NIC in a multihosted PC that links to two different Ethernet networks, such as a PC acting as a gateway or a server.

Major Functions: TELNET, FTP, SMTP (E-mail), TN3270

As the trend toward downsizing and distributed computing with TCP/IP continues, on the surface, the concept is simple, but as with many areas of networking, it is easy to get lost in the details once a solution is introduced. Putting TCP/IP on a PC means more than simply installing the protocol stack. Since networking is all about compatibility and interoperability, the stack must work without interfering with other personal stacks. The benefits of making this work are substantial. A well-designed implementation of TCP/IP on a PC provides users access to information on any other computer (including mainframes, workstations, minicomputers, and supercomputers) that support TCP/IP.

In addition to receiving files from any of these computers, users can send and receive e-mail within their organization or over the Internet. Understanding the elements of TCP/IP software is important when choosing software that will be useful today and in the future. Figure 10.10 illustrates the major elements and interfaces in the TCP/IP software. While a comprehensive explanation was already presented in the previous sections, an overview and how they relate to each other is an excellent first step to understanding the big picture.

The first area of importance is the applications. Most users base their view of TCP/IP on the applications since it is all they see. While many custom applications are possible, TELNET, File Transfer Protocol (FTP), e-mail (SMTP), and 3270 emulation (TN3270) are the most commonly used applications. There are a number of application services which are employed to facilitate internetworking. These are Network File System (NFS), Remote Procedure Call (RPC), and X Window System. In addition, there are a number of utilities such as Ping, Finger, Bind, and a Simple Network Management Protocol (SNMP) agent that are useful complements.

TELNET protocol enables users to login to systems located elsewhere on the network (Figure 10.11). TCP/IP software comes with a TELNET client, which typically emulates at least a VT100 terminal. Any system that has a TELNET server provides desktop users with a prompt to login as if they had a direct serial connection. In a typical scenario, users log in to a specific UNIX system. Once logged onto a UNIX system, they can run an application, look at files, write software using a UNIX editor such as vi, or send and receive e-mail.

TELNET is an application and a protocol. TELNET as an application is both a part of the TCP/IP suite and provides remote logon services. Each TCP/IP protocol suite has a TELNET application. TELNET itself consists of both a client and a server. From an application standpoint, TELNET provides users with the ability to perform remote logons with another host (Figure 10.12). Since TELNET is part of the TCP/IP protocol suite, it works with other components in the suite.

Figure 10.12 depicts a user invoking a raw TELNET client on host A by entering *telnet* at the operating system prompt. Along with *telnet*, a user generally includes the target

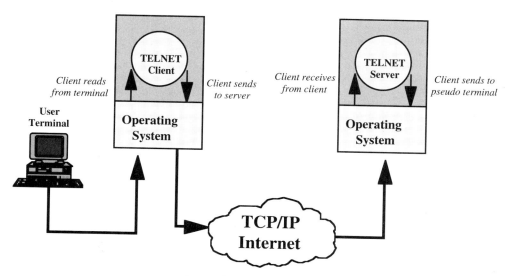

Figure 10.11 A TELNET session.

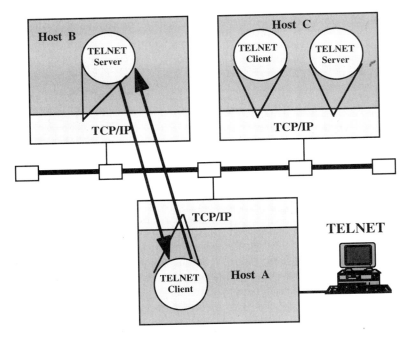

Figure 10.12 Using native TELNET.

host name desired to perform the remote logon. Once executed, the user initiating the *telnet* command receives a logon prompt for the target system. The user can now sign onto the target system and perform tasks as if physically attached. The following commonly used TELNET commands can be executed once logged on:

- Close—closes a current connection if one is established.
- Open— establishes a session with a target host if no valid target host-name was entered.
- Quit—causes the TELNET client to terminate.
- Status—provides information about the connection.

FTP allows files to be transferred among processors of all sizes and vendors that support TCP/IP. A user runs an FTP client on a desktop so files can be downloaded from a UNIX system running an FTP server. One of the best examples how FTP is used is to download software on the Internet. UNIX systems are located across the Internet that have been set up to allow any user to access files. Many sites have become collection points for various types of public domain software. Any FTP client can log in to one of these systems and move through the directories looking for software.

E-mail (SMTP) is the most commonly used application in TCP/IP environments. Numerous e-mail systems are available that are not compatible. The user interface for an e-mail application is not what determines compatibility. However, it is possible for two totally different e-mail packages to be compatible while two similar packages are not. What determines compatibility is the protocol the e-mail uses. The e-mail protocol associated with TCP/IP is Simple Mail Transfer Protocol. This protocol, along with a definition of e-mail message format (RFC 822), forms the standards for TCP/IP networks. An SMTP-based mail system on a desktop lets users send and receive messages on a UNIX system or to anyone on the Internet without going through a gateway.

It is also possible for a user on one e-mail system to send mail to a user on an SMTP-based network through e-mail gateways. These gateways translate between different e-mail systems. For example the gateway takes the e-mail message as it is formatted in a "proprietary system," reformats it for an SMTP-based system, and contacts the appropriate recipient using SMTP. However, features on one e-mail system may not be supported on the other system. As a result, only messages that use common features to both systems will be translated exactly.

As long as the protocol used to set up and transport the e-mail message is SMTP, the user interface can have any "look and feel" that the developer chooses to implement. A command line e-mail system will simply give you a prompt from which you need to enter commands such as to whom the message will be sent. A graphical-based system (such as OSF/Motif) will provide you a template to be filled in with information such as the destination of the message, the subject and content of the message, and to whom the copies should be delivered. Advanced features might include an address book and the ability to attach text from files or save messages in folders and files.

TN3270 is TELNET's ASCII-based data format by default, which does not fit into SNA that is dominated by EBCDIC. The TN3270 client program converts data from ASCII to EBCDIC and vice versa, generating a 3270 data stream as output. Integrating TCP/IP into SNA requires the data stream dilemma to be resolved. The benefit of TN3270 applications is that a 3270 (or 5250 for AS/400 computers) data stream is sent to the SNA-based host; thus data translation is not required on the SNA host. Three possible ways that can be employed to use a TN3270 client are as follows:

- TCP/IP is loaded into a TCP/IP attached SNA host. The data are converted on the host where TN3270 program is located. In this instance, the TELNET server portion of TCP/IP is used only to aid in session establishment (Figure 10.13).
- An SNA network is connected to a TCP/IP network via an SNA-to-TCP/IP gateway, with TN3270 client application in the gateway and the gateway providing the function of a TELNET server. The same functionality of establishing a session occurs on the gateway.
- The TELNET client is loaded onto SNA host, and the TELNET server may be on the SNA host offloaded or on a gateway between the two networks.

Many TN3270 client applications exist in the marketplace, but not all have the same features. Most of these provide terminal emulation and use the TELNET protocol. TELNET originated in the ASCII-based environments, whereas TN3270 was designed to output an EBCDIC data stream, which solved the data translation dilemma. The only difference is where in the network is the data translation performed. To solve this data translation problem, the following three possibilities exist:

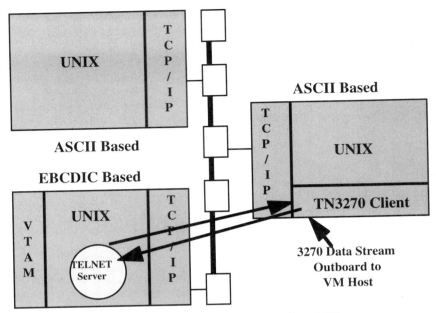

Figure 10.13 TN3270 client interaction with TELNET server.

- On the SNA host.
- On the TCP/IP host.
- On a gateway.

Application Services: NFS, RPC, X Window System

NFS allows a user to make a disk drive on a remote system appear local to the system. NFS runs on many operating systems and hardware platforms. Because of its origins, NFS remains closely aligned with UNIX and the future of the operating system.

NFS is a mechanism for sharing of files on heterogeneous platforms over one or more networks. This sharing is accomplished by allowing users shared access to a set of files called a filesystem. A user's filesystem may be composed of one or more remotely mounted filesystems that appear as a single set of files to the user. NFS is operating system independent. NFS uses a remote procedure call mechanism to accomplish this design goal.

Because every system handles disks differently, it is hard to describe in general terms and causes confusion about what NFS is and how it is used. As an example, in the DOS world, disks have letters: "A" is usually the floppy drive and "C" is usually the local hard drive. If a user wants the disk drive on a coworker's PC to be the "D" drive, it is necessary to network the software in order to make the PC think that the drive is local.

No NFS applications have interfaces similar to TELNET, FTP, or e-mail. NFS works behind the scenes and blends into that system's native environment. In the DOS world, NFS associates remote disk drives with a drive letter, whereas in the Macintosh world, it associates with an icon. As with all other applications, NFS must exist as a client on the user's machine and as a server on the computer whose disk the user wishes to access.

RPC (Remote procedure call) is a session layer protocol. It was especially developed for NFS, but is used in many networked applications. RPC forms the basis for message exchange in all NFS applications. RPC may be used in design and development of network services, which are used in a similar way to subroutine calls or procedures in high-level programming languages. This mode of working eases the programmer's tasks in the design and implementation of distributed programs.

Since the RPC protocol is independent of the nature of the message transport, an RPC program may be executed over both TCP and User Datagram Protocol (UDP). Some servers offer their services over both protocols and leave the choice to the client. As a rule, RPC is used with UDP, since the majority of RPC-based applications are transaction oriented. When UDP is used, the maximum size of the data section of an RPC packet is restricted, since UDP packets cannot be arbitrarily large. However, there is no size limit when using TCP.

If UDP is used, the forwarding of a message is not guaranteed, and the RPC layer must take charge of reliability. When TCP is used, no retransmissions may be initiated at the RPC level since TCP retransmits the message until it reaches the server. If message forwarding is unsuccessful, the RPC layer will be notified which may inform the application program.

The *X Windows* system can be best described as a standardized, client/server architecture that provides the ability to distribute graphics applications. Almost naturally, any such technology must have a conceptual twist. This is especially true with the X Windows system. The client and server roles are reversed when referring to where the application resides. Generally, the X server resides on the desktop (Figure 10.14), and the client process or application program resides on a system that supports X clients somewhere on the TCP/IP network.

X applications on a UNIX system such as spreadsheets, process control displays, text editors, graphic drawing programs, and so on, are clients of the desktop X server. This is why PC and Macintosh products are X servers and can connect to UNIX platforms and use UNIX client processes. The X server is also known as a multiapplication, multiscreen display. Each display manages the functions of a mouse, the keyboard, and the physical monitor or screen. This management involves controlling the tasks of sending the keyboard input to proper applications represented by the display. A nice additional feature of an X server is that it can create windows on multiple screens (physical monitors) of different screen types. This feature is not widely used but has tremendous potential across all industries for training and any area where real-time data can be represented in windows on many screens.

The concept of a centrally located application that can be accessed by terminals out on the network is not new. SNA and 3270 or 3179 terminals employ the same basic concept. The difference with the X Window system is the enhanced ability of the user to

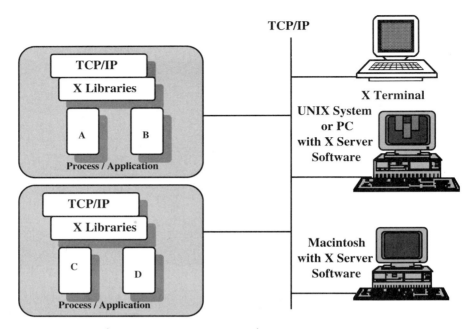

Figure 10.14 Common X window system environment.

manipulate the displayed data in a variety of standardized and intuitive ways. PCs and Macs running X server emulators or pure X terminals can connect to the UNIX servers and access the processes or applications. The end user can monitor several applications simultaneously, cut and paste data between applications, or easily employ a large number of local application interfaces to automate almost any combination of functions interactively.

Figure 10.15 illustrates how X-related systems are used to access applications via centralized 3270 emulators and TCP/IP. Each X terminal can connect to a number of processes on the UNIX system. In this the UNIX process is a TN3270 client. The UNIX system uses the TELNET server on the host. The connection is then passed through VTAM and into the application. The end user can have mixed UNIX and mainframe sessions in different windows on the same X system. A single workstation can display information management system (IMS) and CICS applications and local or remote UNIX applications simultaneously. The ability to simultaneously access multiple hosts, UNIX, and local applications increases end-user productivity tremendously.

With an X-based solution, users have immense flexibility in choosing what applications to run in their windows. Any time they need host access, a window can be opened that has 3270 emulator. The objective in this case is to evolve with the mainframe as a central server and to take advantage of the *POSIX* compliance and associated TCP/IP technology.

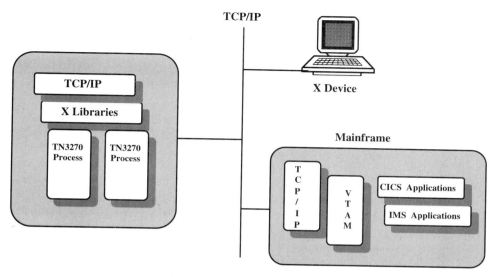

Figure 10.15 X window system access to host applications.

CONNECTING WITH UNIX

A huge number of organizations have made significant investments in DOS- and Windows-based applications. Many of these organizations are now in the process of integrating their DOS applications with their UNIX systems. With millions of DOS- and Windows-based PCs installed worldwide, DOS-to-UNIX, OS/2-to-UNIX, and Novell NetWare-to-UNIX connectivity is a matter of necessity.

Networking capabilities have always been the strongest fare for UNIX. Because of the UNIX's legacy TCP/IP, UNIX and TCP/IP have been catapulted into the enterprise environment, making TCP/IP an important protocol in internetworking. The proliferation of heterogeneous configurations require seamless connectivity between PCs using Window, OS/2-, DOS- and UNIX-based servers. Because of the TCP/IP–UNIX meld, many high data rate (bandwidth) applications are quite amenable to UNIX networks— even multimedia applications. Animation and full-motion video are just a few of the applications that test bandwidth capabilities of the network.

DOS

All DOS applications fall into one of three categories: DOS, DOS in a Window, and Windows. DOS applications were the first to be developed. They are command line oriented and designed to mimic applications found on most UNIX systems. With the popularity of Windows, many of the applications were modified to run in a DOS box under Windows. However, this does not change the command line interface, and the users cannot take advantage of the graphical interfaces Windows provide.

The PC/TCP programs (providing DOS connectivity with UNIX) operate on standard IBM-compatible PCs and PS/2s. PC/TCP network programs operate under DOS operating system for the PC and OS/2 for the PS/2. PC/TCP programs use the end-to-end Internet Protocol and can be used to communicate with any other host that uses that protocol.

Microsoft Windows for Workgroups and Windows NT

Microsoft strategy for providing computing solutions has two distinct product lines. The Windows product line, which includes Windows, Windows for Workgroups, Windows 95, and follow-ons. All of which are intended for desktop environments, and the high-end product line, which is Windows NT, NT Advanced Server (NAS), and follow-ons. Most of the examples discussed in previous sections have been based on Windows and Windows for Workgroups. In this section, we will discuss issues related to providing services in Windows NT and NT Advanced Server environments.

The enterprise model, illustrated in Figure 10.16, consists of Windows clients and UNIX workstations seamlessly accessing shared file resources centrally managed by a mainframe server. Authentication of client users, data security, and data backup are also managed centrally. The model scales upwards to 100's or thousands of PCs. Any preexist-

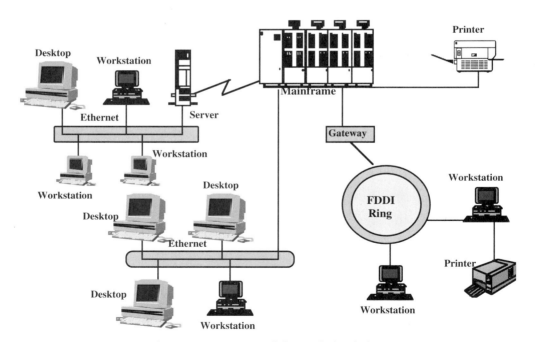

Figure 10.16 Interoperability with the desktop.

ing Windows client interoperability with other NAS servers is maintained. Interoperability with Windows clients for a restricted set of services is attained by supporting the server message block (SMB) protocol using NetBIOS over TCP/IP transport (Figure 10.17).

Windows NT is the first TCP/IP server that automatically configures the IP addresses of attached workstations, freeing net managers and their minions from this laborious task. NT server's autoconfiguration capability with Dynamic Host Control Protocol (DHCP) allows TCP/IP servers to allocate IP addresses automatically. DHCP must be supported on clients and servers whereas Windows NT workstation, the desktop package from Microsoft, includes the client software. It is also bundled with several popular UNIX workstations.

As illustrated in Figure 10.18, when a workstation is attached to the network, it immediately sends the server a DHCP discover message that contains its name and its MAC address. The server maintains a list of available TCP/IP addresses. When it gets the discover message, it checks to make sure it has an unused address on hand and allocates it to the client, and furnishes whatever other information the client may require, such as the address of the network card in the workstation and the server's IP address. The client acknowledges receipt of the information, configures itself, and requests anything else it requires.

Each Windows NT server maintains a logical map of the segments in a TCP/IP network (a segment is a subnetwork separated from other subnetworks by a router). One server can be configured to act as the default Internet gateway for several segments.

When the NT server assigns an address, it updates the database containing user names and IP addresses, which is known as the Windows Internet Naming Service (WINS). However, WINS database structure, at the moment, is not compatible with

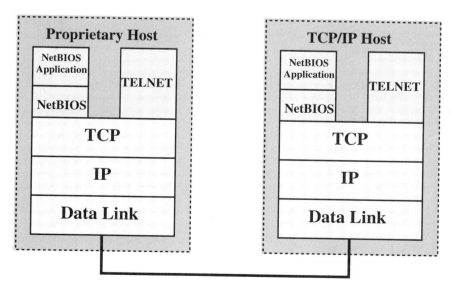

Figure 10.17 NetBIOS over a TCP/IP LAN.

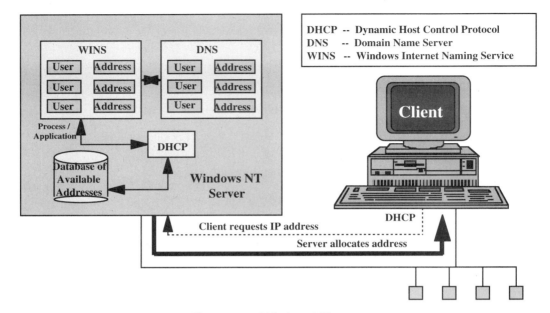

Figure 10.18 Windows NT server.

domain name server (DNS) structure. It means that users who mix NT and non-NT machines on TCP/IP networks must go through the WINS-DNS conversion utility. On the positive side, WINS also keeps track of a parameter time to live (TTL) of a particular IP address. TTL basically tells the server how long that IP address is valid. This feature is particularly useful to remote users who dial into the network for brief periods.

Although DHCP's biggest plus is autoconfiguration for TCP/IP, it also makes it easy for dial-in users of the network, to connect via SLIP (serial line IP) or PPP (point-to-point protocol).

In addition to DHCP and WINS, the NT server also is interoperable with NetWare, via a gateway that allows NT clients to use file and print resources on Novell servers, thus making it possible for remote NetWare clients to access their server over TCP/IP. For users who want to move to NT from NetWare LANs, a special tool is used to translate the NetWare bindery, move the NetWare files, and move the access control lists.

OS/2

LAN Manager/X is a system software that allows PCs running MS-DOS or OS/2 to use a UNIX system as a file server or host for distributed applications. It is specifically designed to run on UNIX systems. Since LAN Manager/X runs on UNIX instead of OS/2, it provides access to additional services such as transparent file access to other network servers accessible only from UNIX and gateway facilities to UNIX services such as printing.

Novell NetWare

NetWare NFS Gateways allow clients on NetWare network to access Network File System files on UNIX systems transparently. UNIX workstations can share files with other NetWare client systems such as Macintosh, DOS, Windows, and OS/2. In addition, the UNIX users may print to any printers on NetWare or UNIX-attached printers. The UNIX clients can also mount and access files from the NetWare server just as they would from a traditional NFS server.

Novell's LAN Workplace can be deployed on all the popular desktops—DOS, Windows, OS/2, and Macintosh—providing direct access to TCP/IP resources (including, file transfer, terminal emulation, and remote printing) with or without NetWare.

Novell's LAN Workgroup is a server-based system allowing full access and management to TCP/IP and UNIX clients on the network. In addition, it supports X Window services, SQL database services, and Windows Sockets API.

Hewlett-Packard HP-UX

HP's desktop integration provides support for a variety of LAN, WAN, and extended LAN connectivity solutions. HP offers connectivity of local and remote DOS, Windows, OS/2, Macintosh, and UNIX clients a choice of NetWare, LAN Manager, AppleShare, NFS, and DCE RPC networking environments. It also offers enterprise networking for multivendor communications (i.e., links between Ethernet, token ring, X.25, and FDDI environments support for TCP/IP, SPX/IPX, OSI, and SNA transport services) and access to HP-UX and MPE/iX server applications, data, and resources.

TCP/IP provides HP users with shared access to heterogeneous systems attached to a TCP/IP internetwork for application services such as FTP, SMTP, and TELNET. HP LAN Manager/X is the center of this interconnection. It transparently integrates MS-DOS and OS/2 PCs with UNIX systems. HP LAN Manager/X is an advanced network operating system and runs on all HP-UX servers and workstations.

With HP LAN Manager/X, users can have access to a wealth of PC applications as well as resources on the UNIX operating system. Users can keep using PC applications on the PC platform with which they are familiar. They can also access UNIX resources, including disk memory systems and high quality printers and plotters. HP LAN Manager/X compliments other HP networking products, such as HP network services and network file system services.

SUMMARY

The phenomenal success of the Microsoft Windows tells us that PC users prefer a graphical, point-and-click, drag-and-drop environment. From within this environment, PC users want to be treated as peers on the corporate network with access to every system that might provide useful information. This access needs to be as easy as possible and requires minimal navigational skills. At the same time, the PC user wants a set of tools for customizing various remote applications. With the new wave of applications "distribution" or "partitioning," that is, presentation, logic, and data, PCs are the primary tool for presentation or graphical user interfaces.

PCs dominate the corporate desktop, and PC LANs, by giving users a first taste of connectivity, are driving the demand for access to applications (logic) and data from other sources.

To meet all these user requirements effectively, there is a simple solution—a multi-protocol PC running Microsoft Windows or a clone software, that is, a single network interface card capable of switching between various protocols effortlessly. For example, a PC might switch between Novell's IPX while using the LAN transport and TCP/IP for integrating the enterprise networks.

With a modular approach to networking at the PC level, transport protocols can be changed or added with minimal impact on the user. The network should be out of the picture as far as the user is concerned. Whether the host is across the hall or halfway around the world, access via the PC should be quick and intuitive.

With the right connectivity software, which includes everything from transport to the user interface, logging to a host application becomes as simple as clicking on an icon. In a typical multivendor environment, the user clicks on icons and starts a UNIX-based inventory control session, a local interface, and a VAX-based financial package.

Because the connectivity software running on the multiprotocol PC is a suite of Windows applications, the users see a familiar frame and can extract information easily. In fact, it can be extended to running multiple remote applications concurrently. For remote file transfers, the software should support drag and drop for one or multiple files, whether the transfer method is *ftp*, *tftp*, or *ftam*.

Eventually, the multiprotocol PC can be a universal client, connecting to everything that the enterprise network has in store for it.

UNIX has survived and grown because of its strong communications protocols. Of these, TCP/IP has proven the most valuable and is fundamental to UNIX. RPC comes in a close second. DOS and Windows do not have communications protocols: their communication solutions are provided by third-party vendors. Of all these, the IPX protocol by Novell is the closest to TCP/IP.

EXERCISES

1. Describe the two methods for integrating PCs and desktops.

2. List the various LAN technologies and their future trends.

3. What is a network operating system and list a few.

4. List the types of microprocessor chips made by the Intel Corporation and used in IBM-compatible computers.

5. When an IBM-compatible PC is said to be an "AT-type" machine, which bus architecture does it have?

11

INTEGRATING UNIX
AND THE PCS (X WINDOWS)

Introduction
Overview
  X Applications
  X and Microsoft Windows
The X Protocol
  The Server/Client Model
  Window Management
  The *xterm* Terminal Emulator
  The Display Manager
  Opening a Session (Starting X)
  Creating a Window
  Mapping a Window
  Closing the Connection
Implementing X Window System
  The X System Components
  The X System
  The X Terminal
  PCs Using the X Window System
  PC Hardware Issues

  PC Software Issues
  Evaluating PC X Server Software
TCP/IP: Network and Serial Connectivity
  Joining the Network(s)
  Using TCP/IP to Maximize the Existing
    Hardware
  Connecting Third-Party Applications to
    the TCP/IP Software
  Other TCP/IP Features
  Serial Connections
Network-to-UNIX Integration
  Installation
  Reliability
Summary
An Example
  Components
  How
Exercises

INTRODUCTION

In today's multivendor and multiplatform environments, enterprises are constantly searching for more effective methods for providing users with easy access to distributed applications residing on host computers. An important consideration is that most users are not at all concerned where the applications reside. Users must have the ability to run distributed applications as easily and seamlessly as native applications.

Users can access applications on a UNIX host (Sun, Digital, Hewlett-Packard, etc.). Users can also transfer information between applications via standard copy and paste procedures.

Most PCs today have an x86 processor and 4 or more megabytes of RAM and are networked in some way. Because there are so many PCs in the market, they play a key role in the developing networked computer environments.

Adding X Windows software to a PC can make it a full-fledged "networked computer." The X server-equipped PC can have all the network's resources at its command. It can run client applications and use storage on any host in the network, with the right TCP/IP software.

UNIX-based mainframes, minis, workstations, PCs, printers, and CD-ROM drives are now within reach. In addition, a PC or a laptop can log on with a modem and gain full network access.

In this chapter, you will be introduced to

- X Windows technology, its features, and its applications.
- The role of X Windows in internetworking.
- Making the right decision in selecting and using hardware/software for integrating PC-UNIX using X Windows solutions.

OVERVIEW

The primary function of PC-UNIX integration is to make host and network resources available to the PC user. Historically, product differentiation has occurred in several areas, such as the level of product complexity, the UNIX-host platforms supported, and the PC platforms supported. Although a variety of solutions exist today for connecting PCs to UNIX hosts, the trend is towards Windows, Windows NT, and OS/2.

Users work more efficiently with familiar tools. Many users regard a desktop computer as the most important tool in their job. The X Window System is a network graphics protocol and windowing system that enables graphical applications to be distributed across the network. X Windows software allows personal computers to run X applications on host computers over a network. X servers provide connectivity from MS Windows, Macintosh, and DOS desktops to UNIX and VMS hosts. Users can switch between their native applications and X Windows applications by simply "clicking into" whichever window they want to use.

Microsoft Windows, Windows NT, and OS/2 PC-UNIX integration provide a new level of integration and connectivity beyond what is offered by network operating systems and other DOS-UNIX applications that execute the DOS command line. Windows-based PC-UNIX integration allows users to manage the complexity of networking computing within a graphical user environment.

Traditional access to network-based applications via terminal emulation and UNIX shells has limited the PC's access to character mode emulation and connection to a single or specific host. However, the new generation of PC-UNIX software integrates the X Window System within the PC environment for DOS, Windows, Windows NT, and OS/2.

X Applications

X Windows implementations are termed as PC X or X display servers and enable users to access applications from many different computer systems, anywhere on the network. Because all variants of the UNIX operating system are based on the X Window System, X provides a common bond facilitating enterprisewide computer interoperability.

X server software allows personal computers to run X applications on host computers over a network. Before any actual implementation, you need to understand what is X and why it has gained respect in the networking environments.

What Is X? Two of the most significant products in the current computer environment are windows and networks. *Windows* provide a modern, graphical, easy-to-use interface to what might otherwise be boring and difficult applications. *Networks* provide the computer users throughout an enterprise with the ability to share their resources. The X Window System is a well accepted and prevalent technology that has managed to merge these two powerful tools.

X Windows is a set of software tools that allows developers and users to create graphics-based hardware-independent distributed applications. X usually runs on UNIX systems. X allows application programs on a variety of computers to display output in separate windows on a single display. X uses a program called a "window manager" to allow the user to create, move, overlap, and destroy windows.

The X Windows system makes full *resource sharing* possible. PCs, mainframes, MACs, UNIX systems, and even DEC's VMS can all work together with X (Figure 11.1.). Using X will allow the average user to work in an environment where the network is almost transparent and everything appears connected directly to their system. Users do not need extensive knowledge of the multiple-vendor product integration. Meanwhile, the enterprise is maintaining its resources by allowing each user the appropriate amount of computing power and performance.

Since X is a network-based windowing system, applications can run in a network of dissimilar operating systems from different vendors.

History of X. During the early evolution of the PCs, in the mid-1980s, the IBM-PC was beginning to populate the desks of corporate America with screens bearing green characters on a black background. The Macintosh was finding a major market for its graphical user interface (based on mouse and windows interface developed at Xerox) in graphic arts and desktop publishing.

About that time, the Massachusetts Institute of Technology (MIT) set out to create software that would allow their computer users to access many kinds of computing resources. These resources may be networks, printers, or computer "hosts" from many kinds of computers using various operating systems. They married a Mac-like windowing

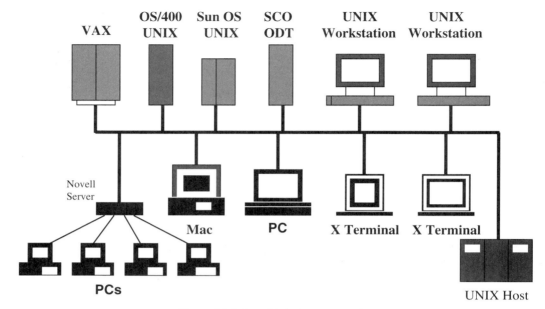

Figure 11.1 A multiple-host network.

system from Stanford University and named it "W" with the UNIX operating system and called it X Window System.

To establish the standard for the X Window System and assure compatibility on many computer hardware platforms, the MIT X Consortium was formed. The consortium set the eleventh version of X, called the X11, as a standard for developers to follow in writing their commercial software programs.

The X Window System today is a very popular standard at corporations, universities, and governments. With thousands of different applications in use, X is the leading network-transparent, platform-independent windowing system in the computing industry. Most of the UNIX operating system developers and vendors support the X Window System, thus providing numerous choices to the users for "internetworking."

Benefits of X. X can provide increased productivity for users and the base for hardware-independent GUIs (graphical user interfaces). Although Microsoft Windows is the most prevalent and extensively used system in the PC world, it is not based on any standard. Therefore, it is not easily portable to other hardware or software platforms.

X is a standards-based windowing *interface* that allows users on multiuser systems to have the same style of interface that workstation users have. Since this interface is a standard, developers can write their applications to run on a virtually unlimited number of platforms. This multiplatform capability has encouraged a large variety of applications to become available. Because of its portability, development of applications in the X environment has become very cost effective.

X's Flexibility and Ease of Use. The X Window System, or "X," is very easy to use because of its friendly graphical user interface. It runs on UNIX as well as many different computer hardware platforms, from desktop to mainframes. With X, a graphics application running on a "host" computer can display information on and receive commands from a user's terminal. The application does not even need to know whether that terminal is a UNIX workstation, a dedicated X terminal, or a PC running X software. In a nutshell, X is

- An open architecture.
- A network graphics protocol.
- Hardware independent.
- Operating system independent.
- Highly portable.
- Network independent.
- Network transparent.
- Vendor neutral—managed by the X Consortium.
- Expandable.

The X Window Standard. The X Window System is an open network software and windowing technology that allows many different types of computing platforms to share information and applications interoperability. The X Window System has revolutionized PC-UNIX integration and connectivity by allowing the PC user to connect to and display applications from many different computers.

X is a software windowing de facto standard. This standard provides the outline for window managed applications to run over a network. X acts as an agent between the display station (PC X server, X terminal, or workstations) and GUI applications. The application is called the client. The client performs the data processing and is not concerned either with the display or the interface to the user.

The X server can take the form of a PC X server, an X terminal, or a workstation. It has special software or "services" that enable the user to run and interface with the client. These X services include functions like letting the client application know when the mouse is activated and the output is displayed within a window on the screen.

X clients (applications) can also be distributed. This means that a portion can run locally on your PC and the remainder can reside on a remote system somewhere on the network. Using this distributed environment, the user does not have to keep track of where an application resides. The user simply clicks on the icon associated with the application, whether it is coming from the desk on their computer or from the host down the hall.

X is invisible to the user. X allows the user to run several different clients at a time, even from different hosts. Each client is displayed in its own window. With the multitasking feature of the operating system, each client can keep working even as the user switches from one application or client to another. Typical "client" applications are

- Word processors and spreadsheets (for example, Microsoft Word, Excel).
- Desktop electronic publishing applications.

- Office automation applications.
- Mechanical and electronic CAD.
- Graphics applications.
- User interfaces (i.e. desktops).
- Databases.

Many companies make the move to X simply to help bridge the gap between PCs, Macs, and UNIX. Microsoft Word and Excel are outstanding desktop applications. For example, using Quorum's Equal, one can run these on a UNIX host under X. This allows the users to share Mac, PC, and UNIX files and data freely. This combination provides the productivity inherent in these applications while benefiting from the power of UNIX and X. X is widely accepted because it provides interoperability and flexibility. X is a networkable, open, and expandable standard.

X and Microsoft Windows

Microsoft Windows is a proprietary windowing system. The graphical user interface, the system's "look" and "feel," is directly tied to the operating system and the underlying hardware. The GUI is a part of the windowing system, which decides how the display should look, where menus pop up or pull down and so on.

With X, the GUI, along with its supporting "window manager" (shown in Table 11.1), is independent of the operating system and display hardware. X provides only basic support for windows. In X, the window manager is essentially a client application with some special capabilities. Like the other X clients, X Window managers can run on any X-supported system. This provides an additional level of consistency and "look and feel" to the user on the entire network, regardless of hardware or operating system. This also saves training and support required in multisystem environments.

There are several GUIs and consequently several window managers for the X environment. For multivendor environments, the most popular is Open Software Foundation's (OSF) Motif. OSF is a nonprofit industry consortium (including Hitachi, HP, DEC, IBM, Siemens, and others). Other GUIs include Sun's OpenLook and DEC's DECwindows.

THE X PROTOCOL

The X protocol is the true definition of the X Window System. It is designed to communicate any or all information necessary to operate X Window application over a single asynchronous bidirectional stream of 8-bit bytes. Below the X protocol, any lower layer of network can be used to deliver "bytes" in sequence between a server and a client process. When a client and server are on the same machine, the connection is based on local interprocess communication. Otherwise, a network connection has to be established between the two.

The X protocol operates asynchronously to gain higher performance. The synchronous operating speed is limited by the time required to make a round trip, which averages

TABLE 11. 1 Comparisons Between Microsoft Windows and X Windows.

DEFINITION/APPLICATION	MICROSOFT WINDOWS	X WINDOW SYSTEM
Runs on	Pcs	Multiple Platforms
Look and Feel	Single built-in GUI	Choice of GUIs (Window Managers)
Applications	Local applications only	Global access
The ability to display multiple applications running together in resizable windows on the desktop	"Windows" runs on Pcs only, using local applications only	Allows "X server"—multi-platform, multi-GUI, network computing
The ability to provide files or other services to the network	Acts as a "server"	Allows as a "host"
The ability to access application software running remotely anywhere on the network or the user's own PC	Not possible	Allows as a "client"
The ability to display data on a user's PC from a centralized program over the network	Acts as a "client"	As an "X server," it allows a single application to handle the users' input/output for all X client applications

5 to 50 milliseconds on a typical local area network (LAN). For example, a client request containing 80 characters with a round-trip delay of 25 milliseconds is only capable of transferring 3200 characters per second synchronously. The server also sends events asynchronously allowing local polling for applications for continuous input.

The Server/Client Model

The use of the terms server and client in X are different from their use in other computing contexts. To X the server *is the software that manages one display, a keyboard, and a mouse.*

A user seems to control the mouse and the keyboard, but only views at the display controlled by the server. X server is unlike a "file server," which is a remote machine with a disk drive from which several machines can read and write files. The term server may seem a little odd. When you sit at a workstation, you tend to think of a server as something across the network rather than a local program that controls your own display. In X, the server is a local system whose displays are accessed across the network by client programs as described in Figure 11.2.

The server acts as an intermediary between user programs (called *clients* or *applications*) running on either the local or remote systems. The server performs the following tasks:

- Allows access to the display by multiple clients.
- Passes user input to the clients by sending network messages.
- Interprets network messages from clients.
- Performs two-dimensional drawings on the display.
- Maintains data structures, including windows, cursors, fonts, and graphics contexts.

Since the X Window System makes the network transparent to clients, these programs may connect to any display in the network. Each user at a server can start applications locally to display on the local server or can start applications on remote hosts for display on the local server.

The essential tasks of the server are to demultiplex the requests from each client and execute those on the display and to multiplex keyboard and mouse input back into the network to the clients. On single-threaded architectures, the server is typically implemented as a single sequential process, using round-robin scheduling among the clients. On multi-threaded architectures, the server could separate elements of its task among separate processors.

The client, *on the other hand, is a program that displays on the screen, accepts input from the keyboard and the mouse.* A client sends information requests to the server. The server returns replies to user requests and error reports to the client. The client may be running on the same machine as the server or on a different machine over the network, as illustrated in Figure 11.2.

The X Window System is not limited to a single client interacting with a single server. Several clients may interact with a single server displaying several applications on the same screen. In addition, a single client may interact with several servers simultaneously. A client may be running on the same machine as the server if multitasking is supported by the underlying operating system. Alternatively, the client may run on a different machine connected over the network, as depicted in the following schematic Figure 11.3.

Window Management

In X, applications actually do not control such things as where a window appears or what size it is. The screen layout or appearance is left up to a separate program, called the *window manager*. The window manager typically allows the user to move or resize windows, start new applications, and control the stacking of windows on the screen. The window manager determines the look and feel of X on a particular system. The Motif window manager allows you to invoke window management functions to

- Create additional windows.
- Hide windows by moving them in back of others.
- Shuffle windows on displays.
- Refresh your screen.
- Restart the window manager.
- Use keyboard keys, pointer buttons, and key and button combinations.

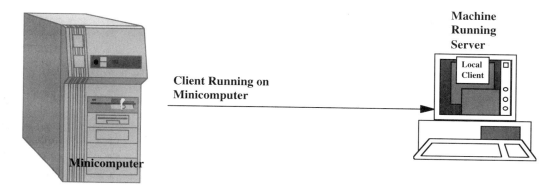

Figure 11.2 X server and X client.

The xterm Terminal Emulator

The X Window Standard (X11) is designed to support only bit-mapped graphics displays. For this reason, one of the most important clients is a terminal emulator. The terminal emulator brings up a window that allows you to log on to a multiuser system and run applications designed to run on a standard terminal.

xterm is the most widely used terminal emulator. Running *xterm* processes is like working with multiple terminals. Since you can bring up more than one *xterm* window at a time, you can run several programs simultaneously. For example, you can run file trans-

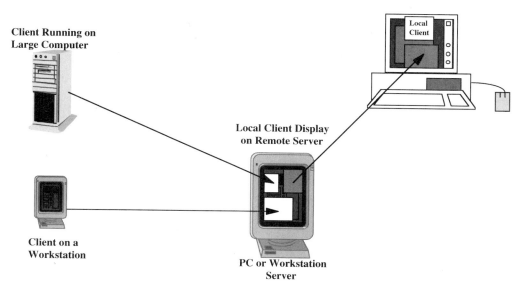

Figure 11.3 Local and remote X environment.

fer process in one window and perform text editing in the other. *xterm* provides you with a terminal within a window. From the *xterm* window, you can also invoke other clients.

The Display Manager

The Display Manager is a client that is designed to start the X server automatically. In its most basic implementation, the display manager puts up the login prompt on a standard terminal, keeping the server running, prompting for a user's name and password, and managing a standard login session.

Opening a Session (Starting X)

On some systems, the display manager may start X and keep it running. While on other systems, you may be required to log in at a prompt displayed on the full screen.

The client permits the user to identify the server it wants to connect by specifying a host and a display number. Since there is only one pointer, one keyboard, and one display connected to a single host, the display number is usually "0" on personal workstations. The client-side library usually provides an easy-to-use method for connecting the client to a server. In the case of Xlib (see the next section on "Implementing X Window System"), the user specifies the server using the host name and server number separated by a colon (for example, xhost:0). The networking utilities usually translate host names into network addresses.

Once the proper address is known, the client starts sending bytes that describe itself. The server responds by sending information describing itself if the connection is acceptable or describing as to what went wrong if the connection is denied. Once the connection is established, the client can start a meaningful session.

Creating a Window

Once the connection to the server is successfully established, the first thing most applications do is create one or more windows. The client issues a *CreateWindow* request by issuing a set of byte streams. The *CreateWindow* has many optional components and attributes. The window attributes control window qualities like background, color, resizing, saving, masks if the events are delivered to the client, what cursors are acceptable, and so on.

The client is not always interested in every type of event. Therefore, each window has an attribute that controls which events are sent over when they occur in that window, thus saving a considerable network traffic.

Mapping a Window

Mapping makes a window eligible for display on the screen. In the simplest case, when the application is alone on the screen, mapping actually displays the window. Once the session connection is established, and the *CreateWindow* session is successful, the *MapWindow* request simply sends the ID of the window that is to be marked for display.

Closing the Connection

There is no request that the client sends to the server to "quit." It is the server's responsibility to be able to clean up after the client is killed. The clients can be killed by a separate X client (for example, *xkill*) or by finding the process ID and killing the process from UNIX shell.

The client library closes the session by simply closing the network connection. The operating system also does this automatically when the client dies abnormally. The application program needs only to free any local structures that may have been created. The server subsequently cleans up after the client by destroying the resources client(s) created.

However, the X protocol does provide a *SetCloseDownMode* request to modify this operation so that the resources created by the client are not immediately destroyed, when the client exits. This allows the client to recover from fatal errors such as broken network connections.

IMPLEMENTING X WINDOW SYSTEM

The X System Components

The X Window system uses the client/server model having the following major components (refer to Figure 11.4.).
The X server

- Controls the user's display and keyboard.
- Draws windows, text, lines, circles, images, and so on.
- Runs as a user program.
- Implements the X protocol.
- Translates the protocol to hardware commands.

    The X client

- Is an application program that uses graphics.
- Interacts with X server locally or via network.
- X library (Xlib).
- Generates X protocol from C language calls.
- Facilitates device-independent code.

The X System

A typical X system requires the X software running on a host from a PC to a supercomputer. It also requires an X client (application) and an X server for a display system. The X server can be a UNIX workstation, an X terminal, a PC, or a Macintosh. If the X system is run locally, the entire X system resides on the workstation or PC.

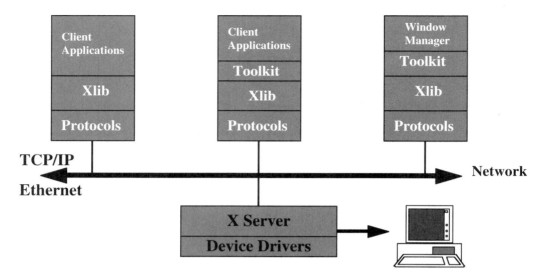

Figure 11.4 X Windows architecture.

X terminals are the most common stations for the end user since they use network resources at minimum cost. X terminals avoid administration and maintenance since all disk storage is on hosts on the network.

A dedicated workstation is required if network access and computing power of the host is essential.

Consider a PC-based X server (if you already own a powerful PC) for using "regular" applications and have access to the network at the same time. The PC application can run locally while the X client applications work over the network. A fast Intel 486 and higher will nicely suffice, in most instances.

The X Terminal

Most users think of terminals as dumb CRTs (for example, IBM 3270s) that are directly connected to host machines, via a wire. However, an X terminal is smart. The X terminal is designed specifically for performance and access to the various network resources. Typically, X terminals offer larger screens at a higher resolution (Table 11.2). X terminals have local memory and computing power to enable them to handle display tasks and produce higher interactivity. These terminals also take advantage of disk storage and computing power somewhere on the network.

One advantage of X terminals is that since there are no local disks, all management (administration, X terminal reconfigurations, data backup and recovery, software upgrades, etc.) can be handled from a central point. When selecting an X terminal, consider the following:

Speed: The perceived performance of running a client on the X terminal depends upon

- The amount of traffic on the network at the moment.
- The X terminal's CPU, clock speed, design, and the amount of local memory (RAM).

Cost: An X terminal can save more than the cost of a workstation if processing is not required locally.

Screen Size and Resolution: The bigger the screen, the more windows and information can be viewed at the same time (Table 11.2).

Ergonomics: Many people find screens with a refresh rate of 70 Hz or higher easier to watch. A tilt-swivel base and antiglare screen etching are helpful.

Local Memory: Get enough memory to suit the applications used. At least 4 megabytes of RAM is necessary for starters. More memory is required for decent performance if using colors, graphics, and opening multiple windows simultaneously (Table 11.3).

Network connectivity: Select the proper network wiring: thicknet, thinnet, twisted pair, or 10BASET. Also make certain of the network protocols supported: TCP/IP is most common.

Interface: Select the proper graphical user interface. The leaders are Motif, OpenLook, and DECwindows.

Administration: Some X terminals have features to make network administration easier. X terminals that have remote configuration let the administrator configure from a central location.

Location: A terminal with Simple Network Management Protocol (SNMP) provides compatibility with many brands of network management software.

Vendor Support: Make certain that the vendor knowledge, service, and support are reliable.

Windowing needs: How many windows will be open at a time, and how much will the user move and resize them?

Color: Most PC users expect at least some color. Sixteen to 256 colors will suffice for most applications. Image processing and multimedia require millions of colors.

Font Sizes: Fonts in X are defined in font libraries. Some X applications require very small fonts. In that case a higher-resolution monitor should be used.

PCs Using the X Window System

X Using DOS: A PC can take advantage of X in several ways. A software X server in the form of a DOS, NT, or Windows application can be installed and run on the PC. A special PC application can also communicate with a special network resident X server. Each X server can communicate with the network via different interfaces, including Ethernet and token ring, using TCP/IP or a serial link.

TABLE 11.2 Display Hardware Requirements of X Applications

MARKET SEGMENT	TYPICAL APPLICATIONS	REQUIREMENTS
High end (scientific/engineering)	Animation, imaging, simulation	17–19″ display; 1280 x 1024 or higher resolution; up to 16 million colors; 16 MB or more RAM
Midrange (professional/technical)	Design/drafting, process control, desktop publishing	16 to 19″ displays; 1280 x 1024 resolution; 256 colors; 8 to 21 MB RAM
Low end (integrated office)	Business and presentation graphics, financial services	1024 x 768 resolution; less than MB RAM; monochrome
ASCII replacement	Accounting, general text processing, word processing	1024 x 768 resolution; less than 4 MB RAM; monochrome

X servers can run on a 286 or a better processor, allowing switching between DOS and the server with both remaining in memory. A limited number of clients can be run simultaneously. A DOS-based X server must have the right drivers to be compatible with the network transport software as well as the PC's graphics controller. A video graphics adapter (VGA) driver is the lowest common denominator, but it is very limited in the resolution and colors it can display.

X Using Microsoft Windows.   An alternative to DOS-based X servers is those designed as Microsoft Windows applications. Due to Windows' graphical nature, most users tend to run X under Windows or Windows NT. The only downside to choosing Windows over DOS is the additional PC power and RAM required to do similar work.

On the plus side, the familiar, "standard" Windows interface is available. There are also several other interface options for X under Microsoft Windows. The user has a choice to use a local window manager (that runs on the user's PC) or a remote window manager. Most PC X servers use the local Microsoft Windows window manager. This is the simplest and most efficient approach, especially for new users of X and those accustomed to Windows.

On the other hand, if the user is more comfortable with X than windows, the user may use one of the X interfaces, such as Motif, OpenLook, or Open Windows. Most PC X servers can run these interfaces remotely where the host not the PC provides "window management." However, more network traffic is created, limiting performance. This option also limits the user to truly combine X and Microsoft Windows. Therefore, some X servers limit the use of only one Windows window while running a remote window manager. Some PC X servers can also run a Motif-style window manager locally on the PC.

PC Hardware Issues

X Server Performance.   Users judge system performance subjectively, usually by the speed with which the system updates displays and reacts to keyboard and mouse inputs.

While benchmark test ratings are useful for rough comparisons, the speed at which users' own applications run in the network are the only real measurement criteria.

In the past, PC-based X servers had a reputation for being slow, particularly compared to RISC-based workstations. A PC-based X server could not perform two-thirds as well as an X terminal. Now that PCs have dramatically increased in power and PC X servers have been improved, the results are very comparable. For acceptable performance, the selection of the right hardware and software is of paramount importance.

One key to great performance is using a 486 or better PC with 8 or higher megabytes of RAM and a good video card in conjunction with 32-bit X server.

Upgrades. Many PCs already have networking and at least 8 megabytes of RAM. This provides the minimum requirements to run an X server. However, upgrades may be desirable or required if more than simple or routine work is done (Table 11.2.).

Such upgrades may involve adding RAM, an Ethernet card, and an accelerated graphics adapter, or installing additional network software with TCP/IP. The cost of upgrading a PC is still less than purchasing an X terminal.

PC Software Issues

The users may continue to run their existing PC software, since a PC X server is just another PC application. However, if the user wishes to continue processing simultaneously with X, more PC power and speed are required to operate with both.

It is more convenient to store fonts for use in X displays on the PC's local hard disk drive. Most PC X servers supply a variety of fonts.

Performance. X servers as a group are generally slow. Some applications are more affected than the others. One of the primary culprits is the "network congestion." The TCP/IP stack also has some effect on performance, because the network communications take time. There is no single solution since most TCP/IP stacks and X servers are different. Each software product has implemented a way to improve performance of their implementations.

X uses several techniques to reduce network traffic. One major technique is to have the server maintain resources such as fonts, windows, and graphics contexts and allocate an integer ID to the client. While performing an operation, only a single integer is transmitted instead of sending an entire structure or string with the request.

In addition, the client programming library that implements the protocol can do several things to improve performance. The careful grouping of requests by the client before sending over the network is one way to improve performance. This makes the network transactions longer and less numerous, reducing the total overhead involved.

The advent of RISC architecture and true 32-bit microprocessors has improved the performance of X servers so that they are now extremely competitive with X terminals. For example, X performance on the PowerPC processor–based Macintosh computer provides an effective solution for both price and performance.

Evaluating PC X Server Software

As a base, the central server might be Novell, Microsoft's LAN Manager, or even a UNIX server. To evaluate PC X servers, at least the following criteria should be considered:

- Relative ease of use.
- Functionality (if it meets the users' needs).
- Depth of features.
- Network administration support.
- Reliability of the software.
- Performance benchmarks.

Desired X Server Features. Among the desired features are the latest version of the X11 server software that is compatible with the underlying central server being utilized. The following guidelines will help in selecting and choosing the desired features in an X server software:

Centralized Management: In a large installation, you can save a lot of installing and update time for PC X server software if it can be installed remotely from the central server.

TCP/IP Compatibility: The X server must be compatible with the already installed TCP/IP software on the PC and/or the host. However, a variety of network communications interface (NCI) modules are available which are often used to translate between the X server and the TCP/IP stack.

Easy Log on: For starting and logging on to a host, the server must support X Display Manager Control Protocol (XDMCP). The system administrator can easily configure users for logon from a single terminal.

For Total Simplicity: The ability of double-clicking an icon to log into a remote X client will add to the ease of use of a system. Some Microsoft Windows–based X servers allow the users to store logon procedures and passwords to execute an "iconic" start-up of an X session.

Graphics Capability: For DOS users, choose an X server that supports all the graphics cards and standards that are or are likely to be installed on the PCs. This is not an issue for Microsoft Windows where Windows drivers are used.

Debugging: It is possible to have compatibility problems between various X servers and X applications. The Xtrace tool helps keep a log of the execution event in X, for later debugging.

Printing from an X Server. Nearly all PC X servers support printing. But all print services are not created equal. Therefore, the printing requirements must be carefully examined. These requirements could include

- Print from host applications locally on the PC's printer. Some PC X servers support this option.
- Print from PC applications to UNIX printers. Practically all PC X servers let the TCP/IP stack handle such printing.

Host-to-PC Printing.   There are two ways to accomplish host-to-PC printing:

- By far, the most popular is for the X server to perform "transparent printing." This is done the same way as the dumb terminals. To start printing, UNIX sends an escape sequence to the PC until it receives another escape sequence to stop printing. This type of printing allows text only. Graphics or extensive formatting use character sequences that could be lost while the PC is looking for the "stop" sequence.
- The second method for printing from the host to the PC (PC X server) uses an interface to the TCP/IP stack. Unlike transparent printing, this method can print text and graphics. This method actually transfers the print job from the host and the PC routes it to the printer.

It is just as easy to print to a NetWare or peer-to-peer LAN printer. This is done by printing to LPT1 or the Windows default printer, using network software to capture the print and put it in a LAN print queue.

In summary, some X servers that use TCP/IP to print accomplish it in one step. However, some transfer the print file to a PC that routes it to the printer in two steps. PC X servers can print to the PC printer, and most can print to the network printers, using one of the following methods:

- Dumb terminal printer emulation (text only).
- TCP/IP interface.
- Separate TCP/IP software.

TCP/IP: NETWORK AND SERIAL CONNECTIVITY

In the beginning, users connected PCs to UNIX hosts via serial lines or modems and by running terminal emulation software on the PC, making the PC appear as a UNIX terminal. One of the primary motivations for PC-UNIX integration was to provide print and file services to the PC user. Terminal emulation enabled the PC user to run UNIX applications to run in character mode and provided the ability to copy files to and from the UNIX host.

Direct serial communication (without modems) and terminal emulation software are the least expensive way to connect PCs to UNIX hosts. Direct serial communication offers limited performance and functionality. However, the Ethernet LAN and TCP/IP model radically increase the performance and functionality of applications and network services. A variety of technologies (including proprietary protocols) exist for transferring files via serial and/or modem. However, the standards for PCs networked via Ethernet and TCP/IP to UNIX hosts are FTP and NFS.

Joining the Network(s)

No PC is an island. Since LANs appeared in the 1980s, sharing files and printers was accomplished by serial connectivity. Consequently, Novell and Microsoft LAN Manager networks became very popular. Even small offices saw the benefits of networking, and peer-to-peer LANs became very popular. Today, by connecting computers more effectively with TCP/IP, the users can maximize the use of a host of computing resources.

TCP/IP is a feature-rich protocol suite that provides interoperability between UNIX systems and other networks. TCP/IP supports UNIX standards such as NFS and the X Window System. Moving from a file-and-printer-sharing LAN to X network computing is a complex project. The primary reason is that TCP/IP adds enormous flexibility to a LAN that has just connected to a UNIX box. Whether or not one uses X, adding TCP/IP software to the PC network and the UNIX system enhances flexibility. It is the TCP/IP software that allows the users to share PC, Novell, and UNIX printers; transfer files; and share files by mounting remote drives.

The X Window System is a vendor-neutral network computing. X runs on local area networks using TCP/IP. TCP/IP is available from several vendors and connects many different platforms. Among the applications using TCP/IP are client/server applications, database servers, and intelligent terminal emulators. To make it possible to communicate beyond the local network, serial versions of TCP/IP have been developed that can move data over serial (through modems, on telephone) lines.

Most TCP/IP networks run over one of the Ethernet standards (discussed earlier). Although less common than Ethernet, token ring networks may be used to carry TCP/IP. To use a token ring network, the users must make certain that the token ring card can handle the installed TCP/IP driver from the TCP/IP stack.

Using TCP/IP to Maximize the Existing Hardware

If the enterprise already has a UNIX network, TCP/IP can make the UNIX resources available to the PCs. With TCP/IP and Network File System (NFS) installed, PCs become full members of the network—and with PC X software, sometimes as hosts running client applications. As discussed earlier, NFS allows the users transparent access to network applications and resources rather than having to deal with File Transfer Protocol (FTP) to transfer files.

The same rules apply, if the PCs are already connected to a LAN having a UNIX host. It does not really matter, whether the network operating system (NOS) is Novell NetWare, Microsoft LAN Manager, LANtastic, Banyan VINES, or even Windows for Workgroups. All such LANs are easily integrated with UNIX via TCP/IP.

A TCP/IP platform installed on the PC is not just a network driver. It also includes network applications and utility software, such as TELNET terminal emulator (for running applications remotely) and a file transfer feature, via File Transfer Protocol (FTP).

Connecting Third-Party Applications to the TCP/IP Software

There are many third-party applications that can use the TCP/IP protocol. These include client/server databases, terminal emulators, and PC X servers. However, these applications use different methods to connect with TCP/IP:

- A hard-coded interface for specific TCP/IP products. The application is aware of that particular TCP/IP, but not every kind of TCP/IP is supported.
- Connecting via interrupt 14 (INT 14) interface. Most TCP/IP products support this interface.
- Connecting applications to TCP/IP via Windows WinSock DLL (Dynamic Link Library) interface. TCP/IP products that support WinSock have the most flexibility. The WinSock DLL is a network programming interface standard. WinSock allows applications to run simultaneously in Windows to share the DLL. This avoids duplication of code and memory requirements. WinSock is portable and is supported by all TCP/IP products.

By installing standard network interfaces (for example, packet driver, NDIS, ODI, token ring), the PC-based TCP/IP-X implementation can coexist with many high-level network protocols, from NetWare to LAN Manager.

Other TCP/IP Features

Printer Sharing. Although most PC X servers support printing, it is generally limited to printing a file from the host to the PC's printer. How this is implemented varies from server to server.

Some offer ease-of-use printing to the printer selected in Window's print manager, and others require transferring the file to the PC and then routing it to the print manager. Some print only on dumb terminals via escape sequences, limiting the printed document to text.

A better way to integrate network printing may be to use the features provided by the TCP/IP stack. However, some TCP/IP-X products may not include printing or file transfer features.

Host-to-PC Printing. Certain TCP/IP packages give users the ability to print from UNIX applications transparently on the PC's printer. For the PC LAN user, this means that a printer on the PC's DOS or Windows-based LAN can be used to print from UNIX.

While new TCP/IP-NFS packages allow the PC to be a file server, many enable the PC to be a print server for the UNIX host as well as the LAN. To the UNIX host, the local printer will appear as a UNIX printer, but transparent to the users. The only drawback is that the configuration of this option on UNIX requires the system administrator to have basic knowledge of the printing mechanism. In fact, the TCP/IP usually allows the user to define the PC's printer as a UNIX printer, making it available to anyone on the network.

Another way to accomplish host-to-PC printer sharing is via TCP/IP remote shell, which comes with some PC X servers and many TCP/IP products. This is the easiest way to print both text and graphics under X. A driver is loaded on the PC, and a UNIX printer is then created that uses a script to redirect the print job to the PC. Some TCP/IP packages include scripts to convert printing data and redirect it to the PC, while others include a sample script but expect the user to customize it for the installation. Depending upon the refinement, printer sharing using a remote shell can be very easy.

From experience, printer sharing is much easier to accomplish under Windows than under DOS. Windows or Windows NT is designed for multitasking, whereas DOS is not.

PC-to-Host Printing. Most full-featured TCP/IP stacks support printing from Microsoft Windows and DOS applications transparently to a UNIX printer on the network. The two methods for doing this are TCP/IP remote shell and printing through NFS.

With the TCP/IP remote shell, one can simply load a driver on the PC that redirects LPT1, 2, or 3 to be a UNIX printer.

Some TCP/IP software packages include NFS, and others offer it as an option. To print from the PC to the UNIX host, one must mount the host as a local drive and then redirect the PC's printer to an established UNIX printer. In DOS, this can usually be accomplished via a simple command. For example, in Microsoft Windows, a printer can be defined as LPT1. With TCP/IP software and NFS, this can be remapped to a remote printer on the UNIX network.

File Sharing. Most PC X servers include the ability to transfer files. Some servers offer a friendly front end to the FTP standard. TCP/IP file transfers come in a variety of flavors. The most common is the UNIX FTP command. Another way to transfer files is to use a command line interface (front end of FTP or TFTP), just like a DOS or UNIX copy (*cp*) command. A typical usage is

ftp	CR
open <hostname>	CR
<login name>	CR
<password>	CR
get file1.xxx	CR
get file2.xxx	CR
get file3.xxx	CR
quit	CR

Microsoft Windows offer a file manager approach, which is more user friendly.

NFS or NFS-like File Sharing. NFS combines the PC LAN with the power of UNIX. It allows PC and LAN operating system users to take their network to the next level. For example, the UNIX host is treated just like a Novell server. NFS makes a defined UNIX directory or volumes look like a local hard disk to the local PC (for example, UNIX directory could be drive E). NFS is used to simplify file storage where PC applications are stored on a UNIX host and actually executed on the PC.

Serial Connections

There are several protocols for serial (non-LAN) connections. These are needed where systems are connected by phone (such as laptop at home connecting to the office network to use TCP/IP and X).

SLIP and PPP. The basic protocol for sending TCP/IP data is Serial Line Internet Protocol (SLIP). Point-to-Point Protocol (PPP) is a more sophisticated successor to SLIP. It is faster than SLIP and has better error correction.

Xremote and Xpress. NCD's Xremote is a proprietary serial protocol that is faster than SLIP or PPP. It maximizes X performance, using dynamic data compression optimized for X traffic to speed X data over slow telephone connections. Xpress from Tektronix is similar to XRemote.

NETWORK-TO-UNIX INTEGRATION

PC-UNIX integration facilitates interoperability between different PC environments. Employing a host application to service PCs enables heterogeneous PC environments to communicate with the network using UNIX host as a gateway. By using a UNIX host for network utility and application services, different PC environments, such as DOS, Windows, Windows NT, OS/2-based PCs and Macintoshes, can share resources and information.

In spite of all the advantages of X, there are thousands of other character-based UNIX applications. Even though most PC X servers and TCP/IP packages include a character-based emulation, these emulations tend to be very limited and are specific to a certain platform. The transport-independent, hardware-independent X server on the PC can run a terminal emulation package that provides other emulations for character applications. The terminal emulation can run in one window and X clients in the others.

Depending on the emulation and TCP/IP suite, you can implement multiple sessions on the PC. With the right character emulation in Microsoft Windows, you can also cut and paste from a character-based application to an X application to a PC or Novell application.

Installation

Particularly for a large enterprise, it is also important that all different pieces of software work together correctly. It is important that the stacks are integrated rather than bundled. When using an integrated stack, the following factors should be considered:

- Predetermine the access required by each user. Given this access, resolve appropriate host names and addresses.
- Evaluate the start-up methods (automatic via xterm or manual) available on the hosts for the required X clients.
- Understand the configurations that are required versus currently implemented.

Reliability

TCP/IP provides a highly visible addressing scheme. Therefore, if your PC X servers use TCP/IP on the network, it is easier to trace network load. TCP/IP standards have been fixed and are stable.

Centralized management and upgrading adds to reliability of the network by providing every user the same level of software. Centralized management also relieves the users from administration tasks and helps them not to worry about their configurations.

SUMMARY

Windows and Networks provide the computer users the ability to share their resources. The X Window System is a technology that has managed to merge these two powerful tools and provide interoperability among heterogeneous hardware and software platforms.

The X Window System can be used to share the full spectrum of network resources, such as files, data, applications, printers, and computing power. PCs, mainframes, Macs, and UNIX systems can all work together with X. X allows the average user to work in an environment where the network is almost transparent without any knowledge of the multiple-vendor product integration.

The X protocol can be implemented using a wide variety of languages and operating systems.

PCs can be used as X servers to communicate with the network via Ethernet or token ring under TCP/IP or a serial link. X servers can be DOS based or Microsoft Windows based. Due to Window's graphical nature, most users tend to run X under Windows.

In large installations, most X terminals are set up and maintained from a central location. This allows for easier installation of software (downloading from central site), compatibility of the server and host software, and makes the operation more cost effective.

Whether or not the enterprises use X Window System, adding TCP/IP software to the PC network enhances the flexibility of sharing resources and the ability to participate in global internetworking.

AN EXAMPLE: HOW TO TURN PC INTO AN X TERMINAL

Components

- Start with any MS Windows or NT PC.
- Add a network card for the PC.
- Select a PC X software that includes TCP/IP.
- Select any standard network (e.g., thick/thin Ethernet, 10BASE T or IBM token ring running any standard protocols like Novell or TCP/IP).

How

- Find the network cable (e.g., thin Ethernet).
- Install the network card.
- Attach the Ethernet to a simple "T" adapter supplied with the Ethernet card and terminate it or run more cable to another PC.

- Load the TCP/IP software on the PC. Make certain, it talks to the UNIX host system(s).
- Load the PC X software. Once installed, the X server software will show up as an icon.

What can the PC do? Now the user can run UNIX applications (multiple connections, if desired to multiple UNIX hosts) and cut and paste any other window programs. Both character-based as well as X programs can be executed concurrently over most existing networks.

EXERCISES

1. How does an X server differ from a file server?
2. Describe an implementation of *xterm*.
3. Can an X client operate on a PC, mainframe, or a supercomputer?
4. Why is X Window System so popular in UNIX-PC connectivity?
5. Can you generate more than one window on an X terminal and how?
6. In case of system failures or forced shutdowns, what must a client do to preserve its resources from not being destroyed immediately?
7. What facilities are available in the X Window System to improve performance?
8. Describe why one should implement X Window System in an enterprise?
9. List most common functions of X servers.
10. How does an X client close the session?
11. List and describe X Window System components.
12. What factors must be considered in selecting an X terminal?

12

INTERNETWORKING WITH MAC

Introduction
Overview
    Terminology and Protocols
    Systems Architecture
    Network Operating Systems
Networking Options
    Networking Features
    LocalTalk
    AppleShare File Server
    Macintosh-to-PC File Transfer
Mac-to-DOS Connectivity
    DOS Emulator on Mac
    Connectivity to Novell NetWare
    Macs as LAN Manager Clients

    Macs as Banyan VINES Clients
    Connecting PCs to Macintosh Networks
Macs and the Enterprise Network
    Mac-to-UNIX Connectivity
    Mac-to-VAX Connectivity
    Mac-to-Mainframe Connectivity
Network Administration and Maintenance
    Administration
    Software and Data Security
    Applications
    Problem Determination
    Troubleshooting
Summary
Exercises

INTRODUCTION

Macintosh computers are widely recognized for their superior graphics capabilities and ease of operation, which are valued in desktop publishing and design applications. For these reasons, the Macintosh has made significant inroads into the corporate environment. This has provided third-party vendors with more incentive to develop link products that tie the Macintosh to every conceivable micro-to-mainframe processors.

Apple Macintosh connectivity has been greatly enhanced since Apple's alliance with Motorola and IBM. However, it is not without a dilemma for the users. The users now must decide if they want to stay with the old bus "NuBus" and continue running the old proprietary operating system or switch to a more powerful PowerPC 604 and use PCI bus to take advantage of the future System 8.0 touting a modified architecture with hardware abstraction layer. OpenDOC, PowerTalk, and QuickDraw GX may be more strategic for those who need server class Macintosh machines.

Traditionally, Macintoshes have not been greatly used on large Ethernet and token ring networks. IBM PCs and other compatible systems have been used in these types of networking environments. However, with a bevy of vendors rallying around the Macintosh and AppleTalk, Apple's status has escalated in networking. Apple's token ring 4/16 NB card, reinforces Apple's strategy for token ring technology support.

Apple has also enhanced its SNA connectivity with 3270 terminal emulation and advanced peer-to-peer program communications (APPC) through logical unit (LU) LU 6.2 support. Even though these links have not produced any immediate, substantial results, they did pave the way for a long-range link to IBM mainframe resources. AppleTalk (Apple's protocol suite) can be used in two types of environments:

- Small networks that use Macintoshes exclusively.
- Large networks of Macintoshes that are connected to larger Ethernet or token ring networks of PCs and mainframes.

The Macintosh's operating system and hardware hide all the details of connectivity from the user. Installation of software is as easy as any other Mac application. However, you still need to understand some of the basics that are applicable to all computers, such as cabling, network configuration, application selection, and protocol compatibility.

Macintosh connectivity can be as basic as transferring and translating files between Macs and PCs or connecting individual Macs to a LaserWriter printer. It can also be quite complex, involving internetworking Macintosh PC and UNIX-based networks or linking local area networks with midrange and mainframe systems. We will consider major Macintosh connectivity alternatives in this section.

This section illustrates the integration of Macs into your existing systems (from PCs to mainframes) on a common network. In addition, we will discuss the general concepts, networking terminology, protocols, and Macintosh's capabilities as to how to handle or share files, e-mail, messaging, and data transfer for efficient use of the Macintosh's networking capabilities.

OVERVIEW

The term "AppleTalk" refers only to Apple's software protocol suite. Apple, most commonly, supports three types of AppleTalk networks: LocalTalk, EtherTalk(Ethernet), and TokenTalk (token ring). Some other vendors support AppleTalk on ARCnet.

AppleTalk was designed to comply with the ISO OSI Reference Model. The protocol set includes modules that address each of the layers of the OSI architecture. It also supports Dynamic Node Addressing (DNA), which automatically assigns network devices node addresses at start-up so that the addressing is transparent to the user. Another feature of the protocol, Distributed Name Service (DNS), lets users read and access resources on the network by name instead of the network address.

AppleTalk supports Apple's proprietary and slow 230 Kbps LAN, LocalTalk, at the data link layer. All Macintoshes come equipped with built-in interfaces to LocalTalk.

AppleTalk also supports links to token ring and Ethernet LANs. Its addressing scheme supports up to 246 devices on LocalTalk, and as many as 16 million devices on token rings and Ethernet LANs. The AppleTalk and Ethernet interface networks are designed to be plug-and-play devices so that inexperienced networking users can install the systems easily. The devices on the AppleTalk network have peer-to-peer relationships, allowing each to retain its individual functionality while simultaneously functioning in a network environment (Figure 12.1).

Terminology and Protocols

As with IBM, Digital Equipment, or Hewlett-Packard, the Mac has a language of its own. If you are a first-time user of the Mac, you will confront the terms AppleTalk, AppleShare, LocalTalk, or AppleTalk filing protocol. The problem with such terminology is its lack of specificity and consistency. In addition, the explanation of the Macintosh implementations appear fuzzy and incomplete.

This is primarily because the Macintosh handles the entire network interface at the level of the users and you do not need the elaborate set up of that of the PCs. The seamlessness of the Mac's networking software has a direct impact on how someone talks about Macintosh networking. All a user sees when connecting to a file server or a networked printer is the name of the network resource and a couple of buttons that complete the process of connecting the computer to the shared resource. Because of all this fuzziness, you need to understand some of the terms used.

- *AppleTalk* is a set of protocols that provide for Macintosh networking.
- *AppleShare* is Apple's file server application.
- *AppleTalk Filing Protocol* (AFP) provides the client interface for server access between a computer and a file server. AFP can be implemented on any PC.

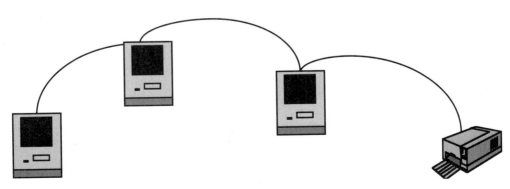

Figure 12.1 A LocalTalk network.

- *LocalTalk* is the physical link or cabling system, constructed using a daisy chain topology (Figure 12.1). It runs at 230.4 Kbps and uses a single strand of twisted-pair wiring with a special adapter.

- *EtherTalk* is the implementation of AFP for the Ethernet wiring standard, regardless of the type of cabling used, such as 10BaseT, Coaxial, or ThickNet. EtherTalk is actually the Ethernet driver that allows the Mac to use AppleTalk on an Ethernet network. It requires an Ethernet card or a built-in Ethernet interface on the Mac.

- *TokenTalk* is the token ring driver that allows the Mac to use AppleTalk on a token ring network.

- *AppleTalk Remote Access* allows connectivity and access to AppleTalk network via a modem or ISDN connection.

- PhoneNet is a physical link scheme similar to LocalTalk. It uses standard telephone twisted-pair cabling, either in a daisy chain or a star topology (Figure 12.2).

- Zone is a grouping of shared resources. A zone is actually established to segment a network and define separate functions, departments, or networks.

Systems Architecture

AppleTalk is the Macintosh's native networking architecture. AppleTalk is a number of layered protocols and is usually referred to as AppleTalk System Architecture. Figure 12.3 illustrates the basic structure of the AppleTalk system architecture, including its layers and how they interact with each other.

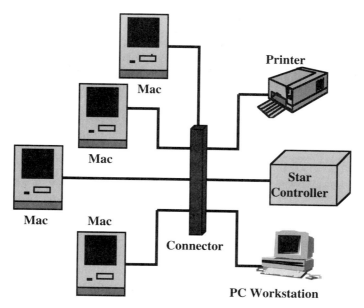

Figure 12.2 A star topology.

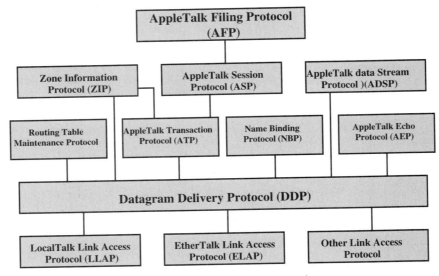

Figure 12.3 The AppleTalk architecture layers.

AppleTalk Session Protocol.   ASP controls all network sessions between a file server and a workstation. The connection between a file server and a workstation is one way where the workstation acts as a client (sending commands) and the file server responding.

AppleTalk File Protocol.   AFP provides the client interface for server access between a processor and a file server. AFP works in conjunction with ASP. AFP can be implemented on any PC, which, in turn, could access the file server as if it were a Macintosh, with all the same capabilities as the Macintosh client.

AppleTalk Data Stream Protocol.   ADSP is a symmetrical protocol that provides a pipeline between two processors on the network with a full-duplex data stream, without the necessity of an intermediate file server. In this set up, one Mac functions as a database server and the other as a client. ADSP can be used for terminal emulation, telephone communications, and other applications that send a continuous data stream between two processors. This is a common protocol used when two Macs are connected together and they both have ADSP installed. However, the programs using ADSP may not necessarily communicate when using a PC or UNIX-based network as a bridge.

Datagram Delivery Protocol.   DDP provides the delivery of data on an AppleTalk network or Internet. DDP is the part of AppleTalk that creates the packets that are sent over the network. DDP is a socket-to-socket delivery mechanism. Each DDP packet contains the packet's address in the form of socket number, node ID, and network number. Any computer on an AppleTalk network can have multiple sockets, so DDP allows for seamless functioning of multiple network-dependent applications. It also allows file server access from any individual machine using AppleTalk.

AppleTalk Echo Protocol. AEP is a client-based protocol that listens for packets sent by another node on the network and then echoes the packets back to the transmitting machine. This is mainly used to check if a specific device is connected to the network.

AppleTalk Transaction Protocol. ATP is used to make sure that the data delivery over the network retains its integrity. It is a transaction-based protocol that is used by the AppleTalk manager. It can be used to transmit data over a network or Internet. It operates like all other data transaction protocols— for sending, receiving, checking, and requesting return receipts, and so on. If a data packet is not received, ATP requests retransmission.

Zone Information Protocol. ZIP maintains a table that contains information about all networks and zone names. This is like a postal zip code directory, where each code is a zone. The only difference is that a zone is a logical determination so that elements of a single network can reside in various networks.

Link Access Protocol. The LAP provides access between a physical connection to the network. There is a different LAP for each type of network cabling and protocols, such as EtherTalk Link Access Protocol (ELAP), LocalTalk Link Access Protocol (LLAP), or TokenTalk Link Access Protocol (TLAP).

Routing Table Maintenance Protocol. RTMP is used by routers on an AppleTalk Internet to forward data packets to the proper network address. The router uses the routing table to determine the shortest possible path to get the packet to its destination. DDP uses the RTMP stub to determine a device's network address and communicate that information to the router.

Name Binding Protocol. NBP binds a device or workstation to the network by entering the network address and the name of each device into a table. Each device that is available on the network is entered into this table. The Internet address in the table contains the socket number, node ID, and network number. NBP is the mechanism that provides one network device with the network address of any other network-visible device, by mapping the client name to the Internet address that is used by DDP to send and receive data.

Network Operating Systems

The Macintosh operating system is simply called the *system*. The software heart and soul of every Macintosh is contained in a folder (*directory*, in DOS terminology) called the *system folder*. Inside the system folder are files that make the Macintosh run. System folder is like the DOS or DOS and Windows directory on a PC. The system file is like DOS SYS.IO file that runs the machine. However, the Mac requires two files—System and Finder. If either of these files is missing or damaged, the Mac will not work. The *Finder* is an application. It creates the desktop, displays the drive icons, allows for file management, and displays the menu commands in the menu bar. The system works in conjunction with the Mac's ROM and contains patches, drivers, keyboard layouts, system level messages, error messages, icons, sounds, and other pieces of code needed to operate the Mac.

Networking Software. *All the networking software is also included in the system.* The only NOS-specific software that needs to be installed on a Mac is the NOS's administration, mail, or chat utility. The specific networking extensions, control panels, and preferences files should be added before you can use it as a workstation. The networking extensions depend on the networking configuration. The extensions may include the following:

- *A/Rose and TokenTalk* extensions allow the MAC to use TokenTalk networking card. TokenTalk is a driver that allows Mac to access a TokenTalk network.
- *AppleShare* extension is critical for Macintosh networking, because it is the component that allows the Macintosh to log into an AppleShare file server.
- *EtherTalk* extension prepares the Mac to use EtherTalk for Ethernet connectivity.
- *File Sharing* extension allows Macs to use the system file sharing. It is basically the driver and controls the Sharing Setup control panel.
- *The Networking Control Panel* extension is used to choose what type of network a Mac is going to use, when the Mac supports Ethernet and/or token ring capabilities. A Mac using LocalTalk or PhoneNet does not need the Network Control Panel installed.
- *The Networking Preferences Files* extensions are files that maintain your network's configuration.
- *The File Sharing Folder* is used to store access rights for shared drives that are read only, like CD-ROM disks.
- *The Chooser* is the application that allows access to printers, serial device drivers, and the network. Once everything for the network is configured, the users will probably use the Chooser to access only the file server and printers.

AppleTalk Protocols. AppleTalk is not really a network operating system but a rather set of protocols compliant with the OSI Reference Model. AppleTalk protocols are designed for peer-to-peer plug-and-play Macintosh networking. The AFP functions as a client software that governs how files are shared over AppleTalk networks. AFP ensures consistent interface regardless of network server software running AFP compliant products.

The AppleTalk architecture supports *LocalTalk* (basic LAN), *EtherTalk* (Ethernet), and *TokenTalk* (token ring) cabling schemes. There is also some third-party support for ARCnet networks. With the acceptance of 10BaseT specifications, Ethernet on AppleTalk networks are becoming more popular. PC, UNIX, VAX/VMS, and other computers can access AppleTalk networks as long as they have AFP-compliant client software and a physical interface to the AppleTalk network.

AppleTalk Internet Router has boosted routing capabilities, by allowing data to be routed along the "best path." The router assigns names to zones, shows all network connections, keeps addresses of other routers in a routing table, and routes between LocalTalk,

EtherTalk, and TokenTalk. The Internet router runs in the background on a nondedicated Macintosh and can connect up to eight AppleTalk networks. Apple also offers a line of interface cards , connectors, and transceivers for AppleTalk networks, in addition to the Internet routers.

AppleTalk Remote Access enables Macintoshes to dial into stand-alone Macs or EtherTalk or LocalTalk networks. It allows the user to set up for either calling out or receiving remote access and specifying whether the remote caller has full access to the network or just to the Macintosh connected to the modem. Several levels of data compression speed up transmission beyond the typical baud rate for remote access. AppleTalk has very limited security features and allows open access to networks and has no central management functions.

There are other options to remote access the AppleTalk networks. Some of these allow Macs to dial into AppleTalk networks without host Macs and also can be used to link remote networks. Some even provide the ability to start up and run a remote Mac via a modem, use applications, and transfer files to or from the Macintosh or an AppleTalk network. Users can control the program from Apple menu, set access privileges, and gain remote access through an icon-based interface.

NETWORKING OPTIONS

When adding a Macintosh to your network, the Macintosh's hardware and operating system hide all the really messy details. You do not have to worry about IRQs, DMAs, or memory addresses as you install the Macintosh hardware. But you still have to be concerned with general networking issues that are applicable to all computers, such as proper cabling, network addresses, and sometimes protocol issues, issues of application compatibility, e-mail systems, security, and all the other networking problems you encounter in your existing environment. On the other hand, if you want to use just the Macs in a LocalTalk, PhoneNet, or Ethernet environment, all you have to do is connect the cables, turn on the networking software, create an access list, and the LAN is ready.

Networking Features

Mac OS offers many enhanced networking features, including peer-to-peer networking capabilities:

FileShare. *FileShare* allows a Macintosh to access files on another Macintosh and vice versa and is fully distributed. FileShare is well suited to sharing files among small groups of Macs.

Inter Application Communications. The two interapplication communications (IAC) features are built into the Mac OS system. The *publish* and *subscribe* is for dynamic file updating; that is, if the changes are made to a shared (published) file, those changes are automatically reflected in all copies (subscribers) of that file. The other feature is

AppleEvents, a protocol set used by applications to communicate between other applications.

LocalTalk

Macintosh has always been a networking computer. Since it was first introduced in 1984, the Mac has come with built-in connection, called LocalTalk, which allows Macs to be networked together. LocalTalk is simple and inexpensive to install and use. It is the primary way that small groups of Macs share printers and files. LocalTalk can handle up to 254 nodes and is generally set up in a daisy chain.

Cabling is simple (shielded twisted pair). LocalTalk is a peer-to-peer network that uses Apple's AppleTalk network protocols, which are built into the Macintosh operating system.

Constraints. LocalTalk can handle *distances* of up to 1000 feet. If a longer network is required, consider a star topology (Figure 12.4) with a hub such as PhoneNet StarController, or use a multiport repeater that amplifies signals to increase network distances. Many repeaters have 12 or more ports therefore a star topology can be easily configured.

Speed is another problem with LocalTalk. Data are transmitted over LocalTalk at the rate of 230.4 Kbps, compared to theoretical 10 Mbps over Ethernet. With graphics and heavy data applications becoming the norm, LocalTalk gets bogged down quickly.

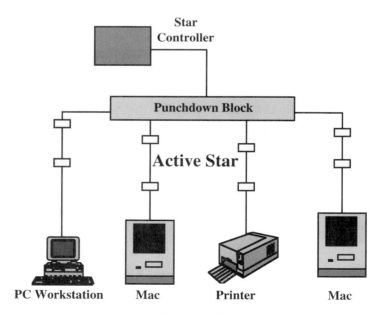

Figure 12.4 PhoneNet star.

Performance degrades quickly with added Macs on the LocalTalk LAN. To overcome this problem, Apple has resorted to "zoning" schemes (Figure 12.5).

Zoning can be accomplished by subdividing the network into zones, using routers. Routers make the network capable of more than one simultaneous session, but they do carry their own overhead on an already slow network. With additions of routers on the network, the network does become more difficult to manage and confusing for the user to navigate through.

The most popular choice for LocalTalk users to alleviate this problem is to switch to *Ethernet*. Relatively, Ethernet networks are faster but are more expensive to install than LocalTalk networks.

Another alternative is to consider using *switches with multiport LocalTalk bridge* that use packet switching to bypass LocalTalk's limited bandwidth. In this case, traffic can be diverted into as many as eight simultaneous "conversations," each with full 230.4 Kbps, and each conversation is broadcast only between the two affected zones, significantly boosting speed.

PC on LocalTalk. While LocalTalk is used primarily for Mac-only networking, there are solutions available to connect PCs into LocalTalk networks.

File Sharing on LocalTalk. There are a number of options for file sharing on a LocalTalk network. For fast, robust file sharing, you can use a dedicated, centralized file server such as AppleShare File Server or one of the Macintosh file server extensions to one of the

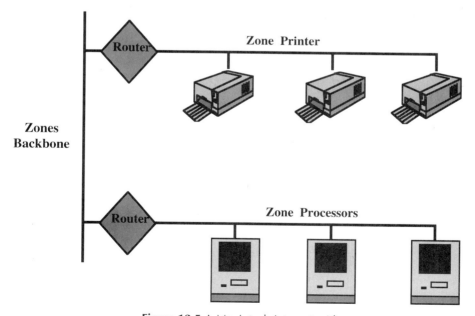

Figure 12.5 A Macintosh Internet with zones.

major multiplatform network operating systems, such as NetWare for Macintosh. In addition, there are a number of options for distributed, peer-to-peer file sharing on a LocalTalk network.

- *Apple's System 7's FileShare* allows peer-to-peer file sharing among up to 10 simultaneous users.
- *MacTOPS* is a popular server for Macintosh networks. It runs in mixed Macintosh, PC, and UNIX environments as a distributed file server and supports aliases and *Publish* and *Subscribe*. The problem is that MacTOPS uses its own proprietary file sharing protocol and interface, requiring special client software for individual Macintosh users on the network.
- *Personal Server Network* runs in a mixed Macintosh and PC environment and uses AppleShare client software.
- *DataClub* is a peer-to-peer server that acts like a dedicated AppleShare File Server.

AppleShare File Server

Any server that can be accessed by a Mac is an *AppleShare* File Server. The AppleShare File Server is the most popular file server for Macintosh networks. Apple makes AppleShare 4.0, which can be used on any Macintosh to turn it into a dedicated file and print server. Requiring a dedicated Macintosh as the server machine, AppleShare File Server runs over an AppleTalk network and supports both LocalTalk and Ethernet cabling schemes. Apple also offers dedicated servers known as Apple Groupware Servers, which provide higher performances for access by workgroups and for multiuser databases.

Macintosh-to-PC File Transfer

The most basic form of Macintosh connectivity with PCs is in the file transfer and translation. The Macintosh has built-in file transfer functionality that can be accomplished with ease. If you need to exchange data among PCs and Macintoshes for use in basic business applications such as word processing, database, spreadsheets, and graphics, you can achieve this level of connectivity with little trouble or expense. However, the files must be in compatible medium.

To move a file, you have to use the Apple File Exchange (AFE) utility, which is part of the Macintosh operating system. AFE utility looks at the contents of a DOS disk and determines the application type that generated the data, translates, and then copies to a Mac disk. It can also copy Mac files to a DOS-formatted disk.

Beyond the physical transfer of a file, the system needs to be able to understand and work with the file. This often requires a format conversion, or file translation. Many popular applications, such as Microsoft Word, Microsoft PowerPoint, PageMaker, and FoxBose+, are written for multiple platforms and have file-compatible counterparts on the Mac and the PC. These programs do not require additional format conversion, and using the AFE alone suffices. If your application does not have Mac and DOS counterparts, you will probably need to use a file translation program. There are a number of utilities that provide such facilities.

MAC-TO-DOS CONNECTIVITY

There are many ways to use a Macintosh when it is connected to a PC network. You can use the Macintosh and provide it with all the capabilities of any PC and connect it to the global networks, or you can isolate the Mac and use the network only for transferring files, or you can provide it with capabilities that fall somewhere between the two extremes. You can even use your Mac as an MS-DOS machine. The only limitation when using a Mac on a PC-based network is that on many networks, such as Novell NetWare or Banyan VINES, you need a PC to access the file server for maintenance or system administration.

There are many options and utilities to suit different environments and needs. Some of these options are described in the following sections.

DOS Emulator on Mac

Through either hardware or software emulation, you can use a Mac as an MS-DOS or even a Windows PC. There are three ways to use your Mac as a PC:

- Add MS-DOS co-processor card to the Mac.
- Use MS-DOS emulation software on the Mac. The emulator creates virtual PCs on the Mac. With RunPC emulator, you can run PC applications on a real PC and control them from within a window on your Macintosh. In addition, RunPC will allow you to mount MS-DOS disks on the Mac's Desktop, print to Mac or MS-DOS printers from MS-DOS applications, use MS-Windowing or multitasking programs to run multiple applications, or connect to host PCs.

   The Timbuktu emulation software allows you to control a Windows PC remotely from a Macintosh over an AppleTalk network or a Macintosh from a Windows PC, including: Controlling a Macintosh from another Mac, or controlling a Windows PC from another Windows PC, or transferring files between machines.
- Connect the Mac to a PC and control the PC from the Mac.

Connectivity to Novell NetWare

Novell NetWare is a complete network operating system, including connectivity with DOS and OS/2 workstations. Novell uses its own format for storing files and is optimized for fast access. Novell has added AFP compliance to its server software, with NetWare for Macintosh module, so that Macs can access NetWare server as easily and transparently as if it were AppleShare on a Mac. NetWare for Macintosh runs under Novell's NetWare operating system as a NetWare Loadable Module (NLM), linking directly into the operating system. It is capable of supporting upwards of 250 DOS, OS/2, UNIX, and mainframe nodes.

Macs as NetWare Clients. The NetWare for Macintosh includes the following features:

- Mac access to NetWare servers throughout the internetwork, using AppleShare client software.
- Ability for Macintoshes and PCs to share files if there are compatible file formats or convertible with utilities. Unfortunately, you cannot access Macintosh volume using Novell NOS from a MS-DOS machine unless the MS-DOS machine has the proper software, like PhoneNet PC, installed.
- Powerful network management and security features, such as password encryption at login, system fault tolerance, support for disk mirroring and disk duplexing, backup, and the AppleTalk network monitoring system.
- Sophisticated print services, which allow users to print on any LaserWriter, or compatible printer that NetWare recognizes, to manage their own print jobs, and to hide devices from other users.
- Ability to act as an AppleTalk Router (Figure 12.6), which can send AppleTalk data across Ethernet, LocalTalk, token ring, and ARCnet networks. It also supports seedability for determining network and zone configuration by analyzing data received from

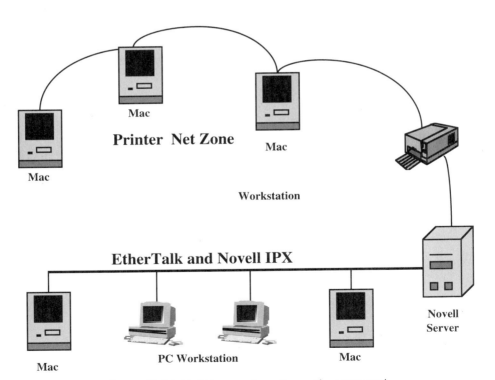

Figure 12.6 A NetWare configuration with router card.

the AppleTalk seed router so that the user does not have to configure network numbers and zone information for each AppleTalk router on the network.

Internetworking with NetWare Server. NetWare offers very fast and powerful mixed-platform networking (Figure 12.7). It also includes print services, a flexible software router for connecting many different kinds of dissimilar networks, and very sophisticated network management and security features that most Mac-only networks do not offer. However, NetWare is expensive and relatively difficult to install. If you need fast performance, a highly secure network environment, and ease in sharing files across platforms, NetWare is a logical choice. On the other hand, if your needs are more modest, or you are concerned with Mac-only networking, or you are running exclusively on LocalTalk, NetWare is probably not the logical choice.

NetWare provides a number of products to enhance Macintosh connectivity. These include the following:

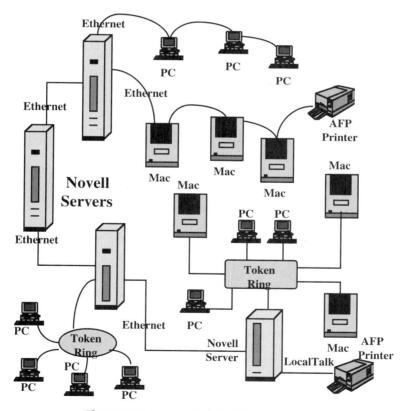

Figure 12.7 A Macintosh-NetWare network.

- NetWare Multi-Protocol Router is a software-only protocol router that supports AppleTalk and runs on a standard Intel-based computer. It consists of several NetWare Loadable Modules plus NetWare Runtime and can be used in non-NetWare networks. It supports any combination of Novell IPX, EtherTalk, TokenTalk, TCP/IP, LocalTalk, and ARCnet protocols.

- NetWare SQL is a version of Novell's data access software for NetWare servers, which supports Apple's Data Access Language (DAL). It provides Mac users running any DAL- compliant application with immediate access to data stored in programs that support NetWare SQL. It also works with off-the-shelf applications such as Excel, 4th Dimension, or Mac query tools such as DataPrism.

- NetWare Access Server allows to launch DOS applications from Mac. It runs on a dedicated Intel-based processor, enables remote users to dial into the NetWare network, and can support upwards of 16 concurrent sessions. Applications can be downloaded from the file server and processed at the machine running Access Server rather than at the workstation. On LAN/Mac, part of the access server, is emulation software that runs on the Mac and connects to the machine running Access Server for DOS sessions.

- NetWare 3270 LAN workstation for Macintosh is terminal emulation software that allows NetWare Macintosh users to access IBM mainframes without leaving the Novell network.

Macs as LAN Manager Clients

Microsoft LAN Manager is Microsoft's network operating system supporting MS-DOS and OS/2 users. The Microsoft LAN Manager for Macintosh gives Macintoshes access to a LAN Manager network's file and print services through an AFP-compatible server volume (Macintosh users need to run AppleShare). Mac can share files with DOS and OS/2 users and print to PostScript printers attached directly to the LAN Manager. DOS and OS/2 users can also print to networked LaserWriters. Figure 12.8 illustrates a LAN Manager Server with Mac and PC clients.

Microsoft LAN Manager for Macintosh is not as full featured as NetWare for Macintosh, but it does provide cross-platform file sharing. It also runs over EtherTalk, LocalTalk, and LocalTalk networks; supports Macintosh system; and complies with AppleTalk protocols.

AT&T's StarGROUP LAN Manager server, a UNIX-based implementation of Microsoft LAN Manager, offers add-on file server software for Macintosh. Called StarGROUP Server for Macintosh, it is AFP compliant, runs on Intel platforms, and allows Macs to share files with DOS, OS/2, and UNIX workstations. Installation is time consuming but simple, and Macs can access server through their Chooser.

Macs as Banyan VINES Clients

Gaining in popularity, Banyan VINES is a high-performance UNIX-based network operating system. VINES for Mac is an add-on for MS-DOS servers running VINES.

VINES for Mac is AFP compatible—Macs access VINES services through their Chooser, as with AppleShare. StreetTalk, a directory service, lets Macs see and access services anywhere on the network without having to log on to another server or switch zones. Macs can print to any PostScript printer on the network. Mac users can also change file and folder privileges and passwords but otherwise cannot perform any network management functions.

VINES Mail for Mac, another add-on, provides mail services for an unlimited number of Macs. VINES for Mac also provides built-in wide area routing, using a feature called tunneling (Figure 12.9), which unifies Mac networks over local or remote VINES TCP/IP connections, encapsulates AppleTalk in IP packets, and sends them over any existing link between Banyan servers. VINES for Mac can run over LocalTalk, EtherTalk, and TokenTalk.

VINES gateway service allows access to any mainframe from a variety of PCs on a VINES network. A single gateway can support PCs running Macintosh, Windows, and DOS computers.

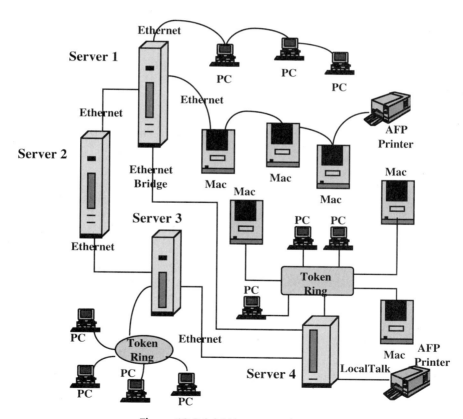

Figure 12.8 A LAN manager Internet.

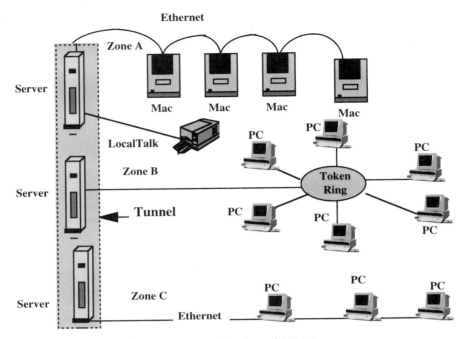

Figure 12.9 Tunneling through VINES server.

Connecting PCs to Macintosh Networks

In addition to the connectivity provided by VINES, NetWare, and DOS emulation on the Mac, the Macintosh networks can be directly connected to PCs and thus internetworks via Ethernet and token ring. Macintosh operating system offers options for PCs to be connected via EtherTalk and TokenTalk.

Via Ethernet. Ethernet is the most popular option for upgrading Macintosh networks that have outgrown LocalTalk capacity. It is good as a backbone for connecting two or more separate Macintosh networks and for networking Macs with DOS, UNIX, and VAX workstations. You can use Ethernet with any Mac from Macintosh Plus on. With a proper adapter, a Mac can fit seamlessly into any network, even to an AppleTalk LaserWriter (Figure 12.10).

Cabling and Topologies: EtherTalk allows Macintoshes to use Ethernet's high-speed backbone to transmit data up to a theoretical speed of 10 Mbps. It supports IEEE 802.2 framing and IEEE 802.3, for a theoretical limit of up to 16 million nodes per network. EtherTalk supports the following cabling and configurations:

- Thick coaxial cable (10Base5) provides excellent shielding and signal integrity, runs up to 500 meters between devices, and is usually configured in a bus topology.

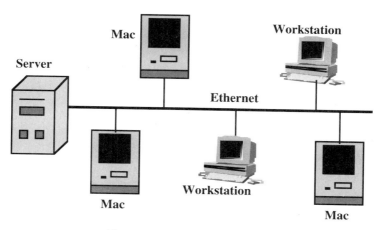

Figure 12.10 EtherTalk with a server.

- Thin coaxial cable (10Base2), often called "thinnet" or "thinwire," is less expensive and can run up to 200 meters.
- Unshielded twisted-pair (UTP) wiring (10BaseT) is the least expensive, but only runs up to 100 meters between devices. It can be used in star topology, where the problems are easy to isolate and detect. However, the expense of a hub at the center of a star topology at least partially offsets the cost savings from using the UTP wiring.

Interface Cards for Ethernet: One way to connect to Ethernet is through interface cards or SCSI devices attached to each Macintosh. Apple has introduced a modular scheme for such connections, by leaving transceivers off of the interface cards, if a lot of Macs need to be connected on the network. This provides added flexibility to handle different Ethernet cabling options at a low cost. If you switch cabling, you only need to change the media adapter that plugs into the interface device. Apple offers a variety of interface cards, transceivers, and cables to facilitate such connectivity.

Mac Classics do not have any expansion slots, so they must also be accommodated. Most interface cards have 10BaseT connectors as well as another Ethernet connection port, typically an attachment unit interface (AUI), which can be connected to an external transceiver for thick or thin coaxial cabling.

To complete the Ethernet connection, you need to install the driver software—EtherTalk. Apple's Ethernet driver software replaces the LocalTalk—the specific part of the AppleTalk protocol to enable Macs to communicate over Ethernet.

Using Routers to Connect to Ethernet: Instead of using an interface card on each Macintosh in an Ethernet network, a single router can be used. Using routers is usually less expensive than using interface cards, which also provide better network management capabilities. Many routers also offer enhanced features, such as gateway functions, dial-up access, and WAN hook-ups. Hardware routers tend to be faster and can generally handle larger capacities. Prior to any router connections, you must install configuration software and provide network specific information to the Internet.

Software routers run in the background, typically on the server. For software routers, connections must be made to the LocalTalk port and to an Ethernet card in one of the Mac's slots, whereas, with a hardware router, connections are to ports in the router box itself.

Ethernet Products: There are many Ethernet products available for the Macintosh and these include

- Apple's Ethernet interface cards and adapters.
- Apple's LocalTalk-to-Ethernet router software.
- AppleTalk Internet router.
- Hubs.
- And others.

Via Token Ring. Connecting to a token ring network is just as easy as connecting to an Ethernet network however, there is no SCSI–to–token ring adapter available. Token ring is more complex than Ethernet, but it offers two advantages: greater speed (up to 16 Mbps) as compared to Ethernet's 10 Mbps and contention-free traffic due to its token passing scheme. Token ring is especially effective for large networks with heavy traffic. If you already have a token ring network and need Mac-to-PC connectivity or Mac access to an IBM midrange or mainframe system, using token ring makes a logical choice.

TokenTalk is a set of drivers allowing Macintoshes on a token ring network to transparently access AppleTalk network services. LocalTalk software comes with token ring interface cards. The AppleTalk Internet router software routes between token ring, Ethernet, and LocalTalk protocols.

Via ARCnet. ARCnet is a PC networking scheme that operates at 2.5 Mbps and supports long distances of up to 20,000 feet between devices, making it conducive for use in industrial settings. It is based on a token passing network access method and generally uses a star topology, although a bus topology is also supported. At the center of an ARCnet star topology is an active or passive hub. Most popular network operating systems support ARCnet.

Via LocalTalk. There may be an occasion when you have an AppleTalk network and want to drop a PC into the network or add a PC without connecting it to an existing NOS. There are a number of solutions available:

PhoneNet Talk allows the user to add MS-DOS or Windows machine to an AppleTalk network. It works by installing an appropriate Ethernet or token ring or AppleTalk adapter card. It will allow access to any AppleShare file server and any networked laser printer or ImageWriter. However, it will not allow the user to share a hard disk on the PC.

Personal MacLAN allows the user to turn a Windows or Windows for Workgroups PC into a true peer-to-peer AppleTalk workstation. With this software, the PC operates just like a Mac with all the networking capabilities of the AppleTalk. The Windows PC can share its drivers and printer resources on the AppleTalk network using LocalTalk, Ethernet, or token ring. In the Windows for Workgroups environment, you can connect to both the Windows for Workgroups and the AppleTalk networks by using WFW and Personal MacLAN adapters, respectively.

MACS AND THE ENTERPRISE NETWORK

Because of the proprietary nature of Apple products, the direct connectivity to the enterprise has been slow. However, with enhanced connectivity to the Novell, Banyan, and Microsoft network operating systems, the Macs are very much part of the enterprise.

Mac-to-UNIX Connectivity

There are three ways to achieve Mac-to-UNIX connectivity: by running UNIX applications directly on the Macintosh or by connecting Macs running the Macintosh OS to UNIX workstations or by making the Macintosh a TCP/IP node.

Installing UNIX on Mac. Apple offers a UNIX operating system that runs on Macintosh II computers. Called A/UX, it is an implementation of AT&T's UNIX System V with Berkeley 4.2 extensions. A/UX is compatible with System 7.0 and the Quadra platform. The later releases of A/UX running on either the Motorola 680x0 chip or the PowerPC RISC chip share the OSF/1 kernel and set of common tools and libraries with A/UX, retaining many features of the A/UX system.

A/UX is a standards-compliant, multitasking, and multiuser operating system. With A/UX you can perform the following tasks:

- Use menu commands and manipulate icons to open, move, rename, or copy files and applications on the A/UX and the Macintosh file systems concurrently.
- Store Macintosh files and applications in the A/UX file system as well as in the Macintosh file system.
- Use the Macintosh files or off-the-shelf Macintosh applications while running A/UX exactly as you use them while running Macintosh operating system.
- Run several applications at the same time, taking advantage of both Macintosh features and A/UX multitasking capabilities.
- Run Macintosh software applications while running UNIX processes simultaneously.

UNIX Applications on Mac. There is a wide variety of software available to run UNIX-networked applications on the Macintosh, however, mostly terminal emulation. Some examples include

- Echo X, an X Windows display server for the Mac, which works with tool kits such as OSF/Motif, OpenLook, and DECwindows to let Macs run X-based applications remotely.

- Multitasking windowing and graphics using X windows commands.
- Xgator, an X Windows system, which allows UNIX workstations running X Windows to run Macintosh applications over TCP/IP networks.
- TCP/connect, which provides TELNET terminal emulation over TCP/IP networks.
- PCIterm, which is a terminal emulation application to let Mac clients run UNIX applications on the server or access other UNIX services directly. This also includes support for RS/6000 RISC UNIX servers.
- PacerTerm, which provides terminal emulation.
- Versions of VersaTerm, which provide file transfer, time synchronization, and terminal emulation offering up to eight simultaneous sessions.

Connecting Macintosh OS to UNIX Workstations. For networking Macs to UNIX workstations and servers, you can make your UNIX server act as an AppleShare server, or you can make the Mac understand TCP/IP. You can also translate AFP and TCP/IP protocols using intelligent network routers. There are a number of choices to make UNIX server act as an AppleShare server:

- AlisaTalk for UNIX provides AFP-compatible file sharing, high-speed file transfer between Macs and UNIX workstations, e-mail, and terminal emulation.
- uShare is software that transforms a UNIX workstation into an AFP-compatible server, while retaining UNIX security and utilities.
- PC-Interface allows Mac, DOS, Windows, and UNIX clients to share a single UNIX-based server and it provides AFP-compatible file services.
- Pacer software provides AFP-compliant file and print services.

Macintosh as a TCP/IP Node. Converting a Mac to a TCP/IP node is not quite as straightforward. Each Macintosh can run TCP/IP protocols itself, or a group of Macs can use a router that supports TCP/IP. On Ethernet, you can install Apple's MacTCP (driver software that allows Macs to communicate using TCP/IP protocols rather than AppleTalk). Some LocalTalk-to-Ethernet routers have TCP/IP routing.

TCP/IP networking is somewhat different from AppleTalk networking by assigning static IP addresses to your workstation, whereas AppleTalk assigns automatically. After you assign an IP address, all configuration is done in a window that looks like a control panel. Then you specify IP address for all host computers you want to connect to. Once the configuration is set, you can run the terminal emulation program and select the *Connect* command from the Terminal menu, select the desired session with a host, and wait for the system to log on to the host.

Mac-to-VAX Connectivity

In 1988, Apple and Digital Equipment formed an alliance to integrate Macs and AppleTalk networks with VAX/VMS and DECnet networks. DECLan WORKS for Macintosh includes file and print server software for the VAX and client software for the Mac.

Digital's DECnet for the Macintosh allows Macs to connect to Digital's Ethernet connection scheme from individual Macs. It does not make the VAX act as an AppleShare device, but it does integrate the Mac into an existing DECnet network.

Macs can connect directly via an asynchronous link through a modem or a direct cable connection, or to a terminal server. Macs can also be directly attached to the VAX Ethernet cable using Ethernet interface cards or SCSI links. An increasingly popular option is to connect to the VAX via gateways.

For the most part, routers are used to make connections between AppleTalk and TCP/IP, UNIX, DEC Pathworks, or VAX terminals.

Mac-to-Mainframe Connectivity

A variety of emulation and protocol conversion gateways are available for the Macintosh. Increasingly, LAN-to-SNA gateways are being used to connect PCs and Macs to mainframes.

IBM Mainframe Connectivity. The traditional way to link a Macintosh and a mainframe is to use coaxial cable and a Macintosh interface card. The coaxial cable plugs into the interface card on the Mac and into an IBM 3174 or 327x cluster controller on the other end.

Gateways reduce communications traffic and generally cost less than coaxial installations. They can link AppleTalk networks to a mainframe via SDLC, token ring, or coaxial connections. Some of the major players in Macintosh LAN-to-SNA gateways include

- Apple's SNA*ps, which uses a Motorola 68000 processor on a NuBus card. SNA*ps software simultaneously supports 3270 terminal emulation and APPC using LU 6.2.
- Avatar's MacMainFrame gateway and MacMainFrame coax gateway; also, the Netway 2000, which uses the proprietary SPARC processor.
- DCA's MacIrma LAN and IrmaLAN/Extended Platform (EP), which is PC based.
- Novell's NetWare 386 Services, a NetWare Loadable Module that gives Macs and PCs, running DFT multisession terminal emulation access to IBM mainframes and AS/400 midrange systems via token ring connection.

There are numerous terminal emulation programs available to run the mainframe applications on the Macintosh. Popular products are as follows:

- Apple's MacDFT offers single-session or five-session emulation using the Mac interface.
- MacMainFrame 3270 from Avatar offers emulation and graphics capabilities. MacMainFrame can be controlled from the HyperCard front end.
- SimWare offers SimMac emulation over asynchronous serial lines.
- Avatar's NetWay Advanced 3270 Workstation client software allows Macs with a LanWay token ring card to emulate 3270.

Many other companies offer 3270 emulation for the Macintosh, each differing in the ease of file transfer to and from the mainframe and in the extent to which they support the Macintosh environments. Most standard 3270 terminal emulation software for Macs does not take advantage of the Macintosh interface. However, more and more vendors are starting to use Apple's 3270 API, in creating mainframe applications.

MacMainFrame and MacIrma support the Macintosh "point-and-click" style of operation using the mouse, which makes for convenient copying of select lines or blocks of text to other Mac applications. Both products also support the Macintosh clipboard facility, which allows the exchange of data between programs in cut-and-paste fashion. Pulldown menus for function keys are offered by both, including the ability to detach the menu bar for placement anywhere on the screen for future reference. MacFrame also offers a unique automatic editing feature that comes in handy when downloading files from the mainframe. *Tab and form feed* characters may be embedded in text files before downloading to the Macintosh so they arrive in a usable format.

IBM Midrange Connectivity.   Traditional connection to an IBM System 3/X or AS/400 is through IBM 5251 terminals using twinaxial cables. However, the most prevalent is token ring LAN connectivity which is faster (4/16 Mbps) and less expensive than a twin axial connection. Most midrange connectivity products support both twin axial and token ring, via a token ring adapter card on the midrange and a token ring interface on the Mac.

For a direct twin axial connection to an IBM midrange system, the Macintosh needs a 5250 emulation card or a protocol converter. There are several 5250 emulators available. Also there are a number of protocol converters on the market, which are boxes that attach to the Mac's modem port, but are significantly slower than emulation cards.

NETWORK ADMINISTRATION AND MAINTENANCE

When dealing with a network of any size, whether it is on PCs or Macs or internetworked, you will need to manage the networks. As with any computer system, certain procedures need to be established and followed.

Administration

A number of administration procedures help ensure the smooth operation of the network, maintenance, performance evaluations, and data integrity. These procedures include, but are not limited to,

- *Backup* to avoid the loss of data on the servers.
- *Archiving* involves copying files to a storage medium and also to free up space from the file server's disk space (or remove it to off-line storage).
- *Disaster recovery* should prepare you for true disasters, fault tolerance, and improper network usage. This is designed to recover the data quickly for bringing the system(s) online without loss of valuable time.

- *Security* allows the user to keep the network secure from unauthorized access and vandalism.
- *Virus protection* has become a necessary evil in today's internetwork environment.

Distributed network management provides for central management of a network or internetwork. The centralized console can communicate with any device on the network, be it a bridge, concentrator, or router on the network, thus providing valuable information. This is also essential for problem determination and troubleshooting. The protocols that facilitate central network management will be discussed in later sections of this book.

Software and Data Security

Network security is one of the major concerns of any enterprise. Security precautions range from letting only registered users on the network to encrypting sensitive company trade secrets. Security techniques can include, but are not restricted to, limiting access to network resources, controlling remote access, and auditing user access.

Depending on the network operating system (NOS), there are two sets of security options: security dealing with PC files and that pertaining to Macintosh files. Regardless of how a NOS deals with its access privileges, an AppleShare volume provides for a specific set of security options. The two major security options are for access to the users to the system and the access rights to specific folders for each user. Most NOSs do not fully implement the security options found on AppleShare file servers.

The access can be granted to the whole volume or to directories (folders) on a volume. With directory access on a volume, the directories are visible in the Chooser as individual volumes. Each volume can be assigned different access privileges, making it available to a specific user or a group of users. Within a volume, access can be restricted to a specific directory and the type of access privileges.

Once a volume is mounted, whenever a directory is created, it belongs to the creating user. To change the access rights, all the user has to do is select the folder and execute the "sharing" command from the Finder's Menu to get an Access Privileges window. The owner of a folder can change any folder within the owned folder. Using the access rights settings, you can provide a user with full access to a directory or volume or totally lock them out, or anything in between.

File Guard is a security application which provides Macintosh network and individual machine security. File Guard allows you to create encrypted directories, set access rights to volumes for specific users and groups, and even specify which printers are visible from specific machines. Its advanced features include an auditing log, copy protecting software and files, and locking of system folders. To be effective, File Guard must be installed on every Mac on the network.

Applications

The primary purpose of internetworking in an enterprise is to be able to exchange data and applications from one platform to another. The most common cross-platform applications with Macintosh environments are among the Microsoft Windows, MS-DOS, and the Mac. The major categories of applications that are commonly employed for such interoperability are the following:

E-Mail

- *QuickMail* started life as a Macintosh e-mail system with MS-DOS and Windows support networked with Macs using AppleTalk. Quickmail requires its own Macintosh as the mail server.
- *cc:Mail* operates on any network and supports Macs, Windows, DOS, UNIX, and OS/2.
- *Microsoft Mail* supports both the Macintosh as well as the Microsoft Windows. However, the MS-DOS/Windows version cannot access the Macintosh Microsoft Mail server.
- *DaVinci eMail* provides cross-platform support for MS-DOS, Windows, Macintosh, and UNIX.

Word Processing

In the word processing arena, there are not very many applications that can run on Mac, MS- DOS, and Windows environments simultaneously.

- *Microsoft Word* for Macintosh is probably the most popular. However, exchanging files between Macintosh and MS-DOS versions is not completely seamless.
- *WordPerfect* is a cross-platform word processor and is available in MS-DOS, Windows, Macintosh, and UNIX versions. The WordPerfect 5.2 format is exchangeable between these platforms. However, when using Macintosh, it automatically saves files in Macintosh format which is incompatible with both the Windows and MS-DOS versions of WordPerfect.
- *MacWrite* saves files in native Macintosh format and is not compatible with any other word processor on the PC.

Spreadsheets:

- *Microsoft Excel* is one of the best examples of a cross-platform application for spreadsheets. Both the Excel for Macintosh and Excel for Windows are seamlessly compatible, and the programs have almost the same interface on the Mac as is on the Windows. Microsoft Excel can read all the standard file formats and is also compatible with Lotus 1-2-3.
- *Lotus 1-2-3* is available for all the three Mac, DOS, and Windows platforms. Lotus 1-2-3 works well when sharing files created by the MS-DOS or Windows versions with other platforms. However, there are some problems with files created on a Macintosh.

Desktop Publishing

The Macintosh is best known for its graphics capabilities. Usually Macs are added to the network for taking advantage of its graphics capabilities. There are a number of graphics applications that were strictly developed for the Macintosh and now have been ported to MS-DOS and Windows environments.

- *Aldus* was one of the first Macintosh software programs to be converted for Windows.
- *Freehand* is a high-end drawing and illustration package. *PageMaker* is the desktop publishing package. *Persuasion* is the presentation application. Files from Mac and Windows versions are basically cross-platform compatible.
- *Adobe* is the company that created the *PostScript* page description language. *Adobe Illustrator* is available for Mac as well as Windows. *Photoshop* is a digital photo editing package. The versions on Macintosh and Windows are compatible.
- *FrameMaker* is probably better known in the Windows world than in the Macintosh world. FrameMaker is designed as a multiuser and cross-platform desktop publishing application. FrameMaker files can be used seamlessly on all platforms supported, including most UNIX operating systems, Windows, and the Macintosh.

Graphics:

- *Microsoft PowerPoint* is the most widely used desktop presentation application. The files created on Windows PC and the Macintosh are interchangeably compatible.
- *CorelDraw and Harvard graphics* files can be interchanged between the Mac and the Windows platforms, in a fashion.

Databases:

A multiuser cross-platform is a requirement in any multiplatform environment. There are a number of database programs that can be used to access data and to create applications that are usable in a cross-platform environment.

- *FoxBase* files can be read on the Mac, DOS, or Windows platforms.
- FileMaker Pro works on both the Macintosh and Windows.
- *Omnis 7* is a high-end database system that allows the applications developed in Omnis to be run both on Windows and Macintosh platforms with no changes to the program code.

Problem Determination

Problem determination is a task that all administrators must perform at one time or another. There are two approaches: using a structured approach or the "shotgun" approach. Using the "structured" approach, you definitely know what the problem was and that you fixed it. However, with the "shotgun" approach, you fix the problem with intuition and trial and error. Experienced administrators usually try both approaches, but novices must stick with the structured approach.

Under normal circumstances, the Macintosh is a stable computing environment. But when things start to go wrong, the first task is to determine whether the problem is with the Mac or the network—that is, whether it is the Macintosh, the physical link, or some other network resource—or keep track of the hardware. Using the structured approach, there is a two-stage process in problem determination:

- *Quick Check:* Many network faults are the result of a component failure or a change to a component (software or hardware). The key here is to collect enough accurate information to decide whether or not that is the case. The key is to identify and eliminate the potential "causes" of the problem. You may need to perform some simple tests to ascertain the severity or scope of the problem.
- *A Closer Look:* The network can be divided into workable segments so you do not have to have the entire network to contend with. Each segment then can be examined and either ruled out or found out to be the culprit. Because more information must be gathered during this stage, specialized equipment, such as a "protocol analyzer," may be needed. Most network problems are directly related to the components, such as workstation, network adapter(s), cabling, server(s), bridges, routers, gateways, newly added applications, and system upgrades. Some of the questions that need to be answered are
  - Are there any user complaints?
  - Have there been any recent changes in software or hardware or upgrades?
  - Is network behavior abnormal?
  - Can the station work in a stand-alone environment?
  - Do any stations work?
  - Is there any traffic on the network?
  - Can the station connect to the network?
  - Is the adapter on the workstation functioning?

Troubleshooting

The process of troubleshooting is essentially that of identification, isolation, and resolution. In addition, there are a number of tools available that can help with the entire troubleshooting process. Hardware diagnostic tools check for hardware problems and malfunctions, whereas software diagnostic tools check for system software and installed application problems.

Identifying the Symptoms. In case of Mac networks, the first task is to run the network-mapping utility. This utility helps identify if the Mac and LaserWriter are in the map and communicating. If the Mac and the LaserWriter are visible in the map, the chances are that the problem is with the Mac. In addition, the utility will identify if all the network zones are up and running. If one of the zones is missing, it is probable that the connecting router is down. By making this simple test, you can isolate many of the possible problems.

Start-Up Problems. There are five basic problems that Macs can have outside of actual hardware problems:

- The Mac does not start because there is no power either because the power supply is blown or the supply is not plugged in.
- The Mac does not complete the boot process because there is a SCSI-ID conflict or the Mac cannot find the start-up disk or a system file is missing or there is a control panel conflict.
- The Mac crashes after it starts up while you are in the Finder probably because of a corrupted system or finder file or there are problems with the hard file.
- The Mac crashes while launching an application is probably due to problems with the system file (either corrupted on a back-level release). If the system file has just been upgraded, then the application may be incompatible with the system.
- The Mac runs properly but there are random system errors. These are the hardest to track down. They can be caused by a corrupted system, low-level hard-disk problems, incompatible hard disk drivers, or an application that is incompatible with some system elements.

If you are having start-up problems, check your cables and make sure SCSI ID numbers are all correct. Also make sure the drives are properly terminated. Boot with the Macintosh Disk Tools disk. If everything works while booting from the Tool disk but not when booting from the hard disk, the problem seems to be with the hard disk. In that case reinstall the system software. After the system has been reinstalled, shut down the Mac, and restart the system.

Chooser Problems. If there are network problems, always check the Chooser first and make sure AppleTalk is active. These problems could surface as

- Cannot see the file server.
- Cannot see the laser printer.
- Zones are not visible.

One of the possible causes of these problems is that the network, a router, or the file server is down. The other possible cause is that the network selection is set improperly. If you have an Ethernet network and LocalTalk is selected in the Network Control panel, you will not see any of the zones or other network resources.

Make certain that the proper network is selected in the Network Control panel and that the AppleTalk is turned on. If needed, reinstall the Apple network software and even the system software in case the Chooser seems to be corrupted.

Printer Problems. Printer problems are more frequent and most annoying. This is because a printer problem is usually network related, even if the problem is actually a Mac problem. Some of these could result because

- The printer keeps getting reinitialized because the printers on the same network have different versions of the LaserWriter drivers.

- The printer consistently fails to finish the print job because the print file is corrupted. Either the file has to be recreated or the printer has to be restarted.
- The Queues back up and the printer fails to receive the output. If a file that is queued is causing the problems, the file may have to be deleted using the server's queue manager.
- If you can print a directory from the Finder, the problems are usually not network or system related, but application related. Therefore, it is very likely that the file being printed is corrupted.
- From time to time, a printer hangs up. This can be alleviated by restarting the printer. You may divert your output to a different printer if there is something physically wrong with a printer. You may need to reinstall the printer software if it is corrupted.

Physical Link and Network Problems. The most common problems are either the routers going down or work intermittently. If a PC suddenly fails to log into the server and everything seems to indicate there is no problem, either the hub is down or the router is down. In this case, rebooting the router may solve the problem. Other type of problems could be with the Ethernet or adapters.

Application Problems. Application problems are rare. Usually, there are three problems you will encounter with mainstream Macintosh software. The fixes are fairly easy. The first could be caused due to a major system upgrade which may cause incompatibilities with the old version. Another could be due to shortage of memory which can be alleviated by allocating more memory to an application. The third problem is usually related to the directory, the partition map and so on. In this case, the hard disk is seriously ill and should be reformatted.

We will discuss "troubleshooting" networks in more details, in later sections.

SUMMARY

Apple has historically been the only real alternative to the often arcane domain of the IBM PC and its networking schemes. It is important to recognize that it was Apple that fostered a vision of the possibilities of truly user-friendly computing based around a consistent graphical user interface (GUI). In fact, the Macintosh's once unique desktop has been the primary reason for the success and longevity of the Macintosh. Even given the advances achieved with Windows, Microsoft has a long way to go before it achieves the kind of consistency of operation across widely divergent types of applications that the Macintosh has always had.

The marrying of the Macintosh with UNIX is the match of a beauty and the beast. While the fair Macintosh may be friendly, easy to use, and network ready, it lacks the gruff UNIX's speed, capacity, and multitasking capabilities. However, PowerMac plays an important role in Macintosh connectivity options and will continue to do so in the future.

For the small network user, Apple provides low-cost connectivity through the venerable but slow LocalTalk hardware included with every Macintosh, or through its newer options. Users with a requirement to connect Macintoshes to Ethernet or token ring or mainframe have the choice of a number of interface cards, routers, or gateway options.

Macintosh-to-host connectivity has been slow. While sophisticated links between PC LANs, wide area networks, and mainframe computers can be forged, Apple has not provided the one-stop organization of a Novell. A high degree of interoperability is possible between Macintoshes, PC networks, and large-scale computing resources, but builders are confronted with the daunting task of assembling pieces from disparate sources.

In this era of desktop integration with the enterprise, the matchmaking trick is to get different platforms to work together. When it comes to UNIX-to-Macintosh connectivity, the user has options ranging from routers to full-fledged network operating systems, complete with a trousseau of file and print services. Integrating Macintosh protocol software with TCP/IP and the UNIX host allows it to act as a server for Macs.

EXERCISES

1. Describe the terms AppleTak and LocalTalk and their relationship.
2. Give a short description of Mac-to-mainframe connectivity.
3. Explain how PCs can be integrated into the Mac networks.
4. What OSI protocols does Macintosh support?
5. Which network operating systems have integrated the Macs?

13

INTEGRATING LEGACY NETWORKS

Introduction
SNA Networking
  SNA Architecture
  SNA-X.25 Integration
  SNA-TCP/IP Integration
  IP Traffic over SNA Networks
  TCP/IP for VM
  TCP/IP for MVS
  TCP/IP for OS/400
  TCP/IP for OS/2
IBM Mainframe to UNIX
  3270 Emulation Using UNIX
  UNIX-to-Host Connections in a
    Traditional SNA/SDLC Network
  Remote UNIX-to-SNA Host Connectivity
    Via X.25
  SNA Host Links for UNIX Systems in
    Token Ring LANs
  Connecting Remote UNIX Systems to
    IBM Hosts over TCP/IP

  SNA Links for UNIX in Client/Server
    Configurations
  Using NetView to Monitor Remote UNIX-
    to-SNA Connectivity
  APIs for Host Applications
  UNIX-to-Host File Transfer Alternatives
  Central Support of Distributed UNIX
    Systems via SNA *rlogin*
VMS-to-UNIX
  DECnet Services
  Internetworking with DECnet
  Bridges
  Routers
  Gateways
  Network Application Services
AS/400-to-UNIX
  Internetworking over an Ethernet LAN
  Internetworking with OS/400
Summary
Exercises

INTRODUCTION

Enterprise systems began emerging as competitive information systems (IS) investments in the face of a dominant trend during the 1980s—decentralization of the IS function in many large enterprises. Most systems being developed were departmental, matching the common hierarchical organization structure. However, ensuring responsiveness to client needs had finally overtaken the earlier emphasis on ensuring economies of scale. Thus a conflict arose on how to mobilize both business and IS resources, which were now owned by powerful departmental managers.

Many IS organizations are turning to client/server technologies in their efforts to keep pace with rapidly evolving business requirements. Corporate downsizing and business process reengineering initiates have created an overwhelming demand for new applications. Highly productive, low-cost client/server tools are no doubt helping corporate developers keep pace with this demand. However, as client/server moves from departmental applications into enterprisewide, mission-critical roles, a key challenge is the need for access to the data and functionality locked behind corporate legacy systems.

Industry analysts estimate that about 80% of all corporate data remains in legacy system environments, including IMS, VSAM, and other proprietary nonrelational databases. Many of these systems are written in a combination of languages including COBOL, PL/I, and Assembler, making enhancements and/or downsizing difficult. Replacing these legacy systems is often not practical. While it is often the most technically desirable solution, the time, cost, and risk associated with replacement of a major operations support system may eliminate the option for many organizations.

One solution is to integrate legacy systems with new client/server applications that provide enhancements such as improved user interfaces, additional data and new levels of functionality. Existing legacy systems data and functionality that continue to meet business requirements may be utilized, while additional needs are fulfilled by client/server applications that are faster to develop and easier to modify. Over time, legacy systems components may be migrated to new technologies based on the need to increase performance or reduce maintenance costs.

SNA NETWORKING

Today's explosive growth of corporatewide computer networks is forcing information systems to look hard at long-term network strategies. There is a serious need to provide access to many different computing platforms from as many workstation platforms. It will take a well-constructed suite of networking protocols, application programming interfaces (APIs) and standard applications to meet these needs. Of all the network protocol suites available, two are most prevalent:

- TCP/IP.
- System Network Architecture (SNA) with the premise of Advanced Peer-to-Peer Networking (APPN).

SNA has been a dominant computer networking architecture since its introduction in the mid-1970s. With more than 500,000 SNA networks currently in operation, they provide the communication functions for enterprise systems that support the mission-critical operations of most major organizations.

During the last decade, organizations have witnessed a growing use of powerful desktop computers connected to LANs. This expansion, and the requirement to share applications and databases on them, has led to the rapid growth of another type of computing network to interconnect these LANs. Originally based on TCP/IP, and having evolved using bridges, routers, and hubs, they are referred to as IP networks.

Despite reports that mainframe computing is being replaced by PC-based client/server systems, most large corporations continue to perform their data processing using large-scale mainframe computers communicating with terminals over SNA networks. Mission-critical applications of these organizations are handled by their SNA networks. These networks, which have been in place for many years, are highly reliable and well tuned to provide optimal performance. Large investments have been made not only in networking equipment, but in trained, experienced personnel to operate and maintain these networks.

Major organizations now face the prospect of supporting both their existing SNA network and a new IP network for LAN interconnection. Since dual networks are expensive, not only to establish but to maintain, operate, and manage, these organizations are seeking solutions that integrate both SNA and LAN traffic over a common backbone network. Most of these organizations want to integrate their SNA and LAN traffic over a common network, but are not willing to replace their SNA network.

SNA Architecture

Systems Network Architecture is a data communication architecture established by IBM to specify common conventions for communication among the wide array of IBM hardware and software data communication products. The manner in which products implement these common conventions, internally, can differ from one product to another. However, the external *interface* for each implementation is *compatible*, different products can communicate without the need to distinguish among the many possible product implementations.

SNA architecture model is divided into a hierarchical structure that consists of seven well-defined layers. Each layer in the architecture performs a specific set of functions. Figure 13.1 identifies seven layers and their major functions.

SNA defines formats and protocols between layers that permit equivalent layers (layers at the same level within the hierarchy) to communicate with one another. Each layer performs services for the next higher layer, requests services from the next lower layer, and communicates with equivalent layers.

Hardware and software components (Figure 13.2) implement the functions of the seven architectural layers. Hardware components include

- Processors such as the ES/9000 family, Application System/400, and older series.
- Communications controllers such as the 372x and 374x series.
- Cluster controllers.
- Workstations.
- Printers.

The software components that implement SNA functions include

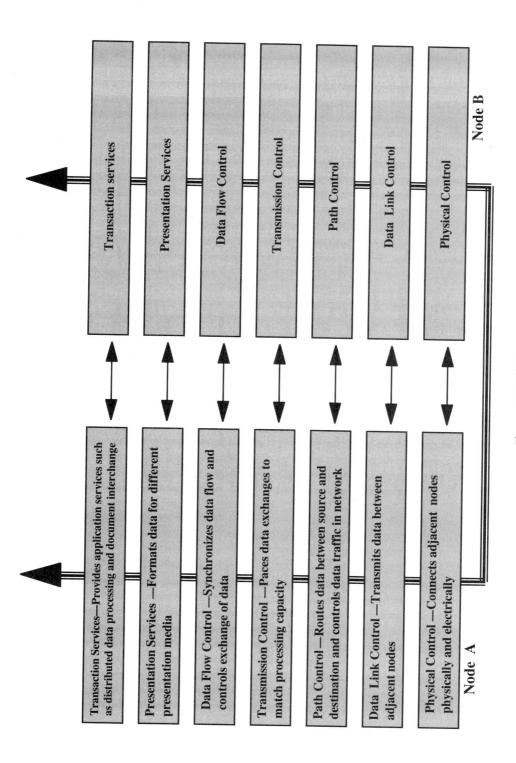

Figure 13.1 SNA layers.

397

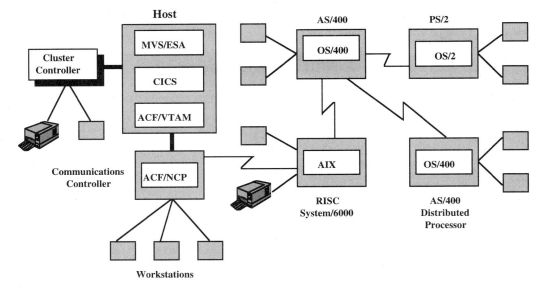

Figure 13.2 Hardware and software components.

- Operating systems such as Operating System/400 (OS/400) and Multiple Virtual Storage/Enterprise Systems Architecture (MVS/ESA) and older operating systems.
- Telecommunication access methods such as virtual telecommunications access method (VTAM) and communications manager/2 (CM/2).
- Application systems such as customer information control system (CICS).
- Network control programs such as the advanced communication functions for network control program (NCP).

Advanced Peer-to-Peer Networking makes any-to-any connectivity possible for large and small networks to communicate over local and wide area networks. APPN provides two basic functions: keeping track of the location of resources in the network and selecting the best path to route data between resources. APPN nodes dynamically exchange information about each other; therefore, customers may never have to deal with complicated system and path definitions. APPN nodes limit the information they exchange, enabling efficient use of network resources (Figure 13.3).

IBM is extending communications architectures to support implementations of multiple protocols (Figure 13.4), as well as integrating these protocols into OSI, TCP/IP, and other standards. Perhaps the greatest accomplishment, as illustrated in Figure 13.4 (multiprotocol networking, termed as CTS or Common Transport Semantics), is that it outlines a manner in which the applications can be separated from the underlying transport network by the implementation of CTS.

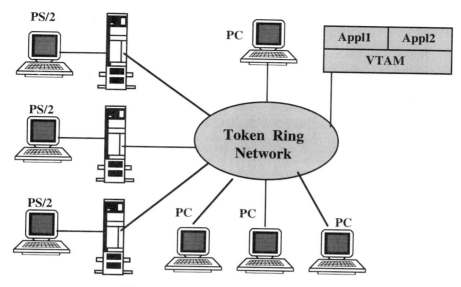

Figure 13.3 SNA peer-to-peer networking.

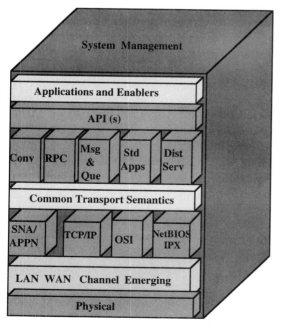

Conv = Conversion Services
Dist Serv = Distributed Services
Msg & Que = Messages and Queues
RPC = Remote Procedure Call
Std Apps = Standard Applications

Figure 13.4 Multiple protocol networking.

SNA - X.25 Integration

When traditional networking protocols such as SNA and X.25 were first designed, 2400 to 9600 bps was considered high speed. The cost of computer memory and computer instructions had a key impact on the design of these protocols. In SNA networks, formatted data streams, that is, 3270, were often used, and a large amount of SNA protocol stack was occupied with achieving a high link utilization. Figure 13.5. illustrates typical X.25-SNA integration.

Although VTAM and NCP generally communicated with each other using large single blocks of data (often around 4096-byte range) when transmitting to peripheral devices, NCP segmented these blocks into much smaller units (about 256-byte range). This was because on the older analog communications lines, there was often corruption of data units, so a *smaller packet size* was advantageous in case of transmission.

SNA relied on the error recovery provided by underlying data link controls such as synchronous data link control (SDLC) and by some application-generated checking mechanisms. X.25 had to account for the poor quality of existing analog services. For this reason, the network layer of X.25 contains end-to-end error recovery mechanisms. Data link

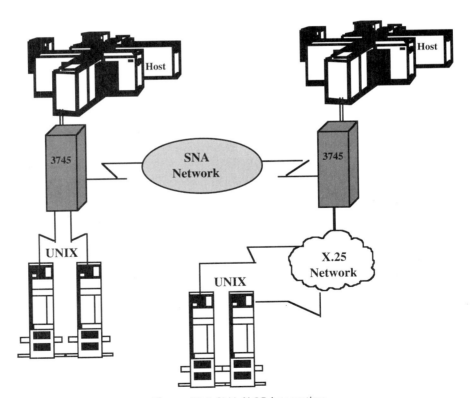

Figure 13.5 SNA-X.25 integration.

controls such as SDLC and link access procedure balanced (LAPB), which are common on current networks, detect errors, and retransmit frames on a hop-by-hop basis. They also help provide flow control by not allowing frames to be transmitted unless both ends of the hop are agreeable. As many links are slower than what current computers can drive, they provide an implicit rate control.

Many WAN schemes are connection oriented with intermediate routing handled by software. With the available link speeds of the 1970s and 1980s, many packet-switching networks can switch only a few thousand packets per second. Both SNA and X.25 are representatives of that era. Users now wish to utilize existing technologies to implement new applications that involve image and graphics processing plus the integration of existing voice, data, fax, and video networks. The traditional (legacy) portion of many modern networks often involves networks of disparate protocols such as SNA, X.25, DECnet, and TCP/IP. While routers provide one solution to multiprotocol data problems, they do not currently allow for the integration of voice and video.

For X.25-SNA integration, IBM has two complementary technical strategies:

- Map virtual circuits into real circuits (NPSI).
- Map virtual circuits into SNA sessions (XI).

For such configurations, the X25 network acts as a substitute for data link control and physical layers of SNA or the SNA network acts as a carrier of X.25 packets.

Network packet-switching interface (NPSI) runs in the 3745 controller and allows SNA hosts to communicate with X.25 DTEs. Qualified logical link control (QLLC) protocols provide part of the SNA to X.25 interface.

X.25 interface (XI) allows the SNA network to act as a packet-switching network. The network provides the X.25 interface and thus can connect UNIX machines using TCP/IP.

Many of the features of the X.25 packet layer, such as the ability to dynamically establish connections using the X.25 virtual circuit capability, are used by stations on a LAN. Many large organizations have their own private X.25 network to which only their systems can connect.

SNA-TCP/IP Integration

Major organizations now face the prospect of supporting both their existing SNA network and a new IP network for LAN interconnection. Since dual networks are expensive, not only to establish but to maintain, operate, and manage, these organizations are seeking solutions that integrate both SNA and LAN traffic over a common backbone network (Figure 13.6).

Recognizing the potential of this LAN/SNA integration market, major router manufacturers have formulated strategies and developed solutions that allow a common backbone network. Their basic approach is to integrate SNA traffic into the framework of their existing IP routers, rather than develop new products that provide routing over an SNA network. The resulting products use standard IP routing procedures augmented with vari-

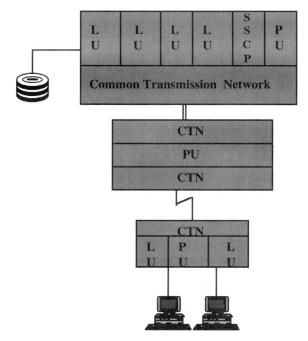

Figure 13.6 SNA overview.

ous techniques to provide routing of SNA data over IP networks. Since this approach is based on IP network, it assumes the replacement of the existing corporate SNA network.

Most of these organizations want to integrate their SNA and LAN traffic over a common network., but are not willing to replace their SNA network. While seeking solutions for routing LAN traffic over their SNA network, they are rejecting solutions offered by major router vendors to route their SNA traffic over an IP network. Despite the compelling need to eliminate their parallel network problem, only a handful of SNA users have switched to IP-based corporate networks. The vast majority still await an SNA-based solution.

Increasingly, SNA-oriented businesses are finding themselves surrounded by islands of TCP/IP-based LANs. In many cases, computing needs are growing exponentially, and user patience waiting for traditional solutions is being overwhelmed by an influx of technology without the benefit of overall corporate planning. Compounding this problem are issues many organizations face integrating newly acquired, geographically dispersed offices into an existing SNA environment. *Figure 13.7* illustrates an SNA-based Dallas office that needs to be integrated with TCP/IP-based LANs in San Jose and New York.

Implementing SNA hosts on LANs.   Let us assume that New York and San Jose have multiple and disparate TCP/IP hosts with 200 plus users and require daily interaction with the Dallas data center. Specifically, the users at New York and San Jose need logon and file transfer capabilities.

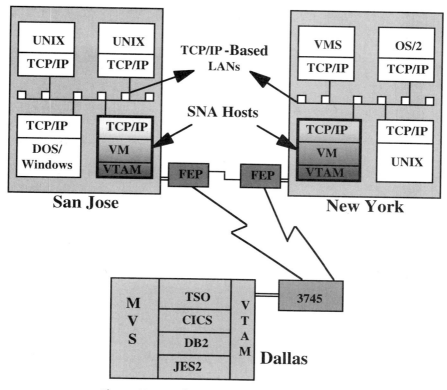

Figure 13.7 Implementing SNA hosts on LANs.

Because of geographic and technical incompatibilities between San Jose, New York, and Dallas, the integration raises a number of technical as well as personnel issues. Integrating TCP/IP into SNA implies merging TCP/IP services into an SNA environment. This means providing TCP/IP-based LAN users with logon, file transfer, and e-mail capabilities with the SNA host. We explore a number of scenarios that not only provide satisfactory integration for the users, but are also cost effective.

- *Implementing SNA Hosts on LANs:* One scenario may include an asynchronous link between remote LANs and the SNA environment, that is, connecting a modem or modem bank to the LAN and providing user access to the SNA. However, this does not provide TCP/IP-to-SNA integration; it merely provides an asynchronous link between the two.

Beyond establishing a link, terminal emulation must be included. LAN-based hosts use ASCII data representation and transmit data asynchronously. In SNA, hosts use EBCDIC data representation and connections are usually synchronous. Therefore, if an asynchronous link is established between LANs and the SNA environment, the issue of data translation must be addressed on the communications controller node where the remote link is made. Hence, additional software must be loaded to the front-end processor (FEP).

If this method of connectivity is implemented, significant expense is incurred because multiple telephone lines, modems, communication packages, and other resources are required. The number of users and the frequency of SNA resource utilization dictates the component requirements to solve link connections between SNA and TCP/IP. This method has only provided terminal emulation connectivity and has not achieved any integration between TCP/IP and SNA services.

Integration can be achieved by installing an SNA host (Figure 13.7) and peripheral equipment on each LAN, implementing TCP/IP on SNA hosts and connecting the SNA hosts via a distributed SNA network. This is probably the most expensive example of achieving integration.

- *Integration by Gateway:* Combining disparate environments may be achieved through a network "gateway" designed to integrate TCP/IP into SNA (Figure 13.8). In this case, the upper-layer conversion must be achieved. Most gateways offer options for link connections from the LAN to SNA environment (by default, the lower-layer protocol conversion is automatically achieved).

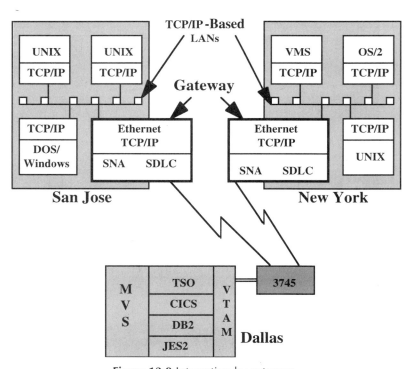

Figure 13.8 Integration by gateway.

An ideal gateway implementation will convert Ethernet to synchronous data link control. The physical link between different sites is achieved over switched or leased lines. Figure 13.8 depicts TCP/IP-to-SNA protocol conversion taking place on the gateway in the physical location of the LAN. It also illustrates Ethernet-to-SDLC protocol conversion occurring on the gateway. As a result, the data stream leaving the LAN is SNA and SDLC, acceptable to the FEP.

According to Figure 13.8, remote logon capability from the LAN is achieved via software on each LAN host and a mechanism on the gateway. Multiple procedures can be employed either for file transfers or exchanging e-mail. Actual requirements to achieve logon, file transfer, and e-mail vary on the implementation of the gateway itself. For example, logons can be attained by a TN3270 client application. File transfers can be achieved with IBM's IND$FILE program or via TCP/IP software located on the IBM host. E-mail can be accomplished different ways as well.

Granted, terminal emulation is required to integrate LANs into SNA, but protocol conversion is fundamental to TCP/IP-to-SNA gateways. Therefore, both solutions must be provided to achieve meaningful integration. However, protocol conversion and data translation do not have to occur on the same device (gateway), but are required.

In short, integrating TCP/IP into SNA requires converting TCP/IP to an SNA protocol and resolving data translation (ASCII-to-EBCDIC and vice versa). True TCP/IP-SNA integration provides, at a minimum, capabilities for bidirectional logons, file transfers, and e-mail, which are commonly used applications in both environments. In addition, there are other services that could include

- Advanced Program-to-Program Communication (APPC) support from LANs to SNA.
- Distributed database support.
- Remote job entry (RJE).
- Other special services.

- *Router and Gateway Implementation:* Another type of solution is based on a router and a gateway. Let us assume that there are three major departments, each having PCs connected to TCP/IP-based LANs. Departmental LANs evolved over time and currently include DOS, UNIX, and OS/2 operating systems. Figure 13.9 illustrates a TCP/IP - SNA gateway providing all LAN host access to the data center.

Assume that a company wants to interoperate between all LANs and that all users need "logon," "file transfer," and "e-mail" capability with the SNA data center, but the amount of interaction with the data center varies from LAN to LAN. The design should include the fact that all users on LANs need independence to sustain operations should problems arise on another LAN or the data center.

In this example, routers help with the network connectivity, whereas the gateway provides the necessary protocol conversions between various operating system characteristics. Software services of routers and gateways remain vendor specific, but provide a fair amount of flexibility. Actual details of the needed software are contingent upon the user needs and the vendor offerings.

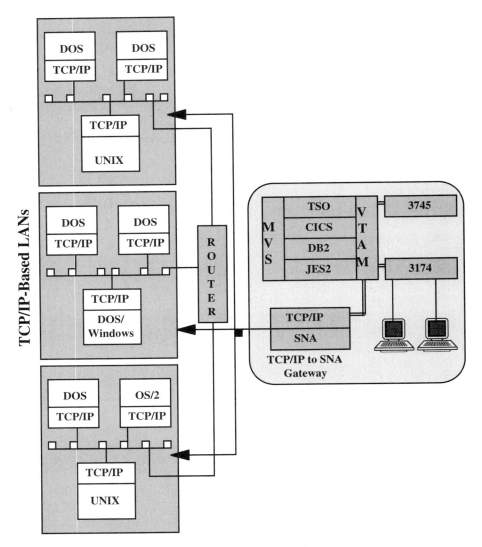

Figure 13.9 Router and gateway implementation.

- *3172 Offload Features:* Another possible solution is by using IBM 3172-3 interconnect controller and implement TCP/IP via the offload feature (Figure 13.10). This solution provides routing services between departmental LANs via the 3172. This indicates that no router is needed. It also provides necessary TCP/IP-to- SNA protocol conversion, permitting TCP/IP hosts on all LANs access to the SNA host. This offload feature, occurring on the 3172 interconnect controller, performs protocol conversion and routing functions on the controller itself, not on the SNA host. However, the TCP/IP offload feature does not eliminate the need for TCP/IP, VM, or MVS on the host.

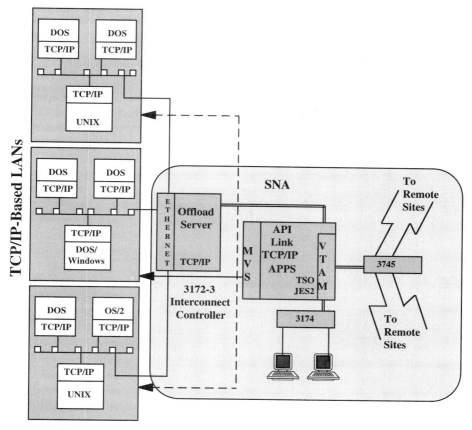

Figure 13.10 3172 offload feature.

In smaller network configurations, the 3172 provides the necessary hardware and software options to support most networked applications. The SNA communication program for the 3172 can coexist with

- OS/2.
- TCP/IP offload for either VM or MVS.
- TCP/IP for OS/2.

Using SNA for LAN Interconnect. There are many reasons why some organizations want to retain their existing SNA network (Figure 13.11). Because,

- SNA networks are more reliable than IP networks. A typical SNA network might have two failures a year, while a comparable IP network could have several failures a month. SNA networks achieve their high availability by using features such as multilink transmission groups (MLTGs),multiple host connections, dynamic reconfiguration, and fail-

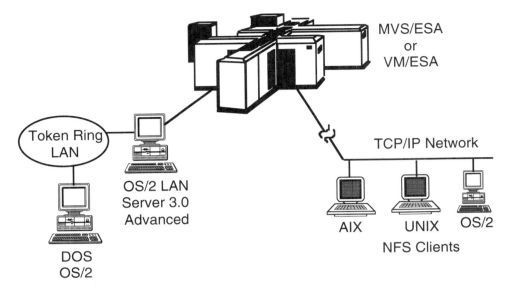

Figure 13.11 Mixed SNA networks.

safe congestion control. On the other hand, none of these is designed into the TCP/IP networks.

- SNA is designed to provide a consistent, predictable level of service to users having stringent performance requirements. SNA consistently delivers guaranteed levels of service to large organizational users.

- The key element in network operation and reliability is the staff that operates, manages, and maintains the network. SNA users do not want to incur the cost of retraining this staff for IP network operation or to hire new people knowledgeable in IP networks.

- SNA networks are significantly less expensive to operate than IP or LAN-based networks.

- APPN can provide most of the IP-type networking features lacking in SNA, but is robust enough to support mission-critical operations handled by SNA.

- Retaining SNA allows the continued use of IBM's NetView network management architecture.

Native SNA Routing. SNA routing has been a standard feature of SNA networks since 1987, beginning with ACF/VTAM. SNA packets are routed to their destination on a point-to-point, peer-to-peer basis using SNA-type PU 2.1 node integration facility. Once a data transfer is initiated, SNA packets are transmitted within SNA sessions without mainframe involvement. This SNA feature leads to a simple approach for TCP/IP-over-SNA routing.

Native SNA routing appears to solve the TCP/IP–SNA network consolidation dilemma. However, IP routers cannot provide native SNA routing. To do so requires these routers to contain an SNA subarea node and appear as a 37x5 communications controller with its NCP. To overcome this difficulty, IP encapsulation is used to route SNA traffic over IP networks. SNA frames are encapsulated within IP datagrams and routed over the IP networks using standard IP routing. However, the IP encapsulation techniques used by router vendors differ, resulting in interoperability problems.

IP routers are not SNA devices and the various techniques they use to handle SNA traffic do not enhance their routing capability or performance in relation to their native SNA routing.

IP Traffic over SNA Networks

It is suggested that IP-over-SNA routing provides a compelling solution to the problem of parallel network integration. This native SNA routing is implemented in TCP/IP-over-SNA routers that attach to one or more SNA lines and also to one or more TCP/IP LANs. On the SNA line, they appear as an SNA Type 2.1 peer-to-peer node and are so defined to SNA in the IBM system generation procedures for NCP and VTAM. On LANs, these routers appear as standard TCP/IP supported devices.

Communications between IP-over-SNA pairs are conducted via standard LU 6.2 sessions. Inter-LAN traffic is intercepted on the originating LAN by the attached IP-over-SNA router, encapsulating into LU 6.2 packets and placed on an SNA line. These packets are routed to the proper destination IP-over-SNA router on a peer-to-peer basis of using the SNA node facility. Upon receipt, IP-over-SNA router removes the LU 6.2 encapsulation and places IP packets on the appropriate LAN containing the destination device. This approach is SNA compatible, utilizes native SNA routing, and uses the existing SNA network.

In addition to using native SNA routing over SNA network, IP-over-SNA routers route LAN protocols on a point-to-point basis over their LAN attached networks. This is performed the same way as regular IP bridge/routers, making use of routing protocols. In essence, IP-over-SNA routers are hybrid in nature. They provide SNA routing by utilizing SNA's native routing over the SNA WAN and provide IP routing over their attached LANs.

Advantages. IP-over-SNA routers provide several other significant features that are supported by SNA, such as:

- Since an IP-over-SNA router assumes the appearance of an SNA Type 2.1 node, all the SNA functionality provided to these devices is available to this router.
- If line congestion is detected, SNA notifies its devices to gradually reduce the amount of traffic they are placing on the line. Lower-priority traffic is reduced before affecting the flow of higher-priority traffic.
- Some IP-SNA routers support data compression. While depending on the nature of the transmitted data, data compression usually provides a compression ratio of at least 2 to 1, increasing the bandwidth from 19.2 KB rate link to 38.4 KB rate.

- Being entirely SNA Type 2.1 and LU 6.2-based, IP-SNA routers are APPN compatible. These routers can be used for multiprotocol LAN interconnection across APPN networks.

Bandwidth Limitation. Most SNA networks run at 9.6 Kbps to 19.2 Kbps as opposed to IP links that generally run at 56 Kbps. Since IP-over-SNA traffic is integrated with the existing SNA traffic, if a large amount of traffic is added, or if SNA circuits are already stressed, the SNA network could become overloaded and adversely affect performance.

Increasing SNA link speeds could overcome this limitation. Most IP-SNA routers can handle that speed. However, with a large number of lines, the cost of 56 Kbps ports in the IBM 37x5 could be a prohibiting factor.

With frame relay, a single 2 Mbps circuit can provide 56 Kbps virtual circuits for 40 or more IP-over-SNA routers and each IP-over-SNA router can have its own 56 Kbps SNA virtual circuit. The cost of a single 2 Mbps port on a 3745 when prorated over 40 circuits loses its significance, thus limiting the bandwidth problem discussed above.

TCP/IP for VM

VM/ESA is a user-friendly, interactive operating system. The conversation monitor system (CMS) that communicates with VM is easy to use. VM supports a guest environment. MVS, VSE, and UNIX operating systems can run as guests under the VM operating system using separate partitions from VM and appearing as separate machines.

For workstation connectivity, VM/ESA (Figure 13.12) extends interprocessing capabilities to PC-DOS, OS/2, AIX/UNIX, Macintosh, SunOS (UNIX), Digital, X.25, and T1 environments with

- LAN Resource Extension and Services (LANRES), as illustrated in Figure 13.12
- TCP/IP.
- Novell NetWare.
- IBM PC LAN.
- IBM OS/2 LAN Manager.

For SNA connectivity, VM/ESA supports LU 6.2, TCP/IP, SNA, VTAM, and T1. Therefore, VM provides complete SNA-TCP/IP connectivity and networking. The addition of TCP/IP to VM's already considerable repertoire of communication software has enabled it to interoperate in multivendor environments over LANs and WANs.

With TCP/IP on a VM host, workstations and terminals connected to UNIX or other hosts (RISC or CISC based) can easily access VM applications and transfer files to and from CMS. If there is media incompatibility (different LAN topology between the workstations and the VM host), an IP router (a PC or PS/2 running a TCP/IP) can provide dozens of sessions to the TCP/IP-based client community. The S/370 computers running VM and TCP/IP blend into this multivendor environment and provide access to many applications they host from terminals, PCs, and workstations alike. The mainframes are

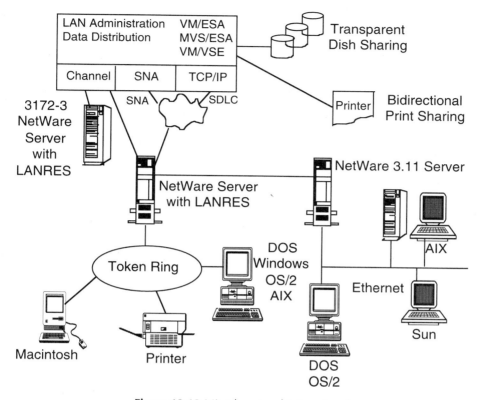

Figure 13.12 Mixed protocol internetworks.

connected to a LAN through a channel-attached network controller to an IBM 3172, eliminating the need for a traditional FEP.

TELNET. PCs and workstations access mainframe applications using the TELNET protocol of the TCP/IP suite. TN3270 can emulate a variety of IBM 327x terminals. Even the traditional dumb terminals can use the same network protocol through various terminal servers that support TELNET. With nonintelligent terminals, multiple concurrent sessions can be supported using terminal servers.

Like most protocols, TELNET has two sides: the client, which initiates a terminal session, and the server, which handles the incoming sessions. TCP/IP under VM supports both sides of the protocol; a user can initiate one or more TELNET sessions on a VM system and, from that host, initiate a TELNET session to a second host. VM with TCP/IP provides easy terminal session access from anywhere in this network and from almost any platform.

FTP. The TCP/IP protocol that provides file transfer between hosts is the file transfer protocol (FTP). The client side initiates the file transfer and the server side provides the file access. Files can be transferred from a PC to a VM system or the session can be initiated from the VM system to a PC if the computer supports the server side of the protocol. For example, a PC can communicate with a local server such as a Novell server while concurrently having a TCP/IP session to another host. Consequently, it is quite simple to transfer files between a VM host and a Novell server or vice versa.

E-mail. VM with TCP/IP supports the Simple Mail Transfer Protocol (SMTP), which is supported on most platforms that support the TCP/IP suite. This allows exchanging e-mail across the Internet, worldwide.

Printers and File Sharing. An important benefit of networked systems is the ability to share resources. Many protocols in the TCP/IP under VM suite of protocols provide sharing of output devices and files, like on a local network server.

The line printing function is provided by the line printer (LPR) and the line printer daemon (LPD) protocols. LPR provides a capability similar to the CMS PRINT command, except that the referenced printer can be attached to any networked system supporting the LPR/LPD protocol. Thus a CMS user not only can print to a VM-owned printer, but also can print to a printer attached to a UNIX system. Likewise, any system supporting the LPR protocol can print to a VM-owned printer. In addition, a user at a remote PC on the network can direct output to a VM-owned printer. Printer sharing devices allow printers to be directly attached to the network and support multiple protocols, permitting printers to be shared among, for example, VM systems, Novell servers, and UNIX systems.

VM provides facilities to share files across many diverse platforms. A separate feature of the TCP/IP product is the Network File System (NFS). Like other protocols, NFS enables VM to be a file server to any networked system supporting the NFS protocol.

Libraries and Toolkits. In addition to standard protocols, TCP/IP under VM also includes a number of libraries and toolkits. One such example is a set of X Window System libraries that allow programs running under CMS to open windows to any workstation on the network supporting the X protocol. In this way, programs on VM can directly interact with a user's screen, keyboard and mouse. Application programs can write high-quality output into client windows based on the Open Software Foundations'/Motif.

One characteristic which VM has shared with TCP/IP and UNIX is the extensive development of tools which include:

- *VMNET*—A product that allows RSCS (remote spooling communication subsystem) to take advantage of the TCP/IP network for RSCS's networking links. The backbone of BITNET, which previously used RSCS bisynchronous serial links, is now almost entirely carried by TCP/IP using VMNET. Several other products running on UNIX and DEC's VMS use the same protocol, allowing VM to interact with and provide services to these systems.

- *VM Gopher*—A VM version of a networked information server allows access to data scattered across an Internet in a user-friendly and transparent manner. In fact, a Gopher user need not be aware that several hosts of diverse operating systems may be providing services.

- *RXSockets*—A REXX function package that provides easy access to TCP/IP protocols from REXX.

- *NetNews*—A worldwide bulletin board system using UNIX's UUCP protocols encompasses many operating systems and protocols, including VM and TCP/IP.

Closer integration of TCP/IP and VM should further exploit more seamless interaction with other operating systems. VM/Pass-Through (PVM) can make good use of TCP/IP for connections between VM systems and to other systems. The VM-TCP/IP integration is a win-win strategy for the multivendor and dissimilar operating system environments.

TCP/IP for VM and Non-IBM Interoperability. For those VM systems surrounded by non-IBM systems, TCP/IP networking is a way of life. The TCP/IP for VM product allows VM systems to offer services over non-SNA networks and to take advantage of services available on almost any computer built since 1983. Basic services include terminal access, file transfer, and e-mail. TCP/IP for VM goes well beyond the minimum requirements and offers such additional services as file sharing and remote database access. CMS users have full access to these services, on both VM and other systems. Users on other systems can partake in many of these as well.

TCP/IP for MVS

MVS operating systems are geared for large-scale installations, especially those needing a great deal of processing power, a multiprocessing operating environment, and built-in security and integrity. MVS requires numerous components for a minimum system, including TCP/IP for connectivity with PCs and workstations on LANs (Figure 13.12).

For SNA connectivity with TCP/IP and other LAN-based environments, MVS provides all the protocols supported under VM, including

- PC systems and linkages, such as PC-DOS OS/2.
- Protocols, such as LU 6.2, VTAM, TCP/IP, and SNA.

TCP/IP for OS/400

Whether by choice, necessity, or demand, the structure of midrange computing is rapidly evolving. Application System/400 (AS/400)-based networks continue to support multiple applications, but the rapid deployment of client/server-based networks is forcing change in traditional midrange environments. Within the client/server-networks, the transmission structure is typically based on one of two technologies (Figure 13.13).

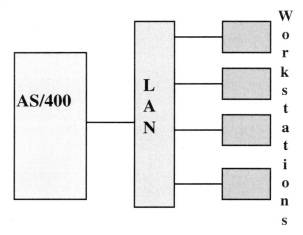

Figure 13.13 AS/400 as a hub.

- Ethernet
- Token ring

Supporting transmission speeds of 10 Mbps (Ethernet) or 4/16 Mbps (token ring), both technologies provide the physical link between the server and its supported workstations, in most cases using TCP/IP protocols for communication.

TCP/IP for OS/2

OS/2 provides a slightly more powerful environment (than DOS) with true multitasking and its installable file system. An example configuration is a PS/2 with a token ring adapter, IBM OS/2 EE, IBM OS/2 TCP/IP, and IBM OS/2 PC Support/400. OS/2 supports 3270 emulation sessions to VM and MVS hosts, VT100 TELNET or ASCII dial-out sessions, and either a TN3270 or 5250 SNA session to an AS/400. OS/2 also supports VM/CMS minidisks on the TCP/IP-attached VM systems mounted as DOS volumes using NFS or on the SNA-attached systems using one of the emulation sessions and enhanced connectivity facility (ECF).

IBM MAINFRAME TO UNIX

During the 1980s, almost all that IBM mainframe connectivity required was straight 3270 terminal emulation, with occasional mainframe-to-PC file transfer via IND$FILE. Support was relatively simple since the dominant end-user computing platform was the single-user DOS-based PC.

Today's environment, however, is much more demanding. Powerful application program interfaces, such as high-level language/application program interface (HLLAPI), provide the means to simplify 3270 applications by masking cumbersome mainframe operations from the end users. Alternatively, with Advanced Peer-to-Peer Communication (APPC/APPN), users can bypass their mainframes and perform program-to-program communications between SNA connected systems.

The most profound change for many organizations has been the switch from DOS-based PCs to multiuser UNIX workstations for distributed computing in mainframe-based networks. Since UNIX systems are more complex than DOS systems, the support requirements are generally greater. As a result, there has been an increased need for remote monitoring and support of UNIX systems from centralized locations.

Vendors specializing in mainframe-to-UNIX connectivity have recognized this need and are stepping up their efforts to build effective remote monitoring and support capabilities in their 3270 emulation packages. The term UNIX encompasses two broadly defined categories:

- Intel-based machines running Santa Cruz Operation (SCO) UNIX, UNIX System V Release 4 (SVR4), Interactive UNIX, Novell UnixWare, and other PC UNIX operating systems.
- Larger and more powerful workstations running a proprietary UNIX operating system. This includes
  - Sun Microsystems' Inc., SPARCstations and SPARCServers running Sun OS/Solaris.
  - IBM's RISC System/6000 (RS/6000) AIX systems.
  - Digital Equipment Corporation's VAX- and RISC-based UNIX Ultrix andOSF/1-based systems.
  - Hewlett-Packard Co.'s HP9000 systems running HP/UX.
- Enterprise-level Hitachi Data Systems mainframes running OSF/1 UNIX operating system.

More and more organizations are selecting UNIX as their preferred platform for distributing host-based applications to remote sites. This is mainly due to UNIX's inherent strengths as a communication server:

- UNIX can be used for remote-to-host connectivity over virtually any network backbone, including SNA/SDLC, TCP/IP, token-ring, and X.25.
- Unlike single-user DOS/Windows, UNIX provides a multiuser multitasking platform for both host and local operations.
- With full-featured emulation packages, UNIX systems can operate in the same way as the 3270 and RJE devices.
- UNIX's built-in utilities facilitate asynchronous terminal connections, remote login, unattended file transfers, and API-driven applications.

3270 Emulation Using UNIX

UNIX has important natural strengths as a communications server. As a true multiuser, multitasking computing platform, it provides the resources needed to

- Run multiple local and host sessions simultaneously.
- Efficiently run API-written front-ends to host applications.
- Run IND$FILE, 3770 RJE, NetView DM, and other file transfer tools, in addition to basic 3270 emulation.
- Route 3270 and 3770 print traffic to spoolers, programs, and disk, as well as printers.

UNIX supports many asynchronous terminals and features the handy "terminfo" utility—a database of terminal characteristics. Terminfo takes 3270 data and automatically determines how it should be displayed on each kind of terminal connected to the UNIX system.

UNIX-to-Host Connections in a Traditional SNA/SDLC Network

In the traditional SNA/SDLC network (Figure 13.14), remote sites interactively link to the host via controllers, modems, dial-up or leased lines, and front-end processors. Such a connectivity is usually termed as "3270."

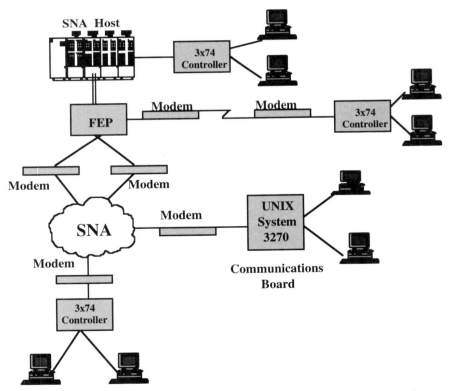

Figure 13.14 UNIX-to-host connections in a traditional SNA/SDLC network.

UNIX-to-SNA via 3270. The traditional way of achieving remote 3270 connectivity is by connecting 327x display terminals and 328x printers to 3x74 controllers, as illustrated in Figure 13.14 (local channel connectivity and a local-site link through the front-end processor). Alternately, users can link their remote systems to the host through the use of 3270 emulation packages.

The 3270 emulator in the UNIX system in Figure 13.14 provides 3x74 controller emulation, in addition to 327x display terminal emulation and 328x printer emulation. There is no need for coax boards and separate controllers in configurations of this type. Instead, the UNIX system connects directly to the synchronous modem or modem eliminator with a synchronous interface board and RS-232 cable. Some boards even have built-in modems, eliminating the need for separate modem boxes at the remote sites.

The 3270 emulators used in this kind of configuration are an efficient way to provide multiuser UNIX-to-host connectivity. With leading 3270 emulation packages for UNIX, users get up to 254 simultaneous host sessions per remote system.

SNA/SDLC Capabilities. UNIX-to-host connectivity in an SNA/SDLC configuration rarely ends with 3270 emulation. Additional capabilities include

- NetView support for central monitoring of remote UNIX-to-SNA connectivity.
- IND$FILE, 3270 remote job entry, NetView Distribution Manager (NDM), and other file transfer alternatives.
- Application program interface tools such as HLLAPI, APPC/CPI-C, and LUA/LU0.
- SNA *rlogin* for central support of remote UNIX systems.

Remote UNIX-to-SNA Host Connectivity via X.25

X.25 can

- Provide multihost connectivity with a minimum of internetworking equipment.
- Route SNA, TCP/IP, and asynchronous protocols over a single backbone.
- Minimize port usage on the front-end processor.

To perform UNIX-to-SNA host connectivity through an X.25 network, you will need to install NPSI in the front-end processor. The remote UNIX will require an X.25 gateway and 3270/3770 emulators supporting the qualified logical link control (QLLC) protocol interface to encapsulate SNA data for transmission over an X.25 network.

X.25 can simultaneously route SNA traffic, TCP/IP, as well as support other X.25-specific network applications (PADs, FTAM, X.400, X.500, etc.). Figure 13.15 illustrates remote UNIX-to-SNA host connectivity via X.25. As in SNA/SDLC configurations, capabilities available include 3270, 3770 RJE, APPC/CPI-C, LUA/LU0, and others.

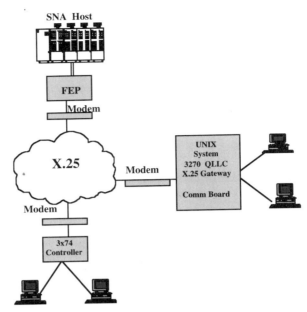

Figure 13.15 Remote UNIX-to-SNA host connectivity via X.25.

SNA Host Links for UNIX Systems in Token Ring LANs

Figure 13.16 illustrates a 3270 token ring adapter (emulator) for connecting UNIX system to the host. LAN-to-LAN connectivity can be achieved with routers or bridges. As in traditional SNA/SDLC networks, other capabilities, besides 3270 emulation, can be utilized for token ring connectivity. These functions include HLLAPI, IND$FILE, APPC/CPI-C, SNA rlogin, NetView DM, and others.

Connecting Remote UNIX Systems to IBM Hosts over TCP/IP

A special connectivity tool called TN3270 can provide UNIX systems in TCP/IP networks with access to IBM host applications and data. A user must install TCP/IP in the host or the front-end processor. Each TCP/IP-linked UNIX system must be equipped with TN3270 client software (Figure 13.17). TN3270 encapsulates 3270 data streams in TELNET packets for remote-to-host communications over TCP/IP. Routers can work with each other to direct the host data to the intended TCP/IP addresses. TN3270's main strength is its cost efficiency because of a software-only solution that uses existing internetworking equipment.

SNA Links for UNIX in Client/Server Configurations

One of the biggest challenges with client/server technologies is defining exactly what it means. Consider the following:

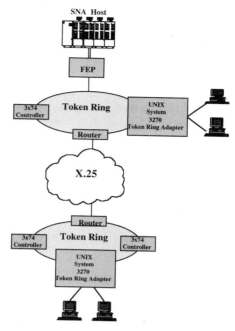

Figure 13.16 SNA host links for UNIX systems in token ring LANs.

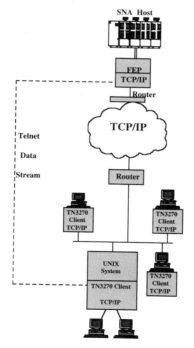

Figure 13.17 Connecting remote UNIX systems to IBM hosts over TCP/IP.

- "An architecture that distributes computing responsibility between a front-end program and a back-end program. Prior to the client/server computing, the burden of data processing was placed on either the client or the server (i.e., mainframe). When two or more machines are involved, client/server can reduce network traffic and thus enhance performance," or
- "A form of shared or distributed computing where tasks and computing power are split between servers (hosts) and clients (workstations or PCs)," or
- Allowing an end user to get access to any network resources, anytime, anywhere, and in any form," or
- "Just about anything that runs on a LAN."

Figure 13.18 depicts a client/server configuration integrating UNIX servers, a variety of desktop clients, and SNA links for LAN access to host applications and data. In this network, each server is equipped with an SNA gateway. Client systems run 3270 emulation software and Ethernet or token ring LAN adapters. Servers and clients communicate with each other via TCP/IP.

In a "split-stack" configuration of this type, where the SNA gateway resides on the server and 3270 emulation runs on the clients, users can perform efficient client-to-host file transfers with the emulator's IND$FILE or RJE utilities. If the emulator, instead, resided on the server, a user first needs to transfer the file from the client to the server and then remotely log into the server for a second file transfer to the host. In addition, this "split-stack" architecture allows the users to run HLLAPI, APPC/CPI-C, and other APIs directly from the client systems, without *rlogins* to the server.

Using NetView to Monitor Remote UNIX-to-SNA Connectivity

NetView—IBM's network management system for SNA—enables operators to monitor and control physical and logical resources in an SNA network. These resources can include 3270, 3770 RJE, APPC/CPI-C, and LUA/LU0 sessions running on remote UNIX systems. NetView operators can monitor these sessions from NetView consoles in the data center. Alternatively, users can access NetView from their remote UNIX systems during 3270 emulation.

To monitor UNIX systems in an SNA network via NetView requires emulation products that support NetView. Some additional NetView support capabilities include

- The ability to issue UNIX commands from NetView consoles, and view output returned from these commands. This helps operators monitor activity on the UNIX systems, diagnose problems, where possible, take corrective action.
- APIs for providing efficient communications between UNIX applications and the NetView host program. An API program can receive complete management messages from NetView and send applications data back to NetView.

APIs for Host Applications

Users at remote UNIX sites in an SNA network can write front-end programs using industry standard application program interfaces, to make host applications faster, friendlier, and more transparent for nontechnical personnel.

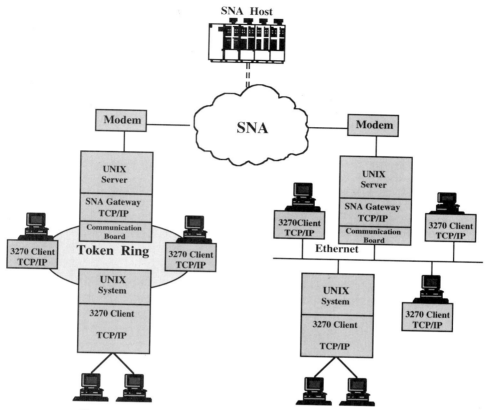

Figure 13.18 SNA links for UNIX in client/server configurations.

Masking Host Operations from Users. Many developers use HLLAPI to automate the start-up of 3270 applications. The front-end programs can supply the necessary keystrokes to log into the host, start an application, and perform any initial transaction procedures including routine data transfers. This especially helps in "transaction processing," where speedy response is crucial.

Front-end programs written with HLLAPI can further simplify host applications by providing menu-driven interfaces and eliminating the need for users to enter long lists of hard-to-remember commands. Figure 13.19a illustrates as to how front-end programs written with HLLAPI can completely mask a user's interaction with the host.

Program-to-Program Links. IBM's APPC and its successor, Common Programming Interface for Communications (CPI-C), offer the latest API technology. They enable separate programs running on the same or different systems to communicate with each other through the LU 6.2 interface.

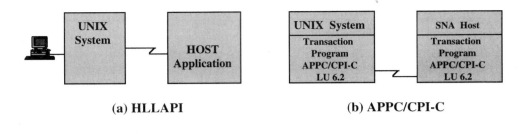

(a) HLLAPI   **(b) APPC/CPI-C**

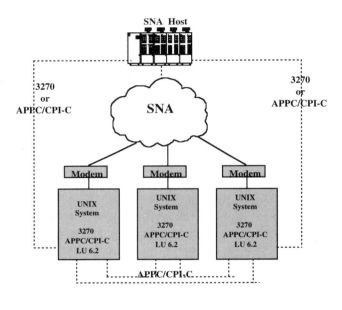

(c)

Figure 13.19 3270 SNA with program-to-program communications via APPC/CPI-C.

Through APPC/CPI-C, separate programs can join to accomplish a single transaction. Program-to-program communication can occur between a remote UNIX system and the central host or between any two systems in the network. In a peer-to-peer situation, the programs can communicate without having to go through the host.

Figure 13.19b and Figure 13.19c depict the relationship between two transaction programs in an APPC/CPI-C peer-to-peer configuration and traditional SNA/SDLC network to expand the range and efficiency of communications.

Low-Level API (LUA). Some UNIX-to-host applications require greater flexibility than that provided by HLLAPI or APPC/CPI-C. Under such situations, low-level API (Figure 13.20), called LUA, provides system links via LU0. LUA/LU0 interface provides control over the SNA messages transmitted between the distributed UNIX systems and central hosts.

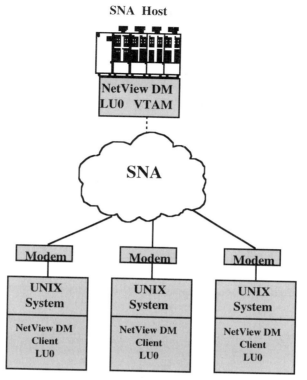

Figure 13.20 Low-level APIs.

UNIX-to-Host File Transfer Alternatives

UNIX and SNA provide a number of tools for file transfer; however, the type of tool used depends on the nature of the application:

- For occasional, unscheduled, user-initiated file transfers, the IND$FILE utility is adequate.
- For UNIX-to-host high-speed batch transfers, 3770 RJE is usually the preferred tool.
- Communication packages using LU 6.2 protocols extend file transfer capabilities by allowing peer-to-peer transmissions between UNIX systems and other processors in the network.
- For distribution of software and data to remote UNIX sites, it can use host-initiated, host-managed file transfer via NetView Distribution Manager (NetView DM).

Host-Initiated File Transfer.   NetView DM host and client software provides the following host-initiated file distribution facilities:

- Provides centralized control.
- Allows file transfers to occur in the background and runs unattended at the remote sites.
- Produces status reports at the host.
- Allows the host to request commands to be executed on the remote UNIX systems.
- Uses existing hardware resources.

The combination of NetView DM host and client software (Figure 13.20) enables operators to perform a variety of file management functions from the host. They can

- Create files on the UNIX systems.
- Transfer host files to the UNIX systems.
- Transfer UNIX files to the host.
- Transfer and execute UNIX command files.
- Send operator messages to their UNIX systems.
- Delete files from their UNIX systems.

Central Support of Distributed UNIX Systems via SNA rlogin

As with host-initiated file transfer, *rlogin* can provide centralized support (Figure 13.21).

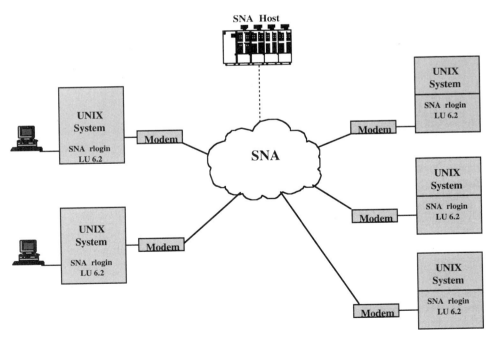

Figure 13.21 Central support of distributed UNIX systems via SNA *rlogin*.

Remote login (rlogin) provides an easy way to support and maintain remote UNIX systems. It does not require dedicated modems or phone lines. The remote login systems include

- Full-screen capability allowing remote users to run UNIX applications in the same interactive, menu-driven mode as local users.
- Native UNIX-to-UNIX connection, where centralized and remote UNIX users can transfer files between master and slave systems.
- Multisession capability, where users can use the same master software simultaneously and can login to a single slave system.
- Security features providing a different level of remote system access for different functional areas.

VMS-TO-UNIX

The DECnet architecture is not hierarchical in structure, a point that differentiates DECnet from SNA. The users linking Digital's systems are more likely to think in terms of Internet connections than host-to-host connections. This makes networking relatively common in DECnet sites. A larger portion of Digital LANs is interconnected than any other type of legacy systems or proprietary LAN environments.

DECnet is second only to TCP/IP in terms of support in routers and third-party tools. For these reasons, Digital has tended to group local interconnection of its LANs into the basic products and architectures of Ethernet, whereas wide-area interconnection of DECnet LANs is supported by digital products using standard leased lines, X.25 networks, and frame relay networks.

The evolution of DECnet LANs and of DECnet itself has resulted in a series of product families within the DECnet. The most advanced products are DEC WAN routers supporting ADVANTAGE-NETWORKS. An older line or the Ethernet/802.3 routers are designed to support DECnet alone.

DECnet Services

DECnet networks are primarily conceived as LANs or WANs. A transition from one type of transmission to another is usually transparent. A range of machines with different operating systems can be DECnet nodes, as illustrated in Figure 13.22.

DECnet nodes have equal privileges. Therefore, each node is addressable and can send/receive requests. Each transaction does not have to pass through central node. DECnet allows a number of service options:

- Shared use of peripherals such as laser printers.
- DECnet/SNA gateway, allowing communication with SNA networks.
- DECnet router/X.25 gateways that can service private and public networks and allow the DECnet supported machines to communicate in the enterprise.

COMPUTER	OPERATING SYSTEM
VAX	VAX/VMS, ULTRIX
MicroVAX I, II	MicroVMS, VAXELN, ULTRIXm
PDP-11	RSX-11M, ESX-11S, RSX-11M-PLUS, RSTS/E, RT 11
DECSYSTEM 20	TOPS 20
DECSYSTEM 10	TOPS 10
Professional 350 PC	P/OS
IBM-PC/XT/AT/	DOS
IBM-PS/2	OS/2

Figure 13.22 DECnet services.

The transition to DECnet Phase V (ADVANTAGE-NETWORKS) has induced some architectural changes in Digital's internetworking strategy, primarily the tristack support of DECnet, TCP/IP, and OSI (Figure 13.23).

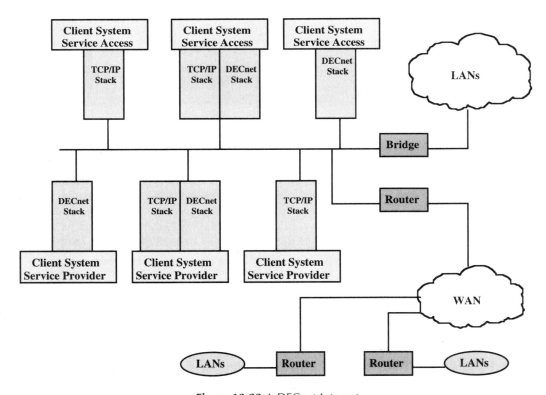

Figure 13.23 A DECnet Internet.

Internetworking with DECnet

DECnet, in many ways, anticipates the peer-to-peer networking developments of other vendors such as IBM. As a result, DECnet interconnection is both a generalized way to internetwork LANs and a specific strategy for host-to-host communications. Digital has assumed that the networks will include DECnet Phase IV and TCP/IP networks with perhaps some ADVANTAGE-NETWORKS nodes in each and that TCP/IP users will primarily want TCP/IP services. Therefore, Digital has established a multistack support, with each stack offering the native application services of the associated protocol, such as TCP/IP FTP, as well as the transport services.

This multistack approach, in most Internet configurations, requires to carry multiple, concurrent protocol flows, one for each stack in use, such as

- DECnet Phase IV protocols, based on Digital's proprietary stack. VMS systems are routing nodes, and ULTRIX systems could be DECnet end nodes.
- TCP/IP protocols used by ULTRIX hosts and possibly by foreign UNIX hosts on the network. These protocols can also be accessed by SCO UNIX users and by PC users who have implemented the Digital TCP/IP on DOS.
- OSI protocols to transport DECnet services associated with ADVANTAGE-NET-WORKS implementations.

Digital supports a wide variety of client systems on DECnet LANs such as

- PATHWORK Clients—PCs and Macintosh systems, ULTRIX, and SCO UNIX clients. The internetworking is strictly a DECnet LAN.
- Access to a DECnet service such as LAT. This allows internetworking using a non-DECnet protocol.
- Sharing media with DECnet but using servers that are not DECnet systems. However, the internetworking of DECnet LANs may not result in internetworking with the other LANs that share the media.

Bridges

Bridges, in Digital's view, are principally high-performance links within local environments to connect Ethernet areas or to create an FDDI backbone. There are three classes of bridges offered by Digital:

- Local bridging of Ethernet LANs, either via private copper or fiber, but not involving carrier service facilities.
- Remote bridging of DECnet LANs of any type.
- Ethernet-to-FDDI bridging, generally conducted locally to create an FDDI backbone for a large Ethernet community.

Bridge congestion can occur in large DECnet LANs unless steps are taken to expedite carrier delivery of the data in transit. The best option for DECnet LAN bridges is a private fiber connection which is capable of supporting the full LAN rate. Where carrier services are required, Digital supports either HDLC over private lines or X.25. Digital also supports frame relay as a bridge protocol to link remote bridges at rates of T1.

Routers

Routers in DECnet LAN interconnection are normally used to connect the routing domains that make up the administrative domain or to create an Internet by linking multiple administrative domains. If the structure is not complex, route selection is trivial. Complex internetworks involve the creation of multiple router domains. This is necessary when the number of nodes is high or if rapid growth is expected. Digital supports virtually every form of network service via routers.

The EtherWORKS Router/DECnet connects PC LANs to DECnet wide area networks. By turning a PC into a DECnet node on an Ethernet/802.3 LAN, you can communicate with other DECnet nodes over asynchronous or synchronous connections that support the DDCMP message protocol. The result is full access to a robust, wide area network for file and print services and for client/server applications such as mail, conferencing, and database access. In addition, the print and file services work transparently over wide area network on other servers. The EtherWorks router performs adaptive routing and has the capability to choose the least cost path or to reroute traffic if there is a line failure. The router also includes network management utility to display statistical and error information, starting and stopping lines, and testing components.

Gateways

Digital offers a series of products to link DECnet users to IBM hosts. Digital's gateways provide for 3270 terminal emulation, LU 6.2 peer-to-peer communications, DISOSS, LU0 peer APIs, printer emulation, and various host data service gateway facilities. Gateways can be accessed by clients in the same LAN, in the same area, or through internetwork routers. Internetwork paths are normally subject to longer delays, which is particularly true for PCs operating through DECnet gateways and using PC HLLAPI facilities.

Digital also offers support for TCP/IP host gateways from DECnet. The VMS/ULTRIX connection, now called TCP/IP Services for VMS, provides *only* DEC VMS users access to ULTRIX NFS files and TCP/IP APIs. X25gateway and X25router provide DECnet users with some access to X.25 services.

The *SNA gateway* provides stand-alone and NetBIOS-compatible LAN-based MS-DOS or OS/2 PCs with concurrent access to multiple IBM hosts, System 3/X, and AS/400 computers using X.25/QLLC or SDLC communications (Figure 13.24). The 3270/5250 terminal emulation packages work with the SNA gateway, providing SNA terminal and printer emulation under the DOS, Windows, or OS/2 environments. Access for Windows (3270 and 5250) can be installed on the same PC allowing them to connect to different host computers using both emulation types concurrently.

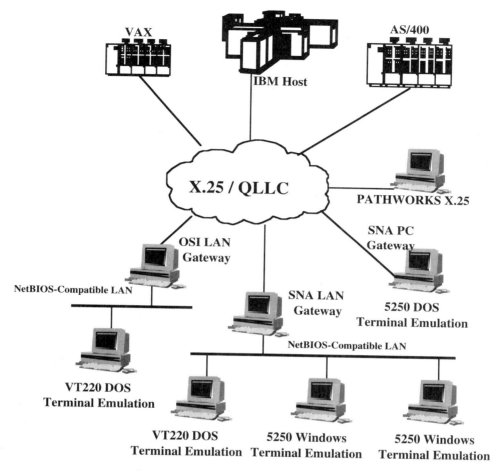

Figure 13.24. Digital's remote PC connectivity.

The *3270 terminal emulation* provides all the standard features of the IBM 3278 display terminal and IBM 3287 printer and supports IBM-PC file transfer (IND$FILE).

The *5250 terminal emulation* allows PC users to connect to IBM AS/400 or System/3X computers emulating 5250 display terminals.

The *WAN PC platform* hardware supports PATHWORKS X.25 (DOS), enabling users to connect a single, remote PATHWORKS for DOS PC client to X.25.

SNA PC Gateway and PATHWORKS X.25 (DOS) can be installed on the same stand-alone PC letting users simultaneously establish a session to remote PATHWORKS server, a 3270 session to an IBM mainframe, and 5250 session to an AS/400.

Network Application Services

NAS is Digital Equipment's implementation of "open systems." NAS is best utilized in a VAX/VMS configuration, for example, desktops from multiple vendors, including PCs and workstations. NAS provides interoperability at some level with IBM, Sun Microsystems, and other platforms, but, not at the same level as with VMS or ULTRIX. It currently supports the following software platforms:

- MS-DOS.
- OS/2.
- Macintosh.
- ULTRIX.
- VMS.
- SCO UNIX.
- SunOS/Solaris.

AS/400-TO-UNIX

Support for TCP/IP on AS/400 allows it to participate in non-SNA networks containing non-IBM computers. This provides users the opportunity for new applications with host-to-host communications. The TCP/IP support on AS/400 contains some of the most commonly used protocols in the TCP/IP family. Besides the low-level functions covered by TCP, IP, UDP, and ICMP, the following functions are included:

- File transfer protocol (FTP), enabling AS/400 to be both a TCP/IP client and server.
- Line printer requester (LPR), enabling to send spool files to any system in the TCP/IP network.
- Line printer daemon (LPD), to accept print requests from other systems in the network and place them in local queues.
- Simple Mail Transfer Protocol (SMTP), which is supported under System Network Architecture Distribution Services (SNADS) via a bridge and interfaces with OfficeVision/400 to handle mail.
- Network terminal protocol (TELNET), which allows access of the resources of another remote system as though the terminal were locally attached to the server remote system.
- Application program interface (API) for both TCP and UDP layers.
- Network file system (NFS), a method of file sharing by providing the same access to remote files transparently. AS/400 can only act as an NFS server.

The AS/400 systems normally participate in the SNA networks and support APPC and APPN connectivity with large mainframes. However, with TCP/IP support on most

IBM processors (OS/2, MVS, VM, RS/6000, AIX RT PC, AIX PS/2, and PC/DOS), AS/400 can participate in nonproprietary networks as well.

Internetworking Over an Ethernet LAN

The AS/400 TCP/IP allows the AS/400 systems to participate in connecting many different environments. It can connect over LANs using Ethernet or token ring topologies, with all IBM systems, such as MVS, VM, OS/2, PC/DOS, and AIX and any non-IBM systems such as DECnet, HP/UX, SunOS/Solaris, and Mac OS.

Figure 13.25 illustrates an AS/400 system as a part of an Ethernet LAN, where it can communicate with IBM and non-IBM systems.

Internetworking with OS/400

The AS/400 TCP/IP allows bridged frame relay and token ring connectivity with IBM and non-IBM systems.

Figure 13.26 illustrates an AS/400 system as a part of a bridged connection between a token ring and Ethernet LANs. The bridge connectivity can be further extended to a WAN connectivity over frame relay.

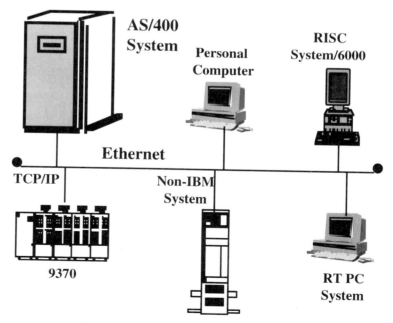

Figure 13.25 AS/400 LAN network.

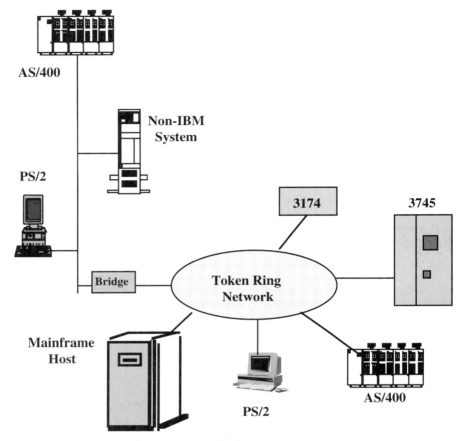

Figure 13.26 Bridged LAN connectivity.

SUMMARY

The legacy systems of past two decades have perpetuated the separation of business units. The explosion of desktop and LAN computing has erected even more barriers to enterprise continuity. Still, the objectives are quite basic. Corporations must be able to rapidly and reliably access and integrate information housed in legacy systems with information distributed throughout numerous workgroup environments.

The challenge is the integration of mainframe, midrange, and compatible systems with multivendor LANs of UNIX systems, DOS and Windows PCs, OS/2 systems, and Macintosh systems. It is a question of connectivity, interoperability, and bidirectional access to mission-critical applications. All translation, communication, printing, and data movement must be bidirectional. Therefore, the protocol conversions, device emulation, programmatic interfaces, data normalization, and communication middleware should be judiciously distributed across hosts, servers, and workstations. Basic network interoperability and integration services include

- Protocol conversion.
- Terminal emulation.
- File transfer.
- Printing flexibility.
- Program-to-program communication.
- Performance.

Achieving TCP/IP and SNA integration is different when the equipment to be integrated is located in the same facility. Although other options are available, those presented here seem to be most feasible, based on the user needs and the hardware installed.

Clarification of departmental and organizational needs should dictate which solution is the best. Having a proactive approach to networking needs, as well as the user computing needs, is the best prescription for healthy organizational networking computing infrastructure. Understanding what equipment currently exists, the types of LANs in use and organizational requirements and goals should be prerequisites to embarking on selecting a solution.

IP-over-SNA routers provide a solution for LAN interconnection with legacy systems, while allowing users to retain their SNA networks. The safest way to consolidate SNA and TCP/IP traffic is to use their existing SNA network as the backbone network and integrate their LAN traffic by using IP-over-SNA routers. SNA was designed as a synchronous linking system, subject to a few if any delays in transmission, whereas TCP/IP was designed as an asynchronous system, capable of responding to variable connection times and speeds without dropping the link. Therefore, encapsulating SNA in TCP to gain ready routability of TCP could introduce network delays beyond the ability of SNA to handle or routing TCP through the SNA network to gain throughput could cost TCP users access when the SNA network goes down even in part.

The two networking systems—SNA and TCP/IP—bear many conceptual similarities when APPC and APPN are taken into account. However, the peer-to-peer connection model as well as dynamic routing were a part of TCP/IP at its inception. SNA has only recently added these capabilities with the introduction of APPN and not yet fully deployed in the field. On the other hand, DECnet is both a generalized interconnection to LANs and specific for host-to-host-communications.

With the advent of TCP/IP modules running on legacy systems, it is possible to construct a network using only TCP/IP that allows access to the mainframe as well as all other TCP devices on the network. Transition paths that preserve the legacy system communication backbones and other communication devices are also available.

EXERCISES

1. List major differences of SNA, TCP/IP, and DECnet architecture principals.
2. List a few ways to integrate TCP networks with SNA.
3. Discuss TCP/IP implementation over VM.
4. List a few applications for mainframe-to-UNIX connectivity.
5. What are the most prevalent techniques/products to interconnect with DECnet systems?

14

INTERNETWORK TROUBLESHOOTING AND MONITORING—I

Introduction
Troubleshooting Methodology
  Initial Steps
  The Problem-Solving Model
  End-to-End Problem Management
Remote Monitoring Tools
  How RMON Management Works
  The SNMP Protocol
  Benefits of RMON

Third-Party Tools and Applications
  Network Test Equipment
  Debugging Tools (Examples)
  Protocol Analyzers
  Protocol Monitors
  Additional Tools
Summary
Exercises

INTRODUCTION

Troubleshooting is a task that all network administrators must perform at one time or another. As industry moves from the decade of the "LANs" to the decade of "internetworks," networks are becoming more and more complex. We will use the term "internetworking" to address both LAN/WAN networks and LAN/LAN as well. When they work, they are marvels of technology. But when they fail, you are in pile of trouble. No matter how troublesome the internetwork problem, with today's technology tools, a thorough analysis should restore it to health. However, before we jump into network troubleshooting, it is important to understand how internetworks became so complicated. The complicity is the result of proliferation of

- Differing protocols (proprietary and standards).
- Dissimilar operating systems.
- Specialized network operating systems.
- Abundant networking devices that cannot interoperate.
- Constantly changing configurations.

- Evolution of technologies.

Network analysis has suffered from the fact that it was performed with rudimentary tools. These tools were of limited value in performing the primary mission: identifying problems and helping to maintain the availability of network. The increasing number, size, and complexity of networks have far surpassed the available tools to manage them. Many network managers live with the daily problems caused by multiple additions and changes to their networks, new applications, new network segments, and new devices. Just keeping track of all this, let alone finding and fixing problems, is a large task. Where do these problems come from specifically? Traditional internetworking problems fall into two major categories:

- Protocol and connection problems and their identification.
- Network performance and tuning analysis.

Analysis designs must keep up with the power of the new networks. Newer, more powerful internetwork devices are being brought on line every day with a trend toward RISC-based, higher-speed switching and routing. Despite the ubiquity of TCP/IP, there are still more, not fewer, protocols that must be managed, saturating the network with a range of problems. Integrating mainframes and client/server environments over internetwork segments, further contribute to this complexity.

Now, more than ever, we need to see network activity as it travels across multiple interconnected network segments. Too often, network management is treated as an afterthought. Only when the network crashes do the organizations realize how essential it is to be prepared. Without the proper systems and tools in place beforehand, a small problem can quickly escalate into a full-scale disaster. There is a jungle of tools available to the network user. Most of these are very specialized and work only in certain environments. In the following sections, we will examine some of these tools and equipment, which could be utilized to solve your specific problems.

TROUBLESHOOTING METHODOLOGY

A network problem can shut down all or parts of your network. In addition, acute slowdowns in response time can result in lost productivity. Network problems typically fall into four major categories, as illustrated in Figure 14. 1.

Initial Steps

To provide end-to-end troubleshooting, it is necessary to gather different information from a variety of devices and systems. To accomplish this task, two significant challenges must be addressed:

SYMPTOMS	CAUSES
INSTALLATION AND CONFIGURATION *PROBLEMS:*	**WORKSTATIONS, PCS, NEW APPLICATIONS**
Slow login Broadcast storms Diskless workstation will not boot	Name service function reading entire database Bridge forwarding broadcast messages File missing boot server
ACCESS TO RESOURCES *PROBLEMS:*	**SERVERS, BRIDGES, ROUTERS, GATEWAYS, APPS**
Slow server access Unable to send output to printer Unable to send e-mail	Too many transmissions Incompatible software versions Router table updated incorrectly
INTEROPERABILITY *PROBLEMS:*	**MULTIVENDOR IMPLEMENTATIONS, STANDARDS**
All traffic on network randomly stopped Diskless workstations takes too long to boot	TCP/IP window bug Workstations dropping packets
HARDWARE *PROBLEMS:*	**CABLES, INTERFACE BOARDS**
Some workstations drop from the network PC intermittently unable to access the network	Faulty section of cable Faulty interface board

Figure 14.1 Typical network problems.

1. Gathering information from such a diverse, multivendor environment often forces the administrator to use multiple, disparate element management systems. Gaining an end-to-end view of the network infrastructure poses a challenge due to the inability to communicate and integrate information between multiple management systems. Effective problem resolution requires a single management system with distributed components capable of monitoring all infrastructure elements. Unfortunately, such a system does not exist today. However, network analysis vendors are currently developing solutions that automate and centralize the troubleshooting process for multisegment distributed environments.

Using a single system to monitor networked resources provides operating efficiencies through consistent command sets and graphical interfaces and standard report formats. In addition, a single system enables the data integration required to gather and analyze end-to-end performance levels and perform event correlation. For example, an integrated system should determine whether response time problems are due to wide area congestion or server overload. Furthermore, the system should provide a deeper level of analysis to determine whether wide area congestion is due to incorrect addressing schemes and a router's failure to filter NetBIOS broadcasts.

2. Network resources are geographically distributed throughout the enterprise, forcing the staff not to monitor the entire enterprise. This actually requires a distributed system for remote management of all locations from a centralized console. A centralized monitoring and analysis of a distributed internetwork can

- Eliminate the need for on-site monitoring.
- Enable an end-to-end view of the enterprise.
- Facilitate problem isolation.

The Problem-Solving Model

The administrators can solve an identified problem in one or two ways:

- Using a structured approach—you will definitely determine what the problem was and confirm that you fixed it.
- Shotgunning—you will make educated guesses and arbitrarily replace components to see if the problem disappears.

We will outline three-stage process in finding the cause of the problem:

1. The first stage involves "quick checks" without any specialized equipment. Such checks often reveal the cause of the problem. But it depends upon how experienced you are, that you know about the configuration and that you recognize the areas that have changed on the network. The network documentation and any historical/audit trail data are very useful in such situations. For example, if users are complaining about large file transfers failing, you may suspect a malfunctioning bridge since you know that other bridges failed recently. It would be a safe bet to suspect the bridge and direct your initial probe toward that device.

The key is to collect enough accurate information. Many network failures occur after something has been changed or modified. Changes in topology, configuration, applications, and users can cause a network to fail. Missing some vital information can easily lead you to an incorrect diagnosis and possibly an inappropriate fix. Most problems on the network have probably happened before. Therefore, you must make certain that you understand the problem. The primary goal is to identify and eliminate potential causes of the problem. Once the suspect problem is apparent, it may be necessary to perform some simple tests to ascertain the severity and the scope of the problem.

2. The second stage involves a closer look at the network for special indicators or symptoms. Specialized tools, such as analyzers, monitors, and diagnostic programs, are often needed to identify symptoms that point to the cause of the problem. In the "bridge" example, if you never had a bridge go bad and this particular bridge has been on the network long enough to be considered stable, you need additional information before

suspecting the bridge. Without the additional data, you could isolate the problem by temporarily bypassing the bridge from the network. If the problem disappears then you can assume that the bridge is the culprit. On the other hand, if the bridge starts dropping frames because of high traffic loads, you need monitoring equipment to help increase the load and measure the bridge's ability to forward frames for malfunction detection.

Problem isolation is easier if the network is divided into workable segments, so you do not have to contend with the entire network at once. Each segment can then be examined to pinpoint the problem areas. Because more detailed information must be gathered in this stage, specialized equipment such as an analyzer, a monitor, or a probe may be required.

3. In Figure 14.2, different analyzers are assigned to different segments of the network, with a central management console (SNMP Manager). The server analyzes and processes the data before transmitting it to the console, thus minimizing the amount of nonuser traffic. In addition, each analyzer can be configured to capture relevant network statistics and transmit them using the SNMP TRAP command to an SNMP Manager on the network. Most network problems are directly related to the components, which could include

- Cabling.
- Network adapters.

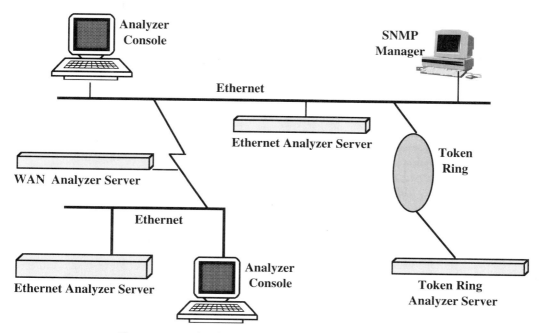

Figure 14.2 A distributed analyzer system connected to a network.

- Wiring concentrators.
- Bridges, routers, gateways, or hubs.
- Host, server, or workstation.
- Protocol stacks.
- The third stage requires either specialized equipment and/or a specialist to interpret the data. The first two stages require some familiarity with normal network operations, so abnormalities will be apparent. It is only after these remedies have been exhausted that you need to move to third stage.

There are many common problems in which you can conduct the same sort of steps to troubleshoot. Some troubleshooting applications and tools can identify these problems and perform the steps without your intervention. Once completed, such tools will notify you that a problem has been fixed or a problem needs special handling.

The ideal way to manage networks is to avoid problems before they occur. But this ideal is rarely, if ever, achieved. In fact, administrators spend most of their time fighting fires while neglecting proactive activities such as network planning and evaluating new management tools that could automate routine problems. Some of these tools and applications are discussed in this chapter to provide you a better understanding.

End-to-End Problem Management

As the number of networked resources grows across a distributed network, the potential amount of data transmitted over the internetwork drastically increases. To avoid stressing the network and burdening the central console with information overload, the network system must utilize intelligent agents to manage the diverse environment. Intelligent agents are device resident applications distributed throughout the enterprise with processing capabilities enabling you to

- Undertake monitoring and thresholding to collect network statistics including memory, protocol, and route path information. Considering these statistics, you can define thresholds, such as early warning, alert, and emergency evaluations and actions.
- Eliminate by filtering excessive network traffic and forward designated information such as alarms, thresholds, and inquiry responses to a centrally designated analysis engine. In addition, filtering can help expedite problem identification and resolution by highlighting the most important information automatically.
- Perform a range of analyses from protocol interpretation to correlation, to offload processing and congestion at the central console, thus expediting the problem-solving process, automatically pinpointing problems requiring attention.
- Maintain historical statistics locally for baselining and minimizing network traffic by passing information to the central console only when you need to view it.

In this fashion, the agents (analyzers, monitors, other tools) can record, manipulate, process, and report the data to the central site. During monitoring, certain conditions drive agent thresholds to activate alarm indicators that can help you isolate and contain the problem and minimize its affect on the entire network.

REMOTE MONITORING TOOLS

RMON is a standard management information base (MIB) specification that provides a consistent format for collecting both Ethernet and token ring statistics. The RMON technology is finding its way into networks of all sizes.

RMON offers standardized mechanisms that allow the administrators to manage both local and remote traffic on the internetworks from a single console. Depending upon the implementation, the hardware may be installed on each segment to be monitored, under the control of an "agent" software application. The agent application analyzes the collected data and reports its findings back to a centrally located management console, via a management protocol, most frequently, Simple Network Management Protocol (SNMP).

Using the SNMP, RMON is an effective tool for monitoring and detecting network changes before they become headaches.

How RMON Management Works

The key to RMON management lies in the interaction between RMON agents and corresponding monitoring applications on network management stations (NMSs). RMON agents are software programs residing within stand-alone probes and/or managed devices (Figure 14.3). Managed devices include routers, bridges, workstations, terminal servers, host systems, PCs, printers, gateways, and hubs, and other devices interconnected to the network.

The role of the NMS is to retrieve, process, present, and act on information from RMON agents. NMSs run network management applications on hosts, workstations, or other CPUs. An NMS application and its hardware can act as a software application under a network management platform such as Hewlett-Packard's OpenView, IBM's NetView 6000, or Sun Microsystems' SunNet Manager.

The RMON standard provides the capability for RMON agents to send statistics and alarms to these network management platforms. The SNMP communications protocol is required to view RMON statistics on an NMS or a management platform console.

The SNMP Protocol

The collection and communication of the RMON-based monitoring data requires the existence of a network communication protocol. A number of proprietary protocols have been developed to address this need. IEEE developed CMIP over LLC (CMOL) for managing layers 1 and 2 defined in a LAN/WAN environment. CMOL provides a means for simple, resource-constrained devices to be managed in an OSI domain.

The most widely known standard communications protocol is SNMP. The SNMP is the de facto standard for the collection and transport of RMON information from distrib-

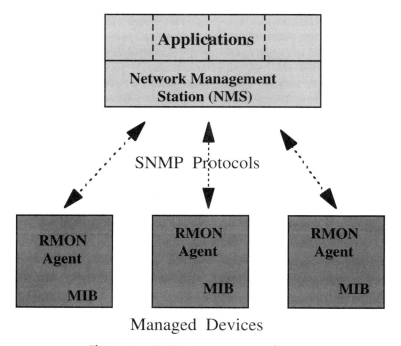

Figure 14.3 RMON management scheme.

uted segments to central locations. SNMP is an application layer protocol running over User Datagram Protocol (UDP) which sits on top of IP in the TCP/IP protocol suite.

The SNMP specifies a "standard" way for RMON agents to communicate with NMS software. The functionality of the NMS, including the manipulation and display of the information, is an important way in which vendors of the network management stations differentiate themselves in the marketplace.

Due to limitations in the security and performance speed, the original SNMP (v1) protocol was revised (v2). The primary differences between the two versions are security and efficiency. SNMP v2 also provides for improved facilities for controlling network devices. In addition, security functions such as user authentication and encryption are also supported. SNMP v2 also features a bulk data retrieval that performs large data transfers faster than SNMP v1—required for transferring collected agent data.

Network Management Station. The SNMP only specifies methods for data collection and communications between the RMON agent (or collector) and the NMS. RMON neither specifies how the information has to be displayed nor the NMS interfaces.

RMON Agents. The SNMP can be used to facilitate the collection and distribution of standard RMON monitoring data. Applications running under an NMS use SNMP to poll network devices (routers, bridges, hubs, and probes) equipped with RMON agents. At the request of the NMS, information is transferred across the network from the agent to the NMS. That information is accessed from the internal memory of the device to produce a map of what information is available and where it is stored.

MIB-I. To facilitate the collection and transfer of RMON information between agents and NMS monitoring applications, the SNMP protocol utilizes a management information base. The MIB provides standard representations of collected data. Considering a tree-structured database, an MIB defines groups of objects that can be managed. MIB I is limited to 114 objects and is organized into 8 groups:

Address Translation Table (ATT) Contains the network address to physical address translation.

Exterior Gateway Protocol (EGP) Collects number of EGP messages received with and without errors, number of locally generated EGP messages, and information on EGP neighbor.

Interfaces Provides single or multiple, local or remote interface (s), and designates the speed of the interface(s).

Internet Communication Management Protocol (ICMP) Tallies the number of ICMP messages received and counts errors.

Internet Protocol (IP) Designates nodes as IP gateways or hosts; keeps statistics on IP datagrams received, discarded, or forwarded; and provides IP routing tables.

System Includes vendor identification and time since the management portion was last initiated.

Transmission Control Protocol (TCP) Provides information about TCP connections, transmissions, and retransmissions.

User Datagram Protocol (UDP) Counts number of UDP datagrams sent, discarded, or undeliverable.

MIB II. MIB II is an extension of MIB I and defines 185 objects in 10 groups. The two additions are

- Common Management Information and Services Protocol over TCP (CMOT).
- Simple Network Management Protocol (SNMP).

With SNMP MIB II, network managers can retrieve information pertaining to the local device served by that agent (for example, bridge statistics). Designed as a supplement to MIB II, RMON MIB provides vital management information on the subnetwork being served (Figure 14.4). This is similar to the functions being carried out by network analyzers that "promiscuously" monitor each frame on the network, gathering traffic statistics.

RMON can be configured either as a dedicated monitor or as a module on a network device with other responsibilities such as a PC or a router. Although RMON defines an MIB, the goal is to specify interface between SNMP managers and remote monitors. RMON reduces the burden on management stations by offloading monitoring and data

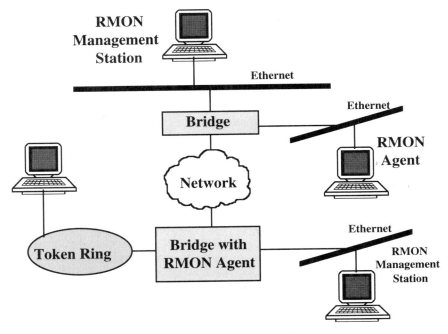

Figure 14.4 The RMON management information base.

analysis functions and provides an approach to effectively monitor remote subnetworks in an internetwork.

RMON MIB Structure. The RMON MIB defines nine functional groupings of both Ethernet and token ring, plus an additional token ring group. Each group can be individually configured through a control table identifying the type of data gathered and stored in the corresponding data table. Each of the functional groups is optional, allowing a monitor to be configured to retrieve and store only necessary data. A monitor may have multiple physical interfaces for connectivity to multiple subnetworks. Each group may contain data gathered from one or more of the attached subnetworks depending on the configuration of that group.

RMON MIB was developed to standardize the basic features of distributed network monitoring products and to provide multivendor interoperability. However, RMON monitoring capabilities can vary drastically from vendor to vendor depending on the other RMON MIBs supported. Since each MIB group is optional, a number RMON MIB agents may each be targeted for different purposes. For example, one RMON agent may be designed for tracing, and another agent may be designed for maintaining a large host table. As a result, individual vendors offer unique interpretations by incorporating different combinations of RMON MIB features.

The standard features of all 10 RMON MIB groups include the following:

Alarms Allows defining value thresholds (such as events) on existing MIB objects and monitors those objects. Generates an alarm when the present threshold is exceeded, typically passing the alarm to the event group.

Events Controls generating and notifying of SNMP events from an agent. Events can be ignored, logged, or used to generate a trap (or alarm), which is then sent over the network for interpretation by a management station.

Filters Creates channels (or arbitrary LAN segment) based on arbitrary filters. The channels then send data to the event or packet capture group, which can generate an alarm.

History Collects and provides general traffic statistics during a user-defined time interval.

Host Table Collects basic statistics about the MAC addresses (such as hosts) on a local segment.

HostTopN Provides reports on a defined number of hosts (N number) that exceed present host group statistical parameters.

Packet Capture Captures all or part of a packet on a LAN segment.

Statistics Collects general traffic statistics about a LAN segment, such as number of bytes, packets, errors, broadcast packets.

Token Ring Provides information on the physical order of token ring stations.

Traffic Matrix Collects basic information about transactions, or conversations, among stations (such as MAC addresses).

Benefits of RMON

The RMON standard allows to proactively monitor activity on every network segment. In the event of a loss of polling from the SNMP manager, the RMON monitor will continue to collect functional management data on the attached subnetworks. The management section then can retrieve the information at a later time. Remote monitors can also be configured to analyze network data collected providing value-added service to the manager. The major benefits to the RMON standard include

Multiprotocol Support RMON monitors the MAC layer of the OSI model and is designed to be protocol independent. Therefore, it can be used in heterogeneous networks supporting dissimilar operating systems. If different protocols are running different protocols, RMON will still monitor and collect data.

Network Configuration Planning RMON helps plan the efficient placement of equipment on distributed segments. For example, by placing application servers on the same subnetwork as application end users, you can minimize traffic through routers where bottlenecks start to develop. RMON also can be used to plan WAN bandwidth requirements between routers, and to help calculate the impact of new applications on the network. By detecting early changes in network performance, RMON can help determine if configuration modifications are necessary.

Proactive Problem Identification   RMON's traffic monitoring and alarm features help pinpoint changes in the network behavior. It allows to set thresholds for key monitoring statistics. When these thresholds are exceeded, an alarm is sent to the NMS from the RMON agent.

Trend Analysis   RMON enables segment and node mapping to determine trends in network performance. This proactive trend analysis helps identify the existence of potential problems on any segment of a distributed network.

THIRD-PARTY TOOLS AND APPLICATIONS

LAN analyzers, baselining tools, response-time monitors, and performance-modeling applications are some of the smorgasbord of tools for troubleshooting and monitoring internetworks. RMON probes and analyzers are supposed to be the one-stop alternative, giving net managers a way to keep a weather eye on their networks from the comfort of the data center. The experience suggests that RMON products fare as well as or better than conventional analyzers in some situations and vice versa.

Almost all major troubleshooting tools/probes count packets accurately at rates approaching wire speed—some generating traffic. Nearly all such products gauge network utilization, both in real time and over days and weeks. Some RMON products even offer baselining and response-time monitoring.

Network Test Equipment

Alarm   A reporting/logging tool that can trigger on specific events within a network.

Analyzer   A traffic monitor that reconstructs and interprets protocol messages that span several packets.

Benchmark   A tool used to evaluate the performance of network components.

Control   A tool that can change the state or status of a remote network resource.

Debugger   A tool that, by generating arbitrary packets and monitoring traffic, can drive a remote network component to various states and record its responses.

Generator   A traffic generation tool.

Manager   A distributed network management system or system component.

Map   A tool that can discover and report a system's topology or configuration.

Reference   A tool for documenting MIB structure or system configuration.

Routing   A packet route discovery tool.

Security   A tool for analyzing or reducing threats to security.

Status   A tool that remotely tracks the status of network components.

Debugging Tools (Examples)

Most of the tools described (that is, arp, DiG, etherfind, ifconfig, netstat, nslookup, ping, traceroute, nhfsstone, nfswatch, and LADDIS) are on the majority of UNIX systems that support TCP/IP. A few, like *traceroute* and *DiG*, are publicly available from Internet archive sites. While others, such as *etherfind*, are found on specific vendor systems. You can only solve some cabling and some physical network problems using specialized equipment such as a protocol Sniffer or a cable fault analyzer, which are especially useful in large complex installations. However, you can track down and isolate many more common problems using the built-in network management tools such as *netstat* and *ifconfig*.

arp Displays and modifies the Internet-to-Ethernet address translation tables used by ARP, the address resolution protocol. The *arp* program accesses operating system memory to read the ARP data structures.

DiG (domain information groper) A command line tool that queries DNS servers in either an interactive or a batch mode. It was developed to be more convenient/flexible than nslookup for gathering performance data and testing DNS servers. DiG is built on a slightly modified version of the bind resolver.

etherfind Examines the packets that traverse a network interface and outputs a text file describing the traffic. In the file, a single line of text describes a single packet: it contains values such as protocol type, length, source, and destination. *etherfind* can print out all packet traffic on the Ethernet, or traffic for the local host. Further packet filtering can be done on the basis of protocol—IP, ARP, RARP, ICMP, UDP, and TCP—and filtering can also be done based on the source, destination addresses as well as TCP and UDP port numbers.

In usual operations, and by default, *etherfind* puts the interface in promiscuous mode. In 4.3 BSD UNIX and related OSs, it uses a network interface tap (NIT) to obtain a copy of traffic on an Ethernet interface.

Minimal protocol information is printed, and can only be run by the superuser. The syntax is painful.

ifconfig Is used primarily to configure the network interfaces at boot time. You can also use it to check the interface configuration and, in particular, the interface broadcast address and network mask.

netstat A program that accesses network related data structures within the kernel, then provides an ASCII format at the terminal. *netstat* can provide reports on the routing table, TCP connections, TCP and UDP "listens," and protocol memory management. *netstat* accesses operating system memory to read the kernel routing tables.

nslookup An interactive program for querying Internet Domain Name System (DNS) servers. It is essentially a user-friendly front end to the BIND "resolver" library routines. This program is useful for converting a hostname into an IP address (and vice versa), determining the name servers for a domain , listing the contents of a domain, displaying any type of DNS record, such as MX, CNAME, SOA, and so on, diagnosing name server problems.

By default, *nslookup* will query the default name server but you can specify a different server on the command line or from a configuration file. You can also specify different values for the options that control the resolver routines. The program formats, sends, and receives DNS queries.

Ping A simple debugging tool. It sends an ICMP *echo request* message to a remote host, which in turn returns an ICMP *echo reply* message to the sender. If a *ping* succeeds, then the two hosts can successfully send and receive IP packets. If the two hosts are on different IP networks, the network routing is also tested.

traceroute A tool that allows the route taken by packets from source to destination to be discovered. It can be used for situations where the IP record route option would fail, such as intermediate gateways discarding packets, routes that exceed the capacity of a datagram, or intermediate IP implementations that do not support the record route. Round-trip delays between the source and intermediate gateways are also reported allowing the determination of individual gateways contribution to end-to-end delay.

Enhanced versions of traceroute have been developed that allow specification of loose source routes for datagrams. This allows one to investigate the return path from remote machines back to the local host. *traceroute* relies on the ICMP TIME_EXCEEDED error reporting mechanism. When an IP packet is received by an gateway with a time-to-live value of 0, an ICMP packet is sent to the host which generated the packet. By sending packets to a destination with a TTL of 0, the next hop can be identified as the source of the ICMP TIME_EXCEEDED message. By incrementing the TTL field the subsequent hops can be identified. Each packet sent out is also time stamped. The time stamp is returned as part of the ICMP packet so a round-trip delay can be calculated.

Some IP implementations forward packets with a TTL of 0, thus escaping identification. Others use the TTL field in the arriving packet as the TTL for the ICMP error reply, which delays identification. Sending datagrams with the source route option will cause some gateways to crash. It is considered poor form to repeat this behavior.

nhfsstone An NFS benchmarking program. It is used on an NFS client to generate an artificial load with a particular mix of NFS operations. It reports the average response time of the server in milliseconds per call and the load in calls per second. The *nhfsstone* distribution includes a script, "nhfsnums," that converts test results into plot(5) format so that they can be graphed using graph(1) and other tools.

nhfsstone is an NFS traffic generator. It adjusts its calling patterns based on the client's kernel NFS statistics and the elapsed time. Load can be generated over a given time or number of NFS calls. *nhfsstone* will compete for system resources with other applications.

nfswatch Monitors all incoming Ethernet traffic to an NFS file server and divides it into several categories. The number and percentage of packets received in each category is displayed on the screen in a continuously updated display.

By default, *nfswatch* monitors all packets destined for the local host over a single network interface. Options are provided to specify the specific interface to be monitored, or all interfaces at once. NFS traffic to the local host, to a remote host, from a specific host, between two hosts, or all NFS traffic on the network may be monitored.

Categories of packets monitored and counted include ND Read, ND Write, NFS Read, NFS Write, NFS Mount, Yellow Pages (NIS), RPC Authorization, Other RPC, TCP, UDP, ICMP, RIP, ARP, RARP, Ethernet Broadcast, and Other. Packets are also tallied either by file system or file (specific files may be watched as an option), NFS procedure name (RPC call), or NFS client hostname.

nfswatch provides facilities for taking "snapshots" of the screen; saving data to a log file for later analysis (the analysis tool is included) is also available. *nfswatch* uses the Network Interface Tap, nit(4) under SunOS 4.x, and the Packet Filter, packetfilter (4), under ULTRIX 4.x, to place the Ethernet interface into promiscuous mode. It filters out NFS packets and decodes the file handles to determine how to count the packet.

LADDIS   A multivendor and vendor-neutral SPEC NFS *Benchmark*. The purpose of the *LADDIS* benchmark is to give users a credible and undisputed test of NFS performance and to give vendors a publishable standard performance measure that customers can use for load planning, system configuration, and equipment buying decisions. Toward this end, the *LADDIS* benchmark is being adopted by SPEC (the System Performance Evaluation Cooperative, creators of SPECmarks) as the first member of SPEC's system-level file server (SFS) "benchmark suite."

In particular, there has been an unexpected interest from some router vendors in using *LADDIS* to both rate and stress-test IP routers. This is because *LADDIS* can send back-to-back full-size packet trains and because it can generate a 90% Ethernet as on simulated "real" NFS workloads, just like routers encounter in the real world. But *LADDIS* is for local Ethernet or FDDI nets only, not WAN. *LADDIS* also generates NFS requests and measures responsiveness of the server.

Protocol Analyzers

Recent trends show that networks and their associated problems will grow faster than the people available to manage them. Network analysis should be about *problem anticipation* and reduction, rather than just resolution. Just as a good physician works to identify the underlying cause of a problem versus treating symptoms, network analysis should do the same in an easy-to-use manner.

Capabilities of the protocol analyzers have been evolving over time. Today's analyzers can decode and process protocols up to and including seven layers and provide a user-friendly interface that facilitates programming and report generation. MANs and WANs encompass layers 1–3. LANs cover layers 1–7 (Figure 14.5). A MAN and/or WAN analyzer must be able to decode the PCI at the physical, data link, and network layers. To diagnose a problem properly between a workstation on LAN A and a server on LAN B connected by a WAN, a LAN analyzer must decode those higher layers.

Features.   Starting at the bottom of the network pyramid, let us examine some analyzer basics required for both accurate problem identification and internetwork performance tuning. To relate analysis information seen on the internetwork, the analyzer tool must be able to correlate events. It also must work at the higher speeds and capacities under which the networks are now operating. The best element to use for correlation is time. Correlation

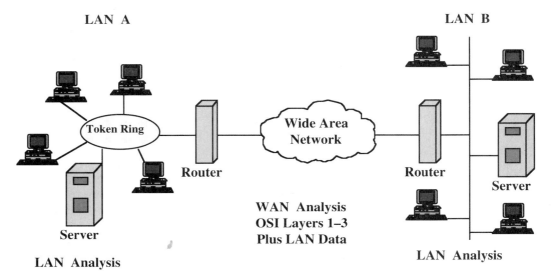

Figure 14.5 LAN and WAN analysis.

of events by time allows the user to accurately measure such parameters as latency, a valuable measurement for determining internetwork capacity and expected performance. Analyzers must have the ability to time synchronize data viewed across two or more segments. To help solve the problem associated with the more powerful networks, the analyzer's interface cards must have an on-board higher-level processing capability, independent of the processor CPU. The basic elements required to deliver the potential of network analysis are

- Processor-enhanced analyzer interface cards that can live within and complement a range of standard platforms.
- Time-synchronized multisegment with simultaneous capture and/or review capability.
- An expert network test, prediction, and problem resolution capability.
- Easy to use and affordable. Ease of use also means providing tracking and presentation mechanisms to show what is happening on the network, on multiple segments, or at whatever level desired.
- Alerting the user as to what may happen if a current condition persists.

Ideally, before you start your new internetwork, you should determine exactly how it will behave under extreme conditions. Apply the existing network analyzer capabilities during the design stage of a network. This will help ward off future problems, helping to catch up on the gap between network problems and available tools to solve them.

Some router-hub-switch devices have some analysis capabilities built into them, but the application of self-diagnosis is limiting when it comes to live networks. Remote

RMON devices also have their place as information gatherers, but have limitations when they are applied to problems outside their original design capabilities.

Today's client/server applications and network devices have not quite achieved the status yet that achieved by the mainframe computing and front-end processors. Applying the new, easy-to-use, proactively smart analyzers of today to traditional lower-level communications as well as higher client/server application level will help enterprises realize greater value. The network analyzer is expanding its horizons to become an easy-to-use tool.

Typical Protocol Analyzers. *Analyzer* is a traffic monitor that reconstructs and interprets protocol messages that span several packets. Some typical analyzers are

LANalyzer

LAN Patrol

LANVista

LANWatch

NetMetrix

NETScout

Sniffer

SpiderMonitor

NetWare LANalyzer Agent is a distributed network analyzer designed to complement Novell's NetWare Management System. While other NMS agents collect data about specific network devices (for example, servers or hubs), NetWare LANalyzer Agent, which resides on a NetWare server, watches the interaction among these devices. It enables you to improve network reliability and performance—from a central location—by proactively detecting and troubleshooting network problems.

NetWare LANalyzer Agent gathers and stores statistics that help you plan for the smooth growth of your network. It locates every networked device—regardless of type— and adds each to the on-screen map of the network's layout. As it monitors network traffic on Ethernet or token ring segments, the NetWare LANalyzer Agent alerts you immediately to potential problems, such as high network utilization, errors, or duplicate IP addresses.

The agent software relays the alert to the centralized NMS console. At the NMS console, you can start each LANalyzer Agent capturing packets, store the packets in server memory, and examine them in interpreted form. This shows you exactly what each station is doing on the network. It provides you with detailed statistics on packet and data rates for the network as a whole, for each station on the network, and for each individual conversation. This information enables you to spot overloaded network devices or segments, determine the heaviest users, and rebalance the load.

The LANalyzer can be installed on any existing NetWare 3.11 or 4.0-based device, or on a PC using the included NetWare Runtime™ software. One copy of NetWare LANalyzer Agent must be connected to each segment of the network you intend to monitor. Two types of NetWare LANalyzer Agents are available: one that can monitor every segment attached to an individual NetWare server and one that can monitor only a single segment. NetWare LANalyzer Agent fully supports SNMP and all nine groups of RMON standards, enabling it to interoperate with a variety of network management consoles, and transmit the information it gathers to them.

The LANalyzer is capable of gathering network specific data, including the following:

- Network statistics, such as network segment utilization.
- Per station statistics.
- Token ring–specific station statistics.
- Per conversation statistics.
- Packet capture.
- Alerts, such as duplicate IPs.
- Ethernet alerts, such as CRC errors, over or undersize packets.
- Token ring alerts, such as receiver congestion, beaconing.
- Lost frame errors.

NetWare Runtime is used to run NetWare LANalyzer Agent software on a dedicated PC. The LANalyzer Agent can run on a NetWare server with Ethernet or token ring interface card and the server ODI driver.

LAN Patrol is a full-featured network analyzer that provides essential information for efficient fault and performance management. It allows network managers to monitor user activity, find traffic overloads, plan for growth, test cable, uncover intruders, and balance network services. LAN Patrol uses state-of-the-art data collection techniques to monitor all activity on a network, giving an accurate picture of how it is performing. LAN Patrol's reports are saved as ASCII files to disk and are imported into spreadsheet or database programs for further analysis.

The LAN Patrol interface driver programs to a standard interface card to capture all traffic on a network segment. The driver operates from the background of a standard PC, maintaining statistics for each station on the network. The information can be viewed on the PC's screen or as a user-defined report output either to file or printer.

Normal operation is completely passive, making LAN Patrol transparent to the network. LAN Patrol can monitor up to 10,000 packets per second on an AT class PC and is limited to monitoring a maximum of 1024 stations for intervals of up to 30 days. Because LAN Patrol operates at the physical level, it will only see traffic for the segment on which it is installed; it cannot see traffic across bridges.

LANVista, CXR/Digilog's LANVista family of protocol and statistical analyzers, provides the tools to troubleshoot an Ethernet and token ring 4/16 Mbps network. LANVista lets you capture frames to RAM and or disk, generate traffic for stress testing, test your network cable for fault isolation, and decode all seven layers of many popular protocol stacks. LANVista offers a wide range of options for LAN management and protocol analysis.

Under Windows, LANVista can be operated in the background, gathering data and alarms as other tasks are completed. Displayed data may easily be cut from LANVista and pasted into other Windows applications such as Excel, Lotus 1-2-3, MS-Word, Harvard Graphics, and so on. The LANVista can also be remotely controlled through the use of PCAnywhere, Commute, Carbon Copy, or other PC remote control packages. This feature allows the use of "co-pilot" mode that enables an operator at the central site to guide and train a remote operator through network management or analysis tasks.

Basic capabilities include network database, statistics based on the entire network and on a node basis, token ring functional address statistics, bridged traffic statistics, protocol statistics, logging of statistics to a printer or file of user definable alarms, hardware precapture filtering, postcapture filtering, playback of captured data, traffic simulation, and on-line context-sensitive help.

Protocol interpreters used for decoding network traffic supported by LANVista include TCP/IP, DECnet, Banyan VINES, XNS/MS-Net, AppleTalk, IBM Token Ring, Novell, 3Com 3+Open, SNMP, and OSI.

LANWatch is a powerful and flexible network analyzer that runs under DOS on personal computers and requires no hardware modifications to either the host or the network. LANWatch is a tool for troubleshooting and monitoring local area networks and for developing and debugging new protocols. Network managers using LANWatch can inspect network traffic patterns and packet errors to isolate performance problems and bottlenecks. Protocol developers can use LANWatch to inspect and verify proper protocol handling. Since LANWatch is a software-only package which installs in existing PCs, it is portable.

LANWatch has two operating modes: display and examine. In *display mode*, LANWatch traces network traffic by displaying captured packets in real time. *Examine mode* allows you to scroll back through stored packets to inspect them in detail. To select a subset of packets for display, storage, or retrieval, there is a set of built-in filters. Using filters, LANWatch collects only packets of interest, saving the user from having to sort through all network traffic to isolate specific packets. The built-in filters include alarm, trigger, capture, load, save, and search. They can be controlled separately to match source or destination address, protocol, or packet contents at the hardware and transport layers. LANWatch also includes sufficient source code so users can modify the existing filters and packets or add new ones.

The LANWatch distribution includes a TCP protocol analyzer, a node-by-node traffic analyzer, and a dump file listing tool.

NetMetrix Protocol Analyzer is a distributed client/server monitoring tool for Ethernet, token ring, and FDDI networks. A unique "dual" architecture provides compatibility with both RMON and X windows. RMON features allow interoperability, while X windows enable much more powerful and intelligent application at remote segments and saves network bandwidth.

With this protocol analyzer, you can decode and display packets as they are being captured. Extensive filters let you sift through packets either before or after trace capture. The capture filter may be specified by source, destination between hosts, protocol, packet size, pattern match, or a complete expression using an extensive filter expression language. Request and reply packets are matched. Packets can be displayed in summary, detail, or hex, with multiple views to see packet dialogs side by side.

It supports full seven-layer packet decodes for all major protocols, including DECnet, AppleTalk, Novell, XNS, SNA, Banyan, OSI, and TCP/IP. The decodes for the TCP/IP stacks have all major protocols, including NFS, YP, DNS, SNMP, OSPF, and so on.

NETScout has the capability to collect wide-ranging statistical data, to display selectively captured and fully decoded network traffic, to set user-defined alarm conditions, and to obtain real-time updates from all segments of a widely dispersed internetwork from a centralized SNMP-compatible network management console.

The NETScout is based on standards so that operation may be realized in heterogeneous networks which constitute a multiprotocol, multitopology, multivendor environment. The fundamental standards upon which NETScout is based are the Simple Network Management Protocol, which defines the protocol for all intercommunications between NETScout devices and the remote monitoring management information base (RMON-MIB). The RMON-MIB defines the type of information that is to be gathered and made available to the user for each network segment. NETScout agents support all nine groups of the RMON-MIB standard. NETScout agents can work with any SNMP-based network management system and currently support Ethernet and token ring.

NETScout clients provide a full array of monitoring and analysis features, including intelligent seven-level decoding of all major protocol stacks. The stacks include TCP/IP, XNS, Novell, NetWare; DECnet including LAT, ISO, AppleTalk, IBM Token Ring,Banyan VINES, NetBIOS/SMB, SNMP including RMON-MIB, and SUN-NFS.

The operation of the NETScout family is divided into two distinctive subcategories. The first is the "client," which is the user console from which operational commands are issued and where all results and diagnostic information are displayed. In a NETScout topology it is feasible to have multiple clients active simultaneously within a single network. The second category is the "agent," which is a hardware/software device and is attached to a specific network segment. It gathers statistical information for that segment as well as providing a window into that segment where network traffic may be observed and gathered for more detailed user analysis. A typical network will have multiple segments and multiple agents up to the point of having one agent for each logical network segment.

For example, a NETScout software package that, when combined in a Sun SPARCstation in conjunction with SunNet Manager running under Open Windows, implements the NETScout client function. RunNet Manager provides the background operational tools for client operation while the NETScout software provides application-specific functions related to RMON-MIB support as well as all software necessary to perform the protocol decode function. SunNet Manager also implements a network map file that includes a topographical display of the entire network and is the mechanism for selecting network elements to perform operations.

Network General Sniffer is a protocol analyzer for performing LAN diagnostics, monitoring, traffic generation, and troubleshooting. The Sniffer protocol analyzer has the capability of capturing every packet on a network and of decoding all seven layers of the

OSI protocol model. Capture frame selection is based on several different filters: protocol content at lower levels, node addresses, pattern matching (up to eight logically related patterns of 32 bytes each), and destination class. Users may extend the protocol interpretation capability of the Sniffer by writing their own customized protocol interpreters and linking them to the Sniffer software.

The Sniffer displays network traffic information and performance statistics in real time, in user-selectable formats. Numeric station addresses are translated to symbolic names or manufacturer ID names. Network activities measured include frames accepted, Kbytes accepted, and buffer use. Each network version has additional counters for activities specific to that network. Network activity is expressed as frames/second, Kbytes/second, or percentage of network bandwidth utilization.

Data collection by the Sniffer may be output to printer or stored to disk in either print-file or spreadsheet format. Protocol suites understood by the Sniffer include Banyan VINES, IBM Token Ring, Novell NetWare, XNS/MSNet (3Com 3+), DECnet, TCP/IP (including SNMP and applications-layer protocols such as FTP, SMTP, and TELNET), X Windows (for X version 11), NFS, and several SUN proprietary protocols (including mount, pmap, RPC, and YP). Supported LANs include Ethernet, token ring (4 Mb and 16 Mb versions), ARCnet, StarLAN, IBM PC Network (Broadband), and Apple LocalTalk Network.

The Sniffer is a self-contained, portable protocol analyzer that requires only AC line power and connection to a network to operate. Normally passive (except when in Traffic Generator mode), it captures images of all or of selected frames in a working buffer, ready for immediate analysis and display. The Sniffer is a stand-alone device. Two platforms are available: one for use with single network topologies, the other for use with multinetwork topologies. Both include Sniffer core software, a modified network interface card (or multiple cards), and optional protocol interpreter suites. All Sniffer functions may be remotely controlled from a modem-connected PC. Output from the Sniffer can be imported to database or spreadsheet packages.

In normal use, the Sniffer is a passive device, and so will not adversely affect network performance. Performance degradation will be observed, of course, if the Sniffer is set to Traffic Generator mode and connected to an active network.

Expert Sniffer® Network Analyzer is a vital network management tool that helps maintain, troubleshoot, fine-tune, and expand multitopology, multiprotocol networks. It observes segments, learns their unique characteristics, and automatically uncovers a wide variety of problems. Once problems are discovered, The Expert Analysis application quickly pinpoints their origins, providing the shortest time to complex problem resolution.

The Expert Sniffer family of analyzers supports all major network types: Ethernet, IBM Token Ring (16/4 Mbps), Internetwork (up to 2.048 Mbps), and FDDI. Protocol interpreters for over 140 protocols are provided, including TCP/IP, Novell NetWare, DECnet, Sun NFS, X-Window, IBM SNA, AppleTalk, Banyan VINES, OSI, NetBIOS, OS/2 LAN Manager, 3Com 3+Open, XNS/MS-Net, and IBM LAN Server.

SpiderMonitor and *SpiderAnalyzer* are protocol analyzers for performing Ethernet LAN diagnostics, monitoring, traffic generation, and troubleshooting. The SpiderMonitor has the capability of capturing every packet on a network and of decoding the first four layers of the OSI protocol model. The SpiderAnalyzer has additional software for decoding higher protocol layers. Protocol suites understood TCP/IP (including SNMP and applications-layer protocols), OSI, XNS, DECnet, and IPX. User-definable decodes can be written in "C."

The SpiderAnalyzer supports multiple simultaneous filters for capturing packets using predefined patterns and error states. Filter patterns can also trigger on not matching 1 or more filters, an alarm, or a specified time. The SpiderAnalyzer can also employ time domain reflectometry (TDR) to find media faults, open or short circuits, or transceiver faults. It can transmit OSI, XNS, and Xerox link-level echo packets to user specified stations and can perform loop round tests.

In traffic generation mode, the SpiderAnalyzer has the ability to generate packets at random intervals of random lengths or any combination of random or fixed interval or length, generation of packets with CRC errors, or packets that are too short, or packets that are too long. Output from the SpiderMonitor/Analyzer can be imported to database or spreadsheet packages. The SpiderMonitor and Spider Analyzer are available as standalone, IBM PC compatible. It is capable of monitoring of up to 1024 stations and buffering of up to 1500 packets.

Protocol Monitors

Net_monitor uses ICMP echo (and DECnet reachability information on VAX/VMS) to monitor a network. It periodically tests whether hosts are reachable and report the results in a full-screen display. It groups hosts together in common sets. If all hosts in a set become unreachable, it makes a lot of racket with bells, since it assumes that this means that some common piece of hardware that supports that set has failed. The periodicity of the tests, hosts to test, and groupings of hosts are controlled with a single configuration file.

Reachability is tested using ICMP echo facilities for TCP/IP hosts (and DECnet reachability information on VAX/VMS). A DECnet node is considered reachable if it appears in the list of hosts in a "show network" command issued on a routing node.

This facility has been found to be most useful when run in a window on a workstation rather than on a terminal connected to a host. It could be useful if ported to a PC (looks easy using FTP Software's programming libraries), but this has not been done. *Curses* is very slow and CPU intensive on VMS, but the tool has been run in a window on a VAXstation 2000. This tool is not meant to be a replacement for a more comprehensive network management facility such as is provided with SNMP.

It requires a host with a network connection, Curses, 4.x BSD UNIX socket programming libraries (limited set), and some flavor of TCP/IP that supports ICMP echo request (*ping*). It runs on VAX-VMS running WIN/TCP and several flavors of 4.x BSD UNIX (including Sun OS 3.2, 4.0, and 4.3 BSD). It can be ported to any platform that provides a BSD-style programming library with an ICMP echo request facility and curses.

Cisco Catalyst offers a unique solution by integrating monitoring functions into its LAN switching platform. Because of the *Catalyst* switch's multiprocessor design (one processor dedicated exclusively for management), it can simultaneously perform as both a LAN switch and a multisegment RMON network probe.

To provide network monitoring and switching performance optimally, Catalyst can be configured to collect network traffic data in two ways. In *standard RMON mode*, Catalyst can collect and forward comprehensive network traffic information from multiple Ethernet segments simultaneously. This allows the network administrator to obtain all the information necessary to help tune or troubleshoot a switched LAN. The benefit of concurrently collecting multiple traffic feeds is obvious for network administrators who attach workgroup servers to dedicated Ethernet segments to improve network performance. If network administrators need to troubleshoot client/server applications, the task is greatly simplified through Catalyst's ability to simultaneously record traffic from both the server's and the client's segments.

Catalyst supports a secondary monitoring mode that provides more focused coverage across all its eight switched Ethernet segments. Called "Roving RMON," this *mode* allows the network administrator to monitor either of two RMON groups across all eight Catalyst Ethernet segments. Roving RMON can be used to collect historical network traffic data (like total switched data including packets, octets, and errors) per port or even per station. The network manager can use this data for various tasks such as capacity planning analysis or network accounting and billing.

Catalyst's Roving RMON also has a unique, user-definable trap feature that lets it reconfigure itself in case it detects specific network events. Network administrators can preconfigure the Catalyst to look out for potentially threatening conditions such as excessive collisions, corrupted packets, or even excessive traffic from a specific station. If the switch detects one of these predefined conditions, it sends an alert (trap) to the network management console and simultaneously initializes a fully configured RMON probes to monitor traffic on the offending network segment. With this function, network administrators can detect and collect troubleshooting data automatically, thereby extending their management capability while also helping to recognize and rectify network problems before they affect users.

The usefulness of a comprehensive switching and monitoring platform is only as valuable as the accessibility of the information available to the network administrator. The ability to centrally configure, control, and manage these RMON agents with an easy-to-use, GUI-based console becomes a necessity as more RMON-capable systems are deployed throughout the network. Leveraging configuration and monitoring functions with semiautomated network traffic recording, configurable alarms, and accounting functions further simplify network administrators' duties while improving their ability to maintain reliable, trouble-free networks. The following paragraphs describe some of the features needed in an RMON GUI.

The console monitor should present RMON data in a format that is easy to view and understand. The network administrator should be able to create customizable "views" of the RMON traffic information coming from specific segments attached to the network analyzer. With customizable views, network administrators can troubleshoot their network applications more effectively by selecting specific elements from the RMON MIB.

Since the RMON MIB can monitor virtually all network traffic, it is also important that the monitor console has the necessary tools to easily manage the myriad bits of information that can be collected from a LAN segment. These tools should let the administrator select specific information provided by the RMON MIB, such as data link statistics, traffic history, host traffic, and host matrix information. If the RMON agent also supports packet capture for protocol analysis, the console monitor should provide the tools to display the various protocol layers contained in the packet. Protocol filter tools should support popular protocols (like TCP/IP, XNS, Novell IPX, or AppleTalk) and should let the administrator view higher-level services as well (like NFS, SNMP, Apple ARP, and DEC LAT, to name a few). Console monitors with comprehensive filter tools can help network administrators save configuration and troubleshooting time. Flexibility in defining custom filters also ensures the long-term value of the console monitor as new systems and protocols are introduced to the network.

The RMON console's ability to automatically capture network traffic data and provide alarms is also valuable to the network administrator for network diagnosis and troubleshooting. A well-designed RMON console should allow the network administrator to define alarm conditions from any of the elements available in the RMON MIB. This level of flexibility helps the administrator address virtually any potential network troubleshooting problem. For example, an event-logging feature, working in conjunction with the RMON alarm, could help track the frequency and timing of network events while also providing information that could help the network administrator track down the cause-and-effect relationships of network-related problems.

To help network administrators track and troubleshoot protocol-related network problems, both the RMON probe and the console should also provide the tools to automatically capture network packet data for off-line analysis. The console manager should let the network administrator limit "packet captures" by using predefined or user-defined filters to help tailor the RMON probe functionality to meet specific troubleshooting needs.

Since fully instrumented RMON probes provide data to track network usage, a full-featured console manager should offer graphing, reporting, and accounting tools that help the network administrator track the growth and usage of the network. Graphing functions are useful for measuring and representing network traffic or server utilization over extended time periods. These graphs can show interesting trends in growth of network or server usage. Similarly, network administrators can use network accounting tools to show network resource usage by functional department. Reporting tools can help organize accounting data so that network administrators can produce usage information for budgeting or departmental billing purposes.

NETScout RMON Console provides an easy-to-use GUI for monitoring RMON statistics and protocol analysis information. NETScout Console also provides extensive tools that simplify data collection, analysis and reporting. The tools include

- GUI RMON monitor (browser).
- Simplified, user-definable RMON configuration and control tools.
- Sophisticated RMON filter editor (domain manager).
- Protocol monitor and analyzer.

- Traffic monitor.
- Alarm manager (Watchdog) and automated data capture.
- RMON grapher.
- Report generator.
- Event logger and database.

These tools allow the administrator to monitor traffic, set thresholds, and capture data on any set of network traffic for any segment. They collect information about all nine RMON groups to isolate and determine problem conditions on the network.

NETScout Console is available on a variety of platforms including SunNet Manager, HP OpenView, IBM NetView 6000, and PC Windows. NETScout Manager can run as a complementary application to Cisco's network management applications (a workgroup director), third-party network management applications (SunNet Manager, HP OpenView), or as a stand-alone application.

As network administrators rely more on switching to improve network performance, they will also require enhanced manageability and monitoring capabilities to ensure the reliability of their high-performance switched networks. Due to the design limitations of existing network monitoring tools, network managers must look at new ways to collect and interpret network traffic data in a switched environment. One cost-effective method is to use the network switch not only as a network performance enhancer, but as a network monitor. Cisco Systems' Catalyst Workgroup switch offers a unique solution, providing high-performance switching, traffic management, and standards-based RMON monitoring functions. Combined with an effective RMON console manager, Cisco's Catalyst switch offers network administrators enhanced management capabilities to ensure high performance and reliability in growing switched workgroup networks.

ChameLAN 100 is a portable diagnostic system for monitoring and simulation of FDDI, Ethernet, and token ring networks— simultaneously. Protocol analysis of multiple topologies, as well as mixed topologies simultaneously, is a key feature of the product family. Tekelec's proprietary FDDI hardware guarantees complete real-time analysis of networks and network components at the full ring bandwidth of 125 Mbps. It passively connects to the network and captures 100% of the data, measures performance, and isolates real-time problems.

The simulation option offers full bandwidth load generation that allows you to create and simulate any network condition. It gives you the ability to inject errors and misinformed frames. A set of confidence tests allows simple evaluation of new equipment. A ring map feature displays network topology and status of all nodes via the SMT process.

Monitoring of FDDI, Ethernet, and token ring networks allows the user to view network status in real time; view network, node, or node pair statistics; capture frames; control capture using trigger and filter capabilities; view real-time statistics; view captured frames in decoded format; and view the last frame transmitted by each station. The following real-time network statistics of FDDI, Ethernet, and token ring networks is displayed: frame rate, runts, byte rate, jabbers, CRC/align errors, and collisions.

Product developers can use the ChameLAN 100 to observe and control various events to help debug their FDDI, Ethernet, and token ring products. End users can perform real-time monitoring to test and diagnose problems that may occur when developing, installing or managing FDDI, Ethernet, and token ring networks and network products. End users can use the ChameLAN 100 to aid in the installation and maintenance of Ethernet and roken ring networks. To isolate specific network trouble spots, the ChameLAN 100 uses filtering and triggering techniques for data capture. Higher-level protocol decoding includes TCP/IP, OSI, and DECnet protocol suites. Protocol decodes of IPX, SNMP, XTP, and AppleTalk are also supported. Development of additional protocol decodes is also under development. The ChameLAN 100 family also offers a Protocol Management Development System (PMDS) that enables users to develop custom protocol decode suites.

The FDDI, Ethernet and token ring hardware interfaces feature independent processing power. Real-time data are monitored unobtrusively at full bandwidth without affecting network activity. Real-time data may also be saved to a 120 MB or optional 200 MB hard disk drive for later analysis. FDDI data are captured at 125 megabits per second (Mbps), Ethernet at 10 Mbps, and token ring at 4 or 16 Mbps.

This portable, stand-alone unit incorporates the power of UNIX, X-Windows, and Motif. Its UNIX-based programming interface facilitates development of customized monitoring and simulation applications. The ChameLAN 100 may connect to the network at any location using standard equipment. Standard graphical Motif/X-Windows and TCP/IP allow remote control through Ethernet and 10BaseT interfaces. Tekelec also offers a rack-mounted model—ChameLAN 100-X. Both models can be controlled remotely via a Sun workstation.

LanProbe The Hewlett-Packard's distributed monitoring system, performs remote and local monitoring of Ethernet LANs in a pro tool and vendor-independent manner. LanProbe discovers each active node on a segment and displays it on a map with its adapter card vendor name, Ethernet address, and IP address. Additional information about the nodes, such as equipment type and physical location, can be entered in to the database by the user.

When the NodeLocator option is used, data on the actual location of nodes are automatically entered, and the map becomes an accurate representation of the physical layout of the segment. Thereafter when a new node is installed and becomes active, or when a node is moved or becomes inactive, the change is detected and shown on the map in real time. The system also provides the network manager with precise cable fault information displayed on the map.

Traffic statistics are gathered and displayed and can be exported in (comma delimited) CSV format for further analysis. Alerts can be set on user-defined thresholds. Trace provides a remote protocol analyzer capability with decodes for common protocols. Significant events (like power failure, cable breaks, new node on network, broadcast IP source address seen, etc.) are tracked in a log that is uploaded to ProbeView periodically.

The system consists of one or more LanProbe segment monitors and ProbeView software running under Microsoft Windows. The LanProbe segment monitor attaches to the end of an Ethernet segment and monitors all traffic. Attachment can be direct to a thin or thick coax cable, or via an external transceiver to fiber optic or twisted pair cabling.

Network data relating to the segment is transferred to a workstation running ProbeView via RS-232, Ethernet, or a modem connection.

ProbeView software presents network information in graphical displays. ProbeView generates reports that can be manipulated by MS-DOS based word processors, spreadsheets, and DBMS.

The HP4992A NodeLocator option can attach to the opposite end of the cable from the HP4991A LanProbe segment monitor. It automatically locates the position of nodes on the Ethernet networks using coaxial cabling schemes.

NetMetrix Load Monitor is a distributed client/server monitoring tool for Ethernet, token ring, and FDDI networks. A unique "dual" architecture provides compatibility with both RMON and X windows. RMON allows interoperability and an enterprisewide view, while X windows enable more powerful, intelligent applications at remote segments and save network bandwidth.

The Load Monitor provides extensive traffic statistics. It looks at load by time interval, source node, destination node, application, protocol, or packet size. A powerful ZOOM feature allows extensive correlational analysis that is displayed in a wide variety of graphs and tables.

NewMetrix allows you to answer questions such as: Which sources are generating most of the load on the network when it is most heavily loaded and where is this load going? Which source/destination pairs generate the most traffic over the day? Where should bridges and routers be located to optimally partition the network? How much load do applications, like the X Windows protocol, put on the network, and who is generating that load when it is the greatest?

NetMetrix NFS Monitor is a distributed network monitoring tool that monitors and graphs NFS load and response time; retransmits rejects and errors by server or client, and breaks down server activity by file system and client activity by user.

A powerful ZOOM feature lets you correlate monitoring variables. You can see client/server relationships, compare server performance, and evaluate NFS performance enhancement strategies. It also allows monitoring of remote Ethernet, token ring, and FDDI segments from a central enterprisewide display. NetMetrix turns the network interface into promiscuous mode to capture packets.

Internet Rover is a prototype network monitor that uses multiple protocol "modules" to test network functionality. This package consists of two primary pieces of code: the data collector and the problem display.

There is one *data collector* that performs a series of network tests and maintains a list of problems with the network. There can be many display processes all displaying the current list of problems that is useful in a multioperator NOC.

The *display task* uses curses, allowing many terminal types to display the problem file either locally or from a remote site. Full source is provided. The data collector is easily configured and extensible.

A configuration file contains a list of nodes, addresses, NodeUp? protocol test (*ping*, in most cases), and a list of further tests to be performed if the node is in fact up. Modules are included to test TELNET, FTP, and SMTP. If the configuration contains a test that is not recognized, a generic test is assumed, and a filename is checked for existence. This way users can create scripts that create a file if there is a problem, and the data collector simply checks the existence of that file to determine if there is problem.

Additional Tools

etherck is a simple program that displays Sun Ethernet statistics. If you have a high percentage of input errors that are due to "out of buffers," then you can run the "iepatch" script to patch a kernel that uses the Intel Ethernet chip ("ie").

hammer and ***anvil*** are the benchmarking programs for IP routers. Using these tools, gateways have been tested for per packet delay, router-generated traffic overhead, maximum sustained throughput, and so on. Tests are performed on a gateway in an isolated test bed. Hammer generates packets at controlled rates. It can set the length and interpacket interval of a packet stream. Anvil counts packet arrivals. Hammer should not be run on a live network.

Distributed Sniffer System, which includes SniffMaster for Windows (SM/W) and SniffMaster for X Consoles, gathers information on network activity from remote Sniffer Servers residing on Ethernet, token ring, and internetwork segments. The console gives network professionals flexible access to vital information from distributed client/server networks. This information can be used to help solve network problems, improve network availability, and increase overall network performance.

The SM/X Consoles integrate seamlessly with Sun's SunNet Manager and Hewlett-Packard's OpenView to expedite network analysis. Intelligent network alarms from Sniffer Servers can be sent to INMSs for trouble ticketing and fault correction. SM/W Consoles fully integrate with Novell's NetWare Management System to expedite network analysis.

As part of the Distributed Sniffer System, Sniffer Servers can provide expert analysis, protocol interpretation, and 24-hour network monitoring of remote Ethernet and token ring segments from centralized locations. Sniffer Servers provide the ability to analyze isolated networks centrally, eliminating the need to travel to isolated network locations. The expert analysis application provides users with automatic identification of common network problems as well as suggested solutions, ensuring fast resolution and minimal downtime.

Foundation Manager® is a powerful and intuitive network monitoring application. It supplies critical information for network performance planning and fault detection. Foundation Manager uses an SNMP remote monitoring (RMON) solution to centrally manage large and geographically dispersed networks. Constant monitoring performed by Network General's Cornerstone Agents and other RMON agents supply Foundation Manager with key information for a clear view of network activity.

Foundation Manager minimizes network traffic in communications with its agents, because a Cornerstone Agent or Cornerstone Probe stores network data locally, thus reducing the need for constant polling. The product conveniently links to other Network General applications such as SniffMaster and Network General Reporter.

Network General Reporter® prepares network management reports using Sniffer analysis and monitoring data. The Reporter documents the wealth of information provided by Network General's Sniffer applications with a range of easy-to-read reports covering network usage over time, error summaries, baseline comparisons, and other important network issues. Use this information in conjunction with all Network General products to make decisions, justify support costs, and plan for the future.

MIB Browser is an X Windows HCI tool that allows you to "browse" through the objects in a management information base. The Browser is generic in that it can connect to a CMIS agent without having any prior knowledge of the structure of the MIB in the agent.

SUMMARY

As networks grow in size and complexity, managing remote sites becomes increasingly more difficult. Enterprise networks often use several network protocols and distributed applications, in addition to hardware and software from multiple vendors. A web of routers and bridges further complicates the mix by tying together this chain of heterogeneous network "islands."

To manage this increasing level of network complexity, network managers need to collect information from the entire network. Information on the status and behavior of all network components is the key—from computer systems, applications, routers, bridges, hubs, and modems to the network protocols that tie them together.

In any internetwork environment, troubleshooting tasks are the most frequently performed. Using monitor and/or analyzers with "expert" or automated capabilities, you can decrease the frequency of these tasks. These devices, tools, applications identify specific types of problems and recommend actions to solve these problems. Basic threshold and alarms will indicate the potential trouble areas, but still require manual intervention to determine the severity and the actions that must be taken.

EXERCISES

1. Describe three stages of problem detection and resolution.
2. What are the most common causes of network problems and failures?
3. What is RMON? How does MIB I differ from MIB II?
4. What different tools are available for troubleshooting networks?
5. List a few most commonly used analyzers and monitors.
6. A *ping* is used to reconfigure a node. True or false?
7. Monitoring network statistics helps the LAN administrator confirm a bottleneck. True or false?

15

INTERNETWORK TROUBLESHOOTING AND MONITORING—II

Introduction
Getting Started
    Problem Determination
    Hands-on Troubleshooting
LAN/WAN Troubleshooting Problem Areas
    Troubleshooting Cable Problems
    Troubleshooting Host-to-Host Connection
    Troubleshooting Application Layer
      Problems
    Troubleshooting Multiple Protocol Stacks
    Problem Isolation in DECnet Connectivity
    Problem Isolation for Gateways in SNA
      Networks
    Problem Isolation in Novell Internetworks
    Troubleshooting AppleTalk Connectivity
Troubleshooting the TCP/IP Internetwork

    Datagram Delivery Problems
    Problem Isolation and Connectivity
      Symptoms in TCP/IP Networks
Measurement and Testing
    Troubleshooting Features
    Common Analyzer Management Features
    Bit Error Rate Testers
    Using a Packet Monitor (Example)
Multivendor Solutions
    OpenView (HP)
    NetView (IBM)
    UniCenter (Computer Associates)
    NetWare (Novell)
Summary
Exercises

INTRODUCTION

Isolating problems in today's distributed enterprisewide network is consuming an increasing share of valuable time and resources. Never before has the Internet consisted of such a complex assortment of LANs, WANs, or MANs. Ensuring an optimal level of performance requires information about the type of traffic on various facilities as well as such critical information as delay, attenuation, and bit error rates. High-level information about packet error rates, packet loss rates, routing tables, and so on, is also needed.

    For example, a packet network often has a large number of logical connections on a small number of physical circuits. In the case of an X.25 or frame relay network, a single link can provide 1000 plus users with simultaneous access to various hosts or front-end processors. To complicate matters, communications protocols associated with each user session are getting more complex, making it more difficult to track down problems. For example, multilayered protocols that are based on OSI often require isolation of a particular layer before troubleshooting that layer to find the source of the problem.

There is a rich assortment of devices on the internetwork. The cause of a performance problem could be the user station, the LAN, the internetworking devices, the WAN, the carrier lines, the carrier service, the remote server, or the application software.

GETTING STARTED

The primary goal in troubleshooting is to identify and eliminate potential causes of the problem. Therefore, before you begin to address a solution, you must make sure that you fully understand the problem. Missing some vital information at the beginning can easily lead to an incorrect diagnosis. An understanding of the problem also helps to determine whether additional checks or data are needed.

Problem Determination

In getting started, you must ask yourself, at least the following questions:

- Is the problem widespread, with several people affected?
- Is only one person experiencing the problem?
- Is the problem preventing users from working at all or whether it is simply a performance problem that is causing delays or interruptions?
- Sometimes, you can get the system running quickly just by replacing a component.
- Is anything about the problem similar to previous problems? Check the statistical data and documentation. Assume that several adapter cards have gone bad in the past. Most problems you encounter have probably happened before. Therefore, you may be able to identify the problem just by going over the network's history.
- Many network failures occur after something has been changed or modified. Changes in topology, configuration, applications, and users can all be the source of network failures.

Changes can also be in the form of adding new components or different versions of applications or management software.

- Did any users change?
- Were new components added?
- Did you reconfigure any connective devices such as routers, bridges, gateways?

When you suspect that the problem may have been caused by recent network changes, verify the correct operation of any suspect components and their connection to the network. Incorrect configurations are often inadvertent. Some problems may occur when any user rather than the administrator makes changes.

Users are the best source to recreate the problem. For example, if a user is having trouble printing a document, the problem could be with the execution of the print command. In any case, you may have to perform some simple tests to ascertain the severity of the problem. But if any of these above measures fails, it is time to start utilizing the data from intelligent tools available, such as monitors, analyzers, probes, and other software diagnostic tools.

Just to reiterate (again), most network problems are directly related to the components. The following components may cause such problems:

- Bridges, routers, gateways.
- Cabling, connectors, concentrators.
- Network adapters, cards, boards.
- Hosts, servers, workstations.
- Others.

To make the problem manageable, it is essential to divide the network into segments. Each segment can then be examined and either rules out or found to be the culprit. Most administrators may feel comfortable by following a system methodology depicted in Figure 15.1.

Hands-on Troubleshooting

During the information/data gathering stage, you should be able to address the following questions:

- Do any stations work?

Check if the other users are also having the similar problems. If that is the case, the problem could be with the server, host, or interconnection devices along the path to the server or host. If not, the focus should be on the workstation, cabling, and any wiring concentrators to which the workstation is connected.

- Is there any traffic on the network?

A protocol analyzer can help by recording the amount of traffic on the network. Little or no traffic indicates a major component failure. It can also pinpoint the type of traffic that does not exist and help in determining the faulty component(s). If the traffic is unusually high, check who is generating that traffic and why. Make sure there are no "chattering" components that are repeatedly transmitting unnecessary data.

- Can the station operate as a stand-alone device?

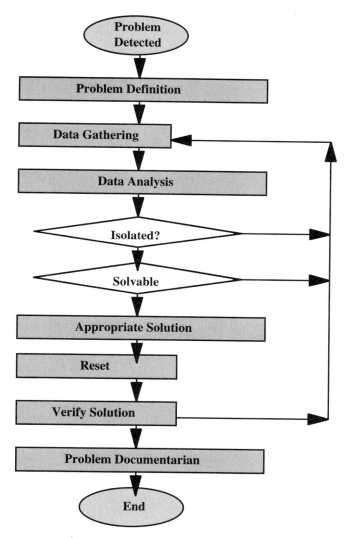

Figure 15.1 Troubleshooting methodology.

This is to determine if you are dealing with malfunction of an actual workstation or a network component. If the workstation can work in a stand-alone mode, the problem may be the adapter card or the network configuration on the workstation. On the other hand, if the workstation cannot operate in stand-alone mode, at least the workstation has the problem.

• Can the station connect to the network?

If the workstation is able to connect to the network, then the problem is neither with the workstation nor the cabling nor the networking software on the workstation. If the workstation cannot connect, the wiring/cabling may be a logical culprit. This can be checked by using a media tester—time domain reflectometer—to isolate a wiring problem. If the wiring tests to be operating normally, then the problem still lies in the workstation.

• Is the adapter on the workstation functioning?

By swapping adapter cards, you can test the adapter cards, provided the workstations and wiring are operational and can connect to the network.

The above information plus symptoms, such as user complaints, recent changes, and abnormal behavior, can get you started on the right path.

LAN/WAN TROUBLESHOOTING PROBLEM AREAS

First there is the challenge of isolating the application from the network. Problems appearing at the end-station or the host computer may be caused anywhere in the communications path between the end-station and the host. The problem symptoms could be intermittent, performance related, or a hard failure, occurring in a component or subsystem of any device on the network. Each protocol network offers a different assortment of challenges. Therefore, we will discuss a few cases. Figure 15.2 illustrates a typically managed internetwork.

First check the basic communication path between devices. Broken cables, loose connectors, and so on can cause what appear to be more complex problems. In a given internetwork, some of the most common trouble areas arise due to mixing multiplatform and multiprotocol environments, including

• Media faults.
• Ethernet/token ring bridging.
• Routing algorithms.
• Routing incompatibilities.
• Lack of routable protocols.
• Timing issues (if encapsulated).
• Early token release.
• Packet sizes.
• Lost packets.
• Corrupted packets.
• Nameservice problems.
• Broadcast storms on ethernets.

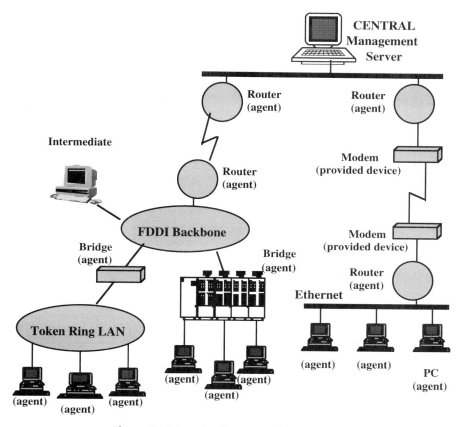

Figure 15.2 A typically managed internetwork.

- FDDI frame formats.
- Frame size.
- Flow control.
- Handshake problems.
- Bandwidth.
- Protocol problems.

Troubleshooting Cable Problems

The cable is the physical medium that carries the electrical signal from a workstation to and from the network server. The transmission line may be a twisted-pair, coaxial, or a fiber optic cable. Often you will come across the terms "balanced" and "unbalanced" in describing transmission lines. In a balanced design, the currents flowing between the generator and the receiver in each of the wires are equal in magnitude but opposite in direction. Twisted-pair and twin axial cables are examples of balanced transmission lines. In an unbalanced design, the current flowing from the signal conductor returns via a ground connection that other circuits may share. Coaxial cable is an example of an unbalanced transmission line.

Twisted-pair cable is the most popular medium for voice and data transmission in the office environment. Telephone cables are an example of twisted-pair cables. Data grade or shielded pairs are used with LANs, principally token ring networks, because the shield reduced interference. But twisted pair is subject to at least two problems:

- *Crosstalk* occurs when adjacent cables interfere with each other's signals. A common example is the background conversation you may hear when you are talking on the telephone. Crosstalk results from the inductive (or magnetic field) coupling of one line into another.
- *Noise* is any unwanted signal that enters transmission line from another source and impairs communication signals. Noise is generally classified in two ways: radio frequency interference from radio and television transmitters and electromagnetic interference from fluorescent lights, fan motors, and light dimmers. However, all systems have a built-in threshold of immunity to noise.

The question is how much interference can a LAN cable tolerate before data errors occur. This questions becomes more significant when you reuse building wiring (telephone cabling) already in place. Because of intermittent nature of noise, the vendors of LAN cabling systems have installed special filters to attenuate noise. For example, ARCnet receiver contains an extremely sensitive filter that passes only the proper frequency. To minimize network maintenance in the long run, the safest approach is prevention. Keep your LAN cables away from potential noise sources, such as AC power or analog telephones.

Coaxial cable gets its name from the center or common axis that the center conductor, shields or braids, and insulating materials share. The shield prevents extraneous signals (noise) from entering the center conductor and prevents the center conductor from interfering with or suffering from noise from another cable.

Both twisted-pair and coaxial cables share similar types of faults and corresponding solutions, such as:

- Faults caused by the connectors, splices, punch-down blocks, terminators, or other mechanical devices.
- Faults caused by the cable itself, such as opens, shorts, crimps, and kinks.

Connectors cause more failures than cables and are fairly easy to spot. A variety of other cable problems, such as shorts, opens, faulty or improper terminations, kinks, bends, crimps, short taps, or impedance mismatches produce a unique signal that can be measured and rectified.

Optical fiber cables do not emit any radiation; therefore, they are immune from electromagnetic and radio frequency interferences. The core of a fiber optic cable is a cylinder that provides a conduit for light and the cladding that surrounds the core reflects the light. Fiber optic cables allow ground isolation between buildings, since the material used for the fiber cable, typically silica, is a non conductor. The small size and light weight of fiber is useful in many installations. In addition, the high bandwidth, hundreds of Mbps, guarantees against the obsolescence of your cable system.

Usually the cause of *broken cable*, or improperly seated or dirty connectors, is excessive loss of optical power. This can be determined by taking the optical measurements and comparing them with the maximum loss allowed for that of system. In addition, consider open or shorted connectors, miswired modular plugs, or open terminators. Also look for cable damage, such as cuts, frays, or breaks in the insulation, and any recent cable or connector additions or arrangements, such as a new Ethernet tap that is shortening the backbone cable.

For suspected fiber optic cable failures, use an optical light source to verify fiber continuity. Verify that the connectors are not dirty. In case of various topologies, look for obvious disconnections for

- *Ethernet:* Connectors, terminators, and transceivers.
- *Token ring:* Media filters used with unshielded twisted-pair cable, or data connectors at the MAUs.
- *FDDI:* Connectors or cables may be plugged into a wrong port.
- *ARCnet, StarLAN:* T-connectors, terminators, modular cords, and data connectors.
- *Switched Multimegabit Data Service (SMDS):* Connects two LANs.
- *Serial Lines:* Connectivity from host-to-host and LAN-to-LAN Serial Line IP (SLIP) and the Point-to-Point Protocol (PPP).
- *Public Data Networks using X.25:* WANs.
- *Frame Relay:* Similar to X.25 for connecting LANs.

The network interface connection is fundamental to any internetwork. If a connector is bad or a network interface card is defective, you must troubleshoot and repair those elements before moving up the protocol stack to analyze the communication protocol layers. Here are some key points to consider:

- First check the basic communication path between devices, since broken cables or loose connectors can cause severe problems.
- Verify, for example, that all workstations on an Ethernet are transmitting Ethernet, not IEEE 802.3 frames. Or verify that all segments have the correct cable type, such as 10BASE2 or 10BASE-T.
- Systematically isolate the problem to a single LAN, MAN, or WAN segment since it is rare for two segments to fail simultaneously.

Troubleshooting Host-to-Host Connection

In TCP/IP networks, there are two protocols that provide end-to-end or host-to-host connectivity. We have learned that UDP provides connectionless service and is typically used for applications that need port identification and basic error control. TCP offers connection-oriented service and rigorously maintains sequence and acknowledgment numbers to guarantee data delivery. Of course, for the TCP reliable service, you pay the price of the additional overhead.

However, if the host-to-host connection fails, the first thing you need to determine is the protocol—TCP or UDP. If the protocol is UDP, verify that connectionless service is adequate for the application. If it is so, then the problems such as multiple transmissions may be the result of improper assumptions by the upper layer protocols regarding the transport mechanism. TCP, on the other hand, is much more complex. In addition to verifying the port number, examine the significant events in the TCP connection, such as three-way handshake (using ACK and SYN flags) and the connection termination (using the FIN and RST flags). During the data transfer phase, also verify that sequence numbers, acknowledgments, and window sizes are appropriate for the application. A setting of window=0 will close the communication path in the opposite direction. Therefore, make certain if the transmitted data are reaching its destination.

Troubleshooting Application Layer Problems

At the application layer, the user interacts with the host to perform application related functions. These functions may include remote host access with the Telecommunications Network Protocol (TELNET), or file transfer using the File Transfer Protocol (FTP) or Trivial File Transfer Protocol (TFTP), or electronic mail using the Simple Mail Transfer Protocol (SMTP), or client/server file operations via Sun's Network File System (NFS). Unlike the host to host, Internet, and the cabling system, which are transparent to end users, the application layer is accessed by users directly via the host's operating systems.

To diagnose the problems related to applications, you begin by determining whether the end-to-end connectivity functions are getting the data to the required destination. If the data are not getting through, then the problem exists in the lower layers. If the data are getting through, then the problem may be at the upper layers. One of the possibilities is that the data are not being properly interpreted, such as conversion between ASCII and EBCDIC. Another possibility is that the two application processes are unable to communicate with each other because of internal implementation differences.

In addition to the protocol analyzer, a number of utilities are available to monitor and diagnose such problems. Some of the standardized monitoring and debugging tools are

etherfind—A traffic monitor.

Internet rover—A network monitor.

netstat—A utility that can report routing table, TCP connections, and traffic statistics.

snmpwatch—A network monitoring utility reporting SNMP variables.

mconnect—A utility to test SMTP connections.

Troubleshooting Multiple Protocol Stacks

Let us examine an environment that mixes DOS, OS/2, and a TCP/IP workstation package. Figure 15.3 illustrates two token rings in two separate locations. One ring supports an OS/2 server and associated workstations and the other ring is connected to an SNA host. The two rings are connected over a WAN via routers. The primary workstation (A) is running Windows and the DOS-based TCP/IP workstation resides on an OS/2 Server.

The TCP/IP workstation program that is required to access the remote SNA host is resident on the OS/2 Server. Since that program is DOS based, you open a DOS Window and start loading a file. The file opens properly, is read from the OS/2 Server, and closes. The Windows workstation A is now ready to connect to the remote host using FTP.

The workstation broadcasts an ARP for the router that can connect it to the host. It finds the router and establishes a TCP connection. But the connection is terminated soon thereafter. It appears that the TCP/IP application is no longer active. The frames sent from Windows workstation indicated receiver congestion, but eventually, the problem was traced to an incompatibility between the DOS application, MS-DOS Window, and the OS/2 LAN Server. The problem was resolved by operating the TCP/IP program from a DOS-based rather than Windows-based workstation.

Problem Isolation in DECnet Connectivity

DECnet network nodes connect to LANs and WANs via separate physical line controllers. The Ethernet network uses the IEEE 802.3 mechanism to provide local communications link for workstations, routers, hosts, and other devices. In the internetwork example, var-

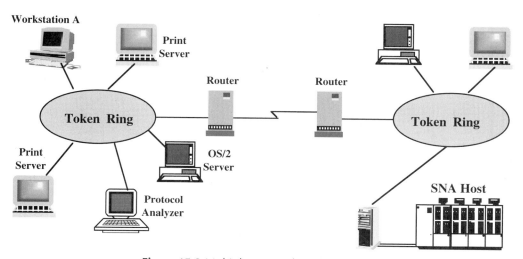

Figure 15.3 Multiple protocol environment.

ious devices and hosts are connected to a backbone (Figure 15.4). A number of protocols are in operation including X.25, TCP/IP, and DECnet.

Sometimes the analyzer on the network indicates an errant signal that generates a number of network errors with degradation of the response times for a while, but then the normal operation again resumes. There are three possibilities of the problem: defective port, a thin wire exceeding the length specification, or something wrong with the segment connected to the print server. To isolate the cause, the network can be conceptually operated in three segments where those components are located.

By disconnecting one component at a time, you will find that the culprit is the segment that connects the print server. Further examination will reveal a severe physical problem with cable close to the server. When the cable is repaired, all operations return to normal.

Problem Isolation for Gateways in SNA Networks

Because SNA environments are so popular, gateways into those environments are popular internetworking devices. The common problem occurs when the gateway is misconfigured

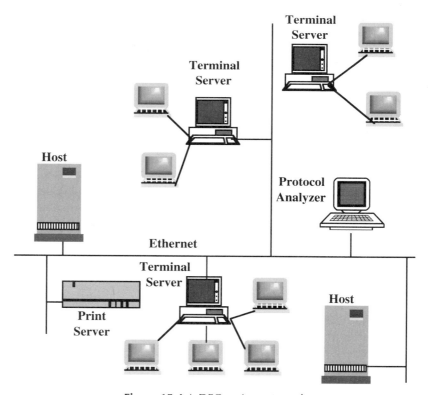

Figure 15.4 A DECnet internetwork.

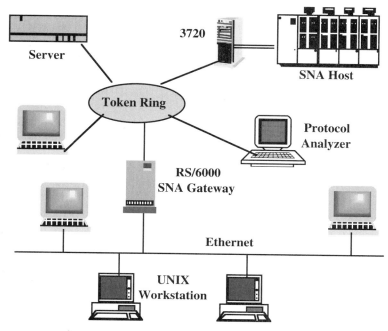

Figure 15.5 Token ring-SNA-RS/6000 gateway.

and cannot handle the sessions as desired. For the gateway and host to communicate, a number of peer-to-peer protocols and parameters must be properly configured. In Figure 15.5, the token ring network includes an SNA host and a number of NetWare workstations. The Ethernet network is primarily running TCP/IP on a UNIX workstation.

During activation, it was discovered that the gateway could only handle one LU-LU session. The gateway was reconfigured for additional LU-LU sessions. The host and the gateway were able to communicate as required.

Problem Isolation in Novell Internetworks

Figure 15.6 illustrates both Ethernet and token ring segments. The NetWare Server provides the internetworking between the two segments via a routing function, using IPX network protocol. Two stations and an analyzer are active on the token ring side. The details of the broadcasts reveal another network (the Ethernet) one hop away, via the server's bus, as the packets cross from token ring to Ethernet subnetwork. This simple exercise has verified a number of internetwork operations: both token ring and Ethernet LANs are healthy, the server is properly configured, and the NetWare internal routing is functioning as expected.

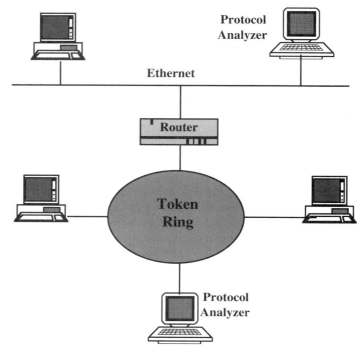

Figure 15.6 A NetWare operation.

Troubleshooting AppleTalk Connectivity

Apple has provided networking capabilities from the very beginning. Therefore, creating a physical network has never been a real problem. Beyond the mess of installing wire and making sure you have the correct cabling adapter, little else is needed for basic connectivity. However, making the jump to cross-platform connectivity has been a problem for a long time, and has been recently addressed. Now it is possible to include Mac either in an Ethernet or token ring network, and consequently in a WAN.

Chances are that you are familiar with and know how to troubleshoot your PC, MS-DOS, and Windows networking problems. However, it is quite likely that Macintosh is not your forte. To make things worse, each NOS uses AppleTalk to communicate with the Macs. Therefore, you must learn the ins and outs of AppleTalk also. Before you embark on troubleshooting Macs, you must be familiar with AppleTalk and the Macintosh networking environment. Before you begin to troubleshoot a Macintosh-centered network, you should examine the tools, the symptoms, and techniques available to isolate and fix the problem.

AppleTalk protocols must never be bridged across a wide area link (Figure 15.7). Since some protocols cannot be routed, you may need to design your network to ensure that some protocols are bridged while others are routed. Consider the following when it is necessary to bridge some protocols:

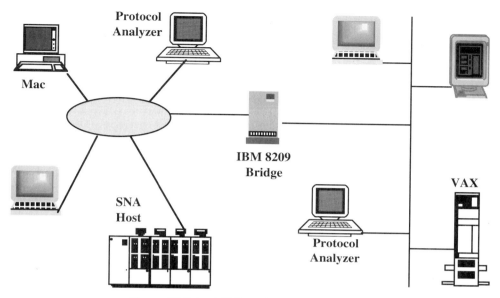

Figure 15.7 AppleTalk and IBM 8209 bridge.

- Use a device that does bridging and routing for your wide area link (Brouter).
- Use a router to isolate AppleTalk nodes from the wide area bridge.
- Whenever possible, group devices using the same protocol onto the same network. Some of the new modular devices make it easier (for example, 10BaseT).

Tools. There are two categories of tools provided with Macs: software and hardware. *Software tools* include system software, virus checkers, hard disk recovery and repair utility, and network mapping utility. The network mapping utility can quickly tell you which network resources are available at a specific time.

Software tools are of three types: hardware diagnostic software, software diagnostic software, and system utilities. Hardware diagnostic software checks for hardware problems and malfunctions. Software diagnostic programs check the Macintosh system software and installed applications. Of course, the utilities such as protocol analyzers and monitors check the network.

Symptoms. There are five basic *start-up problems* that the Mac can have outside of actual hardware problems, namely, the Mac will not start, or cannot complete the boot process, or crashes after it starts up, or cannot launch an application, or has random system errors.

Chooser Problems do not allow any of Mac's networking functions to work for example, you will not be able to use the file server or the laser printer or the zones. One cause of these problems is that the network, a router, or the file server is down. The other cause is that network is selected improperly because of improper zone or address.

Printer Problems are some of the biggest headaches with your Mac network. Printers sometimes keep being reinitialized or consistently fail to finish the print job. Most of the time, these are printer hardware related or the files to be printed have been corrupted.

Problems.   There are a series of steps you can take to isolate and fix the problems. We will concentrate primarily on the network problems.

For *Chooser*-related problems, make sure the proper network is selected. Always check the Chooser and turn AppleTalk on and reinstall the Apple Network Software. The only way to make certain that the Chooser is not corrupted is to reinstall the system software.

Physical link and network problems can occur for a number of reasons:

- Loose cable can cause the network to go down.
- PC suddenly fails to log into the server. This could be if the hub with a port is down or the router is malfunctioning at a very low level.
- Improper network panel could cause Ethernet network to fail.

Troubleshooting is always tedious. But there is not that much can go wrong with the Macs. When Macs are connected to other internetworks, the problems usually are related to internetworking or intelligent devices which are common to all networks.

An Example.   Let us examine the problems you could have by connecting to a file server from a Macintosh where the fix for the problem is the strictly Macintosh related. Because there are several elements to the Mac's networking capabilities, it is easy for one of the control panels or the Chooser to be incorrect. This will result in an inability to access the network.

Usually the first indication of a problem will be when you go to the Chooser and cannot see a file server or a printer when clicking on the respective icons. Another indication is if you do not see any zones. When such a condition exists, you should check the AppleTalk setting in the Chooser. If the AppleTalk setting is inactive, you will have no network access.

If AppleTalk is active and you still do not have network access, and you are using Ethernet or token ring, you should check the Network Control Panel. If you are not using a high-speed network, but relying on LocalTalk or PhoneNet talk, either you are physically disconnected from the network or the network services are down. However, you must make sure the correct network is selected.

TROUBLESHOOTING THE TCP/IP INTERNETWORK

When planning to diagnose internetwork-related problems, it is important to review the functions of the IP layer. The principle function of the IP layer is routing, with desired result being connectivity between two hosts. Associated with the routing are the issues of addressing, subnet assignments, and masks. Because addresses are not always known, protocols such as ARP/RARP may be used. The Domain Name Service may also assist in this effort. Some of the common, human-generated, problems that plague Internet users are

- Failure to log on to a remote host.
- Duplicate IP addresses, because of a duplicate entry in the address database.
- Incorrect address mask can happen when there are duplicate devices on the same network with incorrect subnet mask for a different class network.
- Misdirected datagrams, because the workstations configuration may be incorrect and its initial attempt to communicate with the host fails.
- Confused routers case happens when there are a number of segments on a network and one of them is connected via routers. Workstations wishing to communicate with other hosts are getting confused because two routers want the same datagrams. It seems that both routers had corrupted routing tables. To correct the problem, reconfigure the routers and bring the network back up.

Datagram Delivery Problems

If the problem occurs in the Internet and the network interface layer (basic communication path between devices, connectors, cables, etc.) looks healthy, watch for significant events at the Internet layer. These could relate to datagram delivery. The processes for address assignment, address recovery, communication between routers, and notification of router errors may offer clues about the reason for a problem with the delivery of your datagram.

Intelligent devices such as routers, bridges, and gateways use the addressees to guide that datagram through the Internet. The routers communicate with each other using an Interior Gateway Protocol (IGP), such as Routing Information Protocol (RIP) or Open Shortest Path First Protocol (OSPF). Because the routing mechanism does not always function properly, another protocol intranetwork communications protocol (ICMP) helps the hosts what went wrong.

One frequently used test is the ICMP echo (*ping*) message used to verify connectivity between Internet devices. The *ping* can be used in a sequential manner to isolate a problem. For example, first *ping* a host on your subnet, then *ping* a router, then *ping* a host on the other side of the router, until the faulty connection is identified.

Another maintenance utility, traceroute, is available with some host operating systems. Traceroute uses ICMP messages to verify each segment along a path to a distant host. Traceroute must be used sparingly since it can generate its own traffic and overhead.

Problem Isolation and Connectivity Symptoms in TCP/IP Networks

Any one or a combination of the following are some common symptoms that most TCP/IP networks exhibit:

- Recent changes to the network environment, such as
  - Reconfiguration of components or network operating system.

- New revision of components software, workstation operating system, or an application.
- New user.
- New component.
- User complaints, such as
  - Poor performance or slow response.
  - Lost connection or inability to connect.
  - Failure to execute an application, e-mail, or print.
- The system is exhibiting abnormal behavior, such as
  - Response time is slower than usual.
  - Traffic and server usage is heavier than usual.
  - More protocol errors occur than usual.
  - Different protocol and application mixes occur, causing time-outs or log-outs.
- Host access problems and remedies.
- Path and router network errors and solutions.
- Bridge filtering problems.
- Duplicate addressing.

One of the most obvious addressing issues that must be investigated when joining local area networks with wide area networks is duplicate network addresses. As LANs are added to the internetwork, it should be assured that the rules for network addressing are followed across the WAN. For example, with AppleTalk networks, this includes zone naming conventions:

- All networks must have unique network numbers, even across a WAN.
- Routers must agree on network number and zone name affiliations.
- A zone should never span networks across wide area links.

It is very common for administrators to use nice round numbers when assigning network addresses. If two local area internetworks are to be joined by a wide area link, when two of the networks being joined are using the address, you must be sure to change the router configurations, including specifying which zones are associated with which network numbers.

MEASUREMENT AND TESTING

Interconnection devices, packet switches, and other network equipment typically accumulate usage and performance data that can be retrieved at a terminal connected to the management station. Some provide detailed data on a channel basis. In addition, the high degree of intelligence of these network devices allows them to be remotely instructed to run network tests. For instance, some bridges and routers can verify the path between themselves and an end station attached to the same LAN. At the same time that it is checking the integrity of the local connection and the end station's response to a stream of test packets, a remote interconnect device could check the continuity of the path between it and the local bridge or router. This process can continue until every segment between the end station and a remote host computer is verified as operational.

Troubleshooting Features

The market for LAN and WAN network analysis has expanded because networks are more complex. The analysis tools have become even more complex with the emergence and dependence on microcomputers as a platform for testing software. Today's analysis tools are able not only to analyze LANs but also LAN protocols traveling on wide area links. There are protocol analyzers and monitors for all types of communications circuits, including frame relay, X.25, T1, and ISDN. There are also protocol analyzers that can decode full seven layers of TCP/IP, DEC LAT, XNS/MS-NET, NetBIOS, SNA, SMB, NetWare, and VINES, as well as various LAN cabling, signaling, and protocol architectures, including those for Ethernet, AppleTalk, ARCnet, token ring, and StarLAN.

Protocols are a set of data communications procedures or rules that are used to formalize information transfer and error control between devices. When equipment from different manufacturers uses the same protocols, the different devices can communicate with one another. Communications software formats data for transmission by packetizing it and adding a header and trailer, forming an envelope for the message while it traverses the network. Devices on the network using the same protocol know how to read the envelope so it can be routed over the appropriate link. A *protocol violation occurs when these procedures are not followed.* Then the cause of the problem must be found by reading the headers and trailers attached to the messages or by opening the envelope to read the messages themselves.

The protocols are either byte oriented or bit oriented. Byte-oriented protocols are relatively simple to decode to determine protocol violations. Bit-oriented protocols, such as SNA, X.25, TCP/IP, Ethernet, token ring, and DECnet, are more complicated and require more sophisticated tools. Most of today's analyzers, other monitoring tools, connect directly into the LAN, as if it were another node (Figure 15.8). Many analyzers add features, such as counters, timers, traps, masks, and data capture, to isolate a problem. Some of these features that dramatically shorten the time it takes to isolate a problem, are discussed below:

Monitoring: In a monitoring mode, the analyzer sits passively on the network and monitors both the integrity of the cabling and the level of data traffic, for example, logging such incidents as damaged packets and accessing packet collisions that can tie up an Ethernet LAN.

Filtering: This feature can increase the effective capture size significantly, for example, setting filter criteria so that the analyzer displays only packets that are going to and from specific nodes, formatted according to specific protocols or containing only certain

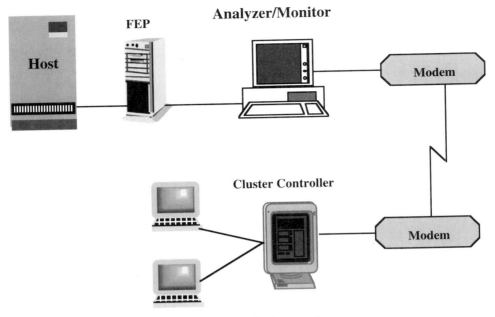

Figure 15.8 Monitoring events.

errors. With this feature, the user can include or exclude certain types of protocol data that require analysis, such as

- Protocol type.
- Destination or source address.
- Errored packets.

Trapping: This feature starts recording data into the analyzer's buffer or to a disk when a specific event occurs. For example, the analyzer could be set up to trap the first incorrect frame it receives. This allows the capture of only essential information. It is common to set performance thresholds according to the type of traffic on the network, setting off alarms when such thresholds are exceeded.

Cable Testing: Cable problems are the source of majority of the LAN network failures. Many protocol analysis tools include the capability to test for cable breaks and improper terminal connections. These devices are capable of pinpointing such faults as shorts, crimps, and water faults, for close-in as well as remote measurements.

Mapping: This feature can save network administrators many hours of work. In automatically documenting the physical location of the nodes, mapping can help rearrange devices (add, delete, move).

Storage: The monitoring device permits the temporary storage of recorded data. Using an integral text editor, the captured data can be edited, and the desired material copied or printed.

Timing: Poor repines time is a frequent complaint of network users. Protocol analyzers contain timers that measure the interval between events. By setting up two traps, one each for transmit and receive paths, you can verify if a *handshake procedure* has exceeded its maximum time interval. Time stamping of the captured events can be a definite asset for relating data to alarms generated by the management system to give total picture.

Traffic Verification: This can be performed by generating packets which allow to test the impact of additional traffic on the network. You can customize the contents of the data field section of packets to simulate real or potential applications. Packets may also be generated to force a *suspected problem to recur.* By loading network from 1 to 98 %, network components such as bridges, transceivers, and repeaters can be stressed to identify any weak links on the network before they become serious problems.

Automatic Reconfiguration: Some analyzers support the device to be automatically reconfigured to the protocol characteristics of the line under test.

Editing: Some analyzers include text editors for manipulating captured data, allowing you to deleted unneeded data, enter comments, print reports, and even create files in desired formats.

Common Analyzer Management Features

- The fault management tool displays a map of the network configuration with node and link state indicated in one of several colors to indicate current status.
- The configuration management tool may be used to edit the network management information base stored in the NMS to reflect changes occurring in the network.
- Graphs and tabular tools are used in fault and performance management.
- Mechanisms by which additional variables, such as vendor-specific variables, may be added.
- Alarms may be enabled to alert the operator of events occurring in the network.
- Events are logged to disk.
- Output data may be transferred via flat files for additional report generation by a variety of statistical packages.

Bit Error Rate Testers

Testers are used to determine whether data are passed reliably over a carrier to provide communications link. The tester sends and receives various bit patterns and data characters. That way, a comparison can be made of what has been transmitted and what has been received. The bit error rate is calculated as a ratio of the total number of bit errors divided by the total number of bits received. Any difference between the two signals an error condition.

Using a Packet Monitor (Example)

Network Operations Center On-Line (NOCOL) is a collection of network monitoring programs that run on UNIX systems, for an IP network. The software consists of a number of monitoring agents that poll various parameters from any system and put it in a format suitable for postprocessing. The postprocessors can be a display agent, an automated troubleshooting program, an event logging program, and so on. Presently, monitors for tracking reachability, SNMP traps, data throughput rate, and name servers have been developed and are in use. Addition of more monitoring agents is easy, and they will be added as necessary. A display agent using curses has already been developed. Work on an "intelligent" module is currently in progress for event logging and some automatic troubleshooting.

All data collected by the monitoring agents follow a fixed (nonreadable) format. Each data entry is termed an event in NOCOL, and each event has certain flags and severity associated with it. The display agent displays the output of these monitoring agents depending on the severity of the event. There can be multiple displays running simultaneously and all process the same set of monitored data.

There are four levels of severity associated with an event—CRITICAL, ERROR, WARNING, and INFO. The severity level is controlled independently by the monitoring agents, and the decision to raise or set an event's severity to any level depends on the logic imbedded in the monitoring agent.

As an example, for the *pingmon* monitor, if a site is unreachable via ping, it would be assigned a severity of WARNING by *pingmon*, which would then elevate to CRITICAL if the site is still unreachable after some time. In the case of *trapmon*, an SNMP trap message of EGP neighbor lost would be directly assigned a severity level of CRITICAL, while an Warm Start trap is assigned a severity of WARNING.

The display agent (and other data postprocessors) would use this event severity to decide whether to display it (or troubleshoot/log it) depending on the user selected display severity level. The software is very flexible and allows enhancements and development with a minimum amount of effort. The display module processes all the files present in the data directory and displays them sequentially. This allows new monitoring programs to simply start generating data in the data directory and the display module will automatically start displaying the new data. The monitoring tools can be changed, and the only element that has to remain common between all the modules is the EVENT data structure.

This monitor presently consists of the following modules:

nocol, which simply displays the data collected by the monitoring agents. It uses the curses screen management system to support a wide variety of terminal types. The criterion for displaying an event is

- Severity level of the event is higher than the severity level set in the display.
- The display filter (if set) matches some string in the event line.

The display can be in regular 80-column mode or in extended 132-column mode. Critical events are displayed in reverse video (if the terminal type supports it). Additional features like displaying informational messages in a part of the window, automatic resizing window sizes, and operator acknowledgment via a bell when a new event goes critical are also available.

ippingmon monitors the reachability of a site via "ICMP" ping packets (ICMP was preferred over SNMP for many obvious reasons). This program can use the default output from the system's ping program, but an accompanying program (multiping) can ping multiple IP sites at the same time and is preferable for monitoring a large list of sites. A site is marked unreachable if a certain number of packets is lost, and the severity level is increased each time that the site tests unreachable.

osipingmon is similar to the ippingmon module but uses the OSI ping program instead. No multiple-ping program for OSI sites has been developed at this time. The only requirement is that the system's ping program output match the typical BSD IP ping program's output.

nsmon monitors the name servers (named) on the list of specified hosts. It periodically sends an SOA query for the default domain and if the queried name servers cannot resolve the query, then the site is elevated to CRITICAL status.

tpmon, for monitoring the throughput (Kbits per second) to a list of hosts, connects to the discard socket on the remote machine (using a STREAM socket) and sends large packets for a small amount of time to evaluate the effective throughput. It elevates a site to WARNING level if the throughput drops below a certain threshold (set in the configuration file).

trapmon converts all SNMP traps into a format suitable for displaying using NOCOL. The severity of the various traps is preset (and can be changed during compilation time).

MULTIVENDOR SOLUTIONS

There are a number of management products by practically every vendor. A few of the major ones are described below which handle multivendor internetworking environments.

OpenView (HP)

HP OpenView Network Node Manager is available on HP-UX, Sun-OS, UNIX/AIX, and other systems. The network Node Manager provides fault, configuration, and performance management for multivendor, TCP/IP-based networks. It is based on the OSF-DME. It automatically discovers maps and continuously monitored all network and system resources as the network changes. It also presents the user with alarms via the network map, an event browser, and an event log.

HP OpenView OperationsCenter enables organizations to manage HP, Sun, IBM, and UNIX servers and workstations as well as coordinate alarms and information gathered by other HP applications and utilities.

NetView (IBM)

AIX SystemView/6000 is available on the RS/6000 family of UNIX-based workstations and servers. AIX SystemView/6000 performs as a distributed or centralized manager when used in conjunction with AIX NetView Service or System/370-390 NetView. The capabilities include troubleshooting capabilities and allows users to directly access historical information.

UniCenter (Computer Associates)

CA-UNICENTER is available for OS/2, UNIX, NetWare, OS/400, Windows NT, HP-UX, IBM RS/6000 AIX, Sun Solaris, and many others. UNICENTER is essentially a system management product but incorporates a variety of tools such as performance monitoring.

NetWare (Novell)

NetWare Management System essentially supports desktop environments. The capabilities include automatic discovery and mapping of network devices, monitoring of network changes, management of alarm information, fault management, address and router management, and SNMP support. This is essentially a planning and analysis tool.

SUMMARY

The monitoring and analysis devices are becoming more and more intelligent, making them suitable for unattended operations. Expert systems are being employed to program the most common type of problems encountered in networks. In fact, some expert systems can either be employed by the enterprises with large networks or as a subscription service that interprets the user's captured data sent to a service center through a dial-up connection. A proper high-performance protocol analyzer can support a broad range of existing and emerging troubleshooting needs. It should be capable of monitoring and decoding all protocols encountered in the field.

For eventual problem solving and troubleshooting, no piece of cable, hardware, software tools, or network analysis can make up for a well-planned design and a thoughtful planning.

EXERCISES

1. List the steps in "hands-on" troubleshooting.
2. List some of the trouble areas on a network.

16

TROUBLESHOOTING A GLOBAL NETWORK (AN EXAMPLE)

Introduction
   Linking Token Ring, Ethernet via FDDI,
     T1, Frame Relay
   UNIX Workstations/Clients; UNIX and
     NetWare Servers
Knowing Your Resources
   Scope and Function of Troubleshooting
   Alarms and Error Messages
Bottleneck Isolation

Looking for Trouble and Remedies
   Misconfigured Workstation
   Server Overloads
WAN Bandwidth Problems
Broadband Troubleshooting
T1 Problems
Summary
Exercises

INTRODUCTION

With the increasing complexity of computer networks, problems are more complex and take longer to solve than ever before. Coupled with the scarcity of experts and the increasing demand on their time, network troubleshooting has become a challenge for every enterprise. Today's internetworks are often global affairs that mix many types of LANs and WANs, making it very difficult to pinpoint the source(s) of problems.

Many vendors manufacture networking products, but not all the products work together properly. With more and more complex relationships between hardware and software, sometimes it is difficult to differentiate hardware from software problems. It becomes even more difficult when a network comprises products from many different vendors or the network has simply evolved over time and the enterprise has grown.

The system programmers who diagnose problems with computer networks must understand the software in multiple components and the protocols used to communicate among them. Different diagnostic tests may need to be performed in various components of the network and then correlated.

Meanwhile, the problems occur daily when changing or adding terminals, lines, concentrators, protocols, or the parameters that govern their performance.

At this time, no single tool exists that provides all the appropriate data to resolve a particular problem. The difficulty is how to locate the problem. The right data must be captured or problems may never be found. Therefore, you must determine the data to gather and then manually correlate and interpret the data to isolate and resolve the problem. The problem may be in the application, a mismatch in the hardware/software specifications, or even a mismatch in interconnected networks.

Linking Token Ring, Ethernet via FDDI, T1, Frame Relay

One of the toughest challenges presented by an internetwork is that it is typically a global affair, with central sites in the United States and abroad. Consider, for example, a global network joining *token ring* and *Ethernet LANs* in Saint Louis with a high-performance *FDDI ring* and a second Ethernet in Boston via a T1 link, as illustrated in Figure 16.1. In addition, token rings in Paris and Munich are linked to the Boston location via a *frame relay* service.

UNIX Workstations/Clients; UNIX and NetWare Servers

These regional subnetworks support a variety of nodes, including both workstation and PC clients, as well as several UNIX and NetWare servers.

KNOWING YOUR RESOURCES

Scope and Function of Troubleshooting

As previously discussed, the key to troubleshooting is efficient fault isolation. And that, in turn, depends on sound knowledge of the scope and function of the network and the use of proper troubleshooting techniques. The place to start is by learning to take advantage of the error and alarm information the network provides. It is also critical to check configuration parameters of the devices involved in the problem and to monitor LAN and WAN traffic for overloaded circuits and devices.

In addition, you need the expertise to evaluate each network segment, perform stimulus/response tests (such as pinging problem devices), and examine and interpret statistical measurements of network traffic. Intelligent troubleshooting tools can help supplement this expertise and lessen the administrator's burdens. Rather than requiring network managers to wade through megabytes of captured frames, an intelligent analyzer can capture and report only significant conditions and events.

Remember that effective troubleshooting requires the administrators to have a feel for the network's normal level of traffic and transmission errors—this could be accomplished by keeping and perusing through historical/statistical data. It is absolutely essential to know who uses the network, under what conditions, what they use it for, and how

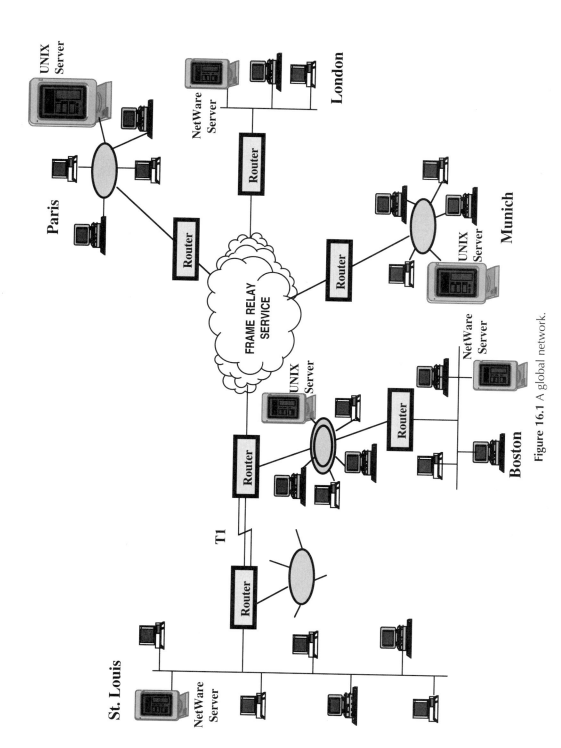

Figure 16.1 A global network.

much traffic they generate. Judicious use of network analysis tools helps to develop this knowledge base.

An intelligent network analyzer can provide a picture of the traffic flows and resource usage when things are running normally. When something goes wrong, this baseline can be used to determine what has changed.

Alarms and Error Messages

The first thing to do when a problem occurs is to take advantage of the free information the network provides. Alarms, error messages, and other notices can help identify and solve problems with little or no additional analysis or data gathering.

It may be axiomatic that such basic information would be considered in any troubleshooting situation, but even the most experienced network managers often overlook the obvious. For example, LED indicators on CSU/DSUs (channel/data service units) can help determine link status and frequency of errors on the WAN circuit. Abnormalities in the self-diagnostic of bridges and routers can alert network managers to impending hardware failures. And standard *ping* and *traceroute* facilities to and from affected workstations can help to narrow the scope of connectivity problems.

BOTTLENECK ISOLATION

Perhaps the most difficult fault to isolate across a WAN is response-time bottleneck, especially if the path between client and server is complex.

Let us assume that an upgrade to the NetWare server in Boston has dramatically improved performance for all users, except those at the remote site in Munich. For them, response time continues to be unacceptably slow. With a total of three routers, a T1 class frame relay circuit, and an FDDI backbone separating these clients, there are several potential points of congestion.

One way to isolate the bottleneck is to use a preconfigured server *ping* test executed by an intelligent analyzer. In this test, the analyzer sequentially pings each router along the path, monitoring and comparing the response times to and from each device. Remember, if the path to the router is unknown, an intelligent network analyzer that offers a *traceroute* utility tool can determine it. These ping messages, which are actually IPX diagnostic request packets, can be issued from the analyzer itself or from one of the Novell end stations.

By measuring the response time to each router and comparing the results, the time delays can also be quickly isolated. With the network analyzer connected at the remote site in Munich, the hypothetical round-trip delays to each of the three routers and to the server are recorded as 20 plus milliseconds to and from the Munich router, 600 plus milliseconds to and from the frame relay-attached router in Boston, 680 milliseconds to and from the router between the FDDI and Ethernet subnets, and 715 milliseconds to and from the NetWare server.

These measurements suggest that most of the delay is through the frame relay link or through the router in Boston. Monitoring the WAN link will quickly reveal any transmission-quality problems, and a quick check of the dropped packet count on the router will reveal any overloaded condition there.

LOOKING FOR TROUBLE AND REMEDIES

Most other networking faults are the result of misconfiguration, in addition to physical device and wiring failures. Many problems that have catastrophic consequences for user data are caused by simple configuration and design errors. Therefore, when any network problem is encountered, it is prudent to check each suspected node to verify that the address and subnet mask are correct. The subnet mask is important since it defines the border between the node and the network, specifying the subnet upon which the node is located.

In addition, it is also prudent to cross-check for duplicate addresses on the network. Routers attached to the LAN where the problem occurs should also be examined. Other parameters that must be the checked are: priority queuing, filtering, and other critical routing parameters.

For example, in case of Ethernet traffic through the router in Saint Louis, if the router reports dropping packets causing slow file transfers and occasional connection timeouts, the problem will result in heavy traffic at times, particularly on the local Ethernet port. The only solution seems to be an upgrade to a more powerful router capable of greater throughput.

Misconfigured Workstation

Upon further analysis, by attaching an analyzer to the local Ethernet segment in Figure 16.1, reveals that there is one additional source of traffic overload on the router. That is one of the workstations is attempting to communicate with a locally attached UNIX file server, by sending data through the router. This can only be ascertained by analyzing the ICMP Event/Alert data shown in Figure 16.2. This is the case of a misconfigured workstation.

By comparing the destination IP address of the file server with its routing tables, the router can determine that the source and destination ports for this conversation are the same. Since the workstation and the server are on the same segment and the traffic does not need to travel to another subnet, according to the router function/design, the router notifies the workstation of the error, using an ICMP redirect message, and forwards the data to the server.

The "culprit" workstation is sending local traffic through the router because of an *incorrectly configured* subnet mask. With the wrong mask, the workstation believes that the server is on another subnetwork. Misconfiguration of networking parameters is a common occurrence, especially in complex networks and where there are lots of users who often copy applications from other users.

```
┌─────────────────────────────────────────────────────────────────┐
│ ICMP Events                                                       │
│                                                                   │
│  ICMP: redirect                    (Warning)    date:......       │
│  Original source:        Workstation IP address                   │
│  Redirect to:            Server IP address                        │
│  For host:               Server IP address                        │
│  Reported by:            Router IP address                        │
│  Frame number:           Data count                               │
│                                                                   │
│                                                                   │
│  ICMP: Unreachable                 (Alert)    date:......          │
│  ............................................................     │
│  ............................................................     │
│  ICMP: Unreachable                 (Alert)    date:......          │
│                                                                   │
│  ............................................................     │
└─────────────────────────────────────────────────────────────────┘
```

Figure 16.2 ICMP redirect message.

On the downside, although the router's ICMP message informs the workstation to redirect its traffic directly to the server, most TCP/IP software does not have the capability of alerting users of the error messages unless the traffic becomes erratic and does not go through. Even if the workstation user were alerted, the users normally ignore such messages as mere warnings since the router does forward the message to the server and communication does occur.

Once the workstation is reconfigured with the correct subnet mask, the router will no longer be burdened by the traffic between the workstation and the UNIX file server, reducing the load to acceptable levels. Since the misconfigured traffic no longer flows to the router, the router is much less likely to drop packets, restoring the internetwork performance back to normal acceptable levels.

Configuration errors like the one just described are hard to diagnose, since the routers do not prevent traffic from the misconfigured workstation to get through to the local server. The workstation continues to communicate with the server, however inefficiently. Each packet sent to the router results in an ICMP redirect message, creating additional traffic, while the router is still forwarding each packet to the server. In this manner, each transmission generates more than twice the necessary data traffic. The delay through the router not only slows each transaction from the misconfigured workstation, but also affects other traffic competing to get on the network.

On a lightly loaded Ethernet network, 10 Mbps of available bandwidth is sometimes sufficient to mask such inefficiencies. However, over a period of time, as the network grows and the traffic increases, the performance penalty of this network error and redundant traffic becomes much more noticeable.

Server Overloads

Simple monitoring and analysis also can help network managers resolve problems across wide area links when devices or resource servers become overloaded. In this case, an analyzer can monitor for traffic congestion and high error rates, automatically reporting abnormal or other significant events. The analyzer can also monitor statistics, connectivity, response times, and other network vital signs which aid in evaluating overall network health.

For example, users in Paris complain of poor response from a NetWare file server in Boston. By examining the traffic (requests/replies) on the server, it becomes obvious that the server is overloaded. This can be done by using an analyzer to selectively monitor traffic to and from the server. The Novell IPX traffic utilization and total packet counts can be compared with total network traffic to get a fast indication of overall network loading. This also shows up in the bandwidth consumed by the Routing Information Protocol (IRP).

It is obvious that any given server can handle only so much traffic (based on communication bandwidth as well as local compute resources), but to distribute network resources properly, the administrator has to know where the service requests originate. To pinpoint the source, local Ethernet traffic will have to be compared with remote server traffic funneling through the Boston router. Another measurement can be the read and write requests to the remote server. In this instance, the most important statistic that the analyzer gathers is the busy-server percentage. This can indicate the number of duplicate service request messages the server has issued as a percentage of total transaction requests. A duplicate service request could be the result of a client time-out, which in turn, indicates a slow response from the server. In normal circumstances, if the busy-server percentage exceeds four percent, the server is probably overloaded.

In this example, the measurement reveals that the server itself lacks the resource necessary to handle the client load with acceptable response times. A number of solutions can be suggested:

- A CPU and memory upgrade for the server may improve performance.
- A second server may be added to split the load.
- Reconfigure the load in such a way that some client access the servers that have more available bandwidth, and so on.

WAN BANDWIDTH PROBLEMS

To identify poor quality or overloaded WAN network circuits, among other parameters, the following data must be measured:

- Line utilization.
- Bit error rate.
- Frame transmissions.

An intelligent analyzer measurements can generate useful information, such as the bandwidth used by each protocol running on the network or by the users who consume most of the available bandwidth. A common problem in an internetwork, connecting LANs and WANs, can be caused by transmission errors in the wide area links. For example, presume that all the users at remote sites in St. Louis complain of poor response times when accessing a database application located on a Boston data center server. Since the users of the same application do not experience any response problems, the administrators automatically assume that the problem could be either with the router in Boston or the T1 transmission line between Boston and St. Louis.

To fully ascertain the cause of the problem, an analyzer has to be employed to monitor the local port. A snapshot of this monitoring reveals that the data throughput on the T1 line is only utilizing 40% of the available bandwidth. Yet a large number of frames transmitted from St. Louis are received with transmission errors. These errors make retransmission of the requests necessary resulting in long response times as reported by the users in St. Louis.

BROADBAND TROUBLESHOOTING

The use of public data networks for wide area transport continues to gain worldwide popularity. One reason is that the carrier services can provide bandwidth on demand to accommodate the bursty requirements of most internetworking connections. Unfortunately, the many benefits of using a public data network are expensive—another layer of complexity for the internetwork manager/troubleshooter.

Let us assume that users at a remote site in Paris complain of poor performance on connections over a frame relay service to another branch office in London. First, the network troubleshooter connects an analyzer to the access link between the Paris office and the frame relay network. The access line to the frame relay network carries several simultaneously active connections. Each active permanent virtual circuit is identified by a data link connection identifier (DLCI). Troubleshooting a problem on any individual connection requires that the analyzer keep track of the data throughput, link error rate, and other statistics for each individual DLCI.

Statistics for the network's active virtual circuits reveal no line-quality problems, but do show significant data throughput on the circuits between Paris and London. The next step is to examine this connection by looking at the frame relay traffic. In this case, an analyzer could be utilized to gather frame counts for both the frame relay link management interface traffic and the user data traveling across the link, which mostly consists of IP traffic.

The analyzer could also monitor forward and backward explicit congestion notification counts, which frame relay uses to keep track of network congestion. A close examination of the notification congestion data will reveal that a congested link from the remote site in Paris to the frame relay network.

The analyzer further reveals that the average data throughput exceeds the committed transmission rate that the line should produce. Since the transmission rate is not a strict limit, it is possible for the instantaneous data throughput over this circuit to vary from time to time. However, on the average, the data throughput over a long period should not exceed the allowable limits. When it does, and the network itself is experiencing congestion, the network begins to discard the excess traffic, causing the end nodes to time out and retransmit. This results in unreliable connections and long response times.

The obvious solution for such a problem is to increase the transmission rate to a level that can accommodate the data throughput required by users at the remote sites. By constant monitoring the throughput for each node and the primary connections, an analyzer can help identify the source of the problem and a possible solution in terms of the required transmission rate for regulated throughput.

T1 PROBLEMS

As mentioned earlier, if there are unusually large number of transmission errors on the T1 framing, it could be attributed to two other reasons:

- The way traffic is prioritized across the T1 link.
- The way traffic is divided.

The errors detected may be attributed to the bit patterns present in the user data, as opposed to the analyzer-generated data. This indicates the total number of packets with a bad cyclic redundancy checks, with the result of at least one bit error in the transmission on that frame.

On the other hand, an active bit error rate test could be run on the T1 link, which will result in repeatable measurement of line quality. The only problem is that the line must be taken out of service since it cannot be active during this test. Therefore, it only makes sense to run such a test when there are strong indications of the T1 transmissions problems. The results of such tests, which use a standard series of bit patterns, report results in a standard format for use by the carrier in fixing the line problems.

In addition, monitoring frame counts according to protocol type (Figure 16.3) could also pinpoint the applications that are consuming the most bandwidth on a T1 leased facility. For example, most of the traffic between Saint Louis and Boston in the sample network uses File Transfer Protocol (FTP) to transmit large data files from a server connected via an FDDI link. Measurements of protocol distribution taken in Boston will reveal the relative bandwidth consumption of the Routing Information Protocol, SNMP, and other types of overhead traffic.

At the same time, a similar set of counts can also be measured for traffic like AppleTalk, DECnet, IPX, XNS, and Banyan VINES. An intelligent network analyzer can monitor such traffic on the Saint Louis site router. By filtering all the frames to and from

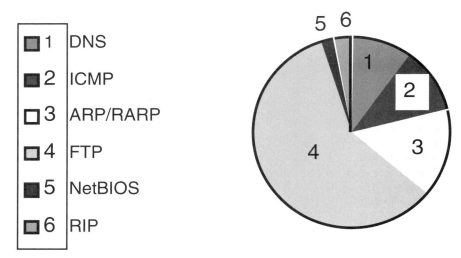

■ 1	DNS
■ 2	ICMP
☐ 3	ARP/RARP
▣ 4	FTP
■ 5	NetBIOS
▣ 6	RIP

Figure 16.3 Application bandwidth usage.

the router, you can determine the protocol distribution for routed traffic in and out of this subnetwork. As illustrated in Figure 16.3, most of the routed traffic generated by the workstations on this subnet is FTP. To reduce such a load on the router, it will be further necessary to breakdown which particular workstations on the St. Louis hub are responsible for generating this traffic.

The capture filter on the network analyzer can be restricted to show only the FTP frames that are going through the router and across the T1 link to Boston. With this filter set, node statistics measurements will easily provide the list of top sources of routed FTP traffic. If a single workstation or workgroup is responsible for the vast majority of the traffic load, most of the traffic on the router and the T1 circuit could be rerouted. This can be accomplished by relocating the "culprit" station or "workgroup" to the same subnet with the FTP server or by establishing a new FTP server on the same subnet as the workstation(s).

On the other hand, if for some reason, the workstation could not be relocated or a new FTP server could not be added, the enterprise has two options:

- Use data compression, which can reduce the data traffic, but may increase processing time for decompression.
- Set up a separate circuit between the workgroup and the server.

SUMMARY

All networking environments are created differently because they support different business needs. Today's organizations are constantly reengineering to keep a competitive advantage. Workers today and in the future must be able to access information wherever it resides.

A basic set of tools is necessary in any global environment to help in the first installation and throughout the daily operational life of a network. Cable testers are used to check the capabilities, reliability, and capacities of the physical cabling plant. LAN and WAN analyzers are a must to troubleshoot many problems. Monitors, especially RMON monitors are becoming a staple in many organizations. RMON monitors allow the network managers to collect statistics, track traffic patterns, capture selected traffic, and perform other tasks under the control of a central management application. Such monitors are available for Ethernet, token ring, and FDDI LANs, the more prevalent subnets in an internetwork.

Troubleshooting internetworks are some of the most frequently performed tasks. Using monitors and/or analyzers with "expert" or "automated" capabilities, you can decrease the frequency of these tasks. These devices and applications identify specific types of problems and recommend actions to solve these problems. Basic threshold and alarms will indicate potential problems, but still require manual intervention to determine the severity and the actions that must be taken.

There are many common problems in which the network managers conduct the same steps to troubleshoot. Some troubleshooting applications can help identify such problems and perform the steps without human intervention. Once completed, these applications send a notification about the completion to the management station.

EXERCISES

1. What types of problems are common in a global network?
2. What are the symptoms of server overloads? How can these be avoided and/or corrected?
3. What type of problems would a "mis-configured" workstation cause?

17

MANAGING NETWORKS

Introduction
Historical Perspectives
Background
Functions of a Management System
A Global Management Architecture
Fault Management
Performance Management
Configuration Management
Security Management
Accounting Management
Components of a Management System
Manager
Agent
Management Information Base
Network Management Protocols
Architectural Overview
Simple Network Management
  Protocol
Common Management Information

Protocol/Services
CMIS Over TCP (CMOT)
**Comparisons of SNMP, CMIP,
and CMOT Protocol**
Implementation
Allocation of Responsibility
Network Load Levels
Management Objectives
Data Definitions
Management Strategies and Products
OpenView (HP)
NetView (IBM)
SunNet Manager (SUN)
NetWare (Novell)
Dimons (NetLabs)
SPECTRUM (Cabletron)
Summary
Exercises

INTRODUCTION

Networks have changed in many respects since the first large-scale use of private data networks in the 1950s. The scale and complexity of networks have increased considerably, as has the variety of equipment and services within them. Networks nearly always carry traffic for multiple applications today, often for multiple computer types, and sometimes for applications using other information media—voice and fax, for example.

Network management can be viewed as managing the network, or managing resources across the network. However, you choose to describe it, network management represents the key to efficiently operating and maintaining a network. In today's world, the concept of a network transcends the classical definitions of local area and wide area; enterprise networks encompass all these network types. Thus, network management capabilities must be applicable across all conventional definitions.

Historical Perspectives

Early networks consisted of terminals linked directly to nearby host computers. Managing such an environment was relatively simple. However, as more organizations move toward distributed computing, the problem of managing such environments becomes far more complex as well as more critical to the health of the network. A number of vendors offered their own solutions by providing management tools specifically designed to manage their own product lines. A solution was needed that could provide monitoring and control across multiple vendors' product lines while retrieving, archiving, and synthesizing management data into a single, consolidated report on the overall status of all network resources.

Currently, the trend is to provide integrated network management systems that offer extensive, in-depth monitoring and control capabilities of multivendor products locally or across the entire enterprise network. Standards play a significant role in allowing third-party management systems to monitor and control network resources. But inconsistency and incompatibility may and often do arise, even when standards are in place.

Background

Before network administrators begin worrying about distributed systems management or remote applications management, they must first take care of managing the physical network. Every network segment, cable, bridge, router, hub, switch, node, and protocol in the entire network is a potential source of management data. And having access to all that management data—along with having more intelligent devices on the network— is allowing administrators to increase network uptime.

Not long ago, 80% of the reasons for user downtime were cabling problems. Now, with devices like intelligent hubs, only less than 20% of downtime can be attributed to cabling. However, the biggest challenge in managing is not cabling downtime, but managing the physical network as to how to handle moves, adds, and changes. Wiring management and connecting PCs or workstations are certainly important issues, but managing change is the most difficult. It is predicted that there are over 6 million network segments worldwide and on the rise. In addition, the heterogeneity of hardware, software, and vendor solutions is increasing—growing the challenge of managing these networks (Figure 17.1).

Most network management systems track and monitor network activity and performance—assisting support staff in various custodial tasks such as fault analysis, performance monitoring, configuration management, accounting operations, and security procedures. However, today's multivendor networks mandate integrated management and control because most of these networks are too complex for a single management solution. A typical network consists of equipment from multiple vendors, with each piece managed

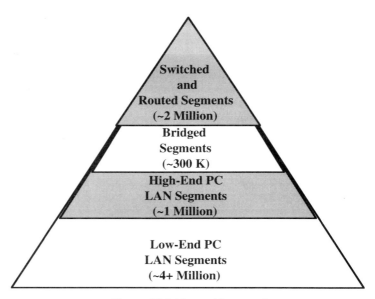

Figure 17.1 Networking trends.

by its own vendor-specific management system; frequently, different products from the same vendor requiring separate management systems.

For a long time, enterprises have struggled to automate the management of extensive worldwide networks. These networks, possessing data access, voice, and video capabilities, are supported by a number of mechanisms including TCP/IP, SNMP, FDDI, X.25, and dial-in modems and contain a variety of different protocols. Citing a lack of comprehensive tools that are compatible with existing infrastructures, many contend complete automated network management for a wide variety of mechanisms is a virtually impossible task.

This section examines the current state of network management capabilities, global management architectures, and the integration of management tools. Network management protocol standards are compared, with particular attention to Simple Network Management Protocol (SNMP) and Common Management Information Protocol (CMIP). We will also examine some management tools from major vendors and their strategic approaches, which affect the network management applications.

FUNCTIONS OF A MANAGEMENT SYSTEM

Most enterprises demand comprehensive network management systems and maintain pace with quickly evolving network technology. As a result, the network management arena is now in a state of flux, as organizations try to find the best possible solutions to these problems. Any network management system should consolidate information from several network elements, element managers, or network management systems into a single system.

A network management system should provide a common user interface that displays information about various network devices in a consistent manner and should support multiple management functions. In addition to fault management, an integrated network management system should support other critical management functional areas defined by the International Standards Organization (ISO), such as accounting, performance, security, and configuration management.

The hierarchy of management systems available ranges from simple element management systems that manage a single product line such as a modem management system to complex integrators that extend management capabilities over multiple differing products and services. Integrated network management cannot happen without standardizing management interfaces between managers and managed elements.

A Global Management Architecture.

In a global management architecture, every computer system and network element implements the same management protocol. A single management protocol can directly manage and control all networked resources, as depicted in Figure 17.2. However, a problem with this approach is the huge installed base of equipment that uses device-specific management interfaces. For this reason, while organizations continue to use established proprietary management interfaces to monitor and control their own products, a number of standards are emerging for different kinds of network and system environments.

Standardized solutions are taking shape, most notably in TCP/IP Internets, where SNMP is widely implemented in bridges, routers, and workstations. The result is that a good SNMP manager can oversee Internet devices from a variety of vendors.

The ISO has broken the network management problem into five distinct functional areas: fault, performance, configuration, security, and accounting, (Figure 17.3). These functions have found broad acceptance as a method of classifying management systems.

No common management strategy can be implemented unless the participants agree on the scope of management activity. The international standards process is providing with

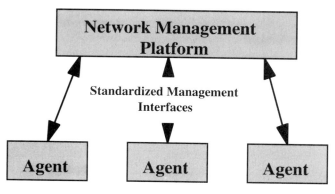

Figure 17.2 A global management architecture.

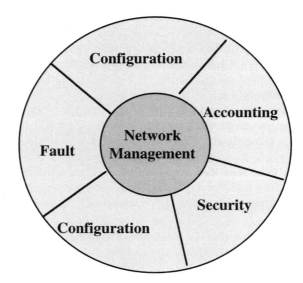

Figure 17.3 ISO network management functional areas.

a blueprint for communications design in the OSI Network Model. Like the OSI Network Model, CMIS is a service-level specification that defines network management functions as fitting into five classifications whose relationship to network tasks is shown in Figures 17.3 and 17.4.

All networks must consider each of these management aspects, but all need not implement them. As networks become more independent and complex, most of these management functions must ultimately be addressed.

Fault Management

Fault management deals with the detection, isolation, and identification of anomalies within the management domain. Depending on the capability of the management software, it may even be able to recommend and take corrective action on the anomaly identified. Open-system fault management provides the ability to log events or errors and to monitor specified events or errors . In fact, a solution should have the capability to anticipate faults as a result of analyzing errors and or events as needed.

On the practical side, individual graphics displays can be customized and stored to accommodate different views or error analysis routines. For example, when a screen displays a certain color (some products already provide such features), a specific situation can be investigated via stored analytical views of the system and appropriate action can then be taken, if necessary, without causing interruptions for network users.

The system should track status following fault correction attempts to ensure that the fault situations are corrected (e.g., by specifying parameters to be tracked) and broadcast and multicast notification of faults. In addition, it should also provide predefined diagnos-

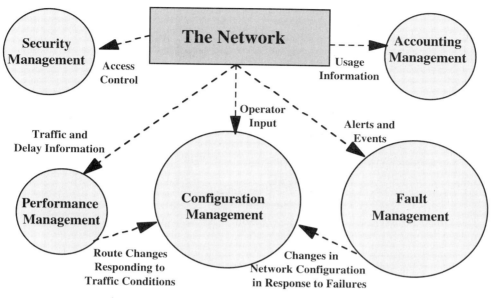

Figure 17.4 CMIS network management classification.

tic and testing procedures for the purpose of determining or verifying where the faults are and for the purpose of testing components before they are put in use. The user can, then, request reconfiguration of all or part of the system, as corrective action in response to a fault.

Fault management can also be viewed as the task of monitoring network conditions to detect *out-of-tolerance* behavior and notifying control points when such conditions occur. Network managers must be notified when any network element has failed, is near failure, or is performing outside the defined thresholds. This is the function of fault management systems and is the most common element implemented today; it is also the one with the longest history of formal support.

Fault monitoring and control are the basis for fault management. Monitoring may use either a monitoring device or software element that analyzes a component's performance and reports when that component fails to meet standards. Data link layer procedures maintain error counters as a part of normal operation. Such counters could also be used as the basis for fault monitoring and reporting.

Both *hard* and *soft* error conditions must be considered in fault management. A *hard* error is a condition that, once it occurs, interrupts service until it is restored. This makes the error relatively unambiguous to interpret. Loss of digital carrier on a T1 line is a hard error. A *soft* error is one that is, to an extent, recoverable, but may interfere with operations if it persists. Excessive bit errors on a T1 line is a soft error. Soft errors are often called "threshold errors" because they are typically acceptable to a point (a threshold value) but are judged unacceptable beyond that point. Because setting thresholds is subjective, users must have some input when defining this type of fault.

A normal response to fault conditions is starting test procedures to isolate faulty elements. Testing is also necessary after a device has been serviced and must be recommissioned. Testing, in the sense of matching observed performance to a standard of correct operation, is normally considered an element of fault management.

Performance Management

Performance management is the task of monitoring the network's traffic, its remaining capacity, the rate of flow, the characteristics of network delay, and other factors relating to the network's connection, congestion control, capacity and planning functions, and traffic flow capabilities.

The solution should provide the ability to monitor performance-relevant events, measures, and resources. Performance management should also allow users to execute predefined performance tests when a performance abnormality occurs. The test results are then used to diagnose network performance-related problems and determine an appropriate tuning strategy. This requires an understanding of the entire network configuration in order to detect where a production bottleneck is occurring. Physical tuning of the network is network-specific (e.g., IBM's NetView) function.

Network traffic can be organized into a large number of small exchanges (e.g., software distribution) or a few high-volume exchanges (e.g., DBMS transaction processing). An optimized network can detect the type of traffic passing through the network and decide on the most appropriate services to deploy (e.g., a X.400 or FTAM). While such solutions can provide management data and analysis that can be used to develop the most effective network configuration, they reside at the application layer and do not exercise control over physical network topology.

Performance management products monitor and control various networked components, optimizing performance critical to current networking requirements. Management software monitors performance issues such as capacity and percent of utilization, throughput, and response time by assigning metrics for actual, real-time analysis. By collecting, correlating, and synthesizing this information, network managers can detect indications of trends leading to performance degradation.

The separation of logical and physical transport networks has its greatest management impact in network performance management and capacity management/planning. Where there are multiple logical networks, congestion can arise through the collision of information traveling on different logical paths. Unfortunately, the cause is invisible to the logical network users and often the managers.

Performance management addresses this issue by monitoring parameters. These parameters provide information concerning the network's information flow rate, residual capacity, and delay statistics. Performance information can be collected and displayed in real time, aiding operators to spot network problems; a utilization percentage histogram is a common management display. It can also be used in analyzing historical conditions or to support network modeling.

For capacity planners, performance data are critical. Network changes naturally affect performance. By analyzing the cause/effect relationships of past changes, planners can often predetermine the network's response to hypothetical changes or problems. This technique can also be applied to infer the change required to cause a desired effect; for example, how fast must a specific trunk operate to increase overall route performance by some factor. This is sometimes dubbed as "predictive" analysis.

Configuration Management

Configuration management is the task of controlling the routes information takes through the network, the relationships between network elements, and how specific system parameters are chosen. Configuration management provides configuration data necessary to startup or shut down the network resources.

Configuration management identifies and controls data in the system for the purpose of initializing, providing the continuous operations of, and terminating system services. It is also concerned with maintaining, adding, and updating system components. Configuration management should allow the user to

- Specify resources and the attributes associated with a resource (e.g., software version, ID) and set and modify the values of a resource attribute (e.g., monitor and adjust buffer allocation).
- Specify relationships, on line (during operations), among users (e.g., add, delete, or modify). For example, a user can dynamically create or adjust an object, which can then be immediately retrieved by another user within the enterprise system on a different platform.
- Develop agents, which are managed objects that represent resources, to communicate to the system manager via CMIS or SNMP.
- Constructed applications that should be automatically enabled for the client/server model, with an objects presentation passed on to the workstation to accommodate any heterogeneity of workstation environments.

Configuration management controls every aspect of network management by allocating initial information paths and network designs. Configuration management permits moving, adding, and removing devices and circuits as well as modifying information routes. It is often invoked to restore a measure of service until a component is repaired or replaced after a network fault.

Many network devices utilize variable parameters to control their operation; for example, modems may allow the selection of different data rates. Configuration management permits changes to these parameter values either on a per parameter basis or through loading "configuration maps"— tables of values. The latter approach is often used for complex nodal devices with many circuits, because per parameter changes are arduous to perform and may delay service restoration.

Because configuration management is often the vehicle through which an operator responds to faults, vendors are focusing considerable attention to developing automatic response tools, often based on artificial intelligence or expert system concepts. In its simplest form, this approach consists of a "script" language following some simple "if-then-else" logic and allowing configurations commands to be stored as a file and invoked automatically under predetermined conditions. More complex systems provide evaluation of network conditions and either suggest or invoke corrective procedures.

Security Management

Security management is the task of controlling access to the network and network-resident services, including the service of network management itself. Security management is concerned with the protection of network resources. Controlling access to those resources often requires passwords, access privileges (e.g., read, write, execute), and possibly encryption methods. Audit trails are a common method of tracking individual users and resources utilized. Audit trails can be the most effective tools in troubleshooting network problems for both hardware and software.

System security should provide the confidentiality, integrity, and appropriate availability of data and data processing capabilities. While security is easily maintained on a single computer, security for the enterprisewide multiplatform system—all operating as a single entity—is much more complex. For this reason, security management is of paramount importance. The security service software layer consists of three parts:

- Authentication.
- Authorization.
- User registry.

There is probably no more complex or disputed area of management than security management. In a broad sense, "network security" in an information technology context is protecting a resource from unauthorized forms of manipulation. Users tend to focus on information resources rather than computational, storage, or transmission resources. Therefore, security is generally applied at the computer level, where information resources are owned and accessed. Network security is applied in three distinct contexts:

- Where the network resources must themselves be protected. This may be to eliminate unauthorized use of a resource or to protect an information or processing resource (such an e-mail system) owned by the network. The network management center is a service resource which must obviously be protected from unauthorized access.
- Where the resources accessed by the user, through the network, are inadequately protected when exposed to network access. A LAN might offer adequate physical security when confined to a single work space but fail to provide acceptable security when internetwork links extend the access potential out of that "friendly environment" and even off premises.
- When user-to-resource relationships are made and broken continually and constantly re-certifying users for access rights becomes intrusive.

Network security may include *interception* protection as well as access protection. This type of protection, normally afforded by encrypting information, prevents an outsider from monitoring network traffic and reading sensitive information. Encryption can also serve as a form of access control: if an information source is encrypted, only clients who have the key can use it. Access security is normally provided by a user ID/password authentication process commonly based on the Kerberos system.

Accounting Management

Accounting management is the task of collecting and distributing information needed to allocate network costs. Accounting management provides service usage measurements and limits, allowing groups to bill for network resources and services utilized. In many businesses, tracking systems may be employed to record group or individual accounts' usage of network resources. Such accounting procedures need to be available to monitor resource utilization, ensuring that adequate resources are available. Tracking resource utilizations provide a mechanism for planning network growth and to justify upgrading or expanding network resources (e.g., adding more storage space to the networked server).

Accounting for network resources and cost is rarely a task sought out by users, yet without some form of accounting, costs tend to rise out of control. The user must agree to some costing basis: fixed allocation costs according to a ratio, usage-based cost allocation, and so on. The network must often collect the data needed to administer it.

Accounting management enables charges to be established for the use of resources, and for costs to be identified for the use of those resources. Accounting management provides cost analysis, tracing network and system usage and user billing of resources. The results of statistical analysis of accounting information can help plan network expansion or the type of existing and new network services.

Accounting management system should allow users to

- Specify the accounting information to be collected (connection time, quantity of data transmitted, etc.) and to set the data collection cycle.
- Access data, stored in a single, in-core relational data cache, through SQL.
- Store enterprise systems management data, based on standard guidelines.
- Define standard accounting metrics such as connection duration, number of bits, characters, blocks, or files.

COMPONENTS OF A MANAGEMENT SYSTEM

Historically, proprietary network management schemes were mainframe based, costing many thousands of dollars and occupying much of the CPU's time and memory. Management standards offer the premise of eliminating mainframe dependence and reducing both the expense and overhead of network management. However, resistance to network management standards by major equipment manufacturers has long plagued the industry. Standards-based approaches must operate in a layered architecture, define the management protocols to be used, and determine what management information will be exchanged.

In the seven-layer hierarchical OSI model, the network management services are provided by the application layer, as illustrated in Figure 17.5. The management software—called the Systems Management Application Process (SMAP)—is local software within a managing or managed system responsible for executing management functions within the local host system.

The application programming interface—system management interface—provides the connection between a network management application and the systems management application entity (SMAE) located in the application layer. The SMAE is responsible for management information exchanges between peer application layer SMAEs in other network resources. In terms of OSI, Common Management Information Protocol (CMIP) provides the mechanism for transporting systems management information between peer SMAEs.

A layer management entity (LME) resides within each layer of an OSI architecture to provide management services specific to that layer. For instance, the physical layer LME would monitor the line error rate, and a session layer LME would monitor the status of currently active sessions. Each LME monitors defined characteristics specific to that

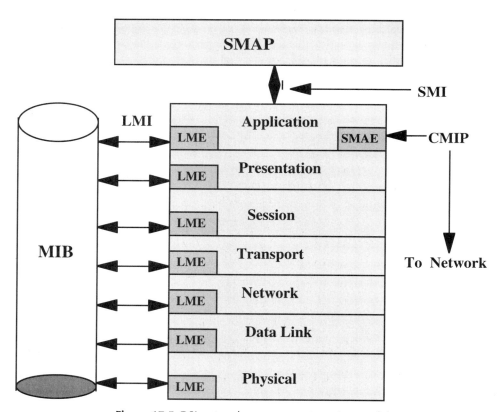

Figure 17.5 OSI network management service model.

layer and archives the data in the local management information base (MIB) using the layer management interface (LMI) to communicate between the LME and the MIB in the local host.

There are three specific components of a network management system: manager, agent, and management information base.

Manager

Vendor-specific managers evolved out of necessity. Until recently, there were no industry-wide accepted standards for management protocols or a management data definition. One path toward integrated, multivendor management is to establish a universal management interface standard.

The management application (*manager*) is the focal point from which management functions are carried out on the network. Accomplishing these varied and often complex tasks typically requires a dedicated computing platform. Depending on the category of management capability, the platform may be a PC or RISC-based workstation. Using a GUI, multilevel network diagrams display the current status of network resources. In the event of a network or system failure within the managed domain, an icon within the network diagram may change color to yellow or red depending on the severity of the alarm. Using a mouse interface, the operator clicks open the failed site, which in turn, opens another network map of the affected site in greater detail, once again highlighting the apparent source of the failure.

The capabilities of the manager application vary from vendor to vendor implementation. Comprehensive manager applications provide extensive, multilevel, detailed information on the current status of the network. Most vendor's management software provides standard functions, such as alarm correlations, that attempt to isolate a single source causing multiple devices to generate alarm conditions. For example, a T-span failure would cause the T1 multiplexer and all connected nodes to indicate an alarm condition. The alarms correlation module within the management application would intercept and attempt to correlate the alarms and highlight the possible failed node on the network map.

Agent

The *agent* can be integrated directly into a network element, or it may be remote from that element. For example, an agent might be a protocol module inside a router that collects management information about the router, or the agent might be a protocol module inside a modem management system. In the latter case, the agent would not collect data about the modem management system; rather, it would collect management information about the modems through the modem management system's services.

Agent software carries out commands issued by the management application. The commands range from status queries to configuration and control operations necessary for the local network device. The agent maintains objects stored in the local MIB by monitoring device operations and conditions and recording that information in the appropriate object record of the local MIB.

Using a particular network management protocol requires that managers and agents support a common protocol stack. This limits direct management to agents that use compatible protocol stacks. To accommodate networked devices that do not support the management protocol, the concept of a proxy was developed. In this scheme, an agent acts as a proxy for one or more networked devices that do not support the common management protocol.

Commonly found in networks using SNMP, a proxy agent provides translation that allows a manager application using SNMP to communicate with an agent module using a proprietary management protocol.

The SNMP manager sends queries to the SNMP proxy agent (Figure 17.6). The proxy agent converts each query into a management protocol used by the agent process. When a reply is received by the SNMP agent, it translates the reply into an SNMP response message and forwards that to the SNMP manager. Most proxy agent software allows simple monitoring and query functions of agents by manager software. Few proxy agent modules allow indirect configuring and controlling of agents.

Management Information Base

The management information base (MIB) is conceptually a database containing all management information related to the local node. Management information—called

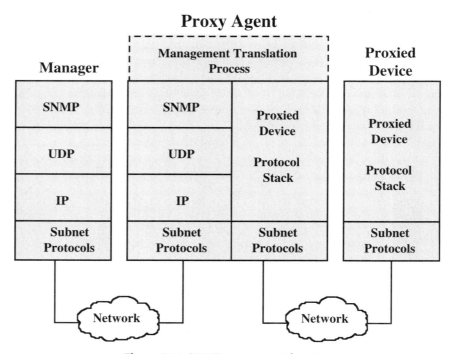

Figure 17.6 SNMP proxy agent function.

objects—contain attributes about certain characteristics of a managed element (e.g., error counters, timers). Therefore, a managed object contain attributes that define the characteristics of the object. A managed object can be defined for any resource that the manager application needs to monitor and/or control. The collection of management data definitions that a manager or an agent knows about is called its MIB.

Each element within the network maintains a MIB containing objects specific to that device. Therefore, the MIB for a LAN bridge would contain different objects than a MIB for a host computer. The manager maintains a MIB containing information about each device in the network. The manager uses its MIB to archive management data for functions such as report generation and trend analysis. A manager sends commands querying for MIB information contained in network elements using a common network management protocol. The station receiving the manager's command queries the local MIB and replies with the requested management data.

MIB definitions are different for OSI and TCP/IP networks. TCP/IP currently has MIB I and MIB II defined for use. MIB II is a superset of the original MIB defining more than 200 objects. The management data definition approach used for the OSI MIB is general but rigorous. It is an object-oriented data modeling technique that defines the elements being managed as *objects*, which are described in terms of their *attributes*. Object definitions also include a list of actions that an object can perform (e.g., modem running a line test) and a list of events (e.g., alarms) that the object can generate.

MIB extensions are vendor-specific objects available only with that vendor's product. A management application can access only the information it knows how to ask for. Thus, for a management station to manage vendor-specific extensions to an existing MIB, the manager must be configured with that vendor's private MIB extensions. Otherwise, the manager application cannot take advantage of those MIB extensions.

NETWORK MANAGEMENT PROTOCOLS

Much attention is being directed at the protocol transporting management information across the network between managers and agents. Standardizing network management protocols have yielded two distinct camps serving different needs within networks of varying complexity: common management information protocol (CMIP) is designed for OSI-based networking environments and simple network management protocol (SNMP) most commonly used for TCP/IP networks.

Architectural Overview

The basic concepts underlying OSI network management are quite simple. Application processes called "managers" reside on managing systems (or management stations). Application processes called "agents" reside on managed systems (or network elements being managed). Network management occurs when managers and agents conspire (via protocols and a shared conceptual schema) to exchange monitoring and control information useful to the management of a network and its components. The terms "manager" and "agent" are also used in a loose and popular sense to refer to the managing and managed system, respectively, as illustrated in Figure 17.7.

The shared conceptual schema mentioned above is a priori knowledge about "managed objects" concerning which information is exchanged. Managed objects are system and networking resources (e.g., a modem, a protocol entity, an IP routing table, a TCP connection) that are subject to management. Management activities are effected through the manipulation of managed objects in the managed systems. Using the management services and protocol, the manager can direct the agent or to perform an operation on a managed object for which it is responsible. Such operations might be to return certain values associated with a managed object (read a variable), to change certain values associated with a managed object (set a variable), or to perform an action (such as self-test) on the managed object. In addition, the agent may also forward notifications generated asynchronously by managed objects to the manager (events or traps).

The terms "manager" and "agent" are used to denote the asymmetric relationship between management application processes in which the manager plays the superior role and the agent plays the subordinate.

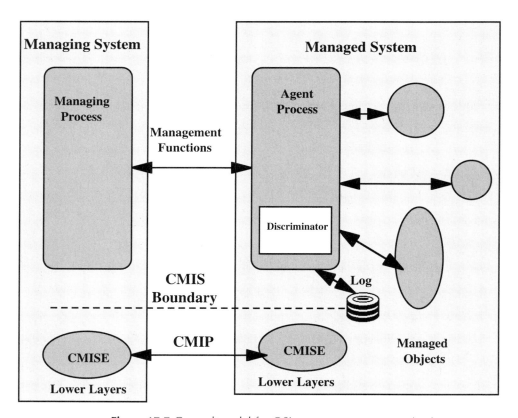

Figure 17.7 General model for OSI management communication.

Simple Network Management Protocol

The simple network management protocol is an application layer protocol designed to facilitate the exchange of management information between network devices. By using SNMP-transported data (such as packets per second and network error rates), network administrators can more easily manage network performance, find and solve network problems, and plan for network growth. Like the Transmission Control Protocol (TCP), SNMP is an Internet Protocol.

There are two versions of SNMP: Most of the changes introduced in Version 2 increase SNMP's security capabilities. Other changes increase interoperability by more rigorously defining the specifications for SNMP implementation. SNMP's creators believe that after a relatively brief period of coexistence, SNMP Version 2 (SNMPv2) will largely replace SNMP Version 1 (SNMPv1). SNMP is part of a larger architecture called the Internet Network Management Framework (NMF), which is defined in Internet documents called requests for comments (RFCs).

Today, SNMP is the most popular protocol for managing diverse commercial internetworks as well as those used in universities and research organizations. SNMP-related standardization activity continues even as vendors develop and release state-of-the-art, SNMP-based management applications. SNMP is a relatively simple protocol, yet its feature set is sufficiently powerful to handle the difficult problems presented in trying to manage today's heterogeneous networks.

SNMP Technology. SNMP is part of the Internet network management architecture. This architecture is based on the interaction of many entities. The internet management model comprises

Agents Software modules that reside in network elements. They collect and store management information such as the number of error packets received by a network element.

Management Information Base (MIB) A collection of managed objects residing in a virtual information store. Collections of related managed objects are defined in specific MIB modules.

Managed Object A characteristic of something that can be managed. For example, a list of currently active TCP circuits in a particular host computer is a managed object. Managed objects differ from variables, which are particular object instances. Using our example, an object instance is a single active TCP circuit in a particular host computer. Managed objects can be scalar (defining a single object instance) or tabular (defining multiple, related instances).

Management Protocol A protocol used to convey management information between agents and NMSs. SNMP is the Internet community's de facto standard management protocol.

Network Elements Hardware devices such as computers, routers, and terminal servers that are connected to networks; sometimes called managed devices.

Network Management Stations (NMSs) Sometimes called consoles, devices that execute management applications that monitor and control network elements. Physically,

NMSs are usually engineering workstation-caliber computers with fast CPUs, megapixel color displays, substantial memory, and abundant disk space. At least one NMS must be present in each managed environment.

Parties Newly defined in SNMPv2, a logical SNMPv2 entity that can initiate or receive SNMPv2 communication. Each SNMPv2 party comprises a single, unique party identity, a logical network location, a single authentication protocol, and a single privacy protocol. SNMPv2 messages are communicated between two parties. An SNMPv2 entity can define multiple parties, each with different parameters. For example, different parties can use different authentication and/or privacy protocols.

Structure of Management Information (SMI) Defines the rules for describing management information. The SMI is defined using ASN.1.

Syntax Notation A language used to describe a MIB's managed objects in a machine-independent format. Consistent use of a syntax notation allows different types of computers to share information. Internet management systems use a subset of the International Organization for Standardization's (ISO's) Open System Interconnection (OSI) Abstract Syntax Notation 1 (ASN.1) to define both the packets exchanged by the management protocol and the objects that are to be managed.

The most basic elements of the Internet management model are graphically represented in Figure 17.8.

SNMP Operations. SNMP itself is a simple request/response protocol. NMSs can send multiple requests without receiving a response. Six SNMP operations are defined:

Get Allows the NMS to retrieve an object instance from the agent.

GetBulk New for SNMPv2. The GetBulk operation was added to make it easier to acquire large amounts of related information without initiating repeated GetNext operations. GetBulk was designed to virtually eliminate the need for GetNext operations.

GetNext Allows the NMS to retrieve the next object instance from a table or list within an agent. In SNMPv1, when an NMS wants to retrieve all elements of a table from an agent, it initiates a Get operation, followed by a series of GetNext operations.

Inform New for SNMPv2. The Inform operation was added to allow one NMS to send trap information to another.

Set Allows the NMS to set values for object instances within an agent.

Trap Used by the agent to asynchronously inform the NMS of some event. The SNMPv2 trap message is designed to replace the SNMPv1 trap message.

Using SNMP. To use SNMP effectively, you must have one or more workstations that serve as a management station for the network and then install management station software that makes the workstation an SNMP management node. Most management software is graphically oriented and designed to allow interactive queries to be sent to network devices. On critical devices, traps can be generated that are captured by the management station.

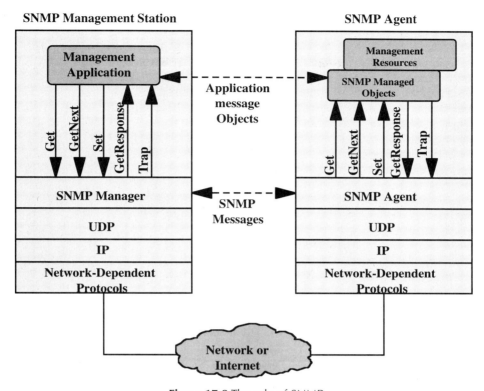

Figure 17.8 The role of SNMP.

On a small network, a single management station usually suffices. Because SNMP uses the User Datagram Protocal (UDP), it is inefficient when retrieving a large table. In addition, SNMP query processing places a load on the network.

On a large network, it is usually a good idea to create more than a single management node, as illustrated in Figure 17.9. This is particularly true when the network is widely distributed and parts of it are under different management authority. The management function is split among different groups, A, B, and C. Each group maintains a management station. Groups A and B represent large LANs, whereas group C represents WAN interconnections. With this separation, management traffic is contained within each group. The only management traffic on the WAN is to monitor the WAN links and routing nodes.

Common Management Information Protocol / Services

The OSI management framework presents the basic concepts and models required for developing network management standards. OSI management provides the ability to monitor and control network resources, which are represented as "managed objects." The fol-

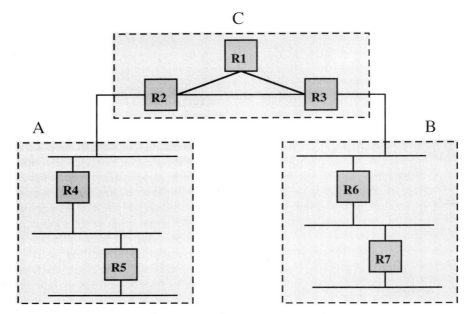

Figure 17.9 A large SNMP network.

lowing elements are essential for the description of a network management architecture and the standardization of a network management system: a model or set of models for understanding management; a common structure of management information for registering, identifying, and defining managed objects; detailed specifications of the managed objects; and a set of services and related protocols for performing remote management operations.

The specification of the management protocol (CMIP) defines a peer protocol relationship that makes no assumptions concerning which end opens or closes a connection or the direction of management data transfer. The protocol mechanisms provided are fully symmetric between the manager and the agent; CMIS operations can originate as either the manager or the agent, as far as the protocol is concerned. This allows the possibility of symmetric as well as asymmetric relationships between management processes. Most devices will contain management applications that can only assume the agent role. Applications on managing systems, however, may well be able to play both roles at the same time. This makes possible "manager-to-manager" communication and the ability of one manager to manage another.

Network management may be modeled in different ways. Three models are typically used to describe OSI management. An organizational model describes ways in which management can be administratively distributed. The functional model describes the management functions and their relationships. The information model provides guidelines for describing managed objects and their associated management information.

The Organizational Model. The organizational model introduces the concept of a management "domain." A domain is an administrative partition of a network or Internet for the purpose of network management. Domains may be useful for reasons of scale, security, or administrative autonomy. Each domain may have one or more managers monitoring and controlling agents in that domain. In addition, both managers and agents may belong to more than one management domain. Domains allow the construction of both strict hierarchical and fully cooperative and distributed network management systems.

The Functional Model. The OSI management framework defines five facilities or functional areas to meet specific management needs. This has proven to be a helpful way of partitioning the network management problem from an application point of view. These facilities have come to be known as the specific management functional areas (SMFAs): fault management, configuration management, performance management, accounting management, and security management.

The Information Model. The OSI management framework considers all information relevant to network management to reside in a management information base, which is a "conceptual repository of management information." Information within a system that can be referenced by the management protocol (CMIP) is considered to be part of the MIB. Conventions for describing and uniquely identifying the MIB information allow specific MIB information to be referenced and operated on by the management protocol. These conventions are called the structure of management information (SMI).

ISO Application Protocols. The following ISO application services and protocols are necessary for doing network management using the OSI framework: ACSE, ROSE, and CMIS/CMIP. All three of these protocols are defined using ASN.1.

In the OSI environment, communication between "application processes" is modeled by communication between application entities. An "application entity" represents the communication functions of an application process. These application service elements may be used independently or in combination. Examples of application service elements are X.400, FTAM, ACSE, ROSE, and CMISE.

CMIS: Common management information service provides the service for exchanging management information. CMIS describes three categories of service as illustrated in Figure 17.10: association, management notification, and management operation.

Peer CMIS (known as CMIS Elements, or CMISE) must establish a connection—called a management association, using the Association Control Service Element (ACSE)—before they can exchange management information. Once a connection is established, peer CMIS entities can send management information whenever specified events occur.

The management notification service is used to convey specified events to a peer CMISE.

The management operation services are used to query and control manageable objects within peer CMISE as applicable to the system management operation.

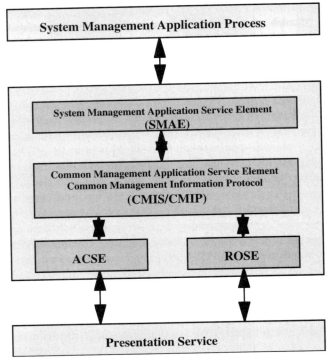

Figure 17.10 The Common Management Information Service.

The functions defined above use CMIS for communications between managers and agents. This service provides the conceptual access to communication mechanisms through which the following operations can be performed and through which notifications are transmitted as event reports:

- Getting data.
- Setting and resetting data.
- Adding data to attributes which are defined as set-valued.
- Removing data from attributes.
- Actions upon objects.
- Object creation.
- Object deletion.

Systems management communications requirements are simple and the service provides the essential characteristics of a *remote procedure call* in which a transmission is requested and, some time later, a response is generated to requester, if desired.

CMISE: The common management information service element is the service element that provides the basic management services. The CMISE is a user of both ROSE and ACSE. The CMISE provides both confirmed and unconfirmed services for reporting events and retrieving and manipulating management data. These services are used by manager and agent application entities to exchange management information.

CMIP: Common management information protocol defines the procedures for transmission of management information and the syntax for the management services of CMIS. CMIP is a connection-oriented protocol that uses the remote operation service element (ROSE) to transfer the CMIP protocol data unit (PDU). CMIP is designed to handle the exchange of management information between two full-scale management systems, each representing a large collection of simpler network elements.

Management communication is affected through the common management information protocol. There is a simple relationship between the elements of the CMIS and the protocol data units (PDUs), which are used to communicate service requests.

CMIS over TCP (CMOT)

The CMOT (CMIP over TCP/IP) architecture is based on the OSI management framework and the models, services, and protocols developed by ISO for network management. The CMOT architecture demonstrates how the OSI management framework can be applied to a TCP/IP environment and used to manage objects in a TCP/IP network.

The use of ISO protocols for the management of widely deployed TCP/IP networks will facilitate the ultimate migration from TCP/IP to ISO protocols. The concept of proxy management is introduced as a useful extension to the architecture. Proxy management provides the ability to manage network elements that either are not addressable by means of an Internet address or use a network management protocol other than CMIP.

The CMOT architecture specifies all the essential components of a network management architecture. The OSI management framework and models are used as the foundation for network management. A protocol-dependent interpretation of the Internet SMI is used for defining management information. The Internet MIB provides an initial list of managed objects. Finally, a means is defined for using ISO management services and protocols on top of TCP/IP transport protocols. Management applications themselves are not included within the scope of the CMOT architecture. What is currently standardized in this architecture is the minimum required for building an interoperable multivendor network management system.

The CMOT architecture provides the foundation for carrying out management in the five functional areas (fault, configuration, performance, accounting, and security), but does not address specifically how any of these types of management are accomplished. It is anticipated that most functional requirements can be satisfied by CMIS. The greatest impact of the functional requirements in the various areas will likely be on the definition of managed objects.

Information Model. There are two different SMI specifications that are important to the CMOT architecture. The first is the SMI currently being defined by ISO. This SMI is important to the CMOT approach because the ISO management protocol CMIP has been designed with the ISO model of management information in mind. The second SMI of importance for use in defining the Internet MIB. This Internet SMI, which is loosely based on a simplified version of the ISO SMI, is important because the managed objects defined for TCP/IP networks to be used by CMOT are defined in terms of it. Thus, to make the CMOT architecture complete, it will be necessary to show how the Internet SMI maps into CMIP in such a way as to enable it to convey the management information defined in the Internet MIB.

Protocol Architecture. The objective of the CMOT protocol architecture is to map the OSI management protocol architecture into the TCP/IP environment. The model presented here follows the OSI model at the application layer, while using Internet protocols at the transport layer. The ISO application protocols used for network management are ACSE, ROSE, and CMIP. Instead of implementing these protocols on top of the ISO presentation, session, and transport layer protocols, the protocol data units (PDUs) for ACSE, ROSE, and CMIP are carried using the Internet transport protocols UDP and TCP. The use of Internet transport protocols is transparent to network management applications, since they are presented with real ISO services.

COMPARISONS OF SNMP, CMIP, AND CMOT

Throughout the late 1980s and early 1990s, SNMP firmly established itself as the standard for management information exchange for LAN and Internet management systems. CMIP is largely viewed as a protocol for interaction between two managers (e.g., IBM's NetView and Digital's DECmcc) rather than a protocol for gathering management information from low-level network elements. Both CMIP and SNMP clearly service a particular network architecture. CMOT is a network management protocol that provides the rich capabilities of OSI-based network management in a TCP/IP environment, but its implementation is slow.

Protocol Implementation

SNMP's simplicity makes it easy and quick to implement with low memory and CPU requirements. Because of greater generality, CMIP or CMOT has made implementation more difficult and lengthy, and can unduly burden high-performance devices such as bridges and routers.

Allocation of Responsibility

CMOT places more load on the network device to support the additional features that allow managing stations to issue complex queries. SNMP queries provide the same basic functions, but normally require several less complex queries and greater amounts of status information to be sent across the network.

Network Load Levels

In a CMOT environment, network devices are better equipped to monitor themselves during normal network operations and send event/trap messages only when experiencing trouble. In SNMP environments, the management workstation must query each network device to retrieve status information. SNMP presents a more predictable load on the network given its polled approach.

Management Objectives

Both CMIP and CMOT provide extensive data retrieval and manipulation capabilities. SNMP data retrieval capabilities are limited and thus is not well equipped to manage larger, more complex networks because of performance limitations of SNMP's polled approach. SNMP does not provide adequate capability to retrieve large data files, such as complete routing tables. SNMP does not support manager-to-manager communications; therefore, one SNMP cannot query another SNMP manager to learn about managed devices and networks.

Data Definitions

The SNMP data modeling approach is not object oriented. An SNMP MIB is a list of data elements, called variables, that can be requested by the protocol. An SNMP MIB is merely a method of standardizing data element identifiers, which is in keeping with the nature of SNMP. In addition, SNMP's MIB is limited and does not easily support applications that make complex management queries. In contrast, CMIP and CMOT use object-oriented data modeling techniques for defining MIB objects.

MANAGEMENT STRATEGIES AND PRODUCTS

The following paragraphs examine the network management offerings and strategies of several of the key vendors in the field.

OpenView (HP)

The OpenView products from Hewlett-Packard provide a consistent user interface and an integrated environment for monitoring, troubleshooting, controlling, and measuring the performance of network components. From a single display, an administrator can see a graphical representation of the network components and their relationships, make configuration changes, and run diagnostic and performance statistics gathering applications. OpenView products include

- OpenView Windows—provides user interface for network management applications.
- OvenView Windows BridgeManager—provides centralized monitoring and control of HP LAN and StarLAN bridges. It can identify and label bridges, access to a variety of

bridge management features, including configuration, monitoring, control, performance management, and problem identification.

- OpenView Data Line Monitor—provides the ability to monitor leased point-to-point analog data lines. It aids in performance monitoring and in fault isolation during troubleshooting operations.
- OpenView DTC Manager—offers centralized and integrated network management for both terminal connectivity and X.25 networking. It configures, monitors, diagnoses, controls, and downloads software. It allows management of local and remote terminal connections.

HP OpenView is arguably the first really comprehensive, off-the-shelf network management system (NMS) to gain wide market use. But, although positioned as an enterprisewide NMS, it (like all the products considered here) really doesn't provide the same functionality provided by management systems specifically tailored for AppleTalk, NetWare, SNA, DECnet, X.25, telecom switches, and other non-SNMP devices. Nevertheless, HP has made great strides in moving OpenView from a development system product primarily for third-party application builders to providing an off-the-shelf product that end users can install and use fairly easily on their own. Its strongest attribute is its wide acceptance among third-party applications developers. IBM has enhanced and extended OpenView in their NetView/6000 product.

OpenView runs on both HP and Sun workstations. Some of the third-party applications developed for OpenView run only Sun or HP systems but not both.

Performance polling is a completely separate activity from status polling. The implication is that if an object fails to respond to a performance poll, it will not trigger an alert—only the status poller can trigger alerts. For example, one may have to wait until the next status poll to find out that a node is down even though a performance poll noticed the node was unresponsive much earlier. It does provide some degree of flexible notification by allowing one to invoke custom programs on an alert or event. However, since there is no dependency mechanism, alert side effects may also invoke these programs.

OpenView uses a commercial, relational database system. This makes it fairly easy for external applications to obtain information being collected by OpenView as well as making SQL searches of the data easy. However, third-party applications are each responsible for storing their own information, which prohibits the sharing of such data.

OpenView has the fault of doing redundant monitoring for devices which are configured to be part of more than one network map. If the total set of devices being monitored is strictly partitioned into separate maps, then no redundant monitoring is done. Further, if more than one operator invokes a display of the same map, then only one of the map instances may be read/write and only the read/write map is kept current. Therefore, to have a device's status accurately displayed to more than one operator, a separate map needs to be defined for each operator, and this will result in redundant monitoring of any of the devices shown on multiple maps.

A big benefit of OpenView is the existence of many third-party applications, more than are available for any other platform. The user interface appears to be clean and fairly flexible. The simple, easy-to-use Motif GUI provides status information and a topological view that most modern NMSs offer.

NetView (IBM)

NetView provides comprehensive end-to-end management that enables administrators to manage IBM SNA and non-SNA resources. It defines five management services that are similar to those provided by OSI (Figure 17.11):

- *Problem management* deals with error conditions, beginning with detection through problem resolution.
- *Change management* provides the planning, control, and applications changes of network resources.
- *Configuration management* controls the information base that identifies network resources and their relationships with other network components.
- *Performance and accounting management* provide network statistical measurements for responsiveness and performance tuning.
- *Operation services* provides security management as well as other operator management functions.

NetView combines the capabilities of several individual management products to provide SNA management services:

SNA Management Services	OSI Management Functions
Problem Management	Fault Management
Configuration Management	Configuration Management
Change Management	
Performance and Accounting Management	Performance Management
	Accounting Management
Operation Services	Security Management

Figure 17.11 IBM and OSI management services.

- Command facility (formerly network communications control facility)
- Hardware monitor (formerly network problem determination application)
- Session monitor (formerly network logical data monitor)
- Additional functions that are part of virtual telecommunications access method (VTAM)

IBM's approach to network management defines a structure consisting of three elements:

- *Focal point* is a host-resident application that communicates with system operators and enables network management capabilities. It provides global viewing and control of the network. NetView is the principal *focal point* application for SNA.
- *Entry point* is an SNA-addressable product having an integrated interface enabling it to communicate with the focal point. Examples of entry point are IBM 37x5 communications controllers and IBM 3x74 cluster controllers. The network management portion of the 37x5 is the network control program (NCP), which provides the distribution point for management information from and to the focal point.
- *Service point* provides monitoring and control capabilities for non-SNA-addressable network components. A service point translates commands from focal point and forwards them to the non-SNA component using the native management protocol format. It also receives management information from the non-SNA components and forwards it to the focal point.

NetView /6000 has become the base to manage large, multivendor or SNA networks by incorporating new management modules to provide distributed management functions and control of SNA networks. System Monitor/6000, running on AIX platforms, can be distributed throughout the network, polling local devices and passing management data back to a central NetView/6000. This software also does SNMP polls of devices on a local LAN and handles traps. It provides all this information to one or more NetView/6000 systems. NetView/6000 incorporates three primary APIs that provide multivendor management application portability. These are

- X/Open Management Protocol, part of the Open Software Foundation distributed management environment (DME).
- End-user interface, which allows applications developers integrate other management applications with NetView/6000.
- SNMP, which allows NetView/6000 to communicate with SNMP agents.

IBM NetView/6000 is a fairly new, comprehensive network management system. It can be used by end users as an off-the-shelf, plug-and-play NMS system as well as a development platform for new network management applications. Although positioned as an enterprisewide NMS, it, like all the products considered here, really doesn't provide the same functionality provided by management systems specifically tailored for AppleTalk, NetWare, SNA, DECnet, X.25, telecom switches, and other non-SNMP devices.

NetView/6000 currently runs only on IBM RS/6000 and Sun workstations. The architecture really does seem to be geared toward managing discrete entities with no knowledge of the overall environment. In a large, heterogeneous environment, this means that a service outage may not easily be distinguishable from a network outage, a major shortcoming.

NetView/6000 uses a commercial, relational database system. This makes it fairly easy for external applications to obtain information being collected by NetView as well as making SQL searches of the data easy. However, third-party applications are each responsible for storing their own information, which prohibits the sharing of such data. NetView/6000 has the ability to filter and correlate information and to use thresholds to reduce the number of SNMP alerts which are treated as actual alarms. Alarms can invoke UNIX scripts or third-party programs.

The NetView/6000 user interface appears to be clean and fairly flexible. The simple, easy-to-use Motif GUI provides status information and a topological view that most NMSs offer. IBM has added an event card display that shows the most recent events in the form of index cards in a separate window.

IBM has a proxy agent for OS/2 Intel platforms which can monitor local devices and communicate via SNMP to a NetView/6000 utility. IBM has made many improvements to HP OpenView, providing a much more complete network management system in their NetView/6000 product suite.

SunNet Manager (SUN)

SunNet Manager (SNM) was the first important UNIX-based network management system. SNM remains primarily a development platform, providing fairly limited capabilities. SNM runs only on SPARCstations.

The two most interesting features of SNM are the proxy agents and the cooperative consoles. SunNet manager is the first product that provides distributed network management. Collection agents can communicate with the manager by RPC routines. (RPCs— remote procedure calls—allow C programs to make procedure calls on other machines across the network.) Proxy agents send back data about what they monitor to the console system. Thus, proxy agents can be distributed across the network as processes on other Suns SPARCstations. Cooperative consoles can share network state information with other SunNet Managers.

Proxy agents are also available for the HP/UX and AIX. A proxy agent can be configured to poll a local subnet, thereby reducing the number of single points of failure, distributing polling responsibility, and reducing overall network traffic. In addition, proxy agents turn unreliable SNMP traps into reliable alerts. The SNMP traps are sent to the local agent, which in turn, attempts to pass information to other manager(s).

Multiprotocol support is provided by the use of proxy agents in the manager/agent services APIs. A third-party agent exists for AppleTalk and IPX. SNM supports SNMP version 2 early adopters' implementation. Cooperative consoles allow multiple SNMs to share network state information.

SNM provides APIs for topology map, management, and agent services, but does not support the XMP open API interface. SNM has a built-in flat-file database. SNM also supports tools for discovery, topology editing, report generation, three-dimensional data analysis, and simple device management. SNM has a ASCII (VT-100) interface for dial-in access and can send mail to alphanumeric pagers.

SNM provides coordinated network management, which is an alternative to centralized hierarchical network management and discrete uncoordinated element management.

NetWare (Novell)

The NetWare Management System (NMS) is Novell's network management solution that enables network supervisors and help desk personnel to centrally monitor and control heterogeneous networks. Designed to provide a modular, open, standards-based platform for enterprise management, the NetWare Management System simplifies the process of managing and optimizing resources in a multivendor network environment. Operating on a single, centralized management workstation running MS Windows, the NetWare Management System integrates management of all the devices and services on your network.

The NMS platform provides many core services, such as the automatic discovery and mapping of network devices, monitoring of network changes, management of alarm information, and SNMP support. In addition to the platform services, NMS 2.0 includes applications to manage the following network resources:

- NetWare 3 and NetWare 4 servers.
- NetWare LANalyzer Agent for distributed network analysis.
- All SNMP devices.
- Routers.
- Hub management interface (HMI)—compliant hubs.
- Network addresses.

NMS provides comprehensive management functions, including

- Asset management.
- Address management.
- Fault management.
- Managing SNMP devices.
- Centralized management of NetWare servers.
- NetWare Management Agent for NetView.
- Management of NetWare Servers from NetView.

Asset Management: NMS automatically maps and displays network devices, with a wide range of configuration information for each device, including such parameters as user name, administrative contact, and system information.

Address Management: Address management automatically finds all the IP and IPX addresses on the network and stores them in its database. Address duplication is one of the most common Internet problems. NMS enables you to determine which addresses are in use and to assign unique new addresses. As a safeguard, the NetWare LANalyzer Agent automatically detects duplicate IP addresses as soon as they go into use and instantly notifies of the potential problem.

Fault Management: With the NMS integrated alarm system, you can view problem reports from each application in a single management environment. All alarm information can be stored in a central database for historical reference. The NetWare Management System incorporates NetWare Expert, a built-in training tool to solve problems and to optimize network performance.

Managing SNMP Devices: NMS also provides a simple network management protocol management information base (SNMP MIB) browser tool. With this tool, you can monitor and control SNMP-manageable devices, such as hubs and routers, regardless of the manufacturer. By automating the management of a heterogeneous network from a single console, you benefit from reduced downtime and maximum network performance.

Centralized Management of NetWare Servers: With NMS, combined with the NetWare Management Agent, you can monitor all of your NetWare servers from a single location. You can access and control any NetWare server and immediately see a display of its status, configuration, performance, and default conditions. By continually monitoring servers for problems and immediately generating an alarm on problem detection, NMS reduces server downtime.

NetWare Management Agent for NetView: The NetWare Management Agent for NetView provides an interface to IBM's NetView network management system. This interface enables NetWare servers to participate more fully in an IBM-host networking environment. Implemented as an NLM, NMA for NetView can run on NetWare servers.

Management of NetWare Servers from NetView: NMA for NetView enables NetView operators to monitor and control NetWare servers from a NetView console. It forwards NetView alerts to the host for errors detected by the NetWare network operating system (NOS). In addition, NMA for NetView includes alert and command forwarding for applications developed to the NetWare Open NetView interface.

DiMONS (NetLabs)

NetLabs DiMONS runs on several platforms including HP and Sun workstations, running under HP/UX, SunOS 4.1.x, and Sun Solaris 2.x. DiMONS runs on a UNIX workstation, can automatically discover devices and gateways on a network, provides an X-Windows interface, can draw various maps of the network which the user can customize, and can be used to detect error conditions and notify personnel of failures. The DiMONS autodiscovery feature provides controls for the type and range of the search, although it appears that it doesn't support IP address range limitations. It provides a flexible notification capability and uses a standard database system for collecting data.

DiMONS provides a single central kernel (server), but supports any number of administrative, security, and operator users. A minimum system would consist of a single kernel and a single administrative user.

The *NetLabs NerveCenter* application provides the systems administrator with the ability to build finite-state models for network elements and services, permitting the creation of fairly sophisticated analysis tools without the need for programming. NerveCenter, as mentioned, is a graphically configurable finite-state machine which allows a user to design how the NMS is to work without the use of any programming. The NerveCenter user specifies *polls* based on a Boolean condition and *triggers* which fire when a polled condition is met or a specified SNMP trap is received. For example, one might have a particular router go from state *green* to state *yellow* when a particular error counter exceeds a specified level. In this *yellow* state, the polling frequency might be increased and variables in the transmission group examined to identify the particular type of error. If the error condition stops, the model would be programmed to return to the normal state. NerveCenter provides a powerful capability in that it makes it possible to provide sophisticated diagnostic tools for inexperienced users.

The *Asset Manager* application is also interesting. It is helpful in dealing with asset inventory tasks through network discovery and polling, and is used to keep track of where specific network devices are located. All information is stored in an extensible database, so that customer and location information can be stored along with the data describing the assets. The assets application monitors network performance and manages faults.

The *MetaViews* application provides the user with graphical summaries and reports of alarm statistics and traffic. When network problems occur, the action router forwards service requests via notification mechanisms such as e-mail, pagers, and so on, based on rules the user has defined.

The *NetLabs CMOT Agent* supports the control and monitoring of network resources by use of CMOT message exchanges.

The *NetLabs' Dual Manager* provides management of TCP/IP networks using both SNMP and CMOT protocols. Such management can be initiated either through the X Windows user interface (both Motif and OpenLook) or through OSI Network Management (CMIP) commands. The Dual Manager provides for configuration, fault, security, and performance management. It provides extensive map management features, including scanned maps in the background. It provides simple mechanisms to extend the MIB and assign specific lists of objects to specific network elements, thereby providing for the management of all vendors' specific MIB extensions. It provides an optional relational DBMS for storing and retrieving MIB and alarm information. Finally, the Dual Manager is an open platform, in that it provides several application programming interfaces (APIs) for users to extend the functionality of the Dual Manager. The Dual Manager is expected to work as a TCP/IP "branch manager" under DEC's EMA, AT&T's UNMA, and other OSI-conformant enterprise management architectures.

The NetLabs SNMP agent supports the control and monitoring of network resources by use of SNMP message exchanges.

SPECTRUM (Cabletron)

Cabletron SPECTRUM is an extensible and intelligent network management system that utilizes an object-oriented, client-server architecture. SPECTRUM is built around an artificial intelligence engine, called the inductive modeling technology (IMT). SPECTRUM provides gateway support for Novell NetWare and Banyan VINES. Native protocol support (AppleTalk, IPX, etc.) could be added to SPECTRUM utilizing external protocol API.

SPECTRUM runs on several platforms including a DEC station running ULTRIX, IBM RS/6000 running AIX, Silicon Graphics' Iris workstation running Irix, and a Sun SPARCstation running SunOS.

The SPECTRUM server allows two types of device polling, automatic (server initiated) and manual (operator initiated). During every automatic poll, the server checks the status of devices and collects the values for specified MIB variables. As with each of the other evaluated NMS systems, the systems administrator can specify which devices are to be polled and at what intervals and which MIB variables are to be collected and logged for report generation. A difference between SPECTRUM and HP OpenView and IBM NetView/6000 is that no redundant monitoring of devices occurs when multiple clients are monitoring the same device on different maps.

The SPECTRUM *generic information block (GIB)* editor permits an operator to generate windows through which rapid polling of specified devices can be initiated by the operator. Operator-initiated polling updates the server state information in the same way that automatic polling does, allowing alarms to be triggered immediately by an operator initiated poll, a feature not found in other NMSs.

Notification capabilities include an alarm screen (displaying list of alarms by severity), sound, electronic mail, and pagers. An additional product allows SPECTRUM to provide a support technician with access to problem information via a voice response system.

SPECTRUM's *Autodiscovery* is quite flexible but is slower than other products. It permits one to discover selected subnets, selected IP address ranges, routers alone, and devices belonging to specific protocols. Both flat and hierarchical discovery is supported.

SPECTRUM uses a integral relational database system that does not directly support SQL access. SPECTRUM's data gateway product adds SAS reporting capabilities to SPECTRUM and provides SQL interfaces to several DBMSs (e.g., Oracle, Ingres, and DB2) through SAS scripts.

In SPECTRUM, network administrators can control what individual operators can view on their console screens, thereby limiting access according to the responsibilities of each part of an organization and local administrators can control access within their domains. However, since there is only one level of administrative privilege, the administrator of one department can access the user profiles of other departments.

Through the SPECTRUM graphical user interface, users can customize their working environment and create navigational shortcuts. There is no on-line help available in SPECTRUM.

SPECTRUM provides the ability to view and control data in the server database from both its X Windows interface as well as a command line interface.

SUMMARY

The emergence of integrated network management platforms such as Hewlett-Packard (HP) OpenView, NetView/6000, Cabletron System's Spectrum, and others have expanded information systems' ability to manage LAN and internetwork resources from a central point of control, along with the ability to focus on operational and availability issues in that environment. They also offer application development and integration tools, along with APIs, to enable third-party vendors to integrate their network applications for greater monitoring, management, and interoperability.

However, vendors have been slow to capitalize on the potential of open systems platforms. To date, most of the integrated applications have focused on component control (e.g., many hub and router vendors have tools for remotely configuring and controlling their equipment only). These applications are generally integrated into the platform by representing their devices on the platform's map and then launching the application based on predefined user or system events.

Simple network management protocol, which controls devices and allows communication of events and information to the central management station, has advanced in step with network management platforms. Early implementations focused on component control and availability, while recent advances such as remote monitoring have begun to provide the roots of the metrics required to address a broader service management spectrum. Even these standards have a long way to go before they can fully address the information needs of managing a new distributed computing environment with the reliability and measurability of traditional and legacy networks. Also, not all devices, on a legacy network can be monitored and reported through SNMP.

Networks are increasing considerably in scale, complexity, and basic value as the variety of available equipment and services within them expands. As organizations commit to distributed and networked computers, they are becoming more vulnerable to network failures. Therefore, network management is changing to reflect greater use of distributed processing and enterprise networks. Users must agree on a common strategy by integrating the network management tools available. One example is ISO's Common Management Information System standard. Other options include SNMP and the major proprietary network management systems. In the long term, as the line between networks and computers changes, managing enterprise information resources will demand a combination approach encompassing both systems management and network management.

The primary challenge is to construct a network management system that is relatively easy to implement, use, and present information in a coherent fashion. By selecting products that can be effectively controlled from a single management system utilizing existing standards, network administrators can avoid many of the problems that plague older established networks.

EXERCISES

1. List and briefly discuss the management protocols employed in network management.
2. List the five functional areas that must be managed by a given protocol.
3. What is SNMP and why is it a preferred protocol employed by most vendors?
4. How does NetView conceptually resemble the OSI management?
5. Briefly discuss the tasks of fault, configuration, and security management functions.
6. Describe three major components of a management system.

18

SUMMARY AND CONCLUSIONS

Introduction
Internetworking Environments
Internetworking Configurations
    Multiple LAN Segments
    Point-toPoint Connections
    Wide Area Network Links
    High-Speed Backbone Interconnections
Minimizing Network Failures
Strategies for Managing Networks
  and Security

Internetwork Management
Protocol Management
Configuration Management
Error Management
Bandwidth Management
Security Management
Future of Internetworking
Finally

INTRODUCTION

Over the last few years, enterprises worldwide have shifted away from "glass house" mainframe environments toward the realm of distributed computing and client/server applications. The basic reasons for this migration are clear:

- Cost-effective ways to make employees more productive.
- Taking advantage of the new technologies to be competitive.
- Process reengineering.

    The industry is responding to the trend of downsizing computer operations. This has increased the importance of LANs, and issues related to telecommunications have become corporate bedroom topics. The processing power of the PCs and intelligent workstations is increasing. In addition, internet, complex graphics, full-motion video, and teleconferencing applications are becoming commonplace.

    Today, an infrastructure of LANs and WANs connect remote resources, giving the users more access to information across the enterprise. Distributed environments provide desktop computers with the intelligence to perform complex tasks quickly. Consequently, the users can gain the technological flexibility to quickly respond to the needs of a changing environment.

The first step in creating an environment capable of supporting internetworks involves building an underlying distributed infrastructure. Unfortunately, the complexity of this new environment does not end with the installation of hubs, routers, multiplexers, and network interface cards. In addition, it introduces complexities associated with the distribution of clients, information, and application processing throughout the enterprise.

Distributed (client/server) applications span *multiple* and *dissimilar* operating systems (DOS, OS/2, Mac OS, VMS, UNIX, MVS, and others), network operating systems (NetWare, NFS, LANServer, VINES, AppleShare, etc.), protocols (TCP/IP, IPX, SNA, AppleTalk, etc.), and transmission technologies (Ethernet, Channels, ATM, FDDI, Token Ring, X.25, etc.). This *heterogeneous mix* presents a new paradigm shifting away from stable, predictable, single-vendor architectures to a multivendor, multioperating system, multiprotocol environment characterized by *variable* demands and *unpredictable* requirements.

INTERNETWORKING ENVIRONMENTS

Designing an efficient internetwork is influenced by several facility-specific issues. These include the business activities of the organization, types of users and their access priorities, size of the network, geographical distribution of network nodes, frequency of use, and a host of other factors. They, in turn, impact the two basic design requirements that are common to all internetworks.

High-Performance Processing: It depends on the design of the network, choice of media and internetworking devices, size of the facility, frequency of use, and security. Users expect on-demand availability of network services from remote locations. This requires efficient traffic management to ensure a bottleneck-free flow of traffic, while providing adequate alternate routes in case of emergencies.

Flexible Configuration: Users' demands, mergers and acquisitions, and a large number of other priorities require frequent network reconfiguration. This has to be done with a minimum of service interruptions and must accommodate a host of network segments that support different architectures, protocols, and media. The network also has to support several additional requirements, including LANs of many flavors, interconnection, WAN topologies, redundancy and alternate paths, transfer speeds, capacity requirements at different loops, selection of suitable devices, and management strategy.

While it is possible to exercise sufficient control over the LAN segments of the internetwork, the WAN portions are usually leased from service providers, including long-distance and regional/local telephone companies. However, the choice of appropriate LAN-WAN services is dictated by a variety of user-specific factors. The overall design of the internetwork should be able to perform the following:

* *Media Support:* Requirements include twisted-pair copper, coaxial cable, fiber optic channels, T1/T3, 56 Kbps, microwave, submarine cables, and satellite.

- *Flexible Bridging and Routing:* Depending on the traffic priorities, the network should be able to bridge or route traffic according to varying transmission demands.
- *Varied Bandwidth Support:* Modern networks should be able to support unpredictable or bursty network traffic of variable bandwidth.
- *High-Speed Packet/Circuit Switching, Frame Relay, Asynchronous Transfer Mode Support:* The architecture and equipment should support varied transmission technologies.
- *Signal Transmission data:* The network entities should be able to collect and maintain traffic data in intermittent nodes.
- *Network Analysis, Monitoring, and Management:* This is an essential element of any efficient internetwork. The *standard tools* must be developed that can assist the enterprise in any dissimilar networking environment.
- *Security Requirements:* The network should be able to protect data from being tapped or corrupted.

INTERNETWORKING CONFIGURATIONS

Currently, internetworks utilize at least four distinct interface models. These are

- Multiple LAN segments connected by bridges or routers.
- Point-to-point, leased line wide area connections between remote routers.
- Wide area network connection using WAN protocols such as HDLC, X.25, and frame relay between two remote routers
- Multiple LAN segments connected by a high-speed backbone.

Multiple LAN Segments

A variety of LAN topologies (including Ethernet, token ring, FDDI, and ATM) can be internetworked using bridges and routers. The bridge or router serves as a segmenting point for network traffic. If the network is designed correctly with respect to traffic load, bandwidth on either side of the bridge or router will be adequate for fast, efficient network operation.

When a router connects LANs together (Figure 18.1), the router interprets the address of each packet at the *network layer*. Then routes the packet to the destination LAN if the address does not correspond to the originating LAN. If a bridge or router is placed between an Ethernet and token ring segment, address translation occurs at the *data link layer*. Generally, it is not necessary to encapsulate packets for movement across interconnected LANs. In this example, the native frame structure that contains the data on the LAN is already optimized for transport within the LAN, and from LAN to LAN.

In a typical LAN-to-LAN internetwork, the medium access control (MAC) address is used on both sides of the bridge or router, eliminating the need for an additional address scheme. Frame size can be optimized for use on the LAN to operate over 802.3

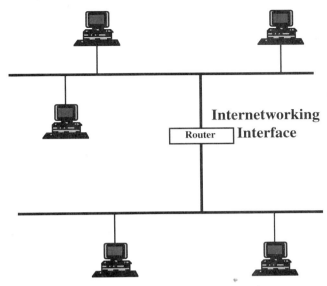

Figure 18.1 LAN-to-LAN connectivity.

(CSMA/CD Ethernet) or over 802.5 (token ring) environments. The transmission times from LAN segment to another are usually short. The transmission media is reliable enough, eliminating the need for additional error checking at the data link layer beyond what the native protocol provides.

Point-to-Point Connections

Figure 18.2 illustrates two routers separated by a circuit provided by a private carrier. The routers repackage the frames received from two remotely located local area connections in a protocol "envelope" appropriate to a wide area connection. In the past, these wide area links have operated at 9600 Kbps. However, the typical speeds today are 56 Kbps, T1 (1.544 Mbps), and even T3 (45 Kbps). This bandwidth allows more traffic from local LAN to be transferred over the wide area link to a remote LAN more quickly.

Bridge or router or high-level data link control (HDLC) or proprietary protocols are commonly used choices for data encapsulation. With proprietary protocols, routers or bridges can communicate more readily with routers and bridges from the same vendor, due to the unique header information that each device appends to the transmitted frame. With HDLC, built-in error checking is available on the wide area link at the data link layer. The error checking may not always be available in the native Ethernet or token ring frame format. When network addresses are not available within a given protocol (for example, NetBIOS, DEC LAT), LAN data is bridged, rather than routed, from the LAN to the wide area network.

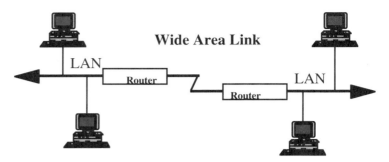

Figure 18.2 Point-to-point connectivity.

Wide Area Network Links

Figure 18.3 illustrates a typical wide area network linked with LANs. The packets passing into the WAN are encapsulated by the bridge or router using common WAN protocols such as X.25, HDLC, and frame relay. The WAN operates between two remote bridges or routers. Frames transmitted from a local router must conform to the same protocol being used by the WAN provider to transfer the frames to a remote router.

High-Speed Backbone Interconnections

Multiple LAN segments (Figure 18.4) can be connected to a high-speed backbone for transfer of data between each segment. Most commonly used high-speed technologies today are FDDI, ATM, and switched Ethernet with data rates in Gbps range. To manage such high-speed connections and protocols, the management device must be capable of capturing traffic from the backbone segment at the local speed.

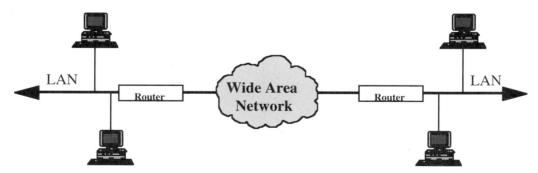

Figure 18.3 Wide area network link.

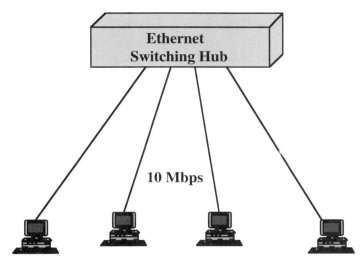

Figure 18.4 High-speed backbone links.

MINIMIZING NETWORK FAILURES

Strategic management tasks are often neglected because managers are spending too much time on operations and five fighting tasks. In the LAN environment, managers neglecting capacity planning risk future problems if inadequate capacity interferes with the organization's ability to conduct business. Instead, the network managers need to monitor and equipment their networks appropriately, allowing for early detection of problems before they impact network users.

As internetworks continue to become distributed, offer higher bandwidth, and support more protocols, network managers must be prepared to adjust their network support with new analysis and monitoring tools. In addition, the development of high-bandwidth connectivity has reduced the economic life of existing network analysis and management equipment.

You need to look for management applications that help you be proactive instead of reactive—those that supply you with information instead of forcing you to dig for it yourself. You can minimize network failures by

- Proper planning.
- Designing (modular) for growth and reconfigurations due to mergers or expansions, for technology changes, and for ease of troubleshooting.
- Utilizing the tools to provide the answers when the failures do occur.

STRATEGIES FOR MANAGING NETWORKS AND SECURITY

As enterprise networks expand, the process of delivering data from one LAN segment to another becomes increasingly complex. From dial-up modems to sophisticated ATM switches, internetworks lay the infrastructure for traffic to move efficiently between nodes, between LANs, and between LANs and WANs. Effective *internetwork management* should support the geographical reach of your distributed network.

Bandwidth management helps ensure sufficient, but not excessive, bandwidth availability to support end-user productivity and minimize line costs. *Protocol management* balances data integrity against data throughput. *Bridge* and *router management* help to ensure that traffic moves along anticipated network paths.

In distributed network environments, with multiple network devices and segments, the process of *error management* is essential to pinpoint the cause of internetwork delays. Finally, *configuration management* helps you keep up to date on the changing nature of devices and applications on distributed internetworks.

Internetwork Management

The goal of internetwork management is to ensure that the connections between LAN segments operate smoothly and cost effectively without impacting the users. In a distributed environment, data often travels across a connection from a service on one LAN segment to a service on another LAN segment, and possibly through a WAN. Effective internetwork management demands knowledge of network traffic patterns.

Ideally, internetwork management consists of central access to all information traveling across a distributed network including segment statistics, devices, and configurations. Network components such as servers, routers, bridges, hubs, switches, cabling, and software (applications as well as network operating systems) also need to be managed across multiple internetwork links. Internetwork management must support this distributed architecture so that the data appears as if it resides on a local connection. To achieve connectivity transparency across internetworks, two critical data translations are necessary.

- Data must be translated from one physical media to another. This may involve a change to any or all of the network types, available bandwidth, and physical interfaces to the network segment.
- The packet often requires translation from one communication protocol to another when a data packet passes across a network interface. This may require (1) an encapsulating protocol to facilitate addressing over the WAN or (2) different frame format may be needed for transmission from one LAN (e.g., Ethernet) to another LAN (e.g., token ring) or vice versa. In general, an encapsulating protocol can enhance the error control and correction capabilities of a wide area link. The communication protocol can be usually translated either from LAN to LAN or from LAN to WAN.

Protocol Management

With LAN-to-LAN internetworks, LAN segments operate using a common media access control layer while theoretically supporting limitless number of upper layer protocols. Traffic on a local LAN has full use of the local segment bandwidth.

Verification of the connection and data integrity is straight forward if the LAN uses native protocols. However, with LAN-to-WAN internetworks, some LAN protocols are far from efficient. For example, NetBIOS takes up a large amount of bandwidth when traveling from LANs to WANs because NetBIOS requires frequent acknowledgments and is prone to broadcasts over the WAN. Unlike traffic on a local LAN segment, internetworks may create noticeable performance and cost penalties for traffic that must be repeatedly retransmitted.

When passing traffic across internetworks, the protocols carrying application data should incorporate maximum connection verification and error checking while adding minimum overhead to the application data. Effective protocol management balances data integrity against data throughput. Protocol management should, at least, address the following problems in any implementation:

* *Session time-outs* can cause response time to degrade. Connection time-outs originate when a connection between two nodes cannot be maintained through the physical media. To minimize time-outs, locate devices closer to the resources used by the devices, or upgrade the processing capabilities of the devices, or migrate to protocol that will automatically reconfigure its acknowledgment time in response to an extended round-trip delay (e.g., TCP/IP).
* Redundant packets may broadcast across the distributed enterprise network, causing excess traffic to affect internetwork links and end-user response times. In majority of the cases, such packets need not travel beyond the local LAN and, therefore, must be filtered out.

Configuration Management

Configuration management includes maintaining an accurate picture of the network's devices, users, addresses, and topologies. Configuration management aids in managing, planning, performance, and troubleshooting a network. Because of the constantly changing and geographically expansed nature of the enterprise internetworks, configuration management can be the most challenging aspect of internetwork management.

Error Management

The application's execution should not affect end-user response time, regardless of whether the application occurs locally or in an internetworked environment. Application delays can result from internetwork device errors and/or media errors. The delays normally manifest as slow performance, application lock-up, or network crash, depending on the seriousness of the error. The types of errors that occur most often are the following:

- Media errors occur when a wide area link introduces multiple physical errors into the bit stream.
- Device hardware errors are generated due to poor physical interface connection or a bad network interface card.
- Device software problems occur due to translation errors resulting in incorrectly addressed packets or packets that contain bit errors.
- Encapsulation protocol errors occur when two internetworking devices are unable to communicate because of differing versions of the same protocol.

Bandwidth Management

Applications that operate over a distributed network and utilize wide area links require sufficient bandwidth to send packets to the intended destination. If available bandwidth on either the LAN or the WAN connection is inadequate, the application may fail. Conversely, access to virtually unlimited bandwidth across a WAN can be both costly and wasteful.

Security Management

Security is a continuing problem. The top areas of concern have been

- Insufficient security.
- Virus and malicious code.
- Unauthorized system access.
- Unauthorized network access.
- Password exposure.

More recently, unauthorized network access has been one of the major security concerns in the internetwork arena. Despite the diversity of security requirements in different organizations, all security management schemes should have the following goals in common:

- Identify valuable *resources* that are worth protecting.
- Identify the *users* who access these resources.
- Establish *access rights* judiciously between users and their resources.

FUTURE OF INTERNETWORKING

Visionaries with ideas about the future of internetworking are not in short supply. In an optimistic and upbeat view, they talk of the expansion of the "data superhighway" and proliferation of enterprise internetworks. The next generations of connectivity devices that will direct the internetwork industry are likely to be systems that integrate three key technologies:

- High-speed switching.
- Virtual networking.
- ATM bandwidth.

Investigating each of these technologies separately and then combining them into a unified framework should provide a future direction of LAN-WAN internetworking.

High-speed switching combines the cost effectiveness and speed of a repeater with the functionality of a router. Many of the high-speed switches integrate multiprotocol routing with a high port density (support for large number of individual LANs). Switching supplies the speed and port density necessary to accommodate bandwidth-hungry and delay-sensitive applications. High-speed switching is primarily a form of layer 2 bridging that delivers full bandwidth to each port.

Virtual networking is a technique that eliminates the logjams associated with a physical LAN topology by creating high-speed switched connections between end nodes on different LAN segments. A switched virtual internetwork is a high-speed, low-latency, broadcast group that unites an arbitrary collection of end nodes on multiple LAN segments. Like all layer 2 schemes, high-speed switching, by itself, cannot establish broadcast and security firewalls. Virtual networking addresses this deficiency by allowing the logical subdivision of switched networks. Because virtual LANs link many segments without a bottleneck, they allow extensive LAN segmentation within workgroups.

ATM bandwidth, which is highly scalable, allows end node connections to support almost any type of bandwidth-greedy, delay-sensitive applications. Switched virtual ATM internetworks can effectively begin to meet the needs of connecting LANs over WAN facilities. As both a LAN and a WAN transport mechanism, ATM can address internetwork requirements as well. Standards-compliant, interoperable switched Fast Ethernet is currently available, ahead of ATM. However, for LAN-WAN internetworking, switched virtual ATM networks are clearly where we are headed.

FINALLY

The majority of this book has dealt with the TCP/IP, SNA, X.25, followed by OSI architectures and protocols because these will be the dominant in the future. But efforts have been made, wherever possible, to show relationships to other architectures and operating systems that make internetworking possible. The past decade has seen a tremendous rate of change in computing technology and specifically in the internetworking of dissimilar operating systems. We expect that this rate of change will continue in the future, however, with greater emphasis on the ease of use for the user.

APPENDIX I

TECHNICAL NOTES

Introduction
Address Resolution Protocol
Bridges
Carrier Sense Multiple Access/Collision
    Detect
Datagram
Domain Name System
Ethernet
FDDI
Filtering
Forwarding
Gateways
Internetworking
Internet Address Classes
Internet Protocol
LAN
LAN Media
Management Information Base
Multiport Bridges
NetView
Network Operating System

Open Systems Interconnection
    The OSI Reference Model
    The Layers
Open Shortest Path First
Packet
Point-to-Point Protocol
Repeaters
Routers
SQL
Simple Network Management Protocol
Token Ring (802.5)
    Token Ring Concepts
    Token Ring Standards: IEEE 802.5
    Token Ring Access Control
Transmission Control Protocol Suite
Transmission Control Protocol
WANs
    Switching Systems
    Frame Relay Systems
    Broadcast Systems
    X.25 Networks

INTRODUCTION

These technical notes are designed to provide a quick review and reference to supplement the information already provided in the text. Some of the key terms mentioned throughout the book are elaborated in this section. Although the comprehensive description of each term makes the technical notes a useful review tool, the applications of these terms is described in more detail in the body of this book. A quick check of the glossary will also help explain the terminology usage, since all terms are not elaborated in this section.

ADDRESS RESOLUTION PROTOCOL

ARP (Figure A1.1) is a LAN data link protocol used by the Internet protocol layer to find the LAN hardware address of a local node, given its IP address. ARP is required on many types of LANs because the hardware address generally cannot be computed from the IP address. ARP is a broadcast protocol. It is used when one node (a router or a host) has a packet to transmit to another node, but does not know the destination hardware address.

The requesting IP layer transmits a LAN broadcast packet indicating the IP address it knows, requesting a response. All nodes on the LAN will receive the packet. The node which has been assigned the specified IP address will respond, giving its hardware address. The response is sent as a "unicast" packet, addressed only to the original requester to minimize the packet processing load by other nodes. When the original requester receives the response, it can then transmit the packet to the destination with the newly learned hardware address.

Once a node has learned the hardware address, matching a given IP address, it will *remember* the two addresses together in order to avoid having to send another ARP packet to the same destination.

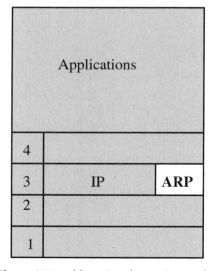

Figure A1.1 Address Resolution Protocol.

BRIDGES

A bridge is a device used to interconnect local area networks. Bridges receive every packet sent on each attached network, and selectively forward packets between LANs, using only the layer 2 (data link) addresses to determine whether to forward each packet. Bridges forward only those packets which are destined for a node on the other side of the bridge, discarding those which need not be forwarded. There are two types of bridges:

- *Local bridges* connect LANs which are co-located adjacent at some point along their length. The local bridge allows a large building or compact campus to have a single "logical" LAN longer than any one LAN cable segment and provides some degree of traffic isolation between segments.
- *Remote bridges* connect LANs which are not co-located. Remote bridges are used in pairs. Each remote bridge is connected to a LAN and another remote bridge via a remote link. Bridges can be used to interconnect LANs via lower-speed telecommunications links because they need not have the same speed link media on both sides.

Most bridges automatically learn the topology of the network by examining each packet they receive and note the source address of each packet. Such bridges are known as *learning bridges*. A source address which the bridge has not seen before is captured and stored in its internal tables for future reference. When a bridge receives a packet with an unknown destination address, it sends out that packet to all other ports to ensure that the packet reaches its destination. At the same time, any packet received from that destination node in the future will allow the bridge to copy its location.

Multiport bridges are simple bridges which have three or more data link interfaces. These links could be either LAN or telecommunication links. Multiport bridges operate basically the same way the smaller two-port learning bridges operate, except that the decision to forward a given packet also includes the choice of which link to use.

Bridges provide better traffic and electrical isolation between LAN segments than repeaters, but introduce some delay. Bridges are simpler to install and manage than routers. However, bridges do not provide as high a degree of isolation between LANs as do routers.

CARRIER SENSE MULTIPLE ACCESS/COLLISION DETECT

CSMA/CD (Figure A1.2) is the algorithm used in IEEE Ethernet (IEEE 802.3) networks to share the use of the LAN media. When a station on the LAN has a packet to transmit, it first listens (*senses* whether there is a *carrier* present) to the LAN to determine whether any other transmission is currently under progress. If not, the station immediately begins transmitting the packet on the LAN. Typically, the packet is transmitted to completion, and the LAN is idle and available for more packets.

If another station also began transmitting at the same time, the two packets *collide*, resulting in an invalid signal on the LAN during the overlap period. To ensure that all stations properly detect the collision, each transmitting node will reinforce the collision by

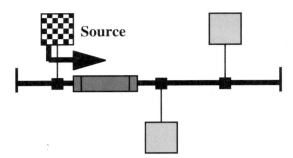

Figure A1.2 CSMA/CD.

sending a special jamming signal for a time interval that all stations can detect the collision.

After the collision, each transmitter backs off and waits for a random time and tries again to send the packet. Because each node picked a random delay interval, one node usually starts transmitting first, while the others wait until the first packet has been transmitted. Often, there are several stations contending for the LAN, causing successive transmission attempts to collide. Each station selects its own random *back off* interval in order to efficiently handle such a case. This mechanism increases the probability that only one station will have the shortest delay time, allowing it to successfully transmit.

DATAGRAM

Datagram (Figure A1.3) is the block of information sent by the IP network layer. The term *datagram* is usually used for IP traffic, while a *packet* refers to the same information after the data link has added its own headers and other control information.

A datagram carries in its header the network level destination address, source address, routing control fields, and other control information.

DOMAIN NAME SYSTEM

The DNS is the means of assigning human-recognizable names to hosts and applications in a TCP/IP network. The domain name system is designed to provide easy-to-use names to the hosts in a large internetwork, while allowing simple and localized management. Domains are registered with a central authority to ensure that two organizations do not choose the same name.

As illustrated in Figure A1.4, the individual parts of a domain name are arranged hierarchically. The rightmost portion (highest) refers to the naming group (*com*), indicating a commercial organization. The next domain level is *hitachi*, indicating Hitachi Corporation. Therefore, all computers in Hitachi will most likely have a domain name ending in *hitachi.com*. The last and the leftmost part is *paul*, which may be the name of a par-

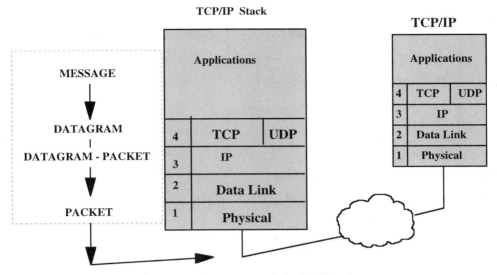

TCP/IP Stack

Figure A1.3 Datagram and the TCP/IP suite.

ticular user. An exact equivalent is represented on the right side of the Figure A1.4, which is the actual address assigned to the network address.

Domain names are used to identify hosts in an internetwork and are used with applications to reach or identify individuals. The most widely used application of this type is electronic mail, as identified in Figure A1.4.

ETHERNET

Ethernet (Figure A1.5) is a baseband LAN specification that was invented by Xerox Corporation. Ethernet LANs employ a bus topology in which each station is directly connected to a common LAN media. Each station on the Ethernet transmits directly to the shared bus, so that all stations on the LAN receive the signal simultaneously.

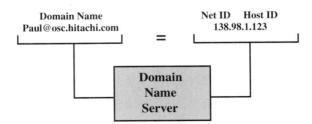

Figure A1.4 Domain name server.

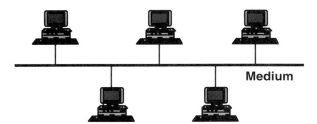

Figure A1.5 An Ethernet LAN.

In Ethernet networks, multiple access is provided by the carrier sense multiple access/collision detect (CSMA/CD) algorithm. CSMA/CD allows a node to transmit a packet as soon as the LAN is available and arbitrates if there is contention for the LAN.

Ethernet networks operate at 10 Mbps using CSMA/CD to run over coaxial cable. Ethernet is similar to a series of standards produced by IEEE and is referred to as IEEE 802.3.

FDDI

FDDI (fiber distributed data interface) is a 100 Mbps data rate local area network standard. The topology is a point-to-point connection of links joined in a logical link. There are two rings with one ring configured as a backup (Figure A1.6). Each station connects to both rings, where each station is daisy-chained to the previous node. There can be up to 500 such stations on the network with a maximum ring size of 200 km. The maximum distance between each node is 2 km. The rule for forming an FDDI network is simple—no greater than two logical paths.

The set of dual rings is referred to as the trunk ring. The dual rings are counterrotating. This allows for easy reconfiguration in the case of a single fault (Figure A1.7). Typically, one ring is used for data transfer and is called the primary ring. The second ring is used as a backup, used only in case of a fault, and is known as the secondary ring.

According to the Open Systems Interconnection Reference Model (OSI), FDDI specifies layer 1 (physical layer) and part of layer 2 (data link layer). The data link layer is responsible for maintaining the integrity of information exchanged between two points. In a LAN environment, because most LANs are shared media networks, the layer 2 is subdivided into two sublayers: logical link control (LLC) and media access control (MAC). The LLC is the same for different subnetworks. Examples of subnetworks are IEEE 802.3 (CSMA/CD), very similar to Ethernet, IEEE 802.5 (token ring), and ANSI FDDI among others. Different LAN subnetworks have different mechanisms for accessing the shared media. The access mechanisms are specified in the media access control (MAC) specification of the LANs. The layer 1 FDDI specification consists of two parts: physical media dependent (*PMD*) and *PHY*. The PHY is independent of the media which can be multimode fiber, single-mode fiber, shielded twisted pair, and so on.

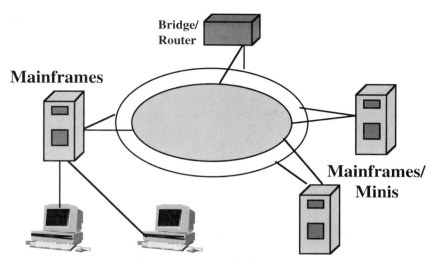

Figure A1.6 FDDI dual ring trees.

- PMD defines the type of media interconnection and its characteristics such as transmitter power, frequencies, receiver sensitivities, and so on. It also specifies the maximum repeater-less distance between two nodes. The first media targeted for FDDI was fiber. To accommodate inter-nodal distances greater than a few kilometers to allow FDDI to be used between campuses and/or buildings and make use of the existing fiber in the public domain. The inter-nodal distances can be extended to 40 km by the use of an alternate media such as single-mode fiber (SMF), but it requires the use of powerful transmitters. The function of the *PHY* is to synchronize the clock with the incoming signal provided by the PMD, encode and decode data and control symbols, and interface with the higher layers and initialization of the medium (fiber, copper). The FDDI PHY bears more similarity to token ring than Ethernet.

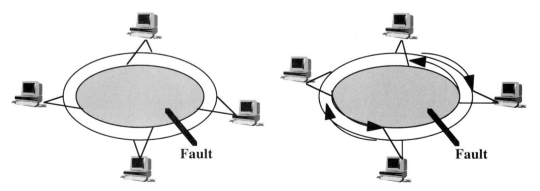

Figure A1.7 FDDI cable fault and reconfiguration.

- The FDDI MAC specifies a class of control frames which are used to execute low-level (MAC-level) protocols such as ring initialization and fault isolation.

Most of the popular networks today are shared media LANs, including FDDI. It was developed to serve as an integrated voice/video/data network. FDDI specifications have been developed by American National Standards Institute (ANSI).

FILTERING

Filtering (Figure A1.8) refers to the decision a bridge makes on every received packet to determine whether it should be discarded or forwarded. A bridge receives all packets transmitted on each of its LANs. For each packet, the bridge first determines whether the packet's destination is on the same LAN as the LAN from the packet was received. If that is the case, the destination and source are judged to be on the same LAN, and the packet is intended for the destination without the help from the bridge. Therefore, such a packet need not be forwarded to another LAN and can be discarded.

A bridge knows which stations are on each of its ports by examining the source address of each packet it receives. If the address is not in its internal routing table, that address is added to its routing table along with its port number and other control information.

Some packets are treated differently at the filtering stage. Packets with a broadcast or multicast destination address must normally be forwarded to the other ports on the bridge, since the packet is supposed to be sent to all stations. Such packets with a destination address not in the bridge's tables must also be forwarded , since the bridge does not know on which LAN that station is installed until it sends a packet.

Some bridges also include a *custom filtering* feature, which allows the network administrator to specify other reasons to drop a packet. For example, to provide high level of security, only certain stations may be allowed to connect to systems outside the workgroup. Therefore, only a controlled access is provided by configuring the bridge to filter out or drop packets except those with specific source and destination addresses. Custom filtering can also be used for traffic control by only allowing packets for selected protocols, such as IP, to be forwarded. Even broadcast packets can be prevented from crossing the bridge with custom filtering.

FORWARDING

Forwarding (Figure A1.9) is used for the process of transmitting packets received by a bridge over one or more of its other data link ports. When a bridge receives a packet, it first filters the addresses to determine whether to drop or forward the packet. If the packet is not dropped, the bridge forwards it by transmitting it on its other port.

Bridges are often compared by their performance in filtering and forwarding abilities. High-performance bridges can filter and forward at the maximum rate at which pack-

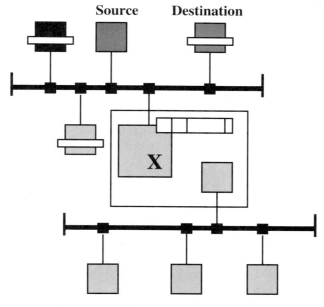

Figure A1.8 Filtering and the network system.

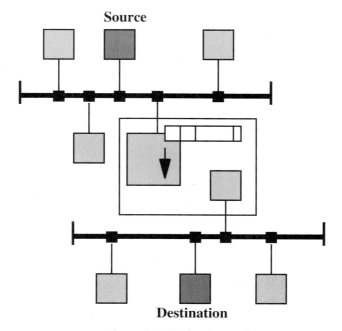

Figure A1.9 Packet forwarding.

ets could arrive. Low-cost or medium-performance bridges may filter and forward at a lower rate if high LAN traffic rates are not expected.

GATEWAYS

Gateways (Figure A1.10) are high-level protocol conversion devices. Gateways enable hosts using a particular protocol suite, such as TCP/IP, to communicate with hosts running a different protocol, such as SNA, DECnet, or OSI-based protocols. There are some gateways which are able to convert from one electronic mail protocol to another.

Gateways, unlike bridges and routers, are not specific to any particular protocol layer. They typically convert data sent by some specific application via the entire protocol stack it uses (for example, ASCII to EBCDIC conversions) to data acceptable to another, related but incompatible, application and protocol.

There are several types of gateways. The most common are *terminal emulation* converters and *electronic mail converters*. Each gateway product is, therefore, specialized to the problem it solves.

INTERNETWORKING

An internetwork (Figure A1.11) is a large communications system consisting of several, possibly many, networks interconnected to a large overall network. Today's internetworks are, typically, combinations of local area networks, telecommunications trunks, public switched facilities, and public data packet networks. One particular Internet is the TCP/IP internetwork. This Internet grew out of the ARPANET in the 1970s.

INTERNET ADDRESS CLASSES

All IP addresses are 32 bits in length, with a portion specifying the network ID, and the rest specifying the host ID. All these classes specify alternatives for the sizes of the network ID versus host ID fields, allowing efficient use of the 32-bit field for different sizes of networks. There are three Internet address classes:

- *Class A* addresses have a zero in the first (most significant) bit, 7 bits of network ID, and 24 bits of host ID. Only a few very large networks are assigned a Class A address.
- *Class B* addresses have a 10 in the first 2 bits, 14 bits of network ID, and 16 bits of host ID. There are a large number of Class B networks, with up to up to 65,000 hosts per network ID.
- *Class C* addresses have 110 in the first 3 bits, 21 bits of network ID, and 8 bits of host ID. A very large number of Class C networks can be assigned, with only up to 255 hosts per network ID.

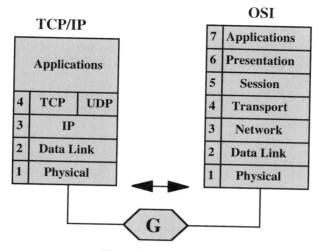

Figure A1.10 Gateways.

INTERNET PROTOCOL

IP is the network layer protocol of the TCP/IP suite. IP provides the addressing and fragmentation functions needed to allow routers to forward packets across a multi-LAN network, often referred to as "internetwork."

IP provides the "best effort" packet delivery service; that is, it attempts to deliver every packet, but has no provision for retransmitting lost or damaged packets. IP leaves such error correction, if required, to higher-level protocols, such as TCP. This trade-off between performance and reliability can be made by the application designer, who can choose a transport-level service meeting the needs of a particular application.

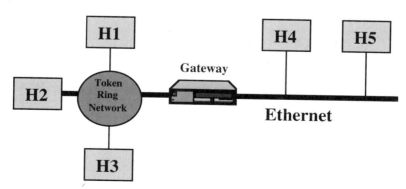

Figure A1.11 Internetworking / Internet example.

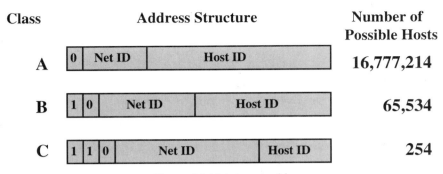

Figure A1.12 Internet address.

IP's addresses, also called Internet addresses, are composed of two parts: the network identifier (Net ID) or network numbering and the host identifier (Host ID) or host address. The network identifier is assigned by a central authority; it specifies the addresses of each network or related group of networks. Each network ID must be unique across the entire Internet. The host identifier specifies a particular host (station, node) within a given network. Host IDs are assigned by the local network administrator. Host IDs need only be unique within their own network, since each network will have a different network ID.

LAN

LANs (Figure A1.13) are high-bandwidth networks designed for geographically local areas, such as a building or a campus. A typical LAN can support hundreds of users from distances of 100 meters to over a kilometer and at speeds in excess of 10 Mbps. These characteristics have made LANs ideal for office and manufacturing applications using microprocessors and workstations.

LANs operate by providing a high-bandwidth channel shared by all processors (nodes) connected to it. Only one node—printer, microprocessor, file server—can transmit at a time. Many nodes can share the LAN, switching from one transmitter to another within microseconds. Many such computers can share a single LAN because most applications on networked computers need the use of the LAN only for a small fraction of time.

The two most common LAN technologies employed today are Ethernet (IEEE 802.3) and token ring (IEEE 802.5). Ethernet was pioneered by Xerox on the 1970s. The token ring was developed and proposed by IBM in the 1980s. Both are IEEE 802 standards and are very widely used.

LAN MEDIA

Regardless of the access method, LANs can use different media as required. LANs can use unshielded twisted pair, shielded twisted pair, coaxial, fiber optic, and even radio signals.

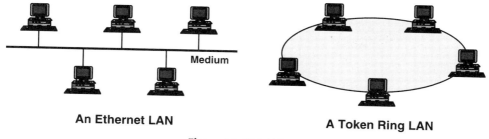

Figure A1.13 LANs.

Each medium has specific characteristics which help in choosing these media for a particular LAN.

- Unshielded twisted-pair cable (UTP) has the poorest signal quality and is limited up to 75 meters. This is the most popular LAN media since UTP is same as the telephone wiring and every modern building already has an elaborate network of telephone lines. UTP is used with wiring hubs, which form a central connection point for a group of workstations, each of which has a UTP point-to-point connection to the hub.
- Shielded twisted-pair cable (STP) is less prone to noise than the UTP.
- Coaxial cable or coax provides the highest noise immunity and longest distances of the metallic media.
- Fiber optic cable has the best noise immunity, can be used for distances over a kilometer, and can support very high data rates.

MANAGEMENT INFORMATION BASE

A MIB is a collection of managed objects residing in a virtual information store. Collections of related managed objects are defined in specific MIB modules.

The management information base is conceptually a database containing all management information related to the local node. Management information—called *objects*—contain attributes about certain characteristics of a managed element (e.g., error counters, timers). Therefore, a managed object contain attributes that define the characteristics of the object. A managed object can be defined for any resource that the manager application needs to monitor and/or control. The collection of management data definitions that a manager or an agent knows about is called its MIB.

Each element within the network maintains a MIB containing objects specific to that device. Therefore, the MIB for a LAN bridge would contain different objects than a MIB for a host computer. The manager maintains a MIB containing information about each device in the network. The manager uses its MIB to archive management data for functions such as report generation and trend analysis. A manager sends commands querying for MIB information contained in network elements using a common network management protocol. The station receiving the manager's command, queries the local MIB and replies with the requested management data.

MIB definitions are different for OSI and TCP/IP networks. TCP/IP currently has MIB I and MIB II defined for use. MIB II is a superset of the original MIB defining more than 200 objects. The management data definition approach used for the OSI MIB is general but rigorous. It is an object-oriented data modeling technique that defines the elements being managed as *objects*, which are described in terms of their *attributes*. Object definitions also include a list of actions that an object can perform (e.g., modem running a line test) and a list of events (e.g., alarms) that the object can generate.

MIB extensions are vendor-specific objects, available only with that vendor's product. A management application can access only the information it knows how to ask for. Thus, for a management station to manage vendor-specific extensions to an existing MIB, the manager must be configured with that vendor's private MIB extensions. Otherwise, the manager application cannot take advantage of those MIB extensions.

MULTIPORT BRIDGES

Bridges with three or more data link interfaces or ports are known as multiport bridges. Such bridges are used to connect more than two LAN segments together at a single point. A single multiport bridge can be used to replace several two-port bridges connected together via a backbone LAN (most commonly an FDDI LAN). The multiport bridge provides higher performance because packets are switched from one LAN to another using an internal I/O bus or memory. Multiport bridges also filter and forward packets like any other bridge.

NETVIEW

NetView is a network management system product from IBM. It runs on an IBM mainframe as well as on RS/6000 workstations. It was primarily designed to manage SNA networks, but now it has been extended to manage non-SNA networks also. NetView includes terminal-oriented display facilities, information gathering protocols, database, and report-generation components. In addition, NetView can accept alarms and other management information from lower-level network management systems.

NETWORK OPERATING SYSTEM

Network operating systems are what finally makes all that hardware function as a network. Originally, NOSs functioned to allow sharing of printers and disk files with limited access by a workstation. However, today's NOSs provide the basis for client/server applications, integrating computers of many types and sizes.

A network operating system functions in the same way as an OS, except that it works to control multiple computers and peripherals. Its mission is to make shared resources (such as hard drives, CD-ROMs, servers and server-based applications, or printers) local. An individual computer's operating system takes requests from application programs and translates them—one at a time—into actions performed by its monitor, hard disk, diskette, or printer. The NOS, on the other hand, takes requests for services from many application programs and individual computers at the same time and satisfies them using the network's resources.

Like the OS, the NOS is a collection of functions and system calls. Some of them provide and control simultaneous access to disk drives, printers, and other devices—these normally reside on the shared network computer, or *server*. Others intercept and redirect requests for service from the computers themselves and send these requests to the appropriate server—these normally reside on the individual PC or workstation.

Since the communication servers support TCP/IP, IPX, NetBIOS, and other technologies, workstations can be attached to LANs running NetWare, Windows NT, LANtastic, Banyan VINES, LAN Manager, PC LAN, or any other popular network operating system.

There are two main types of NOS networks. The most common type is the *client/server network*, in which the individual workstations function as clients and the shared network computers function as servers. The other type of network is the *peer-to-peer network*, which consists entirely of individual PCs that can function either as client—by making requests for resources from other connected computers—or as servers—by providing resources to other connected computers. Although peer-to-peer networks are making inroads in small businesses and workgroups, they are much too slow and cumbersome to be used to connect an enterprise. In addition, they are not as easy to put together as the client/server arrangements. The most popular peer-to-peer systems can link up to larger client/server networks. The best known client/server NOSs are

- Apple Computer AppleTalk/AppleShare.
- Artisoft LANtastic.
- Banyan VINES.
- Microsoft LAN Manager/IBM OS/2 LAN Server.
- Microsoft Windows for Workgroups and Windows NT.
- Novel NetWare and NetWare Lite.
- Digital's PATHWORKS.

OPEN SYSTEMS INTERCONNECTION

Originally released in 1978, the OSI model describes a network architecture that connects dissimilar devices. The original standard applies to open systems, which are open to each other because they use the same communications protocols or standards. The OSI is concerned with the interconnection between systems—the way they exchange information—rather than the internal functions of particular systems.

The OSI Reference Model

In 1984, a revised version of the OSI model was released, and this has since become an international (de jure) standard. Many computer manufacturers have modified their layer network architectures to comply with the layers of the OSI. This seven-layered model is also referred to as the ISO OSI (Open Systems Interconnection) Reference Model. The model has seven layers and the principles that were applied to arrive at the seven layers are as follows:

- A layer should be created where a different level of abstraction is needed.
- Each layer should perform a well-defined function.
- The function of each layer should be chosen with an eye toward defining internationally standardized protocols.
- The layer boundaries should be chosen to minimize the information flow across the interfaces.
- The number of layers should be large enough that distinct functions need not be thrown together in the same layer out of necessity and small enough that the architecture does not become unwieldy.

Each layer of the OSI Reference Model (Figure A1.14) performs a particular, self-contained function. Layering ensures modularity, theoretically allowing a user to substitute one OSI protocol for another at a given layer, without disrupting the protocols/functions above/below that layer. The effect of this is to distribute the work across the layers, which operate in a peer-to-peer fashion. Peer layers are equally ranked layers that communicate with one another by means of peer protocols.

The Layers

Figure A1.14 demonstrates the OSI model layered structure with seven functional levels.
- The *physical layer* (layer 1) is indirectly connected to the physical medium (usually wires) between the systems. This layer controls, among other things, the exchange of individual information bits (relating to transmission rate, bit coding, connection, etc.) over a transmission medium which lies below the physical layer. The design issues here largely deal with mechanical, electrical, and procedural interfaces.

  Examples of the media include fiber optic cable, coaxial cable (thick, thin, and CATV cable), shielded twisted-pair (STP) wire, and unshielded twisted-pair (UTP) wire used for inside telephone wiring as well as LAN connections. Of these technologies, UTP is the least expensive, particularly when using the existing telephone wire for data communications. However, STP and coax are less susceptible to interference than the UTP and can thus bear heavier traffic and higher data speeds.

  Fiber optic cable, the most expensive solution, supports the highest data rates with the least amount of signal degradation. The standards for fiber optic networks, fiber distributed data interface (FDDI), transcend layers 1 and 2.

OSI Model

7	Applications
6	Presentation
5	Session
4	Transport
3	Network
2	Data Link
1	Physical

Figure A1.14 OSI Reference Model.

Computers (minicomputers, workstations, and/or PCs) are often connected over local area networks using thick or thin coax or 10BASET UTP. In some organizations, multiple lower-speed LANs may be interconnected by a higher-speed backbone LAN. Backbone LANs are typically coaxial or fiber optic cables.

• The *data link layer* (layer 2) specifies *how* data are transmitted on one physical link (e.g., between a client and a server). It controls the flow of data and the correction and detection of errors. In local area networks, this includes control of the access to the medium, dictating which system can use the network. The task of this layer is to ensure the reliable transmission of information units (packets or blocks) and to address stations connected to the transmission medium. In other words, this layer provides reliable data transmission from one node to another and shields the higher layers from concern for the physical transmission medium. It is responsible for error-free transmission of frames of data.

The data link layer is divided into two sublayers: the media access control (MAC) and the logical link control (LLC). The lower layer, MAC, provides shared access to the physical layer of the network, while the upper sublayer, LLC, provides a data link service to higher levels of the OSI protocols.

The most popular layer 2 standard in internetworking environment is IEEE 802.3/Ethernet. The other major data link layer technology is token ring (IEEE 802.5). Token ring is more robust and more expensive than Ethernet. Therefore, Ethernet is more prevalent in LAN environments.

FDDI standards at the data link layer include FDDI media control access and logical link control.

Frame relay is another layer 2 standard which is fast and inexpensive for LAN interconnection over the wide area. Frame relay is a packet-switching technology similar to X.25, but without the overhead incurred by intermediate node error correction.

• The *network layer* (layer 3) routes and delivers data from one network node to another. It controls routing, flow control, and sequencing functions. It establishes, maintains, and terminates the network connection between two users and transfers data along that connection. It also does fragmentation and reassembly. Only one network connection can exist between two nodes. This activity includes handing off messages from one segment to another without the need to know the final destination. If there is no direct connection between the two systems that wish to communicate, the network layer finds what intermediate system can relay the messages to their destination.

When a message (packet or block) has to travel from one network to another, many problems can arise: the addressing scheme may be different for each network, or the packet may not be accepted because it is too large or the protocols may differ. Therefore, it is up to the network layer to overcome such problems to allow heterogeneous networks to be interconnected.

The most widely used protocols are the Internet Protocol (IP) and the X.25 packet-switching interface. IP, the "lower half" of TCP/IP, is designed to interconnect LANs over a variety of layer 2 protocols, such as 802.3/Ethernet, 802.5/token ring, RS-232C, and the X.25. In interconnected networks, IP is often used to overcome Ethernet's distance limitations (about one kilometer) by supporting communications over network bridges and routers. X.25 is often used in conjunction with IP to support wide area data networking (7 to 7000 kilometers).

- The *transport layer* (layer 4) transports messages between communications partners and usually controls the data flow and ensures that the data are not corrupted. It is the join between the upper and lower parts of the model. It provides and monitors the quality of service and error rate. It provides data transfer between two users at an agreed-upon level of quality. When a connection is established between two nodes, this layer selects a particular class of service. That class monitors transmissions to ensure that the appropriate level of quality is maintained and notifies users when transmission quality falls below that level.

  The basic function of this layer is to accept data from the session layer (above), split it into smaller units if necessary, pass these to the network layer, and ensure that all the pieces arrive correctly at the other end. Under normal conditions, the transport layer creates a distinct network connection for each transport connection required by the session layer. If the transport connection requires a high throughput, the transport layer might create multiple network connections, dividing the data among the network connections to improve throughput. On the other hand, it may multiplex several transport connections into the same network connection, to reduce cost. In either case, the transport layer actions are transparent to the session layer.

  The transport layer is true source-to-destination or end-to-end protocol. It must recognize both the addresses of the sender and the receiver. In the lower layers, the protocols are only between each machine and its immediate neighbors, not the ultimate source and destinations.

- The *session layer* (layer 5) provides the services necessary to organize and synchronize the dialog that occurs between users and to manage the data exchange. It negotiates "conversation" between the systems. This layer primarily controls when users can send or receive data. A session might be used to allow a user to log into a remote timesharing system or to transfer a file between two machines.

One of the services of the session layer is to manage dialog control. Sessions can allow traffic to go in both directions at the same time or only in one direction at a time, that is, two railroad tracks versus one. A related service of the session layer is token management. For some protocols, it is essential that both sides do not attempt the same operation simultaneously. To manage this problem, the session layer provides tokens to be exchanged. Only the side holding the token may perform the critical operation. This layer initiates and ends communications between processes (i.e., a logical session).

- The *presentation layer* (layer 6) is responsible for presenting information to the network users in a meaningful way. The presentation layers on the two systems agree on a common representation of the data being exchanged. This may include character-code translation, conversion between ASCII and EBCDIC character sets, or data compression and expansion (encryption/decryption). In particular, unlike all lower layers, the layer 6 is concerned with the syntax and semantics of the information transmitted.

  Most applications do not exchange random binary bit strings. They exchange things such as people names, dates, amounts of money, and invoices. These items are represented as character strings, integers, floating point numbers, and data structures. Different computers (hardware architectures) have different codes for representing character strings, integers, and so on. The job of managing these data disparities is handled by the presentation layer.

- The *application layer* (layer 7) provides common application services and allows application processes access the system interconnection facilities to exchange information, including services to establish and terminate connections between users. It is also used to monitor and manage the systems being interconnected and the various resources they employ. This layer contains a variety of protocols that are commonly needed. Users can take advantage of powerful utilities and applications to help them connect disparate systems, including proprietary systems. Many of the protocols are built into the applications and utilities.

OPEN SHORTEST PATH FIRST

OSPF (Figure A1.15) is considered an improvement over the older router information protocol (RIP) in the protocol suite. OSPF's features include least cost routing, multipath routing, and load balancing. OSPF can:

- Compute the best path through a network based not only on hop count, but also on delay, congestion, and other factors.
- Distribute topology changes through the network faster and with better reliability than RIP.

PACKET

Packet is a logical grouping of information that includes a header and user data (Figure A1.16). In TCP/IP terminology, a packet is the unit of information sent by a data link layer.

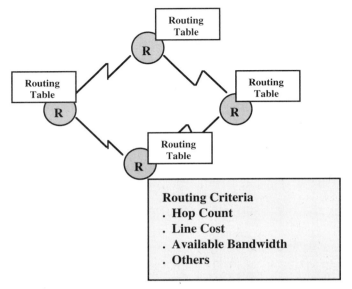

Figure A1.15 Open shortest path first.

Packets typically consist of the contents of a datagram as supplied by the local network layer, with the addition of the data link specific fields, such as link addresses, type field, error control fields, and checksums. Packets on a LAN have lengths dependent on the underlying LAN technology.

POINT-TO-POINT PROTOCOL

PPP can be used on wide area network links such as T1 lines, satellite links, DDS lines, or other non-LAN point-to-point links. PPP is a standard format for use of a serial telecommunications link by routers and other nodes. PPP uses HDLC protocols to define packet boundaries and provides a packet checksum. PPP also includes multiplexing control fields which allow more than one type of protocol to be used over a link, enabling multiprotocol routers to use a PPP link. PPP is significant primarily in providing a multivendor standard over a media which was vendor proprietary.

REPEATERS

Repeaters are hardware devices that operate at the physical layer of the ISO model, repeating all electrical signals from one segment to the other. Repeaters extend the geographic

Figure A1.16 TCP/IP packet with headers.

coverage of a local area network by interconnecting multiple segments. Repeaters also interconnect segments using different physical media such as thick coaxial, thin coaxial, twisted-pair, or fiber optic cables.

Splitting a segment into two or more segments with a repeater allows a network to continue to grow. A repeater connection counts in the total node limit on each segment. For example, a thin coax segment may have 29 processors and 1 repeater, or a thick wire segment can have 5 repeaters and 95 processors.

Remember that at physical layer, there is very little intelligence in any of these units. Repeater units do not know about other repeater units on the network.

Ethernet repeaters are necessary in star topologies. The repeater counts as one node on each segment it connects. A network with only two nodes is of limited use. If the repeater is attached to a backbone, then all computers at the end of the twisted-pair segments can communicate with all the hosts on the backbone.

Repeaters also monitor all connected segments for basic characteristics necessary for Ethernet to run correctly. When a break occurs, all segments in an Ethernet may become inoperable. Repeaters limit the effect of these problems to the faulty section of cable by "segmenting" the network, disconnecting the problem segment and allowing unaffected segments to function normally.

Token ring networks involve three kinds of repeaters: token ring, lobe, and connecting repeater.

- The *token ring repeater* is used when the network has more than one wiring center. This repeater can be used to regenerate both the main ring path and the backup ring path. When the backup path is boosted, it is assumed that the main path is boosted as well.
- The *lobe repeater* boosts the signal only for one lobe attached to a MAU (multistation access units or media attachment units).
- *Connecting repeater* boosts the signals between hubs, usually doubling the distance between hubs.

There are three basic types of repeater units and all three may be intermixed through the use of backbone. These are

- Multiport repeater units, used with 10BASE2 wiring only.
- Multiport receiver units, used with 10BASE5 wiring only.
- Wiring concentrators, used with all types of wiring schemes.

ROUTERS

Routers are devices that interconnect multiple networks, primarily running the same high-level protocols. They operate at the network layer of the ISO model, one layer higher than the bridge. Each network protocol has a routing protocol built into it. Through this, the router accesses the addressing information and shares it with other routers and hosts on the network. Routers have more software intelligence than bridges, provide more sophisticated functions, and are well suited for complex environments or large internetworks.

Unlike bridges, routers support active redundant paths (loops) and allow logical separation of network segments. Routers are also better suited for interconnected network segments using different protocols such as token ring and Ethernet. Because routers are protocol specific, more than one router may be needed to support an enterprise. Some multiprotocol routers can route several protocols simultaneously, thereby approaching the function level of gateways.

The routers are used to route messages through intermediate nodes, not nodes on the same LAN. A router is actually an intermediate station or node. Figure A1.17 demonstrates a router connected to two LANs. Node X on LAN 1 wants to send a packet to node Z on LAN 2. It first sends the message to node Y, the router, The router processes the information embedded in the packet's network layer. Based on that information, node Y forwards the packet to LAN 2 addressed to node Z. This way, the router reads the destination information embedded in the packet and forwards the data to the correct node.

The primary function of a router is to determine the next node to which a packet is sent. To send packets to their destination, a router must perform several functions. When a packet arrives at the router, it holds the packet in queue until it has finished handling the previous packet. The router then scans the destination address and searches in the routing table. The routing table lists the various nodes on the network, the paths between these nodes, and how much it costs to transmit over these paths. If a particular node has more than one path, the router selects the one that is most economical. If the packet is too large for the destination node, the router breaks it into a manageable frame size. This is important in WANs, in which telephone lines provide the link between LANs. With smaller packets, there is less chance that the data will be corrupted by noise on the line.

There are two types of routing mechanisms:

• *Status routing*, where the network manager must configure the routing table. Once these tables are set, the paths on the network never change. This may be acceptable for a small LAN, but it is not practical for wide area networking. A static router may issue an alarm if and when it recognizes a downed link, but it does not automatically reconfigure the routing table or reroute the packet. As new bridges and/or routers are added to the network, the routing tables in the participating network routers or bridges must be manually updated. It is time consuming and frustrating for the administrator to manually update all the routing tables, if a router breaks and is removed from the network. Once the router becomes operational, the routing tables must be updated again to allow other routers to know that this router is again operational.

Source Host

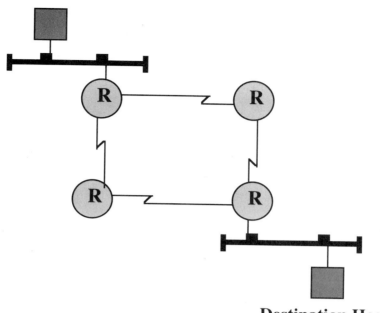

Destination Host

Figure A1.17 A network with routers.

- *Dynamic routing* automatically reconfigures the routing table and recalculates the least expensive path or with the least traffic. Routers periodically send routing tables to one another to identify the routes available to one another. Whenever a new router is added to the network, all other routers will automatically find this router and update their tables as to the new routers' available paths. At the same time, if the routers find a new and better path, the routers will start traversing the new route. Dynamic routing is by far the most advantageous as the administration becomes transparent.

SQL

Structured Query Language (SQL) is a standard relational database access language that facilitates data extraction from client stations (Figure A1.18), regardless of where the required data are located on the network, what database or operating system maintains them, or on what type or vendor computer they are stored on. SQL is well suited for this purpose, since it provides a concise, nonprocedural method of requesting data. Basically, SQL is a specialized programming language in which data are represented as a relational model—where data are held in two-dimensional tables with a simple row and column structure.

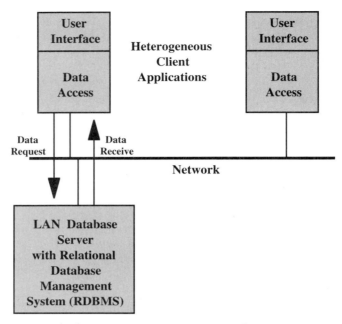

Figure A1.18 How SQL extracts data.

Using SQL as the data access method for client/server applications offers a number of benefits:

- Application programming is simplified for data requests.
- The language is somewhat portable for applications running on different platforms.
- Network traffic is reduced, since only the data request and the requested data are sent over the network.
- Different applications, through standardizing on SQL, can access data stored in the same format—the tables or views maintained by the server.
- SQL makes the task of accessing distributed database servers possible, since the same database access language is used.

With the emergence of an American National Standards Institute (ANSI) standard for SQL, more and more vendors support SQL for their database engines. Because SQL is considered unwieldy in its raw form, software vendors had to overlay it with more user-friendly interface to shield users from having to learn another command syntax. SQL operates in the background, enabling the user to extract data from anywhere on the network.

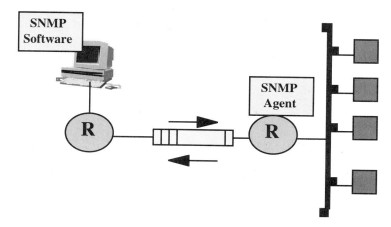

Figure A1.19 SNMP transaction.

SIMPLE NETWORK MANAGEMENT PROTOCOL

SNMP is a protocol defined to aid in managing a network. It provides a means for applications on a network management system (NMS) to get information from another node on the network (Figure A1.19). The information obtained is typically system identification data or counters indicating error rates or performance measures in the node being queried.

SNMP is a transaction (sometimes called query/response) protocol which runs over the UDP transport-level protocol. The management application begins a transaction by sending a packet indicating what action it is requesting either GET data or SET a variable in the remote node to some value). The packet will also include the list of objects (management data variables) requested. The node to which the request is directed will examine the packet and retrieve the requested data. The node will then send back a response packet to the NMS.

Management applications can use SNMP, together with the list of objects which can be obtained, to automatically retrieve and display, save, or analyze data for the network administrator.

TOKEN RING (802.5)

Token ring is another popular approach to local area networking. These networks have become synonymous with IBM, a driving force behind their development at the Zurich Research Laboratory. IBM unveiled the token ring network in 1985.

Token Ring Concepts

The token ring is a series of point-to-point links closed up to form a logical ring that connects the stations (Figure A1.20). Each station is connected to the ring by a repeater, which

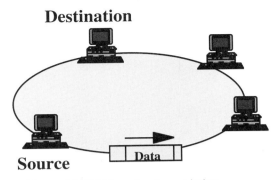

Figure A1.20 Token ring transmission.

is an active device that regenerates all the data flowing on the ring regardless of whether it is in the transmit or receive mode. When a station receives an idle token and has no data to transmit, the token is passed to the next station on the ring. If the station does have data to transmit, the idle token is modified and the information is sent on the network. The destination station then copies the information and passes on the token. All other stations simply regenerate and pass the signal. When the message returns to the originating station, it is removed from the ring and the token is modified to indicate an idle state and forwarded to the next station on the ring.

Token Ring Standards: IEEE 802.5

The token ring architecture is based on the IEEE 802.5 standard. The token ring network uses

- Token passing for access method.
- Shielded and unshielded twisted pair.
- Baseband transmission.
- Star-wired ring technology.
- Transfer rates of 4 Mbps and 16 Mbps.

The token is passed from node to node until a request to transmit data is made. The token, a predetermined formation of bits permits a node to access the cable. The topology is a star wired ring, with the ring formed by the hub. Data flows on the ring only in one direction. The two major versions of token ring have transfer rates of 4 and 16 Mbps, and both use baseband transmission. Both versions use either unshielded or shielded twisted pair. The shielded twisted pair gives better signal reliability and extended signals distances.

A token ring is composed of a number of stations serially connected by a medium. Information is transferred along the ring serially from one node to another. Each station regenerates and repeats each bit and serves as the means for attaching one or more devices to the ring. A station gains transmission access by capturing a token passing on the medium. There are four components that make up the token ring network:

- A network interface card (NIC).
- A multistation access unit (MAU).
- A cabling system.
- Network connectors.

The multistation access unit is the hub of the token ring network. It can connect up to eight nodes. For additional nodes, more MAUs can be added with gross total of up to 72 nodes. The MAUs form the ring portion of the network and the nodes create a star. When the maximum number of nodes on a token ring network has been reached, another network must be established. The MAUs may be in the same physical area or can be separated, but they must be connected to form a ring. The maximum cabling distance from the MAU to the node is from 150 to 500 feet, depending upon the implementation and cable types. Many different types of cabling can be used, including the preexisting telephone wiring.

The IEEE 802.5 standard defines a set of services to be provided by the MAC sublayer of a token ring network. It includes frame transmission, token transmission, stripping, frame reception, priority operation, beaconing, and neighbor notification.

Token Ring Access Control

Token passing is an access method where a node can only transmit on the network when it has the token. The high-speed fiber optic networks also use token passing. Station entry into the ring is controlled by the station itself. The insertion and ring bypass mechanism reside in the trunk coupling unit, which the media interface cable controls.

TRANSMISSION CONTROL PROTOCOL SUITE

The TCP/IP four-layer protocol stack, which began as an experimental approach to connecting networks, was created by the Internet user community in the 1970s to replace the original DOD NCP. The Internet community continues to nurture and augment the protocols today. Much of TCP/IP success is rooted in the Internet community's heritage.

The TCP/IP technology is maturing and vendors can more easily implement it. During the past decade, TCP/IP has come out of the campus lab and into the corporate data center. Commercial users are finding it a quick and readily available way to solve their interoperability problems. TCP/IP has become the "glue" of choice for communicating among dissimilar operating systems. TCP/IP is the most prevalent networking architecture in use today and its implementation is growing.

TCP/IP follows a layered approach to networking (Figure A1.21). Layer 1 is the network access layer, equivalent to both physical and data link layers of the OSI model,

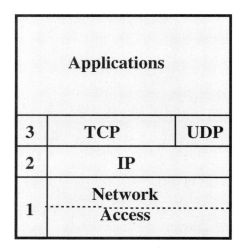

Figure A1.21 TCP/IP protocol suite.

sends data between two processors in the same network. Layer 2 is the Internet Protocol layer (IP), which routes data among more than one network. These networks can be the same or different types. These three layers are also referred to as "lower layers" and essentially perform the networking functions. These layers are functionally equivalent to other networking architectures, such as SNA, OSI, and DECnet.

Layer 3, considered the reliability layer, is the Transmission Control Protocol layer (TCP), in charge of sending the data in sequence and without errors. This layer also includes another protocol, known as User Datagram Protocol (UDP), which allows users to send messages without connection establishment and without any guarantee of delivery or sequencing. Layer 3 is also termed as "transport" layer.

The layers above are termed as "applications" or "process" layers, which provide the services for three types of applications—electronic mail (SMTP), file transfer (FTP and TFTP), and terminal emulation (TELNET). Other TCP/IP protocols, in addition to the four-layer model, include the simple network management protocol (SNMP), developed to manage multiple vendors' products and is considered the de facto standard for managing different devices.

TRANSMISSION CONTROL PROTOCOL

TCP (Figure A1.22) is the primary protocol used in the Internet Protocol suite for reliable transmission of data from one host to another. TCP is a level 4 (of the OSI model) or transport-level protocol. TCP is used by Telnet, FTP, e-mail, and other applications.

TCP provides a reliable data delivery service with detection of, and recovery from, lost, duplicated, or corrupted packets. TCP designed to work with networks which provide a minimal level of service. Two hosts communicate via TCP by setting up a connection

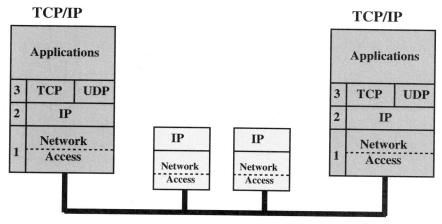

Figure A1.22 Transmission Control Protocol.

(virtual circuit) between them. Establishing a connection results in each host setting aside a small amount of memory to save information about the connection, such as how much data have been received, what data have been acknowledged, and other information.

TCP accepts arbitrary-sized blocks of information called messages from applications. It divides them into smaller blocks called "segments" for transmission across the network. To each segment, TCP adds a header containing certain control fields to be used by the receiver's TCP, such as the sequence number and acknowledgment number. Each byte of data in a segment has a sequence number associated with it. The header sequence number is the sequence number of the first data byte in the segment.

When a TCP module receives a segment from the network, it checks the sequence number to see if the segment contains the next expected sequence of data. If so, TCP retains the data and sends an acknowledgment segment back to the sender's TCP. The acknowledgment field has the sequence number, plus one, of the last byte of data in the received data segment. The acknowledgment number is therefore the sequence number of the next byte of data the receiving TCP module expects to see.

Sequence numbers, combined with acknowledgment ("acks"), are used by most computer network protocols which provide highly reliable data delivery. TCP has a sequence number and acknowledgment field in its header to provide a high level of reliability and integrity in its data delivery service. These fields are used as follows to provide TCP's error control:

- TCP considers the data it sends on any particular connection to be a continuous stream of bytes, with each byte of data having a sequence number. Each segment sent by TCP has a header, which includes a sequence number field. This field contains the sequence number of the first byte of data in the segment. The sequence number of any byte of data in the segment can be computed from its position in the segment. Successive segments continue the sequence numbering, with the first data byte in a segment having a sequence number greater than the sequence of the last byte of previous segment.

- For example, a segment containing 800 bytes of data is sent with a sequence number of 40,000. The sequence number of the first byte is therefore 40,000, the sequence of the second byte in the segment is 40,001, and the sequence of the last byte of data is 40,779. The next data packet transmitted by this TCP module under normal circumstances will have a sequence number field of 40,800.

- The sequence number is a 32-bit field, or about 4.2 billion bytes can be transmitted on a connection before a sequence number will be reused.

- When a TCP module receives a segment it checks the sequence number to see if these data have previously been received. If so, the segment is a duplicate of one previously received and can be safely discarded.

- However, under normal circumstances, the segment will contain new data, so the receiving TCP will deliver the data to its higher-level application and send an acknowledgment segment back to the sender TCP. The acknowledgment field in the header of this segment acknowledges the data just received. The field will contain the sequence number of the next data byte the receiving TCP expects to receive, that is, one more than the sequence number of the last data byte in the segment just received. TCP will also remember this acknowledgment number for checking future packets for duplicate data.

- When the sender receives the acknowledgment segment, it knows that all data numbered lower than the acknowledgment field was successfully received. The next data segment it transmits will therefore start with the data byte whose sequence number equals the just received acknowledgment.

- For example, when the segment of the previous example (sequence = 40,000, length = 800) is received, the receiving TCP will send back a segment with an acknowledgment field set to 40,800, indicating the next data sequence number it wants to receive from the sender TCP. If the sender TCP has data to transmit, its next segment will have a sequence number of 40,800.

WANS

Today's enterprise networks consist of LANs of various protocols, supporting myriad media and architectures, connected to wide area networks consisting of a variety of communication systems. These complex networks span cities, countries, and continents and are being influenced by emerging technologies driven by user demands and vendor innovations.

Designing a LAN-to-WAN internetworking system and managing it successfully demands in-depth knowledge of these technologies. While it is possible to exercise sufficient control over the LAN segments of the network, the WAN portions are usually leased from service providers that offer a variety of control options.

The industry offers several WAN segment options depending on whether the information is to be packet switched or frame relayed once it leaves the source LAN segment and reaches the destination LAN node. The information can be transmitted through physical media such as twisted-pair copper wire and fiber optic lines or broadcast over microwave or satellite.

Depending on the transmission technologies used, available WAN options can be categorized as follows:

- Switching systems (circuit or packet switching).
- Frame relay systems.
- Broadcast systems (satellite or microwave).
- X.25 Newtworks.

Switching Systems

Switching systems are physically connected through nodes using one or more media types. Links are established between nodes to enable the signals to pass through them on their way to the addressed node.

Circuit-switching systems establish dedicated circuits between the nodes before the data signals are transmitted. The data path is established between the source and the destination nodes before the data are sent. Circuit-switching systems send exploratory signals requesting the transmission path to the addressed node. Intermittent nodes examine the request and determine which downstream circuit paths are available for connection. Once all circuits or paths are switched and a source to destination dedicated link is established, the source is ready to transmit the signals. The data signals can be digital, analog, or integrated analog/digital. The circuit is dedicated as long as the connection is required and is disconnected as soon as the transmission is completed.

Packet-switching systems are also known as packet data networks (PDNs). Packet-switching systems combine the advantages of message and circuit switching. The data are broken into small chunks or packets, consisting of header information and user-defined data, and transmitted packet by packet. Different packets can be launched along different network paths and are received at the destination node where they are reassembled to form a complete message.

Packet switching can use two methods to transmit streams of data from source to destination. In the datagram approach, each packet is treated as an independent entity— is received and launched on different links—and the X.25 interface at the receiving end strips the headers and reassembles them in proper sequence, before delivering them to addressed node. The X.25 packet-switching standard uses this approach. The "virtual circuit" approach establishes a logical connection between the source and the destination before packets are transmitted, and the network makes sure that a link is established by exploring the available links, giving the appearance that a dedicated link has been established.

Frame Relay Systems

Frame differs from a packet in its length and header. A frame can be a bit or character oriented. Frame relay uses separate channel for control characters or header/trailer information, while packet switching uses the same channel for both control and user-defined data streams. Frame relaying is performed by setting up a virtual circuit between the source and the destination. Frame relay is a connectionless service that provides flow and error control in addition to other standard services.

Frame relay is particularly suited for bursty traffic, because it offers better routing and error detection. It can be employed in connecting disparate LANs over wide area links. There are number of different services that frame relay technology utilizes:

- Lease line services which operates at 56 Kb ps, primarily from the telephone carriers.
- T1 service, which offers transmission facilities for both voice or data or integrated voice/data signals with a data transmission capability of 1.544 Mb pso.
- T3 service with transmission speeds of 44.736 Mb pso.
- Fractional T1 services that enable the user to lease T1 lines but pay only for required bandwidth; these operate at any multiple of 64 Kb ps up to 768 Kb ps.

Broadcast Systems

Broadcast systems offer several advantages and some disadvantages, over copper wire and fiber optic lines. Broadcast systems can be divided into two main types: satellite and microwave.

Satellite. Satellite systems use geostationary satellites that are positioned 22,300 miles over the earth and maintain the same relative position over the face of the earth. The satellites are in communication with the earth stations that are equipped with large dish antennas. The earth stations act as transmitter/receiver entities with the ability to transmit and receive signals from the satellite. A satellite is a kind of microwave relay station.

Satellite systems have been used for television program distribution, long-distance telephone networks, private networks, and mobile systems.

Microwave. Microwave radio transmissions are used by common carrier service providers for long-distance communication transmissions. Both analog and digital signals can be carried by microwave.

X.25 Networks

X.25 is probably the best known and most widely used protocol. It is also most commonly associated with the ISO model. X.25 was established as a recommendation by CCITT. X.25 has been adopted by public data networks throughout Europe and the United States.

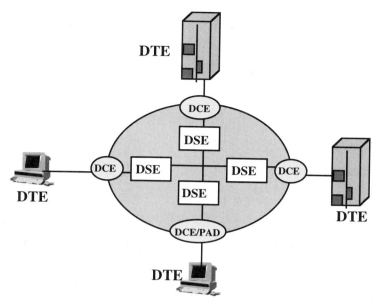

Figure A1.23 X.25 network.

Architecturally, in X.25, a network operates like a telephone system. X.25 network is assumed to consist of complex packet switches that contain the intelligence needed to route packets. Hosts do not attach directly to communication wires of the network.

X.25 is actually a family of protocols that define how a user of the network, known as data terminal equipment (DTE), communicates with the boundary of the network, known as data circuit-terminating equipment (DCE). Once a packet of information is presented to DCE, the X.25 network routes the information to the DCE closest to the destination DTE. Figure A1.23 shows the basic components of an X.25 network.

APPENDIX **II**

ANSWERS TO EXERCISES

Chapter 1 Overview
Chapter 2 Internetworking Basic
   Concepts
Chapter 3 Standards and Protocols
Chapter 4 Network Building Blocks
Chapter 5 Internetworking Protocols–I
Chapter 6 Internetworking Protocols–II
Chapter 7 Internetworking Tools
Chapter 8 Applications
Chapter 9 UNIX Internetworking
Chapter 10 Integrating the Desktop

Chapter 11 Integrating UNIX and the PCs
   (X Windows)
Chapter 12 Internetworking with Mac
Chapter 13 Integrating Legacy Networks
Chapter 14 Internetwork Troubleshooting
   and Monitoring–I
Chapter 15 Internetwork Troubleshooting
   and Monitoring–II
Chapter 16 Troubleshooting a Global
   Network (An Example)
Chapter 17 Managing Networks

CHAPTER 1 OVERVIEW

1.1   a. No, a dumb terminal has no computing power of its own.

     b. No, the PC was not prevalent until the 1980s.

     c. Yes, the mainframe was an important resource for computing.

     d. No, the cluster controller allowed several terminals to access the computing power of the mainframe.

     e. No, the front-end processor allowed a mainframe computer to communicate with other network equipment

1.2   a. No, use of many different devices does not imply decentralization.

     b. No, many users can access the host.

     c. Yes, decentralization means computing power is no longer centralized in one location.

1.3   a. Yes, personal computers can perform independent computing.

     b. Yes, PCs can perform terminal emulation.

     c. Yes, PCs can download host files.

1.4   An internetwork consists of one or more linked networks. These networks may have to traverse diverse operating environments or diverse networking protocols.

Internetworking encompasses the increasingly complex process of delivering data from one network segment to another. In distributed network environments, data traveling across internetwork links can traverse one or more intermediate network (e.g., wide area networks, or WANs) connections. The type of data which travels over internetwork links is rapidly expanding to include client/server applications, fax, video, and voice.

1.5   A hybrid network is an internetwork, sort of global in nature, but utilizes many different access media, transmission media, network protocols, diverse LAN topologies, and transport technologies.

1.6   The term *client/server* has multiple meanings and is sometimes used interchangeably with the term "cooperative processing." In general, client/server computing refers to the situation when some application functions—particularly those which deal with user interfaces—are separated from the internals of application processing. The client systems tend to be of the display-oriented desktop variety, such as personal computers or workstations. Servers range from desktop systems to mainframes or supercomputers. The personal computer revolution of the 1980s brought the realization of client/server computing.

CHAPTER 2 INTERNETWORKING BASIC CONCEPTS

2.1   Internetworking encompasses the increasingly complex process of delivering data from one network segment to another. In distributed network environments, data traveling across internetwork links can traverse one or more intermediate network (e.g., wide area networks) connections. The type of data which travels over internetwork links is rapidly expanding to include client/server applications, fax, video, and voice. Depending on budget and bandwidth requirements, internetwork equipment ranges from inexpensive dial-up modems, to bridges or routers with WAN interfaces, to sophisticated ATM, and like switches.

Today's enterprise networks consist of LANs of various protocols, supporting a variety of media and architectures, connected to wide area networks consisting of a variety of communication systems. These complex networks span cities, countries, and continents and are being influenced by emerging technologies driven by user demands and vendor innovations. Managing these disparate systems can be a formidable challenge.

2.2   Any internetwork is dependent upon the following four basic components:

- Devices
- Network technologies,
- Network architectures/protocols

- Interconnecting devices and networks.

2.3   The major devices used in a network are

- *Terminals* provide the interface between people and the network. IBM 3270-family terminals, ASCII terminals, and personal computers emulating terminals are the most popular types of terminals. Most personal computers are ASCII devices and do not use IBM EBCDIC standards.

- *Protocol converters* are used to translate between terminal's ASCII coding to IBM's EBCDIC coding.

- *Modems* connect a terminal to a network using public telephone lines instead of being hard wired to a network or mainframe.

- *Physical interfaces* such as RS-232, V.35, and RS-449 are used to connect modems to clusters or communication controllers.

- *Communications controllers* improve performance of a host computer by handling communications functions of the hosts and terminals.

- *Cluster controllers* control a cluster of 8 to 32 terminals or printers. A cluster controller is connected to a host using a channel or can be linked to a communications controller.

- *Front-end processors* (FEPs) are placed between a host computer and other communications controllers or cluster controllers.

- *Concentrators* control a number of cluster controllers, terminals, and remote job entry (RJE) devices.

- *Digital switch* is occasionally used as a communications controller and has ports to provide data communication.

- *Multiplexers* combine the data traffic from communications controllers, digitized voice traffic from PBXs, and digitized video traffic into high-bandwidth traffic such as 1.544 Mbps (DS-1) or 435 Mbps (DS-3). These DS-1 or DS-3 facilities are interconnected to provide a backbone network.

2.4   The most common and popular networking operating systems are

- Novell's NetWare
- Microsoft's LAN Manager
- IBM's LAN Server
- Banyan VINES

2.5   The prevalent networks are

- Departmental or workgroup networks
- Campus networks
- Metropolitan networks
- Enterprise networks
- Hybrid networks
- Global networks

CHAPTER 3 STANDARDS AND PROTOCOLS

3.1 *De jure* standards, also known as public standards, exist because they are produced by a legal body to produce standards, usually by consensus. Due to the inevitable combinations of interests involved in reaching a consensus, *de jure* standards invariably take longer to come into use than the industry driven de facto standards. Even though OSI is a well-defined model, all the protocols have not been fully defined yet.

De facto standards do not have to observe the consensus diplomacy in their production. Indeed, many de facto standards are not the result of consensus but a conscious effort to produce a standard, many times from practical implementations (e.g., SNA, DNA). Instead, they originate innovative ideas or attractive products which come to be accepted as standards in the course of time, for example, TCP/IP.

3.2 Multiple vendors implement multiple hardware platforms with multiple operating systems and networking architectures. This makes internetworking very complex if not impossible. Because of competitive pressures, we need standards to implement solutions that are simpler and provide better price/performance.

3.3 DFS is stateful, whereas NFS is stateless.

3.4 TCP/IP is the most popular since it is easier to implement and is well defined.

3.5 Most of them utilize a layered approach and have the following common characteristics:

- Are based on a seven-layer hierarchical model.
- Provide two types of services: connectionless and connection oriented.
- Provide reliable and unreliable delivery of services.
- Provide mechanisms to connect via gateways, routers, or bridges, with incompatible protocols.
- Use the lower three layers of the OSI model as a basis for connectivity and communications.
- Move slowly toward conformance with OSI protocol philosophies.

CHAPTER 4 NETWORK BUILDING BLOCKS

4.1 There are four basic topologies for LAN configurations. The most common topologies are star, bus, ring, and tree topologies. However, in practice, there is no specific topology that must be utilized with any one LAN.

4.2 The bus topology is simple to layout with short cable requirements. In addition, traffic flow is relatively simple to control.

4.3 Define each of the following:

Gateway converts protocols.

Bridge divides LANs into segments.

Repeater regenerates signals.

Router chooses best path to next device.

4.4 DECnet and SNA are examples of PC LANs? False.

4.5 Which of the following devices can be found in modern PC LANs? (Circle all that apply.)

a. Right, mainframe can be integrated into PC LANs.

b. Right, minicomputer.

c. Right, engineering workstation.

d. Right, PC or microprocessor.

4.6 Match each of the following terms to its best description.

a. Downsizing

b. Internetworking

c. Peer-to-peer

d. Client/server

b__ Communication between equipment from different manufacturers.

d__ LAN architecture which stores files on a centralized server.

c__ LAN architecture in which workstations are also used as servers.

d__ Type of application.

a__ Substitution of microcomputer processing for mainframe.

4.7 Write Ethernet's characteristics in the blanks below.

IEEE 802.3_____Standard

10 Mbps _____Data rate

CSMA/CD _____Access method

4.8 Write token ring's characteristics in the blanks below.

IEEE 802.5 _____ Standard

4 or 16 Mbps _____ Data rate

Token passing _____ Access method

4.9 Number the following CSMA/CD events in the proper order.

5___ Retransmit.

3___ Hear collision.

4___ Wait specified time and listen.

1___ Listen for transmission on LAN.

2___ Transmit.

4.10 TCP/IP is described by which of the following? (Circle all that apply.)

a. Right, an example of communication protocols.

b. Right, a protocol suite.

c. Right, contains transmission and Internet protocols.

d. No, not an implementation of the OSI model.

e. Right, allows dissimilar equipment to communicate.

CHAPTER 5 INTERNETWORKING PROTOCOLS—I

5.1 TCP protocols provide reliable end-to-end delivery. TCP uses sequence numbers, checksums, and segment retransmissions after time-outs. TCP also uses elaborate flow control, error checking, and ordered data delivery.

UDP, on the other hand, does not guarantee delivery. UDP allows messaging with minimum of protocol mechanism or overhead without error checking or retransmissions. However, UDP is more efficient for communications such as telephone.

5.2 32 bits or 4 bytes or 4 octets are correct answers.

5.3 The OSI has seven well-defined layers; the lower four, or subnetworking layers, and the upper three, sessions, presentation, application, layers.

TCP/IP combines the upper three layers into application or process layers and leaves the presentation and session services to the application protocols and the user applications.

5.4 TRAP, SET, and GET are the most common commands for SNMP.

5.5 False. IP provides unreliable packet delivery and has no way to provide error checking. IP is also a connectionless protocol and, therefore, does not receive acknowledgments of data. These services are provided by a higher-layer protocol such as TCP. In practice, IP packets travel through the network with minimal errors.

5.6 IP is part of the network layer (layers 3) of the protocol suite. The main tasks of IP are the addressing of the computers (destination and source) and fragmentation of packets.

5.7 False. A file can be accessed by an application without any direct user involvement.

5.8 Connection-oriented service is similar to a telephone conversation. First, you make the connection and after acknowledgments only then the conversation begins. In contrast, the connectionless service is modeled after the postal system. Each message carries the full address and data and is carried through the system independent of all others. Normally, there are no acknowledgments or sequencing.

5.9 TCP protects the destination from being overwhelmed with data through flow control. It ensures that the messages are reliably received at the destination.

No. Although sequence numbers are added to the header, these numbers do not control the path taken to the destination.

5.10 Local area network protocols provide reliable data transmission from one node to another and are responsible for error-free transmission of frames of data. These protocols are defined for the data link layer (layer 2) of the OSI Reference Model. LANs like Ethernet are defined by IEEE in the upper part of the link layer, known as media access control layer.

CHAPTER 6 INTERNETWORKING PROTOCOLS—II

6.1 NetBIOS is a session layer interface, and does not have a definition at the network layer, and provides the following services:
   - Name service
   - Session service
   - Datagram service
   - General services

6.2 Prior to the 1980s, the primary resources used were
   - a. No, not a dumb terminal since it has no computing resources.
   - b. No, not a PC since it was not prevalent prior to 1980s.
   - c. Yes, a mainframe was the primary and important source.

6.3 The trend toward decentralization is best illustrated by
   - a. No, different devices do not imply decentralization.
   - b. No, often many users can access a host.
   - c. Yes, computing power exists at widespread locations. Decentralization means computing power is no longer centralized in one location.

6.4
   - a. Yes, user A computes marketing statistics; user B incorporates these in a report. Distributed processing implies that parts of a computing job are done at various locations.
   - b. Yes, a mainframe at San Francisco downloads manufacturing specification to a workstation in Los Angeles, where they are matched to other data.
   - c. No, there is only one device working on the problem when a programmer in Chicago is entering data.

6.5
   - a. Yes, independent computing is a major benefit of the PC.
   - b. Yes, terminal emulation on a PC can perform as a dumb terminal, if necessary.
   - c. Yes, a PC can download files or data from a host and then process them.

6.6
   - a. Yes, a 56 Kbps line.
   - b. Yes, a T1 line.
   - c. Yes, a fractional T1 line.
   - d. No, a LAN is typically implemented by the enterprise users.

6.7
   - a. No, a message may travel through any one of several routes.
   - b. No, X.25 is not necessarily the most inexpensive option.
   - c. Yes, parts of the message can take different routes and be received correctly.

6.8
   - a. No, connected devices also must be able to communicate.
   - b. No, using just a component of LAN does not imply interoperability.
   - c. Yes, interoperability is communication between devices and applications.

6.9 X.25 is primarily based on the OSI Reference Model and essentially defines the lower three layers of the OSI model. TCP/IP is almost equivalent to the OSI lower layers.

Since SNA is an older standard, the implementation is different and is hierarchical in nature, even though the layering scheme is similar.

6.10 Depending on the transmission technologies, available WAN options can be categorized as

- Switching systems (circuit or packet switching) where systems are connected through nodes using more or more media types.

- Frame relay systems where the information is relayed by setting up virtual circuits instead of direct connections.

- Broadcast systems use satellite or microwave and do not employ any physical media for connectivity between source and destination.

CHAPTER 7 INTERNETWORKING TOOLS

7.1 There are basically five types of devices that facilitate internetworking:

Repeaters are used to enhance the signals so that the network segments can be extended. Repeaters are hardware devices and operate at the physical layer of the ISO model.

Bridges are also hardware devices, but are a little more intelligent than the repeaters. Bridges are used to partition traffic. Bridges filter and forward data packets from one network segment to another. They operate at the data link layer of the ISO model.

Routers are devices that interconnect multiple networks. Routers, as the name suggests, are used to route data packets. These are intelligent devices and keep a map of the nodes connected in the network. Routers operate at the network layer of the ISO model.

Gateways are the most sophisticated of all the tools. Gateways can be hardware, software, or a combination of both. These operate at all seven layers of the ISO model. Gateways are either used for protocol/data conversion or encapsulation.

Brouters are bridges and routers, residing in the same box or functionally used for functions of either.

7.2 The bridge is a simple device, used to filter and forward a data packet from one node to another in a different network. The router is a sophisticated tool that routes the traffic via the most efficient route possible and provides some network management functions.

7.3 An Ethernet LAN will communicate with another LAN on SNA network via a gateway. This gateway will normally provide protocol encapsulation for SNA.

7.4 The repeater works at the physical layer. Its primary function is to enhance the signal so that different segments of a network can be interconnected without degradation. However, there is a limit as to how many repeaters can be used between source and destination nodes.

7.5 Gateways can be both hardware and software devices. Software gateways are the most common since they must provide either protocol encapsulation or conversion at each layer.

7.6   Brouters act as two devices, bridges and routers. These functions can be used interchangeably depending upon the implementation requirements of the network and the device itself.

7.7   Gateway: works at all seven layers.

Router: works at network or routing layer.

Bridge: works at data link layer for transmission of packets.

Repeater: works at physical layer for extending the length of the physical network.

Brouter: is a combination of bridges and routers in a single device. It either works as a bridge or a router, depending upon the specific network requirements.

CHAPTER 8 APPLICATIONS

8.1   The most common network applications include

- Terminal emulation.
- Electronic mail.
- File transfer/exchange.
- Database.
- Directory services.

8.2   A network operating system frequently provides a mail-like utility that allows for basic communication among all the machines on a network. Most network operating systems allow the users to send files. Network security is usually under the control of the network administrator, using services provided by the network operating system. Most network operating systems provide the following services to the users/networks:

- *File services* allow users to share data and storage devices on the network. The network also provides centralized backup, data integrity, and data security resources.

- *Print services* allow workstations to share printers and administer printer sharing by building a queue that serves as a storage zone or buffer on the file server.

- *Administration utilities* include utilities that manage other network services (e.g., file and printer sharing and messaging). The network administrator can use these utilities to optimize network performance.

- *Application programming interfaces* are used to incorporate the services of the network operating system into their program. For example, Named Pipes is a set of calls that allows a programmer to open a pipe, or a channel, from one program to another, for carrying a message or data between the programs.

- *Third-party products* are usually added on to the network operating systems to complement its native functions. Such add-on products provide automated data backup and communication between separate similar or dissimilar operating systems using different types of computers on the network.

There are as many definitions of a network operating system as there are network operating system products, most NOSs have certain features in common. However, all are slightly different in their solutions providing LAN functions.

8.3   Because SQL is a standard across all types of incompatible platforms (e.g., desktops, minicomputers, and mainframes alike), it has the potential to provide access to large databases from PC-based applications. It is also one of the driving forces behind the downsizing movement, where core corporate applications that formerly ran on mainframes migrate to PC-LAN environments. There are a few obstacles, however. Not all database engines speak the same dialect of SQL, and you must solve the universal connectivity problem before you can implement universal database access. In addition, there are basic security problems that must be solved when you try to integrate networks of PCs with corporate data repository. Despite the obstacles, the products such as Microsoft EXCEL and Lotus 1-2-3 are built with the ability to generate SQL queries, and many companies are providing back-end databases that run PC-based LANs.

SQL connectivity solutions make it possible to share a common database engine, but they are not capable of the more general task of sharing processing among all the computers on the network. In other words, it takes something other than SQL to create *network aware* applications. Sharing machine cycles, whether in a peer-to-peer environment or a clientserver arrangement, can greatly increase the power and efficiency of a computing environment. An application can take advantage of the computing power of an entire network and access subroutines that reside on any other machine.

CHAPTER 9 UNIX INTERNETWORKING

9.1   For interconnecting a LAN to a LAN, bridges and routers are the most commonly implemented solutions in the LAN world. LANs can be extended using repeaters. Local LANs can be interconnected with each other using local bridges and/or hubs. However, for LAN-WAN environment, the remote bridges provide one of the means of connecting while ignoring complexities of the upper protocol layers. Remote bridge pairs offer a viable approach for small organizations seeking LAN interconnection solutions for a limited number of applications. These bridging devices filter all packets addressed to the local LAN and forward those packets addressed to remote locations on the other LAN.

Connecting a large number of LANs is a significant undertaking. The task is further complicated if the LANs use different types of media, access methods, and protocols. In these complex, multiprotocol LAN internetworking environments, multiprotocol routers, operating at the network layer, are the preferred approach for interconnection. Routers are more complex than bridges. Increased complexity of these devices stems from the additional functionality in flow control, hierarchical addressing of each source and destination, packet fragmentation/reassemble, and network congestion control.

Gateways provide several different types of internetwork services such as protocol conversion, virtual terminal service, and file access services. Simple gateways called protocol converters provide only basic conversions between various protocols. More robust gateways offer transparent file transfers across different NOS environments. The gateways can translate file structure used in one NOS environment to another network operating system's file structure. For example, a workstation running MS-DOS can transfer files from native Novell IPX to Digital VAX VMS operating system on a DECnet network.

9.2 The major categories of communications utilities and applications typically used in UNIX installations are

- Terminal emulation.
- X Windows.
- Electronic mail.
- File transfer.
- File sharing.
- Remote procedure call.
- Network management.

9.3 UUCP (UNIX-to-UNIX Copy Program), is a batch-oriented system, as opposed to interactive processing, that is typically used between UNIX systems with dial-up telephone lines or systems that are directly connected. Its major uses are for software distribution (file transfer), remote execution, maintenance, administration, and electronic mail. UUCP is still a widely used UNIX networking application. When the CPU is free, UUCP delivers the file to the remote system.

UUCP consists of several commands: *uucp* requests a file to be sent from one machine to another, *uucico* performs the actual transfer of files, *uux* requests execution on a remote machine, and *uuxqt* executes the command. In other words, UUCP is a collection of processes that include both file transfer and remote command execution.

UUCP can be used on standard asynchronous phone lines and modems as well as in LANs and WANs. It is well suited for data transfer over telephone lines. Its major drawback is that it is somewhat slow and not suited for exchanging information in both directions simultaneously. UUCP is bundled with virtually all UNIX systems, so the user has a built-in access to this utility and thus the system.

9.4 File sharing or distributed file access allows users to interactively access files located in specified directories on remote systems. Distributed file systems shield users from details, such as what device the remote file resides on and what file transfer commands that service expects. The most popular standards for distributed file access in UNIX environments are Sun's Network File System (NFS), the Andrew File System (AFS), and AT&T's Remote File System (RFS). File sharing provides the following advantages:

- Maximum use of system resources afforded by distributing the work load among available systems.
- Transparent user access to all computing resources, making it easier to share information quickly.

9.5   There are a number of possible configurations for connecting and implementing LANs.

Novell's NetWare is a full-fledged operating system. NetWare has integrated several protocols, including AppleTalk File protocol (AFP), Network File System (NFS), TCP/IP, and OSI. As a result, it provides seamless, high-speed communications among dissimilar systems. NetWare is capable of providing the network services in the user's native environment for other operating systems, including DOS, Macintosh, and OS/2 applications. At the same time, it provides Macintosh, OS/2, VINES, and UNIX workstations access to NetWare file and print services.

The Microsoft LAN Manager was originally designed to run on top of OS/2, but is also available in a UNIX version. The LAN Manager also supports the client/server version of the Windows/NT and looks as if it is a UNIX implementation with hooks to the Windows graphical user interface.

Banyan VINES is a UNIX-based network operating system intended for large networks where multiple server operation and wide area network integration are of paramount importance. VINES's simple, yet powerful, global naming system, StreetTalk, identifies any network-attached resource. The StreetTalk global naming system provides replication of directories across the network to enhance speed and reliability.

Microsoft LAN Manager is a key component of DEC's PathWorks, allowing PC users to connect to a VAX server. PATHWORKS also supports LAN Manager APIs for OS/2, VMS, and UNIX servers.

IBM supports two implementations of the LAN Manager:

• LAN Server operates under OS/2, allows client/server implementations, and provides services for distributed databases on the network. The OS/2 Extended Edition includes the communication manager and the database manager and supports Advanced Peer-to-Peer Communications for OS/2. LAN Server is similar to Microsoft's LAN Manager, and it adheres to IBM's Systems Application Architecture.

• The PC local area network program is designed for small, DOS-based networks. It permits sharing of disk drives and printers as well as sending and receiving of messages and files.

Even though IBM offers these network operating systems, the emphasis has been on supporting Novell's NetWare.

CHAPTER 10 INTEGRATING THE DESKTOP

10.1   There are basically two approaches for integrating PCs into networks: running an open operating system on a PC and providing access via a network. The physical connectivity choices are synchronous connection via RS-232, X.25 connectivity, token ring, or Ethernet LANs. The integration options are many, but the most common are the following:

• At the low end, the PC, which can emulate an asynchronous terminal such as VT100 and dial into a UNIX server.

- Supporting TCP/IP on a PC, which can allow
  - Virtual terminal and login capabilities.
  - Access to file and print servers.
  - Using the PC as a file/print server.
  - X Window System.
- Using the PC as an application server.
- Emulating PC on a multi-user system.
- Using multiple operating systems on a PC.

10.2 Token ring (802.5) is implemented in versions that run at 4 Mbps or 16 Mbps and can operate on shielded or unshielded twisted-pair wire as well as on fiber optic media. The desktops on a Token ring LAN can be arranged in a star topology, with a hublike device called MAU at the center of the star. Its access method—token passing—makes the physical star arrangement act as if the stations were arranged in a ring, as the token is passed from one workstation to the next in sequence.

Ethernet (802.3) is implemented as a 10 Mbps bus-based network that can run on two types of coaxial cable, on unshielded twisted-pair telephone wire, or on fiber optic media. It uses a random access method carrier sense multiple access with collision detection (CSMA/CD).

ARCnet is a 2.5 Mbps network that can run on coaxial cable or unshielded twisted pair. It is most often implemented in a hub-based star configuration and uses token passing to control access. ARCnet is closest to the IEEE802.4 specification and uses token passing on a bus. Because it uses both active and passive hubs, ARCnet is excellent for elaborate wiring configurations. Active hubs relay messages as well as repeat the signals, whereas the passive hubs can only be used to relay signals. The most common ARCnet network has a limit of 255 stations.

FDDI is a 100 Mbps network that operates over optical fiber or, for limited distances, over shielded or unshielded twisted pair. It is implemented using a dual-ring topology—FDDI concentrators and dual-attached workstations require four separate fiber optic connections—with receive and transmit sides of each ring. Dual attachment provides fault tolerance in case of a cable break. Single-attached stations can also be implemented, where many stations can be attached to a single concentrator in an economical manner. If a cable breaks in a single attached topology, only that workstation will be disabled since workstations are not directly attached to the main ring. However, single attached stations can be directly attached to the ring.

FDDI is a frame-based technology that uses variable-length frames to transport information across the network. This allows it to easily map (translate) packets from other technologies, such as Ethernet and token ring. FDDI II provides the ability to transport limited levels of isochronous bandwidth to support video and multimedia applications. FDDI can operate over both single-mode and multimode fiber optic cable, spanning between 2 and 20 plus kilometers in distance between nodes also.

10.3 Network operating systems are what finally makes all that hardware function as a network. Originally, NOSs functioned to allow sharing of printers and disk files with limited access by a workstation. However, today's NOSs provide the basis for client/server applications, integrating computers of many types and sizes.

A network operating system functions in the same way as an OS, except that it works to control multiple computers and peripherals. Its mission is to make shared resources (such as hard drives, CD-ROMs, servers and server-based applications, or printers) local. An individual computer's operating system takes requests from application programs and translates them—one at a time—into actions performed by its monitor, hard disk, diskette, or printer. The NOS, on the other hand, takes requests for services from many application programs and individual computers at the same time and satisfies them using the network's resources.

Like the OS, the NOS is a collection of functions and system calls. Some of them provide and control simultaneous access to disk drives, printers, and other devices—these normally reside on the shared network computer, or *server*. Others intercept and redirect requests for service from the computers themselves and send these requests to the appropriate server—these normally reside on the individual PC or workstation.

The best known client/server NOSs are:

- Apple Computer AppleTalk/AppleShare.
- Artisoft LANtastic.
- Banyan VINES.
- Microsoft LAN Manager/IBM OS/2 LAN Server.
- Microsoft Windows for Workgroups.
- Novell NetWare and NetWare Lite.

10.4   8086, 8088, 80286, 80386, 80486, and the Pentium and the Pentium Pro.

10.5   ISA.

CHAPTER 11 INTEGRATING UNIX AND THE PCs (X WINDOWS)

11.1   X server is a special software that resides on the user's computer. The X server accepts information from the client application to be displayed on the screen and converts mouse and keyboard actions into data that the client can understand.

On the other hand, file servers are a central repository of data and/or application programs for the network. The file server only performs information retrieval. File servers usually have large-capacity storage devices attached to them.

11.2   X allows you to work with multiple programs simultaneously, each in a separate window. Certain windows accept input from the user: they may function as terminals, allow you to create graphics, control a database, and so on. Other windows simply display information, such as time of day or a picture of particular fonts, and so on. The operations performed within a window can vary greatly.

The windows you will probably use most frequently are terminal emulators, windows that function as standard terminals. In X systems, these terminal emulators are known as xterm. In an *xterm* window, you can do any thing you might do in a regular terminal: enter commands, run editing sessions, compile programs, and so on.

Most window managers will start the root *xterm* when they are initialized by simply typing another "xterm" command, you can create more *xterm* windows. You can even specify the location of a new window using command line options. The new *xterm* window displays a prompt from whatever shell you are using.

11.3   X client is an application program, such as a database package, that can run under the X Window System. A client application may run on the same computer as the X server (as a local client) or on a remote computer which may be mini, mainframe, or a supercomputer.

11.4   X Windows provide a sophisticated, graphical, easy-to-use interface. X is a standards-based windowing interface that enables users on multiuser systems to have the same style of interactive interface that workstation users rely upon. Developers can generate applications for virtually any platform. This allows PC users to integrate their network resources and the capability for a large variety of applications.

11.5   Additional *xterm* windows can be generated by simply typing "xterm" with optional parameters to control the placement of the window. *CreateWindow* command will also create a window based on the parameters specified.

11.6   *SetCloseDownMode* must be specified if the client resources are to be preserved at the close of the connection. If this mode is not specified, the server will clean up by destroying the resources the client created either when there was forced shutdown or the server sent a *xkill* command.

11.7   For acceptable performance, selection of the right hardware and software is of paramount importance. One major technique to enhance performance is to have the server maintain the resources such as fonts and windows and so on. This would reduce network traffic by not transmitting the entire structure or a string with the request.

11.8   The X Window System provides a friendly graphical interface for UNIX as well as a PC running X software. With X, a graphics application running on a "host" computer can display information and receive commands from a user's terminal. This enhances interoperability, increases productivity, and allows the enterprise to utilize its existing hardware.

11.9   The X server is a server that can manage a display, a keyboard, and a mouse. The server acts as an intermediary between user programs (called clients or applications). It allows access to the display by multiple clients, passes user input to the clients by sending and interpreting network messages, and maintains the data structures.

11.10 The X client has no capability to close the session. The server or another client can send an *xkill* command to close the session.

11.11 The X Window System requires X software running on a host, an X client (application), and an X server for a display system. For a local X system, it can reside on a workstation or a PC.

11.12 Among the features, you must consider the speed, the cost, local memory, network connectivity, and vendor support.

CHAPTER 12 INTERNETWORKING WITH MAC

12.1 The term AppleTalk refers only to Apple's software protocol suite. Apple, most commonly, supports three types of AppleTalk networks: LocalTalk, EtherTalk (Ethernet), and TokenTalk (token ring). Some other vendors support AppleTalk on ARCnet.

12.2 Although Apple Computer now offers connectivity products of its own, it has traditionally relied on third-party vendors to develop such solutions. A variety of emulation and protocol conversion gateways are available for the Macintosh. Increasingly, LAN-to-SNA gateways are being used to connect PCs and Macs to mainframes.

The traditional way to link a Macintosh and a mainframe is to use coaxial cable and a Macintosh interface card. The coaxial cable plugs into the interface card on the Mac and into an IBM 3174 or 327x cluster controller on the other end.

Gateways reduce communications traffic and generally cost less than coaxial installations. They can link AppleTalk networks to a mainframe via SDLC, token ring, or coaxial connections.

Many other companies offer 3270 emulation for the Macintosh, each differing in the ease of file transfer to and from the mainframe and in the extent to which they support the Macintosh environments. Most standard 3270 terminal emulation software for Macs does not take advantage of the Macintosh interface. However, more and more vendors are starting to use Apple's 3270 API in creating mainframe applications.

12.3 In addition to the connectivity provided by VINES, NetWare, and DOS emulation on the Mac, the Macintosh networks can be directly connected to PCs and thus internetworks via Ethernet and token ring. Macintosh operating system offers options for PCs to be connected via EtherTalk and TokenTalk.

Ethernet is the most popular option for upgrading Macintosh networks that have outgrown LocalTalk. It is good as a backbone for connecting two or more separate Macintosh networks and for networking Macs with DOS, UNIX, and VAX workstations. You can use Ethernet with any Mac from Macintosh Plus on. With a proper adapter, a Mac can fit seamlessly into any network, even to an AppleTalk LaserWriter.

Connecting to a token ring network is just as easy as connecting to an Ethernet network. Token ring is IBM's official strategy for PCs and PS/2s with IBM midrange and mainframe systems. Token ring is more complex than Ethernet, but it offers two advantages: greater speed (up to 16 Mbps) as compared to Ethernet's 10 Mbps and contention-free traffic due to its token passing scheme. Token ring is especially effective for large networks with heavy traffic. If you already have a token ring network and need Mac-to-PC connectivity or Mac access to an IBM midrange or mainframe system, using token ring makes a logical choice.

There may be an occasion when you have an AppleTalk network and want to drop a PC into the network or add a PC without connecting it to an existing NOS.

12.4 AppleTalk was designed to comply with the ISO OSI Reference Model. The protocol set includes modules that address each of the layers of the OSI architecture. It also supports dynamic node addressing, which automatically assigns network device node addresses at start-up so that the addressing is transparent to the user. Another feature of the protocol, distributed name service, lets users read and access resources on the network by name instead of by network address.

12.5 There are many ways to use a Macintosh when it is connected to a PC network. You can use the Macintosh and provide with all the capabilities of any PC and connect it to the global networks, or you can isolate the Mac and use the network only for transferring files, or you can provide it with capabilities that fall somewhere between the two extremes. You can even use your Mac as an MS-DOS machine. The only limitation when using a Mac on a PC-based network is that on many networks, such as Novell or Banyan VINES network or Microsoft's LAN Manager, you need a PC to access the file server for maintenance or system administration.

CHAPTER 13 INTEGRATING LEGACY NEWTWORKS

13.1 • SNA and DECnet are proprietary architectures, whereas TCP/IP is in the public domain and thus more open. The DECnet architecture is not hierarchical in structure, a point that differentiates DECnet from SNA. The users linking Digital's systems are more likely to think in terms of Internet connections than host-to-host connections. This makes networking relatively common in DECnet sites.

• SNA is a hierarchical architecture, whereas DECnet and TCP/IP are peer-to-peer.

• SNA was designed as a synchronous linking system, subject to a few if any delays in transmission, whereas TCP/IP was designed as an asynchronous system, capable of responding to variable connection times and speeds without dropping the link. Therefore, encapsulating SNA in TCP to gain ready routability of TCP could introduce network delays beyond the ability of SNA to handle or routing TCP through the SNA network to gain throughput could cost TCP users access when the SNA network goes down even in part.

13.2 There are many different ways to integrate TCP/IP and SNA, but any solution depends on the constraints of the installation, available equipment, performance and cost considerations. Some of the solutions explored are

• Implementation of SNA hosts on LANs.

• Integration by using gateways.

• Integration with a combination of routers and gateways.

• Implementation of 3172 offload feature.

13.3 For SNA connectivity, VM/ESA supports LU 6.2, TCP/IP, SNA, VTAM, and T1. Therefore, VM provides complete SNA-TCP/IP connectivity and networking. The addition of TCP/IP to VM's already considerable repertoire of communication software has enabled it interoperate in multivendor environments over LANs and WANs.

With TCP/IP on a VM host, workstations and terminals connected to UNIX or other hosts (RISC or CISC based) can easily access VM applications and transfer files to and from CMS. If there is media incompatibility (different LAN topology between the workstations and the VM host), an IP router (a PC or PS/2 running a TCP/IP) can provide dozens of sessions to the TCP/IP-based client community. The S/370 computers running VM and TCP/IP blend into this multivendor environment and provide access to many applications they host from terminals, PCs, and workstations alike. The mainframes are connected to a LAN through a channel-attached network controller to an IBM 3172, eliminating the need for a traditional FEP.

13.4   UNIX can be used for remote-to-host connectivity over virtually any network backbone, including SNA/SDLC, TCP/IP, token-ring, and X.25. Unlike single-user DOS/Windows, UNIX provides a multiuser, multitasking platform for both host and local operations. With full-featured emulation packages, UNIX systems can operate in the same way as the 3270 and RJE devices. UNIX's built-in utilities facilitate asynchronous terminal connections, remote login, unattended file transfers, and API-driven applications.

There are many techniques for UNIX-mainframe connectivity:

- UNIX-to-host connections in a traditional SNA/SDLC network.
- UNIX-to-SNA via 3270.
- Remote UNIX-to-SNA host connectivity via X.25.
- SNA host links for UNIX systems in token ring LANs.
- SNA links for UNIX in client/server configurations.

13.5   DECnet, in many ways, anticipates the peer-to-peer networking developments of other vendors such as IBM. As a result, the DECnet interconnection is both a generalized way to internetwork LANs and a specific strategy for host-to-host communications. Digital has assumed that the networks will include DECnet Phase IV and TCP/IP networks with perhaps some ADVANTAGE-NETWORKS nodes in each and that TCP/IP users will primarily want TCP/IP services. Therefore, Digital has established a multistack support, each stack offering the native application services of the associated protocol, such as TCP/IP FTP, as well as the transport services.

Digital supports a wide variety of client systems on DECnet LANs such as

- PATHWORK clients—PCs and Macintosh systems, ULTRIX, and SCO UNIX clients.
- Providing access to a DECnet service such as LAT allowing internetworking using a non-DECnet protocol.
- Sharing media with DECnet but using servers that are not DECnet systems. However, the internetworking of DECnet LANs may not result in internetworking the other LANs that share the media.

CHAPTER 14 INTERNETWORK TROUBLESHOOTING AND MONITORING—I

14.1 The *first stage* involves "quick checks" without any specialized equipment. Such checks often reveal the cause of the problem. But it depends upon how experienced you are, that you know the configuration, and that you recognize the areas that have changed on the network. The network documentation and any historical/audit trail data are very useful in such situations. The key is to collect enough accurate information. Many network failures occur after something has been changed or modified. Changes in topology, configuration, applications, and users can cause a network to fail. Missing some vital information can easily lead you to an incorrect diagnosis and possibly an inappropriate fix. Most problems on the network have probably happened before. Therefore, you must make certain that you understand the problem. The primary goal is to identify and eliminate potential causes of the problem. Once the suspect problem is apparent, it may be necessary to perform some simple tests to ascertain the severity and the scope of the problem.

The *second stage* involves a closer look at the network for special indicators or symptoms. Specialized tools, such as analyzers, monitors, and diagnostic programs, are often needed to identify symptoms that point to the cause of the problem. Problem isolation is easier if the network is divided into workable segments, so you do not have to contend with the entire network at once. Each segment can then be examined to pinpoint the problem areas. Because more detailed information must be gathered in this stage, specialized equipment such as an analyzer, a monitor, or a probe may be required.

The *third stage* requires either specialized equipment and/or a specialist to interpret the data. The first two stages require some familiarity with normal network operations, so abnormalities will be apparent. It is only after these remedies have been exhausted that you need to move to the third stage. There are many common problems in which you can follow the same steps to troubleshoot. Some troubleshooting applications and tools can identify these problems and perform the steps without your intervention. Once completed, such tools will notify you that a problem has been fixed or a problem needs special handling.

14.2 Most network problems are directly related to the components, which could include

- Cabling.
- Network adapters.
- Wiring concentrators.
- Bridges, routers, gateways, or hubs.
- Host, server, or workstation.
- Protocol stacks.

14.3 RMON is a standard management information base specification that provides a consistent format for collecting both Ethernet and token ring statistics. The RMON technology is finding its way into networks of all sizes.

To facilitate the collection and transfer of RMON information between agents and NMS monitoring applications, the SNMP protocol utilizes a management information base. MIBs provide standard representations of collected data. Considering a tree-structured database, an MIB defines groups of objects that can be managed. MIB I is limited to 114 objects and is organized into 8 groups. MIB II is an extension of MIB I and defines 185 objects in 10 groups. The two additions are

- Common management information and services protocol over TCP (CMOT)
- Simple network management protocol (SNMP)

With SNMP MIB II, network managers can retrieve information pertaining to the local device served by that agent (for example, bridge statistics). Designed as a supplement to MIB II, RMON MIB provides vital management information on the subnetwork being served. This is similar to the functions being carried out by network analyzers that "promiscuously" monitor each frame on the network, gathering traffic statistics.

14.4   LAN analyzers, baselining tools, response-time monitors, and performance-modeling applications are some of the smorgasbord tools for troubleshooting and monitoring internetworks. RMON (remote monitoring) probes and analyzers are supposed to be the one-stop alternative, giving net managers a way to keep a weather eye on their networks from the comfort of the data center. The experience suggests that RMON products fare as well or better than conventional analyzers in some situations and vice versa.

Almost all major troubleshooting tools/probes count packets accurately at rates approaching wire speed—some generating traffic. Nearly all such products gauge network utilization, both in real time and over days and weeks. Some RMON products even offer baselining and response-time monitoring.

14.5   Analyzer is a traffic monitor that reconstructs and interprets protocol messages that span several packets. Some typical analyzers are

   LANalyzer

   LANPatrol

   LANVista

   LANWatch

   NetMetrix

   NETScout

   Sniffer

   SpiderMonitor

Some of the protocol monitors are

   LanProbe

   Cisco Catalyst

   Net_monitor

   NETScout

   ChemLAN 100

14.6 A *ping* is used to reconfigure a node. False.

14.7 Monitoring network statistics helps the LAN administrator confirm a bottleneck? True. Bottlenecks on a network often cause increased traffic collisions and slow response times. These network statistics can be gathered during network monitoring.

CHAPTER 15 INTERNETWORK TROUBLESHOOTING AND MONITORING—II

1. List the steps in "hands-on" troubleshooting networks.
   Check the gathered data if
   - Any stations work.
   - If there is still any traffic on the network.
   - Can the station operate as a standalone divice?
   - Can the station establish connection to the network?
2. List some of the trouble areas on the network
   - Cable problems.
   - Protocol problems.
   - Frame sizes.
   - Corrupted packets.
   - Broadcast storms.
   - Bandwidth incompatabilities.

CHAPTER 16 TROUBLESHOOTING A GLOBAL NETWORK (AN EXAMPLE)

1. What type of problems are common in a global network?
   - Performance.
   - Data throughput variations.
   - T1 framing.
   - WAN bandwidth and bottlenecks.
   - Down links.
   - Misconfigured network segments.
   - Long/poor response times.
2. What are symptoms of server overloads?
   - Traffic congestion.
   - High error rates.
   - Poor response times.
   How can these be avoided or corrected?

- Determine the busy server percentage. If it exceeds a threshold, there is a potential problem.
- Reconfigure.
- CPU/memory upgrade.
- Split the load.

3.   What type of problems a mis-configured workstation would cause?

Sending data to a local station via a router is usually the primary problem.

Since the server and the workstation are on the same segment, the traffic does not need to be routed via the router.

Check and correct the configuration tables.

CHAPTER 17 MANAGING NETWORKS

17.1   Much attention is being directed at the protocol transporting management information across the network between managers and agents. Standardizing network management protocols has yielded two distinct camps serving different needs within networks of varying complexity: common management information protocol is designed for OSI-based networking environments, and simple network management protocol is most commonly used for TCP/IP networks.

The third protocol, CMOT (CMIP over TCP/IP) architecture, is based on the OSI management framework and the models, services, and protocols developed by ISO for network management. The CMOT architecture demonstrates how the OSI management framework can be applied to a TCP/IP environment and is used to manage objects in a TCP/IP network.

17.2   The international standards process is providing with a blueprint for communications design in the OSI network model. Like the OSI network model, CMIS is a service-level specification which defines network management functions as fitting into five classifications which are the basis for most management protocols and products. These are

- Fault management.
- Configuration management.
- Security management.
- Accounting management.
- Performance management.

17.3   The simple network management protocol is an application layer protocol designed to facilitate the exchange of management information between network devices. By using SNMP-transported data (such as packets per second and network error rates), network administrators can more easily manage network performance, find and solve network problems, and plan for network growth. Like the Transmission Control Protocol, SNMP is an Internet Protocol.

SNMP is a relatively simple protocol, yet its feature set is sufficiently powerful to handle the difficult problems presented in trying to manage today's heterogeneous networks. SNMP's simplicity makes it easy and quick to implement with low memory and CPU requirements. Because of greater generality, CMIP or CMOT have made implementation more difficult and lengthy, and can unduly burden high-performance devices such as bridges and routers.

CMOT places more load on the network devices to support the additional features that allow managing stations to issue complex queries. SNMP queries provide the same basic functions, but normally require several less complex queries and greater amounts of status information to be sent across the network.

17.4   NetView provides comprehensive end-to-end management that enables administrators to manage IBM SNA and non-SNA resources. It defines five management services that are similar to those provided by OSI, as follows:

- Problem management deals with error conditions, beginning with detection through problem resolution.
- Change management provides the planning, control, and applications changes of network resources.
- Configuration management controls the information base that identifies network resources and their relationships with other network components.
- Performance and Accounting management provides network statistical measurements for responsiveness and performance tuning.
- Operation services provide security management as well as other operator management functions.

17.5   Fault management deals with the detection, isolation, and identification of anomalies within the management domain. Depending on the capability of the management software, it may even be able to recommend and take corrective action on the anomaly identified. Open-system fault management provides the ability to log events or errors and to monitor specified events or errors. In fact, a solution should have the capability to anticipate faults as a result of analyzing errors and or events as needed.

Configuration management is the task of controlling the routes information takes through the network, the relationships between network elements, and how specific system parameters are chosen. Configuration management provides configuration data necessary to start up or shut down the network resources.

Configuration management identifies and controls data in the system for the purpose of initializing, providing the continuous operations of, and terminating system services. It is also concerned with maintaining, adding, and updating system components.

Security management is the task of controlling access to the network and network resident services, including the service of network management itself. Security management is concerned with the protection of network resources. Controlling access to those resources often requires passwords, access privileges (e.g., read, write, execute), and possibly encryption methods. Audit trails are a common method of tracking individual users and resources utilized. Audit trails can be the most effective tools in troubleshooting network problems for both hardware and software.

17.6   There are three specific components of a network management system: manager, agent, and management information base.

Manager: The management application (*"manager"*) is the focal point from which management functions are carried out on the network. The capabilities of the manager application vary from vendor-to-vendor implementation. Comprehensive manager applications provide extensive, multilevel, detailed information on the current status of the network. Most vendors' management software provides standard functions, such as alarm correlations, that attempt to isolate a single source causing multiple devices to generate alarm conditions. For example, a T-span failure would cause the T1 multiplexer and all connected nodes to indicate an alarm condition. The alarms correlation module within the management application would intercept and attempt to correlate the alarms and highlight the possible failed node on the network map.

Agent: The "agent" can be integrated directly into a network element, or it may be remote from that element. For example, an agent might be a protocol module inside a router that collects management information about the router, or the agent might be a protocol module inside a modem management system. In the latter case, the agent would not collect data about the modem management system; rather, it would collect management information about the modems through the modem management system's services. Agent software carries out commands issued by the management application. The commands range from MIB and status queries to configuration and control operations necessary for the local network device. The agent maintains objects stored in the local MIB by monitoring device operations and conditions, and recording that information in the appropriate object record of the local MIB.

Management information base (MIB): The management information base is conceptually a database containing all management information related to the local node. Management information—called "objects"—contain attributes about certain characteristics of a managed element (e.g., error counters, timers). Therefore, a managed object contains attributes that define the characteristics of the object. A managed object can be defined for any resource that the manager application needs to monitor and/or control. The collection of management data definitions that a manager or an agent knows about is called its MIB.

Each element within the network maintains a MIB containing objects specific to that device. Therefore, the MIB for a LAN bridge would contain different objects than a MIB for a host computer. The manager maintains a MIB containing information about each device in the network. The manager uses its MIB to archive management data for functions such as report generation and trend analysis. A manager sends commands querying for MIB information contained in network elements using a common network management protocol. The station receiving the manager's command, queries the local MIB and replies with the requested management data.

Appendix **III**

GLOSSARY

10BASET An implementation of IEEE 802.3 Ethernet standard on 24-gauge unshielded twisted-pair wiring, a baseband medium, at 10 Mbps.

10BASE2 An implementation of the IEEE 802.3 Ethernet standard on thin coaxial cable, a baseband medium, at 10 Mbps. This is also known as thinnet because its thin coax cable is about half that of standard Ethernet cable. The maximum segment length is just under 200 meters.

10BASE5 An implementation of the IEEE 802.3 Ethernet standard running on twin axial (thick coax) cable, a baseband medium, at 10 Mbps. This is also known as standard Ethernet. The maximum cable segment length is 500 meters.

1BASE5 An implementation of the IEEE StarLAN standard on a baseband medium at 1 Mbps. The maximum cable length between nodes is 500 meters.

ABI (Application Binary Interface) A specification for executable UNIX program storage. It also specifies the minimum number of system resources that must be present. It describes how the executable code for a given microprocessor can be stored and manipulated by a given version of UNIX.

Access Transparency (local and remote) Objects (e.g,. files) are accessed using identical operations.

ACSE Association control service element—an ISO application-level protocol.

Active Window The window where the input is directed. Sometimes, this is also called "focus window."

Address Resolution The process of determining what LAN hardware address corresponds to an Internet Protocol address. This is used by routers and hosts before transmitting a packet on a LAN.

Address Table The list of host addresses and link numbers maintained by a bridge to determine where to forward packets.

Address A number uniquely identifying each node in a network. There are two types of addresses; the node's hardware address at layer 2 and the Internet address, at layer 3.

AFS (Andrew File System) Originally developed at Carnegie-Mellon University with funding from IBM, which licensed the technology to Transarc Corp., a start-up in 1989. It runs under TCP/IP and provides an NFS/AFS translator to let NFS systems access

AFS files. AFS is the newest DFS with the smallest installed base. Groups of files are organized into volumes. Any file can be located anywhere in the network and can be replicated on many servers.

Agent The part of a system's software that performs information retrieval and exchange on behalf of a client or server application. Software running on a network device or computer system collects and makes available MIB variables.

AIX (Advanced Interactive Executive) A UNIX variant originally developed under contract to IBM by Interactive Systems Corporation for the IBM RT PC. It is an IBM operating system product family that is compatible with AT&T's UNIX.

Alert An asynchronous message, generated by a managed object and sent to an NMS.

ANSI American National Standards Institute is a voluntary U.S.-based organization which defines standards for the information processing industry.

AOW (Asia and Oceania Workshop) Works on behalf of the Asian countries to review ISO's set of OSI Standards to pare down the standards to provide for a better fit within the respective Asian countries they represent.

APA All points addressable.

API (Application Programming Interface) An API is a vendor-provided tool that allows connecting applications running under the same operating environment. Universal API's do not exist. API defines the rules that govern an application's interaction with system software.

APPC Advanced Program-to-Program Communications (LU 6.2). This is the primary protocol for communication in APPN. It is a set of SNA protocols for communication between programs and is also called LU 6.2.

AppleShare Apple Computer's network operating system, which implement its AppleTalk protocols.

AppleTalk A protocol suite defined by Apple Computer for connecting computers and peripherals using shielded twisted-pair wiring and transfer rates of about 230 kilobytes per second. The network and transport level protocols include Datagram Delivery Protocol (DDP), AppleTalk Transmission Protocol (ATP), AppleTalk Session Protocol (ASP), and the Name Binding Protocol (NBP).

Application Generator A product that generates application software from high-level user specifications.

Application Layer A term used in reference to layer 7 of the OSI model. This layer provides the means to access application services such as file transfer, virtual terminal, and electronic mail functions.

Application Software Computer programs that are designed to perform specific user-oriented or business-oriented functions, such as accounting, and word processing.

APPN (Advanced Peer-to-Peer Networking) A distributed networking feature incorporated into SNA. It simplifies the process of adding workstations and supports transparent sharing of applications in a distributed computing environment. It allows direct communication on a network and thus facilitates the development of client/server computing. It is a set of SNA node protocols to enable two systems to communicate on a peer basis.

Architecture Defines parts of a system and the interaction among those parts. Contains technical details, including data formats, rules, protocols, or interface standards, to which hardware and software products must conform.

ARP Address Resolution Protocol is the data link layer protocol used by the IP layer of routers and hosts in a TCP/IP network. It is used to determine the local hardware address of a node on a directly attached LAN, given its IP address. ARP broadcasts a packet with the requested IP address; the node with assigned IP address responds with its hardware address.

AS/400 Application System/400, a series of IBM midrange computers.

ASCII American Standard Code for Information Interchange. A 7-bit code set established by ANSI to achieve compatibility between products manufactured by different companies. ASCII is widely used, especially in personal computers.

Async Asynchronous: a data transmission protocol that does not require a separate clock signal for reception of data.

AT&T UNIX System V Incorporates all major UNIX system implementations (XENIX, SunOS, BSD) for standard open environment. Supports added functionality for real-time processing, dynamic linking, and Sun Microsystems virtual memory. It includes Open Look graphical user interface and does not support OSF's Motif GUI.

AT Advanced technology.

Back-End Functions Those data manipulation functions and procedures performed by a database server in response to directions from an application running on an end-user PC.

Backbone The primary connective cable of a hierarchical distributive system that links individual network segments.

Bandwidth A range of frequencies recommended for safe transmission of data via a transmission medium. The higher the bandwidth, the greater the capacity to transmit data at the same time.

Baseband A transmission that allows only one signal at a time to travel on a cable.

Batch A group of transactions or bulk data that is not processed in an interactive manner.

Best Path The optimal route (series of links) through a wide area network. Routers use a routing protocol to determine the best sequence of links each packet should take to reach its destination with the lowest delay, cost, or other criteria.

Bind An SNA session control command that activates an LU-LU session.

Bisync Binary synchronous communications.

Bitmap A grid of pixels or picture elements, each of which is white, black, or in the case of color displays, a color.

Block A sequence of continuous data transmitted as a unit. It is also referred to as transmission block.

Bridge Number A unique number assigned to each bridge to be used as an identifier.

Bridge A LAN internetworking device used to link two or more local or remote LANs. Bridges use only data link address information to make packet-forwarding decisions. Bridges provide high-performance internetworking for limited size networks.

Broadband A data transmission technique that allows multiple simultaneous signals to share the bandwidth of a transmission medium through the use of radio frequency modulation. Cable TV uses broadband transmission—multiple TV signals are carried on separate channels over a common medium.

Broadcast Storm A LAN software failure mode caused by many stations on the network incorrectly replying to a broadcast packet with another broadcast packet. The result is an extremely high traffic load. A broadcast storm is usually caused by misconfigured network software.

Broadcast A packet delivery system that allows all hosts attached to the network to receive a copy of the sent packet.

Brouter A network device that can perform the functions of both a bridge and a router.

BSAM Basic sequential access method, a software function in the MVS operating system.

BTAM Basic telecommunication access method, an IBM communications software product.

Bus A single connective high-speed link among multiple processing machines where any machine can transmit to any other machine, but only one can transmit at one time. A LAN topology in which all nodes share a single length of cable running between two points.

C Programming Language A powerful but simple systems programming language. Almost all of the UNIX system is written in C.

Cache A storage area, intended to speed up access to data.

CAE (Common Applications Environment) It defines common syntax for major programming languages, common user interface and networking. These are components that need to be standardized for portability, scalability, and interoperability. X/OPEN develops CAE.

Carrier A communication medium used to transmit information in the form of signals.

Cascade A bridged network topology in which LAN segments are connected end to end in order to extend the distance the network covers.

CBX Computerized branch exchange.

CCITT (Consultative Committee for International Telephone and Telegraph) An international organization which sets standards for telephone systems (e.g., X.25 standard for packet-switched networks, X.400 for e-mail). It is organized under the

International Telecommunications Union, which is an agency of the United Nations. Some CCITT developed standards are X.25, X.400, and X.500.

CCS (Common Communications Support) A set of standards for networking communications capability at the low entry networking level. One of the basic elements of SAA, it defines data communications standards for data links, application services, network management, and data streams.

CGM Computer graphics metafile.

Channel A component of the processor complex that supervises the systems' input/output functions.

Checksum An integer value computed from a sequence of bytes or octets. The value of the computed sum is used at the receiver to detect errors that may occur when a sequence of octets is transmitted. Protocol software usually computes and appends the checksum to packets being transmitted across a network.

CICS Customer information control system.

Circuit In telecommunications, it is a physical media connection between two communications devices. In networking (virtual circuit), it is a logical connection between two end points in a network, providing reliable, in-sequence, error-free delivery of the packets sent over the virtual circuit.

CISC (Complex instruction set computing) CISC is one of two types of UNIX microprocessors; RISC is the other.

CLC A cluster controller, a semi-intelligent device that allows several nonintelligent devices to connect to a data link.

Client/Server Model Client/server model is a standard model for networking applications (distributed computing). The server is a process that is waiting for requests from the client. A typical scenario is the following: (1) server is started (sleeps until a client request comes in), (2) client is started (possibly at another system), (3) client sends requests to the server across the network, and (4) server does the required computations and goes back to sleep.

Client/Server Computing Client/server architecture divides an application into separate processes operating on separate CPUs connected by wide or local area network protocols. The goal is to link different applications across multivendor platforms. There are four methods to accomplish this: application programming interfaces, database servers, remote windows, and remote procedure call. Clients and servers may run on different hardware with different operating systems. Client machines execute programs that request services residing on separate server machines. Server machines execute application and system software components that serve clients. An alternative approach for distributed computing is peer to peer. Client /server is preferable when (1) application clearly dictates client and server roles, (2) available compute power is unbalanced, and (3) partial centralization is desirable. Some distributed application systems combine client/server and peer-to-peer distributed processing. However, client/server computing is the model most major vendors have subscribed to.

CMIP Common management information protocol is the network management protocol defined by the OSI specifications. CMIP is used to convey CMIS defined operations over an OSI network.

CMIS Common management information service is a portion of the OSI network management specification which defines the management services available to a network management system. CMIS works with CMIP.

CMISE CMIS Element.

CMOT CMIS over TCP architecture is based on OSI management framework.

CMS Conversational monitor system: a software component of IBM's VM operating system.

CNM Communications network manager.

Coaxial Cable A transmission medium with an outer shield that protects the cable from electromagnetic and radio frequency interferences (EMI/RFI).

COBOL Common Business-Oriented Language.

Compatibility The ability to move applications to successive releases of the same operating system.

Concurrency Transparency Several users can operate concurrently on shared objects.

Connection Oriented Refers to a protocol which uses virtual circuits: the nodes which are the endpoints of the connection, or circuit, maintain state (control information). This allows them to correlate each packet with previously received packets to provide error-free, lossless packet delivery.

Connection A term used in the networking environment to describe the path between two devices. A connection allows the exchange of information between two or more devices. Equivalent terms are "session" and "circuit." The path between the server and the client is known as a "connection." A client usually (but not necessarily) has one connection to the server over which requests and events are sent.

Connectionless Service A protocol or service which does not require that a virtual circuit be established between the endpoints: each packet is processed independently. All commonly used LANs provide connectionless service as the basic packet delivery service mechanism.

COS Mark The "seal of approval" issued by COS for OSI-compliant products.

COS Corporation for Open Systems.

CPI/C Common programming interface for communications. An IBM-SAA component that defines a standard interface for applications for communication services, especially SNA LU 6.2.

CPI Common programming interface. A composite of standardized high-level languages and interfaces for supporting services. One of the basic elements of IBM-SAA. It defines rules for programming and use of system services by applications.

CRC Cyclic redundancy check is an error-detecting code appended to a packet to help the receiver determine if errors were introduced during transmission. The CRC is a specialized checksum computed over the entire packet by the transmitter's LAN controller hardware and is checked for correctness by the receiving station's hardware. Use of the CRC allows the LAN MAC layer to guarantee a very low probability of incorrectly delivering an erred packet.

CreateWindow Is a request of the X protocol that sends a byte stream from a client to the server to create a window. It varies in length according to how much information needs to be transferred.

CSMA Carrier sense multiple access is a process that allows multiple stations to access a transmission medium by listening to find out if it is idles before attempting to transmit packets.

CSU/DSU A channel service unit/digital service unit is a hardware device used to interface a router (or other networking or computing device) to a phone company digital telephone circuit. It provides functions similar to those of a modem except it is used on digital rather than analog telephone circuits and usually at higher data rates.

CUA (Common User Access) This refers to the "look and feel" (e.g., window layout, menu presentations, display options).

DARPA (Department of Defense Advanced Research Projects Agency) Coordinates and funds projects considered vital to national security database servers.

Data Link Layer The network protocol module which defines how packets for a specific type of LAN or network trunk line are addressed, structured, and delimited. The data link layer has an interface downwards to the physical layer and upwards to the network layer.

Datagram Usually refers to a packet sent by a network layer, such as TCP/IP's Internet protocol.

DCE (Distributed Computing Environment) A framework for distributed computing. The components of DCE are threads, remote procedure call, time service, naming service, distributed file system, and security. It is part of OSF's development solution. The other part is DME. *De facto* ("as a matter of fact") standards are the result of successful products accepted as "standards." *De jure* ("according to law") standards are produced by a body with legal status. These standards are public.

De Facto Standard An unofficial standard that exists because it is widely used by companies in the industry.

De Jure Standard A standard that has been officially approved by an organization (for example, IEEE, ISO) established to define and develop standards.

DEC Digital Equipment Corporation.

Decentralize The process of distributing responsibility from a central point to several local points of control.

DECnet DEC's proprietary communications protocol and line of network products. DECnet products are compatible with Ethernet and a wide range of other systems.

Demand-Paged Virtual Memory A technique whereby the limited physical memory of a computer system is made to seem much larger.

Dependency In network monitoring, one object is dependent on another if its state is defined in part by the state of another object. For example, if a host is behind a router, the host's state is dependent on the router's state. If the host cannot be reached because the router is down, the host's state cannot be determined. NMSs which understand network topology can suppress alerts for dependent objects whose state is hidden by another object's failure.

DFS (Distributed File System) Provides transparent access to local and remote files which reside on file servers, It can interoperate with the Network File System (NFS). Files can be shared across systems using incompatible technologies. It allows users access to any file located anywhere in the organization. Most modern DFSs use client/server technology. Major UNIX DFS standards are: (1) NFS, Sun Microsystems, (2) RFS, AT&T, (3) AFS, Transarc Corp. The origin of DFS is the Andrew File System (AFS) from Carnegie-Mellon University.

Digital Equipment ULTRIX Based on Berkeley implementation of UNIX and provides many system and library calls from UNIX System V. It supports distributed computing environment and Ingres Related DBMS. It operates only on Digital hardware.

DLC (Data Link Control) Layer 2 of network architecture, which defines the procedures for exchanging messages using a data transmission medium.

DM Delivery manager.

DME (Distributed Management Environment) Governs system and network management functions. It is part of OSF's development solution. The other part is DCE.

DNA (Digital Network Architecture) DEC's overall architecture. It is designed to connect multivendor products. It is an open-ended architecture designed to absorb new communications technology.

DRDA Distributed relational database architecture.

DTE (Data Terminal Equipment) A machine that is the data source or data sink, which provides communications functions and protocol., A communications path begins or ends at a DTE, commonly used with X.25 networks.

E-mail Electronic mail. A computer application that allows computer users to exchange messages (mail) and documents via e-mail applications on their computers. E-mail is one of the most widely used computer network applications because of its rapid delivery, integration with other computer applications, and the ability to transmit documents.

ECF (Enhanced Connectivity Facilities) An IBM product family that exchanges data between PCs and System/370s, which provides access to host files, disk space, databases, and printers.

Echo The name given to the ICMP packets used to check the reachability of nodes or devices on a network system. These packets are sometimes referred to as *ping* packets.

EDI Electronic data interchange.

EGP Exterior gateway protocol used to advertise the IP addresses of one network system to another. Each individual system must use EGP to advertise their reachability by the routing system.

EIA (Electronic Industry Association) An organization which sets standards for physical connections (e.g., RS-232C interface).

Electo Magnetic Interferences (EMI) Electrical and magnetic signals generated and transmitted by electronic and electrical equipment. Electromagnetic signals from some sources are strong enough to interfere with the proper operation of electronic equipment such as networking devices.

Encapsulate A basic protocol layering technique. The information from a higher-level protocol (data and header) is carried as the data portion of a lower-level protocol, which adds its own header information. For example, IP datagrams are encapsulated in data link packets.

End-to-End An expression used in the networking environment to indicate communication between source and destination nodes on a network system. End-to-end communication is carried out by the transport layer of TCP/IP or OSI.

Entity A device or service being monitored by an NMS.

Error A term used to describe signals with a rate or value below the accepted norms. An error may be caused by mutilation of bits, loss of bits or character, or improper data link control procedure.

Ethernet A widely used local area networking technology. Ethernet is a data link protocol and physical layer specification of a 10 Mbps LAN. Ethernet, closely related to IEEE 802.3, is a baseband LAN using thick or thin coaxial cables or twisted or untwisted-pair (telephone wiring) cables. Ethernet is a bus topology in which nodes can transmit packets immediately if the cable is idle.

EtherTalk AppleTalk protocol governing Ethernet transmissions.

Event Clients are informed of device input or client request side effects asynchronously via events. Events are never sent to a client unless the client has specifically asked the server to be informed of that type of event. However, other clients can force events of any type to be sent to any client.

EWOS (European Workshop on Open Systems) Works on behalf of the European countries to review ISO's set of OSI standards to pare down the standards to provide for a better fit within the respective European countries they represent.

Fault Management One of the five basic network management functions defined by the ISO. It involves the detection, isolation, and correction of faults on the network system.

FDDI Fiber distribution data interface is a network standard based on fiber optics. It was established by the American National Standards Institute (ANSI). FDDI specifies a data transfer rate of 100 Mbps and limits networks to approximately 200 km in length. Access control is provided by the token ring technology.

Fiber Optic Cable A transmission medium made of glass or plastic fibers. Its high bandwidth and low susceptibility to interference make it ideal for use in long-haul or electrically noisy locations.

Field A group of bits (bytes and words) that typically serves a single function. An example is TCP's sequence number—a 32-bit field indicating the number of the first byte of data in a packet.

File Servers A computer which provides file storage for workstations on the network. The workstations can use the disks on the file server as though they were attached to the workstation.

File servers accept requests from user programs running on nonserver machines, called clients. File servers typically maintain hierarchical file systems. Workstations can import/export these file systems, augmenting their local file systems with those located on the servers (thus, different clients may have a different view of the file system).

FIPS Federal Information Processing Standards: Established by National Institute of Standards and Technology (NIST), a standards making U.S. government agency.

File Transfer Protocol FTP is the application-level protocol used to transfer files between two hosts on a TCP/IP based network system.

Filter Used in reference to a function performed by a bridge. It involves comparing each packet received with the specification set by the network manager. Packets are forwarded or rejected according to these specifications. Filtering allows a network manager to conduct several tasks including limiting protocol-specific traffic to one network segment, isolating electronic mail domains, and performing several other traffic control functions.

Firewall A term used in reference to the router's ability to contain a fault to the area of the network that it occurs on.

Flow Control Any of several hardware or software techniques used to prevent a source node's transmissions from overrunning the destination node's capacity to receive and process the information. Flow control can use physical hardware techniques, such as windowing information used by a network protocol such as TCP.

Fragmentation The process of dividing a datagram into smaller datagrams. Fragmentation is required to transmit large datagrams through networks which can only transmit smaller datagrams. The Internet Protocol includes facilities for fragmentation.

Frame A block of data consisting of its own set of control information, including transmission address and data for error detection.

Front End A client application for presenting, entering, and updating data. It operates in conjunction with a back-end application.

FTAM File transfer, access, and management. An ISO-OSI application protocol.

FTP File transfer protocol. It is a reliable end-to-end file transfer protocol. It offers facilities for interactive access, format specification and authentication control. FTP is a set of functions supporting file transfer from one machine to another. It copies entire files across the network. This approach contrasts with NFS, which shares files and allows access to individual bytes within a file.

Gateway A protocol conversion device used to interconnect networks or devices which use different communications protocols. Gateways typically include a full protocol suite (usually seven layers) for both networks, and the software which converts from one to the other. They build on the router concept and perform application level protocol conversion. Many UNIX "gateways" really are routers.

GET The name given to query and reply packets used by SNMP to gather information about devices on the network. These packets are called the GetRequest and GetResponse. GetRequests are query packets sent by the NMS to gather data about the status of a managed device. GetResponse packets are sent by the agent of the managed device in response to queries.

GOSIP Government Open Systems Interconnection Profile, NIST FIPS 146, specifying the eventual use of ISO-OSI protocol by U.S. government agencies. It is the federal government procurement document for computer and networking technology. It encourages vendors to supply OSI-based products. GOSIP defines what OSI will be in government systems.

Graphics Context Various information for graphics output is stored in a graphics context, such as foreground pixel, background pixel, line width, and so on. Everything drawn to a window is modified by the GC used in the drawing request.

GUI Graphical user interface presents a graphical representation of a program through ICONS, pull-down menus and scroll bars, usually manipulated by a mouse. Software that provides the "look and feel" of software as displayed to the user. GUI software is separate from the X server, and there are several types of GUIs. These include OpenLook, DECwindows, and Motif. A GUI determines how windows, menus, icons, and other "objects" on the screen look, behave, and interact with the user.

HDLC High-level data link control is a link level protocol sometimes used by itself. It is also used in the X.25 protocols and Point-to-Point Protocol (PPP). HDLC uses bit-level encoding to define packet boundaries and adds a checksum after each packet.

Header Auxiliary information preceding a transmission block.

Hewlett-Packard HP-UX Based on AT&T UNIX System V with Berkeley UNIX enhancements. It supports added functionally for real-time processing dynamic linking and Sun Microsystems' virtual memory.

Hierarchical Directory A means of storing files which groups those that are common in purpose.

Hop Count A field in the header of an IP packet which counts the number of routers through which the packet has traversed.

Hop Count Limit Specifies the number of routes a broadcast frame may traverse before it will be discarded by a bridge.

Host Provides computing power and the intelligence of the client software running on it.

Hub The central switch in a twisted-pair network. All nodes on the network are connected via point-to-point lines to the hub.

IAB (Internet Activities Board) An organization which drafts standards for TCP/IP.

ICMP Internet Control Message Protocol is a part of the IP that handles error and control messages. It is used by gateways and hosts to report problems worth the datagram to the original source. ICMP also has an echo request/reply feature to test whether a node is alive or dead.

IEEE Institute of Electrical and Electronics Engineers, Inc., of the United States, standards committee for local area networks. It is responsible for standards for logical link control, Ethernet, token bus, token ring, FDDI, and POSIX.

Interface In networking, the boundary between two components, hardware or software, of a network. Hardware interfaces define physical connectors, signal definitions, media, and related issues. Software interfaces define the exact services and means of invoking those services that a lower layer offers a higher layer, or that a protocol layer offers to application software.

Internet A collection of heterogeneous networks interconnected by linking devices such as routers, gateways, and bridges to operate as a single network.

Internetworking The use of linking devices such as gateways, bridges, and routers to connect network systems of same or varied configurations and operating systems.

Interoperability Two computers (systems and/or products) are said to be interoperable if they can communicate and exchange information with each other.

IP (Internet Protocol) The key protocol in TCP/IP which runs over many different lower layer protocols. IP is the network layer protocol. It is connectionless and provides best effort (no guaranteed) delivery of datagrams across an Internet. IP carries TCP and other protocol traffic.

IPC - Interprocess Communications A set of system resources which allows one running program to communicate with another.

ISO (International Standards Organization) Its members are national standards organizations, for example, American National Standards Institute (ANSI). ISO membership is voluntary, and each member country is represented by its national standards organization.

ISO/OSI International Organization for Standardization/Open Systems Interconnection. The ISO/OSI model specifies that seven networking protocols be layered for conceptual simplicity and widest interoperability. A major competitor is TCP/IP.

Open Systems Interconnection, originally established to solve the world's computer communications interoperability problems, defines a collection of protocols in a seven-layer reference model and a set of application services. It was developed by ISO. OSI, while technically defining a set of standards for interoperability, is often used to describe products as well. OSI compliant means the product, whether it is a file server, software program, or a driver, will interoperate with other OSI products. It also means that an OSI-compliant system will interoperate with any other such system.

Kernel A collection of system routines that interact with the hardware. This is the essential core of UNIX.

Layer A conceptual level of network processing function defined by network architectures. Processing thought to take place in layers starting from the physical transmission of data up through to the commands of an end user.

Learning Bridge A bridge which automatically learns the topology of the network by recording the LAN addresses of each node as it receives packets. Learning bridges require little or no setup at the time of installation.

LAN (Local Area Network) Two or more computers, such as network printers or modems, wired together with special hardware and software that allows the computer to exchange information and share resources. Such a network may include PCs, printers, microcomputers, and mainframes linked by a transmission medium such as coaxial cable or twisted-pair wiring. Ethernet and token ring are two commonly used LANs.

Local Client An X application running on the same computer as the X server that is serving it.

Location Transparency Objects are accessed without knowledge of their location.

LLC (Logical Link Control) Defined by IEEE 802 standard as the upper sublayer of the data link layer. It allows higher-layer protocols to operate independently of the LAN being used.

LUs (Logical Units) Network addressable units in the SNA network that support port(s) for communication via the network. LUs perform transmission control, data control and presentation services. Types of LUs are (1) LU 1, host program to keyboard, printer, disk drive; (2) LU 2, host program to 3270 display; (3) LU3, host program to 3270 printer (4) LU4, host program to text processor; (5) LU5, undefined; (6) LU6, general-purpose program-to-program; (7) LU7, host program to 5250 display. The LU is the logical window or port through which end users access the SNA network.

Mach A UNIX look-alike developed at Carnegie-Mellon University. It is at the core of OSF/1. Migration transparency movement of objects does not affect application programs.

Mainframe A large, high-performance multiuser computer, capable of the largest computing tasks and information storage.

Management Information Base (MIB) The set of parameters an NMS can query and modify in an SNMP (or CMIP/MCMIS) agent. Standard, minimal MIBs have been defined and vendors often have private enterprise MIBs. In theory, any NMS which supports SNMP can talk to any SNMP agent with a properly defined MIB.

Management Information Service (MIS) A group or department within an organization that provides the computing and information services needed to operate the company. An MIS professional is one who is involved in the technology, products, and service of making information available to the decision makers who need it.

MapWindow This request sends the ID of the window that is to be marked for display, so that it will be visible when certain listed conditions are met.

MAC (Media Access Control Defined by IEEE 802 standard as the lower portion of the data link layer on a LAN. The MAC layer includes LAN technology specific to parts of the data link layer, such as the mechanism for gaining access to the Ethernet LAN or the token ring LAN.

Message A general term, used to describe one of the transition stages of data as it travels over the different TCP/IP layers.

MIB Browser A software tool which can be used to display arbitrary MIB variables obtained from an SNMP agent, allowing the user to browse through all the information provided about the device or service supported by the agent.

MIB/II A refinement of the original MIB specification.

MMS Manufacturing message specifications.

Monitoring The process of observing the status of network devices and services, either actively or passively.

Motif MOTIF is OSF's graphical user interface that has windows-style behavior and screen appearance. It is based on X Window System. It provides the foundation for many vendor-supplied products, including IBM's AIX windows.

MSNF Multiple systems networking facility. Refer to SSCP.

Multi-protocol A network node which can support more than one protocol simultaneously. A multiprotocol router can forward packets for more than one network layer protocol, for example, TCP/IP, OSI, SNA, DECnet.

MAU (Multistation Access Unit) A device, typically located in a wiring closet, which serves as a connection or distribution point for LANs. A common form is used for token ring LANs, to provide a centralized connection point for all nodes, reducing the problems in managing a ring topology network.

Multistation A network allowing more than one station, or network node, to be attached to the same link.

Multitasking The process of switching from one task to another without losing track of either task. Usually accomplished by time slicing of shared resources—dividing resource use into multiple segments, each of which is assigned to a different task.

MULTICS A predecessor of UNIX designed by MIT and General Electric to provide an interactive computing environment. MULTICS development started in 1965.

NAS (Network Applications Support) NAS is DEC's architecture for allowing the creation of distributed applications across its own operating systems as well as those from other vendors.

NAU A network addressable unit. Network computing system.

NCS This is a major RPC standard and was developed by Apollo Systems.

NMS (Network Management System) A software application, generally running under UNIX, whose purpose is to collect, graphically display, and archive data from devices and services; to detect failures and degradations in the performance of devices and services; to notify people of such failures; and to provide other tools useful in the diagnosis of network and service problems.

NOS (Network Operating System) Software that provides users with a variety of data communication services including file sharing, electronic mail, security systems, and methods for connecting network systems.

Network The set of interconnected computing services and the devices which support communication with those services. In this context, the physical network, hubs, routers, host computers, and processes running on host computers are all part of the *network*.

NFS (Network File System) A networking protocol developed by Sun Microsystems which allows files to be stored and accessed at remote location over a network. It makes remote file systems appear to be local. It provides transparent file access between computers of different architectures via a network. NFS is an example of a network operating system. It is a *de facto* standard for distributed file systems. It allows an arbitrary collection of clients and servers to share a common file system. NFS defines the interface between clients and servers. NFS protocol is a set of procedures that uses the RPC mechanism to contact the appropriate NFS server on the remote node. NFS is designed to support different nodes in any network. Most UNIX systems, including AIX, support NFS. NSF servers are "stateless."

NIS Network Information Service. NIS was formerly known as SUN Yellow Pages (YP). It is a distributed name service for administration of NFS. NIS is a mechanism for identifying and locating objects and resources, uniform storage, and retrieval for network-wide information. It allows the system administrator to distribute administrative databases (maps) and update them from one machine. NIS uses information contained in NIS maps (each map has a map name).

NIST National Institute of Standards and Technology, located in Gaithersburg, MD. It plays an integral part in overseeing and monitoring the OIW's refinement process. NIST also runs the GOSIP program and handles the testing requirements for the Register of Conformance-Tested GOSIP Products.

Node A computer or other device connected to the network which can be directly addressed by other nodes.

NPSI Network packet-switching interface, an IBM software that runs in the 3745 and allows SNA hosts to communicate with X.25 DTEs.

Object-Oriented Framework A service that allows a networked computer and its applications to be represented as a collection of objects, segments of code that represent real entities, such as devices or applications.

Object Any network attached device or service. Routers, hosts, and services running on hosts (e.g., SMTP Daemons) are all considered objects when discussing network monitoring.

OCTET Another term for byte, a group of 8 bits.

OEM Original equipment manufacturers; designation given to firms that make their own hardware.

OIW OSI Implementers Workshop. Works on behalf of the North American countries to review ISO's set of OSI standards to pare down the standards to provide for a better fit within the respective countries they represent.

OLTP On-line transaction processing. Multiple users share common, on-line access to databases.

OMG Object management group. A group that promotes the development of software based on object-oriented technology. It was founded in 1989 by 3 COM Corp., American Airlines, Canon, Data General, HP, and SUN.

ONC Open network computing. A major RPC standard developed by Sun Microsystems. It is an RPC mechanism that can operate on both the TCP/IP and OSI networks.

OOP Object-oriented programming, a programming method allowing more modular and frequently simpler programs to be written to perform a specific task.

OSPF (Open Shortest Path First) A distributed algorithm and routing protocol used by routers to compute the best path to be used to forward packets through an internetwork.

Open System According to Gartner Group, an open system is a compliant implementation of an evolving set of vendor-neutral specifications for interfaces, services, protocols, and formats designed to effectively enable the configuration, operation, and substitution of the entire system, its applications, and/or its components with other equally compliant implementations, preferably available from many different vendors. According to POSIX 1003.0, an open-systems environment supports a comprehensive set of international information technology standards and functional standard profiles that specify interface services and supporting formats to accomplish interoperability and portability of applications, data, and people.

OSF/1 Based on Mach operating system developed at Carnegie-Mellon. OSF/1 is a UNIX alternative. OSF/Motif is a graphical user interface.

OSF Open Software Foundation, an international software development organization that proposes to create a UNIX system separate from AT&T's UNIX System V. OSF was founded in 1988, later expanded by a consortium of vendors, including Bull, DEC, Hewlett-Packard, Hitachi, IBM, Nixdorf, and Siemens. Major products include OSF/1, OSF/Motif, and OSF/DCE. OSF's development solution, which has been in the works for several years, comprises the distributed computing environment and distributed management environment.

OSI/CS OSI Communications Subsystem. It provides connectivity between SNA and OSI.

Packet The basic unit of transfer in local area networks. A packet consists of a block of information with addressing and control information in the header, data is supplied by higher-level protocols or the user, and some error detection code at the end.

Packet Switching A communication technique in which data is packetized and transmitted at variable intervals with other data.

PDL Page Description Language.

Peer-to-Peer Peer-to-peer is an alternative approach to distributed computing. Peer-to-peer gives each computing node access to resources of other nodes. In theory, two peer nodes have symmetric functions. Any function possible using client/server could also be accomplished with peer-to-peer and vice versa. Examples of peer-to-peer architectures are SNA LU 6.2 and IBM's distributed relational database architecture.

Peer   Refers to a system that is equal in function to another. In networking, a balanced relationship between two nodes, which does not use a master/slave approach.

Physical Address   The MAC-layer address of a node, as opposed to the software defined network-layer address. For example, in IEEE 802.3 and 802.5, the physical address is 48-bit field recognized by the LAN controller hardware.

Ping   Network management software used to test if a managed device is reachable. The ICMP packets used for this function are called *echo* packets or *pings*.

Pipe   A UNIX facility which takes the output of one program and makes it input for another program. It is a one-way communication path between processes. An ending process places data in pipe for receiving process to remove.

Pixel   The smallest element of a display surface that can be addressed.

PLU   Primary logical unit. In an SNA LU-LU session, the LU that is responsible for setting the session parameters and for performing error recovery.

PPP (Point-to-Point Protocol Polling)   A standard TCP/IP related protocol used to communicate over a serial point-to-point link such as a T1 trunk between routers.

Polling   The act of periodically querying the state of an object.

Port Number   A field in the TCP or UDP headers that specifies which applications are sending and receiving the messages. The port field is the layer interface that enables TCP and UDP to transfer messages to any application.

Port   A port is a logical communication channel in a host. An access point on a multiuser interconnection device, that is, a physical connector on a hub or a terminal server or on a network.

Portmap   A set of associations between processes and ports.

Portmapper   The Portmapper protocol defines a network service that provides a standard way for the client to look up the port number of any remote program supported by a server. A client sends an RPC call message to the Portmapper. If the remote program is registered with the Portmapper, it returns the corresponding port number in an RPC reply message. The Portmapper provides an inherently stateful service—all RPC services need to be reregistered if the Portmapper is restarted.

POSIX   Portable Operating System Interface for Computer Environments, the IEEE's standard operating system interface specifications. It provides a way of ensuring source-level application code portability. It is broader than just typical UNIX kernel interface—it includes shell (user interface) as part of the specification.

PBX (Private Branch Exchange)   A privately owned telephone switch that provides local communication and access to trunk lines. Originally used for voice communications only, many PBXs now have data capabilities.

Programmer's Workbench   A collection of tools which automate part of the software development cycle.

Proprietary A protocol or communications system developed by a company, as opposed to those emanating from a standards organization.

Protocol The rules or conventions used to govern the exchange of information between networked nodes. For example, the TCP protocol specifies the exact contents and sequence of packets used to send data between two nodes.

Protocol Multiplexing A technique for unambiguously transmitting more than one protocol over the same link. For example, both Ethernet and PPP allow protocol multiplexing.

PUs Physical units, a network addressable unit that controls data link communication between the SNA node and the network. Types of PUs are (1) type 5, System/370 mainframe with a system services control point; (2) type 4 communications controller (3705, 3725, 3745); (3) type 3, undefined, (4) type 2, end nodes with limited routing capabilities (terminal cluster controllers 3274, 3778, or remote batch terminals supporting SDLC); (5) type 2.1, workstations that are able to establish peer-to-peer communications without a mainframe, and (6) type 1, pre-SNA terminals (obsolete). The PU is the manager of the node and cooperates with the SSCP, which acts as a central point for network management.

Refresh Rate The number of times per second the video image is drawn on a display station. Rates below 60 or 70 Hz (Hertz, times per second) may create a noticeable flicker.

Reliable Transport A transport layer, such as TCP, which guarantees reliable, in-sequence delivery of all data.

Remote Bridge A bridge located on a network system separate from the host system.

Remote Client An X application running on a different computer than the X server (the user's computer), and communicating with it over a network.

Remote Login A specific feature which allows authorized users of one TCP/IP system to log into another over a network and interact as if directly connected to each other.

Remote A term used to describe network devices that are managed or controlled from a network system other than the system to which they are directly connected.

Repeater A hardware device that generates LAN signals to extend the length of the network, or converts signals between media at the same speed. Most commonly used in Ethernet technology networks, since ring-based networks regenerate the signal at each node.

Resolution The number of pixels per inch, indicating how densely the pixels are packed on the screen. The number of pixels (points or dots) on a display screen, expressed as horizontal by vertical pixels, such as 1024 x 768. The more pixels, the more information one can see.

RFS Remote file system, a UNIX System V network protocol developed by AT&T which is a distributed file system allowing users to share data and processing capabilities across a network. RFS is designed to support identical UNIX nodes on a reliable network. Like NFS, RFS uses TCP/IP networking. Unlike NFS, RFS (1) retains UNIX features such as named pipes and direct device 1/0, (2) effectively avoids network congestion, (3) provides clock synchronization, and (4) maintains client state information within servers.

Ring A common network topology in which all nodes are connected in a closed loop, or ring. Each node receives packets from its *upstream* neighbor and transmits each one to its downstream neighbors.

RIP (Routing Information Protocol) It is an Interior Gateway Protocol used by TCP/IP to exchange routing information on a small computing network.

RISC Reduced instruction set computing., RISC is one of two types of UNIX processors; CISC is the othe., The first RISC processors were developed by HP in 1983. It is a style of computer architecture that emphasizes simplicity and efficiency.

The concept relies on the empirical observation that a few simple instructions account for almost all computations (e.g., 80% of the computations requires about 20% of the instruction set). RISC must execute those 20% rapidly. The advantage of RISC is the inherent speed of a simple design. The key to performance is single-cycle executions. It also uses pipe-lining (processing of several instructions at the same time). It has a register-to-register design and high-performance memory—at least 32 registers and large cache memories.

Router A network layer packet forwarding device. Routers are software or hardware/software products which receive network layer datagrams and forward them toward their destination based on the network layer address in the packet.

Routers Routers build on the bridge concept and operate at layer 3—network. They are dependent on network protocols (IP, IPX, SNA, etc.). Multiprotocol routers now are commonplace.

RPC Remote procedure call. Gives the interface between the end-user application and the network. It is a mechanism allowing a program executing on one host to call a subprogram on another host. The RPC goal is to allow distributed applications to be written in the same style as programs for centralized systems. An RPC is a code that specifies that portions of a program, called procedures, should run on a remote computer. An RPC enables a compiler to automatically generate the communications code that allows the procedure to be run remotely. It enables client/server communications. Simply stated, the RPC lets a programmer call a subroutine that may be located in a remote machine. The RPC defines a method for a remote client to identify procedure to be executed, machine to be executed on, and arguments required by the remote process. It uses XDR protocol to ensure consistency across different computers.

RT/PC An IBM computer family that uses the reduced instruction set computer architecture and runs the AIX operating system.

SAA Systems Application Architecture, is an IBM architecture that defines tools and techniques for application development. UNIX (or AIX) is not part of SAA.

SAP Service access point.

Scalability The ability to move among different sizes of machines. The ability of an application to run on computers of different sizes (e.g., PCs to mainframes).

SDLC Synchronous data link control. The standard data link control (layer 2) protocol used in SNA; a set of procedures for exchanging information on a data link.

Segment The unit of information formed by TCP when it divides user messages into smaller parts for transmission across the network. TCP gives segments to IP for transmission. IP converts segments to datagrams by further subdividing them and adding IP header information.

Server A program, computer, or network device that provides services for network users. Such services include sharing applications, files, and printer resources.

Session In SNA, a temporary logical connection between two network-addressable units, for an exchange of information, following agreed-upon rules. In OS/2, a group of processes that can occupy the screen, which constitute a single application.

SetCloseDownMode A request issued when the client resources are to be preserved at the close of the connection. This request is used to modify the behavior so that resources created by a client are not immediately destroyed when the client exits.

Shell The program by which the UNIX system implements its standard user interfaces.

SMTP (Simple Mail Transfer Protocol) An Internet electronic mail protocol used for transferring electronic mail messages from one machine to another.

SMTP uses TCP for reliable mail delivery. It focuses on mail delivery across networks, not on the mail interface. Its objective is to transfer mail reliably and efficiently. It is a standard way of exchanging mail. It works with many electronic mail products.

SNA Systems Network Architecture. Developed by IBM, it is IBM's system of proprietary network protocols. It allows users to extend centralized network management from mainframes to LAN-based groups. There are two major types of SNA networks: (1) Subarea SNA networks built round SNA mainframes (mainframes maintain centralized control) may be interconnected using SNA SNI (SNA network interconnect) and (2) SNA low-entry networking or Advanced Peer-to -Peer Networking, limited to PU type 2 and supporting LU 6.2 (APPN can be connected together through an SNA subarea network).

Most networks are subarea networks. SNA defines (1) sets of communications functions that are distributed throughout a network and (2) formats and protocols that relate these functions to one another. Only the key formats and protocols needed for general communications are defined by SNA. It is IBM's master blueprint for communications, which defines sets of communications functions that are distributed throughout a network and formats and protocols that relate these functions to one another.

SNI SNA network interconnection. An IBM software product that provides a gateway between two dissimilar SNA networks.

SNMP Simple network management protocol. Used by network administration applications to monitor network activity. SNMP defines an information model for representing network management information, a protocol for retrieving/setting this information, and a standard set of management information.

Sockets The Berkeley interprocess communication model. It specifies the endpoints of a two-way communications channel connecting two processes so that they can exchange information. Sockets are the basic building blocks for communication. The following types are defined: (1) stream sockets: bidirectional, reliable, sequenced, unduplicated flow of data without record boundaries; (2) datagram sockets: bidirectional, unreliable, unsequenced flow of data (not promised to be unduplicated) with record boundaries; (3) raw sockets: direct access to the underlying communication protocols that support socket abstraction (used mainly for development of new protocols); (4) packet sockets: identical to stream sockets but with record boundaries (not implemented with TCP/IP); and (5) reliably delivered message socket: reliable datagram (not implemented with TCP/IP).

Spanning Tree Algorithm An IEEE 802.1 standard algorithm used by bridges to automatically compute a set of routes between all bridges in the network to avoid loops. It is required in a bridge network if redundant links are needed for backup purposes.

SQL Structured Query Language.

SRPI Server/Requester Programming Interface. A communication tool for connecting PC applications, which act as requesters, to System/370 applications, which act as servers. SRPI is the foundation for ECF.

SSCP System services control point. The SSCP is a special-purpose NAU that performs network management and control functions. An SNA network may have many SSCPs. This is called MSNF (Multiple Systems Networking Facility). SSCP functions include bringing up/down the network, assisting in LU-LU session establishment, scheduling error recovery, executing operator commands, and tracking the status of network resources.

Stack A software module or group of modules, such as one that handles the TCP/IP protocol.

Star A local area network using a star or daisy-chain topology. The star topology consists of a central device (hub) to which are connected other network devices. StarLAN was originally developed by AT&T and is now a part of the IEEE 802.3 standard.

Stateful File Server The Statefule File Server maintains client information from one remote procedure to the next (e.g., server maintains the state of the client's open files—name, mode and position). An example is the remote file system. In the event of a failure, the client needs to detect a server crash.

Stateless File Server The server does not need to maintain any state information about its clients as the client passes all the information in the read request (file name, position, and number of bytes). An example is the network file system. In the event of a failure, the client does not need to know that the server has crashed or that the network went down.

Streams The UNIX System V implementation of interprocess communications. It provides a layered and flexible means for two or more processes to communicate. It provides a standard interface for characters on UNIX systems. User programs are insulated from protocols.

Sublayer A portion of an OSI layer. For example, the data link layer in a LAN has two sublayers: logical link control and media access control.

Subnet A network that has been connected to a larger and more powerful network system. Subnets are connected to a larger net by a bridge or a router.

Suite A related group of protocols, such as TCP/IP protocol suite. The TCP/IP protocol suite includes IP, ARP, ICMP, TCP, UDP, Telnet, FTP, SMTP, and others.

SunOS A UNIX variant developed and marketed by Sun Microsystems.

SVID System V Interface Definition. An AT&T document that outlines what system resources a vendor must implement in order for software portability across System V environments. It distinguishes between base system (system and library calls) and kernel extensions.

Systems Network Architecture IBM's proprietary high-level networking protocol. Used by IBM and IBM-compatible mainframes.

T1 A digital transmission system that sends information at 1.544 megabits per second. T1 links can transmit voice and data.

TCP Transmission Control Protocol. A reliable byte stream protocol, developed by U.S. Department of Defense.

TCP/IP Transmission Control Protocol/Internet Protocol. Rules for exchanging data over a network, more commonly under UNIX.

TELNET A simple remote terminal protocol. It gives the appearance that the user's terminal is attached directly to a remote machine. A character-based terminal emulation protocol available on TCP/IP programs.

TFTP Trivial File Transfer Protocol. It uses unreliable datagram service and time-outs and retransmissions. The receiver acknowledges each block of data (512 bytes). It is a simple file transfer with no authentication.

Thick Ethernet The first 10 Mbps Ethernet which specifies a high-quality, thick coaxial cable. The IEEE 802.3 10BASE5 specification refers to thick Ethernet.

Thin Ethernet The version of Ethernet which uses low-cost, thin coaxial cable, at shorter distances than the original Ethernet specification. It is also called *cheapernet* and 10BASE2.

Thread A thread is a single flow of control within a process. All threads in a process share the same address space and can synchronize with each other. Threads allow parts of the application to execute concurrently. Threads are useful in developing client/server models. Some operating systems support threads, others don't (DCE provides built-in support for threads).

Time-to-Live (TTL) The maximum time an Internet Protocol datagram is allowed to live in the Internet before it is dropped to avoid infinite loop forwarding. A router decrements the TTL field each time a datagram passes through it. If the field reaches zero, the datagram is dropped.

Token Passing A LAN technology which employs tokens as part of the access control mechanism. Both IEEE 802.5 and FDDI are token passing LANs.

Token Ring Network IBM's strategic local area network which uses a star-wired ring topology. The architecture of the token ring is defined by the IEEE 802.5 standard, which is also included in SAA common communications support (CCS).

Token A combination of unique bits that are passed around in the network during the token passing access method used by token ring networks.

Tool Simple programs that perform a particular data processing function.

Trap An asynchronous message generated by an SNMP agent to provide information about an exception condition.

UDP User Datagram Protocol.

UTS UNIX Timesharing System. UTS is a UNIX variant, a mainframe version of UNIX, based on AT&T UNIX System V, which runs on Amdahl mainframes. It supports applications connectivity with VM/ESA and MVS/ESA environments.

UUCP UNIX-to-UNIX Copy Program.

WAN (Wide Area Network) A network which includes nodes distributed over a larger geographic area than can be served by a local area network. Typically used to refer to networks which include telecommunications trunks from common carriers, satellite links, or other long-distance communications links.

Window Manager An X client that allows the user to move and resize windows and controls some aspects of their appearance. It is part of the graphical user interface. It is usually local, but can also be a remote client. The window manager has authority over the management of windows on the screen and the user interface for selecting which window receives input.

Window A function that allows users to divide the screen into multiple independent areas, each containing one panel. An area on a screen in which an application displays data or controls (buttons, etc.). Windows can be scrolled, resized, and moved. Windows are provided by the operating system and related presentation tools or by the application.

Workgroup A small group of computers, typically personal computers and associated file servers, connected via a LAN for departmental-level computing and communications.

Workstation A single-user computer which provides significant graphics processing capabilities. Used in the engineering design and desktop publishing areas.

X Server X server is a special software that resides on the user's computer and provides display services for clients. It accepts information from the client application to be displayed on the screen and converts mouse and keyboard actions into data that the client can understand. X server allows for many "look and feel" varieties.

X Terminal It is a display terminal and keyboard that includes an X server and X clients running remotely on other machines. Some X terminals also support local clients, such as built-in window managers.

X Window System An open window system architecture and protocols first developed at MIT in 1984. It uses the client/server model. X Window System is now a *de facto* standard for graphical interface and window management.

X.25 A standardized application program interface used on a packet-switching data communications network. This protocol is used to encapsulate data for transmission over X.25 network. The encapsulation provides error detection and a means of dividing and reassembling a message.

It is a packet-switched WAN protocol. It is not OS I compatible. X.25 is a CCITT standard that defines a three-layer interface between packet switching data networks and computers or terminals.

X/OPEN Company Ltd A user consortium founded in 1982 by major computer companies, including Bull, DEC, HP, Fujitsu, Hitachi, IBM, ICL, NEC, NCR, Nixdorf, Nokia Data, Olivetti, Open Software Foundation, Philips, Prime, Siemens, SUN, UNIX International, and Unisys to bring structure to open systems standards. A requirement for membership is a commitment to products supporting X/OPEN standards. X/OPEN develops Common Applications Environment. X/OPEN endorses existing technologies as standards and, in some cases, defines its own technology as a standard.

X11 A version of the X Window standard released in 1987 and adopted as an industry standard.

X client An application program (for example, database) that can run under the X Window System. A client program can perform a variety of tasks, including terminal emulation and window management. A client application may run on the same computer as the X server (in local client mode) or on a remotely located computer (in remote client mode).

XDR External Data Representation. It is a standard for passing binary and character data via RPC between possibly dissimilar systems. The calling program translates data into XDR; the called program translates XDR into its own format.

Xenix A UNIX variant marketed by Santa Cruz Operations. It is a stripped-down UNIX targeted for 8086 and 286-based PCs. It was originally a Microsoft product, spun off to SCO.

XI-X.25 Interface IBM software that lets the SNA network act as a packet-switching network.

xkill Terminates a client application.

Xlib A C language interface to the X protocol. Client programs are usually written using Xlib to interface with the X protocol.

XPG3 (X/Open Portability Guide, Version 3) A technical guideline relating to open system products established by X/OPEN Company Ltd. It sets out specifications for realizing a common application environment.

Xstone A graphics performance rating that results from a standard test called Xbench. It does not reflect the performance you may get with a product running your specific application.

xterm The terminal emulator included in the standard release of X.

XTI-X/OPEN Transport Interface An application program interface developed by X/OPEN Company Ltd. that lets applications directly access transport protocols. XTI is already supported by most vendors for TCP/IP.

BIBLIOGRAPHY

Anderson, B., Costales, B., and Henderson, H. *UNIX Communications*. Howard W. Sams, Indianapolis, Ind., 1987.

Andleigh, P. *UNIX System Architecture*. Prentice Hall, Englewood Cliffs, N.J., 1990.

Bach, M. J. *The Design of the UNIX Operating System*. Prentice Hall, Englewood Cliffs, N.J., 1986.

Bates, Bud. *Introduction to T1/T3 Networking*. Artech House, Boston, 1992. ISBN 0-89006-624-8.

Berson, Alex. *APPC: Introduction to LU6.2*, McGraw-Hill, New York, 1990. ISBN 0-07-005075-9.

Beyeda, W. *Basic Data Communications: A Comprehensive Overview*. Prentice Hall, Englewood Cliffs, N.J.,1989.

Black, Uylsess. *Data Networks*. Prentice-Hall, Englewood Cliffs, N.J., 1989, ISBN 0-13-198466-7.

Brambert, Dave. *Guide to Internetworking*. Miller Freeman, San Francisco, 1993. ISBN 0-87930-262-3.

Bureau of Naval Personnel. *Basic Data Processing*. Dover Publications, New York, 1971. ISBN 0-486-20229-1.

Burgard, Michael J. and Philips, Kenneth D. *DOS–UNIX Networking and Internetworking*. John Wiley & Sons, New York, 1994.

Carl-Mitchell, Smoot and Quarterman, John S. *Practical Internetworking with TCP/IP and UNIX*. Addison-Wesley, Reading, Mass., 1993. ISBN 0-201-58629-0.

Claude, J. P. *Advanced Information Processing Techniques for LAN and MAN Management*. North-Holland, New York, 1994. ISBN 0-444-81634.8.

Coffin, Stephen. *UNIX: The Complete Reference*. McGraw-Hill, New York, 1988. ISBN 0-07-881299-2.

Comer, Douglas E. *Internetworking with TCP/IP*, Volume I. Prentice Hall, Englewood Cliffs, N.J. 1991. ISBN 0-13-488505-9.

Comer, Douglas. *Internetworking with TCP/IP: Principles, Protocols, and Architecture* 2nd ed. Prentice Hall, Englewood Cliffs, N.J., 1991.

Comer, Douglas and Stevens, D. *Internetworking with TCP/IP: Design, Implementation and Internals.* Prentice-Hall, Englewood Cliffs, N.J., 1991.

Comer, Douglas E. and Stevens, David L. *Internetworking with TCP/IP*, Volume III. Prentice Hall, Englewood Cliffs, N.J., 1993. ISBN 0-13-474222-2.

Corbin, J. *The Art of Distributed Applications: Programming Techniques for Remote Procedure Calls.* Springer-Verlag, New York, 1991.

Coulouris, G. and Dollimore, J. *Distributed Systems: Concepts and Design.* Addison-Wesley, Reading, Mass., 1988.

Cypser, R.J. *Communications Architecture for Distributed Systems.* Addison-Wesley, Reading, Mass., 1978, ISBN 0-201-14458-1.

Dallas, I. N., Spratt, E. B., and Cabanel, J. P. *Issues in LAN Management.* North-Holland, Amsterdam, 1991. ISBN 0-444-88918-3.

Datapro. *Datapro Reports on UNIX Systems and Software.* McGraw-Hill, New York, 1991.

Davidson, Robert P. and Muller, Nathan J. *Internetworking LANs: Operation, Design, and Management.* Artech House, Boston, Mass., 1992. ISBN 0-89006-598-5.

Dunphy, E. *The UNIX Industry.* QED Technical Publishing, Boston, Mass., 1991.

Enck, J. *A Manager's Guide to Multivendor Networks.* Professional Press Books, Horsham, Pa., 1991.

Fitzgerald, J. *Business Data Communications.* John Wiley and Sons, New York, 1990.

Goscinski, A. *Distributed Operating Systems: The Logical Design.* Addison-Wesley, Reading, Mass., 1991. ISBN 0-201-41704-9.

Grampp, F. T. and Morris, R. H. "UNIX Operating System Security." *AT&T Bell Laboratories Technical Journal*, 1984.

Gray, Pamela A. *Open Systems: A Business Strategy for the 1990s.* McGraw-Hill, London, 1991. ISBN 0-07-707244-8.

Groff, N. *Conceptual Understanding of UNIX.* Que Corporation, Carmel, IN, 1989.

Handel, Rainer and Huber, Manfred N. *Integrated Broadband Networks: An Introduction to ATM-Based Networks.* Addison-Wesley, Reading, Mass., 1991. ISBN 0-201-54444-X.

Hedrick, Chuck. *Introduction to the Internet Protocols.* Rutgers University Press, Brunswick, N.J., 1987.

Hedrick, Chuck. *Introduction to Administration of an Internetbased Local Network.* Rutgers University Press, Brunswick, N.J., 1987.

Helgert, H. *Integrated Services Digital Networks: Architectures, Protocols, Standards.* Addison-Wesley, Reading, Mass., 1991.

Helmers, S. *Data Communications: A Beginner's Guide to Concepts and Technology.* Prentice Hall, Englewood Cliffs, N.J., 1989.

Houldsworth, J., Taylor, M., Caves, K., Flatman, A., and Crook, K. *Open System LANs.* Butterworth Heinemann, Newton, Mass., 1991. ISBN 0-7506-1045-X.

International Business Machines. *Vocabulary for Data Processing, Telecommunications, and Office Systems.* IBM, 1981.

Kapoor, Atul. *SNA: Architecture, Protocols, and Implementation.* McGraw-Hill, New York, 1992. ISBN 0-07-033727-6.

Kauffels, Franz-Joachim. *Practical LANs Analyzed.* Ellis Horwood, Chichester, UK, 1989. ISBN 0-7458-0254-0.

Kernighan, Brian W. and Pike, Rob. *The UNIX Programming Environment.* Prentice Hall, Englewood Cliffs, N.J., 1984.

Kernighan, Brian W. and Ritchie, Dennis M. *The C Programming Language.* Prentice Hall, Englewod Cliffs, N.J., 1988.

Kochan, S. and Wood, P. *UNIX Networking.* Hayden Books, Carmel, IN, 1989.

Kochan, Stephen G. and Wood, Patrick H. *UNIX Networking,* Hayden Books, Carmel, IN., 1990. ISBN 0-672-48440-4.

Kroll, Ed. *The Hitchhikers Guide to Internet.* University of Illinois, Urbana, Il., 1987.

Leffler, S.J., McKusick, M.K., Karels, M.J. and Quarterman, J.S. *The Design and Implementation of the 4.3 BSD UNIX Operating System.* Addison-Wesley, Reading, Mass., 1989, ISBN 0-201-06196-1.

Letwin, Gordon. *Inside OS/2.* Microsoft Press, Redmond, WA., 1988, ISBN 1-55-615117-9.

Linnell, Dennis. "SAA: IBM's Road Map to the Future." PC Tech Journal, April 1988.

Linnell, Dennis. *The SAA Handbook.* Addison-Wesley, Reading, Mass., 1990. ISBN 0-201-51786-8.

Maki, Ken. *Integrating MACS with Your PC Network.* John Wiley and Sons, New York, 1994. ISBN 0-471-30505-7.

Malamud, C. *Analyzing SUN Networks.* Van Nostrand Reinhold, New York, 1992.

Malamud, C. *Stacks: Interoperability in Today's Computer Networks.* Prentice Hall, Englewood Cliffs, N.J., 1991.

Malamud, Carl. *DEC Networks and Architectures.* McGraw-Hill, New York, 1989. ISBN 0-07-039822-4.

Martin, James and Chapman, Kathleen. *Local Area Networks: Architectures and Implementation.* Prentice Hall, Englewood Cliffs, N.J., 1989.

Martin, James and Chapman, Kathleen. *SNA: IBM's Networking Solution.* Prentice Hall, Englewood Cliffs, N.J., 1987. ISBN 0-13-815143-1.

Martin, James and Leben, Joe. *DECnet Phase V: An OSI Implementation.* Digital Press, Burlington, Mass., 1992. ISBN 1-55558-076-9.

McClain, Gary R. *Handbook of Networking & Connectivity.* AP Professional, Boston, 1994. ISBN 0-12-482080-8.

McNamara, J. *Technical Aspects of Data Communication.* Digital Equipment Corp., Maynard, Mass., 1977. ISBN 1-5558-007-6.

McNamara, John E. *Local Area Networks—An Introduction to the Technology.* Digital Press, Burlington, Mass., 1985.

Miller, Mark A. *Troubleshooting Internetworks.* M&T Books, San Mateo, Calif., 1994. ISBN 1-55851-268-3.

Miller, Mark A. *Handbook of LAN Troubleshooting.* M&T Books, San Mateo, Calif., 1993. ISBN 1-55851-268-3.

Miller, Mark A. *Internetworking: A Guide to Network Communications—LAN, LAN-WAN.* M&T Books, San Mateo, Calif., 1992. ISBN 1-55851-268-3.

Miller, Mark A. *Troubleshooting TCP/IP.* M&T Books, San Mateo, Calif., 1992b. ISBN 1-55851-268-3.

Minoli, Daniel. *Enterprise Networking: Fractional T1 to Sonet, Frame Relay to BISDN.* Artech House, Norwood, Mass., 1993. ISBN 0-89006-621-3.

Muller, Nathan J. and Davidson, Robert P. *LANs to WANs: Network Management in the 1990s.* Artech House, Norwood, Mass., 1990.

Naugle, Mathew G. *Local Area Networking.* McGraw-Hill, New York, 1991. ISBN 0-07-046455-3.

Nemeth, Evi, Snyder, Garth, and Seebass, Scott. *UNIX System Administration Handbook.* Prentice Hall, Englewood Cliffs, N.J., 1989. ISBN 0-13-815143-38.

Nunemacher, Greg. *LAN Primer.* M&T Books, New York, 1992. ISBN 1-55851-287X.

Nutt, G. *Open Systems.* Prentice Hall, Englewood Cliffs, N.J., 1992.

O'Reilly & Associates. *Guide to OSF/1: A Technical Synopsis.* O'Reilly & Associates, Sebastopol, Calif., 1991.

Orfali, Robert and Harkey, Dan. *Client/Server Programming with OS/2, 2.0.* Van Nostrand Reinhold, New York, 1992. ISBN 0-442-01219-5.

Open Software Foundation. *Distributed Computing Environment (DCE).* OSF, Boston, Mass., 1989.

Pooch, U., Greene, W., and Moss, G. *Telecommunications and Networking.* Little, Brown, Boston, Mass., 1983.

Prycker, Martin de. *Asynchronous Transfer Mode: Solution for Broadband ISDN.* Ellis Horwood, New York, 1991. ISBN 0-13-053513-3.

Pujolle, G., Seret, D., Dromand, D., and Horlait, E. *Integrated Digital Communications Networks.* John Wiley and Sons, New York, 1987. ISBN 0-471-91421-5.

Ranade, J. and Sackett, George C. *Introduction to SNA Networking.* McGraw-Hill, New York, 1989.

Rose, M. *An Introduction to Management of TCP/IP-Based Internets.* Prentice Hall, Englewood Cliffs, N.J., 1991.

Rose, M. *The Open Book: A Practical Perspective on OSI.* Prentice Hall, Englewood Cliffs, N.J., 1990.

Rosenberry, Ward and Teague, Jim. *DCE and Windows NT.* O'Reilly & Associates, Sebastopol, Calif., 1993. ISBN 1-56592-047-3.

Santifaller, Michael. *TCP/IP and NFS: Internetworking in a UNIX Environment.* Addison-Wesley, Reading, Mass., 1991. ISBN 0-201-54432-6

Schwartz, M. *Telecommunication Networks.* Addison-Wesley, Reading, Mass., 1987.

Shah, Amit and Ramakrishnan, G. *FDDI: A High Speed Network.* Prentice Hall, Englewood Cliffs, N.J., 1994. ISBN 0-13-308388-8.

Sherman, K. *Data Communications: A User's Guide.* Prentice Hall, Englewood Cliffs, N.J., 1990.

Simon, Alan R. *Implementing the Enterprise.* Bantam Books, New York, 1993. ISBN 0-553-09152-2.

Slomon, Morris. *Network and Distributed Systems Management.* Addison-Wesley, London, 1994. ISBN 0-201-62745-0 .

Spencer, Donald D. *Introduction to Information Processing.* Charles E. Merrill, Columbus, Ohio, 1977. ISBN 0-675-08520-9.

Spragins, J. *Telecommunications Protocols and Design.* Addison-Wesley, Reading, Mass., 1991. ISBN 0-201-09290-5.

Stallings, W. *Business Data Communications.* Macmillan, New York, 1990.

Stallings, W. *Data and Computer Communications.* Macmillan, New York, 1991.

Stallings, W. *Handbook of Computer Communications.* Volume 3 Standards. Macmillan, New York, 1988. ISBN 0-02-948072-8.

Stallings, W. *Handbook of Computer Communications, Volume 2, Local Network Standards.* Macmillan, New York, 1988. ISBN 0-02-948070-1.

Stallings, William. *Handbook of Computer Communications Standards—Local Network Standards.* Howard W. Sams, Indianapolis, Ind., 1987.

Stevens, W. *UNIX Network Programming.* Prentice Hall, Englewood Cliffs, N.J., 1988. ISBN 0-13-949876-1.

Stevens, W. Richard. *UNIX Network Programming.* Prentice Hall, Englewood Cliffs, N.J., 1990. ISBN 0-13-949876-1.

Sunshine, Carl A. *Computer Network Architectures and Protocols.* Plenum Press, New York, 1989. ISBN 0-306-43189-0.

Tanenbaum, A. *Modern Operating Systems.* Prentice Hall, Englewood Cliffs, N.J., 1992.

Tanenbaum, Andrew S. *Computer Networks.* Prentice Hall, Englewood-Cliffs, N.J., 1988. ISBN 0-13-162959-X.

Uhlig, Ronald, Farber, David J., and Bair, James H. *Office of the Future Communication and Computers.* North-Holland, New York, 1980. ISBN 0-444-85336-7.

Welch, Frank. *Integrated Computer Network Systems.* Marcel Dekker, New York, 1992. ISBN 0-8247-8742-0.

Wheeler, Tom. *Open Systems Handbook.* Bantam Books, New York, 1992. ISBN 0-553-08954-4.

Wilson, J. *Berkeley UNIX: A Simple and Comprehensive Guide.* John Wiley and Sons, New York, 1991. ISBN 0-471-61582-x(pbk).

INDEX

/bin/sh, 271
100BaseT, 267
100Mb/sec Ethernet, 17
100VG-Any-LAN, 309
3172 interconnect controller, 406
3172 Offload Feature, 406
3270 terminal emulation, 326, 429
3270/3770 emulators, 415, 417
3287 printer support, 326
328x printer emulation, 417
3770 RJE, 416-425
3Com 3+Open, 453
4.3 BSD UNIX, 447
5250 terminal emulation, 386, 429
A/UX, 287, 315
Abstract Syntax Notation 1 (ASN.1), 140, 514
Access security, 507
Access Unit Interface (AUI), 104
Accounting management, 147, 507
ACCUNET, 40
ACF/VTAM, 408
Acknowledged connectionless, 105
Acknowledgment number, 77
Active redundant paths (loops), 223
Ada, 151
Adapter cards, 468

Address Resolution Protocol (ARP), 155, 447, 544
Address Translation Table (ATT), 443
Address-generation circuitry, 314
Adobe, 389
Advanced NT Server, 31
Advanced Peer-to-Peer Networking (APPN), 43,
    177, 288, 396-397, 408, 415-425, 430
Advanced Program-to-Program Communication
    (APPC), 52, 176-177, 305, 405-407, 415-425,
    430
Advanced Research Project Agency network
    (ARPANET), 11, 60, 153
Advantage Networks, 43, 84, 425
AIX, 263, 315
AIX 3270, 289
AIX PS/2, 430
AIX RT, 430
AIX SNA Services/6000, 289
AIX/6000, 288
Alarm correlations, 509
Alarms, 440, 445
Aldus, 389
All-routes broadcast, 218
American National Standards Institute (ANSI), 73
Analyzer, 446
Analyzer console, 439

Andrew File System (AFS), 282-283
ANSI FORTRAN-77, 15, 85, 151
ANSI C, 151, 265
ANSI COBOL 9, 30, 85, 85, 151
Apple File Exchange (AFE), 374
Apple NuBus, 328
AppleEvents, 372
AppleShare, 128-129, 246-247, 319, 366-393
AppleShare file server, 373
AppleTalk, 3, 28, 45, 62, 128-130, 263, 289, 319, 366-393
AppleTalk Data Stream Protocol (ADSP), 368
AppleTalk Echo Protocol (AEP), 369
AppleTalk File Protocol (AFP), 52, 129, 293, 366-389
AppleTalk Link Access Protocol (ALAP), 90, 128
AppleTalk Router, 376
AppleTalk Session Protocol (ASP), 368
AppleTalk topologies, 130
AppleTalk Transmission Protocol (ATP), 91, 129
Application Binary Interfaces (ABIs), 285
Application layer, 66, 137
Application Program Interface (API), 247, 263, 306, 430
Application server, 36
Application System/400 (AS/400), 396
ARCnet (Attached Resource Computer network), 3, 36, 266, 308, 471
arp, 447
Artisoft LANtastic, 319
AS/400, 316
AS/400 TCP/IP, 316, 431
ASCII, 163
Assembler, 395
Association Control Service Element (ACSE), 140, 145, 518-520
Asynchronous link, 403
Asynchronous terminals, 416
Asynchronous Transfer Mode (ATM), 3, 100, 200, 267, 309-310
Attachment Unit Interface (AUI), 381
Authentication, 506
Authorization, 506
Automatic reconfiguration, 483
Autonomous, 5

Backbone, 17, 99, 233-234, 268, 304
Back-end servers, 236

Backoff algorithms, 122
Bandwidth, 244
Banyan VINES, 46, 62, 246, 318, 320
Baseband LANs, 106
BASIC interpreter, 324
Benchmark, 446
Berkeley Software Distribution (BSD) or 4.3 BSD, 154, 273
BIND, 329, 447
Bisync, 325
Bit error rate, 494
Bit error rate testers, 483
BITNET, 41, 412
Bottlenecks, 504
Bourne Shell, 271
Branch processing unit, 314
Bridges, 15, 26, 47, 112, 213-222
Broadband LANs (IEEE 802.7), 101, 104, 106
Broadband troubleshooting, 494
Broadcast services, 116
Broadcast storms, 227, 437
Broadcast systems, 191
Broadcast-data transfer mode, 186
Broken poker chip, 254
Brouter, 49, 113, 227
BSD Pockets, 52
Buffer cache, 261
Bursty requirements, 494
Bus topology, 108
Byte stream interface, 191

C language, 85, 351
C Shell, 272
Calendaring, 254
Carrier Sense Multiple Access / Collision Detect (CSMA/CD), 66, 72, 117, 545
Carrier-band signaling, 126
Cascading bridges, 16
cc:Mail, 388
CCITT, 55, 69
CD-ROMs, 318
Cell synchronism, 200
Central management console, 439
Centralized computing, 12
Centralized management, 12
ChameLAN 100, 459-460
Channel attachment, 325
Chat, 319

Checksum, 76-77, 159
Chooser, 370-390
Chooser problems, 477
Circuit switching systems, 192
Cisco Catalyst, 456
Client/server, 3, 17, 19-22, 29, 60, 98
Client/server computing, 18
Client/server model, 32-36
Clients, 19-22, 31
Cluster controller, 25, 173, 243, 318, 396
CMIP over LLC (CMOL), 441
CMIS Protocol Data Unit (PDU), 519-520
CMISE, 519-520
Coaxial cable, 38, 470
Collision fragments, 120
Collisions, 122
Commitment, Concurrency, and Recovery (CCR), 140, 145
Common Application Environment (CAE), 84
Common Management Information and Services Protocol Over TCP (CMOT), 443, 519-521
Common Management Information Protocol (CMIP), 140, 146, 508-530
Common Management Information Services (CMIS), 140, 146-148, 502, 518-521
Common Operating System Environment (COSE), 273, 318
Common Programming Interface for Communications (CPI-C), 290, 420
Common Transport Semantics (CTS), 398
Communication Manager/2 (CM/2), 398
Communications controllers, 39, 243
Communications server, 36
Complex internetwork, 16
Compute server, 97
Computer Aided Design (CAD), 4, 199, 251, 263,309
Computer Aided Manufacturing (CAM), 4, 199, 251, 263, 309
Concentrators, 39
Configuration management, 147, 483, 499, 505-506
Configuration maps, 505
Congestion, 438
Congestion control, 408
Connecting repeaters, 211, 563
Connectionless service, 16, 139
Connection-oriented, 16, 104

Connection-oriented service, 139
Connectors, 470
Controlling multipoint links, 174
Cooperative processing, 168
CorelDraw, 389
CreateWindow, 350
Crosstalk, 470
Customer Information Control System (CICS), 30, 174, 334, 398
Cyclic Redundancy Check (CRC), 103, 121, 495

Daemon process, 277
Daemons, 276
Data Access Language (DAL), 378
Data bus, 312
Data-circuit Terminating Equipment (DTE), 311
Data collector, 461
Data communication, 4, 26, 65
Data compression, 409, 495
Data Delivery Protocol (DDP), 128
Data encapsulation, 67, 105
Data flow layer, 169
Data formats, 64
Data Link Control (DLC), 203
Data link layer, 65, 128, 135-136
Data management, 84
Data security, 336
Data sharing, 27, 88
Data Stream Protocol (DSP), 129
Data Terminal Equipment (DTE), 174, 179
Data transfer phase, 138
Data transmission, 16
Data warehousing multi-dimensional analysis, 251
Database management, 14
Database Management Systems (DBMS), 19, 243
Database server, 35, 97
Data-cache interface, 314
Datagram, 76, 546
Datagram Delivery Protocol (DDP), 90, 368
Datagram service, 41, 139, 186
Datalink Connection Identifier (DLCI), 494
DataPrism, 378
DaVinci eMail, 388
dBASE, 13
De facto standards, 74, 133
De jure standards, 65, 133
Dead letter notification, 255
Debugging tools, 446-447

DEC OSF/1 AXP, 322
DEC WAN, 425
DECís DECnet, 11
Decentralization, 17
DECLan WORKS, 384
DECnet, 3, 28, 36, 83, 181-187, 289, 425-430
DECnet LANs, 425-430
DECnet Phase V (ADVANTAGE-NETWORKS),
   43, 84, 426-430
DECnet Phase V (DECnet OSI), 183
DECnet router/X.25 gateways, 425
DECnet/SNA gateway, 182, 425
Decompression, 495
DECwindows, 346
Dedicated server-based systems, 245
Delay-sensitive, 310
Desktop publishing, 388-389
Destination address, 67, 77, 120
Destination XNS, 502
Device drivers, 326
Digital Data Communications Message Protocol
   (DDCMP), 181, 428
Digital Data Service (DDS), 198
Digital Equipment Network Architecture (DNA),
   41, 83, 168, 181-187, 292
DiMONS (NetLabs), 527-529
Direct Access Storage Device (DASD), 29
Directory Access Protocol (DAP), 69
Directory Information Base (DIB), 257
Directory Information Tree (DIT), 257
Directory Services (X.500), 69
Directory Services Agent (DSA), 79, 257
Directory Services Protocol (DSP), 257
Directory User Agent (DUA),
Disaster recovery, 35, 386
Discrete systems, 27
Dish antenna, 117
Diskless Support Service (DSS), 88
Diskless workstations, 271
DISOSS, 428
Disparate protocols, 23
Disparate systems, 47
Disparate/dissimilar networks, 23
Display manager, 350
Display mode, 453
Distributed Compute Environment (DCE), 86,
   248, 253, 271, 311

Distributed Database Management System
   (DBMS), 264
Distributed environments, 88
Distributed file access, 282
Distributed file service, 88
Distributed File System (DFS), 89-90
Distributed Management Environment (DME), 88,
   524
Distributed processing, 5, 11, 18, 97
Distributed Sniffer System, 462
Domain Information Groper (DiG), 447
Domain Name Server (DNS), 338, 447, 546
DOS, 10, 23, 326, 405, 415
DOS (TCP/IP) client, 322
DOS and Windows client, 322
DOS-IPX, 263
DTE, 311
DTE-DCE, 193-196
Dual rings, 71
Dynamic Host Control Protocol (DHCP), 337
Dynamic Link Library (DLL), 359
Dynamic reconfiguration, 407
Dynamic routing, 225

EBCDIC, 163, 403
Echo Protocol (ECHO), 190-191
Echo request, 80
ECMA, 140
EDSAC, 8
Electronic Data Interchange (EDI), 256
Electronic Delay Storage Automatic Calculator,
   (EDSAC) 8
Electronic Funds Transfer (EFT), 256
Electronic mail messaging, 143
Electronic Numerical Integrator And Calculator
   (ENIAC), 7
e-mail, 29, 254, 329
Encapsulation protocol errors, 540
End Node (EN), 177
End-to-end troubleshooting, 436
End-user layer, 170
Enhanced Connectivity Facility (ECF), 414
ENIAC, 7
Enterprise computing, 18
Enterprise networks, 27, 53, 304
Entry point, 524
Error Protocol (ERROR), 190-191

ES/9000, 396
etherck, 462
etherfind, 447
Ethernet (IEEE 802.3), 3, 32, 56, 66, 104, 307, 405, 471, 547
Ethernet Analyzer Server, 439
Ethernet bridge, 216
Ethernet LAN, 321, 427
Ethernet repeaters, 211, 563
Ethernet-to-ATM converter, 310
EtherTalk, 366-393
EtherWORKS Router, 428
Event logger and database, 459
Event service, 148
Events, 445, 512
Examine mode, 453
EXCEL, 265
Expansion bus, 314
Expert Sniffer Network Analyzer, 455
Extended High Level Language Application Program Interface (EHLLAPI), 305
Extended Industry Standard Architecture (EISA), 313-314
Exterior Gateway Protocol (EGP),443
eXternal Data Representation (XDR), 282-283

Facsimile, 71, 149
Fast Ethernet, 309
Fault analysis, 499
Fault detection, 253
Fault isolation, 488
Fault management, 147, 483, 502-504
Faults, 470
Fault-tolerant, 88, 309
FDDI backbone, 427
Fiber Distributed Data Interface (FDDI), 3, 17, 38, 99, 198-200, 266, 309, 471, 548-550
Fiber optic cables, 38, 116, 309
File Guard, 387
File server, 29, 97
File services, 247
File sharing folder, 370
File Transfer, Access, and Management (FTAM), 66, 140, 142, 259
File Transfer Protocol (FTP), 36, 44, 75, 82, 259, 280-282, 324, 430, 472
FileMaker Pro, 389

Filter and forward algorithm, 214
Filtering, 445, 550-551
Finger, 329
Firewalls, 275
Flags, 77
Flat file, 260
Flexible bridging and routing, 534
Flexible configuration, 4, 533
Floating point, 314
Flow control, 105
Focal point, 524
Form mode terminals, 141
Forwarding, 550-552
Foundation Manager, 462
FoxBase, 389
Fractional T1, 40, 193
Frame reception, 125
Frame Relay, 17, 21, 100-101, 136, 196-197, 267, 311, 471
Frame transmission, 124
FrameMaker, 389
Front End Processor (FEP), 15, 39, 172, 404-406
Full duplex, 81, 158, 368
Function Management Header (FMH), 175
Functional Redundancy Checking (FRC), 312

Gateway, 15, 26, 49, 79, 113, 228-233, 552
Gateway Access Protocol (GAP), 183
Generic Information Block (GIB), 529
Get, 514
Get service, 148
GetBulk, 514
GetNext, 514
Global internetworking, 41
Global management architectures, 500
Global networks, 16, 54
Graphical User Interface (GUI), 19, 30, 60, 323
Graphics accelerators, 313
graphics-intensive applications, 313
Group-data transfer mode, 186
GTMOSI, 180
Guaranteed delivery, 105

hammer and anvil, 462
Hard and soft errors, 503
Harvard Graphics, 389
Heterogeneity, 60

Heterogeneous mix, 533
Hierarchical file, 260
Hierarchical layers, 43
High Level Language/Application Program
    Interface (HLLAPI), 291, 414, 418, 422, 428
High performance processing, 533
High speed backbone interconnections, 536
High-bandwidth, 6
High-level Data Link Control (HDLC), 46, 181,
    428
High-speed packet/circuit switching, 534
Historical/audit trail, 438
Homogeneity, 27
Hop count, 225
Host computer, 468
Host identifier (host ID), 79
Host table, 445
HostTopN, 445
Host-to-terminal connectivity, 14
HP LAN, 521
HP-UX, 339, 415
Hub Management Interface (HMI), 526
Hubs, 268
Hybrid bridges/routers, 54
Hybrid internetwork, 17, 25
Hybrid LANs, 107
Hybrid topology, 111
Hyper Text Transfer Protocol (HTTP), 36
HyperCard, 385

IBM 3270, 252
IBM 3278 display terminal, 429
IBM 3287 printer, 429
IBM 604, 7
IBM 650, 9
IBM OS/2 LAN Manager, 44, 410
ICMP echo (ping), 448, 456, 479
IEEE 802.1, 104
IEEE 802.10, 104
IEEE 802.2, 104
IEEE 802.6, 104
IEEE 802.8, 104
IEEE 802.9, 104
ifconfig, 447
Imaging, 22
Immediate Network Nodes (INN), 175
IND$FILE, 405, 414-420, 429
Inductive Modeling Technology (IMT), 529

Industry Standard Architecture (ISA), 113, 314
Information Management System (IMS), 174, 334,
    395
Information Systems (IS), 394
Input-output-type devices, 10
Integrated database, 10
Integrated Service Digital Network (ISDN), 21,
    70, 102-103, 133, 148-150
Integration by gateway, 404
Intel processors, 312
Interactive computing, 11
Inter Application Communication (IAC), 371
Interface Message Processor (IMP), 150
Interior Gateway Protocol (IGP), 479
International Standards Organization (ISO), 11,
    133
Internet, 15, 60, 280-281, 330
Internet Communication Management Protocol
    (ICMP), 80, 152, 163, 443
Internet Data Protocol (IDP), 190
Internet Network Management Framework (NMF),
    513
Internet Packet Exchange (IPX), 3, 36, 52, 62,
    289, 91, 187
Internet Protocol (IP), 44, 75, 152-156, 324, 443,
    553-554
Internet Rover, 461, 472
Internetwork, 5, 15, 25, 65
Internetworking, 2, 6, 11, 23, 26, 65, 552
Internetworking management, 27
Internetworking tools, 27, 112, 207-241
Interoperability, 11, 20, 27, 63, 249, 306
Interpacket gap, 119
Interprocess Communications Protocols (IPC), 52,
    137
IP addresses, 552
IP bridge/router, 409
IP header, 156
IP routing table, 512
IP-over-SNA routing, 409
ippingmon, 485
IP-SNA router, 410
ISA, 313
ISDN, 21, 68, 267
ISO Pascal, 85, 151
ISO TP4, 76

JES1, 407

Kerberos, 253, 507
Kernel, 271
Korn Shell, 272

LADDIS, 449
LAN Manager/X, 277, 338
LAN media, 554-555
LAN Patrol, 452
LAN Resource Extension and Services (LAN-RES), 410
LAN server, 51, 321
LAN topologies, 107
LAN Workplace, 339
LanProbe, 460-461
LANtastic, 52, 318
LAN-to-WAN bridge, 309
LANVista, 452-453
LAN-WAN interconnection, 6
LAN-WAN technology, 16
LANWatch, 453
LaserWriter printer, 365, 391
Layer Management Entity (LME), 508
Layered protocols, 26
Learning algorithm, 214
Learning bridges, 545
Leased Line Services, 192
Legacy systems, 23, 395
Line Printer Daemon (LPD), 412, 430
Line Printer Requester (LPR), 412, 430
Link Access Procedure, Balanced (LAPB), 178, 194, 401
Link Access Protocol (LAP), 369
Link-level communications, 36
Link-level error recovery, 174
Load sharing, 28
Lobe repeaters, 211, 563
Local Area Network (LAN), 3, 4, 6, 13, 19, 26, 28, 6, 321, 402, 435, 554
Local Area System Transport (LAST), 84
Local Area Transport Architecture (LAT), 84, 181-182
Local Area Transport Protocol (LATP), 168
Local bridges, 54, 216, 545
Local internetworking, 27
LocalTalk, 266, 366-393
Logical Link Control (LLC), 66, 135, 325
Logical subnets, 226

Lotus 1-2-3, 13, 265, 388
Low entry networking, 177
LU 6.2 (Logical Unit 6.2), 168, 263, 413
LUA/LU0, 417-422
LU-LU session, 174

Mac Bridges, 297
MacDFT, 385
Macintosh, 31, 265, 364-393
Macintosh file server, 373
Macintosh Finder, 323
Macintosh Plus, 380
MacIrma LAN, 385
MacMainFrame, 385
MacOS, 287, 323, 371
MacTOPS, 374
MacWrite, 388
Mainframe-PC connectivity, 13
Maintenance Operations Protocol (MOP), 84
Malfunctioning bridge, 438
Managed devices, 441
Managed node, 147
Managed objects, 512-513
Management Agent, 147
Management application (manager), 509
Management Information Base (MIB), 148, 253, 443, 509-511, 555-556
Management Information Systems (MIS), 1
Management node, 147
Manufacturing Automation Protocol (MAP), 251
mconnect, 472
Mechanical calculators, 7
Media Access Control (MAC), 66, 135, 199, 328
Media Access Unit (MAU), 67, 104, 124, 268,
Media faults, 468
Megabit per second transmission, 55
Message Handling Service (MHS), 53, 140, 143, 255
Message Oriented Text Interchange Systems (MOTIS), 68, 140, 143
Message Queues, 276
Message Transfer Agent (MTA), 69, 144, 255
Message Transfer System (MTS), 69, 144
Message-switched networks, 95
Messaging applications, 256
Messaging services, 321
Metropolitan Area Network (MAN), 53, 96
MIB Browser, 463

Micro Channel Architecture (MCA), 114, 314
Microcomputer, 29
Microkernel, 316
Microsoft Excel, 388
Microsoft LAN Manager, 50, 246-247, 318, 320
Microsoft Mail, 388
Microsoft PowerPoint, 374, 389
Microsoft Word, 374, 388
MicroVMS, 426
Microwave radio transmissions, 37, 116, 117
Military Network (MILNET), 153, 281
Minicomputers, 11, 29
Mirroring, 261
MIS, 1, 19
Misconfigured workstation, 491
Misdirected datagrams, 479
Mission critical systems, 10
Mission-critical applications, 13
Modem management system, 509
Modems, 38, 271
Monitoring parameters, 504
Motif, 265, 331, 346
Motorola 68000, 385
Motorola processors, 313
Mount protocol, 89
Mounting, 88
MS-DOS, 28, 61
MS-DOS PC, 324
Multi Link Transmission Group (MLTG), 407
Multihost network, 13, 173
Multi-layered protocols, 465
Multimedia, 4, 22, 274, 335
Multi-mode, 309
Multiplatform, 27
Multiple bridges, 217
Multiple channels of data, 101
Multiple LAN segments, 534
Multiple Logical Processor Feature (MLPF), 290
Multiple platforms, 61
Multiple Virtual Storage/Enterprise Systems
    Architecture (MVS/ESA), 30, 398
Multiplexers, 39, 157, 243
Multiport bridges, 211, 545, 563
Multi-protocol networking, 227, 241, 398
Multipurpose Internet Mail Extensions (MIME),
    163
Multitasking operating system, 30
Multithreaded, 318

Multivendor, 11, 27, 61
MVS, 10, 28, 61, 245, 406, 430

Name Binding Protocol (NBP), 91, 129
Name discovery, 185
Name registration, 185
Named pipes, 19, 52, 236
National Institute for Standards and Technology
    (NIST), 8
National Science Foundation Network (NFSNET),
    153, 281
NAU services layer, 170
Net_Monitor, 456
NetBIOS broadcasts, 438
NetLabs CMOT Agent, 528
NetLabs Dual Manager, 528
NetLabs NerveCenter, 528
NetMatrix Protocol Analyzer, 453
NetMetrix Load Monitor, 461
NetMetrix NFS Monitor, 461
NetNews, 413
NETScout RMON Console, 454, 458-459
netstat, 447, 472
NetView, 173, 408, 420, 441, 485, 522-525, 556
NetView Distribution Manager (NetView DM),
    416, 418, 423-424
NetWare, 28, 33, 246, 318-319
NetWare 3270 LAN, 378
NetWare 386 services, 385
NetWare Access Server, 378
NetWare Connect, 36
NetWare Directory Services (NDS), 321
NetWare LAN, 263
NetWare LANalyzer Agent, 451-452
NetWare Lite, 319
NetWare Loadable Module (NLM), 375
NetWare Management System (NMS), 486, 526-
    527
NetWare NFS gateways, 339
NetWare Runtime, 452
NetWare SQL, 378
NetWare VMS, 44
NetWare/IP, 321
NetWare-IPX, 263
NetWare-TCP/IP, 263
Network access , 74, 117
Network adapters, 466
Network Addressable Unit (NAU), 171, 175

Network analysis, monitoring, and management, 534
Network Application Support (NAS), 52
Network architecture, 11, 64
Network aware, 250
Network Basic End User Interface (NetBEUI), 62, 183-187
Network Basic Input-Output Operating System (NetBIOS), 3, 44, 90, 183-187, 263, 320, 438
Network centric, 35, 250
Network Computing System (NCS), 283
Network configuration, 467
Network control panel, 478
Network Control Program (NCP), 41, 172, 398
Network CoProcessor (NCoP), 291
Network Driver Interface Specification (NDIS), 328
Network File System (NFS), 46, 52, 86, 260-261, 282-283, 306, 329, 412, 430, 472
Network General Reporter, 462
Network General Sniffer, 454-455
Network Identifier (Net ID), 79, 225
Network infrastructure, 437
Network integration, 54
Network Interface Card (NIC), 124, 111, 228, 326
Network Interface Tap (NIT), 447
Network intrinsic, 250
Network layer, 65, 136
Network layer level, 128
Network management, 22, 25, 436
Network management protocols, 146
Network Management Stations (NMS), 441-446, 513
Network mapping utility, 477
Network Node (NN), 177
Network Operating System (NOS), 50, 225, 318, 556-557
Network Operations Center On-Line (NOCOL), 484-485
Network Packet Switching Interface (NPSI), 179, 401
Network performance, 436
Network resources, 507
Network security, 387
Network segment, 488
Network topology, 54
Network Virtual Terminal (NVT), 162
Network zones, 390
Networking applications, 313

Networking control panel, 370
NeXTstep, 315
NFS Mount, 449
NFS Write, 449
nfswatch, 448
nhfsstone, 448
Nonrelational database, 395
Novell LAN Workplace, 44
Novellís Integrated Computer Architecture (NICA), 52
nslookup, 447
nsmon, 485
NT Advanced Server (NAS), 316, 336, 429
NuBus, 385

Object Linking and Embedding (OLE), 320
Object technology, 274
Office Document Architecture (ODA), 140, 146
OfficeVision/400, 430
Offset, 77
On-line databases, 10
Open Data Link Interface (ODI), 52, 187, 328
Open Network Computing (ONC), 271
Open Shortest Path First (OSPF), 479, 561
Open Software Foundation, 318
Open System Interconnection (OSI), 11, 28, 43, 65, 133, 426, 557-561
Open VMS Macintosh client, 322
Open windows, 354
OpenDOC, 364
OpenLook, 346
OpenView (HP), 441, 485, 521-522
OpenView Data Line Monitor, 522
OpenView DTC Manager, 522
OpenView Windows Bridge Manager, 521
OpenVMS LAN Manager, 322
Operating System/400 (OS/400), 398
Operating systems, 28
Optical fiber cables, 471
Originator / Recipient (O/R) addresses, 256
OS/2, 23, 28, 44, 263, 296, 319, 321, 404
OS/2 EE, 414
OS/2 LAN Manager, 296
OSF/1, 61, 273, 315
OSI Reference Model., 15, 36, 65, 133,
OSI TP4, 294
OSI Virtual Terminal Protocol (VTP), 251
osipingmon, 485

Osiris, 290
OSNS, 180
OTSS, 180
Out-of-tolerance, 503

P1, 144, 255
P2, 144, 256
P3, 144, 256
P6, 313
P7, 144, 255-256
P7, 255-256
PacerTerm, 384
Packet, 561-562
Packet Assembler / Dis-assembler (PAD), 41, 70, 417
Packet capture, 445
Packet error rates, 464
Packet Exchange Protocol (PEX), 190-191
Packet Filter, 449
Packet forwarding, 187
Packet fragmentation, 80
Packet Layer Protocol (PLP), 193-194
Packet loss rates, 464
Packet mode, 311
Packet network, 70
packet sequence checking, 105
Packet stream interface, 191
Packet Switched Public Data Networks (PSPDN), 311
Packet switching (X.25), 15, 69-68, 70, 95, 179-181, 267, 311, 401, 471
Packet switching systems, 192
Packet-switched networks, 70, 95
Page mode terminals, 141
PageMaker, 374
Parallel network integration, 409
Passive broadcast network, 127
Path control layer, 169
Path control network, 172, 175
Path Information Unit (PIU), 175
Path level flow control, 178
PATHWORKS, 51, 84, 295, 322, 385, 427, 429
PC Adapter, 1134
PC LAN, 29, 318, 321
PC network, 321
PC NFS, 261
PC UNIX-host connectivity, 306
PC X windows, 306

PC/TCP, 336
PCAnywhere, 453
PC-DOS, 410
PCIterm, 384
Peer-to-peer, 14, 32, 9, 3057
Pen-based OSs, 316
Performance, 6, 54, 147, 504-505
Performance monitoring, 499
Performance sharing, 28
Peripheral Chip Interconnect (PCI), 313-314
Peripheral nodes, 173
Peripheral sharing, 28
Permanent virtual circuits, 196
Personal MacLAN, 382
PhoneNet, 367
PhoneNet StarController, 372
PhoneNet Talk, 382
PHY, 72
Physical circuits, 464
Physical layer, 65, 134-135
Physical Media Dependent (PMD), 72, 199
Physical Unit (PU), 170, 171
Ping, 80, 329, 448
Pinging problem devices, 488
Pipes, 263, 276-277
PL/I, 395
Point-and-click, 339, 386
Point-to-point, 16, 24, 71, 535
Point-to-Point Protocol (PPP), 198, 338, 471, 562
Point-to-point transfer mode, 186
Portability, 19, 60, 63, 249
Portable Operating System based on UNIX (POSIX), 60, 68 , 334
PostScript Protocol (PSP), 129
POWER (performance optimization with enhanced RISC), 313
PowerMac, 392
PowerPC, 313-314
PowerTalk, 364
Presentation layer, 66
Presentation services, 177
Price and performance, 3
Primary ring, 71
Print server, 36
Print services, 247
Printer Access, 129, 14
Priority operation, 125
Private Branch Exchange (PBX), 46, 311

ProbeView, 461
Problem anticipation, 449
Problem determination, 465
Processor-enhanced analyzer, 450
PROFS, 293
Program-to-program communication, 433
Protocol Analyzers, 449-456
Protocol conversion, 38, 301, 433
Protocol encapsulation, 228
Protocol Monitors, 456- stacks, 440
Protocols, 5, 11, 28, 38, 440
Proxy Agent, 510
Pseudo terminals, 276
Public Data Networks (PDN), 311, 494
Punch-down blocks, 470

Qualified Logical Link Control (QLLC), 401, 417,
    325, 428
Query/response, 82
QuickDraw GX, 364
QuikMail, 388

RARP, 447
RAS server, 36
Rate of flow, 504
Real-time analysis, 504
Reduced Instruction Set Computer (RISC), 274,
    313
Redundant packets, 539
Relational database, 84
Reliability, 3
Reliable packet interface, 191
Reliable stream transport, 166
Remote bridges 54, 216-218, 545
Remote Database Access (RDA), 140, 145
Remote File System (RFS), 282-283
Remote hosts, 252
Remote Job Entry (RJE), 39, 243, 405
Remote login, 100, 162, 276, 279, 245
Remote Procedure Call (RPC), 86, 261-262, 283,
    329, 449, 518
Remote Spooling Communication Subsystem
    (RSCS), 412
Repeaters, 47, 112, 208-213, 563
Repository of data, 24, 29
Rerouting, 244
Resource sharing, 2, 98
Resource utilization, 507

REXX, 413
Rightsizing, 22
Ring PC emulator, 375
Ring Topology, 67, 109
RISC System/6000 (RS/6000), 384, 415, 430
RISC-based bridges, 55
rlogin, 279
RMON, 441-463
Root, 111
ROSE, 518-520
Route path information, 440
Routers, 11, 15, 26, 47, 223-228, 564-565
Routing algorithms, 468
Routing Information Protocol (RIP), 190-191, 449,
    479
Routing nodes, 176
Routing Table Management Protocol (RTMP), 91,
    129
RS-232, 39
RS-449, 39
rsh, 279
RSX-11M, 426
RXSockets, 413

Santa Cruz Operation (SCO), 315, 415, 427, 430
satellite systems, 37, 116, 117, 193
Scalability, 63, 249
Scaleable kernel, 318
Scheduling, 254
Scroll mode terminals, 141
Security management, 6, 64, 88, 147, 506-507
Self configuring, 226
Semaphores, 276-277
Sequence numbers, 76-77
Sequence Packet Exchange (SPX), 3, 52, 62, 91,
    187
Sequenced Packet Protocol (SPP), 190-191
Serial communication ports, 312
Serial connectivity, 357
Serial device drivers, 370
Serial Line IP (SLIP), 198, 338
Serial Lines, 271, 471
Server, 19-22, 31, 438
Service Message Block (SMB), 184, 321
Service point, 524
Session establishment, 185
Session layer, 66, 129, 137
Session termination, 185

Session time-outs, 539
Set, 514
Set service, 148
SetCloseDownMode, 351
Shielded Twisted-Pair (STP), 38, 114-115
Short taps, 470
Shotgunning, 438
Signal strength, 67
Signal transmission data, 534
Signals, 276
Simple Mail Transfer Protocol (SMTP), 13, 44, 75,
    81, 162, 255, 280-281, 324, 412, 430, 472
Simple Network Management Protocol (SNMP),
    44, 75, 82, 140, 145, 253, 329, 439, 443-446,
    500-530, 567
Single fault, 71
Single-mode, 309
Slow login, 437
Small Computer System Interface (SCSI), 313,
    315
SNA for LAN Interconnect, 407
SNA rlogin, 418-425
SNA/DNA gateways, 49
SNA-to-TCP/IP gateway, 228
snmpwatch, 472
Sockets, 276-277, 368
Source Address (SA), 77, 120
Source routing, 217
Source XNS Address, 190
Spanning tree, 218
SPARCServers, 415
SPECmark range, 314
SPECTRUM (Cabletron), 529-530
SpiderAnalyzer, 455-456
SpiderMonitor, 455
Splices, 470
Spreadsheet, 4, 13
SQL database services, 339
SQL interfaces, 306
SQL server, 34
Standardization, 6, 60
Star Topology, 110, 219
StarGROUP LAN Manager, 378
StarGROUP Server, 378
StarLAN, 40, 266, 471
StarLAN bridges, 521
Static routing, 224

Station Management (SMT), 199
Status queries, 509
Store and forward, 68, 143
Stream oriented, 277
Stream Protocol (SP), 129
Stream transmission service, 100
Streams, 276-277
StreetTalk, 295, 379-393
Striping, 125, 261
Structure of Management Information (SMI), 514
Structured approach, 438
Structured Query Language (SQL), 20, 73, 85,
    262, 265, 565-566
Subarea networks, 42
Subarea nodes, 409, 173-181
Subnet mask, 491
Subnets, 24, 79
Subscriber Network Interface (SNI), 197-198
Sun OS/Solaris, 263, 415, 430
Sun SPARC workstation, 314
SunNet Manager (SNM), 441, 525-526
Superscalar PowerPC, 313
SVR4, 61, 317
Switch-based LANs, 107
Switched Multimegabit Data Service (SMDS), 17,
    21, 100, 197-198, 267, 471
Switched Virtual Circuits (SVC), 196
Switching systems, 191
Synchronization, 174
Synchronous Data Link Control (SDLC), 46, 174-
    179, 325, 400, 415-425, 428
Synchronous Optical Networks (SONETs), 248
System 360/370, 10, 29
System Application Architecture (SAA), 52
System Management Application Entity (SMAE),
    508, 518-520
System Management Application Process (SMAP),
    508
System Network Architecture (SNA), 3, 11, 28,
    36, 41, 83, 168-181, 288, 396-410
System Network Architecture Distribution
    Services (SNADS), 430
System Services Control Point (SSCP), 172, 173
System Support program (SSP), 30
System View, 290
System-level File Server (SFS), 449
Systems management, 274

T1, 15, 100-101, 192, 267
T3, 17, 100-101, 193, 267
T-connectors, 471
TCP Header, 158
TCP/IP, 3, 28, 36, 62, 263, 403, 412
TCP/IP for MVS, 413
TCP/IP for OS/400, 413, 430-433
TCP/IP on VM host, 410
TCP/IP-to-SNA, 403
Telecommunications Access Method (TCAM), 41
Teletext, 71, 149
Terminal emulation (TELNET), 44, 75, 81, 251-252, 279-280, 306, 324, 349, 411, 418, 433
Terminal server, 32, 36
Terminals, 11, 38
Terminators, 470
Thickwire (10BASE5), 118
Thinwire (10BASE2), 118
Third generation, 10
Threads, 88
Threshold , 440
Threshold errors, 503
Time Domain Reflectometry (TDR), 456
Time services, 88
Time To Live (TTL), 156-157, 227, 338, 448
Time-synchronized, 450
TN3270, 324, 405, 411, 418
Token, 67
Token Bus (IEEE 802.4), 66, 68, 104
Token ring (IEEE 802.5), 3, 36, 66, 72, 104, 123-126, 445, 471, 567-569
Token ring Analyzer Server, 439
Token ring bridges, 217
Token ring repeaters, 211, 563
Token transmission, 125
TokenTalk, 366-393
TokenTalk Link Access Protocol (TLAP), 369
Topologies, 38
TOPS 20, 426
tpmon, 485
traceroute, 448, 490
Traffic matrix, 445
Traffic verification, 483
Transaction Processing (TP), 290
Transceiver, 121
Transistors, 9
Transmission control layer, 169

Transmission Control Protocol (TCP), 11, 153, 161-166, 324, 443, 569-572
Transmission Control Protocol/Internet Protocol (TCP/IP), 3, 11, 74
Transmission errors, 67
Transmission Header (TH), 175
Transmission media, 27
Transmission system, 118
Transparent access, 167
Transport layer, 66, 129, 136-137
Transport Level Interface (TLI), 52, 84-85, 100, 276-277
Transport-level, 100
Trap, , 482, 512, 514
trapmon, 485
Tree topology, 110
Trend analysis, 446
Trivial File Transfer Protocol (TFTP), 82, 162, 259, 324, 472
Troubleshooting, 22, 389-392, 435-463
Troubleshooting cable problems, 469
Trunk ring, 71
TSO, 407
Twisted-pair (10BaseT), 118, 470
Type 2.1 peer-to-peer node, 409

ULTRIX, 292, 415, 426-430
ULTRIX NFS, 428
Unacknowledged connectionless, 104
UniCenter (Computer Associates), 486
Unidirectional, 108
UNIVAC I, 8
UNIX, 10, 23, 60, 326
UNIX Streams, 275
UNIX System V, 273
UNIX-to-UNIX Copy (UUCP), 281, 413
Unshielded Twisted Pair (UTP), 37, 114-115, 381
Urgent pointer, 77
Usenet, 280
User Agent (UA), 69, 144, 255, 257
User Datagram Protocol (UDP), 75, 152-162, 333, 442-443, 515
User interfaces, 19
User registry, 506
User-centered, 35
User-computer interface, 12
uShare, 384

Vacuum tubes, 7
Varied bandwidth support, 534
VAX/VMS, 44, 415, 426-430
Videoconferencing, 248
Video, 3
Video telephony, 70
Videotext, 70, 149
Virtual circuit, 41, 75, 196, 310
Virtual filestore, 259
Virtual Telecommunications Access Method
    (VTAM), 41, 172, 398
Virtual Terminal (VT), 66, 140, 280
Virus checkers, 477
Virus protection, 387
VisiCalc, 13
VM, 406, 410
VM Gopher, 413
VM/Pass-Through (PVM), 413
VMNET, 412
VMS, 51, 61, 412, 430
VMS SCO UNIX client/server, 322
VMSMail, 293
Voice/data network, 17
VSAM, 395
VT100, 252, 306, 414
VTAM, 173, 413

WAN Analyzer Server, 439
WAN bandwidth problems, 493
WAN PC platform, 429
Watchdog, 458
Wide Area Network (WAN), 3, 14-16, 26, 28, 96,
    100, 19, 311, 572-575
Wide area network links, 536
Window management, 85
Window manager, 346
Windows, 23, 77
Windows for Workgroups, 27, 319
Windows Internet Naming Service (WINS), 337
Windows NT, 51, 292, 322, 336
Windows PC, 375

Windows sockets application programming inter-
    face (WinSock API), 306
Wireless, 116
Wiring concentrators, 211, 440, 466, 563
Word processing, 4, 13
WordPerfect, 388
WordStar, 13
X, 252, 343
X applications, 357
X client, 333, 351
X Display Manager Control Protocol (XDMCP), 356
X display server, 343
X library (Xlib), 351
X protocol, 346-351
X server, 355
X terminal, 252, 334
X Window standard (X11), 344, 349
X Window System, 252, 280, 329
X Windows, 60, 333, 341-363
X.21 BIS, 194-195
X.25 DCE, 180
X.25 DTEs, 401
X.25 Interface (XI), 180, 401
X.25 networks, 193-196
X.25 packet switching protocol, 322
X.25-SNA integration, 400
X.400, 66, 140, 144, 256, 417
X.500, 66, 140, 145, 256-257, 417
X/Open Management Protocol, 524
X/Open standards, 84
X/Open Transport Interface (XTI), 84-85, 151
XENIX, 317
Xerox Network Systems (XNS), 36, 103, 187-191,
    289
Xgator, 384
xkill, 351
xterm, 252, 349
X-Windows, 23

Yellow pages (NIS), 449

Zone Information Protocol (ZIP), 129

1